FROM EMPATHY TO DENIAL

MEIR LITVAK AND ESTHER WEBMAN

From Empathy to Denial
Arab Responses to the Holocaust

Columbia University Press
New York

Columbia University Press
Publishers Since 1893
New York / Chichester, West Sussex

Library of Congress Cataloging-in-Publication Data

Litvak, Meir.
  From empathy to denial : Arab responses to the Holocaust / Meir Litvak and Esther Webman.
    p. cm.
  Includes bibliographical references and index.
  ISBN 978-0-231-70074-0 (cloth : alk. paper)
  1. Holocaust, Jewish (1939-1945)—Public opinion. 2. Jews—Public opinion. 3. Zionism—Public
opinion. 4. Public opinion—Arab countries. 5. Arabs—Attitudes. 6. Antisemitism—Arab countries. 7.
Arab countries—Ethnic relations. I. Webman, Esther. II. Title.
  D804.45.A73L58 2009
  940.53'18089927—dc22
                                    2008028881

∞

Columbia University Press books are printed on permanent and durable acid-free paper.
This book is printed on paper with recycled content.
Printed in India

c 10 9 8 7 6 5 4 3 2 1

References to Internet Web sites (URLs) were accurate at the time of writing. Neither
the author nor Columbia University Press is responsible for URLs that may have expired
or changed since the manuscript was prepared.

CONTENTS

ABBREVIATIONS

ADL	Anti-Defamation League
AFP	Agence France Presse
AHC	Arab Higher Committee for Palestine
AP	Associated Press
AZAR	Association against Zionism and Racism
DFLP	Democratic Front for the Liberation of Palestine
IHR	Institute for Historical Review
ISA	Israel State Archives
IZL	Irgun zeva'i le'umi (National Military Organization)
JHR	*Journal of Historical Review*
JWA	Jordanian Writers Association
LEHY	Lohamei herut yisrael
NGO	Non-governmental organization
NSZ	Narodowe Sily Zbrojne
PLO	Palestinian Liberation Organization
PMW	Palestine Media Watch
PNA	Palestine National Authority
RSHA	Reich Security Head Office
SSNP	Syrian Social National Party
UAR	United Arab Republic (official name of Egypt after 1958)
UNRWA	United Nations Relief and Works Agency
UNSCOP	United Nations Special Commission on Palestine
ZCCF	Zayed Center for Coordination and Follow-Up

PREFACE

The following pages are the culmination of a few years of tedious digging in Arab newspapers, periodicals and books, in search of texts – news items, articles, statements, which refer to the Holocaust. The scope of the work expanded as we proceeded in our research, seeking to grasp the ongoing changes in the Arab Holocaust discourse and reflect its dynamic nature. Until not very long ago, the topic of this study would have been inconceivable. The Israeli academia and public discourse, as well as those in the West, did not evince any particular interest in it. The growing frequent references to the Holocaust in Arab pronouncements and writings, and the increasing public awareness to antisemitism in the Arab world, drew the attention of scholars and students, and motivated us to join forces in researching Arab representations of the Holocaust. Although we were both trained in the discipline of history, our different personal backgrounds brought us to the subject from different directions, which enriched our discussions and we hope that they also benefited our final product. This is the first comprehensive book ever published on the topic, and we believe that it will pave the way for further research.

In transliterating Arabic, we have sacrificed some technical precision for the sake of not scaring away the nonprofessional reader, while following the accepted practice in the field of Middle Eastern history.

We are deeply indebted to numerous people, friends and colleagues, for their advice, encouragement and help. This study was initially supported by a grant of the Tami Steinmetz Institute for Peace Research at Tel Aviv University. We are most grateful to the past and present directors of the Dayan Center for Middle Eastern and African Studies, Prof. Asher Susser, Dr. Martin Kramer and Prof. Eyal Zisser who enabled us to pursue our study and provided us with a platform for discussion of our preliminary findings. Special thanks we owe to Prof. Dina Porat, head of the Stephen Roth Institute for the Study of Antisemitism and Racism, who allowed us to use the Institute's vast database. It is our pleasure to thank Prof. Emanuel Sivan for his thought-provoking and stimulating insights, and Prof. Ami Ayalon for his valuable comments on various chapters of this work. Needless to say, all mistakes and shortcomings are ours alone.

We are obliged to the two readers of the manuscript Prof. Deborah Lipstadt and Dr. Robert Satloff for their constructive comments. We wish to single out Haim Gal, the director of the Dayan Center's newspapers archives for his personal help in complying with our frequent requests for old newspapers, Marion Gliksberg, the librarian of the Dayan Center library and Ilana Greenberg, administrative officer of the Dayan Center for their assistance whenever needed. Thanks are also due to the librarians at Cornell University library who accommodated our dozens of inter-library loans requests.

We are also grateful to the students who assisted us along the road, among them Sarit Ben Ami, Arik Rodnitski, Sami Abu Shahada and Mor Goldberg. Finally, we wish to thank Michael Dwyer for his professional handling of the manuscript and Maria Petalidou for bearing with our capricious requirements in the proofreading process.

And last but not least, we are most obliged to our respective families – Nava, Omri and Adi Litvak, and Adi and Oded Webman, without whose support and love we would not have been able to accomplish this task.

INTRODUCTION

The Holocaust has become a "cultural code" denoting a rejection not only of Europe's deadliest heritage but also of an entire set of ideas and values which no society wants to be associated with.[1] The "pertinent European reference" is extermination, historian Tony Judt asserted, and "Holocaust recognition is our contemporary European entry ticket."[2] Moreover, the representation of the Holocaust has become a major criterion in the examination of attitudes toward the Jews in general, and to Israel in particular. Radical right-wing movements in Europe and the US have adopted the denial of the Holocaust as an integral part of their political platforms. Concurrently, radical left-wing movements in the West came to deny the Holocaust or its uniqueness as a means to assail Israel and to criticize modern capitalism.[3] Both groups have absorbed the Holocaust into their political rhetoric, as both perceive it as a political tool, which Israel exploits. The Holocaust, in their view, created a guilt complex in the West, which played a crucial role in forging sympathetic public opinion in support of the establishment of the State of Israel. Some even argue that without the Holocaust Israel might not have existed at all.

By contrast, "the connection of the Arabs to the history of the Holocaust is indirect," as pointed out by former Arab Israeli Member of Knesset and scholar 'Azmi Bishara, in the first attempt made by Arab scholars to examine Arab attitudes toward the Holocaust.

The scene of the disaster was Europe, and the perpetrators of the extermination acts were Europeans, but the reparations were paid first and foremost in the Middle East by the Palestinians. This is probably the reason that the discussion of the Holocaust in the Arab context always evolves around its political implications, and circumvents

---

1   For the concept of "cultural code," see Shulamit Volkov, "Anti-Semitism as a Cultural Code: Reflections on the History and Historiography of Anti-Semitism in Imperial Germany," *Yearbook of the Leo Baeck Institute*, vol. 23 (1978), pp. 25–46.

2   Tony Judt, "Europe – Rising from the House of the Dead," 25 October 2005, www.theglobalist.com/StoryId.aspx?StoryId=4874.

3   Alain Finkielkraut, *The Future of a Negation: Reflections on the Question of Genocide*, Lincoln, NE: 1998; Elhanan Yakira, *Post-Zionism, Post-Holocaust: Three Essays on Denial, Repression and Delegitimation of Israel*, Tel Aviv: 2006 (Hebrew).

the event itself. The basic Arab anti-Zionist stance determined their attitude toward the Holocaust, as towards anti-Semitism in general. This stance is not the cause of the Arab-Israeli conflict, but its outcome. Anti-Jewish texts were engaged in the justification of the Holocaust and with its denial as a Zionist hoax – a rhetoric which, among other things, was an attempt to deal with the Zionist instrumentalization of the Holocaust.[4]

Bishara's assertions were made in the early 1990s, but they still seem to epitomize the Arab attitude, since its inception after World War II, towards the Holocaust, which stemmed from the viewpoint that the Holocaust does not concern the Arabs. An additional determinant factor in the crystallization of Arab attitudes toward the Holocaust has been the Arabs' view of World War II as an event in which they had no direct connection or interest, while they had to bear its brunt during the war and after it with the loss of Palestine and the displacement of the Palestinians. The proximity of events – the end of World War II, with the urgent need to solve the "Jewish Problem," and the establishment of the State of Israel, led to their convergence and the creation of causality relationships between them.[5] The resistance to the establishment of Israel as the solution to the "Jewish problem" overshadowed the Arabs' ability and willingness to acknowledge and sympathize with the Jewish tragedy. Even Arab intellectuals, who assailed Nazism, did not admit or denounce the Nazi genocide against the Jews, charging Zionism with cynically using the Holocaust or inventing it as a means of financial and psychological extortion. Alternately, the Palestinians are often represented as the Holocaust's true victims. Consequently, we have witnessed the development of an Arab Holocaust discourse encompassing various attitudes partly inspired by those in the West, which range through a spectrum from justification to denial and projection of Nazi images onto Zionism and Israel, who had thus been transformed from victims to culprits.

In Israel, on the other hand, the memory of the Holocaust has become one of the major components of its national consciousness and collective memory.

---

4   'Azmi Bishara, "The Arabs and the Holocaust: The Analysis of a Problematic Conjunctive Letter," *Zmanim*, no. 53 (Summer 1995) Hebrew, p. 54. Bishara's article fueled an intense controversy in Israel between Zionist Holocaust researchers and post-modern, post-Zionist writers. See Dan Michman, "Responses," *Zmanim*, no. 54 (Winter 1995) Hebrew, p. 119; Bishara, "Response," *Zmanim*, No. 55 (Spring 1996) (Hebrew), p. 102; Dan Michman (ed.), *Post-Zionism and the Holocaust*, Ramat Gan: 1997 (Hebrew).

5   The issue of the role of the Holocaust in facilitating the establishment of Israel preoccupied Israeli historiography. Among those who claim a direct causality, see Yehuda Bauer, *Rethinking the Holocaust*, New Haven, CT: 2001, pp. 242–60; and M. N. Penkower, *The Holocaust and Israel Reborn: From Catastrophe to Sovereignty*, Urbana, IL: 1994. For those who dispute this view, see D. Michman, "She'erit Hapletah, 1944–1948: Rehabilitation and Political Struggle" (Review article), *Holocaust and Genocide Studies*, vol. 7, no. 1 (Spring 1993), pp. 107–16.

The Holocaust is perceived as the most tragic event in Jewish history, which had expedited the establishment of the state, and provides a major, though not exclusive, justification for its existence. Israel is regarded as a guarantee for the preservation of the Jewish people, and for the prevention of any possible recurrence of the Holocaust.[6]

The present study seeks to identify and analyze the various characteristics of this discourse and their evolution since 1945. It covers a long and turbulent period in the history of the modern Middle East. It starts at the end of World War II, when the horrors of the Holocaust were revealed, the Jewish–Arab conflict in Palestine intensified and the struggle of the Arab states to gain formal independence from British and French rule was reinvigorated. The 1948 war, launched by the Palestinians and Arabs in order to prevent the establishment of Israel, marked a watershed in the history of the Middle East, with the Palestinian defeat or *Nakba* (disaster or catastrophe) manifested in the loss of around 78 percent of the territory of Mandatory Palestine and the displacement of some 550,000 to 650,000 Palestinians.[7] The Arab–Israeli conflict escalated during the 1950s and 1960s with the rise of the revolutionary Arab regimes, the growing involvement of the super-powers in the region and the rebirth of Palestinian nationalism in the early 1960s, the 1967 and 1973 wars being two important landmarks. The two wars, however, also led some Arab states to favor a political settlement with Israel, culminating in the 1979 Egyptian–Israeli and the 1994 Jordanian–Israeli peace treaties. The occupation of the West Bank and the Gaza Strip by Israel since 1967 exacerbated the tensions and animosities between the two peoples, while, paradoxically, the 1987–93 Palestinian uprising (Intifada) against Israeli rule produced the 1993 Declaration of Principles (the Oslo Accords) between Israel and the PLO. However, the prospects of Palestinian–Israeli peace were dashed in the failed 2000 Camp David summit and the renewed hostilities ever since.

---

6   For the growing importance of the Holocaust in Israeli identity and culture, see *Israel Studies Special Issue: Israel and the Holocaust*, vol. 8, no. 3 (Fall 2003); Eliezer Don-Yehia, "Memory and Political Culture: Israeli Society and the Holocaust," *Studies in Contemporary Jewry*, vol. 9 (1993), pp. 139–62.

7   For analyses of the Palestinian defeat and refugee problem, see Benny Morris, *The Birth of the Palestinian Refugee Problem Revisited*, 2nd edn., Cambridge: 2004; Yoav Gelber, *Palestine, 1948: War, Escape and the Emergence of the Palestinian Refugee Problem*, Brighton: 2001; 'Issa Khalaf, *Politics in Palestine: Arab Factionalism and Social Disintegration, 1939–1948*, Albany, NY: 1991; Baruch Kimmerling and Joel S. Migdal, *Palestinians: The Making of a People*, New York, 1993, p. 147; Danny Rubinstein, *The People of Nowhere: The Palestinian Vision of Home*, New York, 1991, pp. 3–5; Salman Abu Sitta, "Palestinian Right to Return ... Sacred, Legal, and Possible," The Palestinian Return Centre, London: 1 May 1999, www.prc.org.uk.

The Arab Holocaust discourse is, therefore, part of a broader anti-Zionist and anti-Semitic discourse which developed as part and parcel of the Arab–Israeli conflict. While Jews in Muslim lands never suffered the kind of persecutions they endured in Christian Europe, Islamic tradition did contain anti-Jewish themes and the Jews were never considered equal to Muslims.[8] However, manifestations of ideological hostility to Jews were the products of modernity, appearing already in the nineteenth century, before the emergence of Zionism, as a result of the growing European political and cultural penetration of the Middle East. Coupled with the weakness of the Muslim world, they created a sense of deep crisis among Muslims, causing a worsening in their attitude towards the Christian and Jewish minorities, identified as the main beneficiaries of the growing western influence and of various reform efforts carried out by local rulers.[9] The importation of anti-Jewish ideas and anti-Semitic themes along with other ideas, mostly by Christian Arab graduates of European schools, exacerbated the intolerance toward the Jews.[10]

The emergence of Arab nationalism, Zionist immigration to Palestine, which encroached upon the Arab indigenous population during the first half of the twentieth century, and the deep trauma of the 1948 Arab defeat enhanced this hostility and gave it a new momentum. The mere existence of Israel was perceived as contrary to justice and to the natural course of history. As the conflict deepened, anti-Semitism underwent a process of Islamization, using the Qur'an and Islamic traditions to rationalize the negation of Zionism, Israel and the Jews. The polemics against the Jews and the Children of Israel in the Qur'an,

---

8   For analyses of Islamic attitudes towards the Jews, see Bernard Lewis, *The Jews of Islam*, Princeton, NJ: 1984; Mark Cohen, *Under Crescent and Cross: The Jews in the Middle Ages*, Princeton, NJ: 1994; Yohanan Friedmann, *Tolerance and Coercion in Islam: Interfaith Relations in the Muslim Tradition*, New York: 2003. For a much more critical view of Islamic attitudes, see Bat Yeor, *The Dhimmi: Jews and Christians under Islam*, Rutherford, NJ: 1996, c. 1985.

9   For the rise of anti-Semitism in the Arab world, see: Sylvia G. Haim, "Arab Anti-Semitic Literature," *Jewish Social Studies*, vol. 17, no. 4 (1955), pp. 307–12; Yehoshafat Harkabi, *Arab Attitudes Towards Israel*, Jerusalem: 1974; Emmanuel Sivan, "A Resurgence of Arab Anti-Semitism," in William Frankel (ed.), *Survey of Jewish Affairs 1988*, London: 1989, pp. 78–95; Ronald L. Nettler, "Arab Images of Jews and Israel," in William Frankel (ed.), *Survey of Jewish Affairs, 1989*, Oxford: 1989, pp. 33–43; Bernard Lewis, *Semites and Anti-Semites: An Inquiry into Conflict and Prejudice*, London: 1997; Robert Wistrich, *Muslim Anti-Semitism: A Clear and Present Danger*, New York: 2002; Gudrun Krämer, "Anti-Semitism in the Muslim World: A Critical Review," *Die Welt des Islams*, vol. 46, no. 3 (2006), pp. 243–76. For changing attitudes towards Christians, see Leila Fawaz, *An Occasion for War: Civil Conflict in Lebanon and Damascus in 1860*, Berkeley, CA: 1995.

10 The most blatant manifestation of this phenomenon was the 1840 Damascus blood libel raised by monks of the Capuchin order, see Jonathan Frankel, *The Damascus Affair: "Ritual Murder," Politics, and the Jews in 1840*, Cambridge: 1997.

commented British scholar of Palestinian origin Suha Taji-Faruki, "serve as a basis for a negative construction of the Jewish character," and provide "a convincing explanation for Zionist success, for the harm done to Palestine, and for the political and economic Jewish domination in other places of the world."[11] Moreover, enhancing the negative image of the Jews and confronting their "fabricated" religious beliefs with Islam strengthens Islamic self-identity and the Muslim sense of moral superiority.

In a study on the reflection of the Arab–Israeli conflict in Israeli school textbooks, social psychologist Daniel Bar-Tal has shown that societies involved in intractable conflicts develop suitable psychological conditions that enable them to cope successfully with the conflict situation. The beliefs that support the development of these psychological conditions include convictions on the justice of one's cause, delegitimization of the adversary, a positive self-perception and feelings of victimhood. Together, these beliefs constitute an ethos that supports the continuation of the conflict, and they are reflected in language, stereotypes, images, myths and collective memory.[12] As part of the conflict with Israel, Arab societies engaged in a process of raising historical, theological, national, social, cultural and existential reasons to justify their own end goals. Among others, anti-Semitism was drummed up as a means to delegitimize and dehumanize "the other."

The institutionalization of symbols and values in enemies' discourse is not unique to the social dynamics of the Arab–Israeli conflict. At the heart of this process is a split between us–them and good–evil, which polarizes and rigidifies the perception of "the other" and heaps upon it even contradictory traits and allegations, a phenomenon particularly typical to anti-Semitism.[13] Participants in

---

11 Suha Taji-Farouki, "A Contemporary Construction of the Jews in the Qur'an: A Review of Muhammad Sayyid Tantawi's *Banu Isra'il fi al-Qur'an wa al-Sunna* and 'Afif 'Abd al-Fattah Tabbara's *al-Yahud fi al-Qur'an*," in Ron Nettler and Suha Taji-Farouki (eds.), *Muslim–Jewish Encounters, Intellectual Tradition and Modern Politics*, Oxford: 1998, p. 15. The argument that Arabs cannot be anti-Semites because they too are Semites is false, as the term anti-Semitism served as the pseudo-scientific euphemism for animosity towards the Jews, and was applied only to them, see Yehuda Bauer, "In Search of a Definition of Antisemitism," in Michael Brown (ed.), *Approaches to Anti-Semitism*, New York: 1994, pp. 10–24.

12 Daniel Bar-Tal, "Societal Beliefs in Times of Intractable Conflict: The Israeli Case," *International Journal of Conflict Management*, vol. 9 (1998), pp. 22–50; Daniel Bar-Tal, "From Intractable Conflict Through Conflict Resolution to Reconciliation: Psychological Analysis," *Political Psychology*, vol. 21, no. 2 (June 2000) pp. 351–65.

13 Social psychologists and anthropologists, as well as social scientists and historians, vastly explore the issues of prejudice and stereotyping and their dynamics in situations of peace and conflict. See for instance: Robert A. Rubinstein and Mary LeCron Foster (eds.), *The Social Dynamics of Peace and Conflict. Culture in International Security*, Boulder, CO and

conflicts tend to subscribe to ethnocentric "mirror images" of their own country and enemy countries – in which one's own country is believed to be moral, whereas one's enemy is believed to be diabolical. Likewise, the actions of one's own country are attributed to altruistic motives, but identical actions taken by an enemy are perceived as self-serving. "Cognitive consistency" is thus maintained through the application of "double standards" in judging the morality of actions by each group. Ethnocentric beliefs may be maintained by simply ignoring contradictory evidence and by decreasing the salience of information that is inconsistent with a moral self-image and a diabolical enemy-image.[14]

Another factor affecting the Arab Holocaust discourse is the widespread appeal of conspiracy theories in Middle Eastern political culture and their application on Jews and Zionists.[15] Conspiracy theories attribute every development in history to the machination of a powerful group of individuals who master the course of history. The conspirators have common attributes, among these their unusually strong sense of solidarity, which is often aimed against all other groups. Conspiracy theories reduce dissonant perceptions and complexities to seductive patterns of orderliness. They define dangers and bring a welcome rational order to unpleasant and erratic events. They relieve groups or individuals in "stress situations" from the pressure of reality, since they provide an explanation for their suffering, and occasionally exempt them from responsibility for their predicament. Conspiracy theories enjoy great appeal in times of crisis or deep frustration that characterize modern Arab societies. The central role of the Jews in European conspiracy theories served as a source of inspiration and a "factual basis" for applying conspiracy theories to the Jews and Zionism in the context of the Middle East conflict.[16] Thus, the notorious anti-Jewish tract the

London: 1988; Daniel Bar-Tal et al. (eds.), *Stereotyping and Prejudice: Changing Conceptions*, New York: 1989; Ofer Zur, "The Love of Hating: The Psychology of Enmity," *History of European Ideas*, vol. 13, no. 4 (1991), pp. 345–69; Vilho Harle, "On the Concepts of the 'Other' and the 'Enemy'," *History of European Ideas*, vol. 19, nos. 1–3 (1994), pp. 27–34; Robert S. Wistrich (ed.), *Demonizing the Other. Antisemitism, Racism, and Xenophobia*, Amsterdam: 1999.

14   G. N. Sande, George R. Goethals, Lisa Ferarri and Leila T. Worth, "Value Guided Attributions: Maintaining the Moral Self Image and the Diabolical Enemy-Image," *Journal of Social Issues*, vol. 45 (1989), pp. 91–3.

15   For conspiracy theories in the Middle East, see Daniel Pipes, *The Hidden Hand: Middle East Fears of Conspiracy*, New York: 1996.

16   For an analysis of conspiracy theories as a theme of social psychology, see Carl F. Grauman and Serge Moscovici (eds.), *Changing Conceptions of Conspiracy*, London and Berlin: 1987. On the role attributed to Jews, see Henri Zukier, "The Conspiratorial Imperative: Medieval Jewry in Western Europe," in ibid., pp. 87–105; Leon Poliakov, "The Topic of the Jewish Conspiracy in Russia (1905–1920), and the International Consequences," in ibid., pp. 105–14.

Protocols of the Elders of Zion acquired widespread popularity in the Arab world, as it provided a reasonable explanation for the Zionist phenomenon and its successes in the Middle East.[17] Conspiracy theories were also applied to deny the Holocaust as a Zionist hoax, to justify it or to accuse the Zionists of conspiring with the Nazis in killing the Jews.

The Arab Holocaust discourse dealt very little, if at all, with the events of the Holocaust itself. Arab writers were not interested in the processes that led to the Nazi decision to exterminate the Jews, and hardly ever referred to the actual murder act. They were uninterested in the experience of the victims in the ghettoes or concentration and death camps, in the ways the Jews tried to cope with their horrible situation or in the inhuman and insoluble dilemmas which they faced. The only exception was a few books that highlighted cases of actual or fabricated Jewish collaboration with the Nazis. Rather, the Arab Holocaust discourse focused on the political implications of the Holocaust for the Arab–Israeli conflict, on what was perceived as Israeli instrumentalization of the Holocaust and on its ramifications for the status of Israel and Zionism.

The limited interest in the Holocaust per se, or more correctly its instrumentalization in the Arab discourse, is also reflected in the terms used to describe it. The great richness of Arabic notwithstanding, the Arab discourse continued to use the general term "persecutions" (*idtihad*) to describe the Nazi extermination of the Jews, despite the unfolding data about it, thus implicitly minimizing its horror. From the 1980s onward, the transliterated English term "Hulukast" came into frequent use, while its Arabic literal equivalent *muhraqa*, which appeared in the 1980s, became more common only from the 1990s.[18]

However, in addressing the Holocaust as part of the ongoing polemic with Israel and Zionism, writers from all over the Arab world and from all ideological trends adopted a set of terms, ideas, concepts and arguments which fed and reinforced each other since 1948, thereby creating a certain intellectual or ideological climate and a community of discourse. Ever since the 1990s this discourse has been enriched by debates and controversies over Arab attitudes toward the Holocaust.

17 On the Protocols in general, see Norman Cohn, *Warrant for Genocide: The Myth of the Jewish World Conspiracy and the Protocols of the Elders of Zion*, Choco, CA: 1982 and Stephen Eric Bronner, *A Rumor about the Jews: Reflections on Antisemitism and the Protocols of the Learned Elders of Zion*, New York: 2000. On their dissemination in the Middle East, see Esther Webman, "The Adoption of *The Protocols* in the Arab Discourse on the Arab–Israeli Conflict, Zionism and the Jews" in idem (ed.), The Protocols of Elders of Zion: *The One-Hundred Year Myth and its Impact* (forthcoming).

18 The first reference we encountered for the term *muhraqa* appeared in Nizam 'Abbasi, *al-'Alaqat al-sahyuniyya – al-naziyya wa-athriha 'ala filastin wa-harakat al-taharrur al-'arabi, 1933–1945*, Kuwait: 1984, p. 11.

In contrast to the scholarly academic research of the Holocaust that developed in the West, which became a fully fledged field in the general study of history, and the construction of new categories and terms such as victimhood, collective memory and commemoration, the Holocaust never achieved a systematic and comprehensive study in the Arab world, unlike Zionism, Judaism and Israel, which are extensively researched, often with a clear ideological slant.[19] Stemming perhaps from a reluctance to deal with an issue which might arouse sympathy toward the enemy, this phenomenon could also be partly explained by a broader trend of Arab historiography, which hardly deals with non-Arab issues and topics, as manifested, *inter alia*, in the dearth of translations of foreign texts into Arabic.[20]

Aside from writings by notorious Holocaust deniers, such as Robert Faurisson, and subsequently Roger Garaudy, *Les Mythes Fondateures de La Politique Israelienne*, that have been translated into Arabic[21] and have received wide and favorable responses in the Arab media, only a few books claiming the academic mantle have been published on this topic in Arabic. These books deal with only one narrow aspect of the Holocaust – the relations between the Zionists and the Nazis before and during the war – and they suffer from a heavy political bias, reflected in their highly problematic use of historical evidence. One such book is Mahmud 'Abbas's *The Other Side: The Secret Relations between Nazism and Zionism*, published in 1984 and based on his PhD dissertation submitted in 1981 in Moscow.[22] Another book is *Zionism, Nazism and the End of History* by 'Abd al-Wahhab al-Masiri,[23] an Egyptian expert on Judaic studies and a prolific writer on Judaism and Zionism.

Only in the mid 1990s did the first Arab voices challenging aspects of the traditional Arab approach to the Holocaust begin to be heard and a new, more open public discussion on the representation of the Holocaust and its ramifications on Arab political and cultural concepts evolve. Many of those who

19   See Hasan Barari, "Arab Scholarship on Israel: A Critical Assessment," US Institute of Peace: Project Report Summary, 2 May 2007, ww.usip.org/fellows/reports/2007/-5-2_barari.html.

20   For the paucity of translations from foreign languages into Arabic, see United Nations Development Programme, *Arab Human Development Report 2002*, www.undp.org/rbas/ahdr/english.html. For the preoccupation of Egyptian historiography, the most developed one in the Arab world, in domestic issues, see Anthony Gorman, *Historians, State and Politics in Twentieth Century Egypt: Contesting the Nation*, London: 2003.

21   Rober Furisun, *al-Ukdhuba al-ta'rikhiyya: hal fi'lan qutila sitta malayin yahud*, Beirut: 1988; Rujih Jarudi, *al-Asatir al-mu'assisa lil-siyasa al-isra'iliyya*, Cairo: 1998.

22   Mahmud 'Abbas, *al-Wajh al-akhar: al-'alaqat al-sirriyya bayna al-naziyya wal-sahyuniyya*, Amman: 1984.

23   'Abd al-Wahhab al-Masiri, *al-Sahyuniyya, al-naziyya wa-nihayat al-ta'rikh*, Cairo: 1997.

triggered this initial debate were Arab academics and intellectuals living in the West who were familiar with the significance of the Holocaust in post-war western culture, enriching the discourse on the Holocaust in the Arab world. At the same time, Arab scholarship began to deal academically with World War II, focusing mainly on Nazi Germany's relations with the region. Most prominent among them were Wajih 'Abd al-Sadiq 'Atiq on the secret contacts between Egypt's King Faruq and Nazi Germany, the Jordanian 'Ali Muhafaza and the Palestinian 'Abd al-Rahman 'Abd al-Ghani, who had dealt extensively with Nazi Germany's policy toward Palestine while using a wide array of archival sources.[24] However, no original Arab research on the Holocaust had been done, and repeated calls since the 1990s to conduct independent Arab studies remained unheeded.

This lacuna in the study of Arab representation of the Holocaust has not been filled by Western or Israeli historians. Various scholars, among them Bernard Lewis, Yehoshafat Harkabi and Deborah Lipstadt, have treated it only in a fragmentary and cursory manner.[25] Lewis referred to it as part of his work on Arab anti-Semitism and Harkabi within his study on the Arab–Israel conflict, whereas Lipstadt focused on Holocaust deniers in the West. Rivka Yadlin's study on Egyptian anti-Semitism, ten years after the signing of the 1979 Egyptian–Israeli peace treaty, only touched it,[26] and Yosef Nevo discussed few aspects of the Palestinian discourse on the Holocaust.[27] In some of his works, Ilan Gur-Ze'ev touched upon the use of the Holocaust as a metaphor in the Palestinian and Israeli discourses, but minimized the dominant negative aspects of the Palestinian discourse and overemphasized the importance of the new Arab approach.[28] 'Azmi Bishara's article, presented first at a conference in Germany in 1993 and later published in Hebrew, is still the only study that sought to deal with the

---

24   Wajih 'Abd al-Sadiq 'Atiq, *al-Malik Faruq wa-almaniya al-naziyya: khams sanawat min al-'alaqa al-sirriyya*, Cairo: 1992; 'Ali Muhafaza, *al-'Alaqat al-almaniyya al-filastiniyya min insha' mutraniyyat al-quds … wahatta nihayat al-harb al-'alamiyya al-thaniya, 1841–1945*, Beirut: 1981; 'Abd al-Rahman 'Abd al-Ghani, *Almaniya al-naziyya wa-filastin 1933–1945*, Beirut: 1995.

25   Deborah Lipstadt, *Denying the Holocaust: The Growing Assault on Truth and Memory*, New York: 1993; Lewis, *Semites and Anti-Semites*, pp. 15–16, 217–18; Harkabi, *Arab Attitudes*, pp. 277–80.

26   Rivka Yadlin, *An Arrogant Oppressive Spirit: Anti-Zionism as Anti-Judaism in Egypt*, New York: 1989.

27   Yosef Nevo, "The Attitude of Arab Palestinian Historiography toward the Germans and the Holocaust," in *Remembering for the Future*, Oxford: 1989, vol. 2, pp. 2241–50.

28   Ruth Linn and Ilan Gur-Ze'ev, "Holocaust as Metaphor: Arab and Israeli Use of the Same Symbol," *Metaphor and Symbolic Activity*, vol. 11, no. 3 (1996), pp. 195–206; Ilan Gur-Ze'ev, *Philosophy, Politics and Education in Israel*, Haifa: 1999 (Hebrew), pp. 98–122.

Arab representation of the Holocaust in a comprehensive way, although its academic importance was diminished due to the positions he had adopted in the political debate that the article instigated.

The present study aims to fill this gap by analyzing patterns of continuity and change in the representation of the Holocaust in the Arab world since the end of World War II. It examines the evolvement and characteristics of the Arab intellectual and public discourse on this topic and the causes shaping it. It pursues a historical approach, but it draws heavily on the vast literature on the representation of the Holocaust, on discourse analysis, and on the relations between text and context, as well as on studies of prejudices and stereotyping in societies in conflict. However, in view of the vast scope of sources, we have focused on the leading cultural and political centers that produced this discourse: Egypt, Lebanon and the Palestinian–Jordanian arena, with occasional references to other countries.

The study and representation of the Holocaust – a methodological note

The magnitude, horror and unprecedented nature of the Holocaust have produced since 1945 an immense and ever-growing body of scholarship in the fields of history, philosophy, psychology and literature. The Holocaust has also been examined in the context of modernism, modern technology, the structure of modern society and the weaknesses of the human soul vis-à-vis social pressures or totalitarian authority, or even political and ideological disputes unrelated to the Jews. New narratives and new ways of representing Nazism and the Final Solution have emerged, raising new questions on the fragility of human morality, on aesthetics and on the limits of representation.[29] In view of the dimensions of the Nazis' crimes and their efforts to camouflage them, the obligation to record this past seems even more compelling, stated historian Saul Friedlander. Such a postulate implies, naturally, the notion that this record should not be distorted or banalized by grossly inadequate representations. Some claim to truth appears particularly imperative, and it suggests that "there are limits to representation *which should not but can be easily transgressed* "[30] [original emphasis].

---

29   For discussions of these issues, see Neil Levi and Michael Rothberg, *The Holocaust: Theoretical Readings*, New Brunswick: 2003; Omer Bartov, *Murder in Our Midst: The Holocaust, Industrial Killing, and Representation*, New York: 1996. For a philosophical grappling with the Holocaust, see Emil L. Fackenheim, *God's Presence in History: Jewish Affirmations and Philosophical Reflections*, New York: 1970; Berel Lang (ed.), *Philosophy and the Holocaust*, New York: 1984/85.

30   Saul Friedlander, "Introduction," in S. Friedlander (ed.), *Probing the Limits of Representation: Nazism and the "Final Solution"*, Cambridge: 1992, p. 3.

Two broad types of study have characterized the historical research.[31] Comprehensive studies that sought to encompass the Holocaust as a whole have addressed questions such as the essence of the Holocaust, its historical background and causes, the process of extermination as well as its periodization. Most historians who contributed to the comprehensive study of the Holocaust were Jews.[32] The second type has focused on specific aspects and regions, addressing issues such as the processes leading to the Nazi decision in late 1941 to exterminate all the Jews; various aspects of the extermination process; Jewish life under Nazi rule; Jewish responses to Nazi policies – from acquiescence to rebellion; rescue efforts; the relations between the Jews and the non-Jewish population; and the reactions of the free world, including the Jewish communities, to news on the extermination.

Historical studies on the Holocaust have divided their subject matter into three groups: perpetrators, victims and bystanders. Perpetrators were the murderers and persecutors of all kinds, from the Nazi apparatus to collaborators from other nationalities who took part in the actual murder process. The victims were the Jews who were subject to extermination; and the bystanders were all those, inside or outside Europe, who were not involved in the acts of murder but witnessed them or heard of them. Most of them were indifferent; many exploited the situation for economic gain; others helped the victims, risking their lives in hiding Jews; and some even sought to obstruct the killing process. This categorization, initiated by historian Raul Hilberg,[33] created a certain unplanned "division of labor" among historians. German and non-Jewish American historians have focused on the perpetrators, whereas only Jewish and Israeli historians have dealt with the victims.[34]

---

31   For the characterization of Holocaust research, see Dan Michman "'The Holocaust' in the Eyes of Historians: The Problem of Conceptualization, Periodization, and Explanation," *Modern Judaism*, vol. 15, no. 3 (October 1995), pp. 233–64.

32   The most notable among these books are: Leon Poliakov, *Bréviaire de la haine: Le IIIe reich et les juifs*, Paris: 1951; Gerald Reitlinger, *The Final Solution: The Attempt to Exterminate the Jews of Europe, 1939–1945*, London: 1953; Raul Hilberg, *The Destruction of the European Jews*, London: 1961; Lucy S. Dawidowicz, *The War against the Jews, 1933–45*, New York: 1975; Martin Gilbert, *The Holocaust: The Jewish Tragedy*, London: 1986.

33   Raul Hilberg, *Perpetrators, Victims, Bystanders. The Jewish Catastrophe 1933–1945*, London: 1995, pp. ix–xii.

34   Lucy S. Dawidowicz, *The Holocaust and the Historians*, Cambridge, MA: 1981. Jewish historians have studied the perpetrators and bystanders too, but non-Jews refrained from studying the Jews. The volume of German historiography on the perpetrators is too vast to be discussed here. For a comprehensive survey and analysis, see Ian Kershaw, *The Nazi Dictatorship: Problems and Perspectives of Interpretation*, London, which has come out in several editions since 1985.

One segment of Holocaust research, carried out particularly in Israel, dealt with the attitudes and activities of the Zionist movement and the Jewish community in Palestine during the Holocaust. It included issues such as Zionist positions and policy vis-à-vis Nazi authorities during the 1930s; the conduct of the Zionist leadership during the war and its rescue efforts; the Zionist idea and enterprise as a solution to the Jewish problem; and attitudes towards the survivors in the post-war period. All of these issues elicited sharp controversies inside Israel as part of a broader debate between advocates of post-Zionism and Zionist historians, and were reflected in the Arab Holocaust discourse.[35]

The present research, dealing with post-war representations and public discourse, pursues the approach often employed in the study of intellectual history, combining the examination of text and context.[36] We have regarded each text as autonomous, isolating references to and statements on the Holocaust, analyzing its terminology with its symbolic cultural undertones and meanings. Concurrently, we have sought to place them, as much as we could, in the immediate socio-political contexts in which they were produced in order to evaluate them within the background of broader intellectual and ideological context. This has enabled us to overcome the limitations of written texts as sole representatives of the Arab public discourse.

Our analysis in this book is based on several premises. The first is that Arab attitudes have been influenced and shaped by developments in the Arab–Israeli conflict. Another major assumption is that the discourse on the Holocaust is more dominant among the Palestinians as compared with other Arab countries, because they were directly affected by the establishment of Israel, both collectively and individually, and harbor a deep sense of national tragedy. A third proposition is that the peace process launched in the early 1990s may have ushered in changes in the Arab perceptions of the conflict and hence of the Holocaust, which may reflect acceptance of Israel's existence and of the Jewish tragedy.

---

35   For post-Zionist views, see for example, Tom Segev, *The Seventh Million, Israelis and the Holocaust*, Jerusalem: 1991 (Hebrew). For refutations of the post-Zionist allegations, see Tuvia Friling "Ben Gurion and the Holocaust of European Jewry 1939–1945: A Stereotype Reexamined," *Yad Vashem Studies*, vol. 18 (1987), pp. 199–232; T. Friling, *An Arrow in the Mist: Ben-Gurion the Yishuv Leadership and Rescue Efforts during the Holocasut*, 2 vols., Beer Sheva: 1998 (Hebrew); Shabtai Teveth, *Ben-Gurion and the Holocaust*, New York: 1996; Dina Porat, *The Blue and the Yellow Stars of David: The Zionist Leadership in Palestine and the Holocaust, 1939–1945*, Cambridge: 1990, pp. 1–16, 49–63; Yoav Gelber, "Zionist Policy and the Fate of European Jewry," *Yad Vashem Studies*, vol. 13 (1979), pp. 169–210.

36   Quentin Skinner, "Meaning and Understanding in the History of Ideas," *History and Theory*, vol. 8, no. 1 (1969), pp. 3–4.

We examine whether Arab attitudes to the Holocaust form a monolithic, coherent narrative with identical symbols and images, and what factors affected them. Are there differences between the attitudes of conservative and revolutionary or moderate and radical states, or among rival ideological trends – Islamists as opposed to leftists? Is there a divergence between government positions and intellectual discourse? Or between intellectuals living in the Middle East and those residing in the West, who continue to contribute to the ongoing political and intellectual debate in the Arab world? And lastly, have there been any changes in the narrative of the Holocaust since 1945?

We would contend that the Arab discourse did not develop into one coherent narrative. Rather it is more appropriate to speak of a reservoir and a repertoire of references, arguments and images that are scattered and intertwined in the vast literature on the conflict, Zionism, Judaism, World War II, and the history of Arab attitudes toward Nazi Germany and the National-Socialist Party. This reservoir does not represent a specific intellectual trend, but rather serves Islamists, nationalists and leftists, who draw elements from it almost indiscriminately, and incorporate them into their discourse. For example, Arab leftists and liberals distance themselves from Nazi and Fascist ideologies and most of them do not share themes of Holocaust denial, but they do not shun using the Zionist–Nazi equation or the Zionist–Nazi cooperation theme. The existence of the broad repertoire and the situation of an intractable conflict occasionally led writers to employ contradictory claims and arguments, such as denial of the Holocaust and justification of Hitler's measures against the Jews.[37]

Although the Arab–Israeli conflict has undergone significant developments since 1945, and a vast quantity of academic and popular literature has been published on the Holocaust both in the West and in Israel, there is a high degree of continuity in the Arab discourse throughout the period, and many motifs and terms used by authors during the 1950s are still used today. This phenomenon is far from being unique to the Arab discourse, as paradigms and perceptions in situations of conflicts do not keep pace with the reality of changing political circumstances.[38] Only since 1990 have different voices challenged the advisability of this discourse but failed to undermine the dominant Arab approach to the Holocaust. However, we will show that the Arab discourse was attentive to developments in the perception of the Holocaust in Israel and the West. The more the Holocaust occupied a significant role in Jewish and Israeli consciousness,

---

37 For this phenomenon, see Zur, "The Love of Hating," p. 360; Peter Worsley, "Images of the Other," in R. A. Rubinstein and M. LeCron Foster (eds.), *The Social Dynamics of Peace and Conflict. Culture in International Security*, Boulder, CO: 1988, p. 69.

38 Worsley, ibid.

the more it was denied and rejected as a unique Jewish phenomenon – a process which reached its peak in 2001 in the Durban World Conference against Racism, Racial Discrimination, Xenophobia and Related Intolerance.

While this study focuses on the production of the Arab Holocaust discourse, we have sought as much as possible to assess its reception among broader constituencies, despite the difficulty of doing so in non-democratic societies, where tools for evaluating public opinion are not developed. As Gershoni and Jankowski note, authors publish for audiences or "consumers" of ideas. Consumers do not necessarily consume everything presented to them. They sometimes reject the ideas conveyed to them or reinterpret them in terms that suit their norms and values and complement their modes of feeling and expression. Such reconstruction may reverberate back to the producers of texts, thereby creating a dialogue or a "feedback loop" between the producers and consumers of ideas, leading writers to reflect prevalent opinions and adapt their production to meet the demand of their consumers.[39]

The present study is divided into two parts. The first part covers four case studies that were instrumental in the evolution of the Arab Holocaust discourse. In this part, the analysis of the texts is performed strictly against the eventual context, and the discourse reflects the period and its specificities. Chapter 1 discusses the years 1945–1948, the formative years of the evolution of the Holocaust discourse, discerning two broad approaches. One acknowledged to various degrees the Jewish suffering in the war, but argued that the Arabs should not pay its price through the establishment of a Jewish state in Palestine; the second tended to minimize the extent of the Holocaust, particularly as the conflict in Palestine intensified.

Chapter 2 analyzes Arab responses to the 1952 German–Israeli reparation agreement. The initial reaction did not deny the Jewish suffering under Nazi rule, nor the moral case for German reparations to individual Jews, but contested Israel's right to represent the Jewish people and considered the Palestinian refugees as more entitled to compensations for their suffering through the Jews. Failure to convince the Germans and the western powers of the connection between the two compensation issues led Arab writers to denounce the agreement as the epitome of Jewish/Zionist exploitation of the Holocaust – a claim which eventually became a major theme in the representation of the Holocaust.

Chapter 3 deals with the Eichmann affair, which served as a watershed in the crystallization of the Arab Holocaust discourse. After a brief silence over the Israeli announcement of Eichmann's capture, Arab states launched a propaganda

---

39   Israel Gershoni and James P. Jankowski, *Redefining the Egyptian Nation, 1930–1945*, Cambridge: 1995, pp. xii–xiii.

campaign against Israel, presenting it as a violator of international law. The coverage of the affair in the Arab media was extensive, but focused mainly on its political implications and circumvented the accumulated body of evidence about the atrocities committed during the Holocaust. While explicit justification of Eichmann's activities was rare, there was an underlying sympathy with the man. Despite minor nuances by leftist writers, there already existed consensual boundaries which did not allow dissenting voices.

Chapter 4 analyzes the Arab public debate on the Holocaust in relation to the changing Catholic attitudes toward the Jews. While the Holocaust was in the background of the deliberations of the Second Vatican Council, convened from 1962 to 1965, which exonerated the Jews of the murder of Jesus, Arab writers focused mainly on the political benefits that Israel might reap, and addressed the Holocaust only haphazardly. By contrast, Arab reactions to Pope John Paul II's apology for the Church's anti-Semitism that contributed to the Holocaust referred much more to the Holocaust, reflecting the emergence of the new discourse, and at the same time the growing Arab resentment at the increasing importance of the Holocaust in western public and intellectual discourse.

In the second part, we have chosen a thematic analysis of the Arab Holocaust discourse across the period under review, examining patterns of continuity and change. Here, the chronological lines are sometimes blurred, in view of the persistent continuity within each theme, alongside its evolution. Chapter 5 traces the various manifestations of Holocaust denial in the Arab world, from outright denial of any wrong-doing to the Jews during World War II to acceptance of Jewish suffering, with the attempt to minimize the number of Jewish victims or the existence of a Nazi policy to exterminate them. It surveys the various techniques used to deny the Holocaust and the impact of western Holocaust deniers on Arab writings. Arab Holocaust denial stemmed from the belief that the Holocaust was a major factor underlying western support for Israel's existence and its denial would deprive Israel of legitimacy.

Chapter 6 examines expressions justifying the Holocaust, which became less prevalent from the 1970s on, when the conflict with Israel ceased to be perceived by most Arab countries as an existential one. Intrigued by the events of the Holocaust, on the one hand, and by the establishment of Israel on the other, Arab writers sought explanations in Jewish history and in Jewish mentality in order to show that the Jews were responsible for the calamities that befell them. Justification was manifested in three categories: pseudo-historical descriptions of the activities of the Jews throughout history; short-term explanations alleging Jewish conspiracies during the period preceding the war; and retroactive justification based on alleged conduct by the State of Israel.

Chapter 7 discusses the common theme, shared by writers of all political shades, of equating Zionism with Nazism as another means to delegitimize Zionism. The comparisons have two major themes: one claims resemblance between Zionist and Nazi ideologies, contending that both are based on a belief in racial superiority and territorial expansion. The most sophisticated representation of this theme has been made since the mid 1970s by 'Abd al-Wahhab al-Masiri, who purports that both movements are natural outgrowths of the materialist western civilization. The second equates Israel's treatment of the Palestinians to that of the Jews by the Nazis, or describes Israel as worse than the Nazis, thereby indirectly minimizing Nazi crimes.

Chapter 8 analyzes the allegations of cooperation, or even collusion, between the Zionists and the Nazis in the extermination of European Jewry. These claims have been common to all political trends and have become the Palestinian and Syrian semi-official narratives of the Holocaust. The main argument revolves around the joint interest during the 1930s between the Nazis, who wanted to rid themselves of the Jews at all costs, and the Zionists, who wanted Jewish immigration to Palestine.

Chapter 9 assumes that there is a correlation between Arab perceptions of Nazi Germany and World War II and the representation of the Holocaust. Hence, it examines several interrelated themes, such as the shifting attitudes toward Nazi Germany and World War II in Arab historiography and public discourse since the end of the war. Thus, World War II was perceived as a war not between good and absolute evil, but between two equally evil imperialist camps. Particular attention is given to the grappling of Palestinian writers with the collaboration of former Paletinian leader Hajj Amin al-Husayni with the Nazis during the war.

Chapter 10 demonstrates how the terminology and discourse of the Holocaust affected the Palestinian discourse on the 1948 Palestinian Nakba from its very beginning. The Palestinians perceived themselves as the "victims of the victims" and hence adopted the Holocaust as a criterion for many of their political, cultural and artistic decisions. The question of victimization and victimhood, which was crucial for the representation of Jewish experience and identity, became a major component of the Palestinian narrative, and the Nakba was reconstructed, wittingly or unwittingly, like the Holocaust, as a founding myth to shape the memory of the past as well as to serve as a springboard for a hopeful future.

Chapter 11 analyzes the emergence of a new approach to the Holocaust in the wake of the peace process in the early 1990s. The peace process called for revision of the traditional Arab perception and for unequivocal acknowledgement of the suffering of the Jews. Although not set as a prerequisite, this acknowledgement was to be met by recognition of the suffering of the Palestinians on the part of the Israelis, in order to facilitate reconciliation and coexistence between the two peoples. This alternative trend, promoted by a small group of liberal intellectuals highly influenced by western culture, led to a more open discussion of the Holocaust in the Arab media, but also to a more radical identification with Holocaust deniers by its opponents.

The sources we have used – books, newspapers, periodicals and internet sites – reveal the different dimensions of public debate, political, historical, theological and ethical, and reflect the specific attitudes of the various ideological currents. These sources were produced by statesmen, politicians, journalists, publicists, academics and military men. These people could be considered "secondary intellectuals," the cultural agents who mediate between the high rung of intellectuals and the public at large, reproducing and popularizing "high" culture and disseminating it.[40] They were more tuned to the public mood, and echoed the dominant ideological and political trends: mainstream nationalists, Islamists and leftists. We have therefore tried, not always successfully, to characterize each writer in order to identify correlations between certain views and ideological currents. Occasionally, the lines demarcating these three currents are fluid, as many nationalists are devout Muslims and at times incorporate Islamist terminology, and leftists identify as nationalists. Concurrently, writers of all ideological trends advocate similar views and positions.

We have relied heavily on the Arab press – both government and opposition – published in and outside the Middle East, and on a broad array of publicist and historical literature, which dealt with a variety of issues, not only those concerned with the Middle East conflict. We have assumed that the government media reflect the positions of their respective governments and define the limits of the legitimate discourse, shared also by the opposition media. The political and cultural changes in the Middle East following the 1967 war, the declining legitimacy of Arab revolutionary regimes and the emergence of Islamic movements as important social and political players prompted various governments, most notably Egypt, to allow greater latitude on certain issues in the public discourse. The emergence of an opposition press or of Arab newspapers in Europe, and particularly the appearance of new means of communication, such as satellite TV and the internet in the 1990s, added to the pluralism of the Arab intellectual discourse. Yet, this pluralism has functioned within clear boundaries formerly set up by governments and, since the signing of the peace treaties be-

---

40   Gershoni and Jankowski, *Redefining*, p. xxxiii; Edward Shils, *The Intellectuals and the Powers and Other Essays*, Chicago: 1972, pp. 154–6.

tween Israel and Egypt, Jordan and the PLO, by intellectuals who maintained their unrelenting hostility to Israel.

The large number of books which discuss the Holocaust, and the frequent references to it in the media, indicate that the discourse on the Holocaust has struck roots and is far from being a marginal phenomenon. We found out that occasionally books used sharper language and arguments than newspapers, but the recurring terminology, themes and arguments in books, newspapers, TV and the internet indicate the existence of widespread precepts as well as mutual influence that these means of communication exert on each other.

We do not pretend to have covered every single statement uttered or written on the Holocaust in the Arab world. Still, we are convinced that the picture presented in this study is comprehensive and reflects faithfully the Arab discourse and the main approaches that characterize it. The likelihood that major themes or motifs have eluded us is small. The major Arab sources tend to cite each other, and had new or exceptional views emerge they would have elicited responses, as was the case with the alternative discourse that emerged during the 1990s. The wide range of sources and the broad range of topics which include references to the Holocaust reflect the scope of the discourse and the validity of the picture we present. Finally, the criticism of the dominant traditional Arab attitudes toward the Holocaust by proponents of the new approach provided further confirmation to the validity of our account.

The paucity of Arab literature dealing specifically with the Holocaust, and the vast number of scattered references to it, required a meticulous work of digging and choosing the most important and recurring ones, a choice which often depends on personal judgment. There is a subjective dimension in every historical study, and the subject position of the scholar dictates to a great extent his or her writing. There are no methodological tools by which a neutral, objective or transparent account of events can be made. In addition to this general problem, there is another dilemma in our specific case, defined by Israeli scholar Yehoshafat Harkabi as the "blindness of involvement," which may harm the scholar's ability to separate the understanding, assessment and presentation of his material from his emotional and cultural baggage. This is even more so in discussing, as Jews and Israelis, the representation of the Holocaust in the Arab world. Harkabi confessed that in the process of his research he taught himself to empathize with his subject matter. Years later, American Holocaust scholar Christopher Browning attested to a similar process.[41] Aware of our shortcom-

---

41   Harkabi, *Arab Attitudes*, p. xx; Christopher R. Browning, "German Memory, Judicial Interrogation, and Historical Reconstruction: Writing Perpetrator History from Post-War Testimony," in S. Friedlander (ed.), *Probing the Limits*, pp. 22–36.

ing, we have tried to maintain, as much as possible, a dispassionate approach. We have allowed our sources to speak for themselves, and in few cases where we thought that the lay reader might be misled by the distortion of historical evidence, we have confronted them with scholarly studies that present a more accurate account of history. We have tried to interpret rather than to argue with the texts, but there has been no escape from analyzing them within the limits of Holocaust representation, according to universal academic standards.

PART I

HISTORICAL CASE STUDIES

1

RELUCTANTLY INVOLVED "BYSTANDERS": 1945–48

The period 1945–48 was of critical importance to the evolution of the Arab Holocaust discourse, laying its foundations in light of intensive global and regional political developments. The year 1945 not only marked the end of a tragic epoch in world history, and Jewish history in particular, but also stood for new hopes for a better world order. For the Arabs it marked growing expectations for a new dawn of independence and sovereignty. Egypt, which had declared war against Germany only on 26 February 1945, and with a slim parliamentary majority, rejoiced over the victory of democracy and of universal liberal and humanitarian values, while emphasizing its own contribution to the Allies' war effort. Although concerned first and foremost with its domestic affairs and primarily with the attainment of complete liberation from British domination, Egypt was deeply involved in all issues pertaining to the Arab lands, including the Palestine question, especially in view of her leading role in the newly established Arab League.[1]

For the Palestinians this was a period of political reawakening after the crushing of their 1936–39 rebellion and the political stagnation of the war years. Unlike other Arab countries, the Palestinians did not have a formally recognized leadership following the 1937 dissolution of the Arab Higher Committee (AHC) and the deportation of some of its members. After the war few of them were permitted to return to Palestine, and the foremost Palestinian leader Hajj Amin al-Husayni sought asylum in Egypt after having spent the war years in Germany. The major political issue that preoccupied the Palestinians immediately after the war was the intensified Zionist challenge, resulting in the British

---

[1]   For the Egyptian post-war political and social atmosphere, see James P. Jankowski, *Nasser's Egypt, Arab Nationalism and the United Arab Republic*, Boulder, CO and London: 2001, pp. 11–41; 'Izza Wahbi, *Tajribat al-dimuqratiyya al-libiraliyya fi misr*, Cairo: 1985; P. G. Vatikiotis, *The History of Modern Egypt: from Muhammad Ali to Mubarak*, London: 1991, pp. 345–74.

withdrawal from Palestine and the subsequent outbreak of the 1948 war, ending up with a colossal Arab defeat and the disintegration of Palestinian society.

The evolving 1945–48 discourse clearly shows that the Arabs were aware of the scope of the Holocaust. It was during this period that the conceptual foundation was laid and an instrumentalist approach towards the Holocaust was formed. The events of 1948 – the establishment of the State of Israel, the Palestine tragedy and the subsequent intensification of the Arab–Israeli conflict – further contributed to its crystallization, reflecting at the time a high correlation between political developments and certain emerging motifs in the representation of the Holocaust. Moreover, many of the motifs that would dominate the debate in future years appeared already at that time.

Due to the sequence of events, two historical links emerged in the Arab discussion of the Holocaust: one was the causal relationship between the Holocaust that ended in 1945 and the birth of Israel in 1948 – a question which still engages Israeli historians; the second was the association between the Holocaust and the Palestinian defeat, defined as Nakba (catastrophe).[2]

The Arabs, aside from a few political figures who had thrown in their lot with Germany,[3] had been "bystanders" during the war, observing the Jewish tragedy from afar. In the Introduction we proposed to apply the term "bystanders" to the Arabs, a term originally designed to denote those at the scene of the crime who saw "and pretended to see no evil and hear no evil which they confronted."[4] The Arabs were "bystanders" of a different kind. They were not present at the scene and were never part of it, but they were aware of what had been happening, and they reluctantly became involved in the efforts to resolve the problems created by the war. As the solution of the Jewish problem increasingly led to the establishment of a Jewish state in Palestine, Arab preoccupation with the Holocaust focused on its political ramifications, on its perceived political ex-

---

2   On the meaning of the term and its significance to the reconstruction of Palestinian identity, see Esther Webman, "The Evolution of a Founding Myth – The Nakba and Its Fluctuating Meaning," in Meir Litvak (ed.), *Palestinian Collective Memory and National Identity*, New York: 2009 (forthcoming); "Reflections on al-Nakba," *Journal of Palestine Studies*, vol. 28, no. 1 (Autumn 1998), pp. 5–35.

3   Mainly Hajj Amin al-Husayni the Mufti of Palestine, former Iraqi Prime Minister Rashid 'Ali al-Gaylani and their associates, who fled to Germany in 1941 and collaborated with the Nazis; see also below, Chapter 9.

4   "Bystanders Are Not Innocent," *The Wiener Library Bulletin*, vol. 2, nos. 2–3 (January–March 1948), p. 1; Hilberg, *Perpetrators, Victims, Bystanders*, pp. ix–xii. The Maghreb states: Libya, Tunisia, Algeria and Morocco, are excluded from this discussion, as they were under the Axis occupation, and the Arab population's reaction to the persecution of the local Jewish population was diversified. See: Robert Satloff, *Among the Righteous: Lost Stories from the Holocaust's Long Reach into Arab Lands*, New York: 2006.

ploitation by the Zionists and on minimizing its scope. Alongside the discussion on the Holocaust and its effects, there evolved a broader literature, laden with anti-Semitic motifs, on Jewish and Zionist history. Worldwide processes such as the Nuremberg trials of the Nazi leaders provided an additional context which contributed to the evolution of the Arab attitude to the Holocaust.

Terminology

The choice of words and terms to describe an event is always of great importance. Naming is "one of the first hermeneutical moves regarding an event," in James Young's words. The naming "frames and remembers events, even as it determines particular knowledge of the event," and "mold[s] events in the image of its culture's particular understanding of events."[5] Moreover, it can be assumed that changes in the terminology attached to an event reflect transformations in its meaning and perception.

The Egyptian press received and covered the regular news on the course of the war and subsequent political developments. *Al-Ahram*, the leading Egyptian and Arab daily at the time, reported it at length. Alongside these news accounts, information on Nazi brutality in the death and concentration camps arrived as well. The paper described what the Allied troops saw day after day and in great detail, including news items that dealt specifically with the Jews. As such, it had to deal with the variety of terms used by American and European reporters to describe Nazi activities. This vocabulary was well represented in the Egyptian press, which did not resort to euphemisms but rather imported the general and detailed terms from English into Arabic.

As early as January 1945 we can find the terms "massacres of the Jews" (*madhabih al-yahud*),[6] "German atrocities" (*faza'i' al-alman*) with a precise, detailed description of the "death mill" (*ma'mal al-mawt*), which included gas chambers (*ghuraf al-ghaz*) and crematoria to get rid of bodies (*ghuraf al-muhraqa lil-ta-khallus min al-juthath*).[7] Other reports spoke of the "selections" (*'amaliyyat al-farz*), crematoria (*ifran*) in the Nazi "death factories" (*masani' al-mawt*), as well as of the German death camps (*mu'askarat al-i'dam al-almaniyya*), the "camps of horrors" (*mu'askarat al-ahwal*) and "torture camps" (*mu'askarat al-ta'dhib*).[8]

5   James E. Young, *Writing and Rewriting the Holocaust. Narrative and the Consequences of Interpretation*, Bloomington, IN: 1988, pp. 87–8.

6   *Al-Ahram*, 3 January, 9 March, 22 April 1945. See also the articles in *al-Hilal*, August 1944, pp. 462–6, and 'Abdallah 'Inan in *al-Thaqafa*, 20 February 1945, pp. 210–212. The term *madhbaha* (massacre) appears numerous other times as well.

7   *Al-Ahram*, 5 January, 24 July, 14 December 1945.

8   *Al-Ahram*, 15, 29 March, 19 September 1945.

Phrases such as "human carnage" (*majzara bashariyya*), extermination (*ibada*) in crematoria (*mahariq*), or Nazi brutality (*quswat al-nazi*) were also frequent.[9] Nor did the paper ignore the Jewish identity of the victims, speaking of "Jewish martyrs" (*shuhada' al-yahud*) or of the "catastrophe of the Jews" (*nakbat al-yahud*). Reporting on memorial ceremonies held by the Jews in Palestine in March 1945, *al-Ahram* pointed to the "Jewish casualties of the Axis which led to the extermination of a third of the Jewish people." Later it quoted US President Harry Truman saying that 5,700,000 Jews perished by the Nazis.[10]

Even the Islamic monthly, *al-Liwa'*, which was not sympathetic of the Jews, described their fate as a "great blow" (*qar'a 'uzma*). Nazi activities in Buchenwald were described as the "lowest point that humanity has reached" (*asfal ma balaghathu al-insaniyya min inhitat*). Likewise, when the trial of Joseph Kramer, commander of Bergen Belsen camp, opened on 17 September 1945, *al-Ahram* stated that "the most repulsive human tragedy" (*absha' ma'sa insaniyya*) of this generation had unfolded.[11]

All of these phrases were faithful to their English originals and did not differ from those that appeared in the Hebrew press at the time, as there was no broad and universally acceptable term to denote the Jewish catastrophe. Although the terms "Holocaust" and "Shoah" appeared during the war, they acquired their meaning as denoting the Jewish suffering and genocide under the Nazis only years later.[12] The idioms *faza'i'* and *idtihad* became entrenched in Arab terminology at the time, just as their respective English equivalents, "atrocities" and "persecutions," were most common in official documents and journalistic writings, referring not only to the Jews but to all victims of Nazism. However, the term *idtihad* (persecution) was also used in reports concerning attacks on Jews who had returned to Poland after the war.[13] Since *idtihad* in the post-war period did not mean extermination, the continued unqualified use of the term in the Arab discourse might be interpreted as minimization of the gravity of the preceding Jewish tragedy, especially in light of the wealth of the Arabic language.

Concurrently a parallel terminology emerged in reference to the Jewish refugees, which reflected the evolution of Arab attitudes towards the Holocaust and its survivors. In the early reports appearing towards the end of the war the word "refugees" (*laji'un*) was most frequently used to denote Jewish and other dis-

---

9   *Al-Ahram*, 15 March, 8 April, 8 May 1945.

10   *Al-Ahram*, 3, 12 January, 9, 21 March, 15, 31 May, 27 June 1945, 27 February 1946.

11   *Al-Ahram*, 29 April, 19 September 1945.

12   Jon Petrie, "The Secular Word 'Holocaust': Scholarly Sacralization, Twentieth Century Meanings," www.berkeleyinternet.com/holocaust.

13   *Al-Difa'*, 13, 14 January, 24 March 1946.

placed persons in Europe. But once the issue of Jewish immigration to Palestine entered center stage, the term "immigrants" (*muhajirun*) most often replaced it.[14] Still, the use of the term "refugees" rather than "survivors" in discussions of Jews among contemporary European politicians may have also helped to blur the difference between the fate of the Jews as compared with that of other peoples during the war.[15] Occasionally, the survivors were described as "the Jewish remnants in Europe" (*ma baqiya fi uruba min al-yahud*), as "victims of Nazi madness" (*dahaya al-junun al-nazi*), as "survivors of Nazi horrors" (*al-najun min ahwal al-nazi*) and as "the dispersed refugees" (*al-laji'un al-musharradun*).[16] At the same time, refugees who wanted to immigrate to Palestine were merely alluded to as Jews, ignoring the reasons and circumstances behind their situation. Indeed, as the idea of settling the refugees in Palestine acquired support in the recommendations of the Anglo-American Committee of Inquiry and the UN Special Commission of Palestine (UNSCOP) and, finally, in the 29 November 1947 UN Partition resolution (see below), the terminology regarding the refugees became increasingly uniform, with the persecuted refugees turning into "armed" (*musallahun*) and "illegal" (*ghayr shar'iyun*) immigrants. Although "illegal immigrants" was the common phrase used by the British to denote Jewish survivors who sought to enter Palestine despite the British ban, the change in the Arab discourse was not coincidental, as it reflected the transformation of views on the Holocaust and on Jewish immigration.

Factual reports on Nazi atrocities

The question of what Arab leaders and intellectuals, who influenced and shaped the public discourse, knew is critical in examining their attitudes to and representations of the Holocaust.[17] As shown above, the Egyptian press covered the developments in Europe, including the fate of the Jews, quite extensively. The interest in and reference to the Jews under Nazi rule stemmed not only from the narrow prism of the evolving Middle Eastern conflict. What Israel Gershoni has shown in his study of Egyptian attitudes towards Fascism and Nazism during

---

14   *Al-Ahram*, 23 May, 13 July, 6 August 1945, 24, 27, 29 May 1946; Muhammad 'Awad Muhammad, "mas'alat Filastin," *al-Thaqafa*, 10 April 1945, p. 391.

15   *Al-Difa'*, 19 January 1945, 13, 14 January, 24 March 1946; *al-Ahram*, 2 April 1945.

16   *Al-Ahram*, 29 March, 10 August, 15, 28, 29, 30 October, 15, 16 November 1945, 24 May, 19 June 1946.

17   This is also a central question in the study of the Holocaust in general, and particularly regarding the attitudes of the Jews in Palestine during the war; see Walter Laqueur, *The Terrible Secret*, Harmondsworth, UK: 1982; Porat, *The Blue and the Yellow Stars of David*, pp. 1–16, 49–63.

the 1930s[18] was true of the post-war period as well. Egyptian interest evolved, at least among those agents of culture who led the public debate, from a sense of affiliation with the victorious camp and its cultural values, a position which Islamist writers, most notably Sayyid Qutb, often criticized for the unjustified trust placed in Britain and the US.[19] In this atmosphere, reports on the Allies' advances and on the horrors they encountered in the Nazi camps, or coverage of the Nuremberg Trials, were not unusual, and the same could be said of the references to the Jews.

Most of the descriptions cited here came from the Egyptian dailies, mainly *al-Ahram* and *al-Misri*, which published regular news items on the war. The coverage was factual, mostly neutral, usually quoting news agencies or foreign sources. In some cases the dailies dispatched their own correspondents to the scene of events.[20] The number of editorials that reflected a clear political or ideological stance was relatively small. Still, the mere transmission of data was of great importance. The dailies, as Gershoni says, "sought to express the voice of the safe center and the lowest common [political] denominator" in order to reach out to the large literate, but not necessarily intellectual, public.[21] Indeed, they reflected in their coverage the changes in attitudes toward the Jews as the conflict escalated, although they lagged behind the periodicals that were un-equivocally identified with specific political and ideological orientations.

The picture arising from these reports leaves no doubt as to the level of knowl-edge of Nazi atrocities in general and those against the Jews in particular. The Jews had been subjected to persecutions, *al-Hilal* wrote, whenever there were troubles, but in the long history of persecutions, "there were none more com-prehensive and harsh (*shamilan wa muhkaman*) as the German Nazi ones."[22] An *al-Ahram* editorial appealing to Middle Eastern Jews to raise their voice on the question of Palestine (see below) described Hitler as "the greatest enemy of the Jews" (*'adu al-yahud al-akbar*), and "German-Aryan racism" (*al-'unsuriyya al-germaniyya al-ariyya*) as trampling on peoples' rights and blood, adding that the Jews suffered from it more than at any other time in the past.[23]

As Allied forces advanced, *al-Ahram*'s correspondent in London wrote, the amount of evidence of Nazi criminal (*ijramiyya*) acts is increasing, and the Brit-

18   Israel Gershoni, *Light in the Shadow: Egypt and Fascism, 1922-1937*, Tel Aviv: 1999, pp. 120, 128–9, 147, 165, 205–7, 225–6, 238, 264–5.

19   See Qutb in *al-Risala*, 21 October 1946, pp. 1155–7, and 17 February 1947, pp. 190–2; 'Abd al-Majid Nafi', *Baritaniya al-naziyya*, Cairo: 1947.

20   See below the series of articles on the Nuremberg trials.

21   Gershoni, *Light in the Shadow*, pp. 215–16.

22   *Al-Hilal*, January–February 1945, p. 16.

23   *Al-Ahram*, 4 November 1945.

ish press is full of reports and pictures of these atrocities. The paper also produced a report submitted by a delegation from the House of Lords on its visit to Nazi camps, which described Nazi plans to exterminate (*al-qada' 'ala*) all inmates in Buchenwald through hunger and barbaric brutality. It added that 51,572 inmates were killed there, 1,700 in January and February 1945.[24]

Another account, relating to Dachau, spoke of the liberation of 32,000 political prisoners and the discovery of 50 train cars loaded with corpses, torturing equipment and parts of crematoria, which the Nazis had sought to get rid of so that no trace of their activities would be found. What was found in this camp, it added, reflected Germans actions in other centers of crime as well.[25] A small news item on the "Jewish catastrophe in Holland" said that the Germans murdered more than 95,000 Dutch Jews who had been deported during the war.[26]

News on the Holocaust from areas liberated by the Soviets was also reported extensively. A story titled "Jewish massacres (*madhabih*) in Yugoslavia," described in detail the gassing and mass shooting of 16,000 Jews in the Backa camp. The reporter added that out of the 80,000 Jews who had lived in Yugoslavia before the war, only 4,000 survived.[27]

Two other stories in March 1945 cited testimonies by Russian prisoners and women who survived Auschwitz on mass executions in "special gas chambers," emphasizing that Hitler himself was behind the well-organized plan for these murders. The story described the daily schedule of the prisoners, the selection and gassing process, as well as the stench of burning corpses that hovered all over the place.[28] A subsequent story cited from *Pravda*, which described the activities of the SS leader Heinrich Himmler, "the first executioner" (*al-jallad al-awwal*), spoke also of Auschwitz adding that around four million "Russians, Frenchmen, Belgians, Dutch, Czech, Rumanians, Hungarians and Yugoslavs" perished there. The omission of Jews was not incidental, as Soviet sources never regarded the Jews as a distinct group of victims.[29]

24　*Al-Ahram*, 22, 23, 29 April, 3 May 1945.

25　*Al-Ahram*, 1 May 1945. See also the stories on German medical experiments in French prisons, in *al-Ahram*, 5 January, 8 April and *al-Muqtataf*, August 1945, p. 262.

26　*Al-Ahram*, 27 June 1945.

27　*Al-Ahram*, 3 January 1945.

28　*Al-Ahram*, 15, 21 March 1945.

29　*Al-Ahram*, 8 May 1945. In the Nuremberg trials, for instance, the Soviet prosecutors did not distinguish between the suffering of the Jews and that of other civilians in the Soviet Union. For details on the Soviet attitude in the Nuremberg trials, see Michael R. Marrus, "The Holocaust at Nuremberg," *Yad Vashem Studies*, vol. 26 (1998), pp. 5–41. Ever since the 1980s historians have concluded that round 1,400,000 people, most of them Jews, were murdered in Auschwitz.

Al-Ahram also informed its readers of the reactions of the Jews in Palestine to the Holocaust. "The Jews of Palestine declared a week of mourning for the martyrs (*shuhada*) who perished by the Nazi massacre, which led to the extermination of a third of the Jewish people in Europe," it reported in March 1945.[30] A story from Tel Aviv in October said that the Jewish Agency had compiled a list of 60,000 displaced in Europe. The first part of the list, it added, dealt with those who had survived the death camps of Belsen, Buchenwald and Dachau, as well as survivors from cities such as Rome and Milan. The second part contained names of survivors from Poland, the Baltic States, Hungary, Transylvania, Yugoslavia, Czechoslovakia, Holland and Italy.[31]

In comparison to the Egyptian press, the Palestinian press provided little coverage of Nazi policies against the Jews, although it is clear that it was aware of them. *Filastin* reported a story on the conference of the victorious Allied leaders in Potsdam in May 1945, citing a report criticizing the mistreatment in the displaced-persons camps of Jews who had suffered "torture, hunger and disease," in Hitler's "detention camps." *Al-Difa'*, another major Palestinian paper of the time, cited on 23 December 1945 a letter by Anwar Nusayba, a member of the Arab Office in London, that blamed the Jewish Agency for the deaths of 5,700,000 Jews during the war. Another story commending the status of the Jews in Bulgaria noted that "they were not exterminated" during the war. Hence, it appears that *al-Difa'* was aware of the extermination of Jews during the war.[32]

Revelations on the Holocaust from the Nuremberg Trials

The coverage of the Nuremberg trials of the leaders of the Nazi regime between October 1945 and November 1946 sheds additional light on the representation of the Holocaust in the Arab world, even though "the Holocaust was by no means at the [trials'] center of attention."[33] The murder of Jews was not discussed as a distinct subject, but was included in the more comprehensive category of war crimes and crimes against humanity. These were new terms, coined during the course of the trials, and are considered, in a broader historical perspective, among their major achievements. Although the extermination of the Jews was not a distinct category in the indictment, the fate of the Jews did hold "a crucial place" in the trials and was mentioned in each of the indictments' clauses. Thus,

---

30 *Al-Ahram*, 9, 15 March 1945.

31 *Al-Ahram*, 30 October 1945.

32 *Filastin*, 23 May 1945; *al-Difa'*, 3, 22 July, 8 November, 23 December 1945, 13 May, 25 June 1946.

33 Marrus, "The Holocaust," p. 6.

the indictment and the trials were, in Marrus's words, a turning point in the inculcation of Holocaust consciousness in the western world. For the first time, spokesmen of the Allies outlined to a non-Jewish forum the Nazi anti-Jewish policy, backed by comprehensive documentation and ample evidence.[34]

There was a considerable difference in the coverage of the trials between the Palestinian dailies *Filastin* and *al-Difa'*, and the Egyptian *al-Ahram*. In general, the coverage in *al-Ahram* was more comprehensive, in its discussion of the meaning of the trials, in reviewing the charges, and in reproducing the testimonies against and by the defendants. By contrast, we could not find editorials or opinion columns in the two Palestinian newspapers that dealt with the trials. No doubt, part of the difference was due to the fact that *al-Ahram* was a bigger paper and better established financially. Moreover, from reading the various newspapers one gets the impression that *al-Ahram* adopted a moral position vis-à-vis the defendants, both in style and in content, while the Palestinian dailies were more ambiguous. Whereas *al-Ahram* used the phrases "Nazi war criminals," *Filastin* called them "criminals," or occasionally the more neutral "Nazi leaders" (*zu'ama' al-naziyya*). *Al-Difa'* was even less committal, naming them "Nazi chiefs" (*aqtab al-naziyya*). Even more revealing are the headlines given to the various stories: those in *al-Ahram* emphasized the charges against the Nazi leaders, as in "The accusations against Göring and Ribbentrop," "The charges against Frank and Streicher," or "Dönitz accused of waging an inhumane war."[35] The headlines in *al-Difa'* and *Filastin*, by contrast, gave more emphasis to the testimonies of the defendants themselves, saying "Göring's discussions of policy with poets and musicians"; "Kaitel seeks testimonies from Churchill and Field Marshall Alexander, while Göring asks for a testimony from Halifax and Cadogen for the Nuremberg Trial"; "Göring seeks to clear his colleagues by assuming full responsibility"; and so on.[36]

As far as contents were concerned, *al-Difa'* used only news agency reports. It reviewed the charges raised against the Nazi leaders, but devoted more space to the defense arguments of the accused. Equally conspicuous was its emphasis on

---

34 Ibid. According to some estimates, over 800 Nazi documents and the testimonies of 33 witnesses dealt with the Jewish tragedy; Jacob Robinson and Henry Sachs (eds.), *The Holocaust: The Nuremberg Evidence*, Jerusalem: 1976, cited in Marrus, "The Holocaust," p. 41.

35 *Al-Ahram*, 9, 11, 15 17 January 1946. Reichsmarshall Herman Göring was Hitler's No. 2 man during most of the Nazi era and commander of the German air force. Hans Frank was head of the General Government, the German government in Poland, where the largest Jewish community had lived and perished. Ribbentrop was the German foreign minister during 1936–45. Karl Dönitz was commander of the German Navy and Hitler's successor as Führer.

36 *Al-Difa'*, 4 November, 20 December 1945, 19 March, 2, 11, 24 April, 6 June 1946.

the conduct of the defendants rather than on the charges. Thus, it elaborated in depicting Göring's cynical smiles and his ambition to be recognized as the most senior defendant, in describing Rudolf Hess's real or feigned mental illness and the total disregard that the defendants showed towards the testimonies against them. These anecdotal descriptions appeared also in the Egyptian papers, but these contained more substantial details on the prosecution.

Likewise, the coverage of the Jewish issue was much more extensive in *al-Ahram* than in the two Palestinian dailies. Thus, in a report from 3 January 1946 under the secondary headline "mass killing of Jews," *al-Ahram* cited in detail the testimony of the German engineer Herman Friedrich Grabe on the murder of thousands of Jews near the Dubno airport in Poland in October 1942. It also reviewed the charges raised against Ernst Kaltenbrunner, chief of the Reich Security Head Office (RSHA), including a testimony that Kaltenbrunner was present during the gassing of prisoners (not necessarily Jewish) in Mauthausen. *Filastin* reported the charges against Kaltenbrunner briefly, noting that they referred to the murder of Jewish inmates. It also cited the testimony of a "German engineer" that described the execution of 1,000 Jews. The story in *al-Difaʿ*, on the other hand, only mentioned the charges against Kaltenbrunner, and devoted much more space to describing the conduct of the defendants in court. On the following day, *al-Ahram* cited the testimony of Dieter Wisliceny, one of Adolf Eichmann's senior deputies, that reviewed Nazi policy against the Jews and Himmler's 1942 order on the extermination of the Jewish race, and recounted Wisliceny's role in the deportation of Hungarian and Greek Jews to the "death camps" in Poland. In addition, *al-Ahram* reported the testimony by Otto Ohlendorf, commander of Einsatzgruppe D, who confessed that 90,000 Jews "were exterminated" (*ubidu*) under his command in Russia. The coverage in *Filastin* and *al-Difaʿ* was much more succinct. While *Filastin* mentioned Wisliceny's testimony in one sentence, *al-Difaʿ* dedicated one sentence to Ohlendorf's. Both papers omitted the testimony by the Auschwitz commandant, Rudolf Höss, who appeared as a defense witness for Kaltenbrunner, but gave a detailed description of the extermination of the Jews in the camp.[37]

The same phenomenon was repeated in at least two other cases. *Al-Ahram* published an article containing the detailed testimony of a French underground activist about her deportation to Auschwitz. It included descriptions of the gas chambers, sterilization of women and operations conducted on babies born to Jewish mothers, without mentioning whether or not they were Jewish. Both

---

37   *Al-Ahram, Filastin, al-Difaʿ*, 3, 4 January. On Höss's testimony, see Marrus, "The Holocaust," pp. 29–30.

Filastin and *al-Difa‘* ignored the testimony altogether.[38] *Al-Difa‘* did report Göring's admission of his instruction to Reinhard Heydrich, then commander of the RSHA, to carry out "all necessary measures" for the execution of the "final solution" of the Jewish question. It also mentioned the request by Alfred Rosenberg, chief ideologue of the Nazi party, to bring to the court anti-Semitic literature in order to explain his world-view, but both references were extremely concise.[39] *Al-Ahram* devoted a story, albeit a short one, to Julius Streicher, editor of the extremely anti-Semitic daily *Der Stürmer*, whose title was "Enemy No. 1 of the Jews." It used this epithet until Streicher's execution. *Al-Ahram*'s distinct attitude was particularly glaring, during the trials' final days, when reporting the verdicts and the executions of the leading defendants.[40]

Of particular interest in the Egyptian coverage of the trials was a series of articles by an unnamed Egyptian correspondent in Germany, who sent eight stories during February 1946 based on interviews, in addition to his impressions from the Nuremberg trials and from visits to German cities and Nazi camps. Clearly, in these reports the writer allowed himself to express his personal views much more explicitly than in the regular news items. His second story focused on the Nazi leaders. He labeled Göring as "arch-criminal, a criminal of the brutal kind" (*shaykh al-mujrimin, mujrim min al-naw‘ al-qasi*). Rudolf Höss appeared to him as being in "total loss of consciousness as far as human heart and conscience are concerned." Alfred Rosenberg, "the philosopher of Nazism," he wrote, replied to a question on the reasons for the persecution of the Jews that he only wanted to do them good, since his "policy was intended to consolidate Jewish rights in Palestine." Rosenberg, he added, detested Muslims and sought to erect a border between the Germans and "these Asiatic barbarians" that would not be crossed "for a thousand years." He depicted Streicher as the "implacable enemy of the Jews and Judaism," adding that his genius was manifested in the boycott which he organized against Jewish stores and when he shifted from "boycott to a policy of uprooting" (*qat‘ al-dabir*).[41]

In his account of his visit to Dachau, the "grave of the living" (*maqbarat al-ahya*), he recounted how people doubted, during the war, the news coming from Switzerland on the atrocities taking place in that camp, attributed them

---

38   *Al-Ahram, Filastin, al-Difa‘*, 29 January 1946. See also the reference to the massacres of the Jews in Wilna, reported in *al-Ahram* on 1 March and ignored by the two Palestinian dailies.

39   *Al-Difa‘*, 3, 4 January, 4 March, 10, 17 April 1946.

40   *Al-Ahram*, 22 May, 22 October, 20, 24 November, 14 December 1945, 11 January, 2 October 1946. See also *al-Thaqafa*, 12 March 1946, p. 23, and *al-Misri*, 16 December 1945.

41   *Al-Ahram*, 3 February 1946.

to the Jews, or considered them as "figments of the imagination" (*shubuhat*). "I saw with my own eyes that the matter is neither Jewish lies (*akadhib*) nor Anglo-Saxon propaganda," as some people said, but rather "the most horrifying crimes that human beings had ever or will ever commit."[42]

However, the correspondent described the trials as "a dangerous precedent and a revolution in the history of law." If the idea was to try the Nazis for what they had committed after August 1939, that is, "invasion of foreign lands without warning, the destruction of cities and their civilian population, the destruction of countries, the extermination of populations, torturing people, killing of hostages, the theft of treasures and the expertise in methods of killings, then it is the duty of anyone who wishes future generations well." But it would be a "crippled (*'arja'*) justice" if the goal was to punish them for annexing Austria and eliminating Czechoslovakia, without putting on the bench with them those who had enabled them to do so, "sang the praises of their good intentions," and promised to look the other way so long as they left the West and turned their forces eastward.[43]

In the article that followed, the correspondent sharpened his criticism when he divided the charges to three categories: 1) the organized theft of property and money by the Nazis in the lands they had occupied; 2) tortures, deportations and murders; and 3) conspiracies against the peace, including violations of agreements, attacks on neutral countries, accelerated rearmament for the war, and the training of a fifth column. The first were offenses all punishable by accepted laws all over the world; therefore, there was no need to set up a special international military tribunal to try them, since such crimes were committed in all European countries, and each had special tribunals to try them. As for the crimes of the third category, they did not go beyond the traditional and recognized rights of statesmen from the dawn of history, and were not an invention of the Nazis. Could any of the four states which constitute the court, he asked, convince those "members of this generation who had not lost their mind" that they did not commit identical actions of which the Nazis were accused, particularly as they stood idle during the annexation of Austria and had given their consent to the swallowing up of Czechoslovakia in the 1938 Munich Agreement. But supporters of the trials knew that people forget quickly and the "burning desire (*shahwa*) today requires the hanging of the Nazis and the oppression of the Germans."[44]

42   *Al-Ahram*, 7 February 1946.
43   *Al-Ahram*, 4 February 1946.
44   *Al-Ahram*, 7 February 1946.

The writer's criticism of the third category of crimes is not without foundation, since the violation of international treaties and the launching of unjustified wars were very common in international relations for centuries. Likewise,
it is true that the Nazis were not the first to violate agreements. However, these
charges seemed to overlook the true essence of Nazism, which was more than
an aggressive and expansionist foreign policy. Had Nazism been merely that, it
would not have been much different from other types of imperialism that the
world had known since the beginning of history. The real essence of Nazism
was, first and foremost, its racist world-view, which advocated the extermination of "inferior" populations and culminated in the extermination of the Jews
and the Roma, and in mass murders elsewhere. The writer's reservations about
the establishment of a special court for Nazi crimes, the magnitude of which
he realized, show that he seemed to have missed, like others in the West who
argued against the court, the unique and exceptional significance of the Nazi
crimes, which were defined for the first time in history as "crimes against humanity."

The Palestinian newspapers' lack of interest in the Jewish question during the
trials was not coincidental. The difference in interest between the Egyptian and
the Palestinian dailies stemmed perhaps from the increasingly strong Palestinian view that linked the Holocaust to the growing Zionist challenge. Presumably, growing anger among the Palestinians at British and American positions
vis-à-vis the Zionists undermined the willingness of the newspapers' editors to
identify with their other policies. None of the three papers published editorial
comment on the verdicts and their implementation.[45]

Between political and humanitarian positions: official attitudes towards the Holocaust

Alongside the neutral reports described above, the Holocaust became a matter
of growing concern to Arab leaders, due to political developments even before
the war had ended. The Zionist calls for abolition of the restrictions imposed by
the 1939 British White Paper on Jewish immigration to Palestine,[46] invigorated

---

45   *Al-Ahram, al-Difaʻ, Filastin*, 2, 3, 4, 6, 9, 10, 16, 17, 18, 20 October 1946.

46   The White Paper was issued on 17 May 1939 as a statement of British policy in Pales-
      tine. It restricted Jewish immigration to Palestine to 15,000 Jews annually for five years,
      banned the sale of land to Jews and stipulated the establishment of an independent state
      in Palestine after five years, which would have meant an Arab-dominated state. The White
      Paper signified the British withdrawal from the 1917 Balfour Declaration that spoke of
      the establishment of a "Jewish national home" in Palestine and was adopted as the basis of
      the British mandate in Palestine by the League of Nations in 1921; see Michael J. Cohen,
      From Palestine to Israel: From Mandate to Independence, London: 1988, pp. 101–28.

by the emerging problem of Jewish survivors and refugees in Europe, in addition to Zionist demands to establish a Jewish state in Palestine, obliged them to address the Holocaust, directly or indirectly. The issue became increasingly important following President Truman's proposal on 16 August 1945 to allow the immigration of 100,000 displaced Jews to Palestine, the establishment of the Anglo-American Committee on 13 November 1945 and its subsequent recommendations, as well as the formation of UNSCOP on 15 May 1947, which led to the UN resolution on the partition of Palestine on 29 November that year, and the establishment of the State of Israel on 14 May 1948.[47] The Holocaust and "pangs of conscience" in western countries over the failure to help the Jews during the war seemed to play a role in rallying international support for the Zionist solution to the plight of the Jews.

Three basic approaches could be discerned in the Arab leaders' references to the Holocaust. One recognized the Jewish tragedy but sought to separate the issue of the survivors from the question of Palestine and to present it as an international humanitarian problem, in the solution of which the Arabs could take part. Thus, it was possible to express compassion for Jewish pain, together with unequivocal rejection of Jewish immigration to Palestine and of Zionist political goals. Such an attitude was congruent with the aspirations of Arab elites to be integrated in the post-war world order and with their awareness of Arab dependency on Britain and the US. The second approach sought to understate or minimize the meaning of the Holocaust by using ambiguous terms or depicting it as a problem of civil discrimination, going so far as partial or complete Holocaust denial. The third blamed the Zionist movement or the Jews for what befell them.

An early and blatant manifestation of the first approach appeared in the conversation of the Saudi monarch, 'Abd al-'Aziz ibn Sa'ud, with President Roosevelt on 14 February 1945. William Eddy, then US Minister in Saudi Arabia, who served as the interpreter, wrote that Roosevelt started the conversation by raising the need to find a solution to the question of the Jews who "had suffered indescribable horrors at the hands of the Nazis." The King's reply was "give them and their descendants the choicest land and homes of the Germans who had oppressed them." He agreed that the Jews had good reasons for distrusting the Germans, but the Allies, who were about to destroy Nazi power, would be strong enough to protect the victims of Nazism. "Make the enemy and the oppressor pay; that is how we Arabs wage war. Amend should be made by the criminal, not by the innocent bystander. What injury have Arabs done to the

---

47   Martin Gilbert, *Exile and Return: The Emergence of Jewish Statehood*, London: 1978, pp. 258–309; Michael J. Cohen, *Truman and Israel*, Berkeley: 1990, pp. 59ff.

Jews of Europe? It is the 'Christian' Germans who stole their homes and lives. Let the Germans pay." He subsequently went on to say, "This over-solicitude for the Germans was incomprehensible to an uneducated Bedouin with whom friends get more considerations than enemies." The King's final remark was that it was Arab custom to "distribute survivors and victims of battle among the victorious tribes in accordance with their number and their supply of food and water." In the Allied camp there were fifty countries, while Palestine was a small, poor land and had already been assigned more than its quota of European refugees.[48]

Subsequently, in his talk with members of the Anglo-American Committee that dealt with the question of the Jewish refugees, Ibn Sa'ud spoke explicitly about the Jews who had been exterminated during the war, but reiterated his position on the total separation between the Jewish question and the Palestine problem. Significantly, in contrast to his understanding of the Jewish plight during his conversation with Roosevelt, he told the commission that "the hatred between the Jews and Muslims was not born in this generation, but was an old enmity which existed for thousands of years," mentioned even in God's own words in the Qur'an.[49]

Egypt confronted the Holocaust in early 1945, when the representative of the Jewish Agency in Paris, David Shealtiel, asked it to issue 250 visas for 200 children and 50 adults from Europe on their way to Palestine. Initially Egypt declined the request but, following the intercession of the British Ambassador Lord Killearn, it awarded the visas as "an exceptional case." *Al-Ahram* referred apparently to this information when it revealed in May 1945 that Egypt had rejected a request to grant 300 visas to Jewish immigrants from France to Palestine, without mentioning whether they were refugees or Holocaust survivors. The prominent Egyptian journalist Hasanayn Haykal disclosed in 1988 that Egyptian Jews published ads in Egyptian newspapers informing of the formation of transit camps for Jews "persecuted by the Nazis." These camps, he explained were designed for short stays before their arrival in Palestine.[50]

---

48   William A. Eddy, *F.D.R. Meets Ibn Saud*, New York: 1954, pp. 34–5. See also, Charles Bohlen, *Witness to History*, New York: 1973, p. 203. Palestinian writers repeated the same arguments during the 1980s and 1990s; see, for instance, Khalid Shimali in *al-Istiqlal*, 20 December 1989 and 'Azzam Tamimi, an Islamist Palestinian writer who argued that if Europe and the US felt guilty over the Jewish fate in the Holocaust, it would have behooved them morally to give the Jews a state in Europe or America rather than in Palestine at the expense of the Palestinians; Azzam Tamimi, "Questions on the 50th Anniversary of Israel's Creation," www.ptimes.com/articles/htm.

49   Azriel Karlibakh (ed.), *The Anglo-American Commission on Palestine*, Tel Aviv: 1946 (Hebrew), vol. 2, p. 417.

50   Shealtiel to the Egyptian Consulate, 9 February 1945; Consulate to the Jewish Agency,

Concerned by Zionist activities in the US, Egyptian Prime Minister Mustafa Nahhas reported to the Egyptian Senate on 9 August 1944 that he had interceded with senior US officials to avoid making any promises and statements in favor of the Zionist movement. He disclosed that, already in January and March 1943, he had instructed the Egyptian Chargé d'Affaires in Washington to submit memoranda to the US Secretary of State on this issue, when he feared that British–American consultations on finding ways to end the persecution of Jews in Europe and to get them out of Europe might lead to increased immigration to Palestine. He stressed in those letters the need to preserve the status quo in Palestine and to direct European Jews to other countries that could absorb them, according to their economic capabilities.

Nahhas mentioned two other protests to the American government in February and March 1944 following news of the proposals of two US Senators to nullify the White Paper and open Palestine for Jewish immigration. He argued that the proposal was in contravention of the spirit of the Atlantic Charter and would leave negative impressions in all Arab countries. He also launched protests, as head of the Wafd Party, against the 1944 election platforms of the Democratic and Republican parties, arguing that they meant the usurpation of Palestine from its Arab owners and giving it to the Jews.[51] In none of these statements did Nahhas address explicitly the Holocaust or its political ramifications, although it is clear that he was aware of it and of the dilemmas it created. He held the West responsible for its occurrence and highlighted the moral superiority of the Arab and Muslim worlds that had extended their help to the Jews persecuted in the West in the past.

The protocols of the preparatory committee to the Arab League from 7 October 1944, of which was Nahhas the first signatory, expressed the "deep sympathy as every other person would, with the sorrow of the Jews over the atrocities and suffering they had endured in Europe due to the activities of certain dictatorial states." However, the committee warned against confusing the Jewish issue with Zionism, since "nothing would be more arbitrary or unjust than solving the problem of the Jews in Europe by creating another injustice in which the Arabs of Palestine ... shall be the victims."[52]

Paris, 23 February 1945; from the British Foreign Ministry to the Ambassador in Cairo, 25 April 1945; Killearn's statement on the approval, 6 June 1945, enclosed in FO 371/51198, WR 985/985/48, WR 1682/985/48; *al-Ahram*, 23 May 1945; "Mohamed Hassanein Heikal: Reflections on a Nation in Crisis, 1948," *Journal of Palestine Studies*, vol. 18, no. 1 (August 1988), p. 113.

51   *Al-Balagh*, 10 August 1944; HZ/21/2566, "Nahhas Pasha on his actions in favor of the Arabs of Eretz Yisrael," 25 August 1944 (Hebrew).

52   FO 371/45237, Resolutions of the Preparatory Committee to the General Arab Confer-

'Abd al-Rahman al-'Azzam, Secretary General of the Arab League, espoused a similar view in his response on 19 August 1945 to President Truman's proposal to enable the greatest possible immigration of Jews to Palestine in coordination and understanding with the British and the Arabs. "We thought that the fall of the dictatorship in Europe and Asia would enable the great democracies to provide a just treatment to the problem emanating from the persecution (*idtihad*) of the Jews." The Arabs reject unlimited immigration that would put an end to their "national entity" in Palestine. Such immigration would harm Arab interests and lives and would be a "pointless factor" in solving the universal Jewish problem, he said, adding that "the persecution (*idtihad*) and oppression of the Arabs in order to help persecuted Jews is not a moral or practical solution."[53] By using the same term "persecution" to describe both the fate of the Jews during the war and the future fate of the Arabs, should a Jewish state be established, 'Azzam, wittingly or unwittingly, minimized the significance of the Holocaust to expulsion and discrimination of minorities. Returning from Europe in November, 'Azzam further blurred the extent of the Jewish calamity during the war by saying that the Jews were not the only people who had suffered in Europe, and that the entire continent – men, women and children – were experiencing "hard times."[54]

British Foreign Secretary Ernest Bevin's reference to the Holocaust in his announcement on 13 November 1945 regarding the establishment of the Anglo-American Committee obliged the Arab leaders to confront the Holocaust issue once again. Bevin maintained that the Jewish issue was a major humanitarian problem, as one "could not accept the view that the Jews should be driven out from Europe" or would not be allowed to live there free of discrimination. The Palestine problem was different, he contended, and consequently, the commission's main duty was to study the political, economic and social conditions in Palestine in all matters concerning Jewish immigration and settlement there; to study the state of the Jews in European cities where they had been victims of Nazi and Fascist persecution; and to listen to the views of influential Jewish and Arab representatives in order to formulate recommendations which the

---

ence, 7 October 1944. On 10 March 1945 Prince 'Abd al-Ilah, the Iraqi Crown Prince, sent a personal letter to British Prime Minister Winston Churchill which presented Iraq's position on the Palestine question. 'Abd al-Ilah attacked Zionist claims that link the persecution of the Jews and the demand for the establishment of a Jewish state. He depicted the injustice that could befall the Palestinians in such a case as the "greatest tragedy of the twentieth century." FO 371/45237/E 2090, Oriental Department to Dickson, 26 March 1945.

53   *Al-Ahram*, 20, 24 August 1945. See also the letter of Syrian President Shukri al-Quwatli to President Truman, *al-Ahram*, 13 November 1945.

54   *Al-Difa'*, 5 November 1945.

British and American governments would have to implement.[55] The framing of the commission's goals created a linkage between the Jewish and the Palestine problems, despite the British position that portrayed them as two separate issues. Consequently, the Arabs viewed the commission with grave suspicion. They refrained from officially recognizing it, and even contemplated a boycott, but eventually Arab officials and representatives of various organizations did appear and testify before it.[56]

In response to Bevin's statement, the AHC, the Palestinian leadership body, insisted that there was no reason why the Arabs should be held responsible for the outcome of the Jewish problem, which had emerged due to the rise of the Nazi and Fascist regimes in Europe. Downplaying the uniqueness of the Holocaust, it added that this persecution was not different in essence from what other peoples had endured during the war. Therefore, it was only logical that it would be solved once these regimes were gone.[57]

The official response of the Arab League to Bevin's announcement of 13 November 1945 was the first case of official implicit or partial denial of the Holocaust. The League expressed Arab appreciation of the humanitarian desire to help the Jews of Europe and others who had been persecuted during the Nazi and Fascist period. Concurrently, it warned against dealing "with one case of oppression by perpetrating a new one," and replacing one oppression by another. "Should Zionism attain its goals it would lead to the dispossession of the Arabs from their homeland and from their national rights," which is "no less cruel than the oppression of the Jews which the world complains about." Fortunately, it concluded, the victory of the democracies over Nazism and Fascism would enable the solution of the Jewish problem on a democratic basis and the return of the persecuted Jews to their homelands from which they had been expelled by Nazi and Fascist fanatic actions.[58] Thus, the fate of the Jews was reduced to mere expulsion from their homeland and was even less serious than the anticipated dispossession of the Palestinian Arabs. Moreover, the statement cast a certain doubt as to the scope of oppression which the world "complains" about. Both arguments would become central themes in the future Arab argumentation.[59]

---

55   J. C. Hurewitz, *The Struggle for Palestine*, New York: 1951, pp. 236–7; *al-Ahram*, *al-Misri*, 16 November 1945.

56   *Al-Ahram*, 25 November 1945.

57   *Al-Difa'*, *Filastin*, 12 December 1945.

58   *Al-Ahram*, 27 November, 7 December 1945.

59   See a similar insinuation by Michel Kafuri, *al-Sahyuniyya: nishatuha wa-atharuha al-ijtima'i*, Cairo: 1947, p. 19, who charged the Jews with exploiting "the persecutions attributed to some states against the Jews living in their midst during the war."

The Anglo-American Committee heard various Arab statesmen, most notably Iraqi representative Fadil al-Jamali and Syrian Speaker of Parliament Faris al-Khouri, in addition to Egyptian and Palestinian politicians and representatives of various political and social organizations. They presented a unified position that rejected Jewish immigration to Palestine, fearing that it would turn it into a Jewish state. The Egyptian press gave particular coverage to the statement by 'Abd al-Majid Ibrahim Salih, a member of the Egyptian parliament, who said that the only solution was to adhere to the 1939 White Paper so that Jewish–Arab relations would revert to what they had been in the past as "loving brothers and respected citizens." The Arabs had always treated the Jews with respect and appreciation, while in Europe they were subjected to "crimes and atrocities" (*jara'im wa-faza'i*), he explained, but this "crime should not be washed at the expense of the noble Arabs." Salih further emphasized that the Arabs had been friends of the Jews, but "Zionist policy forces us to become their enemies," and that a "national home" for the Zionists meant "a cancer in the Arab body."[60]

In a similar vein, Faris al-Khouri declared that the "Jewish refugees and their bitter fate in the world is something that all people with human feelings address with sympathy," and that the Arabs "share this sympathy." Yet he explained that the situation of the Jews in Europe should not be linked to the Palestine question, since the latter was a political issue while the former was a humanitarian problem, "and it would be unjust for [Palestine] and the Arabs to merge the two." He expressed his hope that the United Nations, particularly Britain and the US, would "seek to give satisfaction to the Jews and heal the mortal wounds inflicted upon them during the war" and find a solution for them elsewhere rather than in Palestine.[61]

Presumably, Khouri's sympathetic tone was influenced by the identity of his interlocutors. Thus, he expressed his sorrow that "the history of the Jews was always accompanied with difficulties, tragedies and persecutions," even though the Jews were "intelligent," and among them were "professors, scholars and philosophers." Yet, he held the Jews responsible for this hatred, which stemmed from their "wish to live their life in isolation" and their "inability to assimilate in other people," and from their belief that they were "God's Chosen People." The Jews "practice racism," and insist on "purity of blood" and racial discrimination, he went on to say, revealing some entrenched anti-Semitic views.[62]

---

60   *Al-Ahram*, 6, 7 March 1946.
61   Karlibakh, *The Anglo-American Commission*, vol. 1, pp. 262–3. See also the statements by George Hazim, Representative of the Arab-American Office in Washington, ibid., p. 136 and by Albert Hourani, of the Arab Office in London, ibid., vol. 2, pp. 486–92.
62   Karlibakh, *The Anglo-American Commission*, vol. 1, pp. 262–3.

The Arab League, in its letter to the Committee, stated that Palestine could not absorb new Jewish immigration so long as the immigrants who were sent there for humanitarian reasons sought to transform the Arabs into a minority. It was unjust that those who wished Palestine to absorb Jews should refrain from taking Jews into their own land, it added. The letter accused the Zionist movement of exploiting the persecution in Europe for its own political purposes, saying that the Zionists arrived in the Middle East with materialistic western ideas, and with the western and European concepts of colonialism, control and civilization (*tamaddun*). Undoubtedly, the Zionists who took advantage of oppression were the last to assist in eliminating that phenomenon. The letter also stressed the motif that Jewish–Arab relations in the past had never been afflicted by systematic racism and persecutions and that these were western inventions.[63]

The AHC reiterated its position, rejecting any new Jewish immigration to Palestine, in a memorandum submitted on 22 January 1946 to the Anglo-American Committee saying that the Arabs did not feel that they should accept "from a humanitarian point of view" a people (*qawm*) that sought to break their national existence in their homeland. Moreover, "the humanitarian aspect itself deserves reexamination, since the age of oppression for the Jews in Europe had ended," and their state of affairs was good, despite Zionist claims to the contrary. Jamal Husayni, secretary of the AHC, spoke to the Anglo-American Committee in the same vein. Referring to "the terrible problem of the displaced persons" from many nations who were wandering throughout Europe, he also reduced the Holocaust to expulsions and displacements.[64]

Implicit denial of the Holocaust, and the equating of Nazi policy against the Jews with the treatment of other groups was incorporated into the statement of Sami Taha, secretary of the Arab Workers Union in Haifa, to the Anglo-American Committee. The Arab workers sympathized with "members of the Jewish faith" persecuted in Europe, he said. They knew that "these persecutions against the Jews and the Catholic Church" were part of a broader phenomenon emanating from racism and religious fanaticism, thereby blurring the distinction between the extermination employed against the Jews and Nazi hostility towards the Church, which was manifested in various ways.[65]

More explicit denial, coupled with the accusation of Holocaust exploitation by the Zionists, appeared in the memorandum submitted by the Syrian Students

63   *Al-Ahram*, 3 March 1946.
64   Karlibakh, *The Anglo-American Commission*, vol. 1, pp. 354–5, 362.
65   *Al-Difa'*, 31 March 1946. For Nazi policies against the Church, see Ronald J. Rychlak, *Hitler, the War, and the Pope*, Indiana: 2000, pp. 76–8.

Association to the Committee, and in the response of the Iraqi government, made on 19 June 1946, to the Committee's proposals. Both accused the Zionist leaders of "shedding tears" in order to attain the world's support, and of inflating the universal Jewish problem caused by Nazi oppression when they realized that their arguments in justification of their invasion of Palestine were refuted. The Zionist movement was continuing with this plan in the most blatant way following the end of the war and the demise of Nazism, while Europe was trying to restore democracy and the oppression of the Jews had ended. There was no Jewish problem in Europe in the full sense of the word, but rather a problem of an anguished Europe ruined by the war and worried by the residues of Nazism, the Syrian memorandum concluded.[66]

The Anglo-American Committee published its report, containing ten recommendations, on 30 April 1946. It concluded that Palestine alone could not solve the immigration needs of victims of Nazi and Fascist persecutions, and that the whole world should share responsibility for their resettlement. Concurrently, it proposed granting 100,000 entry permits to Palestine to Jewish victims of Nazi and Fascist persecution and expediting implementation in 1946.[67]

The Egyptian government discussed the Committee's report on 14 May 1946, and government member Fikri Abaza's statements quoted by *al-Ahram* the following day epitomize the Arab mainstream reaction. The Committee chose to nullify the White Paper and transfer 100,000 European Jews to Palestine "even though there is no linkage between the problem of the Jews in Europe and the Palestine question," he said. "It needed courage to tell Britain to relocate the Jews in Australia or another place in its vast empire, but it did not find a solution except that of bringing a catastrophe (Nakba) on Palestine." If the problem of European Jews was a universal one, the whole world should have decided on the means to resolve it. "The evil acts perpetrated in Palestine by the Zionists are threatening all Arab countries," he added. Abaza expressed his disappointment at the disappearance of the "noble principles that we have heard during the war from the allies," and concluded, "Hitler died, but in his place 100 Hitlers have emerged."[68]

---

66 *Al-Difa'*, 20 March 1946. Both the Iraqi government and the All-India Muslim League in their responses to the Anglo-American Committee recommendations used the term *Anschluss*, which referred to the German annexation of Austria in 1938, to describe Jewish immigration from Germany. CO 733/463/17/1570, A letter from the Government of Iraq to the Foreign Office, 19 June 1946; CO 733/463/17/1534, *Dawn*, 1 August 1946.

67 *Memorandum of the Institute of Arab American Affairs on the Recommendations of the Anglo-American Committee of Inquiry*, New York, August 1946, p. 22.

68 *Al-Ahram*, 15 May 1946. See similar objections in the memorandum presented by the Egyptian Foreign Ministry: 20 Juin 1946, CO 733/463/17/1538, 1549, Ministère des

On 7 July 1946, the AHC issued another statement, suggesting to President Truman that if he felt such great compassion towards the Jews, he should open to them the gates of the White House and of other American cities that could absorb not only 100,000 Jews, but millions of immigrants.[69] Reiterating similar views on several occasions, 'Azzam Pasha asserted that the Arabs felt special compassion towards the Jews "and never hesitated to express it each time they were persecuted." Both he and Prince Faysal ibn 'Abd al-'Aziz declared that, should each country in the world take in a number of refugees according to its size and population, the Arabs were committed to doing their share.[70]

The speech of the Egyptian MP 'Abd al-Majid Ibrahim Salih at the session of the International Parliamentary Union in Switzerland that debated the question of Jewish immigration in September 1946 summarized the official Egyptian and Arab position vis-à-vis the Committee's report. He insisted that any talk of the migration of groups to the Near East was tantamount to a disaster (ma'asa) for Palestine. "Had it not been for Hitler, and without the forced persecutions of the Jews in Central Europe as well as Nazi and Polish persecutions, the number of immigrants would have been limited and Zionist propaganda would have failed." After reviewing the statistics on Jewish immigration by countries of origin, he maintained that they proved beyond any doubt that the Jews did not arrive in Palestine out of ideological, religious or emotional motivation. They fled from racist persecutions in their countries. Hence, immigration was insignificant before 1932. It accelerated only following Nazi persecutions and peaked in 1939, when Hitler's influence in Europe was at its highest. The Zionist movement, he charged, hid the facts that did not suit it. The National Home was only a cover-up, and Zionist propaganda, aimed at the Jews to return to Palestine, "the promised land" and the land of their forefathers, did not appeal to the Jews of Britain, France, the US, Switzerland and Egypt, who sought to stay where they were and did not wish to become Palestinians. "Where Zionism failed, Hitler and the persecutions succeeded," and since 1932 the symbolic National Home had become a shelter to the victims of hatred of the Jews, and had caused hardships and catastrophe (Nakba).[71]

Affaires Etrangères, Departement des Affaires Arabes, Observations et Remarques au Sujet des Recommandations de la Commission Anglo-Americaine, Le Caire.

69   Al-Ahram, 23 January, 8 July 1946.

70   CO 733/463/17/1642, Arab News Bulletin, 17 May 1946; al-Ahram, 24 May, 28 July, 10, 13, 29 September, 16 October 1946.

71   While Salih was correct in his statistical analysis and in his references to attitudes towards Zionism among Western European Jews, he ignored the fact that providing a shelter to persecuted Jews, most of whom had lived in Eastern Europe before the war, had been one of Zionism's major goals since its inception.

Salih denounced the claim of historical linkage between a people and the land from which their ancestors had been expelled a thousand years ago as "a dangerous and destructive view," reminiscent of Mussolini's statements on the Mediterranean as *mare nostrum* ("our sea"), because it had been part of the Roman Empire. Moreover, espousing the equation of Zionism with Fascism and Nazism – which was to become ever more popular in the Arab argument through the years – he contended that the advocacy of rights for the Jewish people was by itself a racist view, which "Hitler invented and relied upon in persecuting the Jews in Germany," in holding them to be distinct from the German people, as foreigners (*ghuraba'*) and invaders (*dukhala'*).[72]

The unity of the Arab position regarding the separation of the Jewish and Palestine problems notwithstanding, it appears that the tone of the Palestinian and Syrian representatives was harsher than that of the Egyptians.[73] While the war was raging, Faris al-Khouri of Syria asserted that "Zionists are Nazis."[74] In his testimony to the Anglo-American Committee Fadil al-Jamali, Deputy Foreign Minister of Iraq, insisted that Zionism was "a reactionary movement, based on race, national homeland and fanaticism," and therefore "there was no difference between Zionist and Hitlerite fanaticism to which the Allies put an end." Speaking in 1947 to UNSCOP, Jamali equated Zionism with Nazism because both were founded on myths and on racial superiority mixed with religious beliefs. Zionism, he added, used the same means of propaganda and aggression as Nazism.

Palestinian spokesmen were almost unanimous in equating Zionism with Nazism. Sami Taha explained that establishing a Jewish state, on the basis of a new nationalism, by members of different nationalities holding the Jewish religion reflected a racist approach, presupposing that they were members of the Semitic race. This view, he went on, was equal to the Nazi ideology that was based on racial divisions and on the superiority of the Aryan race. Ahmad

---

72   *Al-Ahram*, 4 September 1946. See a similar view of Jewish immigration by Egyptian politician and writer Muhammad Husayn Haykal in *al-Ahram*, 9 October 1947. The British, too, saw no reason why the displaced survivors – estimated at 200,000–250,000 Jews – would not stay in Europe following the demise of Nazism. They rejected the survivors' argument that they did not wish to remain in Europe, which had become the "graveyard of their people," pointing to Western European Jews who did not wish to leave and saying that non-Jews had suffered as well. British officials attributed Jewish aspirations of emigration to Palestine to economic hardships and renewed anti-Semitism that stemmed from harsh economic conditions and the conduct of Jewish black marketeers; see FO 371/61956/ E 0456, Wilkinson to Billan, 30 September 1945.

73   Karlibakh, *The Anglo-American Commission*, vol. 1, pp. 354–5, 362; *al-Ahram*, 12 September 1946.

74   Freya Stark, *The Arab Island*, New York: 1946, p. 141.

45

Shuqayri of the Arab Office, formerly a leader in the Palestinian Istiqlal party, compared the Zionist assertion of being more capable in developing the land to the Nazi claim "to rule over Europe because they know what good order is." 'Abdallah Khalaf, head of the rural regional council in al-Bira, told the Anglo-American Committee that "the Zionist assault on a peaceful people is not different than the Nazi attack on Poland." But then the whole world rose up "and shed the blood of its best youth in defending the same rights and principles that we demand for ourselves." How can you reconcile "your struggle against Nazi and Fascist aggression with this arbitrary dictatorial takeover of this country," he asked.[75] Undoubtedly, these assertions directed at a western audience were intended to undermine support for the Zionist movement among those who saw Nazism as the enemy of humanity. Alongside the ideological comparisons, Arab spokesmen attributed Nazi imagery and characteristics to individual Zionist leaders. Thus, Jamal Husayni explained to the Anglo-American Committee that when he heard David Ben-Gurion talk, it was as if he heard "Hitler's voice from the grave – the same tone the same spirit."[76]

The Holocaust in the early public discourse

Expressions of recognition of the Jewish tragedy, coupled with rejection of any link between it and the immigration of Jewish refugees to Palestine, were not confined to political statements addressed to western ears, but were also voiced consistently in the internal Arab discourse during 1945–46.

Arab intellectuals were mobilized by a deep conviction when writing about the Palestine problem, the intentions to turn part of Palestine into a Jewish state and the dangers posed by Jewish immigration. The first references to the Holocaust appeared as part of this public debate and laid the ideological, moral and religious foundations of the Arab Holocaust discourse. Unlike the earlier, matter-of-fact reports during 1944–45 about the horrors that were revealed by the liberation of the Nazi camps and by the Nuremberg trials, described above, the ensuing references to the Holocaust became highly charged and their point of departure was that of conflict and confrontation between the Arabs and the Zionists. The Holocaust was no longer viewed as a neutral fact, but as a catalyst to a political course of events and a major justification for the enemy. At this stage, there was no coherent narrative, but arguments that were mostly a reaction to Zionist assertions or to specific clauses in documents published by vari-

75   *Al-Ahram*, 7 December 1945, *al-Difa'*, 6, 31 March 1946; Karlibakh, *The Anglo-American Commission*, vol. 1, pp. 354, 356, vol. 2, pp. 450, 486; *al-Misri*, 9 September 1947; *al-Ahram*, 7 October 1947.

76   *Al-Ahram*, 13 November 1945; Karlibakh, *The Anglo-American Commission*, vol. 1, p. 356.

ous international committees. The public debate evolved alongside the official governmental positions, although it was often more radical.

The journalistic writings at the beginning of the period under discussion were preoccupied with the question of Jewish immigration and saw it as a genuine danger to the future of Palestine and the entire Arab region. Yet, they did not deny the existence of a Jewish problem that needed to be resolved. "Undoubtedly, a solution has to be found for the Jewish problem, but colonizing Palestine is not a solution to the universal Jewish problem, and it would be unjust to demand solely from the Arabs to solve it at their expense," al-Hilal wrote, adding that opposition to Zionism did not contradict Arab compassion for past Jewish plight.[77]

Egyptian writer Salah al-Dhahani anticipated that with the end of the war and of Nazism the highly educated people who had left Germany and Europe would return to their countries. After all, he maintained, they left under the pressure of Nazi persecution, and not for any national idea. Even the German Jews wish to go back to Germany.[78] Another Egyptian intellectual, Muhammad 'Awad Muhammad, raised the same point too. Only a few Jews wanted to come to Palestine, and those Jews of Polish or German descent who were in Palestine were interested in returning to their countries of origin, he wrote. The emigrants from countries that had been subjected to "Nazi oppression and Hitlerian tyranny" were looking for a safe haven anywhere, be it Palestine or elsewhere, until the spirit of tyranny came to an end in their countries.[79] Al-Misri and al-Ahram also pointed to the many Jews living in Palestine who dared, despite the "terrorist-Nazi Zionist regime" prevailing there, to express their desire to emigrate to the United States. Al-Misri cited "numerous sources," confirming that the number of Jews seeking to leave Palestine exceeded 75,000 and that the Jewish Agency sought to save the situation by producing international resolutions calling for the establishing of a Jewish state. The war, he concluded, enabled the Jews in Palestine to get rich at the expense of its victims.[80]

Egyptian intellectual Ibrahim 'Abd al-Qadir al-Mazini explained Arab opposition to the Jewish immigration, pointing to the fear that, with the entrance of more Jews, the Arabs would become an alien minority in their own land.[81] The discussion on immigration, as seen from Mazini and others, fol-

---

77   *Al-Hilal*, January–February 1945, p. 16. See also *al-Thaqafa*, 20 February 1945, p. 197.

78   *Al-Thaqafa*, 6 March 1945, p. 258.

79   *Al-Thaqafa*, 10 April 1945, p. 391.

80   *Al-Misri*, 1 September, cited in HZ/21/2566, the Egyptian Press, 25 August–10 September 1945.

81   *Al-Risala*, 11 February 1946, p. 150.

lowing the establishment of the Anglo-American Committee, was detached
from its historical context. It was no longer a matter of refugees or displaced
persons, as had appeared in the early reports by *al-Ahram*,[82] but a question
of Jewish immigrants, seen only from a political vantage point. What were
the Jews lacking in other countries, wondered Muhammad Farid Abu Jadid
in *al-Thaqafa*. They lived in the United States and Britain, enjoying all the
liberties and generosities, and "thank God, the tyranny of the tyrants (*tughyan
al-tughat*) was eliminated in Europe, so that nothing endangers them any-
more." Nothing justified their coming to Palestine to shed blood and expel its
inhabitants, he claimed, warning that there was a real danger in gathering all
Jews in one place. "I am not an enemy of the Jews … God is my witness, but
I am wise and I warn them of the danger of their gathering in one place," he
concluded.[83]

In the Palestinian discourse one can discern the blurring of the uniqueness of
the Jewish issue, which was represented as a refugee problem no different from
the broader refugee question in Europe. AHC member Musa al-'Alami, while
commenting on the British-American discussions on the Jewish refugees, contended that the refugee problem was a universal one. The Arabs were willing to
contribute their share to solving it, but they could not do so before they knew
their political rights. The UN should have rehabilitated the refugees, he added,
but Palestine had done more than its share. 'Alami also accused the Jews of
exploiting their suffering in Europe for their own political purposes and argued
that most legal and illegal immigrants that had arrived in Palestine during the
war did not come from Europe but from Middle Eastern countries, implying
that Jewish immigration was unrelated to Europe and was solely motivated by
political considerations.[84]

Filastin stated that "if it is argued that the goal of establishing a [Jewish] national home is to attend to the persecution of the Jews in Europe, then Palestine
is not responsible for these persecutions," adding that the Jewish argument on
the need for immigration due to Nazi persecutions was invalidated by the disappearance of the Nazi regime. *Al-Difa'* praised the proposal, raised by the British
Spectator magazine, that Britain and the US should each take in 50,000 Jewish
refugees, saying that the problem should not lose sight of its universal humane

---

82 Reports on the Jewish refugees, their lives in displaced persons camps and the debates in
the US Congress and British parliament on their problem, as well as reports on Jewish
legal and illegal immigration to Palestine, appeared regularly in *al-Ahram*; see 29 March,
10, 26, 28, 29 October, 15, 19, 20 November, 13, 18, 19 December 1945, 27 January
1946.

83 *Al-Thaqafa*, 13 November 1945, p. 1261.

84 *Al-Difa'*, 7 November 1945.

nature and turn into a racist program that meant aggression against another people, i.e., the Arabs. The overall refugee problem, not just the Jewish one, was a humanitarian problem that the entire world should resolve.[85]

Following the publication of the Anglo-American Committee's recommendations, the Egyptian press, while stressing the need to distinguish between the Palestine and the Jewish problems, agreed that the recommendations meant a "death sentence for Arab Palestine." Tying the two issues together was perceived as a crude political mistake, which proved the indecent intentions of the international community of unjustly imposing upon Arab Palestine the burden of the Jewish problem. The Islamist thinker Sayyid Qutb, who advocated terror activity against the British at the time, concluded that the Jews had achieved their goals in the war.[86] His point gradually took a central place in the Arab discourse, which presented the Jews as the real victors of World War II.

The reactions to UNSCOP's recommendations published on 31 August 1947, calling for the partition of Palestine into two states, Jewish and Arab, were unequivocal in their rejection. Although the committee's report emphasized the humanitarian aspect of the Arab–Jewish dilemma and the difficulties in finding a solution to a problem related to humanitarian issues and political rights, the Arab public debate focused more on the political ramifications of the recommendations for the Arab world. Maintaining, with few exceptions, that Jews had lived harmoniously with the Arabs in the past, it ceased to express any compassion for past Jewish suffering. Two points assumed ever-growing importance: first, the accusation of inflating the scope of the persecution of the Jews in Europe by Zionism to justify the claim over Palestine and to extort universal conscience; and second, the argument that a Jewish state would not provide security to the Jews in general and to Middle Eastern Jewry in particular.[87] The recommendations were seen as "a further violation of the principles of justice and [legitimate] right," and a "mark of disgrace on the forehead of human justice." Could the world, which fought the Nazi tyranny and founded the United Nations, agree "to the results of that awful partition," wondered Egyptian writer

85   *Filastin*, 7 October 16 December 1945; *al-Difaʻ*, 23 May, 30 July 15, 29 November, 12 December 1945, 24 January, 23 May 1946.

86   *Al-Ahram*, 3, 4, 5, 11, 12 July 1946; ʻAbdallah ʻInan in *al-Thaqafa*, 28 May 1946, p. 2, 9 July 1946, pp. 759–60, 25 February 1947, p. 2; Sayyid Qutb in *al-Risala*, 17 February 1947, pp. 190–2.

87   *Al-Ahram*, 3, 29, 30, 31 August, 1, 2, 9 September, 3, 5, 9, 29 October, 25 November 1947; *al-Misri*, 9, 10 September, 25 November 1947; CO 733/482/1/9,11, *Arab News Bulletin*, nos. 43, 44 (8, 22 August 1947); CO 733/482/1/15, *Arab News Bulletin*, no. 46 (19 September 1947); *Liwaʼ al-Islam*, November 1947, p. 4, December 1947, p. 4.

Ahmad Hamza.[88] Christian writer Nicola Haddad, who portrayed the Jews in negative terms, accused them of taking advantage of the humanism and compassion of the Christian Europeans following the recent persecutions, which he defined as expulsion and expropriation of their property.[89]

Implicit and explicit Holocaust denial

The evolving association in international forums of the survivors issue and the question of Palestine produced an increasing tendency in the Arab discourse to downplay the significance of the Holocaust as genocide. It employed ambiguous or softer terms to describe the fate of the Jews, representing it as merely a case of civil discrimination, and blurring the difference between the fate of the Jews and that of other peoples during the war.

Palestinian papers *Al-Difaʿ* and *Filastin* dismissed the underlying causes of the emergence of the Jewish refugee problem and its unique significance. The victorious states were in control of events in Europe and they were capable of preventing anti-Semitic activities, one editorial commented. Why, then, "the hue and cry" and "the gross exaggeration" of the difficult situation of the Jews alone. Tens of millions had suffered, but the Jews alone were referred to. Why was it that when misery and loss were mentioned, they are attributed only to Jews? The truth, concluded one article, was that the propaganda over the situation of the Jews in Europe is "an unparalleled plot of modern times."[90] *Al-Difaʿ* conceded, on another occasion, that the Jews were scattered and persecuted, they suffered a lot and were victims of many tragedies and terrible deeds in Europe. But these disasters were not unique to them, as they happened to "millions of Christians in the continent" who were dispersed from Russia to the Mediterranean and were "facing the harsh winter without proper clothes." Seeking to show that the Jewish problem was far less serious than the way Zionist propaganda portrayed it, the paper reported that many Jews were returning to Germany and "already many can be seen in the newly opened nightclubs." Concurrently, it also acknowledged manifestations of hostility towards the Jews in Germany.[91]

While speaking of the trials of those responsible for the horrors committed in Bergen Belsen, and of the circulation of stories about other Nazi atrocities, *Filastin* conceded that Jews had indeed suffered. But it cautioned that these

---

88   *Al-Ahram*, 3, 29–31 August, 1, 2 September, 2 December 1947; *al-Thaqafa*, 25 November 1947, p. 1193; Ahmad Hamza, *Liwaʾ al-Islam*, November 1947, p. 4.

89   *Al-Risala*, 22 December 1947, pp. 1395–6.

90   *Al-Difaʿ*, 19 and 30 July, 7 November, 31 December 1945.

91   *Al-Difaʿ*, 9 May, 9 July, 5 November 1945, 12 April, 22, 29 July, 15 August 1946.

sufferings had taken place in the past and were not unique to the Jews, since all Europeans suffered hardships.[92] In another article it criticized the British and American position vis-à-vis the Jewish refugees who did not wish to return to their homelands, saying that it did not stem from sympathy and sincere compassion, since both states were indifferent to the plight of other peoples in Europe. The reason for their solidarity with the Jews was the influence of international Jewry in the fields of finance and propaganda. This sympathy, it concluded, "did not come from the heart, but from the pocket."[93]

Another motif that had emerged already, before the end of World War II, and became more prominent after the war in Palestine in May 1948, was the equation between the fate of the Jews and that of the Palestinians, thereby minimizing the scope of the Holocaust and transforming its victims into criminals equal to or worse than the Nazis. "Imposing a Jewish state on Palestine exceeds in its tyranny and aggression the greatest crimes (*atham*) carried out by the Axis states," Muhammad 'Awad contended in April 1945.[94] An *al-Ahram* editorial which appealed to Middle Eastern Jews wondered whether anyone could imagine a time when the Jews, "who had been subjected for generations to harshest oppressions and tyrannies," would do the same to others. The Zionist efforts to dislodge people from their homes and disperse them "constitute the same disaster (*ma'asa*), which the Jews had experienced." The whole world, the writer went on, denounced German Aryan racism that shed human blood, particularly of the Jews. Why, then, did Zionism seek to operate as the Germans did and implement their methods in Palestine, which would lead to the perdition (*fana'*) of a people, its deportation and destruction, he posed.[95] The new imperialism was one of eviction (*izaha*) and extermination (*ibada*), stated *al-Hilal*, which hitherto had taken a moderate approach toward the Jews. "The Jews inflict upon the Arabs what Hitler did to them, and perpetrate what he dared and even dared not do. They sterilize men so that they would not have any descendants and they torture them so that no trace would remain of them."[96] An editorial in *al-Thaqafa* depicted the Jews as a "spoiled people." The Zionists regarded themselves as "God's Chosen People" based on myths which passed through the generations. As a result of Zionist aggression, hundreds of thousands of Arabs were displaced. The great powers were shocked by the displacement of

92   *Filastin,* 30 September 1945.

93   *Filastin,* 20 October 1945.

94   *Al-Thaqafa,* 10 April 1945, p. 391.

95   *Al-Ahram,* 14 November 1945, 11 January 1946. See also Muhammad Rif'at, *Qadiyyat Filastin,* Cairo: 1947, pp. 98–9.

96   *Al-Hilal,* June 1948, p. 5.

one group of Jews (*fariq min al-yahud*) in Europe, while the displaced Arabs of Palestine did not get any attention. "How wide is the distance between what the criminal Jews get and what the poor Arabs get?" it concluded.[97]

Filastin was blunt in understating the scale of Jewish suffering, as early as two weeks after the end of the war, stressing the instrumentalization of the victims for achieving political goals:

The Jews have grossly overstated the number of their victims in Europe in order to gain the world's support for their imagined catastrophe (*nakbatihim al-maz'uma*). Time will show that the Jews were those whose casualties were the lowest compared with other people, and that their propaganda and their 'haggling' [quotation marks in source] (*musawamatihim*) over 'these victims' (*hadhihi al-dahaya*) was a means to establish a Jewish state in Palestine.[98]

Mixing denial with other motifs, the Egyptian *Akhbar al-Yawm* charged that Zionism managed to mislead the world into believing that the Jews had been persecuted in Germany. "Indeed there was Nazi tyranny, but it did not harm the Jews any more than Germans. All they were required to do, as an alien people that betrayed Germany in the previous war, was to live their lives separately, to set up their own institutions and carry a special badge." Nazism had been eliminated, but Zionist propaganda continued, it concluded.[99] Other writers, too, attacked Zionism for succeeding in drawing attention to the Jewish tragedy, leading to the decision to allow the emigration of 100,000 displaced Jews to Palestine, while neglecting over 100 million Europeans who were still suffering from disease and hunger.[100] An article on the "extermination, the suffering, the persecutions and the deportations" throughout Jewish history did not ignore the "great disaster and the worst possible catastrophe" (*al-tamma al-kubra wal-qar'a al-'uzma*) that Hitler had inflicted on the Jews. This was indeed a "sign of shame that would not be erased from their history," but it was also the reason for the catastrophe in Palestine. Yet, it concluded that what had happened to

---

97   *Al-Thaqafa*, 26 October 1948, pp. 5–6.

98   *Filastin*, 17, 23 May 1945.

99   *Akhbar al-Yawm*, 2 September 1945, cited in HZ/21/2566, From the Egyptian Press.

100   The Arab press remained preoccupied with Jewish immigration even after the establishment of the State of Israel on 14 May 1948, and repeatedly demanded its cessation. It saw Jewish immigration as a subversive Jewish attempt to take over not only the lands of Arab Palestine but also the entire Arab region, arguing that Palestine alone could not solve the problem of displaced Jews. Thus *al-Misri* explained that the Zionist movement concealed its true intentions and exploited Nazi extermination policy in its lobbying before the nations. *Al-Ahram*, 1 June; *al-Misri*, 29 June 1948. See additional discussions on Jewish immigration in *al-Ahram*, 4, 5, 6 July, 3, 16, 17 August, 2, 8, 9 September 1948; *al-Misri*, 14 August, 4 September 1948.

the Jews simply affirmed what had been written about them in the Qur'an, namely "humiliation and misery shall be their fate."[101]

Three elements are contained in all these arguments: Zionist exploitation and exaggeration of the Holocaust; relativization of the Holocaust in comparison with the sufferings of other peoples in the war; and justification of the Holocaust as a German reaction to Jewish treason. All of these elements would acquire a more central place in the future Arab Holocaust discourse. While it may be too early to attribute to these arguments the broader meanings that emerged later, there is no doubt that the first seeds had been sown in response to what was perceived as an Arab predicament requiring an answer. However, the public debate contained, as the official discourse, a moral aspect toward the Jewish problem that stressed the good-neighborly relations between Arabs and Jews through previous centuries. Arabs opened their doors to Jews fleeing persecution, and nowadays Europeans and Americans sought to get rid of the Jews in their midst by turning Palestine into a national Jewish homeland.[102]

Equating Zionism with Nazism

Al-Difa' criticized President Truman and other westerners who often spoke about the Jewish tragedies and attacked Nazism, but were unaware of the "Nazism, which they support in Palestine." An editorial on the smuggling of Jewish refugees by the Jewish Brigade in Europe referred to the "Fascist spirit dominating the Jewish camps in Germany."[103] Likewise, the Palestinian *al-Sha'b* described plans attributed to the Zionist IZL (Irgun zeva'i le'umi – National Military Organization) to plant bombs in London in retaliation for the deportation to Germany of the Jewish refugees from the *Exodus* immigrant ship as "Hitlerite operations."[104]

In a somewhat different vein, *Filastin* criticized the American calls for continuing Jewish immigration to Palestine as a blow to democracy, seeking to

---

101   *Liwa' al-Islam*, November 1948, pp. 33–8.

102   *Al-Ahram*, 22 October 1945.

103   *Al-Difa'*, 1 January, 28 February, 8 April 1946. The Jewish Brigade was a British army unit of Jewish volunteers from Palestine who had fought on the Italian front. During their stay in Europe after the war's end, they smuggled Jewish refugees from Germany to Palestine through Italy as part of the Zionist campaign defying the British ban on Jewish immigration to Palestine.

104   *Al-Sha'b*, 9 September 1947. The *Exodus* was a ship carrying 4,515 Holocaust survivors that was intercepted by the British in July 1947. After they refused to land in France, the British returned the passengers to Displaced Persons camps in Germany. The affair brought widespread support for the Jewish immigration in the US and some European countries. See: David C. Holly, *Exodus 1947*, Boston: 1969.

impose the minority over the majority. When American democracy spoke in such a language, it went on, it committed crimes against democracy "that neither Hitler nor Mussolini perpetrated." A powerful country such as that, which came out against others in such a criminal assault, was "the one closest to Nazi Germany."[105]

Other writers, such as Mahmud Muhammad Shakir, warned that the Arabs would no longer have any compassion towards the Jews. "We pitied them when they were persecuted. We provided them with shelter when they were expelled, and opened our lands to them when they were driven out like leper dogs by the ancient Christian peoples. But they denied and forgot it all, and they had bitten the hand that healed their pain and wounds throughout history." Still, the same Shakir described the Jewish immigrants as "the scum (hathala) of the Jews," as "the lowest (ardhal) creatures," and as "human carcasses," and charged the great powers with committing an unprecedented crime by imposing them on another people.[106]

'Abd al-Jabir Jo Mard raised a new argument against Zionism in relation to the Holocaust, which would also become more popular in later years. The Zionists were those behind the pogroms against the Jews, seeking to encourage immigration to Palestine. They incited various peoples to persecute the Jews and instigated hatred against their own brethren, in order to force them to leave their countries and immigrate to Palestine. The "Hitlerite persecutions were no more than a spark of Zionist incitement and propaganda," even if the Zionists "did not expect it would reach such proportions."[107]

Egyptian 'Abbas Mahmud al-'Aqqad, one of the leading liberal Islamic thinkers, who had been a harsh critic of Nazism before and during World War II, made a more systematic effort to equate Zionism with Nazism in a series of articles written during May–June 1948, which were obviously influenced by the war atmosphere. 'Aqqad noted that the Jews had been among the first victims of the "gangs famous for their brown shirts," and the "irony of history," he added, was that "this type of gang regime had disappeared from Germany and all other parts of the world, except for Palestine among the Jews."[108] Aren't the "gangs of the Irgun and Stern and Hagana[109] Nazi gangs in their organization, conduct

105   Filastin, 20 December 1945.

106   Al-Risala, 20 October 1947, pp. 1140–1, 6 October 1947, p. 1085, 11 December 1947, pp. 1313–15.

107   Al-Thaqafa, 24 June 1946, p. 659.

108   'Abbas Mahmud al-'Aqqad in al-Asas, 17, 26 May, 20 August 1948 cited in 'Abbas Mahmud al-'Aqqad, al-Sahyuniyya wa-qadiyyat Filastin, Beirut, Sidon: n.d., pp. 83, 176.

109   The "Irgun" refers to the IZL and Stern is the British pejorative for LEHY (Lohamei

and reliance on terrorism in order to obtain their goals?" he asked, adding that "treachery is the only law (*shari'a*) those Nazi Zionists are accused of." In another article he equated the Nazi and Zionist desires for world domination and warned the Zionists, who knew more than anyone else what the Nazis did in order to take over the world, and how they ended up, of a similar fate.[110]

Still, there remained in 1948 few voices that continued to acknowledge the Holocaust while rejecting the Jewish aspirations in Palestine. Hasan Lutfi al-Manfaluti took an exceptional approach in 1948 as he discussed in detail the destruction of the various Jewish communities in Europe by the Nazis and conceded the loss of five million Jews. However, he concluded that most Jews did not wish to immigrate to Palestine and stressed that they were suffering, just as all others who suffered from the destruction wrought by the war, suggesting that the UN should ensure that these Jews lived safely in their various countries. The Arabs, he said, oppose the arrival of Jews "whose only link [with Palestine] was the religious claim that is unreasonable in the twentieth century."[111] His argument implied the belief that the war had created new universal circumstances which left no place for nationalist identities based on religion. 'Ali Rifa'a al-Ansari also recognized the destruction of six million Jews, but drew comfort from the small number of Jewish immigrants to Palestine, which had not exceeded 280,000 since Hitler's rise to power. These numbers, he believed, showed that the Jews did not take their state very seriously. However, he accused the displaced persons who cried so bitterly over their suffering of losing all human feelings and of cruelly killing women and children in Palestine.[112] Al-Ansari raised here another motif, namely that the long-suffering Jews should be more attuned to the suffering of others.

A broader and a more coherent picture of the attitudes toward the Holocaust is provided by the few books published in the post-war period on the Palestine question and Zionism. The writers discussed below belong to the national camp, with two of them having Islamic leanings.[113] Before the war, Najib Sadq explained in 1946, Zionists focused their propaganda in the US on Biblical stories and on promoting compassion for the millions of Jews persecuted in Germany,

herut yisrael – Fighters for the Liberty of Israel), named after its founder Avraham Stern. Both were right-wing Zionist organizations. The Hagana (Defense) was the mainstream organization of the Jewish community under the British mandate.

110 *Al-Asas*, 26 May, 20 August 1948, cited in al-'Aqqad, *al-Sahyuniyya*, pp. 83, and 176.

111 *Al-Thaqafa*, 21 September 1948, pp. 5–7.

112 *Al-Thaqafa*, 10 August 1948, p. 26.

113 Najib Sadq, *Qadiyyat Filastin*, Beirut: 1946; Rif'at, *Qadiyyat*; Kafuri, *al-Sahyuniyya*; 'Abd al-Ghaffar al-Jiyar, *Filastin lil-'Arab*, Cairo: 1947.

Poland and other Eastern and Central European countries. They described the lives of the scattered Jews in European ghettoes, stressing the duty and justice in compensating them for the acts of their fathers and forefathers. Today, the Nazi and Fascist persecutions were over and the western democracies, the friends and allies of the Jews, had won. The Jews could no longer reiterate their old tunes so they invented new ones, far more influential on sensitive British and American souls. Nowadays, they asserted that the Jews suffered in the war more than any other people in history. Of all those millions in Europe, only a few thousands survived, and all the rest were killed, burned or tortured in concentration camps. They were tired of their lives "in the service of democracy!" Was it not the duty of democracy to "pay its debts to them," as the Jewish Agency claimed? The Jewish communities in Europe today demanded to go back to their old homeland in Palestine because they could not find employment and they feared additional persecutions from those groups still influenced by Nazi propaganda. But Sadq believed, like other writers, that the establishment of two states in Palestine would not resolve the Jewish problem in the world, and asserted that the "disease" should be fought in Europe, and that the Arabs' interest required them to make sure that Jews there led a peaceful, secure life.[114]

The prominent Egyptian historian Muhammad Rif'at, writing a year later, adopted a harsher tone towards the Jews. The Jews joined the Allies during the war, he contended, with a long-term view and used it "in order to conceal their criminal intentions." They trained and equipped themselves with weapons, and even channeled the aid given by UN organizations to the refugees, to those that were secretly sent to Palestine after the war in order to join the Zionist undergrounds.[115] In describing the Jewish predicament, Rif'at conceded that the Jews in Eastern and Central Europe suffered "unimaginable horrors" from the Nazis and Fascists, and that the Germans exterminated them with gas, microbes and other barbarian means until the number of those killed reached around six million.[116]

Both Sadq and Rif'at began their historical narrative with the 1917 Balfour Declaration and the British Mandate in 1921, and both reflected the growing Arab fear of Jewish immigration. Although they did not ignore Zionist activity before the war, both more than implied that the combination of the Holocaust – which they accepted as a fact – and Zionist efforts had turned the scale in favor of Zionism. Therefore, the Arab official and intellectual debates rejected the linkage between the Jewish and the Palestine problems because they realized

---

114   Sadq, *Qadiyyat*, pp. 294–301.

115   Rif'at, *Qadiyyat*, pp. 94–9.

116   Rif'at, *Qadiyyat*, pp. 95, 103. See similar argument in al-Jiyar, *Filastin*, p. 77, and in *al-Thaqafa*, 16 December 1947, pp. 1–2.

that the Holocaust could add moral and emotional leverage to a problem they saw as political in essence, and presented Zionism as a cunning, manipulative and unscrupulous movement.

In addition to these books, historian Muhammad Fu'ad Shukri published in 1948 a research on Nazi Germany, in which he also referred to the Jews. Shukri, who abhorred Nazism, described in detail the tenets of its ideology and the Jews' centrality in it, as well as the measures taken against them since Hitler came to power.[117] In contrast to the other books, his analysis was not affected by events in the Middle East, and he adopted a factual approach toward the Jews, although he did not deal with their systematic genocide during the war. This book also proves that in the Arab world there was abundant supply of information on the persecution of the Jews in Nazi Germany. However, due to political developments, this information had been repressed in the public consciousness, and led to the emergence of a discourse that opted not to remember, so that it would not stand in the way of the campaign against the Zionist enemy and its state.

By 1948, compassion toward the Jews had faded in both the official and the public discourses, giving rise to two additional motifs: (1) the Arabs were not responsible for the Holocaust; and (2) if they would pay the price of the Holocaust, it would be a tragedy no less serious than the Holocaust. In the coming years all the themes which were identified in this formative period were developed and came to typify the Arab discourse on the Holocaust. Although they did not constitute a systematic, coherent narrative, one can discern a trend moving from recognition of the event as a human disaster of which the Arabs, and especially the Egyptians, were ready to share the burden, to alienation, relativization and denial. The diversity of voices was substituted by a more monolithic discourse that increasingly used the Holocaust as a tool in a rhetoric of conflict. This trend was a clear outcome of the developments in Palestine that instilled the feeling that Arabs had to bear the brunt of deeds perpetrated in Europe by Europeans, causing what they considered an even greater disaster. During the following years references to the Holocaust were made in various contexts, but it was not until the signing of the reparations agreement between West Germany and Israel in September 1952 that the Holocaust came again to the fore, giving prominence to the theme of Zionist and Israeli exploitation of the Holocaust.

---

117   Muhammad Fu'ad Shukri, *Almaniya al-naziyya. dirasa fi al-ta'rikh al-urubbi al-mu'asir (1939–1945)*, Cairo: 1948, pp. 14, 19–25, 153–71.

2

THE REPARATIONS AGREEMENT BETWEEN
GERMANY AND ISRAEL, 1951–53

The question of German reparations payments to Israel for some of the damages the Jewish people had suffered at the hands of the Nazis was another issue which brought the Holocaust to the attention of the Arab states and compelled them to refer to it. They viewed it, like the problem of the displaced Jews who came from Europe, as linked to the question of Palestine, and therefore they felt obliged not only to express their opinion but even to intervene to prevent the payments. The first contacts between West Germany and Israel regarding reparations began in 1951, and direct negotiations began on 12 March 1952 in Wassenaar, Holland. They ended on 10 September of the same year when the agreement was signed in Luxembourg; both houses of the German Parliament ratified it on 18 March 1953.[1]

During those years, the internal situation in Arab countries was simmering. Most of them were seeking to rid themselves from the remnants of the colonialist grip, suffering from instability in the wake of the defeat in Palestine. Egypt, for example, reached a dead end in her talks with Britain concerning the evacuation of British forces, and the Egyptian economy was in distress. There was general dissatisfaction with the regime's corruption and helplessness, and a strong sense of disappointment with the great powers and the international institutions, which, after the war, were supposed to have laid the foundation for a more just and equal world, that culminated in the revolution of the Free Officers' Movement in July 1952.[2] While taking its first steps in power, the

---

1   Kurt R. Grossman, *Germany's Moral Debt: The German-Israel Agreement*, Washington: 1954; Nana Sagi, *German Reparations: A History of The Negotiations*, Jerusalem: 1980; Ronald W. Zweig, *German Reparations and the Jewish World. A History of the Claims Conference*, London: 2001; Wajih 'Abd al-Sadiq 'Atiq, *al-Siyasa al-duwaliyya wa-khafaya al-'alaqat al-misriyya al-almaniyya, 1952–1965*, Cairo: 1991, pp. 21–71, 347–416.

2   On the perception of the new world order see, for example, the editorial in *al-Ahram*, "The United Nations for Spreading Oppression" (*Al-umam al-muttahida li-nashr al-zulm*), 10

new regime had to deal with the issue of the reparations agreement. The affair provides an opportunity to examine continuity and change in the Arab public discourse and in the response of two types of regimes to a specific event related to the Holocaust. The Arab response to the issue also sheds light on the Arab world's relations with Germany and on its perceptions of Germany, as well as on the issue of the German experts in Egypt, some of whom were Nazis who had found refuge there after the war.

Three basic premises underlie this chapter. (1) The reparations agreement became a test case for the young regime, which had to demonstrate its ability to deal with a problem in both the inter-Arab and the international arenas, especially since it was related to the Arab–Israeli conflict. However, all its attempts to differentiate itself from the old regime notwithstanding, the steps it took were in essence the same as those of its predecessor and, in the end, pragmatic internal political considerations determined its conduct. (2) The Holocaust continued to pose a moral dilemma for Arab decision makers, particularly the Egyptians. They did not deny it, but they tried to shift the focus of the discussion onto their conflict with Israel. Thus they could support reparations for the Jewish victims of Nazism on an individual basis, while regarding the transfer of funds to Israel as a political, economic and military action which threatened the Arab states' security. (3) The question of reparations reinforced the motif of the comparison between the Palestinian Nakba and the Holocaust.

The official stance: hesitant steps against implementing the reparations agreement

Only a small amount of information was published in Arab newspapers about the Jewish and Israeli demands for reparations from West Germany before the agreement was signed in September 1952. Reports about the peace treaties between the Allies and the Germans mentioned reparations to the Jews, but they did not awaken any particular interest because no specific mention was made of the Jewish demands in the decision of the Paris Conference of July 1946, which dealt with compensation claims from Germany. On 7 August 1946, *al-Ahram*, reporting from Paris, noted that the World Jewish Congress was meeting there and that it demanded the inclusion of certain articles in the peace treaties. These related to the right of the Jews to defense in the countries in which they had been persecuted, the return of nationalized and stolen Jewish property to its owners, or payment equal to the value of the property of those killed, for the re-

---

December 1951; and *Ruz al-Yusuf*, 4 February 1952.

settlement of Jewish survivors.[3] The State of Israel had not yet been established and the report was factual. Only in January 1951, quoting a London *Times* article on the Palestinian refugees, did *al-Ahram* refer to the question of reparations. It was argued that "after Israel demanded reparations for refugees from Germany, logic dictates that the same principle should be applied to settling the Arab refugees."[4] Another initial response came from an Arab journalist who attacked the Erich Lüth's Peace with Israel movement in the daily *Hamburg Zeit* on 13 December 1951, warning that if the payments were a result of "moral support for the Israeli plan to conquer Arab territory," the Arab world would re-examine its traditional friendship with Germany.[5]

The statements made by German Chancellor Konrad Adenauer[6] on Germany's readiness to pay reparations, on 11 November 1949 and 27 September 1951, which were milestones in preparing the way for talks between Israel and Germany about the agreement, and Israel's three official appeals[7] to the Great Powers during 1951 and the March–September talks at Wassenaar, were not reported in the Arab newspapers, despite their wide coverage of other foreign affairs. According to Israeli scholar Nana Sagi and Egyptian historian Wajih 'Atiq, the Arab states thought the negotiations would end without conclusive results and thus did not express strong objections to them. They also did not expect that Germany, with its traditional friendship with the Arabs, would accede to Israeli demands, and they never imagined the agreement would include so many economic advantages for Israel which would threaten Arab interests. 'Atiq also

---

3   *Al-Ahram*, 8 August 1946. For Jewish actions regarding reparations during and after the war, see Grossman, *Germany's Moral Debt*, pp. 4–7; Sagi, *German Reparations*, pp. 7–27; Zweig, *German Reparations*, pp. 11–18.

4   *Al-Ahram*, 27 January 1951.

5   *The Wiener Library Bulletin*, vol. 6, nos. 1–2 (January–April 1952), p. 6. Erich Lüth, who was in charge of the government press bureau in Hamburg, was head of a popular movement which wanted peace with Israel. *Al-Ahram*, 2 January 1953; Grossman, *Germany's Moral Debt*, pp. 11–12.

6   Two months after Adenauer became Germany's first Chancellor, on 11 November 1949, he stated that the new German government was determined to remedy the injustice done to the Jews and that it was a duty to pay reparations. On 27 September 1951 he officially stated in the Bundestag that Germany intended to remedy the injustice done to the Jews under the National Socialists and to accede to the material demands made of it. Grossman, *Germany's Moral Debt*, p. 14; Zweig, *German Reparations*, pp. 18–22; 'Atiq, *al-Siyasa*, pp. 30, 421–3; Eliezer Shinar, *Under the Burden of Necessity and Emotions, on a National Mission. Israeli-German Relations, 1951–1966*, Tel Aviv: 1967 (Hebrew), pp. 20–21.

7   On 16 January, 12 March, 20 November 1951, Israel appealed to the great powers to intervene with West Germany to accede to its demands for reparations. Grossman, *Germany's Moral Debt*, pp. 7–10.

suspected that one reason the negotiations were conducted in secret and out-side Germany was to fool the Arab states and prevent them from impeding the talks.[8] Undoubtedly, the lack of clarity regarding the extent of the agreement contributed to the hesitancy of the Arabs' reactions.

When the information about Israel and Germany holding talks leaked out, the governments of Syria, Lebanon and Jordan individually protested to their various British, French and American ambassadors as early as March 1952. Lat-er, Iraq, Yemen and Egypt also lodged protests.[9] Syria was the first Arab state to bring the agreement-in-progress to Arab attention. On 2 March 1952, it sent a long memorandum to the Egyptian government about the issue, expressing its concern at the Israeli receipt of German reparations, and stressed the impor-tance of a joint Arab action to prevent it.[10] It raised the following claims: the proposal to pay Israel reparations was tantamount to legally recognizing it as the representative of the Jews in the world; the damage was inflicted on German Jews and not on Israeli citizens, since Israel did not exist at the time; the Israelis had already received reparations at the expense of the Arab residents in Pales-tine; the Arab refugees who lost their houses and property were more entitled to compensation from Israel, which bore the responsibility for the expulsion of a million refugees; reparations would enable Israel to arm itself and become a greater danger to the neighboring Arab countries; Britain, the United States and France should intervene and use their influence to confiscate the reparations to Israel and turn them over to the Arab refugees.[11]

Similar contentious observations were raised in the Lebanese Foreign Min-istry appeal to the British government on 4 March 1952. However, according to the British ambassador's report, unlike the Syrian government, the Lebanese "did not deny that the claim of many Jews in Israel against Germany is liable to be strong, but stressed the fact that those Jews in turn expelled Arabs from

8   'Atiq, al-Siyasa, pp. 31, 40; Sagi, German Reparations, p. 180.

9   Despite its independence, Germany could not at that time conduct foreign relations. Only toward the end of 1952 could it establish diplomatic relations, and Egypt was the first Arab state with which it did so, in October of that year. Egypt was also the first state to terminate the state of war with Germany, in May 1951. Al-Ahram, 17 May 1951.

10 A memorandum from the Syrian consul in Cairo to the Egyptian government, 2 March 1952, in the "Arab States and German-Israeli Reparations Agreement" file in the Egyp-tian Foreign Ministry archive, quoted by 'Atiq, al-Siyasa, p. 42.

11 FO 371/98518 (E18210/7), Minutes by Wardrop, 3 March 1952; FO 371/98518, H[er] B[ritannic] M[ajesty's] Legation, 3 March 1952; FO 371/98518 (E18210/8A), U.S. Sug-gestion on Form of Answer to be given in conversation with Arab Countries on the sub-ject of the utilization of any indemnification from Germany to Israel for Arab refugees, n.d.; FO 371/98519 (E18210/27, 31), Despatch No. 89, 26 May 1952; FO 371/98519 (E18210/34), Despatch No. 102, British Legation, Damascus, 19 June 1952.

Palestine," who became the "final sufferers."[12] The Western Powers coordinated their response, which boiled down to formally stating their inability to intervene in the issue of reparations because it had nothing to do with them. They expressed their understanding of the question of compensation for Palestinian Arab refugees, and made it clear to the Arab representatives that they saw no connection between the reparation payments to the Jews and the Arab demands for compensation.[13] According to the report made by the British representative in Damascus, the Syrian foreign minister, who again raised the issue on 25 July 1952, fully understood that officially no connection could be made between the two,[14] and that conditioning the establishment of diplomatic relations with Germany on settling the Arab demands for compensation at the expense of the payments made to the Jews was considered "ridiculous" and "unrealistic" by the British representatives.[15]

In the end, those individual protests also roused the Arab League to action. On 17 May, Philip Takla, the Lebanese foreign minister, sent a memorandum to the members of the Arab League and the representatives of the Arab states in his country regarding the outcome of the talks with Britain, France and the United States about the reparations. The memorandum demanded that the money be used as compensation for the Arab refugees and asked the Arab governments, should an agreement be reached, to intervene directly with the Germans.[16] On 16 July, a few days before the Free Officers' revolution, the Lebanese government sent an additional memorandum, this time to the Egyptian government, proposing the establishment of a joint Arab delegation composed of Arab League members, which would be sent to confer with the German

---

12   FO 371/98518, Telegram No. 134, Beirut to Foreign Office, 4 March 1952. See also FO 371/98518, Aide Memoire, No. 5089/4P/408. For the appeal of the Jordanian government, see FO 371/98518, Telegram No. 86, Furlonge to Foreign Office, 5 March 1952. For the appeal of the Iraqi government, see FO 371/98518, Ministry of Foreign Affairs, Arab Affairs Department, Baghdad, 29 March 1952 (No. 1415/1415/13). For the oral appeal of the Yemenite government, see FO 371/98518 (E18210/18), Bowker, Israel-German Negotiations, 16 April 1952.

13   FO 371/98518 (E18210/18), Beirut, Knight to Foreign Office, 19 April 1952; FO 371/98519, AC207, Knight to Foreign Office, 6 May 1952.

14   FO 371/98519 (E18210/36), Ross, Arab claims against Israel, 25 July 1952. For the response to the Lebanese government, see FO 371/98518, British Legation, Beirut, No. 62, 31 March 1952. For the response to the Jordanian government, see FO 371/98519, Furlonge to Foreign Office, 16 April 1952. Similar responses were sent to the governments of Iraq and Yemen on 29 March and 16 April 1952 respectively.

15   FO 371/98518 (E18210/13), Beirut, No. 79, Chapman Andrews, 7 April 1952; FO 371/98518 (EE18210/13), London, Ross, 29 April 1952.

16   *Al-Nahar*, 18 May 1952 – Summary of Arab broadcasts, Daily Survey, No. 754, 18 May 1952 and Appendix no. 12, 21 May 1952.

government, directly and without intermediaries, to convince it to change its position.[17] However, the other Arab states apparently did not attach the same importance to the issue.[18] Egypt did not bother to appeal to the Great Powers. *Al-Misri* noted that it was characteristic of Syria and the League secretariat to be active in matters relating to Israel. Egypt, it claimed, was concerned about its own internal affairs and relations with Britain, and therefore not active in the matter.[19] Nevertheless, after the Syrian appeal, on 23 April the Egyptian government instructed its ambassador in Holland to lodge a protest with the representatives of the German government in the name of the Arab states, and ask the Germans to examine the possibility of freezing the reparations until the problem of the Palestinian refugees could be solved. According to the government's memorandum, the Palestinian Arabs expelled from their country by Israel had been exposed to the worst sort of persecution, and had the right to demand compensation before Israel received reparations on behalf of the Jews. On 4 June, Egypt sent an appeal written in the same spirit to the United States, asking it to intervene and stop the Germans from sending reparations until Israel paid reasonable compensation to the Palestinian Arabs, and to pressure Israel to settle the Arab compensation claims.[20]

After Adenauer presented the draft of the agreement to the German government for ratification on 17 June, *Filastin* reported that Germany was offering the Jews compensation "for damages in souls and properties inflicted on them during the Nazi era." *Al-Ahram*, on the other hand, elaborated that the compensations were to be granted to Israel "for crimes committed by the Nazis against the German Jews" in the form of merchandise valued at three billion German marks over the next 12 years. The report also quoted a warning to the German government, issued by the AHC in Cairo on 7 June, demanding that the Arab refugees be compensated for the crimes Israel had committed against them. "The Jews who claim the right to demand compensation for the damages and hardships to which German Jews were exposed," it said, were those who

17 A memorandum sent on 16 July 1952 by the Lebanese Foreign Ministry to the Egyptian Foreign Ministry, in the "The Arab states and the German reparation agreement with Israel" file in the Egyptian Foreign Ministry archive, quoted by 'Atiq, *al-Siyasa*, p. 44.

18 FO 371/98519 (E18210/25), Wardrop, German Compensation to Jews, 12 May 1952; FO 371/98519, Amman, Furlonge to Ross, 17 May 1952; FO 371/98519 (E18210/36), Jedda, Riches to Ross, 14 July 1954.

19 *Al-Misri*, 5, 12 March 1952, cited in HZ/41/10, 24 March 1952.

20 Memorandum no. 12, 12 April 1952, and Memorandum no. 28, 4 June 1952, "The problem of German reparations" file in the Egyptian Foreign Ministry archive, quoted by 'Atiq, *al-Siyasa*, pp. 42–3.

had imposed "barbaric aggression and treacherous persecution" of the worst possible sort on the Arabs of Palestine. Paying reparations to Israel would give it new tools for aggression against the Arab states, which would be a dangerous threat to the peace and order of the entire Middle East.[21]

According to 'Atiq, the Arabs did not in principle oppose the German reparations to Israel, only that the payments would be made before Israel had compensated the Palestinian refugees. That position, he added, reflected the Arab point of view, linking German reparations to Israel and Israeli compensation to refugees, and granting both affairs the same humanitarian implications, but the Arab states did not correctly assess the "enormous imperialist and Zionist power supporting Israel, which used different criteria to deal with the compensations of Jews and Palestinians."[22] However, in contrast to 'Atiq's assertion, that attitude was characteristic of the initial Egyptian position, while Syria, for example, rejected Israel's right to reparations. There was no direct reference to the Holocaust in the various memoranda presented by the Arabs, but there was recognition of the "injustice" and "damages" done to the Jews under the Nazi regime. Those mainly reflected a deep fear of the political, economic and military implications the reparations would have for Israel's situation and standing. The 1948 defeat was still fresh, and Israel continued to be perceived as a genuine threat to the entire region.

The central theme reflected in the general Arab approaches was the analogy between what had happened to the Jews and what had happened to the Arabs of Palestine, and indirectly between the actions of the Nazis and those of the Jews. This analogy relativized the Holocaust and minimized its horrors by emphasizing the injustices done to the Palestinians, even portraying Israel's actions as worse than those of the Nazis, and by limiting their scope to German Jews or referring to them as mere damage. Arab discourse did not make the distinction, which existed in international discourse, regarding the terminology for the kinds of reparations, using only the word *ta'widat* (compensation), which denotes "instruction to get rid of a debt while giving up the demand and the recognition that money will fix the injustice." That was how the agreement was eventually perceived in the Arab discourse, whereas the use of the term "reparations" in Israeli discourse meant to deny such recognition.[23]

---

21 *Filastin*, 19 June, *al-Ahram*, 20 June 1952. For approval of the draft by the Bonn government, see Grossman, *Germany's Moral Debt*, p. 25.

22 'Atiq, *al-Siyasa*, p. 43.

23 English correspondence and research literature have made a distinction between *reparations, restitution* and *indemnification*, which express different ideas: material reparation for bodily harm, restoring property and returning taxes. According to Tom Segev, the term reparations in Hebrew (*shilumim*) was introduced by Moshe Sharett "to present the Ger-

As was only natural, the new Egyptian regime was busy with problems more pressing than the German–Israeli agreement. Thus, until it was signed, press reports about it were scarce. In August, information on an Arab League memorandum to the German government, transmitted by the Egyptian consul in Bonn, had been published. It warned that the traditional friendship between Germany and the Islamic world might be harmed if Israel were paid reparations for the "so called persecution" of the Jews at the hands of the Germans during and before World War II. It noted that Israel was still at war with the Arab states and that a million Arabs had been expelled from their country, and their property confiscated by the Jews. It also questioned Israel's right to represent world Jewry and claimed that, in such a case, Jews living in other countries would have to give up their citizenship. It stressed the fact that the Bonn government owed nothing to a state hostile to the Arabs which had been established after a war on Arab land. "The Arab League does not object to Germany's paying compensation to private citizens or to the members of their families, but not to Israel." The report also quoted the Arab League secretary, 'Abd al-Rahman 'Azzam as saying that the League was about to transmit another memorandum to the United States, which would state that Germany had been sufficiently punished for its bad deeds in the past and was already bankrupt. The Arab League, therefore, considered German reparations to Israel as indirect American aid to Israel and as an unfriendly act toward the Arabs.[24]

A few days before Adenauer went to Luxembourg to sign the agreement, a Syrian delegation headed by Ma'mun al-Hamawi arrived in Bonn in a last-ditch effort to keep him from signing. Al-Hamawi managed to meet with the Chancellor's special political advisor, Walter Hallstein.[25] The Egyptian consul in Frankfurt joined al-Hamawi in his efforts to convince Hallstein that only 100,000 Jews had fled the Nazi regime to Palestine, and not the number claimed by Isra-

---

man payments as a kind of punishment and fine." The term *compensatiom* (*pitzuyim*) was used in Hebrew to refer to the money received by private individuals. Segev, *The Seventh Million*, p. 179, note; also see Shinar, *Under the Burden*, pp. 13–16, 56.

24 The memo had already been presented on 6 August and reported on by Radio Beirut and the East Jerusalem newspaper *al-Difa'*, but only toward the end of the month did *al-Ahram* see fit to report it; Radio Beirut, 7 August 1952 – Summary of Arab Broadcasts, no. 823, 8 August 1952; *al-Difa'*, 7 August, *al-Ahram*, 26 August 1952.

25 Beginning in June the Syrians tried strenuously to influence German public opinion against the agreement. BBC, 9 June 1952. FO 371/98519 (E18210/33), Arab Bid to Transfer German Compensation to Arab Refugees. According to Radio Damascus, a formal protest was lodged with the German foreign minister on 5 September. On the same day a similar telegram was sent by the Jordanian foreign minister. Radio Damascus, Radio Ramallah, 6 September 1952 – Summary of Arab broadcasts, no. 848, 7 September 1952; *Filastin*, 10, 13 September 1952.

el.[26] He reiterated that paying reparations to those 100,000 would not anger the Arabs. Postponing the agreement's signing, he said, would force Israel to pay $250 million in compensation to the Arab refugees, otherwise it would exploit the German reparations for military rather than humanitarian purposes.[27]

Syria sent a second letter of protest to the German government on 2 October, written in the same spirit and again cautioning that reparations to Israel were liable to damage Germany's relations with the Arabs. A report in *al-Misri* about a month later presented the letter's main points, which reflected the kind of narrative being constructed around the events occurring from the rise of the Nazi regime in Germany to the establishment of the State of Israel. It stressed the tiny number of Jews who had left Germany for Palestine since 1918 and during the war. In February 1946 the number of refugees and displaced persons was, according to the data supplied by the Anglo-American Commission, only 152,000 Jews, and not all of them had gone to Palestine. Thus there was no basis in fact for Israel's claim that half a million displaced persons had emigrated there. In addition, the claim that they had been expelled by the Nazis was "a terrible distortion of the facts." When the Nazi regime ended, its policies of persecution also ended and, thanks to the Allies, the Jews began enjoying full rights, so there was no reason for them to immigrate to Palestine, which was not "a country without people for a people without a country." German Jews who had lost their property received compensation after the war, and the Jews who came to Palestine from Europe took the houses and property of the Arabs who had been expelled. How, therefore, could the expenses of a family of four reach $12,000, and how could a reckoning of a billion and a half dollars be made, when the UN Committee asked for only $250 million to settle a million Arab refugees? The report made no attempt to deny what had happened to Jews "who had been harmed" personally by the Nazis' "cruel behavior," but it rejected out of hand Israel's right to receive any sort of compensation, both because it did not represent the Jewish people and because it ignored the international law and its duty to compensate the Arab refugees.[28] The newspaper did not take a stand, which was the case for most of the reports concerning Egyptian and Arab activity regarding the agreement. Since the initiatives and efforts for counteraction came from other Arab states, the importance of the information published

---

26   Reparations to Israel were calculated according to the absorption needs of 500,000 Jews.

27   Memorandum no. 61, 12 September 1952, from the Consul General in Frankfurt to the Egyptian Foreign Ministry, "The Problem of German Reparations" file, Egyptian Foreign Ministry archive, in 'Atiq, *al-Siyasa*, pp. 44–5; *al-Ahram*, 7 September 1952.

28   Radio Damascus, 11 October 1952 – Daily summary no. 874, 13 October 1952; *al-Ahram*, 12 October; *al-Misri*, 1 November 1952.

about them in the Egyptian papers stemmed from the inherent message that in the future would shape the perceptions of the Holocaust. The same was true for the reports about reactions to the agreement in other parts of the world, especially Germany.

Immediately after the agreement was signed on 13 September, the Arab League's political committee met in Cairo to discuss it, and two days later sent another memorandum to the German government. Its claims were not significantly different from those appearing in previous Arab protests. The committee also decided to send a delegation to Germany to prevent ratification by the German Parliament.[29] The Arab press reported widely about the concern, discomfort and fear among German diplomats and businessmen that economic steps would be taken against Germany. It stressed the opposition to the agreement and consent with the Arab point of view, prevalent in Germany itself. Those who opposed the agreement, it had been said, even welcomed the threat of an Arab boycott and used it in their struggle to prevent the ratification of the agreement.[30]

Following the decision to send an Arab delegation to Germany, the Egyptian government's involvement in the reparations affair increased and so did the interest of the Arab media. The Egyptian cabinet deliberated on the subject on 30 September, and for the first time since the affair had started an Egyptian minister announced the Egyptian government's support for the efforts made by the Arab states to delay ratification and implementation of the agreement. Fathi Radwan, a former member of Young Egypt who had joined the Free Officers and was a member of the government, reiterated the Arab states' post-war aspirations to renew relations with Germany.[31] Despite the tension that the agreement caused in Arab–German relations, Egypt was the first Arab state to institute diplomatic relations with Bonn, and when Gunther Pawelke, the first German ambassador, arrived in Cairo in October, Egypt became the center of Arab activity with Germany.[32]

During the second week of October the Egyptian government sent a memorandum to Germany. The Egyptians were convinced that public opinion in Germany was ready to react favorably to the Arab viewpoint. According to

---

29   Radio Cairo, 13, 16 September, Radio Damascus, Radio Baghdad, 13 September, Radio Beirut, 21 September 1952 – Summary of Arab broadcasts nos. 854, 856, 859 from 14, 16, 22 September 1952; *al-Ahram*, 15 September, *al-Misri*, 16, 17, 25 September, *Filastin*, 20 September 1952.

30   *Filastin,* 16 September, *al-Misri*, 18, 27 September, *al-Ahram*, 23 September 1952.

31   Radio Cairo, 30 September – Summary of Arab Broadcasts, no. 865, 1 October 1952; *al-Ahram*, 1 October 1952.

32   'Atiq, *al-Siyasa*, p. 61.

'Atiq, the memorandum adopted a new approach based on Egyptian objection to Israel's receiving reparations, stating that:

The Egyptian government had no objection to the Jews' receiving restitution for what the Nazis had done to them. "It is a matter about which there is no argument, and it is required by international conventions." It objected to the payment of reparations to the State of Israel, especially since the Nazis had committed crimes against individuals and not against the state. In addition, Israel was not the legal heir of the Jews who died under the Nazis.

The large sums which would be paid to Israel and support the Israeli economy would undermine the Arab boycott of Israel.

The reparations would enable Israel to allot large amounts of its budget to military purposes, since it was still at war with its Arab neighbors.

The Egyptian government was of the opinion that the affair of reparations for German Jews who had moved to Israel had been settled both practically and legally, since the State of Israel had nationalized German property in Palestine.

Morally speaking, Israel, which was asking for reparations, had carried out the same acts as the Nazis against the Arabs in Palestine, and the reparations would enable it to continue its policy of expulsion and to plan new aggression.

The Arab protest against compensation for Israel was not in any way motivated by anti-Semitism, as Zionist propaganda claimed, but from the right to self-defense and the threat that Israel's expansionist policies posed to Arab interests.

Egypt proposed that the UN take upon itself to determine the amount of compensation for both the Palestinians and the Jews. Israel was asking for compensation while itself denying it to the Palestinians.[33]

In effect, this was the first document detailing the Egyptian position regarding the reparations agreement. In contrast to other Arab states, Egypt did not threaten to take any step against Germany. In addition, it corroborated a news item which appeared in *al-Ahram*, according to which on 13 October the Egyptian consul in Frankfurt had dissociated himself from the remarks made by Ahmad Sulayman Isma'il, chairman of the German–Egyptian Economic

---

33   *Al-Misri*, 14 October, *al-Akhbar*, 15 October 1952. Memorandum no. 75, 17 October 1952, from the Consul General in Frankfurt to the Egyptian Foreign Ministry, "The Problem of German Reparations" file, Egyptian Foreign Ministry archive, in 'Atiq, *al-Siyasa*, pp. 48–51. It should be noted that the Arabs demanded compensations while rejecting a peaceful settlement of the conflict, as well as recognition of the right for compensation of Jews from Arab countries whose property had been confiscated upon their immigration to Israel.

Association in Cairo, who had earlier warned that if the German parliament ratified the agreement, the Arab countries would sever diplomatic relations with Germany.[34]

On 19 October the Arab League delegation, headed by Faris Ahmad al-Da'uk, the Lebanese ambassador to France, arrived in Bonn for talks with the German government and with supporters of the Arab position on the agreement. The German government did not show any particular interest in the delegation and restricted its movements, almost expelling its members as *personae non gratae* because of the pressure they exerted in political circles.[35] The delegation's report, which was sent to the Arab League on 30 October, emphasized that "if the German government feels it is its moral duty to repair the damage done to the Jews of Europe by the previous regime, the Arab governments have no objection because it is an internal matter [they] have nothing to do with." The report also raised an additional argument, specifically relating to the Holocaust, which had not appeared previously in relation to the reparations, although it was already a typical theme in the discourse on the Holocaust. The Arabs, it stated, "did not know what anti-Semitism was, however, they had to pay the price for persecutions inflicted on European Jewry in the modern age." That report also referred to the Holocaust as an accepted historical fact, and none of the claims raised as motives for the Arab objection to the agreement was different from the various protests that had already been lodged, especially the Syrian protest from the beginning of October, noted above.[36]

Apparently the Arab League delegation's failure motivated the Egyptian government to act separately and to direct its efforts against the reparations agreement at the German public, many of whom opposed it for various reasons. Dozens of letters arrived at the Egyptian consulate in Frankfurt and at *al-Ahram*'s offices, identifying with the Arab position. The Egyptian legation distributed flyers with a direct, personal appeal "from the Egyptian citizen to the German citizen," presenting the Egyptian point of view and the reasons for its opposition to the agreement, but to no avail. Adenauer refused to succumb to Arab

34   *Al-Ahram*, 12, 14 October 1952; Radio Beirut, 12 October 1952 – Daily Survey, no. 874, 13 October 1952.

35   *Filastin*, 22, 28 October, *al-Ahram*, 23, 26 October, 2, 4, 7, 10 November, *al-Akhbar*, 3 November, *al-Difa'*, *al-Misri*, 4, 12 November 1952. Memorandum no. 78, 24 October 1952, from the Egyptian consul in Frankfurt to the Egyptian Foreign Ministry; Telegram no. 11, 29 October 1952, from the Arab League to the Egyptian Foreign Ministry, "Arab League Matters 1952" file in the Egyptian Foreign Ministry archive; report of the joint Arab delegation 30 October 1952 to the Egyptian Foreign Ministry, "Arab League Matters 1952" file in the Egyptian Foreign Ministry archive, in 'Atiq, *al-Siyasa*, pp. 57–9.

36   *Al-Misri*, *Ruz al-Yusuf*, 10 November, *al-Akhbar*, 12 November 1952. Also see the report of the joint Arab delegation, 30 October 1952, 'Atiq, *al-Siyasa*, p. 59.

threats.[37] However, according to the report of the British High Commissioner in Germany, Germany was surprised by the Arab reaction and even requested British intervention to defuse Arab opposition, sending Alexander Böker of the Foreign Ministry to Egypt at the beginning of October to explain Germany's position and motives. The Egyptians received him cordially and played down the delegation's importance, describing it as a formal gesture while expressing understanding for the German federal government's moral need to make the gesture of reparations.[38]

On 30 October, Egyptian President Muhammad Naguib (Najib) called an urgent government meeting to discuss the agreement and to refute rumors that the Egyptian and other Arab governments were not serious about their objection to it.[39] After the meeting Naguib lodged a protest with the German ambassador in Egypt and asked to convene the Arab League's political committee. That protest also, which was essentially no different from those that preceded it, did not contain a threat to the German government. It was in fact the last protest letter sent by the Egyptian government, which had apparently reached the conclusion that the endeavor was useless. The change had been effected by the German ambassador in Cairo, who managed to convince Naguib that it would be better not to ruin relations between the two countries because of the agreement. Rather than Germany's backing down and abandoning the agreement, Egypt backed down and abandoned its protests.[40]

In fact, starting at the end of October, the Egyptian government ignored the agreement and focused on planning the German aid promised to overcome the economic difficulties faced by the revolutionary regime. Germany was perceived as a model country which had changed its economy from agricultural to industrial, a transition Egypt was eager to make.[41] However, Egypt continued its activities in the Arab League, seeking to channel it into adopting its approach. On 4 November, the League's Political Committee convened in Cairo and Naguib took an active part in the deliberations. At the same time, he maintained close contacts with German Ambassador Pawelke and updated the committee.[42] The League's meeting had been convened to determine a united

---

37   *Al-Ahram*, 17 November 1952; 'Atiq, *al-Siyasa*, pp. 60–1; Sagi, *Reparations*, p. 181.

38   FO 371/97867 (C1041/3), Kirkpatrick to Eden, 10 November 1952. Also see 'Atiq, *al-Siyasa*, p. 67.

39   *Al-Ahram, al-Akhbar, al-Misri*, 31 October 1952.

40   'Atiq, *al-Siyasa*, pp. 62–3.

41   Ibid., pp. 69–70.

42   *Al-Misri*, 1, 2, 5, 6 November, *al-Ahram*, 1, 3, 6 November, *al-Difa'*, 3 November, *al-Akhbar*, 4, 6 November 1952.

Arab position regarding the agreement and Germany, based on an analysis of its political and economic aspects. Subsequently, a sub-committee was appointed, aided by professional and military experts.[43] The political committee completed its deliberations on 9 November but issued its final report a few days later.[44] The reparations agreement remained firmly on the Arab public agenda and its media exposure reached new heights in November, when the UN General Assembly met in New York and provided another platform for the discussion of the issue.

Naguib expressed the dilemma facing Egypt and the Arabs by pointing to two dangers: the reparations agreement with Israel and the possibility of severing diplomatic relations with Germany.[45] He had to navigate, he said, between those two dangers without harming Arab interests, and had therefore influenced the committee not to rush to announce its decision and issue warnings to Germany. He sent a personal letter to Adenauer, again asking Germany not to implement the decisions regarding the agreement and to discuss positions with the Arab League.[46] The reports in the papers on his answer, submitted on 10 November, related to German willingness to ask the UN to supervise the shipments of merchandise to Israel to ensure that they did not contain strategic materials. *Filastin* even boasted that, due to the Arab unified stance and persistence, ratification of the agreement had been postponed. The German government adhered to its view that the reparations were a moral duty, and announced that it had done everything it could to mend fences with the Arabs regarding the agreement. Until ratification of the agreement by the Bundestag, it searched for ways to soothe the Arabs' anger and proposed sending a delegation to Cairo to negotiate with Egypt and with each of the other Arab states to find a solution satisfactory to both sides.[47]

---

43 *Al-Ahram*, 6, 7 November, *al-Akhbar*, 6 November 1952; Radio Monte Carlo, 1 November 1952 – Daily Survey, no. 896, 7 November 1952.

44 *Al-Misri*, *al-Ahram*, *al-Akhbar*, 10 November, *Filastin*, 20 November 1952.

45 *Al-Ahram*, *al-Akhbar*, 8 November 1952.

46 Radio Ramallah, Radio Baghdad, 7 November 1952 – Daily Survey, 9 November 1952; *al-Ahram*, *al-Akhbar*, 9 November 1952. For the report of the conversation with the Egyptian Ambassador in London, who submitted the Egyptian memorandum to the British Foreign Office, see FO 371/97867 (C1041/4), Minutes by Foster, 14 November 1952. The ambassador made the same points against the agreement and said that perhaps the solution to the problem could be found in solving the problem of the Arab refugees, meaning to transfer some of the reparations payments for that purpose. FO 371/97867 (C1041/15), Roberts to Central Department, 6 December 1952.

47 *Al-Difa'*, 10, 11 November, *Filastin*, 11, 16 November, *al-Ahram*, 11, 12 November, 24 December, *al-Misri*, 11, 12, 13 November 1952; Radio Ramallah, 12 November 1952 – Daily Survey, no. 899, 12 November 1952.

The Arab League's 11 November decision was transmitted to Germany (and to the United States, Britain and France) before it was publicly announced. It again stated that, in light of the enormous amounts of aid Germany would give to Israel, the Arab states would be "forced to defend themselves in every way possible." Since protests and diplomatic intercourse were of no avail, the only road open to them was the immediate severing of economic relations with Germany and preserving their right to take the appropriate steps to defend their interests once the agreement had been ratified. Naguib expressed his sorrow that the steps about to be taken were liable to harm the German people, who "we know does not want the agreement to be ratified, since it is against its own best interests." Al-Ahram reported that the memorandum contained "resolve and a warning," and other sources reported that the decision contained a 48-hour ultimatum.[48] In practice, however, the wording was far less emphatic than that of previous protests, and it left the door open for broad diplomatic action to balance the German aid to Israel with similar aid to Egypt and other Arab states.

Following the Egyptian-led activity, the Egyptian and Jordanian press wrote about various German and American initiatives intended to prevent the Arab states from actually taking steps against Germany, and widely quoted from editorials that appeared in the German newspapers which were critical of the agreement and raised claims the same as those of the Arabs.[49] The reparations agreement continued to be a focus for joint Arab interest and activity throughout the first quarter of 1953, especially in light of the efforts to come to an understanding with the German government before its ratification in the two German Houses of Representatives. When it became known that the date for ratification was the middle of January, the Arab League's Political Committee called an urgent meeting. The minutes of the meeting were not made public, but it was clear from reports that an essential change had occurred in the Arab approach. The threat of an economic boycott of Germany was still viable, but it had been considerably moderated and gave every state the freedom to determine its position regarding Germany and the kinds of demands it would make.[50] The Egyptian press reported the agreement's ratification on 18 March 1953 and gave a detailed account of Adenauer's statement, which stressed the agreement's importance in closing "the worst chapter" of Germany's history and "regaining

---

48   *Al-Misri, al-Akhbar, al-Difa'*, 13, 16 November, *al-Ahram*, 14, 16, 17 November 1952; Radio Baghdad, 13 November 1952 – Daily Survey, no. 900, 13 November 1952.

49   *Filastin*, 15, 19 November, *al-Misri, al-Difa', Ruz al-Yusuf*, 17 November, *al-Ahram*, 21, 23, 28 November 1952.

50   *Al-Ahram*, 13 December 1952, 1, 6, 8, 10 16 January 1953; *Filastin*, 31 December 1952; Radio Damascus, Radio Monte Carlo, 5 January 1953 – Daily Survey, no. 945, 6 January 1953.

respect in the eyes of the free world." The German government issued a special statement expressing its desire to strengthen relations with the Arab states, but ignoring the threats.[51]

The Arab League adopted the Egyptian approach, based on the realization that it would be impossible to prevent implementation of the agreement and that Arab countries might lose more from an economic boycott of Germany. Hence, besides the joint activities, each Arab state pursued its own independent policy vis-à-vis relations with Germany.[52] Saudi Arabia was the first Arab state to actually stop negotiations with a German company (which was supposed to establish a wireless communications network), and took steps to end economic and commercial projects with it.[53] In September, Syria postponed signing new contracts with German companies,[54] and the Lebanese government decided to stop all contacts with Germany concerning the establishment of diplomatic relations.[55] Egypt, on the other hand, continued its attempts to influence the German government and public opinion by exploiting the diplomatic relations it had established in October 1952.[56]

Naguib made statements and gave interviews to the German news agencies to explain that the agreement was "an unfortunate event," and expressed hope that the disagreements with Germany would come to an end and that it would find a way to compensate the Arab states.[57] In addition to propaganda activity, Egypt took a small number of steps in protest: in October 1952 it scrapped an

51   *Al-Ahram*, 6, 20, 22 March, *al-Difa'*, 11, 20, 22 March, *Filastin*, 20, 30 March 1953.

52   *Al-Ahram*, 25 March, 2, 6 April, *al-Difa'*, 23, 24 March, *Filastin*, 1 April 1953. Also see remarks made by al-Shuqayri in discussions with two members of the British Foreign Office: FO 371/103955 (CW1041/19), McCarthy to Baker, 12 March 1953.

53   Radio Baghdad, 20 September 1952 – Daily Survey, no. 859, 22 September 1952; Radio Damascus, 31 October Radio Monte Carlo, 1 November 1952 – Daily Survey, no. 891, 2 November 1952; *Filastin*, 21 September, 7 November, *al-Misri*, 2, 5, 13 November, *al-Akhbar*, 16, 17 November 1952. Also see FO 371/97867 (C1041/3), report of the British High Commissioner in Germany, 10 November 1952.

54   *Filastin*, 10, 13 September 1952. Radio Ramallah, 27 September, Radio Cairo, 7 November 1952 – Daily Survey, nos. 864, 867, 30 September, 9 November 1952.

55   Radio Beirut, 5 November 1952 – Daily Survey, no. 859, 6 November 1952. Lebanese, Jordanian and Syrian commercial offices even sent warnings to German commercial offices about the implications of the agreement. Contracts estimated to be worth tens of millions of German marks had reportedly been cancelled. *Al-Difa'*, 5, 12 November, 18, 25 December, *al-Ahram*, 12 November, 30 December 1952. Radio Ramallah, 13 November, Radio Damascus, 21 December 1952 – Daily Survey, nos. 901, 903, 14 November, 22 December 1952.

56   *Al-Misri*, 14, 29, 30 November, 5, 7 December, *al-Ahram*, 20 November 1952.

57   'Atiq, *al-Siyasa*, pp. 68–9; *al-Ahram*, 8 October, 11 December 1952; Radio Beirut, 1 December 1952 – Daily Survey no. 916, 2 December 1952; *Akhir Sa'a*, 20 May 1953.

agreement for the establishment of a branch of a German institute in Egypt and cancelled both its participation in an international trade fair in Germany and a German industrial exhibition which was supposed to open in Cairo in January 1953.[58] Egypt's careful steps were also the result of intensive diplomatic activity in which Ambassador Pawelke played an important role. In a gesture of goodwill, Germany donated 100,000 marks to UNRWA, the UN refugees fund, and throughout his posting in Egypt, the ambassador himself donated his monthly allotment as a wounded veteran to the organization of disabled Egyptian veterans.[59]

At the beginning of February 1953, an eleven-man economic delegation, headed by State Secretary of the Department of Economics Ludger Westrick, arrived in Egypt. The delegation symbolized Egypt's acceptance of the reparations agreement. *Al-Ahram* editorialized that deliberating with the delegation was a way of implementing the Arab viewpoint, which saw no connection between the German reparations and economics, and enabling the Arab states to receive, like Israel, equipment and raw materials to strengthen their industries and economies and to raise their technological level.[60] However, official Egyptian spokesmen continued to refer to Arab bitterness over the agreement and consistently objected to it because of the Arab refugee problem.[61] At the press conference convened before the German delegation returned to Bonn, Westrick was forced to relate to points raised by Mahmud Fawzi, the Egyptian foreign minister, and expressed his solidarity with the refugees' distress and the "terrible catastrophe" which had befallen the Palestinians.[62] However, Germany refused to link reparations to Israel with compensation for the Arab refugees.[63] The general impression after the visit was that the negotiations had been unsuccessful and achieved no results, especially when the delegation returned and learned that Egypt had signed a trade agreement with East Germany.[64]

---

58   *Al-Ahram*, 4 October, 19 November 1952; Radio Beirut, 29 November 1952 – Daily Survey, 30 November 1952.

59   Radio Baghdad, 3 October 1952 – Daily Survey no. 867, 5 October 1952; *al-Ahram*, October 4, *al-Misri*, November 4, 1952.

60   *Al-Ahram*, 18, 29 January, 1, 2, 3, 5, 8, 9, 11, 12, 13, 15, 16 February, *al-Misri*, 19 February 1953; *Majallat al-Azhar*, 15 February 1953, pp. 772–3. See also FO 371/103955 (CW1041/16), Trevelyan to Allen, Foreign Office, 12 February 1953.

61   See the remarks of Foreign Minister Mahmud Fawzi, who headed the Egyptian delegation at the talks, *al-Ahram*, 4 and 11 February 1953.

62   *Al-Ahram*, 11 February, *Filastin*, 4 March 1953.

63   FO 341/103955 (CW1041/19), McCarthy to Baker, 12 March 1953. Also see Shinar, *Under the Burden*, p. 50.

64   *Al-Akhbar*, 17 October 1952; *Manchester Guardian*, 19 February 1953; FO 371/102842

It can safely be said that the official Egyptian attitude toward the matter of reparations for Israel was, in the final analysis, pragmatic, and that there was nothing essentially different in the new regime's response or in its claims against the agreement. The new Egyptian regime exploited the reparations agreement to prove that it conducted its affairs differently from its predecessor, especially when it was a question of guarding national interests.[65] However, as compared to the old regime, it led intensive activity against the agreement, which climaxed in November 1952, and even used threatening language toward Germany, but it took no real steps which might harm Egypt and its needs. Naguib's approach was more balanced and moderate than that of his Arab League colleagues, explained a member of the British Foreign Office,[66] and Moshe Sasson, the Israeli representative in Athens, was of the same opinion. The reaction to the reparations agreement was viewed as an outburst of anti-Israeli sentiment "needed to reinforce his internal position."[67] The gap between the vehement rhetoric and its translation into practical language led to the assumption that the threat of a boycott was "an empty threat and an attempt at blackmail."[68]

The reparations agreement in public discourse

As in the case of the discussion on Jewish immigration to Palestine, there was a difference between the official references to the reparations agreement and the discourse evolving around it in journalistic writings. The editorials in the large Egyptian newspapers, al-Ahram, al-Misri and al-Akhbar, and in the various periodicals which continued to be published after the revolution, reflected the official line to a great extent, although a critical tone, directed primarily at the functioning of the old regime in the affair, could be discerned in a number of them. The Egyptian press preceded the government and was more militant in its representation of the agreement and the Holocaust than were official spokes-

---

(E11318/2), Stevenson to Foreign Office, 12 February 1953. Also see Sagi, *German Reparations*, p. 184; Shinar, *Under the Burden*, p. 50.

65   Ahmad Taha al-Sanusi, "al-siyasa al-duwaliyya fi usbu'," *al-Thaqafa*, 17 November 1952, p. 6.

66   FO 341/103955 (CW1041/19), McCarthy to Baker, 12 March 1953. The American Ambassador in Cairo had a similar impression. See LM 089, Roll 37, 1950–1954 International Relations (674.84A/8–2853), Caffery, Egyptian Policy on Palestine, 28 August 1953.

67   HZ/2548/18, Athens, Sasson to the Director of the Research Department, 18 February 1953.

68   *Al-Misri*, 22 November 1952; *Manchester Guardian*, 19 February 1953; *The Wiener Library Bulletin*, vol. 7, nos. 3–4 (May–August 1953), p. 24.

men.[69] When details of the first appeals made by Israel and Jewish organizations regarding reparations became known between 1951 and the signing of the agreement in September 1952, the number of references was fairly limited. However, as official Arab activity concerning the agreement intensified, it appeared on the public agenda more frequently, and became the subject of editorials and long articles, some of which were printed on the front pages.

Although *Filastin* did not publish editorials and refrained from exposing its particular views on the agreement, it closely followed Arab diplomatic activities and reported them daily, stressing the Syrians' adamant oppositional position, and naturally focused less on the special Egyptian role. In some cases it even preceded the Egyptian papers. Already on 10 September 1952 it introduced the major articles of the agreement, hardly mentioning the reason for the compensation of "international Jewry."[70] In other cases it related aspects that were completely ignored by Egyptian papers, such as the internal controversy raging in Israel regarding the reparations, and attempts on Adenauer's life. A small item on 12 September 1952 quoted "Jewish information agencies" on the opposition of the Herut party leaders, defined as "the extreme party" headed by the "terrorist" Menahem Begin. The paper emphasized that they vowed to fight the agreement by all means, but did not dwell on the reasons. A week later it reported the death of a German policeman in Munich in an explosion of a letter bomb sent by "extremist Jews" to the Chancellor, and in November it revealed another plot to assassinate him, exposed by American intelligence.[71]

Beyond the official complaints manifested in Egyptian and Arab analyses, the starting point of the discussion was chiefly a matter of moral principles, explained 'Atiq, who described the Arab reaction as emotional and derived from interpersonal relations, whereas relations between countries were dictated first and foremost by interests. The spokesmen projected values of interpersonal relations onto the relations between nations, he asserted, and therefore perceived the agreement above all as Germany's alienation of its friends, exposing a whole set of attitudes toward Germany and the German people. However, projecting the blame for Germany's behavior onto external factors, such as American and British pressure and the intrigues of world Jewry, enabled them to adhere to their belief in the friendship of the German people and even contributed anti-imperialist, anti-Jewish rhetoric to the discussion.[72]

---

69   FO 371/96848 (JE1013/40), Cairo, Stevenson, Report from 22 October, 4 November 1952.

70   *Filastin*, 10 September 1952.

71   *Filastin*, 12, 19 September, 8 November 1952.

72   'Atiq, *al-Siyasa*, p. 41.

References to the Holocaust in the mainstream discourse were indirect, and did not dispute its being a historical fact. Nor was Germany's right to compensate Jews on a personal basis denied, but Israel's right to represent and receive reparations in the name of those Jews was rejected out of hand. A large part of the discussion about the agreement evolved around its political aspects and implications for the balance of power between Israel and the Arab states. The assertion that the Arab refugees were more entitled to compensation, which implied an equation between the suffering of the Palestinians and the suffering of the Jews under Nazi persecutions, also seemed to stem from political considerations rather than from an intention to minimize the Holocaust. However, there were a number of manifestations of Holocaust denial in the public discourse which did not appear in official pronouncements. Those were especially characteristic of the writing and statements of Islamic circles. Several recurrent themes evolved:

1. *Germany has the right to compensate the Jews, but not the State of Israel, for the actions of the Nazis.* The Germans are entitled to compensate their Jewish countrymen for what happened to them at the hands of the Nazis, but the agreement ignores the fact that Israel was established on land taken from the Arabs. If the persecution of the Jews justifies their being given reparations, then those who were personally victimized by the Nazis should be compensated, not the State of Israel, which is a spearhead of imperialist aggression against the Arabs.[73] Egyptian leftist journalist Ihsan 'Abd al-Qudus, on the other hand, claimed that the Jews in Israel did not deserve reparations even if those living in Israel were the same Jews who had been persecuted by Hitler in Germany, since Hitler persecuted them as Germans.[74] In challenging the right of Jews for reparations as individuals, the claim revealed a lack of understanding of – or the lack of a desire to understand – the special place anti-Semitism held in Nazi ideology, which persecuted the Jews as Jews and not as German citizens. It also ignored the fact that not only German Jews were targeted, but all Jews, wherever they were. However, it seems to reflect an attempt to dispel the idea of the Jews as a nation more than it intended to deny the Holocaust.

2. *Jews unjustly instill guilt feelings in Germans.* Paying reparations to Israel is like a German admission of guilt.[75] This claim was contrary to the official German position, which did not recognize either guilt or direct responsibility for

---

73   *Al-Misri*, 28, 29 October, *al-Ahram*, 29 October 1952.

74   *Al-Misri*, 12 November 1952.

75   *Al-Ahram*, 15 December 1952.

the crimes of the Nazi regime.[76] An article based on journalistic investigation carried out in Germany by an *al-Musawwar* reporter tried to explain why Germany was making such an effort to satisfy the Jews and claimed that the Jews "invented well-constructed stories about how their children died, and about how they were tortured" in Hitler's concentration camps. Moreover, they repeated "that tune again and again, and everywhere, until they managed to make many Germans feel guilty." Every German, the article added, had a personal guilt complex and felt it his duty to apologize to every Jew he met for Hitler's behavior and actions, and to compensate him for his sufferings. The Allies were horrified by the Jews' stories and in their desire to avenge themselves they fostered Germans' guilt feelings so that they might purify themselves of Hitlerism.[77] The Jews "distorted the reputation of the Germans in the world through their false claims," explained an article in *Filastin*, and hence they were forced to pay compensation now that they were building a new life.[78] There is no doubt that the claim was meant to draw a demonic image of the Jews as individuals who possessed the power to concoct plots, instigate conflicts and dictate conditions because of their political and economic might. Like the previous motif, this one also expressed the prevailing discourse regarding Jews and showed the developing connection between denial of the Holocaust and the perception of Jews in the spirit of *The Protocols of the Elders of Zion*.[79] The motif of "fostering guilt feelings" among Germans and the West in general and exploiting them materially would, in the future, develop into one of the main themes in the Arab representation of the Holocaust.

3. *Germany succumbed to pressure exerted by the western powers and world Jewry.* It was American–British pressure that pushed Germany to take the enormous financial burden on itself, wrote Ibrahim al-Shanti. Promises were made to encourage it to finish the affair and to rid itself of the attacks made by world Jewry and its spies. Those who forced Germany to pay Israel more than $800 million were those who rejected paying anything to the Arab refugees.[80] It also became apparent, claimed another editorial, that the Jews who controlled

---

76   See, for example, Segev, *The Seventh Million*, p. 233; Roni Stauber, "*Realpolitik* and the Burden of the Past: Israeli Diplomacy and the 'Other Germany'," *Israel Studies*, vol. 8, no. 3 (Fall 2003), p. 116.

77   *Al-Musawwar*, 21 November 1952. For the Arab claims as they were reflected in the German and Swedish press, see HZ/2545/8a, Stockholm, Ben-Haim to the Department of Western Europe, 23 September 1952, 14 April 1953.

78   *Filastin*, 4 November 1952.

79   See also, Dina Porat, "*The Protocols of the Elders of Zion*: New Uses of an Old Myth," in Wistrich (ed.), *Demonizing the Other*, pp. 325–7.

80   *Al-Ahram*, 26 September 1952.

German policy were the same Jews who were expelled by Hitler's government, and had now returned to decide the fate of West Germany.[81] Al-Shanti also claimed that the Jews in Germany held high-ranking positions in the judicial system, the universities, the press and other professional fields. Despite the fact that they were pleased with the situation, they were still upset with the "former era," and therefore the German government had proposed to pay Israel $830 million to satisfy its 24,000 Jews. The American government had brought its influence to bear to close the deal, he added, and it would repay Germany what it gave Israel.[82] Bakri al-Nasir quoted a German journalist who tried to explain how the hatred and revulsion Germans felt for the Jews and the reparations agreement could be reconciled. He doubted whether the reparations would eliminate the hatred between the two peoples, claiming that actually, Germany was not a sovereign country, its affairs were managed by three powers and all it could do was comply with their demands.[83]

Ihsan 'Abd al-Qudus also, in a very critical article entitled "Egypt First," claimed that the United States was the force behind the agreement and thus there was no reason to boycott Germany. A boycott of German goods would only serve American and British interests, since a void would be created in the Egyptian market which they would rush to fill.[84] Germany was in difficult straits, explained Husayn Kamil Salim. It was compelled to honor the agreement so as to preserve its reputation, and to satisfy the western countries and "the Jewish interests behind them."[85] A four-part series was published in *al-Ahram* between 31 December 1952 and 3 January 1953, exposing what it claimed was the secret of the German reparations agreement. It also tried to show how the "Zionist plot" had been conceived with the aid of the occupying powers ever since "the Allies forced the German army to surrender unconditionally." It described the German de-Nazification and demilitarization laws, the appointment of prisoners liberated from the concentration camps to high-ranking positions, and the imprisonment of high-ranking officers in the German army as war criminals. Prominent figures, including key Americans such as General MacCloy and Morgenthau, were described in great detail as

---

81 *Al-Ahram*, 31 October 1952.

82 *Al-Ahram*, 9 November 1952. See also *al-Musawwar*, 21 November 1952.

83 *Al-Misri*, 2 November 1952.

84 *Al-Misri*, 12 November 1952. See also *al-Misri*, 13 November 1952; Ahmad Suwaylim al-'Umari, *al-Sharq al-awsat wa-mushkilat filastin*, Cairo: 1954, p. 104.

85 *Al-Musawwar*, 21 November 1952. The article was extensively quoted by *Filastin*, 21 November 1952. Also see Fathi al-Ramli, *al-Sahyuniyya a'la marahil al-isti'mar*, Cairo: 1956, pp. 138, 240.

Zionists, pro-Zionists and Jews, some of them accused of being involved in the activities of the Organization of Nazi Victims and in preparing the ground for the payment of reparations. Zionists had taken control of the propaganda media, radio stations and newspapers, and strove to starve the German people and destroy the German economy and industries, claimed the series. It also stressed the Jewish financial support of Adenauer, his pro-Zionist leanings and his sole responsibility for signing the agreement. That situation, as well as the threat of an Arab boycott, increased unemployment and the anger of the German people against Zionism. Arab protests and claims were received with understanding by the Germans, who found in them an expression of their own views, which they had been forbidden to express since 1945, the series concluded.[86] The theme also reflected the increase in classic anti-Semitic images in Egyptian public discourse.

4. *The Arab refugees are more entitled to compensation.* In the discussion of the Israeli demand for reparations, as early as September 1951, *al-Ahram* had referred to the fate of "the victims of Zionism, the Palestinians, who were expelled by Hitlerite Israel," and wondered whether "the Arabs aren't more deserving [of reparations]."[87] How could the German people forget that humanism obliged them to show more compassion for the Arab refugees, who were also more worthy of their mercy, asked another editorial.[88] *Al-Misri* published the text of the agreement on 27 and 28 October, with a short introduction which again expressed disappointment at the way the Germans treated the Arabs and apprehension concerning Israeli intentions. "While it is true that the Jews suffered under the Nazis, compensation for their suffering should not come at the expense of the Arabs and their interests. What the Jews have done to them in Palestine is far worse than what the Nazis did to the Jews."[89] The theme appeared again and again in later pronouncements. *Al-Ahram* referred to "hair-raising atrocities," and an Arab Monte Carlo Radio commentator said that the reparations should be given to the Arabs in compensation for the "great loss and suffering" the Jews had caused the Arabs of Palestine.[90] *Filastin* quoted a letter to the *New York Times* in December 1952 in which two professors criticized Israel's attitude to the refugees' problem. Although the paper did not express its view, the publication of the letter was significant in reflecting it, especially

---

86   *Al-Ahram*, 31 December 1952, 1–3 January 1953.

87   *Al-Ahram*, 12 September 1951.

88   *Al-Ahram*, 16 November 1952.

89   *Al-Misri*, 27, 28 October 1952.

90   Radio Monte Carlo, 13 November 1952 – Daily Survey, no. 901, 14 November 1952; *al-Ahram*, 15 December 1952.

through the inserted question and quotation marks. "The tragedy of the six millions Jews (?) [sic] killed by the Nazis could be compensated by Germany's payments," the writers claimed, but it was absolutely unjust to compensate the Jews on the Arabs' account, while "Israel" shunned its responsibility to compensate the Arab refugees.[91]

5. *The agreement was a blow to German–Arab friendship.* Egyptian columnists assumed that Germany was taking action hostile to the Arabs and creating a dangerous precedent for other European governments, and that sooner or later Israel would present similar claims to other countries where large Jewish communities had lost their property and lives. Germans had a good reputation in the Arab states, they claimed, and after the war they had quickly gained the Arabs' trust because they were perceived as supporting Arab rights and independence, especially the rights of the Palestinian Arabs against the Israeli occupiers. "Moreover, they follow with wonder the victory of the defeated and Germany's rise from its ashes, and look forward to its return to a large, unified country serving science, culture and humanism."[92] There were those who advised Germany to weigh its compliance with the agreement against the damage caused by Arab anger. Germany had to decide, they said, between a moral consideration, which it had announced with the decision to pay reparations, and the economic and international implications resulting from it.[93] Quoting a Syrian paper, *Filastin* considered the payment of compensation by Germany "a bigger crime" against the Arabs than the "crucial mistake" committed by Hitler against the Jews.[94]

6. *The Islamic discourse.* Unlike the nationalist mainstream press, the Islamic discourse was notorious for its denial of the Holocaust. *Majallat al-Azhar*, the monthly magazine of al-Azhar University, which reflects official Islamic positions, dealt with the topic of reparations more than the other periodicals surveyed. In October 1952, *al-Ahram* reported the resolutions passed at a conference of the Young Muslim Association (*jam'iyyat al-shubban al-muslimin*) in Alexandria, which related to the demands of "the Jewish authority of occupied Palestine" for "so-called compensation." "They claim that they were oppressed in Germany and that they suffered heavy losses, and therefore they deserve compensation which they will use to oppress the Arabs and cause them even worse

91   *Filastin*, 28 December 1952.
92   *Al-Ahram*, 29 October, 9, 16 November, *al-Misri*, 28, 29 October, 8, 16 November 1952, 1 January 1953.
93   *Al-Thaqafa*, 17 November 1952, p. 6; *al-Ahram*, 15, 18 December 1952.
94   *Filastin*, 20 March 1953.

damages." Therefore, the Association demanded that the Arab and Muslim states should strive to convince the German government to freeze the payments to the Jews until they compensated the Palestinian Arabs, and to explain that payment of reparations was considered an aggressive measure against the Arab nations.[95] According to the Egyptian daily *al-Balagh*, the greatest danger of the agreement was that it posed an international precedent which the "Jews" would exploit to make further demands on other European countries where Jews had been harmed in World War II.[96]

Another editorial in *Majallat al-Azhar* summarized the claims against the reparations agreement, and shed light on the entire Islamic perception of the events that had occurred since Hitler's rise to power. The article began with a short history, beginning in 1937, when, it said, Hitler took over the government. When his government determined its plan "to liberate itself from the Jews and their intellectual, social, economic and political power over Germany," it collected their books and burned them. Then the Jews began to leave for other countries and most of them, 300,000, came to Palestine. The Zionists "exploited and inflated the event [the book-burning]" and raised a great outcry. From there the editorial passed directly to the reparations agreement, completely disregarding the developments of the war years. While ignoring international law, the western countries compelled West Germany to compensate the Jews "who alleged that Hitler expelled them from his country," and Germany's political situation forced it to comply. The Arab governments viewed the agreement as a threat, that was likely to lengthen the life of the Israeli government by ten years or more, and serve as a precedent for similar demands on other countries, in which the Jews also claimed they were persecuted.[97]

Similar statements, implying doubt about the Jewish claims of Nazi persecution, were also made by the dean of al-Azhar University, Shaykh Muhammad al-Khadr Husayn, in an interview with *al-Ahram*. Although he did not directly mention the Holocaust, the way he represented the Palestinian catastrophe incorporated certain relativism and denial. When they would write about World War II, historians would find that "the most despicable event visited upon humanity and its values in the twentieth century" was the expulsion of the legitimate Palestinians from their homes to settle alien Jews from all over the world in their stead, he said, suggesting that the Holocaust was an act less grave than the expulsion. Now, he added, Germany was starting a new chapter in "this humiliating story for human conscience." He concluded with a call to return

---

95   *Al-Ahram*, 4 October 1952.
96   Radio Cairo, 8 November 1952 – Daily Survey, no. 897, 9 November 1952.
97   *Majallat al-Azhar*, 19 November 1952, p. 386.

the Jews to Germany, where Nazism no longer existed, and the Arab refugees to their Palestinian homeland, otherwise the western countries' claims of human rights would be exposed as the greatest lies told in history.[98]

7. *Opposition to the agreement in Germany.* Many articles dealt with the opposition to the agreement in various German circles, and introduced motifs of Holocaust denial, exposing the potential of the connection between former Nazis and the Arabs. An editorial entitled "The Friendly German People" stated that many letters had been sent to *al-Ahram* from various places in Germany voicing objection to imposing on Germany the duty to compensate Israel for what Hitler had done to their Zionist kinsmen. The false claim that Hitler and his followers had persecuted the Jews had long since evaporated, said the letters, and "the Jews in Israel were never harmed by the Germans. So what is the connection between the Germans and compensating them? And how did the burden of compensation fall upon the Germans when they were innocent of any crime?"[99]

On 19 January 1953, *al-Misri* published a letter from Berlin signed by intellectuals, students, workers, businessmen and political party leaders, expressing support for the Arab position and demanding that an investigation be made of Adenauer's mistakes concerning the issue of reparations to Israel.[100] Syrian newspapers reportedly published an open letter by the Organization of Free Germans, a pro-Nazi group in Brazil, stating that the agreement was not commensurate with the aspirations of the German people, "which has sentiments of friendship and brotherhood for the Arab nation."[101] Similarly, *al-Akhbar* reported on a group of Nazi lawyers who believed that Germany had been betrayed a second time during World War II, a statement which was characteristic of German public discourse on the eve of Hitler's rise to power, and thus the article was entitled "Another Hitler Needed!"[102]

8. *German experts in Egypt.* The issue of the arrival of former Nazis in Egypt, their motives and activity is not within the scope of this chapter (see below,

---

98   *Al-Ahram*, 21 January 1953. The interview was also published in *Majallat al-Azhar*, 15 February 1943, pp. 722–4. Also see FO 371/103956 (CW1041/9), Cairo to Foreign Office, 22 January 1953.

99   *Al-Ahram*, 17 November 1952. The question of whether the Jews living in Israel were in Germany in the past was raised a number of times. For example, see *al-Ahram*, 15 December 1952.

100   *Al-Misri*, 19 January 1953; Radio Damascus, 19 January 1953 – Daily Survey, no. 957, 20 January 1953. The article did not mention names.

101   Radio Ramallah, 30 November 1952 – Daily Survey, 1 December 1952.

102   *Al-Akhbar*, 6 November 1952.

Chapter 9), but the extent of their influence on the Egyptian position toward the reparations issue and perhaps even the representation of the Holocaust are relevant to the discussion. The connection between former Nazis and the Middle East aroused particular interest in both Israel and the West. They followed their activity in the Arab states, especially Egypt, where they were reportedly received with favor and great esteem. In January 1951, *al-Ahram* published a survey on the perception of foreigners by the Egyptians, which revealed a clear preference for German experts and a great affinity for Germans.[103] Muhammad 'Abdallah 'Inan, writing in *al-Thaqafa*, expressed admiration for Germany's achievements and rehabilitation after the war,[104] and the Egyptian press prided itself on the fact that the German experts viewed Egypt as a second home.[105]

The issue of German experts in Egypt had already been mentioned in the Egyptian media during the monarchy. In many instances this had resulted from protests by Israel or Britain, who were apprehensive regarding German military activity in Egypt and the convergence of Nazi ideology and hatred for the Jews with the Arab effort against Israel. As early as June 1949, *al-Ahram* quoted Syrian sources denying the "Zionist rumors" that former Nazis were being recruited by Egypt to establish a military unit of foreign nationals.[106] Israel and various Western states suspected that the German experts – many of whom opposed the reparations agreement – were inflaming Arab opposition to it. Ambassador Pawelke implicitly confirmed this and warned that by opposing the agreement after it had been signed, they were damaging Germany's relations with Egypt.[107] Hjalmar Schacht, German Minister of Finance and Chairman of the Central Bank during the Third Reich, who was one of the senior Nazi leaders acquitted at Nuremberg, and was also critical of the reparations agreement, arrived in Cairo on 22 September 1952, at the invitation of the new government, to provide advice about agricultural reform and other economic matters.[108]

The agreement exposed the identification of the German neo-Nazi right with the Arab side in the conflict with Israel, and the possibilities for cooperation

---

103   *Al-Ahram*, 1 January, 1951. For a survey of the activities of German experts and the connection between them and the industrialization of the Egyptian military between 1948 and 1964, see 'Atiq, *al-Siyasa*, pp. 143–78.

104   *Al-Thaqafa*, 18 February 1952, pp. 7–8.

105   *Akhir Sa'a*, 25 March, *al-Ahram*, 19 May 1953.

106   *Al-Ahram*, 20 June 1949.

107   *Al-Ahram*, 18 November 1952; *Ruz al-Yusuf*, 29 December 1952; *Hatsofeh*, 29 December 1952; HZ/2445/8a, Ben-Horin to Eisler, 4 May 1954; 'Atiq, *al-Siyasa*, p. 71.

108   *Al-Ahram*, 21, 23, 26, 29 September 1952. Also see *La Bourse Egyptienne*, 4 January 1952 – Selection of News, no. 136, 22 January 1952; *al-Akhbar*, 14 December 1952.

between the two, which were reflected in their joint opposition to the agreement. Otto Ernst Remer,[109] leader of the Socialist Reich Party (outlawed in 1952), who had been in Egypt from the beginning of 1953, also condemned the agreement as "a brutal robbery" and "a national shame" in an article in *Der Weg*, a neo-Nazi periodical appearing in Buenos Aires. He described the Germans and Arabs as those who had been oppressed by "world Jewry," and said that if the agreement were put to a referendum it would garner 10 percent support at best.[110]

After the ratification of the agreement in 1953, interest in it declined and it was no longer on the public agenda, though occasionally it reappeared. Through the offices of the Arab Boycott of Israel, the Arabs continued to monitor its implementation, the merchandise sent to Israel and the German companies doing business with Israel, and sometimes these activities were reported in the press.[111] Among the reports were background articles which ostensibly divulged additional secrets behind the German reparations. One such article, based on a report prepared for the Arab League's Political Committee, appeared in *al-Musawwar* in December 1953, and later in *al-Ahram*. It ascribed great importance to the manipulations of the Allied powers, which convinced the Germans that their former leaders had been criminals. The article in *al-Ahram* also mentioned the political capital Adenauer had made from the agreement and enormous amounts in bribery paid to the head of Adenauer's office,[112] but did not reflect an essential change in the discourse, nor did it actually reveal any fact that had not been reported on in the past.

The matter of reparations returned to the Egyptian agenda after the Suez Campaign in 1956, when Egypt demanded that Germany stop the payment of reparations to Israel because of what it called "aggression," and even submitted a legal appeal against Germany in March 1957. The idea of boycotting Germany

---

109   Remer was the Nazi officer who played a key role in foiling the attempted coup against Hitler on 20 July 1944, and after the war became a symbol among neo-Nazis in Germany.

110   *Ruz al-Yusuf*, 20 April 1953; *The Wiener Library Bulletin*, vol. 7, nos. 3–4 (May–August 1953), p. 24. Remer was also quoted by *al-Musawwar* on 25 December 1953. Similar sentiments were expressed in a conversation held by Ralph Dibi, a representative of the German–Arab Friendship League, with a member of the *al-Ahram* staff when he visited Egypt at the beginning of 1956. See *al-Ahram*, 16 February 1956.

111   See, for example, *al-Ahram*, 14 May, 9 August, 5, 30 September 1953, 13 March 1954; *Akhir Sa'a*, 1 July, 30 September 1953; *Ruz al-Yusuf*, 3 August, 7 December, *al-Difa'*, 27 December 1953; HZ/2517/19, HZ/2593/3, Shinar to Eitan, 11 February, 9 March 1955; HZ/2530/3a, Legation in Berne to the Department of Western Europe, 18 June 1956.

112   *Al-Musawwar*, 25 December 1953; *al-Ahram*, 3, 5 January 1954.

arose again;[113] however, there was no significant public discussion concerning it. The agreement had been frequently mentioned in articles and books about Israel and the conflict since the early 1960s and presented as the major factor which rescued Israel from destruction, stabilized its economy, turned it into a military power and enabled it to continue oppressing Palestine.[114] Those material advantages reinforced the claims that the Holocaust had been exploited by Israel and blown out of all proportion, and increased the urge to diminish its dimensions so as to dispel Israel's demands.[115]

The Israel–West German reparations agreement epitomized, in Arab discourse, the Jews' emotional exploitation of European guilt feelings, which were translated into material gains, and the debate over it never actually ceased. Repeated attempts were made by Arab representatives to change articles of the agreement, to prevent various consignments which might be used in military manufacture from reaching Israel, and to rouse public opinion against it in Germany. In March 1957, the Israeli legate in Bern, Yesha'yahu Avi'ad, reported that Egyptian students were spreading inflammatory propaganda against Israel which related to the Holocaust also, exploiting a prevailing sentiment that Germany was not obliged to atone and pay such amounts of compensation to Israel and the Jews.[116] After Ben-Gurion met Adenauer in the United States on 14 March 1960, the Egyptian and Arab press raged at their joint statement, which insinuated future German commitment to supporting Israel.[117]

---

113 *Al-Ahram*, 7, 9 March, 10 August 1957; *al-Difa'*, 21 March 1957; HZ/3100/1, Shinar to the Assistant Director of the Department of Western Europe, 7 April 1957; HZ/3100/1, Joachim Joesten, Germany and the Suez Crisis, No. 34 (January 1957). See also 'Atiq, *al-Siyasa*, pp. 135–42.

114 See, for example, *Filastin*, 20 January 1962; Muhammad Fa'iz al-Qusari, *Harb filastin, 'am 1948: al-sira' al-siyasi bayna al-sahyuniyya wal-'arab*, Cairo: 1961, p. 41; 'Ali Muhammad 'Ali, *Isra'il wal-sharq al-awsat*, Cairo: 1963, p. 416; 'Ali Muhammad 'Ali and Muhammad Hina'i 'Abd al-Hadi, *Dawlat al-irhab*, Cairo: n.d [probably 1963], p. 110.

115 For later references to the agreement which emphasize the American influence on its acceptance and its contribution to Israel, see Kenneth M. Lewan, "How West Germany Helped to Build Israel," *Journal of Palestine Studies*, vol. 4, no. 4 (Summer 1975), pp. 41–64; Kamal al-Din Rif'at, *al-Isti'mar wal-sahyuniyya wa-qadiyyat filastin*, Cairo: 1967, p. 56; Galina Nikitina, *Dawlat isra'il. Khasa'is al-tatawwur al-siyasi wal-iqtisadi*, Cairo: n.d., pp. 125–7, 274; Jamal al-Din al-Rimadi, *al-Sahyuniyya al-'alamiyya wa-ma'rakat al-masir al-'arabi*, Cairo: 1968, p. 9; Muhammad Kamal al-Dissuqi and 'Abd al-Tawwab 'Abd al-Raziq Salman, *al-Sahyuniyya wal-naziyya. Dirasa muqarina*, Cairo: 1968, pp. 149–54; *Rabitat al-'Alam al-Islami* (October 1978) pp. 36–40.

116 *Al-Ahram*, 16 August 1954, 7 January, 5 February, 7 May, 10 June, 30 October 1955, 15 January, 18 August 1960; *Arab Observer*, 5 August 1963, p. 8. HZ/3112/22, Avi'ad to the Department of Western Europe, 7 March 1957.

117 *Al-Ahram*, 15 March, 22 May, 30 September, *al-Akhbar*, 22 May, *al-Nahar*, 16 March 1960.

The Arab approach to the agreement focused on the benefits Israel reaped from the payments, as it had done since the eve of its signing. As far as the Arabs were concerned, wrote the *Arab Observer*, "the money finances the Zionist plundering of Palestine."[118] The main points of the narrative were, in effect, those that had appeared from the beginning: the United States had pressured West Germany to pay moral compensation "for the damage done to the Jews under the Nazis"; the compensation was not paid to the real victims or their heirs but was, rather, intended to prevent the economic collapse of Israel; Israel was putting the money to military uses; and West Germany needed it to clear its name. Long articles reiterated the same claims and many books were written about them as well, sometimes without mentioning the reason for the payment of compensation.[119] While the United States allowed the Arabs to be expelled from Palestine and Israel to be established, it forced Germany to pay reparations to Israel for the losses the Jews sustained under Hitler, claimed 'Ali 'Alluba, while 'Ali Muhammad 'Ali and Muhammad Hina'i 'Abd al-Hadi in the 1960s maintained that the "official" Germans still had guilt complexes regarding the Jews because of the propaganda campaign the Jews were waging against the Nazis for what they had done to them.[120] Germany apologized to the Arabs for paying reparations to the Jews to atone for what the Nazi era did to them, wrote *Filastin* in 1962, but the question was, what apology and atonement would it offer to its friends "now that the compensations took part in turning Palestine's Arabs, not Europe's Jews, into the real victims of the Nazi era?"[121]

One of the articles which incorporated all of the themes in an original fashion was published in *al-Hilal* in 1956. It was written by Egyptian historian Muhammad Rif'at in the form of a historical drama, in which Israeli and Arab representatives were judged by the ancient Greek gods. The very fact that the issue of Israel and its right to Palestine were a matter for a trial indicated its importance and how widespread the issue was. Clio, the Muse of History, tells Zeus the history of the conflict and specifies the aid and support received by Israel, including the German reparations based on "the myth that it represents

118   *Arab Observer*, 22 January 1962, p. 19.
119   *Al-Hilal*, January 1956, pp. 35–7; *Majallat al-Azhar*, 29/3, 25 September 1957, pp. 251–2; al-'Umari, *al-Sharq al-Awsat*, pp. 104, 233, 236; Muhammad 'Ali al-Zu'bi, *Isra'il. Bint baritaniya al-bakr*, Cairo: n.d., p. 13; 'Ali Muhammad 'Ali, *Isra'il*, p. 416; Ahmad 'Abd al-Qadir al-Jamal, *Min mushkilat al-sharq al-awsat*, Cairo: 1955, pp. 313–14; Hasan Mustafa, *al-Musa'adat al-'askariyya al-almaniyya li-isra'il*, Beirut: 1965, pp. 17–22.
120   Muhammad 'Ali 'Alluba, *Filastin wa-jaratuha*, Cairo: 1954, p. 166; 'Ali and 'Abd al-Hadi, *Dawlat al-irhab*, p. 110.
121   *Filastin*, 20 January 1962.

Jews all over the world." Zeus asks to know what justification there was for reparations to Israel if it hadn't existed during the Holocaust, and Clio answers that "in fact, reparations were supposed to be given to the Jewish families persecuted in Germany, Austria and the other countries occupied by the Nazis. But the United States, which established the State of Israel, ordered them to pay [Israel] the reparations to save it from bankruptcy." The Arab representative interrupts and claims that Israel uses the money it receives to stockpile weapons. The trial does not end in a verdict, but the words of the Arab representative remain hanging as the logical conclusion: the various western countries should stipulate that some or all of the compensation should go to the Arab refugees whom Israel expelled from their houses just as Hitler expelled the Jews from theirs. However, Zeus allows the Muse of History to take her own course.[122]

A long article written in 1959, which claimed to be "the full story of the Jewish campaign to steal funds from West Germany," appeared in *al-Ahram* on the eve of the Arab League conference to discuss America's direct and indirect funding of Israel. Next to a detailed explanation of the terms of the agreement and the conditions which prepared the ground for it, beginning with the end of the war, Ibrahim Tantawi raised a claim which had not been made in the past. He contended that in addition to what the German government paid, Hitler had paid $200 million in compensation to the Jews as part of the "transfer agreement." A German Jewish firm called Transfer, he explained, was responsible for the disassembling of the property of 200,000 Jews and the transfer of its value to Mandatory Palestine. After listing all the sums Germany paid to individuals, Israel and Jewish organizations, he recounted the story of a Jew who had received reparations even though he had immigrated to Argentina in 1933, lived there peacefully throughout the war and made a large profit. Therefore he had hung a picture of Hitler in his room under which he had written, "Thanks to our leader, who took us out." The compensation affair turned into a great campaign of exploiting German property, Tantawi added, and Jews all over the world began looking for reasons to justify the receipt of reparations.[123] The implications of such a narrative go far beyond the reparations and their contribution to Israel: to a certain extent the narrative releases Germany from all responsibility for its past.

---

122   *Al-Hilal*, April 1956, pp. 69–74.

123   *Al-Ahram*, 28 February 1959. The same stories were echoed in al-Quwwat al-musallaha: Qiyadat al-jaysh al-awwal, *al-Sahyuniyya*, Cairo: 1960, p. 276. For the transfer agreement and the circumstances leading to it see Francis R. Nicosia, *The Third Reich and the Palestine Question*, London: 1985, pp. 41–9.

Within the framework of this discussion there was no room to sympathize with the Jewish tragedy. Moreover, there is not even room to discuss the raging controversy that broke out in Israel around the contacts with Germany and the agreement, the mass demonstrations in the streets and the tossing of a hand grenade at the Knesset. Even when Wajih ʿAtiq mentioned them in retrospect, he only viewed them as an additional means to wring larger sums of money out of the Germans.[124] The Palestinians, who were initially more aware of this issue, also presented the controversy as one of Israel's tactics in its negotiations with Germany in a 1966 publication issued by the PLO research center. Although Israel initiated them, it delayed its answer until the beginning of the talks "artificially, using the excuse of the sensitivity of conducting direct contacts." It was said that a bitter argument erupted in the Knesset, and Menahem Begin, leader of the extremist "Stern Gang" [sic], headed the opposition to the agreement. Thus Israel wanted to strengthen its position in the talks and force Germany to accept its demands.[125]

The representation of the Holocaust, reflected indirectly and by implication in the public discourse on the agreement, was an additional stage in the development of trends which were discerned in earlier references to Jewish emigration to Israel. It strengthened the linkage between the discourse surrounding the Holocaust and the Israeli–Arab conflict, and placed the Arabs on one side of the barricade and Israel on the other when dealing with the events of the Holocaust. Political, economic and military considerations emanating from the conflict formed the way in which the Holocaust and every event of World War II were related to. The Arab states were afraid of the contribution of the reparations to Israel's resilience, and therefore rejected its right to receive them. However, at least initially, the official discourse recognized the right of Jews who had suffered at the hands of the Nazis to receive compensation as individuals, and distinguished between their right and the right of the State of Israel to reparations. It is possible that Egypt's hesitant and more moderate position toward the agreement stemmed partly from a recognition of the Holocaust, and perhaps as a result of its pragmatic approach to the conflict, which was first and foremost dictated by its vital needs, and its concern for the

124 ʿAtiq, al-Siyasa, pp. 27–8.
125 Asʿad ʿAbd al-Rahman, al-Musaʿadat al-amrikiyya wal-almaniyya al-gharbiyya, Beirut: 1966, p. 53. For the controversy in Israel regarding the agreement, see, for example, Segev, The Seventh Million, pp. 187–208.

relationship with Germany.[126] Criticism of Egypt's delayed response confirms that hesitation.[127]

The Arab press devoted front-page headlines to the agreement as soon as it was signed and intensive Arab diplomatic activity started. Most of the reports reflected the official position. The matter was rarely discussed in periodicals and the number of analytical articles and editorials was generally limited, especially in the Jordanian/Palestinian papers. Although the agreement's implementation was perceived as an action hostile to the Arab states, it was not a focus of public attention. However, the agreement and the discussion concerning it contributed a great deal to the formulation of motifs in the representation of the Holocaust, beginning with its relativism by the implied comparison between it and the Palestinian catastrophe; linking the reparations to the compensation for refugees; through accusing Israel and the Jews of fostering feelings of guilt in Germany; and Holocaust denial. The agreement provided additional "proof" of how Israel and Zionism "profited" from the Holocaust politically and materially. "The German guilt complex is the goose that lays golden eggs for Israel, while at the same time it is a knife at the throats of the German politicians. Looting West Germany, its government and people, in the name of that guilt complex has turned into a hobby for Israel the same way the slogan 'anti-Semitism' has become a tool to destroy and deter anyone who tries to oppose its will."[128] The attitude to the agreement in the public discourse, as in the official discourse, was not determined by a latent approach to the Holocaust, but rather by the perception of the conflict with Israel and the fear of its gathering strength.

---

126   Radio Beirut, 4 October, Radio Cairo, 19 November 1952 – Daily Survey, nos. 867, 905, 5 October, 19 November 1952; *al-Ahram*, 21 November 1952; IHZ/3753/6, Dibon to Shiloah, 1 February 1953; *Haaretz*, 20 July 2001.

127   For example, see *al-Ahram*, 26 September 1952, 1, 3 January 1953; *al-Misri*, November 12, December 30, *al-Akhbar*, 15 December 1952.

128   'Atiq, *al-Siyasa*, p. 92.

3

THE EICHMANN AFFAIR, MAY 1960 TO MAY 1962

Chronologically, Israel's capture, trial and execution of Adolf Eichmann, which came to be known as the Eichmann affair, was another landmark in the encounter between the Arab world and the Holocaust. Eichmann was an SS officer who in 1939 was appointed head of the Jewish Department of the Gestapo. From then until the end of the war he played a central role in the deportation of European Jews to the death camps and in the implementation of the Final Solution. Captured by the Allies at the end of the war, he managed to escape from a PoW camp. Using his connections with underground organizations which helped Nazis, he reached Argentina in 1950, where he settled and lived under the assumed name of Ricardo Klement.[1] On 10 May 1960 he was captured in a Buenos Aires suburb by Israeli Mossad agents and brought to Israel. On 23 May, David Ben-Gurion, who was then prime minister of Israel, announced in the Knesset that Eichmann had been caught and would be tried in accordance with the Nazi and Nazi Collaborators Punishment Law of 1950. The trial, which began on 11 April 1961, marked the beginning of a dramatic change in the way Israelis viewed the Holocaust and was a milestone in establishing the perception of the Holocaust in the collective Israeli, Jewish and world memory.[2] At the trial, wrote Israeli Holocaust scholar Hanna Yablonka, "there was a meeting between the two most important chapters in modern Jewish history: the Holocaust and the founding of the State of Israel."[3] That meeting had occupied Arab

---

1   For Eichmann, his activities, kidnapping and trial, see Peter Papadatos, *The Eichmann Trial*, London: 1964; David Cesarani, *Becoming Eichmann: Rethinking the Life and Trial of a "Desk Murderer"*, Cambridge: 2006; Hanna Yablonka, *The State of Israel* vs. *Adolf Eichmann*, Jerusalem: 2001 (Hebrew), pp. 307–59; Israel Gutman (ed.), *Encyclopedia of the Holocaust*, New York: 1990, pp. 426–32. See also Hannah Arendt's highly controversial *Eichmann in Jerusalem. A Report on the Banality of Evil*, New York: 1963.

2   For example, see Anita Shapira, "The Eichmann Trial: Changing Perspectives," *The Journal of Israeli History*, vol. 23, no. 1 (2004), pp. 18–39.

3   Hanna Yablonka, "The Eichmann trial and Israelis, 40 years later," *Bi-Shvil Ha-Zikaron*, no. 41 (April–May 2001) (Hebrew), p. 24.

public discourse since Israel's establishment. Following the trial, awareness of the Holocaust heightened in the Arab states, but whereas the Israeli and western societies underwent processes of internalizing the Holocaust and its lessons, the Arabs developed a growing sense of alienation from and rejection toward it.

The affair took place at a time when the Arab–Israeli conflict was prominent on the Arab public agenda and pan-Arabism, propagated by the charismatic Egyptian president Jamal 'Abd al-Nasir, was at its peak. At first glance, the Eichmann affair was an internal Jewish matter. It raised historical, legal, philosophical and ethical questions which had nothing to do with the Arabs, as opposed to the Jewish immigration to Palestine and the reparations agreement issues, whose connection was more obvious. The first led to the establishment of the State of Israel, and the second contributed to its consolidation. The trial, on the other hand, would seem only to have given the Jewish people a forum to settle accounts with its executioners. Why, then, were the Arab media so interested? Which issues were raised in the public debate, and was the Holocaust at the center of it? Was it influenced by the worldwide discussion of the trial, and if so, how? What were its implications for the representation of the Holocaust in the Arab public discourse?

In view of these questions it can be argued that the Arab media could not ignore the affair because it had captured the world's attention. Eichmann's kidnapping on sovereign Argentinian soil provided a legitimate opportunity to attack Israel. However, since Israel was quickly forgiven, following a UN Security Council resolution, and it seemed that the trial was playing into Israel's hands, Arab governments and media embarked on a smear campaign against the trial and Israel to minimize, as far as possible, what was perceived as an Israeli propaganda success. The widespread reporting of the affair was not the result of any particular Arab interest in the Holocaust and did not reflect a coherent approach toward it. On the contrary, it reflected a prevailing unease, and therefore, as in previous affairs, the main emphasis of the discussion was diverted to political aspects which could be used to attack Israel and Zionism. However, due to the topics raised at the trial, public discourse gradually turned to issues related to the Holocaust, such as the alleged Zionist–Nazi collaboration, which became a central theme in the Arab discourse of the Holocaust and in the wider discourse of the Arab–Israeli conflict. There were two other prominent themes: the equation of Zionism and Nazism, implying a comparison between the Holocaust and the Nakba, or between Jewish suffering and Palestinian suffering; and the accusation that Israel and Zionism were exploiting the Holocaust while fostering feelings of guilt among the Germans for material and political gains.

94

The Arab press did not deviate from the official Arab stand, and expressed similar sentiments toward the trial and Israel, yet differences could be discerned between the Lebanese, Jordanian/Palestinian and Egyptian presses. Despite the fact that the Egyptian press had been nationalized and had become a tool of the regime for the dissemination of its views, there remained room within the limits of consensual discourse for nuances in representing the Holocaust.[4]

Writing about the affair focused on its four crucial time periods: the end of May to June 1960, when Eichmann was captured and the UN Security Council held its deliberations; April to June 1961, the first stages of the trial; December 1961, the end of the trial and pronouncement of the verdict; and Eichmann's execution at the beginning of June 1962. These periods typified the foreign and Arab media as well as the public debate of the affair in Israel.[5] There were two separate categories of articles: informative articles based on information received from international news agencies covering the trial, and editorials and analytical pieces. The first category attests to the flow of information and knowledge, whereas the second to the way that information was interpreted and perceived.

DAY-TO-DAY REPORTING OF THE AFFAIR

From capture to trial: May 1960 to early April 1961

The first mentions of the capture of Adolf Eichmann appeared in the Lebanese and the Jordanian papers almost immediately after Ben-Gurion made his announcement to the Knesset. On 24 May, *al-Hayat* reported Ben-Gurion's announcement and issued daily in-depth accounts of developments, while the first report in *Filastin* appeared on 25 May.[6] The Egyptian media were more hesitant, and almost a week passed before *al-Ahram* published its first report.[7] The Arabic broadcasts of Radio Cairo, which served the regime as an anti-Israeli propaganda tool, mentioned it for the first time on 26 May.[8] Avoiding the issue

---

4   Regarding the criticism which infiltrated the press within the limits imposed by the regime, Hopkins noted that in the field of foreign affairs there was a greater margin for interpretation and opinion. Harry Hopkins, *Egypt the Crucible: The Unfinished Revolution of the Arab World*, London: 1969, p. 348

5   See the American Jewish Committee's study of the press, The American Jewish Committee, Institute of Human Relations Press, *The Eichmann Case in the American Press*, New York: 1962; Yosef Gorni, *Between Auschwitz and Jerusalem*, Tel Aviv: 1998 (Hebrew), pp. 35–69.

6   *Al-Hayat*, 24 May, *Filastin*, *al-Nahar*, 25 May 1960.

7   *Al-Ahram*, 30 May 1960.

8   Radio Cairo, 26 May – Daily survey, 27 May 1960.

of the capture and subsequent kidnapping was not surprising, because the Lebanese press was free and independent compared to the Egyptian press, which had been nationalized exactly one day before information about Eichmann's presence in Israel was revealed. It can be assumed that the Egyptian press was still suffering from the trauma of nationalization and was perhaps waiting for instructions on how to report. Moreover, it would seem that response had been postponed until it could be determined in which direction the affair would develop, perhaps because of its connection to the Holocaust. Arab reporting struggled with the problem of how to report the kidnapping and condemn Israel without seeming to identify with Eichmann or defend him, and how to present a factual, reliable report without arousing the slightest identification with the Holocaust, which might lead readers to pity or feel empathy for Israel and the Jewish people. In addition, during the first days after the kidnapping, rumors were rife and it was unclear how the affair would evolve and the sides involved would react: Argentina, Germany, the international community and Israel. When it looked as though the situation between Argentina and Israel was growing tense and criticism was heard of the kidnapping and Israel's intention to try Eichmann, a kind of legitimization was given to taking a stand and introducing the affair from an Arab perspective, which hurt Israel on the one hand, but remained within the limits of consensual international discourse on the Holocaust on the other.

The kidnapping of Eichmann and his transfer to Israel raised many questions concerning international relations, legislation and criminal law. They were a violation of the sovereignty of an independent state and were viewed as a negative precedent in international relations and a threat to world order. On 1 June, the Argentinian government demanded from Israel an explanation regarding the place of Eichmann's capture and the way he had been brought to Israel. On 6 June, Israel answered that Eichmann had been captured by a group of volunteers who had been hunting for him for years and that he had expressed his willingness in writing to be tried in Israel and to set down everything he knew for posterity. Israel also expressed its regret at having violated Argentina's sovereignty. Two days later, Argentina demanded that Eichmann be returned within a week and threatened to bring the subject to the UN Security Council should Israel refuse. At the same time Ben-Gurion sent a personal letter to the president of Argentina, Arturo Frondizi, explaining the motives and high moral aspects of bringing a war criminal to be tried in a court of the people whom he had wanted to annihilate. Argentina's answer came on 13 June, and despite Frondizi's understanding, he made it clear that he had no choice but to bring the matter to the Security Council. Argentina's complaint, which asserted that the kidnapping was a "gross violation" of international law and a threat to world peace and security, was deliberated on 22 and 23 June. The crisis in Israeli–Argentinian relations did not end with the Security Council resolution demanding an Israeli apology and "fair compensation." Argentina rejected Israel's response of 4 July, withdrew its ambassador from Israel and expelled the Israeli ambassador on 22 July. However, a month later the matter was smoothed over and in October of that year the ambassadors returned to their posts. According to Robert Kempner, who was a member of the American prosecution staff during the Nuremberg trials and an advisor to Israeli Attorney General Gideon Hausner, Argentina did not pursue the matter further because it had joined the London Agreement of 8 August 1945 regarding the punishment and extradition of war criminals, and no other country had requested Eichmann's extradition for trial.[9]

How were those developments reflected in the Arab press? On 30 May, *al-Ahram* printed a short article at the bottom of the front page containing a report from its New York correspondent to the effect that diplomats who had returned from the celebrations marking Argentina's 150 anniversary of independence said that Adolf Eichmann, "who was accused of the mass murders of European Jews," had been kidnapped in Buenos Aires on 11 May and taken to an Israeli submarine which had entered Argentina's territorial waters. Eichmann, it said, quoting a false German account, had worked as an agent in Damascus in 1959 and fled to Argentina long before his capture with the aid of the Nazi secret police. His wife and three children had left Austria in 1952, and when she returned to renew her passport, Austrian officials gave that information to Israeli agents who had spent years unsuccessfully looking for Eichmann. That enabled them to kidnap him on 11 May. The article also reported that the government of Israel was discussing the arrangements necessary for trying him, and that it wanted to extract information from him about Hitler and other German leaders who had disappeared under mysterious circumstances at the end of the war.[10] The article ended with another bit of information, according to which Eichmann was responsible for the safety of Hajj Amin al-Husayni, the Mufti of Jerusalem, when he visited Berlin during the war.[11] In that way *al-Ahram* avoided having to quote Ben-Gurion, but the information about the kidnapping and the reasons for it were given. The details presented in the article were incorrect,

---

9   *Skira Hodshit* (Monthly Survey), June 1960, pp. 3–7; Robert Kempner, *Profession: Annihiliation – Eichmann's Way*, Jerusalem: 1963 (Hebrew), p. 10; Yitzhak Oron (ed.), *Middle East Record*, London: 1960, vol. 1, pp. 283–6.

10   Kuwait was mentioned as being involved in the affair because in 1959 Fritz Bauer, the Hessian Jewish attorney general, suspected Eichmann of being in Kuwait at the time. *Al-Nahar*, 25 May 1960.

11   *Al-Ahram*, 30 May 1960.

and were gradually clarified in subsequent accounts. However, what is important is the fact that the article gave information about the annihilation of the Jews without using a hostile tone toward Israel, and did not hide or question the charges against Eichmann, although it was extremely laconic. In general, the reports in *al-Ahram* hid more than they revealed. In contrast, the Lebanese dailies' accounts were more factual and comprehensive, and did not hesitate to detail the accusations leveled against Eichmann, as reported by Israeli sources. While *al-Ahram* and *Filastin* were publishing articles about the kidnapping, the Lebanese dailies exposed details of the annihilation, Eichmann's responsibility for carrying it out, the plans to try him in Israel and Germany's reaction, as well as the attitude toward the trial of the Jordanians, who thought it should not be left in Israeli hands lest it be exploited to influence international public opinion. *Al-Hayat* reported on 29 May that deliberations to demand that Eichmann be tried by an international court were taking place in Amman in order to provide a precedent for bringing Ben-Gurion to trial for crimes against the Arabs of Palestine.[12] The Saudi newspaper *al-Bilad*, which reported the kidnapping a week later, ran the following headline: "Arrest of Eichmann, who had the honor of killing 5 million Jews." "It is said," continued the article, that he escaped from Germany 15 years earlier to avoid being tried as a war criminal, and that he suggested suffocating Jews in gas chambers instead of shooting them, which took too much time. That, said the article, was called "the operation to annihilate the Jews, the final solution to the Jewish problem." Eichmann was quoted at the Nuremberg trials as someone who liked to boast to his commanders that he was satisfied with himself for having killed five million Jews, said the author of the article, Hilmi Abu Ziyad, and he finished by stating that "most people hate Hitler not because he caused a war in which millions were killed, but because he was defeated before he finished killing all the Jews in the world."[13] Thus, informative articles were laced with themes reflecting the developing Arab approach to the Holocaust, such as its exploitation by Israel to enlist public opinion and gain other advantages, and the equation of Ben-Gurion's actions with those of Eichmann as part of a broader comparison between Zionism and Nazism, and even justification of the annihilation of the Jews.

Another week passed before the Egyptian press referred to the subject again, but it limped behind the developments. On the other hand, *al-Hayat* published more concrete information about Kempner's willingness to advise the Israeli prosecution, and about Argentina's admission that Eichmann had been kid-

12   *Al-Hayat*, 24, 25, 26, 28, 29, 31 May, *al-Nahar*, 25 May 1960.
13   *Al-Bilad*, 31 May 1960; Lewis, *Semites and Anti-Semites*, p. 162.

napped from its territory.[14] On 7 June, both *al-Akhbar* and *al-Ahram* reported baseless accounts of Eichmann's suicide attempt, and incidentally mentioned the preparations being made in Israel for the trial, the tension between Israel and Argentina and the incidence of defamatory graffiti and other anti-Semitic manifestations in London, including the inscription, "I like Eichmann."[15] The gap between reports in the Egyptian and Lebanese newspapers continued after the Argentinian–Israeli crisis began, although a fairly clear picture of the exchanges of diplomatic notes and the deliberations in the Security Council emerged from the Egyptian press. As expected, *obiter dicta* found their way into the information, whether as parts of headlines or within the text, which indirectly reflected an argumentative position. The press tended to emphasize aspects contradicting Israeli explanations. For example, an *al-Ahram* headline referred to Israel's admission to the kidnapping as an admission of "the piracy" carried out on Argentinian soil, and to the memorandum presented to the Argentinian government explaining Israel's actions as "a great international lie," transparent and unreasonable. *Al-Akhbar* reported the memorandum and its details under the headline, "Israel tries to hide its crime of kidnapping Eichmann claiming that he asked to be tried." The Lebanese *al-Hayat*, on the other hand, wondered whether Argentina would recall its ambassador in the wake of the crisis caused by the kidnapping, which was "considered an act of aggression" against its sovereignty, and described the circumstances of the kidnapping as they appeared in the memorandum.[16]

The reports about the Argentinian government's answer to the memorandum, which rejected Israel's claims, can be viewed in the same light. Small differences existed between the reports of *al-Akhbar* and *al-Ahram*. While both stressed that Argentina had threatened Israel with diplomatic sanctions if Eichmann were not returned, neither presented Israel's claims. *Al-Akhbar* quoted Argentina's reservation concerning "the crimes of extermination carried out by Hitler's agents during the Nazi regime," whereas *al-Ahram* chose to ignore it. *Al-Hayat*, on the other hand, did mention Israel's point of view, quoting Ben-Gurion's remark about "historical justice," and reported the general tendency in Israel against returning Eichmann to Argentina.[17] Those differences could be seen almost daily during June in the articles concerning the Israeli–Argentinian confrontation, gradually diminishing as the trial approached.

14   *Al-Ahram*, 4, 5 June, *al-Hayat*, 2, 3 June 1960.
15   *Al-Ahram*, *al-Akhbar*, *al-Hayat*, *Filastin*, 7 June 1960.
16   *Al-Ahram*, *al-Akhbar*, *al-Hayat*, 8 June 1960.
17   *Al-Ahram*, *al-Akhbar*, *al-Hayat*, 10 June 1960.

Information about the Holocaust was revealed in news reports regardless of their point of view. Reports about Ben-Gurion's letter to Frondizi and the Security Council deliberations repeatedly mentioned that Eichmann had been responsible for the murder of six million Jews during Hitler's rule. On 12 June, *al-Ahram* quoted the *New York Herald Tribune*, which defined the kidnapping as illegal but justified Israel's right to try Eichmann "because he held a high-ranking position in Nazi Germany which caused the annihilation of many Israelites [sic]." That report and one in *al-Akhbar* also quoted attorneys in various parts of the world who disputed Israel's right to try Eichmann. Neither expressed an opinion, and only the two exclamation points after Ben-Gurion's claim that Eichmann had agreed of his own volition to go to Israel revealed the reservations of the reporter or editor.[18] Doubt about Eichmann's actual deeds and their minimization could be seen in a report dealing with a wave of anti-Semitic acts in Uruguay after the kidnapping. A short *al-Ahram* article, which quoted foreign sources, reported that a Mexican association had sent a telegram to Pope John XXIII, stating that the kidnapping was "a crime worse than anything Eichmann had done, if what they say about him is true."[19] In presenting a summary of the Security Council deliberations, *al-Ahram* cited Golda Meir, then Israel's foreign minister, Henry Cabot Lodge, Jr., the American representative to the United Nations, and other speakers. The Eichmann affair, explained Meir, "can be summed up by saying that people who were exposed to his crimes arrested him and are going to try him." She also claimed that the violation of Argentinian law should be viewed "in the light of the unusual nature of the crimes attributed to Eichmann," and the British representative, Sir Pierson Dixon, stated that "the years which have passed have not wiped out the memory of the terrible things that happened then."[20] The Tunisian representative was also quoted, saying that "it is impossible to deny that the Israeli aggression against Argentinian sovereignty was the result of its desire to punish what is considered one of the most heinous crimes in history."[21]

One of the articles that retold the story of how Eichmann was tracked down, adding and correcting details which had since become known, portrayed the man and his deeds. He was described as "a detached individual," powerless and without influence, whose ardent faith had stirred Israel's lust for revenge and motivated it to trace him. He believed that "Zionism had to be uprooted because it meant evil and treason, and the final solution to avoiding its damage was

---

18   *Al-Ahram*, 11, 12, 29 June, *al-Akhbar*, 12 June 1960.

19   *Al-Ahram*, 15 June 1960.

20   *Al-Ahram*, 23, 29 June 1960.

21   *Al-Ahram*, *al-Akhbar*, 24 June 1960.

to annihilate it." The Nazis put him in charge of the Gestapo's Department of Jewish Affairs and instructed him to carry out the Final Solution, which he did with "a strange zeal." Most of the organized acts of annihilation he supervised, added the article, had been carried out in Auschwitz, Poland. Clearly, presenting Eichmann as an "enemy of Zionism" and not as an enemy of the Jews allowed identification with him. A different article recounted how Eichmann had reached his position, adding information about his Jewish physiognomy, as it were, about his absorption with the Jewish problem, which led him to learn Hebrew and read about Jews and Zionism, and about the emigration policy he implemented in Austria. After the conquest of France, the article continued, he believed in the Madagascar Plan but the Vichy government refused to support it. In April 1945 he was on his way to Theresienstadt, the show camp erected by the Nazis for Red Cross visitors "to refute the claims of the Jews that the Nazis do not treat them well. The Jews in the camp lived normal lives far removed from cruelty and persecution."[22]

The first time the name of Rudolf Kasztner, a representative of the Zionist movement in Hungary, was mentioned in connection with the Eichmann affair was in the report of the weekly *Ruz al-Yusuf*, quoting an interview of Ben-Gurion with *Le Monde*. He was asked about attempts made by political figures in Israel to prevent the trial from taking place in order to avoid revelations on the negotiations the accused had held with Kasztner regarding the rescue of Hungarian Jewry.[23] The article presented the facts without being judgmental or critical of Ben-Gurion or the Kasztner affair, which had not been covered when it exploded on the Israeli scene in 1954, but would return later during the trial and was exploited afterwards in the Arab discourse on the Holocaust (see Chapter 8).

Even during the initial phase of the Eichmann affair, when the debate focused primarily on the kidnapping and the UN deliberations, the Arab press discussed the issue of Israel's right to bring him to trial and punish him, but for the most part it relied on foreign sources and statements by Jewish and non-Jewish jurists and well known figures.[24] During this period the Jordanian/Palestinian paper *Filastin*

22   *Al-Ahram*, 10 June, 5 August, 1960. The information appearing in the 5 August article about Eichmann was mostly true, although life in Theresienstadt was far from being normal and most of the Jews were sent to Auschwitz. For Theresienstadt, see Kempner, *Profession*, pp. 47–9. The Madagascar Plan was discussed as a solution for the "Jewish question" by the Nazis in the 1930s. See Yehuda Bauer, *Jews for Sale? Nazi-Jewish Negotiations, 1933–1945*, New Haven: 1994, pp. 56–8. For other articles relating information about the kidnapping, see *al-Ahram*, 18, 30 June 1960; *Ruz al-Yusuf*, 4 July 1960.

23   *Ruz-al Yusuf*, 4 July 1960.

24   In general, those quoted were experts in international jurisprudence who questioned Is-

avoided any direct mention to the Nazi atrocities against the Jews, and preferred to concentrate on developments in the crisis between Argentina and Israel.[25]

From trial to execution: April 1961 to June 1962

The trial began on 11 April 1961. The prosecution presented its witnesses until 20 June, the defense until 14 August. On 11 December the court reconvened to announce its verdict, and the sentence was handed down on 15 December 1961. Eichmann's defense attorney, Robert Servatius, filed an immediate appeal, which was under consideration from 22 to 28 March 1962. On 29 May the appeal was rejected, as was an appeal to the president for clemency. Two days later at midnight on 1 June, Eichmann was hanged.

Throughout the trial, doubts were continuously voiced all over the world by both Israel's supporters and its detractors concerning Israel's right and authority to try Eichmann. Even the United States and Britain questioned the legality of the trial, and according to a secret Associated Press circular, instructed the media to restrain themselves and be careful in their coverage of it, especially with regard to testimonies relating to people outside Israel. Apparently, they were primarily concerned about the exposure of former Nazis who now worked for the West German government, which could play into the hands of the Soviet Union and affect their relations with Germany.[26] The main legal questions focused on the retroactivity of the Israeli law, and hence Israel's right to punish Nazi criminals, since the State of Israel did not exist at the time the crimes were committed and because they were not committed on its territory or against its citizens. Other reservations were raised by Servatius regarding the objectivity of the Israeli judges, the impossibility of bringing witnesses for the defense and the question of the responsibility of those who followed the orders of their superiors.[27] However, despite all their reservations, the western countries, especially the United States, expressed their understanding for Israel, and when Argentina's complaint to the Security Council had been settled,

rael's right to try Eichmann and regarded the trial as a violation of international law or who warned Israel against executing him. For example, see *al-Ahram*, 12 July 1960, 7 April 1961. Other articles noted recommendations that he be tried by an international tribunal such as the Nuremberg tribunal. *Al-Ahram*, 17, 24 June 1960.

25   *Filastin*, 29 May, 3, 8, 10, 12, 16, 23, 25 June 1960.

26   FO 953/2023, British Embassy, Bonn to Albert, 1 March 1961; FO 953/2023, U.S. Information Agency, Infoguide No. 61-43, The Eichmann Trial, 6 March 1961; FO 371/157811 (ER 1661/12), Memorandum on Legality of the Eichmann Trial, 7 April 1961.

27   Gavriel Bach, "Thoughts and Reflections 30 Years after the Eichmann trial," *Bi-Shvil Ha-Zikaron*, no. 41 (April–May 2001) (Hebrew), pp. 4–9; Kempner, *Profession*, pp. 31–8; Papadatos, *The Eichmann Trial*, pp. 40–78.

the moral questions about the period of the war, and in particular the Allies' reaction to the information about the annihilation of the Jews and the degree of their responsibility, resurfaced.[28]

Unlike the western press, but to a great extent similar to the position of the Eastern Block, the Arab media consistently opposed the trial and had no sympathy for Israel or the victims of Nazism. Their viewpoint was primarily political, emanating from their stance toward Israel and the Arab–Israeli conflict. The trial was perceived as "theatre," "a farce," "a political act from beginning to end," and "another tool of Israeli propaganda."[29] The Arab regimes, apprehensive about the effect the trial might have on public opinion, discussed the trial and two secret decisions were reportedly made by the Arab League's Information Committee in February 1961.[30] In April, it had reportedly issued a brochure of expert international legal views regarding the Eichmann trial and the "massacre" at Qibya and Deir Yasin.[31] The linkage made between the trial and the two incidents, which was in effect a comparison between the crimes of the Nazis and the actions taken by Israel against the Palestinians, became a central theme in Arab discourse during the trial. The Egyptian People's Assembly raised the issue of Eichmann's kidnapping as a query to the Foreign Ministry, and Egyptian Deputy Foreign Minister Husayn Dhu al-Faqar responded and even referred to the trial in his address to the Security Council in May 1961. It was not the Arabs' intention, he said, to pose the question before international institutions,

---

28 *The Eichmann Case in the American Press*, pp. 6–8, 67–8. Also see Oron (ed.), *Middle East Record 1960*, vol. 1, pp. 280–2. The Soviet Union reacted differently. It attacked Argentina for not having tried Eichmann when he was there, but also accused Israel, particularly for a plot to hide evidence during the trial that could embarrass the German government, which employed former Nazis in important government offices. In return, claimed the Soviets, Ben-Gurion expected financial support and arms from Germany. Yitzhak Oron (ed.), *Middle East Record 1961*, vol. 2, Jerusalem: 1961, pp. 323–4. Justice Bach wrote in the previously mentioned article that Servatius refused to allow the testimony of witnesses who wanted to testify on Jewish collaboration with the Nazis, Bach, "Thoughts," p. 8. Arendt, *Eichmann in Jerusalem*, pp. 14–16; Segev, *The Seventh Million*, pp. 321–3; Liora Bilsky, "Like a Phoenix: Arendt in Jerusalem, 2000," *Bi-shvil Ha-Zikaron*, no. 41 (April–May 2001) (Hebrew), p. 21.

29 *Al-Jihad*, 11 April, *al-Hayat*, 11, 28 April, 4 June, *al-Musawwar*, 14, 21 April 1961.

30 Oron (ed.) *Middle East Record 1961*, vol. 2, p. 115. Also see *Egyptian Gazette*, 19, 24 February 1961. Details on these decisions are not known.

31 *Al-Ahram*, 18 April 1961. On 9 April 1948 IZL and LEHY, in collaboration with the Hagana, raided the village of Deir Yasin, and on 14 October 1953 the Israeli army raided Qibya in retaliation for the killing of two Israeli children by Jordanian infiltrators (Operation Shoshana). In both cases innocent Palestinian civilians were killed. Deir Yasin founded a myth in Palestinian historiography and became a symbol of their catastrophe. See Benny Morris, "The historiography of Deir Yassin," *The Journal of Israeli History*, vol. 24, no. 1 (March 2005), pp. 79–107.

since they did not recognize the legality of the existence of Israel, but it was their duty, he added, "to expose every disgraceful Zionist and Israeli act using every means" they had at their command. He retold the story of the kidnapping and denied the charge that the Nazis had killed six million Jews. Completely distorting demographic data, he claimed that, according to Zionist information, there were eleven million Jews in 1939 but sixteen million in 1948. Therefore, it was clear that the number was inflated and neither Eichmann nor Germany had killed even one million, he asserted.[32]

When the details of the indictment became known, *al-Ahram* published the changes adopted by the Knesset concerning the Lawyers' and Court Law Act (crimes punishable by death) to facilitate the death penalty. The paper also referred to the astonishment of observers at the scope of the indictment, which went far beyond crimes committed against German Jews. Israel, *al-Ahram* explained, had appropriated the right to try Eichmann in the name of international society and the Jewish people. The indictment contained fifteen points, including crimes committed against the Roma, Yugoslavs, Poles and Czechoslovakians, and twelve of them carried the death penalty.[33] Shortly before the trial began, *al-Ahram* published a long, comprehensive article about the entire affair: the man and his deeds, the surveillance and kidnapping, the indictment, the preparations for the trial, its goals and related unanswered questions. Written anonymously, it included pictures of Eichmann, Servatius, Gideon Hausner, the courthouse, and the glass booth in which the accused was seated. Like articles about the kidnapping, it had pretensions of being factual, but the headline and opening paragraph revealed the newspaper's point of view: "In two days the strangest trial in history will begin ... The accused, Adolf Eichmann is German, the courtroom and all the witnesses are Jewish. The crime is 15 years old but Israel is no more than 12 years old. For the sake of the trial, Israel mustered every means of propaganda at its disposal both within the country and abroad." That opening paragraph contained a number of essential

---

32   *Al-Ahram, al-Jumhuriyya*, 3 May, *al-Hayat*, 4 May 1961; Oron (ed.), *Middle East Record 1961*, vol. 2, p. 591. Dhu al-Faqar's attitude was also reflected in Palestinian Fayiz Sayigh's lecture to the American Friends of the Middle East in New York in April 1961. *Al-Ahram*, 7 April 1961. Political circles in Jordan as well feared Israel would exploit the affair in its propaganda, and in April 1961 they demonstrated their position toward it by presenting the Argentinian representative to the UN, Mario Amadeo, with the Jordanian Medal of Independence on the occasion of UN Day, since it was he who had lodged the Argentinian complaint over Eichmann's kidnapping. *Al-Difa'*, 28 April 1961 – Daily survey, 1 May 1961, No. 1148/685.001; *al-Hayat*, 29 May 1960.

33   *Al-Ahram*, 3 February 1961. For the legislation related to the special requirements of the trial, see Yablonka, *The State of Israel*, pp. 146–58.

issues concerning the trial, while the headline still referred to how Eichmann was tracked down and kidnapped.[34]

It was not a question of executing a 55-year-old man accused of killing six million Jews, the article began, but rather it was "the most profitable robbery Israel has committed since its establishment to realize as many aspirations as possible." In that spirit, it listed several goals: presenting itself as judge on behalf of all the Jews of the world; planting fear in the hearts of Nazis holding important positions in every country, including Germany; embarrassing Adenauer's government by presenting Germany as a country unable to protect its citizens; convincing world public opinion that Arab nationalism was a racist movement with the same roots and nature as Nazism, by trying to show that the Arabs collaborated with the Nazis, not only during the war but today as well, by the employment of German experts who ostensibly had connections with the Nazi party;[35] and enlisting world compassion "for the myth of the persecuted Jewish people," in preparation for a new round of fund-raising "that will save their country from collapse."

The article questioned the legality of the trial, which "the Jews themselves dispute," and listed the arguments prevalent against holding it. Even if the Jews had the right to demand revenge on the Nazis, it asserted, it should be the prerogative of the countries whose citizens they were. Israel kept quoting the words of Ben-Gurion, who said that the country was the only political authority representing world Jewry, and that therefore it had the exclusive right to try him for his crimes against Jews. The Jews of the United States objected and were of the opinion that Eichmann should be tried not only in the name of the Jews but in the name of all humanity by an international court.[36] Yet the problem, continued the article, was not only Israel's right to try him but how he was kidnapped, in violation of international law and the diplomatic code. Thus it returned to the theme that put the claims against Israel on firmer ground, and for which it was condemned by the UN.

The article dealt with two other aspects in addition to new details about the circumstances leading to the identification and tracking of Eichmann: Germany's "Nazi complex" and the Kasztner's trucks deal. West Germany's policy, it said, was dictated by its Nazi complex, and as a result it shrank from defending

---

34   Al-Ahram, 6 April 1961.

35   The activities of the German experts caused a great deal of worry in Israel, especially from the middle 1950s. It viewed their presence, in conjunction with statements about the destruction of the State of Israel, as proof of the Nazi orientation of the Egyptian regime. See a detailed discussion in 'Atiq, al-Siyasa, pp. 143–79.

36   The decision to try Eichmann did in fact cause dissension among American Jews. See Gorni, Between Auschwitz and Jerusalem, pp. 35–48, 54–69.

one of its own citizens lest it be accused of defending Nazism; every discussion on the subject, feared Adenauer, would rouse anti-German sentiments. Therefore, he had asked Israel not to embarrass his government during the trial, and Israel provided the names of Germans which had come up in the investigation, so as to dispel his fears. Thus the threads were spun and Eichmann was entrapped in the web. In a discussion of Eichmann's memoirs which appeared in *Life* magazine,[37] described as forged, reference was also made to the truck deal which Eichmann, encouraged by Himmler, tried to close with Kasztner. According to the article, in return for 10,000 trucks and other merchandise, one million Jews would be released from the camps. Moreover, Kasztner ostensibly agreed to calm the Hungarian Jews and encourage them to comply with the Nazi instructions. However, the deal fell through because the representative of the Jewish organization [Joel Brand] was arrested and imprisoned in Egypt by the British, who staunchly rejected the deal.[38] The article did not take sides in the truck issue, which would later reappear in Arab discourse on the Holocaust as solid proof of the collaboration between the Zionists and the Nazis.

The various aspects discussed in this article were reflected in many other Arab reports and editorials during the trial, and in the literature about Zionism and the Arab–Israeli conflict published after it. Although the press continued to follow Eichmann and the trial, most of the news was watered down. The daily newspapers' interest in the trial waned after a few days, but increased as the verdict approached and when the appeal was rejected. Shortly before the trial, the reports emphasized the attacks made on Israel in the international and particularly the western press, the tight security measures at the courthouse, the courtroom and the communications system installed in it, Servatius' reservations and the inability to prove Eichmann's "imaginary crimes."[39]

---

37 After his capture Eichmann gave the copyright for his memoirs based on the interview to Sassen, a Dutch journalist with a Fascist past. They were only supposed to be published after his death and were brought in evidence at the trial. See Kempner, *Profession*, p. 17; Bach, "Thoughts," pp. 13–14.

38 For this deal, nicknamed "goods for blood" or "trucks for blood," which was supposed to rescue some of Hungarian Jewry, and a discussion of its chances of materializing, see Kempner, *Profession*, pp. 353–4; Bauer, *Jews for Sale*, pp. 145–95. *Al-Hayat* gave a factual report of the deal when it was brought up during the trial. *Al-Hayat*, 13 June 1961. At a press conference in March 1961, the Mufti also referred to it, noting that the Zionists had refused to accept old people, women and children and insisted, because of their military calculations, on only young people. "That truth shows how much the Zionists were willing to sacrifice … for the sake of building up their military force in Palestine." *Al-Hayat*, 5 March 1961.

39 *Al-Ahram*, 10, 11 April, *al-Jumhuriyya*, *al-Akhbar*, 11 April 1961.

The reports in *al-Akhbar* were more factual and neutral than those in either *al-Ahram* or *al-Jumhuriyya*, and it did not print sensational headlines attacking Israel. For example, in reports printed on 11 April, while *al-Ahram* attacked Israel in its headlines and avoided specifying the crimes Eichmann was accused of in the body of the article, *al-Akhbar* reported that he had been accused of killing Jews and of being responsible for formulating the plan known as the Final Solution of the Jewish problem, and even referred to a number of witnesses for the prosecution, some of whom had testified to having met Eichmann during the Holocaust. Moreover, it quoted Adenauer's radio speech to the German people of the previous evening, in which he claimed that there were no relics of Nazism in Germany, and expressed his desire that "the trial reveal the truth and serve justice."[40] A similar distinction could be made between the two Jordanian/Palestinian papers *al-Jihad* and *Filastin*. While the first revealed its harsh criticism of Israel in its headlines, from the beginning of the affair, the second was more restrained.[41] Describing the first day of the trial, *al-Ahram* and *al-Jumhuriyya* printed some of the accusations, but most of the articles dealt with Servatius, who had refused to recognize the choice of judges and described the trial as purely an act of vengeance and Eichmann as a "scapegoat." Yet, they quoted Hausner as having said that there would be no mercy for Eichmann, and that the Jewish people would not forget that he had partially succeeded in implementing the Nazi plan to kill eleven million Jews.[42]

Al-Ahram presented Eichmann as an "offering" sacrificed by Zionism on Memorial Day for the Jewish victims of Nazism, in a report dealing with Zionist organizations' continued surveillance of 20,000 Germans, whose "only sin was to be part of Hitler's regime." It was not, as it might seem, only their desire to revenge the deaths of the Jews in the war, the report made clear, but "a purely political act" by which Zionism was realizing its goals.[43] Similar matters marginal to the issues of the trial continued to occupy the pages of the Arab daily papers: the German defense counsel's demand to present witnesses for the defense; the British Nazi party's offer of £10,000 to whomever would kidnap Menahem Begin and Nazi hunter Tuvia Friedman; Eichmann's forced confession; Eichmann's life from his escape after the war until the kidnapping.[44] *Al-Akhbar*

---

40   *Al-Ahram, al-Akhbar,* 11 April 1961.

41   See for instance, *al-Jihad,* 11 April, *Filastin,* 12 April 1961.

42   *Al-Jihad,* 11, 12 April, *Filastin, al-Ahram, al-Jumhuriyya,* 12, 13 April, *al-Difaʻ, al-Hayat,* 13 April 1961.

43   *Al-Ahram,* 14 April 1961.

44   *Al-Ahram, al-Jumhuriyya,* 15, 16 April, *al-Akhbar,* 25 April, *al-Jumhuriyya,* 5, 12, 19, 16 May, *Filastin,* 22 April 1961. For other reports in the same spirit, see *al-Ahram* 7 June, 21

and *Filastin* reported a document that was submitted to the court, written by Joseph Kennedy, President Kennedy's father, when he was the American ambassador in London, about the deteriorating conditions of the Jews in Germany and the actions of the Nazis. *Al-Ahram*, on the other hand, reported *Pravda*'s approach to the trial, regarding it as a "farce" serving Israeli propaganda, and attacking the West German government for collaborating with Israel and pressuring Eichmann to protect the ex-Nazis who were a part of it.[45]

The Egyptian press reflected the Arab positions but, as in previous cases, its tone was not as blunt and aggressive as that of the Jordanian/Palestinian and Syrian presses. The headlines and photographs accompanying the texts left no doubt as to the editors' opinions. For example, on the first day of the trial a headline in *al-Jihad* read, "Who are the criminals? Today the Jews are trying Eichmann ... When will the Arabs try the murderer Ben-Gurion?"[46] Next to pictures of Eichmann there were pictures of dead Palestinians and refugees. A subhead in the Syrian daily *al-Ayyam* stated that "The trial is legally invalid because Eichmann was carrying out orders," and wondered, "Were the crimes of the Allies less barbaric than those of the Nazis?"[47] The Jordanian/Palestinian press presented most of the accusations but, like the Egyptian press, preferred to focus on Servatius' claims and Eichmann's answers to questions, and to grant more exposure to his wife and son. As opposed to the aggressive nature of those papers, the Lebanese press remained fairly balanced, affording equal space to the prosecution, Eichmann and the defense. Moreover, the reports were fuller and more up to date. On the other hand, reports of the testimonies of Holocaust survivors were not published in any of the Arab newspapers, suggesting that there was an attempt to cut off the flow of information about the Holocaust so as to prevent the generation of empathy for the Jews, Zionism or Israel.

Conspicuous by its absence from the Egyptian and Jordanian/Palestinian papers was any direct reference to Hajj Amin al-Husayni, whose relations with Eichmann and involvement in sabotaging the rescue of 10,000 Jewish children had been revealed in Eichmann's interrogation and by two testimonies given on 26 April 1961. It can be assumed that Husayni's relations with Eichmann and Hitler were problematic for Egypt, especially in light of his function as an

---

August, 14 October 1961; *al-Musawwar*, 4 August 1961; *Ruz al-Yusuf*, 22 August 1961. *Al-Hayat* reported that in view of the trial, the National British Party demanded that Britain try Begin. *Al-Hayat*, 23 April 1961.

45   *Al-Akhbar, Filastin*, 28 April, *al-Ahram*, 29 April 1961.

46   *Al-Jihad*, 11, 12 April 1961.

47   *Al-Ayyam*, 11 April 1961.

ing a movie." The trial had failed to achieve its objectives, he asserted, among

intermediary between Germany and King Faruq.[48] In addition, he had fallen out of favor with the revolutionary regime, principally because of his support for 'Abd al-Karim Qasim, the Iraqi ruler, and had been forced to move from Cairo to Lebanon in August 1959.[49] The issue was even more complex for the Palestinians in Jordan, who distanced themselves from the Mufti at the time. (For further discussion of the Palestinian attitude to the Mufti, see Chapter 9.)

When the first part of the trial ended in August, al-Ahram published a page-long article in its Friday section, "The significance of the events", written by Sami Mansur. Its subheads were "The Eichmann trial play recently ended," "Prosecution witnesses testified in Israel and defense witnesses in Germany," and "Eichmann to write a book about Nazism after the verdict." However, stated the article, it had not realized even one of its goals, and Ben-Gurion's party had lost five Knesset seats.[50] As part of the representation of the trial as a staged show, Mansur claimed that some of the witnesses who testified to Nazi atrocities had done so "in a clearly literary way and as though they were making a movie." The trial had failed to achieve its objectives, he asserted, among other things, because while Israel had hoped to make the front page of all the newspapers in the world, it had barely managed to hold readers' interest for more than a week, and Yuri Gagarin's voyage in space had taken its place.[51] Moreover, Europe, "which suffered the horrors of war more than others," had shut its ears to the story of Nazism that it had remembered in the past and wanted to forget today. Even in Israel itself the trial had missed the point. The youth to whom Ben-Gurion wanted to teach a chapter in history had rebelled and asked difficult questions about activities to save the Jews, and their fathers

48   For a discussion on the German contacts with the Egyptian monarch during the war, see 'Atiq, al-Malik faruq.

49   Zvi Elpeleg, The Grand Mufti: Haj Amin al-Hussaini, Founder of the Palestinian National Movement, London: 1993, pp. 130–2. The Egyptians instituted a fierce campaign against the Mufti, see HZ3766/32, Appendix to collection no. 653, 28 August 1959. Husayni's activities with respect to the Holocaust, which have been the subject of a great deal of research, are beyond the scope of this study. Although he denied all involvement in acts of killing Jews or any connection with Eichmann, he gave conflicting evidence. See al-Hayat, 5 March, 27 April, 17, 23 May, 28 June 1961. 'Abd al-Karim al-'Umar (ed.), Mudhakkirat al-hajj Muhammad Amin al-Husayni, Damascus: 1999, p. 19, and below, Chapter 9.

50   On 15 August 1951, elections were held for the Fifth Knesset. Mapai, Ben-Gurion's party, won 42 seats (34.7 percent), down five seats from the 47 it had (38.2 percent) in the Fourth Knesset.

51   Yuri Gagarin, the first Russian cosmonaut, reached space on 12 April 1961, the day after the trial began, and his voyage aroused great interest and was widely reported by the international press, especially since it was considered a great Soviet achievement in the Cold War with the United States.

saw no benefit in opening old wounds. Even the attempts to convince world public opinion that the Arab nationalist movement was racist and similar to Nazism had turned into a double-edged sword, and during the trial names were mentioned of Zionist leaders who had collaborated with the Nazis despite the persecution of the Jews.[52]

In describing the main issues raised during the trial, Mansur also mentioned the attack on the Allies, and particularly Britain, for their refusal to respond to the Zionists' request to bomb the concentration camps. The truth was, he said, that had they done so, Zionism would have accused them of acting like Nazis. Touching upon a controversy in Israel over the question of what the Jews in Israel knew about the Holocaust in real time and what they had done to help European Jewry, Mansur mentioned the testimony of Joel Brand, who allegedly expressed his disappointment with the representatives of the Jewish Agency he had met in Istanbul, claiming that they had no interest in the fate of Hungarian Jewry. Although they had not known a lot about the Holocaust (ma'asa), he was quoted as contending, they had received reports and they should have believed them. However, the greatest surprise of the trial, according to Mansur, was Germany's agreement to take the testimonies of eight former Nazi defense witnesses in a court in Germany, due to the prosecution's warning that they would be arrested if they set foot in Israel. The article ended with the defense made by Eichmann himself and presented the controversy in Israel as to his execution. It also emphasized the alleged lack of interest in the trial in the West and the lack of identification with Israel, according to an undated Gallup poll conducted in the United States and Britain.[53]

Arab press reports on Eichmann's conviction on twelve of the fifteen charges that carried the death penalty varied in detail. Some referred to the major charges, such as the annihilation of millions of Jews and the perpetration of war crimes against the Jewish people and humanity. They even noted that the court had admitted the illegality of the kidnapping, but explained that there was no

52   *Al-Ahram*, 25 August 1961. Undoubtedly, international events clouded the trial, and it was only natural that the longer the trial lasted the less interest was shown in it, but it seems that the Arab press was happy to report the waning interest in the trial. *Al-Difa'* reported the indifference of British public opinion on 16 May 1961, and *al-Hayat* only a month later, on 20 June 1961. Also see *Arab Observer*, 15 January 1962, p. 21.

53   According to the survey, only 44 percent of those participating supported the Israeli court; 13 percent knew nothing about the trial; 60 percent of the Americans and 70 percent of the British thought the trial was fair; only 25 percent sympathized with Israel and the Jews and 32 percent thought Eichmann should have been tried by an international court. *Al-Ahram*, 25 August 1961. Reports on the testimony in Germany were published by *al-Hayat*, 4 May, 30 June 1961; *al-Jihad*, 4, 9, 16 May 1961.

other way to establish Eichmann's identity.[54] Two days later, Eichmann was quoted as saying that he had lost his hopes of justice and that he did not recognize the legality of the Israeli court nor admit his crime of mass murder, which was the responsibility of the political leadership. Servatius was quoted as well, repeating his assertion that Eichmann had only been following orders and was nothing but a small cog in a big wheel.[55] Until the end of December a few more accounts were published, among them the statements made by Eichmann's son Klaus and an interview with Eichmann's wife, Veronica. *Al-Hayat*, on the other hand, also printed the appeal by three noted Israeli intellectuals of German origin, Martin Buber, Hugo Bergmann and Gershom Shalom, to Israeli President Yitzhak Ben-Zvi to reduce Eichmann's sentence, and described Buber as a great philosopher who had immigrated to Palestine in 1938.[56] Until the execution on 1 June 1962, the press reported the deliberations concerning Eichmann's appeal and its rejection,[57] his last meeting with his wife,[58] and the last-minute request to President Ben-Zvi to reduce the sentence.[59]

A tone of sympathy and perhaps even admiration crept into the reports describing Eichmann's conduct as he went to his death. "Eichmann faced death bravely," refused to cover his head with a hood and with a smile bid farewell to his friends, cheering Germany, Argentina and Austria, quoted the reports. *Al-Jihad* added that "the oppressors burned his body and scattered his ashes at sea."[60] The Arab press also dealt with the world's reactions to the execution and with the violence perpetrated against Jewish institutions in Argentina and various places in Europe. They quoted Klaus Eichmann as saying that history would judge Israel's crime, and that his father had been the victim of Israel's demand for reparations from Germany. They emphasized the distress felt in Germany, where there were those who were stunned by the affair, especially in view of the fortune the German government had paid and was paying in reparations, and quoted observers who noted that the trial had a political objective and therefore the reactions were political. Israel, they stated, wanted to use the trial to remind

54 *Al-Ahram, al-Akhbar, al-Jumhuriyya, Filastin, al-Jihad, al-Hayat, al-Nahar,* 12 December 1961. For additional reports of the verdict see *al-Hayat, al-Nahar,* 14 December, *al-Jihad, Filastin,* 14, 16, 17 December 1961.

55 *Al-Jumhuriyya,* 14 December 1961.

56 *Al-Ahram,* 15–18 December, *al-Hayat,* 21 December, *Akhir Sa'a,* 27 December 1961; Segev, *The Seventh Million,* pp. 340–2.

57 *Al-Ahram,* 23, 18 March, 30 May 1962. Also see *al-Jihad,* 22, 29 March, 31 May, *al-Hayat,* 30 May 1962.

58 *Al-Ahram,* 5 April 1962.

59 *Al-Ahram, al-Jumhuriyya, al-Hayat, al-Nahar, Filastin,* 1 June 1962.

60 *Al-Ahram, al-Jumhuriyya, al-Jihad, Filastin,* 2 June 1962.

not only the younger generation in Israel but the whole world that "some of the Jews had been persecuted" in various countries, and in that way to justify its own crimes.[61] "After a three-ring circus of a trial, 'authorized' and conducted by those responsible for the murder, rape and displacement of most of the Arab population of Palestine, Eichmann was found guilty of responsibility for the killing of nearly 6 million Jews during World War II," wrote the Egyptian English-language weekly, *Arab Observer*. The article also recounted for the first time that Eichmann had visited Mandatory Palestine, a short time after 1933, to inflame the Jews against the Arabs before the Nazi conquest, but had been captured by the British and expelled within less than a week – a completely fictitious story which would later be used to demonstrate Zionist–Nazi collaboration.[62]

The affair in the public discourse

Editorials and radio commentaries reflected the Arab point of view of the trial even more than the informative articles. There were no restrictions on either thoughts or vocabulary in their interpretation of the events, which contained severe and often vicious criticism of Israel and abundant references to the Holocaust. The first and strongest reactions came from the Egyptian broadcasts in Hebrew, which served anti-Israeli propaganda. As early as 26 May 1960, in the first broadcast referring to Eichmann's capture, the radio commentator warned that "the rulers of Israel as well will not escape punishment, and capturing Eichmann will teach them a lesson."[63] The following day, he suggested that Eichmann might reveal anti-Jewish secrets about the Zionist representatives who had collaborated with him, a point which leaked into the press only later, as was seen above. It is possible that the lack of correlation between the press and the radio came from the gap between information and knowledge. Information kept streaming in, but it made no sense to the Egyptian reader, and commentaries aimed at the Israeli ear justifiably assumed that it was more aware of the problems involved in the affair. Another theme which appeared in the first broadcasts was denial and minimization of the Holocaust. Eichmann was liable to destroy "the myth of the slaughter of six million Jews," said the Radio Cairo

61   *Al-Ahram*, 2, 3 June, *al-Hayat*, 2 June, *Filastin*, 3 June, *al-Jihad*, 6 June, 3 July 1962.

62   *Arab Observer*, 4 June 1962, p. 13. In October 1937 Eichmann was in fact on his way to visit Palestine as part of his job as responsible for the Department of Jewish Affairs and in coordination with Zionist activists in Germany to examine the possibility of Jewish emigration to Palestine. However, the British did not permit him to enter and he went to Egypt instead, where he conducted part of his investigations. Kempner, *Profession*, p. 25; Arendt, *Eichmann in Jerusalem*, p. 57.

63   Radio Cairo, 26 May 1960 – Daily survey, 27 May 1960, No. 3380/583.03.

commentator, adding that "he could prove that no more than 100,000 Jews had been killed throughout Europe during the Nazi regime." Radio Damascus's Hebrew commentator also described the annihilation of six million Jews as "a ridiculous, untruthful myth that no one believes, not even the Zionists."[64]

Another theme which appeared in radio broadcasts at an early stage was the equation of Israel's deeds with those of the Nazis. The Israeli rulers, it was said, committed worse crimes against the Arabs than the Nazis did against the Jews. "Is it just to bring one type of criminal to trial and to leave the others alone? We are absolutely certain that the day is not far off when the Arab people will bring the leaders of the Zionist crime to trial."[65] In response to the report on Eichmann's alleged suicide attempt, understanding was expressed for his motives, because "he had fallen into the hands of war criminals," "more barbaric and worse" than he was, and "it was the only way he could escape the claws of the Jews and Zionists." However, the Egyptian commentator, 'Adil al-Qadi, added that "we do not have pity for Eichmann and we do not identify with him," but wondered how "one criminal tries another for the same crime he himself committed."[66] The theme of Israel's exploiting the Holocaust also appeared in radio commentaries which explained that Eichmann's kidnapping was nothing more than a Jewish plot whose objective was political, to wring money out of world Jewry and divert the attention of the Israeli people from their own difficulties.[67]

Editorials, as were to be expected, elaborated on themes which also appeared in informative articles, but reflected the complexity of the discourse, serving as a more fitting forum for discussing the affair and arguing with Israel, and sometimes with the western countries because of their relations with it. Egyptian liberal intellectual Mustafa Amin wondered what would have happened if the United Arab Republic had kidnapped Ben-Gurion during his visit to the United States (which in fact took place a few days after Eichmann was brought to Israel) and brought him to Cairo for trial. He described a situation in which the whole world rose against Egypt, revealing a prevalent Arab belief that the international

---

64   Radio Cairo, 27 May 1960 – Daily survey, 29 May 1960, No. 3381/586.03. Radio Damascus, 12 June 1960 – Daily survey, 13 June 1960, No. 3393/586.03.

65   Radio Cairo, 5 June 1960 – Daily survey, 6 June 1960, No. 3387/586.03.

66   Cairo (Voice of the Arabs), 7 June 1960 – BBC, 9 June 1960. The theme of relativism was evident in a Radio Baghdad broadcast, which stated that Eichmann was a Nazi German Jew who killed Jews and non-Jews. Radio Baghdad, 23 June 1960 – Daily survey, 24 June 1960, No. 3403/586.03.

67   Radio Cairo, 13, 15 June 1960 – Daily surveys, 14, 16 June 1960, Nos. 3394/586.03, 3396/596.03. UAR Broadcasts to Israel, 7–13 June 1960 – BBC, 16 June 1960. The same was true for Radio Beirut, which claimed that Israel was trying to capture world sympathy and support by exploiting an affair which was, in effect, an open robbery. Radio Beirut, 7 June 1960 – Daily survey, 8 June 1960, No. 3389/586.03.

community had a double standard for dealing with the Arabs and the Israelis, and indirectly comparing Eichmann with Ben-Gurion. Amin viewed the trial in Israel as contrary to international law, and for that reason demanded UN intervention, otherwise there was no reason for its existence and for the human rights it was supposed to protect.[68]

In his *Ruz al-Yusuf* column "Yesterday, Today and Tomorrow," leftist Ihsan 'Abd al-Qudus asserted that the Nazi leader "did not deserve to be defended by us." Fearing lest the Arab reaction to the kidnapping be interpreted as defending Eichmann, he explained that "we defend humanity from Israeli hatred." Israel, he said, was using this hatred to take over the world, and had founded an international organization, whose task was to track down war criminals and bring them to trial. On the list of war criminals were the names of all its enemies, as was everyone who stood in the way of Israel's aspirations. The war had ended 15 years ago and Hitler's persecution campaign against the Jews had ended. "Today the world needs mercy, forgetfulness and quiet," he concluded, wondering "why those who persecuted the Jews are considered criminals while those who persecuted other peoples are not criminals and are not brought to justice?!"[69] Kamil Zahiri pursued a similar theme in the same journal. Why was the persecution of the Jews the only Nazi-inflicted wound which had not healed? West Germany was trying to forget the past, and was using its activities and economic delegations to make others forget it as well, but Israel kept raising the subject of Nazi crimes, especially since the reparations agreement was supposed to end in 1966, apparently in order to extort financial, political and material support from Germany again and justify renewal of the agreement.[70]

In another long, detailed article about the kidnapping, also published in *Ruz al-Yusuf*, Mamduh Rida wrote that Israel was tracking down former Nazis with the intention of kidnapping them for their participation in the killing of six million Jews. It was also pressuring Germany to bring those living there to trial. What was the objective, and why now, asked Rida, answering that Israel was making internal and foreign "material and propaganda gains." Reminding the Israeli people of the atrocities committed against the Jews meant diverting their attention from internal problems, he said; to educate younger Israeli generations about them; to close ranks behind Ben-Gurion and turn attention away from the failures of the Tawfiq campaign,[71] the struggle for a passage

---

68   *Akhbar al-Yawm*, 11 June, *al-Hayat*, 12 June 1960.

69   *Ruz al-Yusuf*, 13 June 1960.

70   *Ruz al-Yusuf*, 20 June 1960. For another article in the same vein, see *Ruz al-Yusuf*, 10 April 1961.

71   In an operation carried out on 1 February 1960, Israeli forces raided Hirbet Tawfiq in

through the Suez Canal and the campaign against the Arab boycott. Its foreign objectives were to issue a reminder to world public opinion so as to wring its sympathy; to strengthen the link between Jews abroad and Israeli citizens; to bring the two world blocks closer by hunting Nazis; to stress Nazi persecutions and anti-Semitism so as to overshadow Arab claims concerning the Palestinian refugees and their persecution; to exert pressure on Germany to establish diplomatic relations, and on the Austrian government for reparations; and to reveal the capabilities of Israeli intelligence to raise morale and cover up the Israeli espionage failure in Egypt.[72] Thus, the article linked the Eichmann affair to current events in the Israeli internal arena, the Arab–Israeli conflict and Israel's foreign relations.

The denial of Israel's right to try Eichmann, despite recognition of his crimes, was also characteristic of editorials appearing in *al-Hayat*. On 12 June 1960, Basil Daqqaq expressed his astonishment that Germany had renounced "its right and perhaps obligation" to try him, an aspect which had not appeared in the Egyptian press.[73]*Al-Ahram* was more blatant in its commentary on Israel's conduct.[74] Viewing the trial as "a personal campaign" against Eichmann, the paper accused the Israeli government of inflating the charges to justify the kidnapping. In conclusion, the article noted that some of the Zionist voices disagreed with Ben-Gurion's government and proposed that Eichmann be tried by an international tribunal.[75]

Habib Jamati, an *al-Musawwar* columnist, believed the affair deserved the Arabs' attention because of its worldwide echo, and should be used as a springboard for launching a counter-offensive to raise world awareness to Israel's crimes in Palestine, which were no less atrocious than those of the Nazis. In describing Eichmann's past he did not deny that he had been one the perpetrators of the annihilation plan against the Jews, who were considered "enemies of humanity." He stressed that he had not been working alone and was not the "chief planner," but rather subordinate to Himmler, who carried out Hitler's will. The Zionist insistence that six million Jews had been killed was "an exaggeration" to "re-arouse hatred for the man and other Nazis scattered around the

---

response to Syrian fire on border villages.

72   *Ruz al-Yusuf*, 4 July 1960.

73   *Al-Hayat*, 8, 10, 12, 24 June, 1 July 1960, 13 April 1961. A detailed analysis of the legal aspects of Israel's right to try Eichmann was written by the president of the civil court of appeals in Beirut, Zahdi Yakan, in response the British Judge Barry O'Brien. *Al-Hayat*, 21 June 1960.

74   *Al-Ahram*, 16 June 1960.

75   *Al-Ahram*, 24 June 1960.

globe, and to rouse pity – and contributions – for the Jews." He also questioned the right of Israel, "the alien nation in Palestine," to try him. That, he claimed, was the right of the countries which had defeated Germany, and only after Argentina had agreed. "There is no doubt that Eichmann was a murderer, but he is imprisoned by a group of murderers who are no less dangerous. He participated in mass killings and Ben-Gurion and his gang have been engaged in the mass killing of Arabs for 12 years. Zionist terrorism is judging Nazi terrorism!"[76]

The comparison between the Holocaust and the Palestinian Nakba, describing the incidents at Deir Yasin, and Kafar Qasim during the Suez Campaign in 1956, and the assertion that Israel's actions were worse than those of the Nazis, were motifs that appeared in another article in the same issue of *al-Musawwar* by Sabri Abu al-Majd. Headlined "Who will judge a million Eichmanns?" it cast doubt on the probity of the Israeli legal system. In *Akhir Sa'a*, Muhammad al-Tabi'i also claimed that if Israel had appropriated the right to try Eichmann, it was the UAR's right to kidnap and try the killers among the Israeli leadership, and it would not be a violation of international law because the UAR did not recognize Israel and its sovereignty. The articles were accompanied by three cartoons. One depicted Ben-Gurion standing in a pool of blood, his hands dripping. The caption was a play on words, using Eichmann's name to denote disgust: "Ich mann." The second showed Ben-Gurion, carrying Eichmann on his back, arriving at the "Israeli kidnapping warehouse," in which were packages labeled "The rights of the Palestinian people," "War property," "Palestinian property." It was captioned, "This week's movie, 'The Return of the Kidnappers.'" The third showed Golda Meir standing at a bus stop looking over her shoulder at a man reading a newspaper and taking his wallet out of his pocket. The caption read, "Golda Meir is collecting contributions in the United States through Eichmann."[77]

The few editorials in *Filastin* were no less vicious toward Israel and the Jews. Under the title "Between Eichmann and Joshua," columnist Yahya Hawwash made a direct link between Nazism and the Jewish Scriptures. "The Nazi heroes," he claimed, "studied the ways of Joshua, the Jewish prophet, in Jericho and adopted from him the idea of people annihilation, but [they were] more lenient than the Jews." Hawwash, who stressed his denunciation of Eichmann and Nazism, concluded his column with a clear anti-Semitic remark, referring to the ungrateful trait of the Jews, demonstrated in their attitude to Jesus.[78] In another column presenting the Jews as war criminals, he resorted again to a

---

76   *Al-Musawwar*, 17 June 1960.
77   *Al-Musawwar*, ibid.; *Akhir Sa'a*, 8 March 1961.
78   *Filastin*, 29 May 1960.

classical anti-Semitic motif, accusing them of being behind every war, "like a snake which stings and hides."[79] It should be noted that although anti-Semitic manifestations were already abundant in Arab writing, in the context of the trial they were especially typical of the editorials of this paper.[80]

One editorial by noted leftist intellectual Lutfi al-Khuli, entitled "Eichmann between Nazism and Zionism," discussed the Israeli criticism of the Arab position on the trial. "The Zionist propaganda," he wrote, "describes Arab condemnation of the kidnapping as a defense of Eichmann," but "by virtue of our revolutionary opinions regarding colonialism and racism, we would never defend Eichmann and Nazism because of their hostile and racist position on the Jews." Moreover, he noted, "we are hostile to all the inhuman principles and views Eichmann and Nazism symbolize," and the same logic lay behind the Arab position on Ben-Gurion and Zionism. In Arab history, claimed al-Khuli, there were no cases of racist persecution of Jews, who remained Jews and did not link their fate to Zionism in the 1948 war or during the "triple aggression" in 1956. He was also of the opinion that, as a Nazi and an international war criminal, Eichmann should be tried by an international court, and described the trial in Israel as a caricature. He emphasized that Israel feared an objective trial because it was liable to expose Zionist crimes "as a continuation of Nazi crimes," and expected that some day Zionist leaders would be tried for crimes not only against Arabs but also against Jews, whom they "seduced with the slogan of the national homeland and undermined their stability and security all over the world."[81]

Inspired by the Soviet perception of Zionism and Nazism, al-Khuli, who expressed the Arab left's position, viewed Zionism as "an aggressive colonial movement which fed on racism," although he recognized the Holocaust but saw no difference between Eichmann's deeds and those of Ben-Gurion. "The crime is of the same kind in both cases," he concluded, noting that, "it is insignificant to compare the amount of blood spilled in Nazi Germany and the amount spilled in Zionist Israel. Killing one man is like killing a

---

79   *Filastin*, 9 June 1960.

80   Also see, *Filastin*, 29 March, 14 April 1962.

81   *Al-Ahram*, 12 April 1961. The British historian Arnold Toynbee contributed his share to the equation and was often quoted by the Arab press, *al-Hayat*, 7 February 1961. Hajj Amin also raised that point at a press conference in March 1961. The traces of the Nazis' actions against the Jews had already been erased and now belonged to the past, while Zionist aggression was continuing, he said, and it was no less ugly than the Nazis', "as admitted by Prof. Toynbee and large, neutral international circles." He also stated that the Palestinians had decided to pass a law "for bringing to trial the Zionists responsible for the crimes committed in Palestine, like the law according to which the Nuremberg trials were held and the Zionists themselves were trying Eichmann." *Al-Hayat*, 5 March 1961.

thousand."[82] He reiterated the equation between Zionism and Nazism in another article, in which he tried to prove that the Zionist hostility to the Arabs and the acts of slaughter carried out against them were the result of Zionism's fanatical, racist world-view.[83]

However, it should be noted that Khuli criticized the Egyptian ban on the screening of a movie that showed Nazi persecutions of the Jews. The truth, he said, was that Zionism and Israel were dangerous, but that the movie presented the persecution of the Jews as part of Aryan racism, which harmed every other race, including the Arab. And while accusing the censors of damaging Arab interests, he stressed that it was the Arab nationalist movement's hostility toward racist fanaticism which led him to identify with the movie. The fear that the movie would make western viewers sympathetic to Israel, he claimed, reflected a lack of understanding of Israel and the Allies. Israel, he explained, had not been founded out of pity but in realization of an imperialist force's strategic plan. Banning a work of art because it was Jewish or because its producer had visited Israel would isolate Egyptian society from the scientific, cultural and artistic trends of the world.[84]

The English-language weekly *Arab Observer* also referred to the movie, claiming that it was being shown in Cairo and that it had stirred a controversy because of its Zionist orientation. The article, which described the movie as an indictment of Hitler and even more of Zionism, insinuated denial and the relativization of the Holocaust, which had not previously been mentioned. There was no doubt that Hitler had killed Jews, it noted, but there was also no doubt that he had killed millions of others in the death camps and other places. Most Germans had been unaware of the crimes until the Allies exposed them at the end of the war, but in any case, many Germans had also been killed by the bombings of the large cities during the war, and no one had been tried for that. Why had no one made a movie about that? And why had no movies been made about the other people the Nazis had killed, wondered the writer.[85]

82   *Al-Ahram*, 12 April 1962. The claim that killing one person is the same as killing a million, which contains relativization of the Holocaust, became more common later on, especially in Islamist discourse on the Holocaust, and was presented as a moral Islamic perception.

83   *Al-Ahram*, 18 May 1961.

84   *Al-Ahram*, 1 February 1962. By the beginning of May 1961, the Egyptian Minister of Culture and National Direction, Tharwat 'Akkasha, answering an enquiry posed in the Egyptian People's Assembly, said that the screening of "Zionist movies" had been banned as rousing sympathy for the Jews and presenting them in a positive light. *Al-Ahram*, 9 May 1961.

85   *Arab Observer*, 5 February 1962, p. 16.

'Abbas Mahmud al-'Aqqad expressed a different approach, attacking other aspects of the Eichmann affair. What would Zionism say about Eichmann in another 1,000 years, and which of its many myths would it foster about its sworn enemy "who was worthy of its malice, as it was worthy of his," he wondered. It was reasonable to assume, he stated, that it would be said that the God of Zion had come down to earth and taken Eichmann to Tel Aviv as "a present for the chosen people and a palatable sacrifice for the feast of the Exodus from Egypt." He also claimed that Eichmann looked Jewish and had been insulted because of it. Therefore, he was amazed at the interest Eichmann had shown in the people he would come to annihilate, and "why he bothered to learn their language, the Talmud and Jewish history."[86] In his indirect reference to the affair, 'Aqqad recognized the fact that the Holocaust had occurred, but did not hide his antipathy toward the Jewish victims, and perhaps there was a hint of justification in his assertion that they deserved the hatred they aroused in their enemies. However, he was consistent in his hostility to Nazism (see also Chapters 6 and 9).

In a column entitled "When the enemies of humanity speak about humanity," 'Aqqad rejected the legitimacy of the Israeli court and focused on the mentality of groups who viewed themselves as chosen people. The Aryans thought they were the people most entitled to "purify humanity from this scheming gang," he said. If the Nazis wanted support for their claims, they could find them in the Zionists' faith, because they also believed they were the chosen people. While Jews were God's chosen people in antiquity, the Nazis were in modern times. Since they denied Eichmann the basic right of calling witnesses for the defense, 'Aqqad recommended that he admits to one thing, that he was a gentile, and then three billion people on earth would share his crime. Thus the Zionist court would have to explain the difference between his enmity for humanity and the Zionist enmity for humanity. 'Aqqad, like many other Arab commentators, claimed that Zionism aspired to the idea of Jewish nationalism from its perception of the Jews as the chosen people, and often did not make the distinction between Jews and Zionists.[87]

---

86 *Al-Akhbar*, 12 April 1961. He referred to the Talmud and the books on Jewish history as "sahyuniyyat," deriving the term from "Isra'iliyyat," the term for the forged narratives from Jewish sources believed to be implanted in Islamic sources. For the significance of the "Isra'iliyyat," see Ronald L. Nettler, "Early Islam, modern Islam and Judaism: The Isra'iliyyat in modern Islamic thought," in Ronald L. Nettler and Suha Taji-Faruki (eds.), *Muslim–Jewish Encounters. Intellectual Traditions and Modern Politics*, Amsterdam: 1998, pp. 1–14.

87 *Al-Akhbar*, 26 April 1961. Also see Habib Jamati's article in *al-Musawwar*, 21 April 1961.

Akhir Sa'a columnist Mazin al-Bunduk stressed that this Arab viewpoint did not reflect an inclination toward Nazism or pity for Eichmann. He repeated the claim made earlier, that it was the Arabs' bad luck that Hitler and Nazism had come to power, because they pushed many Jews into the ranks of Zionism. He denied the numbers of the victims, a theme which had not been prominent until then. Israel, he said, was interested in painting a "horrifying and exaggerated picture of the Jewish victims of Nazism." Its claim that six million Jews had been killed was "entirely untrue." Moreover, the number of non-Jewish victims in the European countries under Nazi occupation was far greater than that of Jewish victims. In addition to claims made by others, he added two other objectives Israel hoped to gain from the trial: to place the responsibility for the persecution of the Jews squarely on the conscience of the West, so that the only way of dealing with the past would be to offer aid to Israel; and to prove to the Jews that they would have peace only by emigrating to Israel and supporting its existence.[88]

The theme of Israel's exploitation of the trial for the realization of material goals appeared in several articles. Israel was accused of terrorizing West Germany, which "was very sensitive to its history of Nazism." All the signs, concluded an article in *Akhir Sa'a*, indicated that Germany had decided to give Israel more reparations "to prove to the world that Nazism was a thing of the past."[89] It linked the Holocaust and the establishment of the state by saying that the persecution of the Jews in "yesterday's" Germany was one of the factors which brought about the conquest of Palestine as a safe haven for the persecuted, and attacked Israel's attempt to involve the Arabs by force in "that filthy affair," as participants in the annihilation of the Jews. It was doing so, it claimed, to cover up its extermination policy against the Arabs of Palestine.[90] The trial was perceived as flawed in every legal sense and as a political step which went beyond its goal of demanding Eichmann's head. Echoing arguments raised previously by Nazi defendants, *al-Musawwar* asserted that the man sitting in the witness box was "a clerk doing an official job," adding that his government and country and citizens did not view his acts as justifying a trial or condemnation.[91]

Shortly after the trial began, the Syrian *al-Ayyam* printed a column entitled "The Eichmann trial – denying justice and exploiting [the trial] to extort addi-

---

88   *Akhir Sa'a*, 12 April 1961. See also *al-Akhbar*, 14 April 1961.

89   *Akhir Sa'a*, 26 April 1961. See also *al-Musawwar*, 21 April 1961; *Arab Observer*, 5 February 1962, p. 18.

90   *Al-Musawwar*, 21 April 1961.

91   *Al-Musawwar*, 14 April 1961.

tional reparations," about a workshop held by the Political Science Association (*Jam'iyyat al-'ulum al-siyasiyya*) in Cairo which dealt with the Eichmann trial in light of international law. It was attended by Egyptian professors of political science and economics, among them Hafiz Ghanim, Egyptian expert in international law at 'Ayn Shams University, and Butrus Butrus-Ghali, who then taught political science at Cairo University and later became deputy foreign minister and Secretary General of the UN, and 'Ali Muhammad 'Ali, the representative of the Palestinian Administration in Gaza. The findings presented in the article show that in academic circles also, the discussion of the trial was not elevated above the political and propagandist level. Ghanim questioned the trial's legality, stressing the fact that the judges were Jewish and therefore were biased and incapable of fairly judging a man accused of "annihilating the Jewish race." The trial, he said in conclusion, was fundamentally illegal, since the political factors behind it overshadowed the legal aspects. Butrus-Ghali also viewed the trial as Ben-Gurion's attempt to further his political goals within Israel after the decline in his power following the Lavon affair.[92] The same motifs typified the few editorials in the Jordanian/Palestinian papers.[93]

After the execution, Mahmud Dhahani reported from Denmark on the Egyptian view of the Eichmann trial, as it was presented in a press conference there given by Deputy Foreign Minister Dhu al-Faqar. He did not raise new points, but stressed the theme of Zionist–Nazi collaboration, which became a main Arab theme after the affair. He accused Israel of organizing "Jewish gangs" whose job was to kill other Jews so as to foster sympathy in world public opinion, and contended that Ben-Gurion headed such a gang and that Kasztner, Eichmann's only defense witness, who had been killed in Israel a few days before the trial, was one of its members.[94] Reflecting on the lesson to be learned by the Arabs from "Israeli justice," Salih Jawdat concluded that it allowed them "to kidnap Israeli leaders and bring them to Cairo or any Arab capital, hang them, burn their bodies and scatter their ashes at sea."[95]

Lebanese commentator Basil Daqqaq summarized the lessons of the trial from the Arab point of view and indicated two "historical truths": the affair would always remain "a symbol in history of the triumph of politics over jus-

---

92   *Al-Ayyam*, 25 April 1961. It should be noted that no report of the workshop appeared in the Egyptian press. The Palestinian speaker also raised the claim that the accused and the judges were one and the same, since Israel had committed the same crimes against the Arabs in Palestine.

93   *Al-Jihad*, 11 April, *Filastin*, 13 April, *al-Difa'*, 16 May 1961.

94   *Ruz al-Yusuf*, 11 June 1962. Kasztner was murdered in 1957, three years before Eichmann was kidnapped.

95   *Al-Musawwar*, 15 June 1962.

tice," regardless of the executioners' success "in arousing the sympathy of the world for the hundreds of thousand of Jewish victims during the Nazi era"; and it would serve "as a precedent related, as far as the Arabs were concerned, to the chain of murders and expulsion of the Palestinians ... on the altar of the Jewish state."[96]

A number of articles and editorials showed sensitivity to the involvement of Arabs in the trial, implied in Ben-Gurion's remarks on the connection between Nazi criminals and some of the Arab rulers,[97] and in the allusion to the Mufti as a collaborator in the annihilation of the Jews and an obstacle to rescuing them. They rejected any involvement in the annihilation, but the writers' national vantage point was never in doubt, even when they were left-ists, like al-Khuli, who spoke in the name of revolutionary, anti-Fascist, anti-imperialist values.

In writing about the trial there was a tendency to quote western and Jewish sources, as if to give further validity to the claims that had been raised. For example, *al-Ahram* quoted the *Chicago Tribune*'s attack on the trial because of the retroactivity of the Israeli law and because the judges were "victims of the crimes he [Eichmann] was accused of."[98] American Jewish representatives and Jewish professors of law who had reservations about the trial and Israel's pretensions to representing world Jewry were also quoted.[99] A firmly anti-Nazi stance was taken by spokesmen for the Egyptian left, such as Lufti al-Khuli in the article quoted above.[100] Others, speaking from a nationalist point of view, such as Mazin al-Bunduk, expressed bitterness with Nazism, which had led to the flourishing of Zionism.[101] *Al-Difa'*, too, said Nazis deserved the most severe punishment possible for what they had done, although it defined them only as "stupid," and the Jews as a "plague" who were, apparently, worthy of purifica-tion.[102] West Germany was presented as suffering from a complex because of its Nazi past, and was attacked for renouncing its responsibility to defend one of its citizens out of fear of being accused of defending Nazism and exposing former Nazis in its government.

---

96   *Al-Hayat*, 2 June 1962.
97   The *New York Times* interview with Ben-Gurion is quoted in Arendt, *Eichmann in Jerusa-lem*, pp. 8–10; Segev, *The Seventh Million*, p. 311.
98   *Al-Ahram*, 7 April 1961.
99   *Al-Ahram*, 22, 23 June 1960, 28 February 1961; *al-Hayat*, 10, 12, 19 June, *al-Akhbar*, 30 June 1960; *Ruz al-Yusuf*, 10 April, *Filastin*, 23 May, *al-Jihad*, 13 September, 6 November 1961; *Arab Observer*, 15 January 1962, pp. 14–15.
100 *Al-Ahram*, 12 April 1961.
101 *Akhir Sa'a*, 12 April 1961.
102 *Al-Difa'*, 13 April 1961. Also see *al-Ahram*, 8 April 1961.

The affair's contribution to Holocaust discourse

The representation of the trial in the Arab media and research literature has so far been depicted in Israeli and western research literature, and hence in Israel's public awareness, as one-dimensional. Based on a small number of articles and cartoons repeatedly quoted, and on Arab propaganda against the trial, it has not reflected all the dimensions of the discourse. That distortion was amplified by the preoccupation with Husayni's connections with the Nazi regime and his influence on them. Moreover, the political and ideological use of the trial by Israel fanned the fires of its instrumentalization by Egypt and other Arab states.

Jewish and Israeli scholars who dealt with the trial claimed that the theme of regret that the annihilation had not been complete was particularly characteristic of Arab discourse concerning the trial. Robert Wistrich wrote that the Arab reactions were "a concrete expression of the Arab position on the issue – not feelings of regret for the Jewish Holocaust but rather sorrow that the Germans had not managed to finish the job."[103] Yehoshafat Harkabi noted condemnations of Israel in the Arab press and sympathy for Eichmann. He gave the example of a cartoon appearing in the Lebanese paper *al-Anwar* which showed Ben-Gurion and Eichmann facing one another and shouting. Ben-Gurion says, "You deserve the death penalty for having killed six million Jews," and Eichmann answers, "There are a lot of people who claim I deserve the death penalty for not finishing the job."[104] Bernard Lewis referred to the headline in the Saudi paper mentioned above, "The capture of Eichmann, who had the honor of killing five million Jews,"[105] as characteristic of Arab writing, and Hannah Arendt asserted that the Arabs did not conceal their sympathy for Eichmann.[106] The Israeli press also reported two instances in which Israeli Arabs identified with Eichmann's actions against the Jews, and *al-Hayat* reported the case of a young Arab from the Galilee who was brought to trial for doing so.[107] The Israeli Foreign Ministry briefings on the Arab press reinforced those evaluations and gave prominence to the Arab claim that the trial was morally a torture for Eichmann, reminiscent of trials held under Stalin and Hitler.[108] Those evaluations were based on what

---

103 Robert Wistrich, *Anti-Zionism and Anti-Semitism in Our Time*, Jerusalem: 1985 (Hebrew), p. 14.

104 Harkabi, *Arab Attitudes*, p. 257.

105 Lewis, *Semites and Anti-Semites*, p. 162. See note 13.

106 Arendt, *Eichmann in Jerusalem*, pp. 8–10.

107 Yablonka, *The State of Israel*, p. 205; *al-Hayat*, 30 April 1961.

108 HZ3757/12, Loya to Ouman, A memorandum about "the position of Arab broadcasts and the Arab press concerning the Eichmann trial," 16 April 1961.

had been written, but were far from reflecting the entire scope and the nuances of the discourse about the trial and the Holocaust.

The Arab debate on the trial stemmed from the premise that the Holocaust did not concern the Arabs but they had to deal with it because of what was perceived as its detrimental political ramifications for the Arab cause and its exploitation by Israel. The justification of the Holocaust and regret that the annihilation had not been completed was a marginal theme and even absent from Egyptian writing on the trial. Moreover, Egypt's position toward the trial partially expressed identification with Eichmann, primarily out of its desire to strike a blow at Israel and Zionism. Indeed, *al-Jihad* reported that Eichmann was suffering from hypertension, had a nervous breakdown and had been tortured into confessing,[109] whereas *al-Ayyam* regretted Eichmann's bitter fate, comparing it (and thus minimizing his deeds) to the luck of Raoul Salan,[110] a rebel French general who was pardoned the same week that Eichmann was hanged.[111] However, the implied identification with Eichmann was not necessarily identification with his past.

References to Eichmann as a small cog in a big wheel and as a clerk who was merely following orders from his superiors, sitting at his desk during working hours and then going home to his family like everyone else,[112] was not the exclusive province of Egyptian and Arab discourse. Those arguments were part of an intensive international public debate over the trial. Moreover, intellectuals such as Egyptian leftists Lutfi al-Khuli and Ihsan 'Abd al-Qudus noted that their criticism of the trial and of Israel did not stem from a desire to defend Eichmann or his deeds. There is no doubt that these two expressed the position of the communist left, which was not common but was prominent in the Egyptian intellectual and public discourse. Thus, attitudes toward Eichmann were varied and reflected different approaches, from pity for the individual, identification with him and understanding for his deeds, to reservations about him and about what he symbolized.

The way the Arab press related to the Holocaust during the trial revealed a wide spectrum of motifs which were not new in the discourse on the Holocaust. There were aspects of denial, the Holocaust's exploitation by Israel, the equation between Zionism and Nazism and between the Holocaust and the

---

109   *Al-Jihad*, 23 May 1961.

110   Salan opposed the French pull-out from Algeria and was one of the leaders of the army rebellion against De Gaulle. He was brought to trial for his attempt to assassinate De Gaulle.

111   *Al-Ayyam*, 20 June 1962.

112   For example, see *al-Hayat*, 21 June 1960.

Palestinian Nakba. Two additional themes emerged: Zionist–Nazi collaboration, which had been negligible until then, and the creation of a causal linkage between the Holocaust and the establishment of the State of Israel. Eichmann was viewed as "an old friend of Israel," who had visited Palestine as "a guest of the Haganah," and had signed an agreement with world Zionism according to which he committed himself to expelling the Jews from Germany and the Zionists committed themselves to receiving them in Palestine. "If it weren't for the myth of Nazi persecution," Israel would not exist.[113] Eichmann's alleged visit to Palestine and the Jewish contacts with him served as evidence for the claim of Zionist–Nazi collaboration. That claim was also used by the only official Egyptian spokesman who referred to the trial. Husayn Dhu al-Faqar, who has been quoted above, claimed that Hitler "was a victim of the Zionists" and that they had forced him to carry out crimes which in the end were supposed to bring about the establishment of the State of Israel.[114] The Jewish German newspaper *Deutsche Rundschau* regarded the statement as a result of the influence of former Nazi Johann von Leers, who had settled in Egypt and served as a propaganda advisor.[115]

The allegation of Zionist collaboration with the Nazis was not only an attempt to repel and contradict the Israeli claim of Arab–Nazi collaboration. It exploited an issue which was fiercely debated in Israel during the Kasztner affair and in response to Arendt's reports during the trial. Moreover, the claim was compatible with and even reinforced the themes of the equation between Zionism and Nazism and the connection between the Holocaust and the establishment of the State of Israel. Zionism was represented as striving to realize one goal, the establishment of a Jewish state, and the end justified the means (see Chapter 8).

The public debate over the trial indicated that the Arab discourse was attentive to other discourses, and was particularly responsive to the development of the discourse on the Holocaust in Israel. The Eichmann affair again highlighted the subordination of the discourse on the Holocaust to the political struggle against Israel and Zionism. It was perceived as a good opportunity for the Arabs to call world attention to the alleged crimes committed in Palestine and to reveal "the

---

113   *Al-Jumhuriyya* as quoted (no date) in Oron (ed.), *Middle East Record 1961*, vol. 2, p. 187; *Arab Observer*, 4 June 1962, p. 13. See footnote 62.

114   *Al-Jumhuriyya*, 3 May 1961; *al-Hayat*, 4 May 1961; Arendt, *Eichmann in Jerusalem*, p. 17. Eichmann's son, Klaus, had reportedly accused the Jewish leaders of giving the instructions for the killings. *Al-Ahram*, 15–18 December, 2, 3 June, *al-Hayat*, 9 July 1961.

115   *Wiener Library Bulletin*, vol. 15, no. 3 (1961), p. 48.

ugly face" of Zionism.[116] Exploiting the Holocaust to attack Israel and Zionism increased as the Holocaust played a more central role in Israeli identity and collective memory. The polemical literature published about Zionism, both in the first years after the trial[117] and more than 30 years later, fixated on the same claims and themes which had appeared in the public debate during the trial. Even before it had ended, the trial was mentioned in a book by Najm Halumi and Ahmad Muhammad Saqr called *Zionism Past and Present*.[118] The book, which was published as part of the national books (*kutub qawmiyya*) series by the Egyptian Ministry of Information and contained many anti-Semitic motifs, did not deny Eichmann's crimes, but attacked Israel for kidnapping him, for its actions against the Arabs and for its political use of the trial. The book *The Terror State* also stressed the kidnapping and arguments against the trial. It quoted Arnold Toynbee, Charles Whitman and Jewish historian Oscar Handlin, as well as Jews who denounced the trial. Israel was using the trial, concluded the authors, to warn the entire world that the fate of anyone who opposed Zionism would be like Eichmann's. The book, which was published close to the end of the trial, had no specific insights other than those appearing in the press.[119]

Historian Wajih 'Atiq referred to the Eichmann affair in an analysis of Germany's commitment to support Israel, and he, too, adopted the narrative that Israel's policy was aimed at plundering Germany by exploiting its guilt feelings toward the Jews. He pointed to the personal motive that played a central role in Germany's surrender to Israel following the affair, namely, fear of the exposure of wanted Nazis who had become key figures in the federal government, such as Hans Globke, one of Adenauer's close advisors, who had participated in drafting the Nuremberg Laws in 1935. In return for not "looking too closely at the past of German government members," Israel received military aid. Thus, 'Atiq reinforced the claim that the Nazi past was effectively used by Israel as a means of extortion.[120]

---

116   *Al-Musawwar*, 17 June 1960.

117   According to the introduction to the edition of *The Protocols of the Elders of Zion* published in 2002, fifty books on Zionism and the Arab–Israeli conflict were published between 1956 and 1967. Husayn 'Abd al-Wahid, *Brutukulat hukama' sahyun*, Cairo: 2002, p. 12.

118   Muhammad Najm Halumi and Ahmad Muhammad Saqr, *al-Sahyuniyya Madiha wahadiruha*, Cairo: 1961, pp. 51–60. Also see Muhammad Nimr al-Madani, *Hal uhriqu al-yahud fi afran al-ghaz?* Damascus: 1996, pp. 41–50.

119   'Ali and 'Abd al-Hadi, *Dawlat al-irhab*, pp. 71–80. Also see 'Abd al-Munsif Mahmud, *al-Yahud wal-jarima*, Cairo: 1967, pp. 92–100, which quotes whole paragraphs from their book. For Handlin's position, see Gorni, *Between Auschwitz and Jerusalem*, pp. 39–40.

120   'Atiq, *al-Siyasa*, pp. 108–10. For the theme of the use of the trial as a weapon by "world Zionism" and Israel, see also Mustafa, *al-Musa'adat*, pp. 22–3.

Three years after the trial, Egyptian leftist Ahmad Baha' al-Din published a book which included a chapter dealing with the trial that was based on Moshe Perlman's book about the kidnapping.[121] His discussion of the power of world Zionism led him to the Eichmann trial, where he saw proof of Israel's exploitation of Diaspora Jews. As far as he was concerned, the trial was illegal and an unjustified act of revenge. He discussed the connections between the Nazis and representatives of the Zionist movement and the negotiations for the truck deal, but the chapter's main insight was his assessment that the clash between Zionism and the German racist movement was unavoidable (see Chapter 7).[122]

Baha' al-Din's thesis was further developed into a well-formulated perception in the writings of 'Abd al-Wahhab al-Masiri, an Egyptian scholar and specialist in Jewish and Zionist studies who during the 1970s became known for his Islamist tendencies. In 1997 he published a book called *Zionism, Nazism and the End of History*,[123] at the same time that a new approach toward the Holocaust was emerging in the Arab world (see Chapter 11). He devoted only a very short chapter to the Eichmann trial. Reading between the lines made it obvious that he had based it on Arendt's book; but where she wondered, he drew definite conclusions. He noted, for example, that Eichmann had studied Yiddish, Hebrew and Judaism, while Arendt made it clear that that was only a lie Eichmann liked to tell so as to impress his colleagues and Jewish victims.[124] He adopted the erroneous version that Eichmann arrived in Palestine at the invitation of the "Jewish settlers" to learn about the Zionist experiment there.[125] The fact that Eichmann had read Herzl's book and was supposedly enchanted by Zionist ideology suited Masiri's thesis. His views and those of the Zionist movement were no different from each other, he claimed. They both "believed the Jews should immigrate to a special country, since they were an abandoned organic people." Eichmann was influenced by Zionist thought and especially by Buber, asserted Masiri, who referred to Servatius' reflections as to whether there was something in the character of the Jewish people that led to its persecution and displacement everywhere, quoting him in an ostensibly neutral way: "Is it not possible that this people is responsible for the evil inflicted upon it?"[126] While Arendt viewed such statements as manifestations of anti-Semitism along the lines of *The Protocols of the Elders of Zion*, which led directly to the assertions of

121   Moshe Perlman, *How Eichmann Was Caught*, Tel Aviv: 1961.

122   Ibid., p. 170.

123   Al-Masiri, *al-Sahyuniyya*.

124   Ibid., p. 120; Arendt, *Eichmann in Jerusalem*, p. 25.

125   Arendt, ibid., p. 57.

126   Al-Masiri, *al-Sahyuniyya*, p. 121.

Dhu al-Faqar quoted above, Masiri left them as an open question for the reader to answer.

Arendt served as a source for the Eichmann trial in another study on Zionism and racism, prepared by three Egyptian scholars: Shihab al-Din Mufid, head of the department of international jurisprudence at Cairo University, intellectual al-Sayyid Yasin, then the director of *al-Ahram*'s Center for Strategic Studies and historian Yunan Labib Rizq. The study was carried out after the adoption in 1975 of the UN resolution which determined that Zionism was a type of racism. Like other studies, it indicated that Israel had exploited the trial and the Holocaust, but from a different angle: the part they played in constructing Israeli identity or personality. They claimed that the trial exposed the efforts of Israel's ruling élite to construct an Israeli personality based on the one hand on a racist perception, preaching suspicion of and hatred for non-Jews, especially Arabs and, on the other, on the belief that Jews were superior because they were the chosen people. The trial's objective had been to judge Eichmann not as a man but rather as a symbol, not only of the Nazi regime but also of anti-Semitic ideology throughout history, in order to display the Jewish fate before the world, to rouse guilt feelings among nations, to show Israelis the meaning of life as a minority in the Diaspora and to convince them of the justice of the Zionist solution. In addition, the trial had attempted to reinforce Jewish identity among Israelis and to strengthen the bond between them and Diaspora Jews out of the Zionist belief that anti-Semitism was immortal.[127] Notwithstanding the flaws in the authors' analysis, they seemed to identify the most important implications of the trial, i.e., the changes in the relations between Israel and the Diaspora and the place of the Holocaust in Jewish and Israeli identity.[128]

From the Arab point of view, "the Eichmann trial was useful to the Arab side during the psychological battles of the 1960s as a way of exposing Israeli callousness to the Arabs, and not especially as an attempt to acquaint Arab readers with details of the Jewish experience," explained Palestinian-American intellectual Edward Said. Indeed, his remarks support our claim that the Holocaust was not the focus of the Arab public discourse regarding the trial. The newspaper reports and commentaries that recognized the Holocaust as a crime against humanity, counterbalanced it with the Palestinian tragedy, perceived as a crime that was no less serious and perhaps even more severe. Said quoted the findings of a study on Egyptian and Lebanese press coverage of the trial carried out by Usama

127   Shihab al-Din Mufid, al-Sayyid Yasin and Yunan Labib Rizq, *al-Sahyuniyya wal-'unsuriyya: al-sahyuniyya ka-namat min anmat al-tafriqa al-'unsuriyya*, Cairo: 1997, pp. 69–72.

128   For the contribution of the trial in that respect, see for example, Gorni, *Between Auschwitz and Jerusalem*, pp. 24–34.

Maqdisi, which confirmed that conclusion but determined that there was no attempt to compare the Holocaust and the Palestinian tragedy, but rather to view them as "two great, despicable crimes."[129] That assertion perhaps contains the kernel of the difference between the subject positions of researchers. Putting both events on the same plane diminishes the Holocaust and denies its uniqueness. That is not to deny the Palestinian tragedy, but between it and the events of the Holocaust there is no room for comparison.

---

129 *Al-Hayat*, 5 November 1997. The article appeared in English in *al-Ahram Weekly*, 6 November 1997. Also see Gur-Zee'v, *Philosophy*, p. 110. Gur-Ze'ev distorted what Said had said by translating "exposing Israel's cruelty toward the Arabs" as "exposing the closeness between Jews and Arabs," an interpretation which was completely unsuitable for the spirit of the times.

4

ARAB VIEWS ON THE CATHOLIC CHURCH
AND THE HOLOCAUST

Arab references to the Holocaust in reaction to developments in the Catholic Church's attitude toward the Jews, as reflected in the deliberations of the Second Vatican Council in 1962–65 and in Pope John Paul II's statements in 1998, shed additional light on the evolution of the Arab Holocaust discourse. Christian doctrines which castigated the Jews for rejecting Christ's message, culminating in the charge of deicide, i.e. the murder of God through the crucifixion of Jesus, played a central role in the dissemination and perpetuation of anti-Semitism. The nineteenth century ushered in an additional kind of anti-Semitism, based on race rather than on religion, leading to the Nazi brand of genocidal anti-Semitism. While Christian anti-Semitism resulted in discrimination and sometimes violent persecutions, the Church, in contrast to Nazi anti-Semitism, rejected the extermination of the Jews, since their survival in humiliation was the divine proof of Christian supremacy. Moreover, Christian doctrine offered the Jews conversion as a way out of their predicament, whereas racial anti-Semitism left no way out, since people cannot choose or change their race. Still, Christian anti-Semitism played a major historical role in bringing about the Holocaust by facilitating the acceptance of Nazi anti-Semitism by Germans (and European public opinion at large), with the dehumanization of the Jews, and by fostering preconceived animosity towards them merely for being Jews.[1]

The conduct of the Catholic Church during the Holocaust became another thorny issue in Christian–Jewish relations. While various priests and monasteries throughout occupied Europe saved Jews from the claws of the Nazis, many others were indifferent in either turning Jews away, or actively assisting

---

1   For an analysis of the different kinds of anti-Semitism, see Jacob Katz, *From Prejudice to Destruction: Anti-Semitism, 1700–1933*, Cambridge, MA: 1982. For the role of Christian anti-Semitism, see David Kertzer, *The Popes Against the Jews: The Vatican's Role in the Rise of Modern Anti-Semitism*, New York: 2001.

the Nazis. The most notorious example was the Catholic priest Joseph Tisso, who headed the pro-Nazi Hlinka regime in Slovakia during the war.[2] Quite a few senior German churchmen, who had shown great courage in attacking the Nazi policy of euthanasia and in resisting the Nazi campaign to remove crosses from public buildings, failed to demonstrate the same moral strength when the persecution and extermination of the Jews were concerned.[3] Most problematic was the conduct of Pope Pius XII (1939–58) vis-à-vis the plight of the Jews during the war, which became subject of heated controversy among historians and members of the two communities.[4] In the aftermath of the Holocaust, various circles within the Christian Churches – Catholic and Protestants alike – who acknowledged the contribution of Christianity to anti-Semitism, as well as their indirect responsibility for the tragic fate of the Jews, held a series of conferences to re-evaluate their theological attitude toward Judaism and the Jews. For the first time in history, Catholic, Protestant and Jewish delegates from nineteen countries met in August 1947 in Seelisberg, Switzerland, in order to debate and approve a document denouncing anti-Semitism.[5]

The turning point in Catholic attitudes toward Judaism and the Jews followed the election on 28 October 1958 of Angelo Guiseppe Cardinal Roncalli as Pope John XXIII. During the war, he distinguished himself in saving the lives of hundreds of Jews who had escaped Nazi terror, in his capacity as Papal Pronuncio in Istanbul. Shortly after his nomination he instructed the Church to delete the reference to the Jews as "perfidious" from the Good Friday prayer. In 1962, after a two-year preparation period, Pope John XXIII inaugurated Vatican II, the ecumenical council attended by more than 2,600 Catholic bishops from all over the world, in order to discuss a series of doctrinal and organizational reforms. The Holocaust stood in the background of Vatican II debates as a major event which required the Church to rethink some of its doctrines. In

---

2   Yeshayahu Jelinek, *The Parish Republic: Hlinka's Slovak People's Party, 1939–1945*, New York: 1976.

3   Robert P. Ericksen and Susannah Heschel (eds.), *Betrayal: German Churches and the Holocaust*, Minneapolis, MN: 1999; Michael Phayer, *The Catholic Church and the Holocaust, 1930–1965*, Bloomington, IN: 2000; Daniel Jonah Goldhagen, *A Moral Reckoning: The Role of the Catholic Church in the Holocaust and its Unfulfilled Duty of Repair*, New York: 2002.

4   For criticism of the Pope's conduct, see John Cornwell, *Hitler's Pope: The Secret History of Pius XII*, New York: 1999; Carol Rittner and John K. Roth (eds.), *Pope Pius XII and the Holocaust*, London: 2002; Susan Zuccotti, *Under His Very Windows: The Vatican and the Holocaust in Italy*, New Haven, CT: 2000. For writers defending the Pope, see David G. Dalin, *The Myth of Hitler's Pope: How Pope Pius XII Rescued Jews from the Nazis*, Washington, DC: 2005.

5   Arthur Gilbert, *The Vatican Council and the Jews*, Cleveland, OH: 1968, pp. 25ff.

addition, the Church's deliberations followed Adolf Eichmann's trial, which heightened world attention on the Holocaust. One of the most important and controversial issues debated in it was the document submitted by Augustin Cardinal Bea, head of the Pontifical Council for Promoting Christian Unity, which advocated a reassessment of the Church position on the Jews. The document sought to remove the religious causes of anti-Semitism by narrowing the responsibility for the crucifixion to a small group of Jewish leaders at that time, while absolving the rest of the Jews, particularly those of later times, of any guilt. Pope John XXIII died on 3 June 1963 and his more conservative successor, Paul VI (d. 6 August 1978), proceeded with the Vatican II reform program, though more cautiously. At stake were serious theological issues regarding the Church's fundamental positions on the Jews and other religions, as well as their political ramifications.[6]

The doctrinal debate was also linked to the Church's political stance vis-à-vis Israel and the Arab states. The Vatican had opposed Zionism from its inception, primarily because its realization contradicted the Christian dogma that the Jews were punished with loss of sovereignty and dispersal from their homeland for rejecting Christ's message. It also feared that Jewish sovereignty might impinge on its own rights in the Holy Land, and that recognizing Israel might affect the status of Christians in Arab countries. Pope John XXIII was the first to take measures which signaled de facto recognition of Israel, when Church officials held unpublicized meetings with the Israeli ambassador in Rome. Pope Paul VI pursued this approach, but was careful lest it be interpreted as granting Israel de jure recognition. The Vatican established diplomatic relations with Israel only in 1993, following the signing of the PLO–Israeli Declaration of Principles.[7]

Arab states and public opinion reacted with indignation to the Vatican II debates on the "exoneration of the Jews from the Messiah's blood." Representatives of the Uniate Eastern Churches that were part of the Catholic Church were active inside the Church corridors to forestall the ratification of the document in two crucial sessions of November–December 1963 and September–November 1964. Concurrently, Arab governments exerted diplomatic pressure on the

---

6   Gilbert, *The Vatican Council*, pp. 88ff; F. E. Cartus, "Vatican II and the Jews," *Commentary*, vol. 30, no. 1 (January 1965), pp. 19–29. For general discussions of Vatican II, see also Henri Fesquet, *The Drama of Vatican II: The Ecumenical Council, June 1962–December 1965*, New York: 1967.

7   For discussions of the Church's policy toward Israel and the Arab–Israeli conflict, see Sergio I. Minerbi, *The Vatican, the Holy Land and Zionism, 1895–1925*, Jerusalem: 1985 (Hebrew); Andrej Kreutz, *Vatican Policy on the Palestinian–Israeli Conflict: The Struggle for the Holy Land*, New York: 1990; Marshall J. Breger (ed.), *The Vatican–Israel Accord: Political, Legal, and Theological Contexts*, Notre Dame: 2004.

Vatican. The Arab media, which was initially slow to realize the significance of Vatican II, was much more vocal during the two crucial sessions. Overall, the joint efforts of conservative church circles and Arab pressure led to a diluted final document, approved on 28 October 1965 under the name *Nostra Aetate* (Our Times). Yet, the document's long-term historical significance should not be underestimated.[8]

The politicized nature of Arab reactions led to the subordination of Islamic religious principles to politics, in view of the fact that Islamic doctrine categorically rejects the crucifixion as a historical fact. Speaking of the Jews who supposedly claimed "we slew the Messiah, Jesus son of Mary," the Qur'an (IV: 156–7) states that "they did not slay him, neither crucified him, only a likeness of that was shown to them" (*walakin shubbiha lahum*). Muslim traditions differ as to whether Christ was replaced by a double, or whether it was Simon the Cyrene or one of the apostles (Judas), who was indeed crucified. Jesus himself ascended to heaven to be with God, and his resurrection refers to that which will take place on Judgment Day.[9] However, the fear that any improvement in Christian attitude towards the Jews and Judaism might serve Israel's interests led the Arab states and media to overlook their own religious principles and protest the exoneration. The references to the Holocaust in the Arab public debate on Vatican II were not numerous, reflecting a difficulty to comprehend or accept the Holocaust's increasing effect on European and American culture and political discourse, which were unrelated to Israel per se. Rather, the discussion focused on the political ramifications of the Church's new theological stand, on benefits Israel might gain from the presentation of the Jews as victims, and on alleged Israeli scheming behind the scenes of the affair.

The entire spectrum of Arab arguments against the ratification of *Nostra Aetate* is beyond the scope of this study. Arab governments argued that the "exoneration document" (*wathiqat al-tabri'a*) meant submission to Zionist efforts to push the Vatican into granting Israel official recognition, while maintaining that the Arabs did not harbor any ill feelings towards the Jews as a people or Judaism as a religion. Consequently, this position contained only a few implicit references to the Holocaust.

The Eastern Churches, Catholic and Orthodox alike, raised religious arguments, saying that absolving the Jews contradicted the explicit statements of

---

8   For the politics surrounding the resolution and its meaning, see the sources cited above in note 6, and Michael McGarry, "*Nostra Aetate*: The Church's Bond to the Jewish People: Context, Content, Promise," in Marvin Perry and Frederick Schweitzer (eds.), *Jewish–Christian Encounters Over the Centuries*, New York: 1994.

9   "'Isa" *Encyclopaedia of Islam*, 2nd edn., Leiden, vol. 4, pp. 81–4.

the Christian Scriptures, and that Vatican II had no authority to change such enshrined principles. Occasionally the doctrinal arguments were accompanied by strong anti-Jewish statements. In addition to theological considerations, the Orthodox Churches seized the opportunity to score points against the Catholics by presenting themselves as the true keepers of Christian ideals and to signal to the Muslims their loyalty to the Arab cause.

The public discourse, on the other hand, incorporated into the debate broader accusations against Zionism, including a whole array of references to the Holocaust, accompanied by anti-Jewish themes borrowed from European anti-Semitism.[10]

The Arab League's Arab Information Center, near the UN headquarters, reiterated in a press communiqué on 1 July 1963 the same points regarding the Holocaust and Zionism that were raised during the 1945–48 period. It rejected the claim that Arab opposition to the Vatican's deliberations was due to anti-Semitism, insisting that the Arabs were only anti-Zionist. As proof, it cited the 1944 Alexandria Protocol that served as the foundation of the Arab League, which "unequivocally" denounced anti-Semitism and stated that the founding committee "declares that it is second to none in regretting the woes which have been inflicted upon the Jews of Europe by European dictatorial states," during the war.[11] However, in a statement to Arab constituencies discussing Arab diplomatic efforts vis-à-vis the Vatican in April 1964, the League came much closer to Holocaust denial. The resolution maintained that approving the "exoneration document" would pave the way for the Vatican's recognition of Israel "even though Israel's crimes against the Arabs were crueler than Nazi crimes against the Jews."[12] Since the League always accused Israel of dispossessing or expelling the Palestinians, but not of exterminating them, the implication for the meaning of the Holocaust was fairly clear.

Denial of any link between the Church's doctrinal attitude toward the Jews and Nazi anti-Semitism was raised mainly, but not solely, by Arab Christians, who for obvious reasons felt the need to absolve the Church of any wrongdoing. Occasionally, this view contained implicit Holocaust denial or justifica-

---

10   The broader issue of Arab theological and public reactions to Vatican II has not been thoroughly studied. For some short references, see Gilbert, *The Vatican*, pp. 61–3, 85–7, 100–3.

11   Arab Information Office, New York, 1 July 1963 in HZ/7/3544. While denying anti-Semitism, the Egyptian embassy in Rome, according to the Italian police, donated $3,000 to the Fascist organization Ordine Nuovo to publish an anti-Semitic tract called *Plot Against the Church* that was distributed to the Council's participants. HZ/10/217, Rome, Fisher to Levavi, 10 December 1962; Cartus, "Vatican II," p. 21.

12   *Al-Hayat*, 1 April 1964.

tion of anti-Semitism, including that of the Nazis. Bishop Najib Quba'in, head
of the Arab section of the Anglican Church in Jordan, Syria and Lebanon, who
criticized the exoneration of the Jews on theological grounds, and denied any
link between Christian doctrines and modern (including Nazi) anti-Semitism,
attributed the convening of Vatican II to Jewish plots which, he explained, had
originated in the *Protocols of the Elders of Zion*.[13]

Seeking to allay Arab anger over the Church's new course and prevent an Arab
conflict with the Vatican, the Melchite (Greek Catholic) Patriarch Maximos IV
of Antioch issued a statement on 31 November 1964 which acknowledged the
Holocaust as a historical fact, while describing the Jewish question at large as a
"silk ball in a pile of thorns" which would injure the fingers of those who would
try to deal with it. The Patriarch explained that "personal interest" had guided
the vote of many Council Fathers, particularly the Americans. These were "dictated by a sentiment of pity due to the massacre of Jews by Nazism" and the fact
that most Americans had commercial interests with the Jews. He defended the
Council's denial of Jewish collective guilt for the crucifixion, but maintained
that "a stain of shame" would "certainly remain on the forehead of the Jewish
people as long as it remains far from Christ the Redeemer." Thus the collective
Jewish crime was not the murder of Jesus, but his continuous rejection, and this
stain could be removed only by the conversion of the Jews to Christianity. He
also accused the Jews of always trying "not to differentiate between the heavenly
Jewish religion, which gave the prophets, and criminal Zionism in order to at-
tract world sympathy," adding that through their propaganda skills and their
control over the media, the Jews managed to portray reality in any way they
wanted. Finally, stressing the loyalty of the Christians to their Arab countries,
he warned that "one cannot defeat Israel by becoming an enemy of the Holy
See because everyone knows the strength of the Vatican's power in the balance
of forces of the world."[14]

The Arab media was much more forthright in its reactions to Vatican II,
often fusing anti-Semitic accusations with the anti-Zionist arguments. For obvious reasons the Palestinian press in East Jerusalem (which was then under
Jordanian rule), paid the greatest attention to the affair. The Christian-owned
Lebanese press was equally adamant in rejecting the Council's resolutions, although it advocated a more cautious response, reflecting reluctance to part ways
with the Church, the historical backer of the then dominant Maronite community in Lebanon. The Egyptian press did not cover the affair extensively. Only
a few articles discussed the resolutions in some depth, while most news reports

13   *Al-Jihad*, 5 October, *Filastin*, 2 December 1964.
14   *Al-Safa'*, 1 December 1964.

focused on the reaction of the Egyptian Coptic Churches, with only minor attention being given to the other Middle Eastern Churches. Overall, however, three broad positions can be discerned in the media discourse: implicit or "soft" Holocaust denial; justification of anti-Semitism, including the Nazi type; and Zionist manipulation of the German guilt complex.

The document prompted the Lebanese columnist Salim Nassar to discuss anti-Semitism, which he attributed to "economic, social and beastly causes," and which became a source of profit and internal unity for the Jews. The Poles, he asserted, suffered much more than the Jews during the war, but their "screams did not rise after the war had ended." As for Germany, he contended that "German nature and its unique vision of the Jews" drove the Nazis to commit evil, in addition to Jewish machinations in igniting World War I when they incited the Christian powers against each other.[15] Similarly, the Egyptian author Mahmud Na'na'a attributed the Nazi persecution of the Jews to their siding with the enemies of the Third Reich and their declaration of war on Germany.[16]

The Christian-owned (Greek Orthodox) *Filastin*, which devoted the greatest attention, relative to other Arab newspapers, to Vatican II deliberations, blamed the Jews for arousing animosity against themselves all over the world. It was Zionism that forced the Jews to live in closed and secluded ghettoes, isolating them from the rest of society and making them lose their sense of true citizenship and loyalty to the states they resided in, it maintained. It was clear, *Filastin* concluded, that what was at stake was not Nazism or anti-Semitism, but "genuine feelings of vengeance for Zionist conduct, treachery, lies and deceptions" that stood at the heart of European attitudes toward the Jews throughout history. *Filastin*, wittingly or unwittingly, anachronistically predated political Zionism to the early days of the Jewish Diaspora, and adopted the arguments of traditional European anti-Semites.[17] The Arabs who were displaced from their homeland and persecuted by the Jews deserved greater compassion than the Jews who suffered "persecution," it added elsewhere.[18] The Muslim-owned Jeruselamite *al-Difa'* contended that the US and Britain drove the whole world to war against Hitler, who, they alleged (*za'amata*) persecuted the Jews. Yet both

---

15   *Al-Safa'*, 26 November 1964. See a similar accusation against Zionism for actively fomenting anti-Semitism and of conspiring against Germany in *al-Safa'* editorial on 1 December 1964.

16   Mahmud Na'na'a, *al-Sayhuniyya fi al-sittinat: al-fatikan wal-yahud*, Cairo: 1964, p. 10.

17   *Filastin*, 18 July 1962.

18   *Filastin*, 24 November 1964. *Filastin* used the term "persecution" to denote both Nazi policy toward the Jews and Israeli policy vis-à-vis the Arabs, but always inserting quotation marks when referring to the former, insinuating its questionable credibility. See a somewhat similar argument in *al-Manar*, 13 November 1963.

called Hitler the "Number One Enemy of Christ" in the modern age. Hence, the crucifixion was not the reason for the persecution of the Jews, but rather the latter's "opposition to the nations in which they lived, their constant efforts to conspire against them, and their refusal to assimilate."[19]

Several Egyptian and Lebanese writers attributed the deliberations on the Jews to German guilt complex over Germany's "sins" (original quotation marks), even though, as the Egyptian Muhammad al-Tabi'i concluded, Nazi crimes were grossly exaggerated.[20] The Egyptian priest Ibrahim Sa'id pointed to the German urge to "hide the past" as a result of an "inferiority complex" due to Hitler's deeds, by changing the Church's theological position. He also considered "American capital" as a major driving force behind the Council's meetings. He warned the Arabs not to allow such devious policies to destroy the Christian faith. As "one of those Germans who carry the guilt complex toward the Jews," Cardinal Bea mistakenly believed that animosity toward the Jews was religiously motivated, while in fact it was political and economic. Years later, Shaykh Ahmad Kuftaro, the Grand Mufti of Syria, attributed to Bea a non-existent Jewish descent as the reason for his conduct.[21]

The Christian Lebanese *al-Ahrar* charged that the Council's deliberations showed that the exoneration was a purely political move that had nothing to do with the doctrines of Christianity and its natural tendency of forgiveness and tolerance. The cardinals who pushed for the exoneration came from the US, Britain and other countries that were all subject to political and economic Zionist control. Their position reflected the impact of the false Zionist propaganda, which presented the Jews as a persecuted victim, whereas Zionism was the usurper of an Arab land and its dispossessed inhabitants. These cardinals justified their stance by the need to show pity for Jewish suffering and persecutions under the Nazis, who destroyed all of Europe, as if Jewish suffering justified revenge on an Arab people.[22] Reflecting on the constraints and pressures surrounding the Christian Arabs, the British Catholic periodical *The Tablet* reported that Christian Arabs expressed hope that they would not have to pay the price in their countries for the European atonement for the crimes of the Nazis.[23]

---

19   *Al-Difa'*, 30 September 1964. The Arabic verb *za'ama* usually means a false allegation.

20   *Al-Ahram*, 25 September, 2 October 1964; *Akhbar al-Yawm*, 3 October 1964; Salim Nassar in *al-Safa'*, 27 November 1964; *The Tablet*, 20 June 1964, p. 688.

21   *Al-Nahar*, *al-Safa'*, 27 November 1964; *Ruz al-Yusuf*, 2 December 1963; Ahmad 'Abd al-Wahhab, *Isra'il harrafat al-anajil*, Ba'abdin: 1972, p. 31; "Nida' lil-'alamayni al-islami wal-masihi min ajl al-quds," 16 June 1996, www.kuftaro.org/Arabic/Kuftaro_Book/4-2-2.htm.

22   *Al-Ahrar*, 22 November 1964.

23   *The Tablet*, 20 June 1964, pp. 688–9. Overall, the veiled threats to harm Arab Christians and the latter's own fears did not materialize.

Israel and the Zionist movement were accused of being the driving force behind the convocation of Vatican II in order to "manipulate" the Church into adopting a more favorable policy towards Israel, and in order to rob (*ibtizaz*) Europe and the West financially. The Zionist trump card, according to this view, was the "false" accusations against Pope Pius' role during the Holocaust as a means of arousing guilt feelings among Churchmen or of outright extortion. Indeed, Jews did play a role in persuading Pope John XXIII to convene Vatican II. Various Jewish organizations, mainly in the US, lobbied the Council members, particularly the American bishops, to secure a favorable resolution for the Jews.[24] Likewise, the Israeli government sought to influence the Council's outcome, and the Israeli ambassador in Rome, Morris Fisher, held numerous contacts with members of Cardinal Bea's staff. However, it would be a gross exaggeration and total disregard of the internal processes within the Church and Pope John's own personality to claim that Vatican II was convened due to Zionist or Jewish "manipulations." Likewise, while the Israeli government definitely sought recognition by the Vatican, it is evident, from the correspondence of the Israeli ambassador in Rome, that it gave higher priority to securing the "exoneration," in view of its greater historical and moral importance for Jewish–Christian relations.[25]

Mahmud Na'na'a explained Zionist efforts to convene the Council as a way to extricate Israel from the predicaments that beset it in the early 1960s, when the initial euphoria from the establishment of the state was fading. The Zionists had realized that Israel failed to fulfill the hopes of the Jews, that instead of serving as a refuge for them, it was in fact a "farcical entity" threatened by the Arabs, who were getting stronger day by day. In an attempt to improve their international standing, the Zionists had resorted to rewriting the history of Christian–Jewish relations in order to win over the Protestant and Catholic Churches to their side.[26] Adopting the exoneration in order to appease the Jews who had criticized Pope Pius XII for not helping them during the Nazi "persecution," *Filastin* concluded, was tantamount to defending the head of the Catholic Church against false accusations by fabricating history.[27]

Finding the Vatican document somewhat positive from an Arab point of view, Ahmad Baha' al-Din discerned in it three important aspects: the reli-

---

24 *Al-Ahram*, 11 September 1964. See Gilbert's *The Vatican*, which covers the Jewish efforts extensively.

25 See for instance, HZ/10/217, Jerusalem, Levavi to Katz, 19 November 1962; HZ/5/217, Rome, Fisher to Levavi 16 November 1963; HZ/6/217, Rome, Fisher to Pratoo and Levavi, 15 October 1964.

26 Na'na'a, *al-Sahyuniyya*, pp. 3–8.

27 *Filastin*, 24 November 1964.

gious, the racial anti-Semitic and the political. Had the document carried only religious meaning, the Muslim Arabs would not have been concerned with it, as Islam denied that the crime of crucifixion was ever committed. The racial aspect reflected the significant difference between European and Middle Eastern cultures and histories, as racial persecutions and wars were a recurrent phenomenon in Europe, and what Hitler did to the Jews was not the first such thing under the shadow of European culture. By contrast, racism and anti-Semitism had never existed in the Arab world, even when the Arabs had become the victims of "fanatical Jewish Zionist aggression." Pursuing a common theme in the Arab Holocaust discourse, he concluded that the "tolerant Arabs have paid the price of centuries of racist European fanaticism culminating in Hitler's activities." These persecutions had two historical solutions: Zionism, which sought to gather the Jews in a state of their own, or assimilation. The Arab interest was to encourage assimilation and to fight anti-Semitism so that Jews would not come to Israel.

However, moving to the political aspect, Baha' al-Din spoke of the "weapons of guilt complex and plundering" which the Zionists employed. The "Hitlerite regime" had exterminated more atheist Soviets, Catholic Poles and Orthodox Balkan [people] than Jews, he said. Yet, all of these historical accounts of massacres were closed and sealed, except for the Jewish account that remained open, because the Jews were the only ones who had continuously exploited and transformed this historical account into a guilt complex that required atonement through reparations. Although Baha' al-Din is correct regarding the higher number of Soviet casualties, by blurring the distinction between Nazi genocidal policy against the Jews, which targeted an entire people, and the vicious terror exercised against non-Jewish civilians under their rule, he engaged in an implicit denial of the Holocaust as a premeditated genocide. Baha' al-Din described the Vatican affair as another expression of the Zionist plunder and exploitation, particularly the accusations against Pope Pius XII's silence during the Holocaust. Israel, he added, employed vis-à-vis the Vatican the same "type of terrorism" it had used against Germany, that is, the threat to any politician or official to expose his past connections in order to destroy his future, as part of its effort to associate the issue of "liberation" from Nazism with Zionism and Israel. In conclusion, Baha' al-Din called for the separation of the religious issue, which was of no concern to the Arabs, from the racial and political aspects. Tolerance and the struggle against racism were Arab principles, he claimed, while Israel was the product of a racist movement, which in itself was born out of European, not Arab, persecutions. Hence, Arabs should always be ready to expose Israel's actions to exploit religion, but refuse to pay the price for the outcome of European racism.[28]

Taking a more vehement view of the Jewish or Zionist "machinations," Anis Mansur, who was a senior leftist journalist at the time, and later became a confidant of President Anwar al-Sadat, published a series of articles from Rome in which he described the Vatican Council as the "final and decisive phase" of a Jewish campaign that had started shortly after World War II to "settle scores" with the entire Christian world. The Jews used their money and expertise to "indict" Germany first and then all other countries that had helped Germany to exterminate millions of Jews. The Jews had decided that revenge would be carried out by others, rather than by themselves. They tried the Germans through the Americans, British and French,[29] and had abducted, tortured and executed Nazi officials. Concurrently, they influenced philosophers and writers to write favorably about them and to remove anyone who dared stand up to them. Dozens of stories and books had come out, he said, all describing the Germans as criminals, the Nazis as brutish and the Jews as an oppressed people who deserved pity and sympathy. They had also produced dozens of movies and plays telling imaginary heroic stories of children who were tortured in Nazi camps, the most famous of which was Anne Frank's diary.

While acknowledging the magnitude of the Holocaust, Mansur attributed the active role of US bishops in promoting the exoneration to Jewish financial pressures or dealings with the Church rather than to the impact of the Holocaust. He expressed his surprise that the US bishops took such a position vis-à-vis the Jews, precisely when a Jew had assassinated President Kennedy (see below). Mansur criticized the Jewish demand to absolve all the Jews throughout all ages of the guilt of deicide while they insisted on denouncing all Germans as guilty for Hitler's killing of millions of Jews. Why didn't they absolve the Germans from Jewish blood, he asked, particularly when not all of them were Hitlers or Nazis. While ignoring the differences between German complicity with the Nazi regime and the alleged Jewish collective role in the crucifixion, he also disregarded the historical ramifications for the two peoples involved in the two events.[30]

The 1964 *Year Book of the Palestinian Problem*, issued by the newly established PLO, reviewed the whole affair in a rather mild tone. It explained that the fall of the Axis powers and the Nazi war-crime trials which revealed the "Nazi

28   *Al-Musawwar*, 11 December 1964.
29   Mansur failed to mention the Soviets, who were part of the Nuremberg Court, presumably because they were Egypt's allies at the time.
30   *Al-Musawwar*, 6 December 1963; *al-Akhbar*, 1 October, 9, 24 November 1964

atrocities" against the Jews, together with a sense of guilt among Catholics for the "sin" of the Church's "silence" over the fate of the Jews during the war and over "anti-Semitic" persecutions in Christian countries, had created feelings of compassion toward the Jews. Moreover, it claimed, the Eichmann "trial" as well as the war-crime trials held in Munich and Frankfurt during 1964 had generated a "guilt complex" within the Vatican. The Zionist movement had reaped political and financial fruits with the establishment of Israel and in getting reparations, and now it sought to foster a similar "guilt complex" among the Catholics by associating anti-Semitism with the Church's teachings. The mild tone notwithstanding, the writer's frequent use of quotation marks around numerous terms regarding the Holocaust could appear to the readers as casting doubt on their veracity or creating the impression of a sinister manipulation behind the entire affair.[31]

Some writers pointed to the opening in Berlin on 20 February 1963 of the play *The Deputy* (*Der Stellvertreter*), written by the [Protestant] German playwright Rolf Hochhuth, which strongly criticized the conduct of Pope Pius XII during the Holocaust, to prove the alleged Jewish–Zionist conspiracy against the Church.[32] Muhammad Haqqi of *al-Ahram* conceded that the play had emerged as a result of internal German predicaments, particularly historical Protestant–Catholic splits and the divisions among liberals and conservatives within each Church. But he also described the play as part of an ongoing "witch hunt," reminiscent of the Spanish Inquisition, against various German officials who were accused of having a Nazi past. Therefore, he focused his criticism on the Zionists who, he said, were using the play to pressure and "terrorize" the Catholic Church and Germany in order to bring about the exoneration of the Jews from the guilt of the crucifixion and to extort greater financial compensations from Germany. The Zionists supposedly provided great support and publicity to the play, in accordance with their continuous policy of introducing new stories on Jewish suffering, such as the Eichmann trial and the Anne Frank diary, aiming at keeping alive the memory of World War II and Jewish suffering, as both served to legitimize Israel's existence.[33]

31 Mu'assasat al-dirasat al-filastiniyya, *al-Kitab al-sanawi lil-qadiyya al-filastiniyya, 1964*, Beirut: 1966, pp. 167–72. See similar assertions of Zionist manipulations in *al-Mawsu'a al-filastiniyya*, vol. 3, "al-Fatican," pp. 417–21; Markaz filastin lil-dirasat wal-bahth, *al-Fatikan wal-sira' al-'arabi al-sahyuni*, Gaza: 2000, p. 34.

32 *Al-Hayat*, 21 November 1964; *al-Musawwar*, 11 December 1964; Hamid Mahmud, *al-Di'aya al-Sahyuniyya: wasa'iluha wa-asalibuha wa-turuq mukafahatiha*, Cairo: 1966, p. 65.

33 *Al-Ahram*, 21 March 1964.

According to Na'na'a, the Zionists used their control over the world media in order to instigate public interest in the play, while Basil Daqqaq of *al-Hayat* commented that whenever the uproar around the play subsided, "Zionism took care to reignite it." Typically, he added, the Zionists preferred others [i.e. Hochhuth] to speak for them in expressing their hatred of the world. Alluding to the criticism of Pope Pius XII, he accused them of injuring world figures who did not cave in to their conspiracies, while refusing to allow anyone to put them in their proper place or to respond to their abusive propaganda.[34] Anis Mansur went further and linked the play with the murder of President John Kennedy, as two prongs of the Zionist campaign designed to force the Church to grant Israel official recognition.[35]

In an official PLO publication Anis al-Qasim denied that the Arabs or Palestinians opposed the Church's condemnation of religious or racist persecutions, but asked why those statements were confined to the Jews, whereas the Palestinians were the oppressed people who deserved the Vatican's support. Fusing together several themes of the Arab Holocaust discourse, such as implicit denial, equation of Zionism with Nazism and blaming the Jews for their past predicament, al-Qasim rejected the rationale behind Vatican II, i.e., the notion that anti-Semitism had contributed to or facilitated the Holocaust, by insisting that the Zionist "acts of murder and mass killings" in Palestine were as brutal as those of the Nazis against the Jews. Furthermore, he claimed, Zionist organizations and leaders had taken "a significant role in the acts of persecutions, torture and killings against the Jews [during the Holocaust] as demonstrated in trials held inside Israel itself."[36]

Turning to alleged Zionist conspiracies against the Church, Qasim maintained that, prior to the Council, the Zionists had operated on several complementing levels: by putting *The Deputy* on European stages, they did not intend to generate a sincere historical debate on Pope Pius XII's role, but to

---

34 Na'na'a, *al-Sahyuniyya*, pp. 52–4. In contrast to the Arab allegations, the Israeli Foreign Ministry exerted heavy pressure on the Israeli national theater, Habima, not to show the play, fearing it would alienate Pope Paul VI, who had been Pope Pius' secretary during the war. See HZ/5/217, Fisher to Levavi, 13 November 1963; *Ha'aretz*, 29 March 1963.

35 *Al-Musawwar*, 6 December 1963. Various Arab newspapers described Kennedy's assassination as a Zionist plot in view of Jack Ruby, Lee Harvey Oswald's assassin's Jewish origins. See *al-Jumhuriyya*, 28 November, *al-Akhbar*, 29 November, 12 December 1963; *Filastin*, 13, 19 February 1964. See the same argument raised 36 years later in 'Abd al-'Aziz Kamil, "Ziyarat baba al-fatikan: khutuwat jadida 'ala tariq al-ikhtiraq," www.islamweb.net/aqeda/big_religen/crist/13.htm.

36 Anis al-Qasim, *Nahnu wal-fatikan wa-isra'il*, Beirut: 1966, pp. 8–10. He probably refers to the trials held against several Holocaust survivors during the early 1950s, who were accused of serving as Kapos in Nazi camps.

denounce him and issue a warning to all Church officials as to the measures that would await them should they oppose the Zionist scheme. The Zionists had set out to distort the Christian Scriptures in order to rewrite the role of the Jews in the crucifixion and the persecutions of the early Christians. The crucial point, he concluded, was not whether the Pope had made mistakes, but the Zionist effort to persecute any Catholic, regardless of his rank, if his policies displeased them.[37]

Ilya Abu al-Rus, who emphasized "Jewish insolence" and "vile attack" on Pope Pius, conceded that Hochhuth was not Jewish, but described him as a close disciple of the famous "leftist radical Jewish" playwright Bertold Brecht. Moreover, the producers of the play in the world stages were all Jewish and "the entire theatre industry in Europe and the US stood on Jewish financing."[38] By contrast, the Greek Orthodox priest Ikram al-Lamaʿi found some fault in the failure of [the Catholic] Pope to condemn the extermination of the Jews, even though he knew it was against religion and humanity. But, while acknowledging that the Church's animosity toward the Jews had reached its peack during World War II, Lamaʿi laid greater responsibility on the Jews themselves, whose conduct throughout history and manipulation of Christianity were the major reason for their miserable fate.[39]

Retrospective references to Vatican II from the 1990s onward reflect the increasing Arab awareness of the importance of the Holocaust in Western cultural discourse, demonstrating the evolution of the Arab Holocaust discourse as a mirror image of the Western one. As on previous occasions, a large spectrum of terms, attitudes and representations of the Holocaust within implicit boundaries emerged which contributed to the evolving but fairly consistent discourse. Most common among them was denial of the magnitude of the Holocaust as genocide. Various Arab writers mentioned Nazi measures against the Jews, but usually referred to them as "persecutions," while using the same terms to describe Israeli policies against the Arabs or asserting that there was much exaggeration in the descriptions of the Nazi acts. Occasionally, they qualified these measures to the Jews of Germany, ignoring the scope of Nazi policies against the Jews throughout Europe. In addition to implicit justification of anti-Semitism as a logical response to Jewish conduct, there were a few allegations of Zionist collaboration with the Nazis in killing the Jews.

---

37   Ibid, p. 29.

38   Ilya Abu al-Rus, *al-Yahudiyya al-ʿalamiyya wa-harbuha ʿala al-masihiyya*, Beirut: 1993, pp. 19–22. Brecht was a communist, but not Jewish.

39   Ikram al-Lamaʿi, *al-Ikhtiraq al-sahyuni lil-masihiyya*, Beirut: 1991, pp. 10, 12, 65, 83–7.

"We remember: reflections on the Shoah"

The question of the Church's attitude toward Judaism and the Holocaust re-emerged in the late 1990s in view of the advancing rapprochement between the Church and the Jewish people and Israel. The two cornerstones of this rapprochement were the 16 March 1998 declaration of Pope John Paul II, "We remember: reflections on the Shoah," and the subsequent document, "Memory and reconciliation: the Church and the faults of the past," of 12 March 2000, which acknowledged the uniqueness of the Jewish tragedy and addressed the role of the Papacy and the Church during the Holocaust. As in the early 1960s, they elicited a broad range of Arab responses, reflecting most of the themes prevalent in the Arab Holocaust discourse. Many of these resurfaced after the Pope's death on 2 April 2005.

Most Arab writers viewed the "We remember" document as the culmination of the Church's conciliatory measures towards the Jews, which had started with Vatican II. However, unlike the 1960s debate, the Holocaust assumed a more direct place in Arab reactions, even though they continued to revolve mainly around the document's political implications for the Arab–Israeli conflict and the broader historical context of Muslim–Christian relations. The change was not only due to the fact that the Pope addressed the Holocaust explicitly, but also because the Arab Holocaust discourse had changed (see also Chapter 11). For many Arab writers the document was yet another gain for the Jews and Zionists, demonstrating the extent of Jewish–Zionist influence in the West, the weakening of the Eastern Church and its Arab representatives in the Vatican and, even worse, the unequal western treatment of Jews and Arabs. Consequently, they reflected Arab frustrations over the broader historical East–West encounter and the perceived western mistreatment of the Arab and Muslim worlds.

While the West Bank [Palestinian] press under Jordanian rule reacted vociferously to Vatican II, the semi-official press under the Palestine National Authority (PNA) kept almost complete silence over the 1998 document. Only the privately-owned *al-Quds* published a short informative item on 16 March. In the early 1960s the Jerusalem press was in opposition to the Jordanian government, which was anxious to preserve cordial relations with the Vatican. Conversely, in 1998 it complied with an apparently conscious PNA decision to avoid any public disagreement with the Vatican. The Jordanian press, by contrast, was much more vocal, as many journalists there are of Palestinian descent.

A widespread initial response expressed surprise, if not indignation, at the Pope's decision to apologize to the Jews, attributing it to the ongoing Zionist onslaught on Europe to disseminate the myth of the Holocaust and to ter-

rorize anyone who dared challenge its veracity. According to the Syrian Han-
nan Hamad, the Israeli demand for apology over past oppressions perpetrated
against the Jews was nothing but an opening for further financial plundering of
Europe under the guise of compensations. Particular anger was expressed at the
Church's "caving in" to "unwarranted" Zionist accusations against Pope Pius
XII. Proponents of this theme expressed greater anger at the Jewish "exploitation" of the Concordat, which he (then Cardinal Pacelli) had signed with Nazi
Germany in 1934, than at the agreement itself, which they viewed as a perfectly
reasonable act serving the Church's interest.[40]

Reactions amounting to outright denial were particularly strong in Lebanon,
where a delicate balance in Christian–Muslim relations has been barely maintained. Shaykh Muhammad Mahdi Shams al-Din, President of the Supreme
Shi'i Council in Lebanon, maintained that the Church had no reason to apologize because the Holocaust was "a myth fabricated by the Jews and Zionists."[41]
In a somewhat similar vein, Shaykh Muhammad Husayn Fadlallah, considered
the spiritual leader of Hizballah and Shams al-Din's political rival, maintained
that the Jews were not Hitler's only victims but that they succeeded in focusing
the spotlight on themselves and they continue to arouse the world's conscience
in order to extract political and cultural concessions.[42] Lebanese foreign minister
at the time, the Maronite Faris Buwayz, who considered the document detrimental to Arab and especially Lebanese interests, deplored Israel's exploitation
of the Holocaust during his visit to the Vatican at the beginning of April 1998.
He wondered why the Pope had apologized for the deeds of Nazism, which had
victimized even more Christians than Jews. Buwayz explained that "Hitler acted
for political reasons against the Jews because they conspired against the state and
created a state within a state." Hitler's reaction was thus similar to the behavior
of the Spanish Queen Isabella in the fifteenth century and Czar Nikolai II in the
nineteenth century, he insisted, thereby justifying Hitler's actions as a legitimate
act of self-defense and reducing them to mere persecutions or, at the most, mass
expulsion of the Jews.[43] The document regarded the story of the Nazi mass murder of Jews as a universally accepted fact, the Jordanian columnist Kamal Rashid

40   *Tishrin*, 16 March 2000; *al-Sha'b*, 7 April 2000; Anon, "al-Kanisa al-kathulikiyya bayna
     al-mumana'a wal-ikhtiraq al-sahyuni," www.balagh.com/islam/4q0vkqaa.htm; Nafidh
     Abu Hasana, "al-fatikan wal-quds," www.Palestine-info.info; Shirbil Bu'ayni, "al-Fatikan
     wal-i'tidhar min al-yahud," www.elaph.com/ElaphWriter/2005/1/36397.htm; *al-Mujta-
     ma'*, 30 April 2005.

41   Agence France Press (AFP), 22 March 1998.

42   *Al-'Ahd*, 20 March 1998.

43   AFP, 2 April, *Ha'aretz*, 3 April, *al-Nahar*, *Akhbar al-Khalij*, *al-Safir*, 6 April 1998.

complained, even though quite a few scholars, such as Roger Garaudy (see Chapter 11), had refuted it.[44]

Unlike the Arab Church leaders of the early 1960s, who had vehemently opposed any Jewish–Christian rapprochement, the Latin Patriarch of Jerusalem, Monsignor Michel Sabah, adopted a much more conciliatory position, which in addition to his own personal traits probably reflected a broader impact of the changing Catholic position vis-à-vis the Jews, and also his delicate position as a Patriarch under Israeli rule. In a meeting with the Israeli Chief Rabbis on 23 March 1998, which dealt with a host of Jewish–Christian issues, he explained that the Church could not be accused of the Holocaust, because it did not commit it. In his public statement following the meeting, Sabah referred to the Pope's document indirectly, saying that "relations between the Catholic Church and the Jewish people stem from a past history of persecution of the Jewish people on the part of Christians, not only the Catholic Church but all the Christians in the West."[45]

In similar vein, various writers denied any link between Christian doctrines and Nazi actions. Why, they asked, did the Church apologize for crimes for which it was not responsible, thereby implicating the entire Christian world? However, unlike in the early 1960s, Muslim writers too came to the defense of Christian doctrines. The Greek Orthodox and leftist journalist Jurji Haddad castigated Cardinal Cassidy, who conceded that anti-Jewish Christian doctrines had created an atmosphere of apathy and hostility towards the Jews that facilitated the Holocaust. Such statements, Haddad charged, present the Jews as angels while blaming Christ and his religion as the cause of their persecution and dispersal.[46] Why should the Christians apologize for Hitler's crimes that derived from Nazi ideology, and not from Christian doctrines, and aimed at humanity as a whole, not just at Jews, he asked?[47] Going along the same line, various writers reiterated the distinction between European guilt and the absence of any Arab link to the Holocaust. Kamal Rashid complained that while apologies usually come from the criminals, the Pope's document came out as if the Church had sinned and took the blame for the Holocaust upon itself and the entire Christian world. Even if these crimes were true, what have the Chris-

---

44   *Al-Dustur*, 30 March 1998. See a similar theme in Anon, "Shakhsiyyat sana'at al-ta'rikh: al-baba yuhana Bulus al-thani," www.alshamsi.net/man/mel/yohana_bolls.html.

45   *Jordan Times*, 24 March, *Jerusalem Times*, 27 March 1998. The Arabic language Palestinian newspapers that covered the meeting omitted the reference to the Christian persecution of the Jews and only mentioned his criticism of Israeli policies vis-à-vis the Palestinians. *Al-Ayyam*, 24 March 1998.

46   *Al-Dustur*, 21 March 1998.

47   *Al-Ra'y*, 20 March 1998.

tians all over the world, and particularly the Eastern and Palestinian Christians, sinned that they have to apologize to the Jews? It was inconceivable that Arab Christians should apologize to the Jews for past sins, while they saw their land taken from them on a daily basis, wrote another.[48] Whereas Hitler did not represent all Christians in Europe, added Shaykh Fadlallah, Israel's crimes reflected its Jewish nature, which typified world Jewry as a whole.[49]

Quite a few writers, particularly Islamists, failed to understand why the Church showed such benevolence towards the Jews, while the latter persisted in their arrogance and defiance vis-à-vis Christianity. According to the Lebanese Shirbil Bu'ayni, writing on the otherwise liberal website Elaph, the Pope's apology amounted to a second crucifixion of Christ, since the Jews had committed crimes against the Church. If the Pope's apology eased the pain of the Holocaust, the Jews too should apologize for their persecution of the early Christians. What Hitler had done to the Jews was an unforgivable crime, but Israeli policies, such as the Qana massacre, were unforgivable too, he concluded,[50] thereby equating the accidental and tragic killing of 105 civilians in battle to the Holocaust.

Much more pervasive was the rhetorical question why the Church confined its apology to anti-Semitism and the Holocaust and did not address other crimes and cases of injustice perpetrated by Christians and the West, such as the millions of Vietnamese killed by the Americans, or the Koreans and Iraqis killed by western countries, not to mention the Algerians killed by France. Why didn't he apologize for the victims of Hiroshima and Nagasaki, "who perished in a Holocaust, which humanity had never experienced before"? Was it because the victims were not "God's chosen people and their price" was not bargained under "Zionist influence and Jewish plundering," Sulayman al-Azra'i wondered.[51]

Reflecting greater bitterness was the charge against the Church's apology to the Jews, while it failed to do the same to the Muslims for past injustices which Christianity had committed ever since the eleventh-century Crusades. This point, part of the "politics of victimhood" or the "competition over victimhood" between Jews and Muslims, assumed ever-growing weight, particularly for Islamists, up to the Pope's death in 2005. The Islamists saw the document in the broader context of Christian–Muslim rivalries throughout history, reflecting the deep sense of humiliation, frustration and anger felt by Muslims in the modern age over their painful encounter with the West.[52] In Germany people only talked

48   *Al-Dustur*, 30 March, *al-Hayat*, 27 July 1998. See also *al-Ra'y*, 26 March 1998.

49   *Al-'Ahd*, 20 March 1998.

50   Bu'ayni, "al-Fatikan." See also *al-'Ahd*, 20 March 1998.

51   *Al-Ra'y*, 20 March 1998. See also *al-Dustur*, 30 March 1998; *al-Ahram*, 22 March 2000.

52   See the debate in al-Jazeera network "I'tidhar al-fatikan 'an al-hurub al-salibiyya," held

about the compensation of millions of dollars to the Jews, Shaykh 'Ikrama Sabri, Mufti of the PNA complained, whereas many more Muslims were killed during the Crusades than Jews under Nazism. But nobody talks about the Crusades or compensation for Muslims.[53] According to the Egyptian Ibrahim al-Qaʻud, Europe employed double standards towards the Jews and Arabs. The Pope exonerated present-day Jews from the crimes of their ancestors against Christ and the Church, while he did not apologize for the massacres and atrocities which the Crusaders had perpetrated in the Arab East under the guise of the Cross.[54] Another Islamist writer, Yahya Abu Zakaria, expressed his anger that the "Zionist entity" had succeeded in getting an official apology from the Vatican although they knew that the Western Churches had killed a million Muslims in Spain, expelled another million and forced a third million to convert to Christianity. The Canadian Islamic Congress sent a formal letter to the Vatican asking for recognition of errors committed by the Church against Muslims, alleging that four million Muslims had been victims of genocide during the Crusades (1095–1272) and the Spanish Reconquista and Inquisition (912–1834).[55] Dr. Zaynab 'Abd

---

on 25 January 1999, www.aljazeera.net/channel/archive/archive?ArchiveId=89739; the open discussion in the Islamic website Islamonline.net, "I'tidharat al-fatikan wa-mawqifihi min al-quds mawduʻ al-hiwar," www.islam-online.net/livedialogue/arabic/Browse. asp?hGuestID=y680k4, 14 March 2000; 'Abdallah al-'Aliyan, "al-Fatikan bayna al-i'tidhar lil-yahud wa-'adam al-i'tidhar lil-'arab wal-muslimin: dirasa fi al-khalfiyat al-thaqafiyya al-idi'ulujiyya," www.islamicfeqh.com/almenhaj/Almen26/min26001.htm; Ridwan al-Sayyid in *al-Hayat*, 3 July 2004; *al-Sharq al-Awsat*, 12 April 2005; Abu Islam Ahmad 'Abdallah, "Baʻd rahil Jan Paul al-thani," http://albayan-magazine.com/bayan-212/bayan-21. htm. In a debate following the election of Pope Benedict XVI, held on 29 April 2005, the two Muslim participants, Dr. 'Azzam Tamimi and the political scientist Hashim Salih, rejected the argument raised by the Christian participant Dr. Shafiq Abu Zayd, that Islam and Muslims were not passive victims of Christian aggression but powerful rivals that conquered Christian territories. They claimed that, unlike the West, the Muslims fought for the sake of religion in order to spread God's divine message and justice, and by their conquests they brought the light of civilization to the conquered territories – arguments that were almost identical to the nineteenth-century European justification of imperialism under the guise of *mission civilisatrice*. Anon, "al-Baba al-jadid wa-mustaqbal al-infitah wal-hiwar," www.aljazeera.net/NR/exeres/29633E6E-2196-4CF0-9DB2-DA4D-C000B8B7.

53 *La Republica*, 24 March 2000 – Palestinian Media Watch (PMW) Special Dispatch, no. 82, 29 March 2000.

54 *Akhir Saʻa*, 3 November 2004; *al-Hayat*, 3 July 2004.

55 "The Canadian Islamic Congress Bulletin," 9 October 1999, http://msanews.mynet.net (this website no longer exists, but the authors have a printout of the document). While the Crusaders massacred the Muslim and Jewish inhabitants of Jerusalem upon conquering the city in 1099, the number of Muslim casualties in the Crusades which the Islamists cite seems to be inflated; see Joshua Prawer, *The Crusaders' Kingdom: European Colonialism in the Middle Ages*, London: 2001.

al-'Aziz concluded that the Pope's apology was not religious at all, but was more a mockery of the Arab regimes and a political ploy aimed at Islam.[56]

Although the publication of the "Memory and reconciliation" document in March 2000 addressed the Church's misdeeds towards Muslims, Arab commentators criticized it as "a selective apology," expressing dismay at the Pope's failure to properly mention the Arabs or Muslims.[57] The moderate Islamist writer Fahmi Huwaydi argued that the Pope "gave precedence to the Jews over all others, as 'first class' victims." The document was "shameful" on two counts, for "not only failing to condemn and apologize for what had been done, but also in denying responsibility for it." Hizballah's organ, al-'Ahd, was also concerned by the imbalance in the Pope's attitude and contended that he spoke in two languages, one for the Jews and the other for the Arabs.[58]

Pursuing a similar line, Egyptian journalist Muhammad 'Abd al-Mun'im argued that, whereas western states had closed their borders to the Jews who had fled the Nazis, the Arabs had welcomed them "with open arms." Yet, the Jewish victims had responded to this generosity by insisting on having a state of their own in Palestine, which had led to the dispossession of the Arabs and the occupation of their lands. When would the world acknowledge Arab tolerance and generosity, and when would it apologize for the wrong-doing it had committed against the Arabs, he wondered.[59] 'Afif Safieh, the PLO representative to the Holy See, commended the Pope for initiating "a thorough soul-searching exercise," but asked him to use his moral authority to invite the Israelis and Jews to "make their own self-examination," thereby implying a moral equivalence between the Jewish and Palestinian tragedies. Other Palestinian writers wished that the Pope's apology would prompt Israel to admit the injustices it had inflicted on the Palestinians and issue a historical apology to pave the way for peace and reconciliation (see also chapter 10).[60]

---

56   Cited in 'Aliyan, "al-Fatikan."

57   *Al-Ahram Weekly*, 16 March 2000.

58   *Al-Ahram*, 22 March, *al-'Ahd*, 24 March 2000.

59   *Al-Ahram*, 22 March 1998. See also, *al-Dustur*, 30 March 1998. 'Abd al-Mun'im ignores the adamant opposition of the Palestinians to Jewish immigration during the 1930s, which led to its restriction by the British. Semi-independent Egypt and Iraq, as well as French-controlled Syria and Lebanon, did not take in any significant number of Jewish refugees during the 1930s. See a similar claim by D. Yuhana in "Hiwarat hayya: i'tidharat al-fatikan wa-mawqifihi min al-quds," islamonline.net, 14 March 2000.

60   *Jerusalem Times*, 27 March 2000. See also, *al-Ahram*, 23 February, *al-Hayat*, 18, 19 March, 8 April, *al-Hayat al-Jadida*, 20, 22, 23 March, *Ha'aretz*, 21 March, *al-Sha'b*, 21 March, 14 April, *al-Ahali*, 29 March, *al-Ahram Weekly*, 30 March, *al-Sabil*, 11 April, *al-Liwa'*, 27 September 2000.

Since most Arab writers found it difficult or refused to acknowledge the enormity of the Holocaust as a historical event and could not understand its significance in western cultural discourse, they could not envisage the Pope's initiative as a genuine one reflecting his own personality and the internal changes which the Church had experienced since 1945. Some of them resorted to conspiracy theories which described the *Nostra Aetate* as the beginning of the Church's "collapse" vis-à-vis the Zionists and the 1998 document as yet another gain for Jewish and Zionist influence and machinations. These views, which were raised shortly after Vatican II, mostly by Christians, acquired greater weight in subsequent years in Islamist circles.[61]

The most common conspiracy theory attributed the document to a long-term and meticulous Jewish–Zionist effort to infiltrate (*ikhtiraq*) the Church, take it over from within and Judaize (*tahwid*) it, thereby leading to the abandonment and distortion of the Church's sacred, centuries-old doctrines. Among other proofs, these writers often cited the *Protocols of the Elders of Zion*.[62] Some writers claimed that Pope Paul VI was descended from a Jewish family, while others alleged that he was a converted Jew who had joined the Church in order to advance Jewish goals.[63] Various writers focused their attention on Pope John Paul II, whom they presented as one of the most vocal and influential of the bishops who had promoted the "exoneration of the Jews" during Vatican II (while he was actually a young bishop). Others attributed his conduct to his close ties with the CIA. Summing up Pope John Paul's tenure after his death, the Hamas organ *al-Risala* concluded that the document "We remember" was his "greatest crime" (*a'zam jarima*), setting the seal on his life "in the service of Zionism."[64]

---

61   For the interim period see, Lama'i, *al-Ikhtiraq*; Abu al-Rus, *al-Yahudiyya*, p. 7; Suhayl al-Thaghlabi, *al-Sahyuniyya tuharrifu al-injil*, Damascus: 1999; Michel Munir, *Kanis fi al-kanisa: al-'alaqat al-masihiyya al-yahudiyya*, Damascus: 2001; Anon, "Qissat al-ikhtiraq al-yahudi lil-fatikan," www.khayma.com/hedaya/news/fat-his.html; Kamil, "Ziyarat"; Suhayl Kasha, "Al-turath al-babili al-dini: sirqatuhu wa-tashwishuhu," www.ssnp.info/thenews/daily/Kasha.htm.

62   *Al-Dustur*, 30 March 1998; "Tahwid al-nasraniyya: qissat al-ikhtiraq al-yahudi lil-fatikan," www.alsaha.com/sahat/Forum1/HTML/003888.html; Kasha, "al-Turath al-babili al-di-ni"; Shaykh Dr. 'Abdallah Hallaq, "Nahwa jabha masihiyya-islamiyya li-muwajahat al-sahyuniyya," www.alwahdaalislamyia.net/13th/jabha.htm; Anon, "al-Kanisa"; al-Watan, 16 April 2005; "Ya shaykh al-azhar al-istiqala akram bika," www.marsad.org.uk/arabic; Kamil, "Ziyarat"; "Qissat al-ikhtiraq," ibid.; 'Abdallah, "Ba'd rahil."

63   'Abdallah, "Ba'd rahil"; Dr. Mahmud 'Abd al-Rahman Qadah, "Mujaz ta'rikh al-yahud wal-radd 'ala ba'd maza'imihim al-batila," www.iu.edu.sa/Magazine/107/5.htm; Dr. Riyad ibn Muhammad al-Musaymiri, "al-Baba fi qubdat al-malik," http://saaid.net/Doat/almosimiry/15.htm.

64   *Al-Risala*, 7 April 2004. Commenting earlier on the political rapprochement between the Vatican and Israel, the other Hamas organ, *Filastin al-Muslima*, of January 1998 men-

Other criticisms were directed against the Jews, who were never satisfied with the concessions that the Christians and the Church had made and demanded a formal apology.[65] The Jews had blamed the whole world, not just the Germans, for Hitler's crimes against many peoples, even though they had been the only ones to exact a price for these crimes. They compelled other peoples to apologize to them, while they refused to forgive the Germans for a crime that only some of them had committed in the past. Although they were guilty of the killing of Christ, they denied any link between present-day Jews and the crime of the past. Yet, they insisted on continuity with the past in other issues, such as making false claims on Palestine.[66]

Few voices dissented from the overall consensus. *Al-Hayat* columnist 'Abd al-Wahhab Badrakhan accepted the reasoning behind the Church's apology to the Jews, but argued that "apologizing to Israel is something totally different." The Christian Palestinian-Jordanian journalist Rami Khouri went even further, considering the document "constructive and timely," not only for contributing an "appropriate theological perspective on the ugly political events of the recent past," but for providing "constructive moral and political guidelines" as a standard of behavior and universal morality for all human beings.[67] As on other occasions, Khoury's response was part of his broader approach to the Holocaust and to the settlement of the Arab–Israeli conflict. Overall then, the past and even antiquity could not be separated from contemporary political considerations.

Conclusions

Arab reactions to the change in Catholic attitudes toward Judaism demonstrated once again that the Arab Holocaust discourse was responsive to the development in the status of the Holocaust in Western cultural discourse. During the Vatican II deliberations, references to the Holocaust were secondary to the broader theological debate and its political ramifications. However, once the Holocaust became the focal point of the Church's apology to the Jews in 1998 and 2000, Arab writers focused more on it, revealing a striking persistence of the Arab Holocaust discourse, despite its evolution, where ideas and themes keep appearing in different contexts and periods.

---

tioned the age-old blood libel on Jewish use of Christian blood for ritual purposes as an example of Jewish treachery towards Christians.

65   *Al-Hayat*, *al-Sha'b*, 17 March, 27 July, *al-Ahram*, 22 March 2000; Yuhana, "Hiwarat hayya."

66   *Al-Hayat*, 7 May, *al-Ahram*, 18 August, *Akhir Sa'a*, 3 November 2004.

67   *Al-Hayat*, 22 March, *Jordan Times*, 21 April, *Ha'aretz*, 23 April 2000.

While it is difficult to find a clear correlation between the various themes of Holocaust denial or other charges and particular ideological or national affiliation, one such correlation does appear. Christian writers were adamant in rejecting any link between Christian theological positions on the Jews and modern anti-Semitism which played a role in facilitating the Holocaust. Islamist writers, on the other hand, felt less compunction in voicing clear anti-Semitic views, but were particularly angry at the Church's focus on the Holocaust while ignoring what they saw as Christian wrong-doings to Muslims throughout history. Both groups, however, articulated similar views on the Holocaust, ranging from outright denial to minimization of its scope or historical significance.

PART II

PROMINENT REPRESENTATION THEMES

5

DENIAL OF THE HOLOCAUST

"The Jewish Holocaust – a historical lie," and the "greatest Zionist lie history had ever known" are but two of the numerous expressions that appeared in the Arab discourse to deny the historical veracity of the Holocaust. Such pronouncements were conveyed in a manner reflecting the passionate involvement and self-conviction of the writers.[1]

Denial of the Holocaust began once the Nazi camps were liberated toward the end of the war and the extent of Nazi crimes became evident. Its early propagators were extreme right-wingers, isolationists and anti-Semites in the US who had opposed America's joining the war and who had viewed Communism as a greater enemy than Nazism. As part of their effort they strove to relativize Nazi crimes and claim that the Allies had committed equal if not worse atrocities. Thus, they alleged that the reports, photographs and films on the Nazi camps were "propaganda" released in order to instill unnecessary vengeance against the German people. In Europe, some Germans and French Fascists also tried to minimize Nazi wrong-doing, insisting that they were not as immense as the Allies had charged. Moreover, some of these first-generation deniers also sought to vindicate the Nazis by justifying their anti-Semitism. While they argued that the Nazi atrocities were exaggerated or falsified, they also contended that whatever had been done to the Jews was justified because the Jews had been Germany's enemies. Within a few years, the effort to minimize the scope and intensity of the Nazi crimes was overtaken by the claim that the death of six million Jews was not only greatly exaggerated but a fabrication.[2]

---

1   See, for instance, Ahmad 'Abd al-Ghafur 'Attar, *al-Yahudiyya wal-sahyuniyya*, Beirut: 1972, p. 157; Rafiq Shakir Natshe, *al-Isti'mar wa-filastin: isra'il mashru' isti'mari*, Amman: 1984, p. 147; *al-Jumhuriyya*, 5 August 1986, 3 January 1988; *al-Bilad*, 1 June 1996; *al-Sabil*, 27 April 1999.

2   For a review of early efforts at denial, see Lipstadt, *Denying the Holocaust*, pp. 41ff; Sarah Rembiszewski, *The Final Lie: Holocaust Denial in Germany: A Second Generation Denier as a Test Case*, Tel Aviv: 1996.

Denial of the Holocaust in the Arab world started independently of its development in the West, primarily in order to counter Zionist arguments. Whereas manifestations of Holocaust denial that appeared prior to the 1948 war were mostly implicit and indirect, they became more forthright from the 1950s on, as the Arab–Israeli conflict intensified. The 1961 Eichmann trial, which ended the relative indifference in Europe and the US towards the Holocaust, also marked a qualitative as well as quantitative landmark in Arab responses. The third phase in the evolution of this discourse was the adoption from the late 1970s onward of the arguments articulated by western "professional" Holocaust deniers. It may be possible to speak of a fourth phase toward the end of the twentieth century, with the appearance of books fully dedicated to denial or to the personal exoneration of Hitler alongside the emergence of the new approach toward the Holocaust (see Chapter 11). The intensification of the denial theme in the Arab Holocaust discourse was largely a "mirror image" of the growing significance of the Holocaust in Israeli collective identity and in the western cultural and political discourse.[3]

As in the West, denial in the Arab discourse was articulated in several ways, most important of which were: total denial of the event as if nothing had happened to the Jews during World War II and its depiction as a Jewish–Zionist hoax designed to extort funds and political support from the West, particularly Germany; acknowledgement of the death of Jews – a few hundred thousand at the most – during the war, coupled with the allegation that it was part of the overall loss of civilian life during the war due to hunger, disease and random Nazi terrorism, while rejecting or ignoring the Nazi policy of targeting the Jews or exterminating them as a group; minimizing the number of Jewish casualties in order to deprive the Holocaust of its meaning as a genocide; acknowledgement that the Nazis "persecuted" Jews, mostly the German ones, similar to the way in which they had treated the French or the Dutch peoples, but did not exterminate them. At times denial was implicit, when various writers noted that the number of Jews declined after the war, without ever mentioning the reasons.

Denial in the Arab political and intellectual debate aimed primarily at demolishing the moral–historical basis of Zionism. The most blatant manifestation of the instrumentalization of denial is its occasional appearance with the claims that Hitler was right in killing the Jews and/or that the Zionists collaborated

---

3   For the shift in European attitudes toward the Holocaust from disinterest and suppression to acceptance of a collective European guilt, see Tony Judt, "Epilogue: From the House of the Dead an Essay on Modern European Memory," in his *Postwar: A History of Europe since 1945*, New York: 2005, pp. 803ff.

with the Nazis in mass-murdering the Jews. The prevalent view in the Arab world has been that Zionism – lacking any moral or historical justification – is based on a series of unfounded historical myths and outright distortions. Arab deniers, therefore, view the Holocaust as one of the major myths that Zionism invented in order to create a guilt complex in the West, which consequently played a crucial role in forging sympathetic public opinion in support of the establishment of the State of Israel. "Not a single country in history was founded by turning fiction into fact, save for the country of the Jewish enemy," leftist Jordanian journalist Muwaffaq Muhadin wrote in Jordan's *al-'Arab al-Yawm* in 1997. "The beginning of that country was by making up or creating the Holocaust. That fiction was what truly brought about the foundation of that country." Some even argue that without the Holocaust myth Israel might not have existed at all, as put by Mahmud al-Khatib in the same paper in 1998: "the entire Jewish state is built on the great Holocaust lie."[4] Hence, the premise behind Holocaust denial is that refutation of the "lie" would totally undermine Israel's international status and legitimacy. "As one of the ideological bulwarks of Zionist power the 'Holocaust' must be exposed," says the Palestinian-Jordanian Islamist Ibrahim 'Allush (Alloush), who is one of the leading advocates of denial in the Arab world since the late 1990s. In addition, deniers sought to present Israel as an unscrupulous state that resorted to any means in order to extort western financial and political support. Sa'id b. Salih al-Ghamdi, Director of the Global Center for Strategic Consultation in Riyad, charged that the term Holocaust has become "an industry to extort the others, in conformity with the Jewish mentality, which is based on plunder."[5]

In view of the Holocaust's importance in shaping Israeli collective identity and psyche, its denial was perceived as demolishing the broader historical and ideological edifice on which both stood. Moreover, precisely this centrality of

---

4   *Al-'Arab al-Yawm*, 12 April 2007; Sayyid Ahmad Rif'at, *Qissati ma'a ukdhubat al-hulukast*, Cairo: 2005, cited in www.terrorism-info.org.il/malam_multimedia/English/eng_n/pdf/egypt_e_ind.pdf, 29 October 2006. See also *al-Ahram*, 13 July 1986; *al-'Arab al-Yawm*, 27 April, *al-Quds al-'Arabi*, 22 April, *al-Ahram Weekly*, 24 September 1998; *al-Hayat*, 31 July 1998, 31 January 2000; *Akhir Sa'a*, 24 May 2001; *al-Liwa' al-Islami*, 24 June, 1 July 2004; Faysal Darraj, "al-Talfiq wal-'udwaniyya fi al-idiulujiyya al-sahyuniyya," www.wahdah.net/zionideology.html, and a series of statements in the Syrian press during 2006 in www.terrorism - info.org.il/malam_multimedia/English/eng_n/pdf/syria_as0506e.pdf.

5   Sa'id b. Salih al-Ghamdi, "Preface," in Muhammad Jarbu'a, *Tabri'at hitler min tuhmat al-hulukast*, Riyad: 2004, pp. 6, 11. See similar statements in Ibrahim 'Allush, "Man hum al-mu'arrikhun al-muraji'un wa-limadha ta'nina 'al-muhraqa' al-yahudiyya," www.free-arabvoice.org/arabi/index.htm; Mamduh al-Shaykh 'Ali, "Nahwu ru'ya 'arabiyya jadida lil-hulukast: Inkaruha khata' wa-ihtikaruha khati'a," 12 May 2004, www.islamdaily.net/AR/Contents.aspx?AID=2115; Husayn Salama, "al-Mazhar al-hulukasti: al-'aql al-qurbani lada al-yahud," www.alwahdaalislamyia.net/53/salamah.htm.

the Holocaust made it more difficult for Arabs to accept it, since it implied acceptance or certain legitimization of Israeli identity. Acceptance of the victimhood of the "other," the enemy, even by a third party unrelated to the conflict, is a rare phenomenon in any conflict, since it could mean granting the adversary some moral authority or justification, and undermine one's own status of victimhood. The Holocaust myth, according to Faysal Darraj, serves the Zionist argument that the Jews were perpetual global victims in history. Hence, acknowledging the Nazi systematic extermination of Jews might give implicit credence to Zionist claims that the Jews were a persecuted people who, therefore, had a right to statehood.[6]

Another reason for denial may have been the Arab difficulty in reconciling the absolute helplessness of the Jews during the World War and their victory over the Arabs only three years later, in 1948. Admitting the weakness of the Jews would have required a deep, soul-searching analysis of the causes of the Arab defeat, beyond the standard explanations given at the time in the Arab world. It was, therefore, easier to present the Jews as a much more powerful force than they had actually been, by "showing" how they had manipulated the world into accepting the Holocaust myth.[7] Such an approach fits the broader tendency in modern Middle Eastern political culture to adopt conspiracy theories which simplify a complex and often perplexing reality by attributing every development to the intended machination of a group of individuals.[8] According to an anonymous Palestinian-Israeli writer, denial emerged as part of the broader Arab belief in a worldwide Jewish conspiracy in an attempt to explain the 1967 Arab defeat.[9]

Many Arabs saw the common practice of Israeli leaders, of invoking the memory of the Holocaust when referring to threats Israel faced from its Arab neighbors, as a cynical means to justify its own conduct – immoral and unacceptable in their view – vis-à-vis the Arabs. As Robert Fisk, a sympathetic British observer of Arab affairs, contended, the peace process that started in the 1990s hardened the Arabs' refusal to accept Jewish suffering, since the process itself appeared as serving only Israel. No Muslim had any difficulty in acknowledging the massacres of Armenians by the Turks during World War I, he maintained,

---

6   Darraj, "al-talfiq", see also, 'Allush, "Man hum"; Anon, "Akbar ukdhuba ta'rikhiyya yuhawilu al-yahud tamriruha: hiyya ukdhubat al-hulukast aw al-muhraqa fa-hal laha asl? http://3asfh.net/vb/showthread.php?t=40811.

7   For discussions of Arab grappling with past and present failures, see Emmanuel Sivan, *Mythes Politiques Arabes*, Paris: 1995, chapters 2–3; Fouad Ajami, *The Arab Predicament*, New York: 1998, pp. 24–73.

8   For conspiracy theories in the Middle East, see Pipes, *The Hidden Hand*.

9   www.arabs48.com/display.x?cid=44&sid=178&id=41622, 14 December 2006.

even though the Turks were Muslims too. By contrast, accepting the Holocaust entailed empathy with the enemy, and hence the greater difficulty.[10]

Conceivably, denial among the Palestinians reflected frustration over the refusal of western countries to recognize their national tragedy as equal to if not greater than the Holocaust. Denial of the Jewish tragedy may have been a reaction to Israel's refusal to recognize the "historical sin" that its very existence constituted for the Palestinians. It could have also been a means of emotional bargaining with the Israelis' stance of "I will not recognize your tragedy as long as you do not recognize mine." Historian 'Abdallah Hourani, for example, charged that "instead of talking about the so-called Holocaust," Palestinians should speak about "the massacres perpetrated by the Israelis against the defenseless Palestinian people."[11]

Denial was often accompanied by sharp condemnation of the Allies' conduct during the war, mainly the claim that they had committed war crimes far worse than those attributed to or committed by the Nazis. It may also reflect deeper resentment toward the perceived dominant western discourse regarding the history of the region, typical of Middle Eastern Islamist and nationalist trends. Ibrahim 'Allush explained to the editors of the *Journal of Historical Review*, the leading organ of Holocaust deniers in the US, that exposing the Holocaust myth is associated with resisting "imperialist western hegemony."[12]

Consequently, denial appeared among all political trends, from Islamists to leftists, albeit with different emphasis and arguments. It emerged in a variety of forms and contexts with no set pattern. It was raised as part of a long polemic against Zionism or Judaism, when the Holocaust was presented as one link in a series of lies and distortions by the Jews going back to alleged Jewish distortions of the Scriptures, and appeared in discussions of various Israeli policies or issues totally unrelated to the conflict.[13]

---

10   *Independent*, 30 August 1996. For an example of the different attitudes towards the Armenian and Jewish cases, see Egyptian historian Mahmud Rif'at al-Imam, "Ibadat al-jins: nash'at al-mafhum wa-mu'adalat al-tatbiq," *al-Siyasa al-Duwaliyya*, no. 151 (January 2002), pp. 62–5; *al-Sharq al-Awsat*, 25 April 2005; Jurji Haddad, "al-Qadiyya al-armaniyya," *al-Hiwar al-Mutamaddin*, 25 April 2005, www.rezgar.com/debat/show.art.asp?aid=36126.

11   *Al-Istiqlal*, 20 April 2000. See a similar statement as early as 1960 in Nasir al-Nashashibi, *al-Hilal*, January 1962, p. 112; and years later by Islamic Jihad activist Nafiz 'Azzam and historian Dr. 'Isam Sisalem, in Memri, Special Dispatch Series, no. 187, 21 February 2001; and by Wasif al-Shaybani of the Islamic movement in Israel, in *Sawt al-Haqq wal-Hurriyya*, 30 April 1993.

12   "A Conversation with Dr. Ibrahim Alloush," *Journal for Historical Review* [*JHR*], vol. 20, no. 3 (May/June 2001, all citations are from the electronic edition).

13   See for instance an assertion or denial during an interview on the activities of the PNA

There are major differences between Holocaust deniers in the Arab world and their counterparts in the West. Most deniers in the West belong to the extreme right that seeks to redeem the reputation of Nazism or of Hitler personally and rehabilitate the past as part of the latter-day political battles in their countries. Few belong to the radical left that views the Holocaust as a Western alibi to exonerate the crimes of capitalism. In post-Communist Eastern Europe deniers seek to embellish the collaboration of certain leaders and movements with the Nazis during the war, as part of constructing an alternative national past to the Communist era.[14] By contrast, Arab deniers are mostly uninterested in Nazism per se and their main focus is the attack on Zionism and Israel. Some of them regard themselves explicitly as anti-Nazi and denounce Nazism as blatant racism.

Deniers in the West are often racists who detest Jews as well as other foreign ethnic groups, including Arab and Muslim immigrants. The academic establishments in western countries reject their arguments as patently false and as undeserving of serious scholarly consideration except by way of refutation. They are often shut out of the major media and, consequently, they often constitute a "community" of like-minded fanatic believers. Conversely, in the Arab world most of those who deny the Holocaust belong to the intellectual and political mainstream. They include academics, respectable research institutes and journalists. Consequently, they are able to promote their views in the major media, including leading newspapers and TV channels.[15] Their views, which form part of the dominant intellectual and political discourse, are seldom challenged, and

National Institutions Office in *al-Hayat al-Jadida*, 8 December 1998.

14   For denial in the West, see Lipstadt, *Denying the Holocaust*; Michael Shermer and Alex Grobman, *Denying History: Who Says the Holocaust Never Happened and Why Do They Say It?* Berkeley, CA: 2000; Yakira, *Post-Zionism*; Rembiszewski, *The Final Lie*; on denial in the radical European left, see Finkielkraut, *The Future*. See also Yehuda Bauer, "'Revisionism' – the repudiation of the Holocaust and its historical significance," in Yisrael Gutman and Gideon Greif (eds.), *The Historiography of the Holocaust Period: Proceedings of the Fifth Yad Vashem International Conference*, Jerusalem, March 1983, Jerusalem: 1988, pp. 697–708. For an extensive bibliography see, John Drobnicki et al., "Holocaust denial literature: a bibliography," www.york.cuny.edu/~drobnick/holbib.html#general. For denial in Eastern Europe, see Michael Shafir, *Between Denial and "Comparative Trivialization": Holocaust Negationism in Post-Communist East Central Europe*, ACTA, no. 19, Jerusalem: 2002.

15   The most glaring example is the The Zayed Centre for Coordination and Follow-Up (ZCCF), which was established as an independent think-tank by Deputy Prime Minister of the United Arab Emirates, Shaykh Sultan bin Zayd Al Nahyan, in order to facilitate and serve Arab solidarity and cooperation. The Center hosted several Holocaust deniers, and published reports denying the Holocaust in addition to other extensive anti-Semitic activity. It was shut down on 27 August 2003 following sharp criticism in the West for these actions. See, Memri, Special Report no. 16, 16 May 2003.

the Arab public is rarely if ever exposed to the more historically valid discourse of the Holocaust.

Moreover, politicians and statesmen also took part in denial of the Holocaust. A very early pronouncement by an Arab official was Lebanese Foreign Minister Charles Malik's statement during the 1955 Bandung Conference of Third World Countries. In response to Indian Prime Minister Jawahar Lal Nehru's mentioning the "five million" Jews that were murdered during World War II, Malik contended that the massacre of the Jews was a mere "Zionist propaganda."[16] Similarly, Egyptian president 'Abd al-Nasir told the German *National Zeitung*'s editor in 1964, that "no person, not even the simplest one, takes seriously the lie of the six million Jews that were murdered."[17] While such expressions by senior public figures were rare, they were repeated in later years by officials such as Jamil Barudi, Saudi ambassador to the UN, Mahmud 'Abbas, then member of the PLO Executive Committee (see below), Lebanese Foreign Minister Faris Buwayz, Syrian President Bashar al-Assad;[18] by senior clerical leaders – Shaykh Muhammad Mahdi Shams al-Din, head of Lebanon's Shi'ite Council, Shaykh 'Ikrima Sabri, Shaykh Muhammad Khidr of al-Azhar University in Cairo, and Pope Shannuda III, head of the Coptic Church in Egypt.[19]

Unlike the European racists, the Arab deniers see themselves as members of the Third World who are hurt by the racism of the radical right in the West. Still, often due to their shared enmity toward Israel, many of them tend to ignore the racist views of Western Holocaust deniers and of the radical European right and cooperate with them. Similar to western deniers, many of the Arab deniers tend to relativize the Holocaust by claiming that both sides in World War II carried out atrocities against civilians, e.g., bombing of cities, thereby denying its essence as an act of wholesale extermination. Not only do they argue for the moral equivalence between the Nazis and the Allies, but some portray the Allies as the more brutal party in the war.

Arab denial was also aided by the post-war Soviet and Communist historiography, which blurred the Jewish identity of the victims and the unique circumstances of their death by presenting them as part of the overall civilian casual-

---

16   G. H. Jasen, *Zionism, Israel and Asian Nationalism*, Beirut: 1971, p. 257.

17   *National Zeitung*, 1 May 1964; on Barudi, see Bauer, "Revisionism," p. 702; AFP, 22 March 1998.

18   For 'Abbas, see below; for Buwayz, see *al-Nahar*, 6 April 1998; for Assad, see SyriaComment.com, 29 March 2006.

19   AFP, 22 March 1998; *October*, 23 April 2000; AP, 25 March, *Ha'aretz*, *New York Times*, 26 May, *al-Akhbar*, 27 May 2001.

ties.[20] Such influence is evident mainly, but not solely, among writers of the left. It also suits the broader view in the Arab world, which rejects the distinct Jewish ethno-national identity as serving the Zionist case.

Arab Holocaust denial is not a consequence of ignorance of historical facts, as shown by the immediate post-war Arab discourse. It is often the product of selective reading and borrowing of material published in the West. The publicity given in the Arab press to western news items dealing with Holocaust deniers shows that Arab writers are well aware of the western discourse on the subject, but prefer to ignore the vast scholarly literature dealing with it, since it does not suit their ideological convictions. Egyptian historian Muhammad Kamal al-Dissuqi, who completed a doctoral dissertation in Germany during the 1960s on Hitler's policy in the Middle East, demonstrates such selective reading. Dissuqi boasted that he had read "thousands of pages" in German archives related to the war. Yet, he claimed that the "Zionist" figures of Jewish losses were "imaginary and fantastic" (*wahmiyya wa-khiyaliyya*), as there is not "even one document which confirms them."[21]

Contexts: denial and the conflict

The "fabrication" of the Holocaust by Zionism, according to the Arab deniers, stemmed from several motives: Zionist or Jewish desires to extract western political and financial support; domestic political considerations in Israel; and psychological needs, which the Jews developed due to their abnormal historical situation. The direct linkage between denial and the Arab–Israeli conflict appeared in the writings of most deniers, and received official blessing.[22]

Nazi persecution of the Jews, according to Dissuqi and Salman, writing shortly after the 1967 war, has become the "wailing wall" for the Jews to which they turn each time when their "treasures are depleted and their economic plight

---

20   Yitzhaq Arad, "The Holocaust in Soviet Historiography," in Gutman and Grieff (eds.), *The Historiography of the Holocaust*, pp. 187–216; Dawidowicz, *The Holocaust*, pp. 68–87. *The History of the Great Patriotic War (1941–1945)* by Boris Tepulchowski, which represents official post-Stalinist Soviet historiography, mentions the gas chambers and the extermination as it was practiced in Auschwitz, Maidanek and Treblinka, and refers to the number of six million Polish citizens (a figure that includes the Jews), but does not specify the Jews among the victims. Two lines explain that the entire Jewish population on occupied Soviet soil was exterminated, cited in Pierre Vidal-Naquet, *Assassins of Memory: Essays on the Denial of the Holocaust*, New York: 1992, p. 94.

21   Muhammad Kamal al-Dissuqi, *al-Harb al-'alamiyya al-thaniya: sira' isti'mari*, Cairo: 1968, pp. 282–4. See a similar selective view in *al-'Alam*, 5 April 1997.

22   See, Musa Zayd al-Kaylani, *Sanawat al-Ightisab: Isra'il 1948–1965*, Amman: 1965, p. 128. The introduction, endorsing the book, was written by then Jordanian Prime Minister Wasfi al-Tal.

worsens." It is on this basis that world Zionism inflated the so-called "guilt complex" among the Germans and the need to "atone" continuously for their sin through compensation and aid. Western historians "fell under the influence of Zionist propaganda" and adopted its claims. Zionism, they charge, exploited the Nazi persecutions in the "vilest way" in order to mislead and to commit the most vicious crime that modern history has ever witnessed – the usurpation of Arab Palestine.[23] A former Egyptian diplomat, Mustafa Sa'dani, also contended that the Holocaust was invented so that Arabs would pay its price with their blood, and Germans with huge financial compensations.[24] Years later, other writers explained that Israel invented the Holocaust lie in order to justify its own persecution and oppression of the Palestinians, and regain the support it had lost in Europe following the massacres it committed against the Arabs.[25]

Dr. 'Abdallah al-Khatib of Jordan attributed the invention of the Holocaust myth to Israeli domestic needs. The [Holocaust] "massacre and horror stories" which then Prime Minister Yitzhaq Shamir (1983–92) was talking about were "a figment of his imagination, part of the *Protocols of [the Elders] of Zion*." These were intended to unify the Jews by fomenting fears of the recurrence of such "imaginary massacres." The invention of the Holocaust, Husayn Salama added, was necessary in order to build a new "wailing wall" that would enhance Jewish self-imposed isolation from other societies based on the racist Zionist ideology.[26]

The Iraqi leftist Nuri al-Muradi attributed in 2002 the Jewish invention of the Holocaust to the murderous heritage of the Bible, which speaks repeatedly of the extermination of the ancient people of Canaan. If God-ordained genocide was an inherent part of the Bible, it was easy for the Jews to accept the false claim that it actually happened during the war, particularly as the number six had particular sanctity in Judaism.[27]

---

23   Dissuqi and Salman, *al-Sahyuniyya*, pp. 94–5.

24   Mustafa Sa'dani, *al-Fikr al-yahudi wal-siyasa al-yahudiyya*, Cairo: 1971, pp. 266–7. See similar arguments by the Algerian writer 'Abd al-Hamid ben Ashenhu, *Usul al-sahuyniyya wa-ma laha*, Algiers: 1974, p. 111; and the Moroccan *L'Opinion* cited in *Le Monde*, 2 June 1982.

25   *Al-Sha'b*, 22 August 1995; *October*, February 1996. Among many other examples, see Shamil 'Abd al-Qadir in *Alif Ba*, 7 May 1995; *al-Bilad*, 1 June 1996; *al-Siyasa*, 15 June, *al-Sharq*, 24 October 1997; *al-Watan al-'Arabi*, 14 April 2001.

26   *Al-Ra'y*, 17 February 1988; Salama, "al-Mazhar al-hulukasti." See similar arguments by Dr. Muhammad Ahmad al-Nabulsi, secretary general of the Arab Psychological Association in his "al-Sahyuniyya wal-harb al-nafsiyya," www.bahethcenter.org/arabic/sahyouniyyat/almasonya_alnfsia.htm and in *al-Bayan*, 1 March 2002, and Hamid Maw'id, *al-Sahyuniyya ta'lim al-hiqd: qira'a fi tashkil al-'aql al-sahyuni*, Nicosia: 1993, pp. 34–6.

27   Nuri al-Muradi, "al-Hulukast (madhabih al-yahud) – haqiqa am khiyal," 31 October 2002, www.alkader.net/Man_alkader/Alholakost.htm.

Syrian writer Rim Arnuf in 1990, and years later the Palestinian writer Ismahan Shurayh, added the US as a party to the "fabrication of the gas chambers."
Without the hoax of the "Jewish genocide" they claimed, Allied activities, particularly the bombing of Dresden and the nuclear bombing of Hiroshima, would
have been regarded as the greatest crime of the war, and fingers would have been
pointed at "the American barbarian" instead of at the "German barbarian."[28]
'Allush took an argument employed by European deniers from the radical left
in order to argue that "many of those who claim to be anti-Nazi have colonial
and racist track records that surpass that of the Nazis by any objective standard."
Furthermore, he said, many use the banner of anti-Nazism today to "spread
their colonial tentacles across the globe." In other words, the Holocaust serves as
an instrument to exonerate the crimes of capitalism and the West itself.[29] Denial
also appeared in other contexts unrelated to the conflict.[30]

Western Holocaust deniers as the authoritative source

The major change in the denial of the Holocaust since the 1980s was the growing reliance on the so-called professional western deniers, and the translation of
their works to Arabic. In this way denial acquired a pseudo-scientific backing,
as if these were serious historical studies based on documents and verifiable statistics. That these deniers came from the West, which is supposedly captive to
the Zionist myth, "in the midst of the very house where the massacres allegedly
took place," in the words of the Palestinian journalist Khayri Mansur, gave their
arguments greater importance and respectability.[31] Conceivably, this reliance
reflected subtle or unconscious esteem for, despite the resentment towards, the
West or western sources.

The most prominent example of reliance on western deniers is Mahmud 'Abbas' book, based on his doctoral dissertation that was submitted in 1982 to the
Oriental Institute in Moscow. The book itself was devoted to "showing" Zionist–Nazi collaboration in the extermination of the Jews (see below, Chapter
8), but in his introduction 'Abbas deals with the number of Jewish victims and
quotes the notorious French denier Robert Faurisson to refute the gas chambers

---

28   Rim Arnuf, "al-Khadi'a allati sahamat fi sun' isra'il," *Balsam*, no. 181 (July 1990), pp.
      69–75; Ismahan Shurayh, "al-Hulukast iquna urubiyya," www.alhourriah.org/?page=Sho
      wDetails&table=articles&Id=469&Issue=.

29   'Allush, "Man hum"; *JHR*, "Conversation."

30   Ramadan Lawand, *al-Harb al-'alamiyya al-thaniya*, Beirut: 1965, pp. 513, 516. See also
      the entry on Hitler in a small Egyptian lexicon on famous personalities by Magdi Sayyid
      'Abd al-'Aziz, *Mawsu'at al-mashahir*, Cairo: 1996, vol. 2, pp. 164–5.

31   *Al-Hayat al-Jadida*, 21 April 2001. See also, *JHR*, "Conversation."

"myth," as well as the Canadian denier Roger DeLorme to contend that the number was significantly lower than six million.[32]

DeLorme also serves as a major source for Rafiq Natshe, member of al-Fatah Central Committee during the 1980s and later minister in the PNA, to refute the "imaginary" (*maz'um*) mass murders. Citing Delorme, Natshe discusses in depth the 1958 discovery in Eastern Poland of mass graves of tens of thousands of Jews brought there from Nazi camps near the towns of Zegan and Sviet-Ostrow, using some true facts but totally distorting them and their meaning. It turned out, Natshe contends, that the causes of death of these people were hunger, cold, contagious diseases and maltreatment at the end of the war, but not execution during the war.[33] Examination of the corpses and their clothes showed that they were British, French, Belgians, Italians, Yugoslavs, Poles and Russians, but there were no Jews among them. It also turned out, he says, that they did not die of gassing, "of whose existence no proof or evidence has been found to date." On the contrary, the vast number of corpses buried in the pits shows the absence of facilities and means to cremate such a large number of people, and hence the proof that there was no Nazi extermination plan. Natshe explains that he has no intention to belittle the extent and scope of Nazi crimes, but only to show how "the Zionists exploited in the most despicable way ... a whole series of myths and fables to attain financial and political remunerations."[34] He concedes that Hitler did kill some Jews, "only the old and those opposed to Zionism." The young people were sent to Palestine "with their pockets filled with money," while the killing and emigration were under Zionist supervision.[35]

---

32   'Abbas, *al-Wajh al-akhar*, "Introduction," pp. b, g. On Faurisson, see Vidal-Naquet, *Assassins*, pp. 19, 21–4, 44–5, 113–15, 125–6. Delorme was a Montreal TV personality who ran for the Progressive Conservative Party in a Quebec by-election in May 1977 and failed. He publicly doubted whether the number of Jewish victims exceeded one million, http://books.google.com/books?id=DMaS5cb7s8QC&pg=PA328&lpg=PA328&dq=delorme+holocaust+canada&source=web&ots=PPcnQdsi5T&sig=emm2jtxk4TS8cR-Mh7Uww2Uw_Qk.

33   See a similar claim by the Egyptian columnist Lutfi Nasif, citing an unknown "German expert" who "proved" through demographic data that the decline in the number of Jews during the war was due to "natural causes," thereby "refuting" the accusation that Hitler could destroy "the imaginary figure" of six million. *Al-Jumhuriyya*, 12 December 1987.

34   Natshe, *al-Isti'mar*, pp. 147–8. Our attempts to locate the two towns mentioned in the text failed to produce any results. However, the fallacy of this description is evident. The Nazis did not imprison Britons in concentration camps, and Dutch underground activists were sent to concentration camps in Germany rather than Poland. Likewise, they did not bring prisoners from Yugoslavia to camps in Poland but murdered them in Yugoslavia or imprisoned them in the notorious Yasenovac camp in Croatia. By 1945 all prisoners in Nazi camps wore rugs and there was no way to tell their nationality from their clothes.

35   Natshe, *al-Isti'mar*, pp. 147–51.

Robert Faurisson, a professor of literature in France, is a most eminent western denier in the Arab discourse. His writings were translated to Arabic,[36] and he was cited extensively in the Arab press. A year after the publication of his first articles in 1980, the Jordanian government newspaper *al-Dustur* published in three installments the interview Faurisson had given to the Italian journal *Storia Illustrata*. In the introduction attached to each part, *al-Dustur* explained that the "eminent" French historian "refuted decisively and emphatically in a clear scientific analysis and decisive proofs the existence of gas chambers and crematoria for burning corpses. This is a major legend, which the Jews launched at the end of WWII, and the Allied media supported and disseminated." *Al-Dustur* turned his readers' attention to the "vile" manner in which the questions to Faurisson were raised, the "obvious intention" of which was to embarrass Faurisson and challenge his arguments. But, it added, the "eminent historian" refuted the attack.[37]

The 1986 approval by the University of Nantes in France of Henri Roques's doctoral thesis that "proved" the "hoax" of the gas chambers as a means to exterminate the Jews caused a public and intellectual scandal in France, prompting then Minister of Higher Education Alain de Vaquet to instruct its withdrawal and the repeal of Roques's title.[38] In the Arab press, on the other hand, the dissertation received positive acclaim, and it was subsequently published in Arabic. *Al-Dustur*, for instance, reported the affair on its front page, bringing Roques's side of the story, but without mentioning the arguments against him.[39] An elaborate report in the Egyptian weekly *al-Musawwar*, which described Roques as "a new victim of a Zionist campaign in France," stated that Roques had "proved" that the gas chambers shown in various post-war documentaries were in fact used for fumigating clothes. Likewise, the photographs of naked prisoners were designed to humiliate them, but not to kill them. Obviously, the article's author Salwa Abu Sa'da explains, the Zionists would not allow such an event to pass respectfully, since Roques's work serves as the cornerstone of an effort to bring the truth to the western world's consciousness. Abu Sa'da expressed her fear that

---

36   See, Furisun, *al-Ukdhuba*.

37   *Al-Dustur*, 14–16 January 1980. Interestingly, another story on Jewish racism that appeared in the 14 January issue claimed that Eichmann himself took pride in killing six million Jews. See also the interview with Faurisson in *al-Sha'b* (Cairo) 17 May 1994, and three articles dedicated to him and his arguments in Shamil 'Abd al-Qadir's series in *Alif Ba*, 14, 21 and 28 June 1995.

38   On the affair, see Vidal-Naquet, *Assassins*, pp. 114–15, 118–19.

39   The translation with an introduction and appendices by Andre Shaylan appeared under the title *Usturat ghuraf al-ghaz al-naziyya: utruhat nant wa-qadiyyat ruk*, Beirut: 1997, tr. Ramadan al-'Abbasi; *al-Dustur*, 14 June 1986.

Roques would not be the last victim of such a campaign, criticizing the French response to the entire affair as reflecting "the fear nesting in the West's mind and soul in view of Zionist aggression."[40]

Dr. Lutfi Nasif, a columnist in the Egyptian government daily *al-Jumhuriyya* who had frequently dealt with the Holocaust, expressed satisfaction that Roques's study reflected major changes in European public opinion on Israel and Zionism, since formerly the charge of anti-Semitism prevented any serious discussion on the role of the Jews during the war. "Our duty as Arabs," he stated, is to publicize the book as much as possible since the issue is directly linked "to our continuous existential struggle against Zionism." Nasif pointed to his personal experience and "research" carried out during his journalistic work in Germany in 1967–70 to validate Roques's claims. He had visited, he says, all German and Polish concentration camps, where German journalists, and even former camp inmates, provided him with documents affirming Roques's thesis. The documents proved that "the Zionist movement and the Jewish Agency planned most of the massacres against the Jews in Europe" during the war, while simultaneously, the "Jewish Agency exaggerated the role of the Nazis in torturing Jews, and invented crimes and massacres against the Jews." I have no intention, he adds, to deny the mass murder which Hitler committed in those camps and the inhuman tortures of Russian, Polish, French and other prisoners, but the number of Jews among them was negligible.[41] Both the official PLO organ *Filastin al-Thawra* and the government daily *Syria Times* praised Roques as a serious historian and as "a renowned French thinker" who exposed the Zionist deceptions and was therefore ferociously attacked by the French media.[42]

Writing in *Balsam*, organ of the PLO-affiliated Palestinian Red Crescent Society, Rim Arnuf gave by far the most passionate endorsement of Roques and Faurisson. She opens with a statement by Faurisson refuting the existence of the gas chambers. The war caused terrible catastrophes to many peoples, and the French, British and Soviet peoples paid a heavy price in life and property. In particular, she stressed the German losses by Allied bombing, which in Dresden alone amounted to 135,000 persons, an inflated number which according

---

40   *Al-Musawwar*, 6 June 1986; see also 'Arafa 'Abduh 'Ali, "Usturat al-hulukast: ta'awun mashbuh bayna al-sahyuniyya wal-naziyya," *al-'Arabi*, No. 498 (May 2000), pp. 108–14, which discusses the dissertation and criticizes the French minister for rejecting it.

41   *Al-Jumhuriyya*, 12 December 1987. Nasif reiterated the same argument in his columns on 3 January 1988 and 4 March 2000.

42   *Filastin al-Thawra*, 5 July 1986; *Syria Times*, 6 September 2000. See also the long and sympathetic interview with Roques under the title "A Man under Siege," *al-Ahram*, 13, 15 July 1986. For additional praises for Faurisson and other deniers, see *al-Bilad*, 1 June, 1990; *al-Shira'*, 26 January 1998.

to more accurate historical accounts ranged from 25,000 to 35,000. Likewise, she claims that the Japanese casualties of the nuclear bombing of Hiroshima and Nagasaki reached around one million, whereas the official Japanese figures stand at 140,000 dead in Hiroshima and 70,000 dead in Nagasaki.[43] Arnuf substantiates her claims with Faurisson and Roques's allegations, describing in detail how Faurisson had "proved" through elaborate "scientific" and "technical" examinations the improbability that Jews were executed in gas chambers. She endorses his conclusion that while Israel and world Zionism benefited from this "historical lie," their two main victims were the German and Palestinian peoples. In addition, Faurisson himself became the victim of a major campaign by "illustrious Jewish organizations" that accused him of distorting history, assaulted him physically and threatened to kill him.[44]

Arab newspapers welcomed the 2001 Arabic translation of the "Leuchter Report," by Fred Leuchter, a self-proclaimed expert on gas chambers in US prisons, which denied the gassing of Jews in Auschwitz and Maidanek on spurious technical grounds. The report was submitted to a Canadian court in 1989 by the defense attorneys of the German-Canadian Holocaust denier Ernst Zündel.[45] In a long, two-part report al-Ahram al-'Arabi praised Leuchter, Zündel and Faurisson for their work. Ever since the end of World War II the victors had imposed their hegemony on history and invented the "Holocaust lie" to extort the whole world, it claimed. Each time that scholars voiced the truth, the western democracies had treated them in the same way that the Catholic Church had treated Galileo Galilei. Zündel, it added, had joined Galilei "as one of the victims of truth facing the forces of ignorance, lies and deceit." So moving was the story that the Palestinian al-Manar reproduced it verbatim under the title "The myth and the truth."[46] Al-Dustur, which produced long excerpts from the translated report, lamented the loss of truth and the suppression of freedom of expression when confronted with the "Jewish taboo" of the Holocaust myth. The report itself was subsequently on sale at the 2001 Cairo International Book Fair.[47]

---

43   James S. Corum, "Inflated by Air: Common Perceptions of Civilian Casualties from Bombing," Alabama, Air War College: 1998, pp. 18, 20.

44   Arnuf, "al-khadi'a," pp. 69–75.

45   On Zündel and the report, see Lipstadt, Denying the Holocaust, pp. 157–63; Shermer and Grobman, Denying History, pp. 129–31.

46   Al-Ahram al-'Arabi, 24 April, 1 May, al-Manar, 3 May 1999; al-Sha'b, 16 May 2000; al-Istiqlal, 14 June 2001. See also the TV series A Study of Israel's History on Nile Culture TV, 27 November 2005, www.memritv.org clip No. 943 and al-'Arab al-Yawm, 23 February 2006, which uses the Galileo metaphor for Zündel and David Irving.

47   Al-Dustur, 28 March, 3, 8 April 2001; Yedi'ot Aharonot, 23 February 2001.

Little wonder that the Arab writers praise the deniers for having left an imprint on European society that began to cast doubt on the truth distorted by the Zionists.[48] Reacting to the Stockholm International Conference, convened by the Swedish prime minister in January 2000, that discussed means to combat Holocaust denial and incorporate Holocaust studies into school curricula, the Syrian editor Muhammad Khayr al-Wadi expressed his satisfaction over the achievements of Holocaust deniers, who "establish the truth that was distorted by the Zionists," despite the latter's "attempt to repress them." The stream of Holocaust deniers had "cast fear in the hearts of the Zionist movement" that had hastened to convene an international conference on the Holocaust "in order to turn the Zionist lies into common knowledge."[49]

Following the masters

Arab writers and spokespersons did not only quote western deniers, but also adopted their arguments and methodology. One such tactic was the distortion of the content of authentic documents or their presentation out of context. A prominent example is a two-part article in the Palestinian journal *al-Istiqlal* in 1989 titled "How the raucous Zionist propaganda silenced reason and science ... the cremation of Jews in the Nazi ovens is the hoax of the 20th century in order to justify the new Nazism." Although the author, Khalid al-Shimali, emphasized that he had based his account on his own impressions of the Sachsenhausen concentration camp and on his technical knowledge of incinerators, his arguments were probably inspired by the western deniers. Shimali described his sadness when he and his friends entered the camp, since they had all been influenced by "exaggerated Zionist propaganda." However, the more he saw of the camp, the more he realized that the living and hygiene conditions were far better than those of Palestinian prisoners in Israel. Zionist propaganda, he went on to say, "filled the world with screams and yells" about Nazi massacres and tortures against the Jews, whereas in fact the Nazis had supplied them with nutritious food and housing. The Nazi concentration camps, he went on to say, were not different than other detention camps in the twentieth century, as they were used to detain political rivals and minorities during the war.[50]

---

48 Arnuf, "al-Khadi'a," pp. 74–5; Lutfi Nasif in *al-Jumhuriyya*, 12 December 1987, 4 March 2000.

49 *Tishrin*, 31 January 2000.

50 *Al-Istiqlal*, 13, 20 December 1989. Sachsenhausen served as a concentration camp for tens of thousands of prisoners during the war, but was not used for extermination. Death camps were set up only in Poland. Nasir Nashashibi, also, was unconvinced during his

The 1990s marked a new phase in Arab Holocaust denial with the publication of several books fully devoted to denial and to the personal exoneration of Hitler.[51] The change was probably in reaction to the growing efforts in Europe to establish the Holocaust as a central event in universal collective memory, which were manifested in the establishment of Holocaust museums and international ceremonies of commemoration. Although this process sometimes led to a distinction between the Holocaust as a universal symbol and the specific Jewish tragedy, the fear that this trend would benefit Israel, coupled with deep-seated resentment against the West, particularly on the part of Islamists, prompted an enhanced effort of denial. It may have also been in response to the new dissenting discourse that began to emerge in the Arab world itself. Reflecting this approach was 'Allush's conclusion that the Arabs needed a "coherent, principled, cognizant response to the campaign to Zionize the Arab mind. Therein lay the promise of historical revisionism for us Arabs." Moreover, 'Allush explained that

[p]ainstaking research findings are not enough: revisionist findings should be popularized in pamphlets and articles directed to the average person, who has neither the time nor the background to delve into thick volumes. The research findings of historical revisionism can only become politically effective if they reach the people. Therefore, revisionist work should proceed along two parallel lines: the serious academic work of debunking the "Holocaust" myths, and the even more important work of popularizing revisionism.[52]

Muhammad Nimr Madani's *Were the Jews Burned in the Gas Chambers?* summarizes all the motifs in the Arab discourse: starting from allegations of Zionist–Nazi collaboration, laying responsibility for the Holocaust on the Jews, presenting the Allies as the true war criminals and, finally, in outright denial. Throughout his discussion Madani focuses on the writings of the various deniers, particularly Faurisson, Roques, Leuchter and Roger Garaudy, praising them for their heavily documented "meticulous scientific research," by which they refute the great historical lies and allegations that the Jews were exterminat-

---

1962 visit to Dachau by the "false stories" (*abatil*) of killing and torturing in the camp. *al-Hilal*, January 1962.

51   Among these books, see Madani, *Hal uhriqa al-yahud fi afran al-ghaz?* Damascus: 1996; Yasir Husayn, *Bara'at hitler wa-tazwir al-ta'rikh*, n.p.: 1995, which also appeared in an electronic edition as *Hitler wa-tazwir al-ta'rikh*, electronic book 2148.54KB www.kotobarabia.com/BookDetails.aspx?ID=2970; Jarbu'a, *Tabri'at hitler*, which appeared in two editions in Beirut 2002 and Riyad 2004; Sayyid Ahmad, *Qissati ma'a ukdhubat al-hulukast*; Nuri Muradi claims in his article "al-Hulukast," that he had written a book on the subject, but the ISBN number (9163018314) that he provided failed to produce any results.

52   *JHR*, "Conversation."

ed.[53] The book's introduction, "Israel's end will start here," points to the direct link between denial and the delegitimization of Israel. Madani states that "the final solution" to the Jewish problem was indeed one of the major Nazi plans, in full harmony with the Zionist wish to concentrate all Jews in Palestine. It was carried out through a joint agreement on mass emigration of Jews from Germany and Europe to Palestine. Hitler, in his words, had done great service to the Jews, and in return the Jews supported him when he launched the war. However, the Jews betrayed Hitler during the war and started publishing the lie that he was exterminating their people. Madani agrees that Jews were detained in German camps, as were members of other nations, but claims that there is ample documentary evidence showing that Germany employed those Jews, like all other prisoners, in armament production, rather than murdering them. As proof, he cites the cynical and misleading emblem written on the gate to Auschwitz and other camps *Arbeit macht frei* [work liberates]. Not only was there no extermination, as the Zionists claimed, but the post-war years were a period of Jewish prosperity and success, manifested in the establishment of Israel. What happened in the war, then, was far from extermination, but rather a stimulant (*tanshit*) for the Jews.[54]

Techniques of denial

Similarly to their western counterparts, Arab deniers resort to various pseudo-historical or a-historical arguments to justify their claims. Several writers, particularly since the 1990s, have taken issue with the term "Holocaust" and its implied religious or theological meaning in order to deny the event and to deprive it of any historical meaning. These writers contend that the use of this term carries with it sinister theological and political aims intended to portray the Jews as an innocent collective, whose death constituted a sacrifice to God and therefore carried with it some deeper theological reasoning, such as presenting them as "the holiest nation," or entitling them to moral or historical remuneration. Since these writers view Zionists as inherently evil and some of them espouse strong anti-Jewish sentiments, they reject this characterization of the event. In other words, proving that the Jews were malevolent by their nature and activities or that the Zionists supposedly collaborated with the Nazis in exterminating the Jews would not only deprive the Holocaust of its moral or political significance, but would also refute its foundations as a historical

---

53   Madani, *Hal uhriqa*, pp. 24–30.
54   Madani, ibid., pp. 151–2.

event.[55] Thus, the Syrian *al-Thawra* concluded that "what is left to say is that there was no Holocaust and no hatred between the Nazis and the Zionists. On the contrary, there was an alliance and an agreement to carry out the ugliest crimes against humanity."[56]

A common pseudo-scientific claim is the absence of a written order by Hitler for killing the Jews, or of any other written document showing an explicit and comprehensive Nazi extermination plan. Neither the Arab nor the European deniers ever ask themselves why the Jews, who supposedly fabricated so much evidence, did not forge this one document.[57] The common conclusions are either that no extermination plan and policy ever existed, or that the Jews were not the prime victims of Nazi atrocities. The absence of German pictures or newsreels showing the gassing of Jews in the Nazi death camps was considered as a "proof" that extermination never took place – ignoring, as all deniers do, the vast amount of documentary evidence on the extermination that does exist.[58]

Another ploy of denial is the dismissal of existing evidence as false and fabricated – particularly that pertaining to the use of gas chambers for killing Jews – often by focusing on or referring to concentration camps in Germany which were not used for mass extermination, rather than to the death camps in Poland. The resort to pseudo-technical explanations of the burning capacities of crematoria in various camps to contend that six million Jews could not have been burned, or that the Germans could not have hidden the vast amount of ashes of the burned victims is also a common tactic of denial. Khalid al-Shimali claims that, as an engineer who examined the crematoria at Sachsenhausen camp, he concluded that it would take 1,300 years to burn the three million Jewish victims whom he falsely attached to that camp, and therefore at the most 30,000 Jews were killed during the war rather than six million. The Iraqi nationalist

55 Jarbu'a, *Tabri'at hitler*, p. 11; Shaykh 'Ali, "Nahwu ru'ya"; Salama, "al-Mazhar al-Hulukasti"; Abu Hamza al-Jaza'iri, "al-Hulukast: al-ukdhuba allati saddaqnaha," www.maktoobblog.com/abuhamza_aljazairi?post=80368; Ghazi Khalaf, "al-Hulukast: 'muhraqa' naziyya am 'muhraqa' naziyya-sahyuniyya mushtaraka," www.alwahdaalislamyia.net/40/ghazi%20khalaf.htm.

56 *Al-Thawra*, 12 December 2002; *Tishrin*, 31 January 2000 – Memri Special Dispatch Series, no. 71, 2 February 2000. Michel Kilu, "al-Hulukast: 'arabiyyan," www.moqawama.tv/arabic/articles/holocost.htm, June 2000.

57 See, for instance, Nasir Ghalima, *Saytarat isra'il 'ala al-wilayat al-muttahida al-amrikiyya*, Beirut: 1981, pp. 44, 61, 136–7; Natshe, *al-Isti'mar*, pp. 147ff; Isma'il al-Baqqawi in PNA TV, 27 May 2003, and 'Allush to *JHR*, vol. 20, no. 3 (May–June 2001). On the fallacy of the "lack of written order" argument, see Shermer and Grobman, *Denying History*, pp. 194–7.

58 Hamid Maw'id, *al-Sahyuniyya*, p. 36. The Nazis did not film the gassing process because they kept the entire extermination operation a secret.

Nuri al-Muradi, on the other hand, questions the existence of death camps by asserting that the Nazis could have shot the Jews on the spot. In addition to the spurious scientific validity of these explanations, those deniers ignore the fact that more than two million Jews were shot or starved to death and their bodies were never burned in crematoria. Another tactic is to deny the existence of evidence, even when it is found: for instance the argument that no mass graves or ashes of Jews were discovered.[59]

Dr. Yusuf Ziedan, of the New Alexandria Library, developed a more sophisticated approach of dismissing evidence in his scholarly article on epistemology and the meaning of knowledge. Discussing the difference between information, knowledge and empirical reality, particularly in view of the "information explosion" of the internet era, he insists that millions of people "know" things from news (*khabar*) but not from actual experience (*khibar*). He agrees that information or news stem from a certain reality, but cautions that there is a major gap between this knowledge and reality based on personal experience, and he refers to the Holocaust as the prime example. When Hitler's atrocities are mentioned, he says, people "immediately point out the cremation of the Jews in the gas chambers." This happens because of the knowledge that is passed on regarding the Holocaust via diverse sources of information, from journalists' reports, historical research, the "unceasing buzz in the media," and films such as *Schindler's List*. Yet, he insists that empirical reality is very different from the image created by these sources, since, as he claims, out of the fifty million victims of the Nazis, only one million were Jews. Moreover, "an analysis of samples from the purported gas chambers has proven that these were sterilization chambers, without a sufficient quantity of cyanide to kill." "Had Hitler wanted to annihilate the Jews of Europe," Ziedan concludes, he would have done so, as he had the opportunity.[60]

Ziedan addresses, wittingly or unwittingly, an important issue in the study of the Holocaust regarding the gap between information, knowledge and awareness. There was a need for a critical volume of data on the mass killing of Jews for the Jewish communities in Palestine and the West during the war to overcome psychological barriers of denial and repression and for the information to be fully internalized and become knowledge and awareness.[61] Ziedan turns the

---

59   Madani, *Hal uhriqa*, pp. 55, 157–8, 162–74; *al-Istiqlal*, 13 December 1989; Muradi, "al-Hulukast"; Salama, "al-Mazhar al-hulukasti." See similar claims by Muhammad Salmawi, editor of *al-Ahram Hebdo*, in *al-Ahram*, 2 February 1998; *al-Ahram Weekly*, 24 September 1998.

60   Yousef Ziedan, "WWW and the informatics plexus," in www.ziedan.com/English/memory.asp. The article is not dated, but was probably written in the late 1990s, based on references to 1997.

61   Hanna Yablonka, "The Development of Holocaust Consciousness in Israel: The Nurem-

argument upside down by insisting that knowledge does not necessarily reflect reality, citing as a prime example the availability of vast amounts of data on the Holocaust. The more knowledge there is in the modern age, he argues, the less it fits historical reality, thereby he demonstrated the power of psychological and ideological barriers which prevent the acceptance of knowledge by the deniers.

Unlike their western counterparts, some Arab deniers attribute false statements to renowned western scholars of the Holocaust. Most notable is the false citation by Mahmud 'Abbas from Raul Hilberg's *The Destruction of European Jews*, supposedly saying that the number of the victims did not exceed 896,000 Jews. Needless to say, the figure does not appear in the page cited by 'Abbas (p. 670), and Hilberg himself estimated that around 5,100,000 Jews perished.[62] Similarly, Madani falsely attributes conflicting low figures to eminent historians of the Holocaust such as Raul Hilberg (1,250,000 and 1,000,000), Leon Poliakov (2,000,000) and Lucy Dawidowicz (1,500,000) in order to substantiate his own claims of the low number of Jewish losses during the war and of supposed Jewish fabrication of statistics. A 2006 Lebanese TV program went so far as attributing to Hilberg the figure of 50,000 Jewish casualties. All three scholars, however, estimated the number of victims at around six million.[63] While western deniers might have feared libel lawsuits for making such false citations, the Arab deniers probably feel secure in view of the lack of awareness in the West of their allegations and are confident that in their countries no court would convict them.

Some deniers distort authentic historical evidence. One example is Shamil 'Abd al-Qadir's citation in the official Iraqi weekly *Alif Ba* from a witness named Kagan during the Eichmann trial, allegedly testifying that all the Jewish inmates at Auschwitz were criminals, imprisoned there for various crimes they had committed. A witness called Ra'ya Kagan did appear in the trial, but her testimony was completely different.[64]

---

berg, Kapos, Kasztner and Eichmann trials," *Israel Studies*, vol. 8, no. 3 (Fall 2003), p. 1. See also Deborah Lipstadt, *Beyond Belief: The American Press and the Coming of the Holocaust 1933–1945*, New York and London: 1986, p. 240, which discusses the impact of these psychological mechanisms on American press reports regarding the Holocaust.

62   'Abbas, *al-Wajh al-akhar*, pp. b, j (preface), 30; Hilberg, *The Destruction*, p. 767. See also Khalid al-Shimali's article in *al-Istiqlal*, 13, 20 December 1989, which attributes false data to *Encyclopedia Britannica*.

63   Madani, p. 15; www.memritv.org, clip no. 682, 21 June 2006. Dawidowicz, *The War*, pp. xxxv–xxxvi; Poliakov, *Brévaire*, p. 386. Poliakov even says that the Jewish demographic deficit in the war approximated eight million.

64   Shamil 'Abd al-Qadir, "Shahadat gharbiyya: qatl al-yahud fi almaniya kidhba kubra," *Alif Ba*, 5 July 1995. For Kagan's authentic testimony, see The State of Israel, *The Attorney General of the State of Israel vs. Adolf Eichmann: Testimonies*, Jerusalem: 1974, vol. I2I, pp.

Deniers sometimes refer to true evidence, but distort its meaning. For Naji Sam'an, who relies on the British Holocaust denier Richard Harwood, and for Rafiq Natshe, documentary films that show Jewish victims of Nazi killings are in fact a historical forgery, since they "actually" show German physicians treating civilian German casualties of the cruel Allied bombing of Dresden in February 1945. As another proof for the absence of crematoria, Natshe recalls that, following the death of 30,000 civilians in an Allied bombing of Munich in September 1944, the city's Archbishop Michael Cardinal von Faulhaber asked the German authorities to cremate the corpses in Dachau, but they declined because Dachau had only one crematorium and could not cremate so many corpses. How could the Germans then burn 2,380,000 corpses, as the Zionists claim, and where did the tons of ashes disappear, he asks. As before, he conflates outright distortions of the films with correct facts regarding Dachau so as to substantiate a fundamentally false case. Dachau, which was a concentration camp and was not used for mass killings, may have had few crematoria, but the gassing of Jews took place in the death camps in Poland and not in Germany.[65]

Nasr Shimali takes the true fact that Auschwitz also served for slave labor to create a fictitious story of the Holocaust as a whole. Accordingly, the Germans were "obliged" to transfer the Jews to concentration camps after the Warsaw Ghetto rebelled against German rule, thereby endangering the German war effort.[66] Shimali, who did not indicate the reason for the rebellion, added that Auschwitz was a peaceful, pleasant working camp with vocational training courses for prisoners. Auschwitz 2 or Birkenau simply contained old and infirm persons who became ill due to the general, harsh war conditions throughout Europe and their wandering around. Children were brought to the camps because the Nazis complied with the demands of their allies not to separate families. Shimali concedes that Hitler committed war crimes, but insists that he never ordered the killing of the Jews. Moreover, none of the Nazi war crimes compares with those of the Israelis in Palestine and the Americans in Iraq.[67] Shimali also refers to the revelation that around 1,200 "half Jews" served in the Nazi army,

---

1183–202.

65   Naji Sam'an, "Banuramat al-'unf al-isra'ili wa-'unf al-gharb," *al-Fikr al-'Arabi*, nos. 85–6 (Summer–Fall 1996), p. 244; Natshe, *al-Isti'mar*, pp. 14ff.

66   The Warsaw Ghetto rebellion started on 20 April 1943, when the Germans decided to liquidate the ghetto, after sending more than 350,000 of the Jews there to the Treblinka death camp. By that time, over 3,000,000 Jews had perished by the Nazis.

67   *Tishrin*, 2 March 2006. Nasr Shimali, "al-Fariq bayna mu'askar abu ghurayb wa-mu'askar ushwitz," www.voltairenet.org/article136329.html.

in order to claim that Jews were not persecuted in Germany for being Jewish, but only if they opposed the regime, just as any other person.[68] 'Abd al-Qadir regards statements by former Nazi officials as absolutely reliable. Thus, he accepts the assertion by Hitler's foreign minister Joachim Ribbentrop at his trial in Nuremberg, and those of other senior Nazi officials, that they knew nothing about the killing of the Jews, as a convincing proof that such killings did not take place. Likewise, the Lebanese *al-Bilad* cites Louis Darquier de Pellepoix, the official responsible for Jewish policy in the collaborationist Vichy French government, who "proved" that the "imaginary massacres in the gas chambers and the imaginary extermination," were nothing but a "great historical lie."[69] In both cases the authors ignore the possibility that Ribbentrop and Pellepoix lied in order to avoid punishment. In contrast to the "reliable" Nazi assertions, Arab deniers, like their western colleagues, totally reject testimonies by survivors as being utterly fabricated and distorted.

By the same token and using the same arguments, Western and Arab deniers dismiss admissions by Nazi officials of their crimes. The Saudi writer 'Abdallah Kahtany contended in 2000 that the only evidence for the killing of Jews in Auschwitz was based on the confession of the camp commander Rudolf Höss, who was executed in 1946. But such testimony, as well as all confessions of other camps commanders, are totally unreliable and should not be used, he insists, explaining that they were extracted under severe torture, and they contradict the reports of professional and impartial experts such as Holocaust denier Fred Leuchter. Similarly, the Egyptian weekly *October* questioned Eichmann's admissions of his activities in his diary pending his execution, by referring to Holocaust denier David Irving.[70]

As their western counterparts, several Arab deniers rely on partial or invented statistical data to provide their claims a pseudo-scientific aura. In 1998 Wajih Abu Dhikra, a columnist and later editor of the Egyptian *al-Akhbar*, concluded from "UN statistics" that the number of Jews had actually increased by 300,000 during the war, while *al-Sharq al-Awsat* raised this figure to two

68   Nasr Shimali, "al-Qada al-yahud fi al-jaysh al-almani al-nazi," 6 May 2004, www.ara-brenewal.net/index.php?rd=AI&AI0=4073. See also readers' responses to 'Abd al-Wahhab al-Masiri's article on this issue, which view it as a decisive proof that the Holocaust was a hoax "Junud Naziyyun yahud," 16 January 2007, www.aljazeera.net/NR/exeres/1F29F6E0-0D3E-4332-B82E-31044645E852.htm.

69   *Alif Ba*, 5 July 1995; *al-Bilad*, 1 June 1990.

70   Abdallah Kahtany, *Zionism*, Riyad: 2000, pp. 30–3, 35, 95–7; Sa'd Khalif al-Balwi, "al-Hulukast: ukdhuba qamat 'alayha isra'il," www.adabihail.com/pages.php?pageid=61; *October*, 7 November 1999. An earlier article in the same weekly on 26 July 1992 described Irving as a historian who exonerated Hitler in his "well-documented" book from any responsibility for the Nazi crimes.

million. Neither of them produced these imaginary documentary sources.[71] Shaykh Muhammad Khidr questioned the "dubious" six million figure, based on an absurd demographic logic. If we assume, he contended, that each one of these millions had five family members, then the number of Jews alive during the war would have reached thirty million. Moreover, applying the same absurd calculation to the surviving Jews, he concluded that around sixty million Jews were supposed to have lived at the time, more than the overall German population. His conclusion, therefore, is that even if we divide the number of six million alleged victims by ten, it would still be a gross exaggeration.[72] Some Islamist writers explain the disappearance of European Jewry by conspiracy theory, according to which the Jewish leadership, which had planned World War II in advance, secretly removed the Jews, with their property, to the US, Palestine and other countries.[73]

Contradictory claims are not uncommon among deniers, stemming from their tendency to heap all possible accusations against Zionism and Israel. Natshe concludes his long exposé denying the extermination of the Jews by accusing the Zionists of collaborating with the Nazis in sending "hundreds of thousands" of Hungarian Jews to a sure death in Auschwitz. Muhammad Daud of the *Syria Times*, who describes the Holocaust as a lie, simultaneously accuses the Zionist leaders of refusing to allow Jewish immigrants to enter Palestine, thereby sentencing them to death "without hesitation" in the Nazi death camps.[74] Several writers who justified the Nazi persecution of the Jews contend in the same breath that the Jews exaggerated and overstated the severity of Nazi measures against them. Ahmad 'Attar, a prolific writer against Zionism who describes at length the immoral conduct of the Jews in Germany as the reason for German enmity towards them, maintains that "Hitler killed at the most several thousand Jews," but nowhere is it said "that he killed their children."[75]

71   *Al-Akhbar*, 24 July, 25 September 1998; *al-Sharq al-Awsat*, 2 May 2001. See also, 'Abdallah al-Najjar and Kamal al-Hajj, *al-Sahyuniyya bayna ta'rikhayn*, Beirut: 1972, pp. 57; Muradi, "al-Hulukast"; Dissuqi, *al-Harb al-'alamiyya*, pp. 249–51, 281, 283–4.

72   *Al-Akhbar*, 27 May 2001. Khidr disregards the basic fact that the six million figure included whole families, therefore his statistical extrapolation is groundless, and his attempt to refute the number of perished Jews based on an imaginary number of Jews defies any logic.

73   Sa'id Banaja, *Nazra hawla al-mu'amarat al-duwaliyya al-yahudiyya wa-asl al-thawrat*, Beirut: 1985, pp. 124–8; see a similar description in Sa'dani, *al-Fikr*, pp. 268–70.

74   Natshe, *al-Isti'mar*, p. 151; *Syria Times*, 6 September 2000. See also Kamal Sa'fan, who denies the Holocaust but accuses the Zionists of collaboration with the Nazis in the killing of 700,000 Hungarian Jews in *al-Yahud: ta'rikh wa-'aqida*, Cairo: 1988, p. 104. Lutfi Nasif in *al-Jumhuriyya*, 12 December 1987, 4 March 2000.

75   'Attar, *al-Yahudiyya*, pp. 159, 162–3. See similar justification and denial in Dissuqi and

Links between Arab and western deniers

Although western deniers have been interviewed and cited in the Arab media, institutionalized relations between them and political groups in the Arab world are rare. The most celebrated case was the reported contribution of £250,000 by Syrian President Bashar al-Assad to British Holocaust denier David Irving, according to the account of Ahmad Rami, a former officer in the Moroccan army of Islamist orientation who has lived as a political refugee in Sweden since 1973.[76] In 1987 Rami set up Radio Islam in Sweden, apparently enjoying Libyan and Iranian financial support, and disseminated anti-Semitic messages, including Holocaust denial. Radio Islam acquired great publicity outside Sweden, even though it was a local station. Following numerous denunciations in the Swedish press, Rami was tried in 1990 and sentenced to six months in prison for racial incitement. After his release he was invited to lecture in front of anti-Semitic and Holocaust denier groups in Europe, Canada and the US.[77]

During his December 1991 tour to the US Rami gave an interview to the heads of the Institute for Historical Review (IHR), the flagship of Holocaust deniers, subsequently broadcasted on Radio Islam. Both parties agreed that the Holocaust was a Zionist myth, and that World War II had broken out in order to advance Zionist goals. They also agreed on the need to liberate the West, the US and Germany from Jewish domination, which grew to a large extent from the memory of the Holocaust. Such liberation, achieved by debunking the Holocaust myth, would advance the liberation of Palestine. Rami did not only express his admiration for western deniers, but maintained that the Arabs should take an active part in it. In the early 1990s he was a lone voice. A decade later many more shared his view.[78] In November 1992 Rami attempted to convene the first 'Antizionist [sic] World Congress' in Stockholm. Among those invited were the notorious Holocaust deniers Faurisson, Zündel, Leuchter and David Irving. Following an uproar in Sweden, he was obliged to cancel the entire plan.[79]

Salman, *al-Sahyuniyya*, pp. 94–5; *al-Jumhuriyya*, 18 December 1985; Jarbu'a, *Tabri'at hitler*, throughout his book.

76   *Il-Folio*, 2 August 2001, cited in *Ma'ariv*, 2 August 2001.

77   *Ma'ariv*, 22 November 1997; Rami to *Maroc Hebdo International*, n.d., http//:abbc.com/mh/mh-eng.htm; Esther Webman and Sara Rembiszewski, "The unholy alliance between Muslim fundamentalists and Holocaust deniers," Occasional Paper, Tel Aviv: October 1993. Following his trial, Rami visited Iran and spoke before the Iranian parliament.

78   Radio Islam Broadcast, 13–14 December 1991, Swedish Committee against Anti-Semitism – Nizkor Project: Shofar FTP Archive File: people/d/duke.david/rami-interviews-ihr.

79   Nizkor Project: Shofar FTP Archive File: people/r/rami.ahmed/antizionist-congress.

In 1993 Rami was appointed as special correspondent for *al-Sha'b*, organ of the Egyptian opposition *al-'Amal* (Labor) party, which formerly had been associated with the ultra-nationalist Young Egypt Party and since the 1980s had assumed an Islamist line. In that capacity, he published interviews with Faurisson on 31 August and 14 September 1993, and with the Nazi general Ernst Otto Remer, who was also engaged in Holocaust denial.[80] Forced to shut down his radio station, Rami opened a 10-language internet website named Radio Islam dedicated to Holocaust denial.[81]

Rami was not the only Arab activist to hold contacts with the IHR. Magdi Husayn, editor of *al-Sha'b*, sent a congratulatory letter to IHR in 1998 expressing his appreciation for the institute's activity to "reassess and revise the historical record."[82] Issa Nakhle, a Palestinian lawyer residing in the US, former representative of the defunct Palestinian leadership body the AHC, and author of the *Encyclopaedia of the Palestinian Problem*,[83] published in *JHR* an open memorandum to then President Ronald Reagan urging him to change his policy towards Israel, which he compared to Nazi Germany. The IHR served as a distributor of Nakhle's encyclopedia.[84] In his response to Arab intellectuals who opposed the convening of a Holocaust denial conference in Beirut in 2001 (see Chapter 11), *JHR* editor Marc Weber specifically pointed to Nakhle and to the Palestinian writer, Sami Hadawi, as two Arab intellectuals who collaborated with his institution.[85] Likewise, the *Palestine Times* published an article written by the German Holocaust denier Michael Hoffman on "Zionist terrorism" in which he mentioned his book denying the Holocaust as part of the struggle against "intellectual Zionist terrorism."[86]

More important were the contacts between the IHR and Arab deniers in 2001 for convening a denial conference in Beirut and later Amman. 'Allush, who served as the organizer in Amman, gave an interview to the *JHR* in which he urged his interlocutors to make their research more accessible to the Arab public. He also

80   Webman and Rembiszewski, "The unholy alliance."

81   http://abbc.com/islam.

82   *JHR*, November–December 1994.

83   Published in New York, 1991.

84   Issa Nakhle, "Memorandum to the President," *JHR*, vol. 3, no. 3 (Fall 1982).

85   www.ihr.org/conference/beirutconf/010410mwletter.html.

86   *Palestine Times*, November 1996; *Arab News*, 16 July 2002, and IHR's response in www. ihr.org/news/newstoc.html. Weber's articles also appeared in the Arab website http:// ashahed2000.tripod.com/drasat/222–11.html, and were cited by the Bahraini daily *Akhbar al-Khalij*, 3 September 2005, and the Hamas website www.palestine-info.net/arabic/ terror/sijil/2005/malame7.htm. See also praise for the IHR in the semi-official Palestinian daily *al-Hayat al-Jadida*, 2 July 1998.

disseminated articles from the *JHR* on his website.[87] Whereas Rami and Nakhle were active among the Arab diaspora, 'Allush propagated his views in an Arab capital, and the relationships he forged with the IHR were not only as a private individual but as an activist in the Jordanian Writers Association and the Jordanian-based Association against Zionism and Racism (AZAR). Although Rami, Nakhle, Hadawi and 'Allush represent a limited phenomenon in the Arab world, they are not insignificant. By institutionalizing ties with the IHR, Rami served as an intermediary and a channel between western deniers and Arab audiences as well as an intermediary to European public opinion.

These trends created a common denominator between neo-Nazi movements and some Islamist circles, even though their origins were very different. For the neo-Nazis, this was a modern manifestation of age-old anti-Semitism, for the Islamists it stemmed from anti-Semitism born largely out of the Arab–Israeli conflict. During the 1990–91 Gulf crisis neo-Nazis held joint demonstrations with radical Islamists in some European cities, and some of them called for a change in the traditional right-wing views against the Arabs.[88]

Films and cinema

The power of the cinema to convey information and moral messages was perceived by participants in the Arab Holocaust discourse as an important component in the concerted Jewish/Zionist effort to produce, cultivate and control the myth of the Holocaust. Consequently, all Arab countries banned the screening of foreign films that dealt, even indirectly, with the Holocaust. Moreover, they criticized the West for showing and publicizing such movies. For Naji Sam'an, who reviewed the history of the "Zionist film industry," the American TV series *Shoah* shown in Europe and the US in 1978–79 had far greater influence on western public opinion, the main constituency of Zionist propaganda, than any documentary film on the fate of the Jews. The Egyptian weekly *October* described the series as part of a widespread propaganda effort conducted by Israel and "all Jewish production companies" on its thirtieth anniversary, in order to help then Prime Minister Menahem Begin to raise money during his visit to the

87   See *JHR*, "Conversation," and "An Anti-Holocaust Intifada Grows Among the Arabs," *JHR*, vol. 20, no. 3 (May/June 2001).

88   Goetz Nordbruch, "An Attempt to Internationalize the Denial of the Holocaust," *SICSA Annual Report* 2001, p. 9. See also the invitation of the neo-Nazi activist William W. Baker to be the keynote speaker at the Islam Awareness Week held by the University of Pennsylvania's Muslim Student Association on 9 October 2003; *FrontPage Magazine*, 9 October 2003.

US, which took place at that time.[89] All Arab ambassadors in Greece, except the Egyptian, protested the screening of *Shoah* on Greek TV in April 1979.[90]

After watching the documentary French film *Shoah* by Claude Lanzmann, the Egyptian columnist Muhsin Hasan reached the conclusion that the Israeli intelligence services were behind the film's production in providing the necessary financial backing and technical equipment. He also enumerated *The Diary of Anne Frank* (1959), *Sophie's Choice* (1982) and the TV series *Shoah* among similar films behind which Israel allegedly stood. Hasan challenged the facts shown in the film, accusing Lanzmann of using "sophisticated techniques" to force the viewers to shed tears, to convince them that six million Jews had indeed been killed and that the Jewish problem was still pertinent. He also charged the director of diverting the viewers' anger against the Palestinians, rather than against Hitler, expressing his frustration that the extermination of the Jews received so much coverage even though it was totally outdated and highly exaggerated, whereas the Palestinian problem, which was very much alive, did not get any cinematic coverage at all.[91]

Egypt, for its part, banned in 1984 the screening of Edward Dimitryk's documentary on anti-Semitism *The Human Factor* and the movie *Sophie's Choice*, for representing "the same themes which the Zionists use to describe persecution of the Jews."[92] Steven Spielberg's movie *Schindler's List* was also banned in all Arab countries, including Egypt, for containing numerous "scenes of violence and seduction." The *Egyptian Gazette* explained that the film defended the Jewish claim so as to justify the occupation of Arab lands. Most critics described it as a racist and biased movie, part of the Zionist war effort to influence world conscience. The Qatari daily *al-Sharq* contended that *Schindler's List* sought to make the West believe that Hitler had indeed "burned the Jews in the crematoria," thus rendering the lie of the Jewish tragedy a concrete reality.[93] For Moroccan Islamist leader 'Abd al-Salam Yassine [Yasin], the film was a prime example of the pro-Israel Hollywood bias, where "Jewish production," "Jewish money"

89   Sam'an, "Banuramat al-'unf," p. 245; *October*, 14 May 1978; Ra'uf Tawfiq, *Sinimat al-yahud: dumu' wa-khanajir*, Cairo: 1997, pp. 7–11, 21–45.

90   Lewis, *Semites and Anti-Semites*, pp. 16, 218.

91   *Al-Masa'*, 5 January 1986. See a similar criticism in Muhammad 'Abidu, "al-Sahayina wal-hulukast cinima'iyyan," *al-Hiwar al-Mutamaddin*, no. 1534, 28 April 2006, www.rezgar.com/debat/show.art.asp?aid=63372.

92   *Al-Wafd*, 29 March 1984. The documentary's name in Arabic was *al-Aswad al-sighar* [The Little Blacks].

93   Esther Webman, "Arab countries and the Maghreb" in Dina Porat and Roni Stauber (eds.) *Anti-Semitism Worldwide, 1994*, Tel Aviv: 1995, p. 160; *al-Sharq*, 11 March 1999. See also *al-Bayan*, 1 March 2002.

and Jewish talent joined together to honor the mythological Schindler, while ignoring his widow's protests.[94]

Filastin al-Muslima, Hamas official organ, compared *Schindler's List* to Spielberg's *Jurassic Park*, in which he sought to re-enact the past by combining imaginary story and invented scientific background with true historical events. In *Schindler's List*, the reviewer said, Spielberg had invented a "new dinosaur" to keep the world attracted for a whole year. He had entered this adventure in order to "re-enact the vision of a Holocaust, which exists in western imagination (*khiyal*)." He presented the Holocaust, the writer complained, as if it were a singular event, ignoring other holocausts such as in Bosnia and Kurdistan. Still, the writer drew one positive lesson from the film, worthy of imitation by the Palestinians – the importance of memory in the human experience. As an example of Jewish control, Naji Sam'an complained that no film describing the massacres of the Roma was ever produced, even though the number of their victims by far exceeded that of the Jews.[95] Egyptian movie producer Munir Radi announced in March 2001 the production of a motion picture based on the best-selling book *Matzah of Zion*, as the "Arab response" to *Schindler's List*. Written by then Syrian Defense Minister Mustafa Tlas in 1973, it describes the 1840 Damascus blood libel against the Jews as a true historical event.[96]

Roberto Benigni's 1999 film *Life is Beautiful* was also banned in all Arab countries, and some newspaper columnists accused it of presenting the Jews as Hitler's sole victims. Egyptian film critic Samir Farid, who cautiously criticized the prevailing Arab approach toward such films, agreed that the undue preoccupation with Jewish victimhood was intended to justify Israel's existence, but he opposed banning them. The proper Arab humanist attitude should denounce the persecution of Jews as well as any religious or racial persecution and the ban

94   Bruce Maddy-Weitzman, "Islamism, Moroccan-Style: The Ideas of Sheikh Yassine," *Middle East Quarterly*, vol. 10, no. 1 (Winter 2003), p. 50.

95   *Filastin al-Muslima*, April 1994. Sam'an, "Banuramat al-'unf," p. 245. The latest (1997) figure from the U.S. Holocaust Memorial Research Institute in Washington puts the number of Romani [Gypsies] murdered by 1945 at between 500,000 and 1,500,000. See Ian Hancock, "Genocide of the Roma in the Holocaust," in www.geocities.com/~Patrin/holcaust.htm.

96   *Ruz al-Yusuf*, 24 February 2001 – Memri, Special Dispatch Series no. 190, 1 March 2001; *al-Hayat*, 21 October 2002 reported the publication of the book's eighth edition. Tlas denied the book was anti-Semitic, insisting it described a well-documented historical fact of Jewish ritual murder. See *al-Sharq al-Awsat*, 10 August 2003 – Memri, Special Dispatch Series, No. 566, 4 September 2003. For an historical analysis of the Damascus blood libel, which preceded Zionism by 50 years, see Frankel, *The Damascus Affair*.

did not serve the Arab cause. The Arabs would do better to produce their own movies so as to debunk Zionist propaganda, he concluded.[97]

Jewish control over knowledge of the Holocaust

A recurring theme in Arab writing is the alleged Jewish effort to control the flow of information on the Holocaust, and the Jews' success in constructing and disseminating their false narrative throughout the world, thanks to their control of the world media.[98] In a case of psychological projection of their own activities, some deniers accuse the Jews of employing the cynical slogan of the Nazi propaganda minister Joseph Goebbels, that the repetition of a lie would eventually lead people to believe it. The Holocaust became a "European icon," Ismahan Shurayh concluded, while Jarbu'a complained that the Jews were so successful in their propaganda that they managed to instill in the minds of the Germans that Hitler was a criminal.[99]

One of the major means which the Zionists used to create the Holocaust lie, the United Arab Emirates' *al-Bayan* stated, was a "literary cultural framework" in order to make it "a continuously living idea." They exerted great efforts to endow the Holocaust with cultural importance and a central place in European and world history by imposing Holocaust literature on schools and universities throughout Europe and the US.[100] According to the Zayed Center, the Zionists produced dozens of literary and artistic works on the Holocaust by famous Jewish and non-Jewish authors that dealt with the topic in accordance with the Zionist point of view. Even the Nobel Prize was used to serve the Zionist Holocaust industry when it was awarded to Nellie Zachs for her poetry on the Holocaust in 1968 and to Elie Wiesel for his books on the same theme in 1986. Art in general and the theater in particular had become important means in this Zionist effort, the Center claimed. These effective means turned the myths, the

97   *Al-Jumhuriyya*, 31 March 1999; Esther Webman, *Anti-Semitism Worldwide, 1999/2000*, p. 185.

98   See for example Michael Saba, an Arab-American lawyer, who while challenging the six million figure complained that Jewish pressures were so successful that the Holocaust became as important as sports lessons in Illinois schools, *al-Hayat*, 21–22 October 1989.

99   Shurayh, "al-Hulukast"; Jarbu'a, *Tabri'at hitler*, p. 23. See also 'Abd al-Rahim Nasrallah, *Imbiraturiyyat al-fawda wa-hulukast al-'iraq* reviewed in http://iraqk.com/modules.php?name=News&file=article&sid=3321.

100   *Al-Bayan*, 1 March 2002. The article reviews the pirate translation and publication by the ZCCF of Ben Ami Feingold's book *The Holocaust in Hebrew Drama*, Tel Aviv: 1989. The Zayed Center changed the book's name to *Zionist Literature and the Holocaust Industry* and added an introduction explaining the motivations and means used by the Zionist "industry." Memri, Special Report, no. 16, 16 May; Memri, 20 May 2003 (Hebrew), www.memri.org.

lies and the false Israeli claims into faked facts that influence the mind so much that viewers and readers become prisoners of the ideas implanted there.[101]

Moreover, according to this view, the Zionists fought with all their might against anyone who dared to cast doubt on the Holocaust, and succeeded in blocking all authentic data that would challenge their narrative. Muhammad Khayr al-Wadi, editor of *Tishrin*, accused Israel of resorting to "ideological and physical terrorism" by using the myth of the Holocaust "as a sword hanging over the necks of all those who oppose Zionism." For Fayiz al-Sayigh, director general of the Syrian News Agency, the 2000 Stockholm Conference "turned the Holocaust into school textbook material for the coming generations of [the participant countries] and set an annual memorial service in which they would kneel in front of the Holocaust memorial, despite the problematic historical nature of the Holocaust."[102] Similarly, 'Abd al-Wahhab Badrakhan, an editorial board member of *al-Hayat*, resented the fact that the excessive appearance of the Holocaust in the media would be transferred to the schools. Considering the conference a rebirth of the "Holocaust business," he depicted Holocaust studies as "an injection in the blood or brains" of the students, and expressed his concern that the Holocaust would be taught in European schools without allowing the children to "ask questions, to examine the data, and use their common sense to accept or reject them."[103] Concurrently, 'Abdallah Al Malihi reported in *al-Watan* that "hundreds of people" were incarcerated in the West for "exposing the truth about the fabricated Jewish propaganda," while the Iraqi 'Abd al-Rahim Nasrallah claimed that "historians and scholars" were actually murdered or destroyed psychologically for questioning the Holocaust.[104]

Praising Lebanon's Foreign Minister Faris Buwayz for accusing Israel of intolerable commercialization of the Holocaust, the Bahraini columnist 'Abd al-Malik Sulayman accused Israel and the Zionists of "launching a terror campaign" against anyone who avoided visiting the memorial sites of the "so-called Holocaust," whether in Israel or elsewhere. Arab leaders complained, he added, that they were forced to participate in Holocaust-related ceremonies, despite

101   Cited in *al-Bayan*, 1 March 2002.

102   *Al-Hayat*, 1 February, Syrian News Agency, 31 January; *al-Thawra*, 2 February 2000; *al-Ba'th*, 7 February, in Memri, Special Dispatch Series, nos. 71 and 72, 2, 14 February 2000; *al-Ushu' al-Adabi*, 24 February 2000.

103   *Al-Hayat*, 30 January 2000.

104   *Al-Watan*, 9 December 2001, 28 December 2005; Darraj, "al-Talfiq." See also *al-Hayat*, 30, 31 January, *al-Ayyam*, 2 February, *October*, 10 December 2000; Haytham al-Kaylani, *al-Irhab yu'assisu dawla: namudhaj isra'il*, Beirut: 1997, p. 11. Nasrallah, *Imbiraturiyyat al-fawda*. The writers apparently refer to a series of laws passed in Europe banning Holocaust denial.

their "grave doubts about the veracity of the crime."[105] Other writers called for a concerted Arab effort to publish and distribute those studies that refuted the Holocaust myth, and to set up internet websites that would "highlight the truth," as opposed to the Zionist websites that spread lies and fabrications.[106]

Even writers who are partially critical of the deniers' methodology present them as freedom fighters, treated unjustly by intolerant governments. Zayd Nabulsi, a Jordanian lawyer working in Geneva, expressed reservations about the deniers' haggling over the number of Jews who had perished, when most of them conceded that "hundreds of thousands of Jews" died as a result of German "siege," "deportation" and maltreatment. Yet, he complained that in France, Germany and Switzerland "any slight deviation outside the officially scripted version of this episode in history" [i.e., the Holocaust] would end up in court. Describing the measures taken against Holocaust deniers as "a medieval form of censorship," he stated that the persecution and silencing of revisionist historians in the West would be remembered as one of the most "shameful blemishes to ever tarnish Western liberal democracies."[107]

Parallel to accusing the Jews of silencing all challenges to the hegemonic narrative on the Holocaust, various Arab circles sought to foil efforts to commemorate it in international events, dubbing them as Zionist propaganda. In 1978 Iraq issued a formal protest to the Communist Polish government, itself an opponent of Zionism, for holding ceremonies for the "so-called Warsaw Ghetto revolt," and the death of Polish Jews during the war.[108] Various Egyptian newspapers denounced British Prime Minister Margaret Thatcher for visiting Israel's Holocaust memorial in June 1986. Muhsin Muhammad, in *al-Jumhuriyya*, ridiculed Thatcher for publicly "shedding tears," so rare an occasion for her, precisely at her visit to the Yad Vashem Museum, which preserves, "according to Israel's allegation," the "memory of Jewish extermination." *October* criticized her kneeling in front of "what they call the memorial for Holocaust victims" as the "epitome of hypocrisy."[109]

When the New York City Council decided in 1992 to include Holocaust studies in its school curriculum, Dr. Muhammad Mahdi, president of the American–Arab Relations Committee, denounced the decision as a Zionist attempt to

105 *Akhbar al-Khalij* cited in *Mideast Mirror*, 6 April 1998. See similar claims in *al-Jumhuriyya*, 5 June 1986; *al-Hayat*, 8–9 July 1989; *al-Watan*, 9 February 1995; *al-Ayyam*, 2 February 2000; and *Akhir Sa'a*, 25 April 2001.
106 Al-Balwi, "al-Hulukast"; Anon, "Akbar ukdhuba ta'rikhiyya."
107 *Jordan Times*, 26 May 2001.
108 Lewis, *Semites and anti-Semites*, p. 218.
109 *Al-Jumhuriyya*, 9 June, *October*, 15 June 1986.

use the New York educational system for cheap propaganda purposes.[110] In May 2001, the Egyptian pharmacists' association declared a boycott on the products of the American pharmaceutical company Elie Lillie for supplying free medication against schizophrenia to Holocaust survivors living in Israel.[111]

The Palestinian Hamas movement issued an official condemnation against the 2000 Stockholm Conference, aimed at "fabricating history by hiding the truth" about the unfounded so-called Holocaust. The Zionist entity used "psychological and ideological terrorism" through the conference and the "Nazi Holocaust story," the statement asserted, and urged the participating states to renounce their "sympathetic understanding of Zionist arrogance and continuing blackmail." It further called upon all "the free scholars of the world" not to fear "the Jews and their ideological terrorism," through which "they shut mouths and prevent objective, unbiased scholars from exposing the Zionist claims as lies."[112]

Relativizing Jewish suffering

A subtle expression of denial raised by spokesmen of all political trends, which appeared even prior to 1948, did not deny the persecution or massacres of the Jews, but blurred the uniqueness and significance of the Holocaust as a genocide, presenting Jewish suffering as nothing worse than that of other peoples during the war. Thus, in a speech in March 1965 Egyptian President 'Abd al-Nasir pointed to allegations that Jews had suffered at the hands of Germany during World War II, but immediately asked rhetorically, "Did only the Jews suffer? The Czechs suffered, the Yugoslavs suffered, the French suffered." Since it was obvious to him, and probably to his audience, that the French or the Czechs were not exterminated, the clear message was that the same was true for the Jews.[113]

---

110   Kenneth Stern, *Holocaust Denial*, New York: 1993, pp. 49–50.

111   Elli Wohlgelernter, "In a state of denial," *Jerusalem Post*, 10 June 2001.

112   Press Release, on the "Stockholm Conference Concerning the so-Called Jewish Holocaust," 3 February 2000; Reuven Paz, "Palestinian Holocaust Denial," *The Washington Institute: Policy Watch*, no. 255, 21 April 2000. The original article appeared in Arabic on the Hamas official website, Palestine-info.org, and was not translated into English, presumably because the editors realized it could harm Hamas' reputation among non-Arabs. See also the article by 'Abd al-'Aziz al-Rantisi, Hamas leader in the Gaza Strip, a few months before his assassination in March 2004, denying the Holocaust. *Al-Risala*, 21 August 2003.

113   Cited in Harkabi, *Arab Attitudes*, p. 278. *Al-Ahram* correspondent Kamal Naguib raised a similar claim following his visit to Auschwitz in 1955, when he described the mass extermination that took place there without mentioning that most victims had been Jews. *Al-Ahram*, 31 May 1955. See also Dr. Sayyid Nawfal of the Academy of Islamic Research in D. F. Green (pseudonym) (ed.), *Arab Theologians on Jews and Israel: Extracts from the*

Butrus Butrus-Ghali took in 1960 a more relativist approach. Sharing his impressions of his visit to Auschwitz with al-*Ahram* readers, he described it as "the biggest Nazi detention camp, which Communism had turned into a propaganda museum," showing Nazi atrocities and crimes against humanity. However, in response to a question from the Auschwitz museum director about his impressions, Butrus-Ghali replied that he had read many books on the Nazi detention camps, and now saw them live, but wondered why there were no similar museums to commemorate British and French detention camps in Kenya or Algeria, and the tortures that took place there. He added that he saw no reason to get into a futile argument with the director, who insisted that there was a significant difference between those camps and Auschwitz, which had been designed for mass extermination.[114]

Filastin al-Thawra and *al-Hurriyya*, the organ of the DFLP, adopted from the 1970s onward the Soviet position of blurring the Jewish identity of the victims in a series of articles on the victory over Fascism. A story on Maidanek reported that the Nazis imprisoned men, women and children from fifty-one cities in the camp, without mentioning that they were Jews. Another story dealing with the Nazi attack on the Soviet Union told that the Nazis carried out genocide, but the implication was that they aimed at the Soviet people, totally ignoring the Jews.[115] In a somewhat different vein, *al-Hayat* attached the famous picture of a fearful Jewish boy from the Warsaw Ghetto raising his hands in front of armed SS men to a story on the 1944 Warsaw rebellion of the Polish *Armia Krajowa* (The Homeland Army) against the Nazis. Setting the picture in this context obliterated its association with the Jewish tragedy, thereby denying the specificity of Jewish suffering and presenting the fate of the Jews as part of the general Polish suffering.[116]

Mahmud 'Abbas explained that forty million people from various nationalities were killed during the war. "The German people *sacrificed* [emphasis added] ten millions, the Soviet people twenty million people," and other nations smaller

proceedings of the Fourth Conference of the Academy of Islamic Research, Geneva: 1971, p. 55; 'Abd al-Wahhab al-Masiri, *Nihayat al-ta'rikh: dirasat fi bunyat al-fikr al-Sahyuni*, Beirut: 1979, p. 29; Tamimi, "Questions"; *al-Hayat*, 20 March 1997; 'Abd al-Malik Sulayman in *Akhbar al-Khalij*, cited in *Mideast Mirror*, 6 April 1998 and Khayr al-Wadi in *Tishrin*, 31 January 2001.

114   *Al-Ahram*, 17 March 1960.

115   *Filastin al-Thawra*, 13, 20 April, 18 May 1981, 13 October 1984; *al-Hurriyya*, 1 February 1987. See also DFLP leader Naif Hawatima, "al-Sahyuniyya wa-sina'at al-karitha," *al-Hiwar al-Mutamaddin*, no. 1204, 21 May 2005, www.rezgar.com/debat/show.art. asp?aid=37761; *al-Masa'*, 6 April 1990.

116   *Al-Hayat*, 4 October 1999.

figures. Yet, he added, after the war it was announced that six million Jews were among the victims, and that the war of annihilation had been aimed first of all against the Jews, and only then against the rest of the people of Europe.[117] In other words, not only did he put German casualties as higher than those of the Jews (which they were not), but he placed them on an equal if not a higher moral standing by describing them as a sacrifice, while Jewish losses were only alleged.

Masiri, who zig-zagged over the number of Jewish victims, accepted in 1983 the claim that the Nazis exterminated Jews, but qualified it in two major points. The Nazi plan, he argued, echoing to some degree the neo-Marxist Franz Neuman, was aimed originally at "superfluous Slavic elements," in accordance with their Darwinian world-view, and consequently, the Nazis had to deport or eliminate millions of Slavs. Masiri insisted that the extermination of the Jews was not one of the Nazis' strategic goals during the war, but rather a by-product of their anti-Slavic policy. Therefore, he concluded, millions of Slavs were murdered, in numbers far exceeding those of the Jews, "even if we believe the false number of 6,000,000."[118]

In a subsequent book, published in the 1990s, Masiri rejected the excessive preoccupation with the number of Jewish victims, but argued that their extermination was no different than any other massacre which the West had carried out against Third World peoples. He described the relationships between the Jews in the Warsaw and Terezienstadt ghettos and the Germans as similar to the relationships of any Third World country with imperialist countries, and those of the Palestinian Authority with Israel.[119] Elsewhere, Masiri explained that the western focus on the killing of the Jews by the "gentiles" and the omission of the deaths of others at the hands of the Nazis was part of a broader conspiracy against the Arabs, designed to legitimize the West's decision, through the UN, to compensate only the Jews by usurping Palestine from the Arabs and giving it to the Jews.[120]

---

117 'Abbas, al-Wajh al-akhar, pp. b, g., where he claims that only around 800,000 may have perished. See also Fa'iq Fahim, "al-'Alaqat al-khassa bayna almaniya wa-isra'il," www.aleqtisadiah.com/article.php?do=show&id=1021, who also presents the Germans as the true victims of Hitler, because they had lost nine million people as a result of his policies.

118 'Abd al-Wahhab al-Masiri, "al-Ibada al-jima'iyya lil-yahud: asbabuha al-ta'rikhiyya wal-hadariyya," Shu'un Filastiniyya, no. 183 (June 1988), pp. 60–1. Idem, Nihayat al-ta'rikh, p. 29. In his later article "al-I'lam al-'arabi," he once again rejected the number of six million as a Zionist lie. For Neuman's views, see Shlomo Aronson, Hitler, the Allies, and the Jews, Cambridge: 2004, p. 96.

119 Masiri, al-Sahyuniyya, pp. 160–3.

120 Cited in Shurayh, "al-Hulukast."

188

'Abd al-Salam Yassine espoused a similar line. Yassine does not deny the enormity of the evil perpetrated by Hitler. He even acknowledges that Jews experienced a "massacre." However, he complains bitterly that the Jews somehow managed to manipulate the world through guilt into giving them special treatment. In doing so and turning on those who defeated Germany and accusing them of complicity in the massacre of Jews, the Zionist leadership "proved their Hitlerian parallel". Why is Hitler seen only as the murderer of Jews, he demands to know, when fifty million persons died in World War II, twenty million in the Soviet Union alone?[121]

Ismahan Shurayh pushed the relativization of the Holocaust a little further by putting it into a global context. In addition to disputing the six million figure, she insisted that Hitler's policy against the Jews was not genocide because it did not differ from what Western imperialists had done in the past 500 years to the native peoples of America and Africa, who had perished in much greater numbers than the Jews.[122]

As an implicit competition for victimhood was part of the Arab–Israeli conflict, the Islamist Tijani Bul'awali applied the usual statistical manipulations to claim that the Jews had inflated their losses, while insisting that they were dwarfed as compared with the Muslim victims of massacres and genocides throughout history. Among the latter he contended that 500,000 Muslims perished during the Crusades; one million in the 1258 Mongol conquest of Baghdad; three million under British and French imperialism. While most of his data on Muslim casualties cannot be verified or were patently false (e.g., one million in the rebellions against the Ottoman Empire), he blurred the difference between casualties in wars and victims of genocides.[123]

In a scholarly article on the legal and historical definitions of genocides, Muhammad Rif'at al-Imam acknowledged the Holocaust as genocide. Yet he complained of the "tyranny of the Holocaust" and its "sanctification," whereby any attempt to compare it with other, even worse cases of genocide, was subject to accusations of "betraying Jewish history."[124] In a more passionate vein,

121 Maddy-Weitzman, "Islamism," p. 50. See also, *Tishrin*, 31 January 2000 – Memri, Special Dispatch Series, no. 71, 2 February 2000.

122 Shurayh, "al-Hulukast."

123 Anon, "Mantiq al-ibada aw al-khuruj 'ala al-fitra," www.alqlm.com/index.cfm?method=home.con&contentID=305. See similar claims in Dissuqi, *al-Harb*, pp. 283–4; Dissuqi and Salman, *al-Sahyuniyya*, pp. 94–5; Nawfal in Green, *Arab Theologians*, p. 55; 'Abd al-Malik Sulayman in *Akhbar al-Khalij*, cited in Mideast Mirror, 6 April 1998; Tamimi, "Questions."

124 Mahmud Rif'at al-Imam, "Ibadat al-jins: nash'at al-mafhum wa-mu'adalat al-tatbiq," *al-Siyasa al-Duwaliyya*, no. 151 (January 2002), pp. 63–5.

an article on the PNA website lambasts the Zionist "pimps of Holocaustism," whose focus only on the suffering of the Jewish people" reveals "what are the racist, exclusivist, self-absorbed sentiments which form the operating ideologies of their agenda."[125]

Implicit denial

Denial sometimes appeared implicitly in various contexts. Occasionally, it appeared when attributing Nazi conduct to Israel or to the US, coupled with condemnation of the Nazis and their activities, while in fact it belittled the evil of Nazism and its actual policies. Muhammad al-Sammak, a columnist in *al-Ahram*, raised doubts over the "crematoria theory," contending that [death camp] Treblinka may have existed, but al-Khiyam camp (where the Israeli-backed South Lebanese army held prisoners under tough conditions prior to the Israeli pull-out from Lebanon in June 2000) certainly existed. It was possible that Auschwitz witnessed great massacres, he added, but so did Qana in South Lebanon.[126] Thus, Treblinka, where around 730,000 Jews were gassed, became no more than a harsh detention camp, while Auschwitz was transformed into a massacre site not much worse than an accidental shelling of a Lebanese village. For the Syrian *Tishrin*, Israel, which presented itself as the heir of the Holocaust victims, carried out much graver atrocities than the Nazis, who never drove a whole people to exile nor buried people alive, as the Zionists supposedly did.[127]

Even more forthright was Egyptian pro-Islamist columnist Dr. Rif'at Sayyid Ahmad, a contributor to the Lebanese Islamic periodical *al-Liwa'*. Describing the US military base Guantanamo, where al-Qa'ida prisoners were held following the US war against the Taliban in Afghanistan, as the "Auschwitz of the American era," he charged that by its maltreatment of the prisoners the US carried out worse crimes than those committed at the original camp and had created "another Auschwitz, at the beginning of the new century." Auschwitz, he reminded his readers, "is the detention camp in which, allegedly, Hitler burned Jews in gas chambers during World War II." The senior Egyptian journalist Anis Mansur also regarded the US treatment of the Afghan prisoners as "worse

---

125 Mark Glenn, "One less than six million," www.ipc.gov.ps/ipc_e/ipc_e-1/e_Articles/2004/articles-008.html. Although the author is not a Palestinian, the inclusion of the article in an official website renders it part of the Palestinian discourse on the Holocaust.

126 *Al-Ahram*, 16 February 2000. Qana is a village in southern Lebanon where more than 100 Lebanese civilians were accidentally killed during an Israeli shelling in 1996.

127 *Tishrin*, 31 January 2000. See a similar argument in *al-Akhbar*, 2 April 1999; *Sawt al-Haqq wal-Hurriyya*, 30 April 1993.

than what Hitler had done to his Christian and Jewish rivals," implying that the Jews merely suffered from harsh prison conditions.[128]

Omission also plays a role of denial. A Lebanese history textbook for high school students published in 1980 excluded any discussion on the Nazis, their ideology and policy towards the Jews in its short reference to World War II. Another history textbook discusses the nationalistic racist and violent essence of Nazism, but only mentions briefly that the Nazi party advocated the electoral disenfranchisement of the Jews. Concurrently, it provides a lengthy description of Nazi persecution of the Catholic Church in Germany and Catholic resistance to Hitler. The sections devoted to the war do not mention the Jews at all, while the section on Zionism explains only that the war gave a significant economic boost to the Jewish community in Palestine and enabled the Zionist movement to advance its political aims.[129]

Conclusions

Denial has been the most pervasive theme in the Arab Holocaust discourse since the 1950s, with the aim of delegitimizing Zionism and Israel. Therefore, it has appeared in all Arab countries and among all political trends with varying nuances. Likewise, it has been articulated in a variety of techniques and multiple contexts, not all of them associated with the conflict.

The arguments which the Arab deniers have employed have become more sophisticated over the years, borrowing heavily from western deniers with the aim of lending them a pseudo-scholarly aura. Yet, as is the case with the western deniers, Arab denial is not the product of ignorance, but is rather, based on distortion of existing data or the fabrication of non-existent evidence. It is often voiced together with dismay, frustration and anger at the growing importance of the Holocaust in western political and cultural discourse, attributing this development to all-pervasive Jewish or Zionist manipulations and power.

In recent years, two seemingly contradictory developments in the denial discourse have become more salient. The first saw the publication of books and pseudo-scholarly studies fully devoted to denial and containing a wide range of arguments and so-called "proofs," alongside the articulation of a coherent ideology whose main spokesman was the Palestinian-Jordanian Ibrahim 'Allush, explaining the necessity of denial. Concurrently, a growing number of Arab writers acknowledge the Holocaust as a historical fact, while raising qualifica-

---

128   *Al-Liwa'*, 21 February, *al-Ahram*, 26 January 2002.

129   Husayn 'Ali Khallaq, *al-Wajiz fi ta'rikh al-'alam al-mu'asir*, Beirut, 1980, pp. 85–7; Dr. Bishri Qubaysi and Musa Makhul, *al-Hurub wal-azamat al-iqlimiyya fi al-qarn al-'ishrin: uruba, asia*, Beirut: 1997, pp. 77–88, 188, 192–3.

tions as to the number of Jews who perished, the Nazi policy of targeting the Jews for extermination, and the distinction between the nature and scope of the Jewish tragedy and the suffering of other peoples during the war. Yet, it should be stressed that in the historical and philosophical scholarship of the Holocaust, all of these reservations are tantamount to denial.

A crucial point is the measure of popular reception and acceptance of the denial theme. A major factor facilitating widespread reception has been the absence for many years of counter-arguments acknowledging the Holocaust, except indirectly, by justifying Hitler's policies or by blaming the Zionists for the Holocaust. Conversely, the Arab media indulged in disseminating Holocaust denial, thus making the public at large oblivious of the historical facts. The scope of Holocaust denial, the variety of means of dissemination and the multiple contexts in which they appear are in themselves an indication of reception, as the various Arab writers repeat earlier arguments reflecting their own reception and convictions. While readers' letters in the press regarding the Holocaust are extremely rare, internet forums may serve as an indicator, although exposure to the internet in the Arab world is not widespread and those who participate in such forums may represent more radical views than the mainstream. One important indication is the survey of Arab public opinion which Hilal Kashan, political science professor at the American University of Beirut, conducted in 1999 among 1,600 Lebanese, Syrian, Jordanian and Palestinian interviewees on their attitudes toward Israel and peace. Of the 1,291 persons (82.3 percent), who stated that they felt no empathy toward the Jews, particularly victims of the Holocaust, 634 (53 percent) justified their position by denying that the Holocaust ever took place.[130] Moreover, in a 2007 survey of Palestinian Israelis, who are much more exposed to the Israeli discourse on the Holocaust, over 28 percent denied its occurrence.[131] In other words, the psychological barrier to recognizing the victimhood of the adversary in a situation of protracted conflict is still powerful, despite massive exposure to data.

---

130   Hilal Kashan, *Arab Attitudes toward Israel and Peace*, Washington Institute Research Memorandum no. 40, Washington: August 2000, p. 44.

131   Reuters, 20 March 2007.

6

THE UNFINISHED JOB – JUSTIFICATION
OF THE HOLOCAUST

The retrospective justification of the Nazi extermination or, to use the more common Arab term, persecution (*idtihad*) of the Jews, represented the opposite extreme to denial in the range of themes of the Arab Holocaust discourse. It was also one of the most radical expressions of animosity towards the Israelis, projected on the Jewish people as a whole in the post-1948 Arab "culture of defeat" – a sense of humiliation and an urge for revenge against the enemy developed by nations and societies that suffered serious military defeats. By portraying the Jews as a diabolical and all-powerful Machiavellian force, such description also helped the various writers and their readers comprehend or explain the 1948 defeat.[1]

As a result, there was a growing perception in the Arab world during the 1950s and 1960s of the conflict as an existential one that necessitated the elimination of Israel as a state. The theme of Holocaust justification stemmed from the need to explain and rationalize such a radical position. The basic premise was that only a people who were inherently malicious and whose culture and historical roots were immersed in evil could commit the grave injustice of usurping Palestine from its rightful inhabitants. Therefore, the logical conclusion was that the Jewish fate in the Holocaust was a just and deserving punishment for past and present deeds. It also served to further refute Jewish claims to Palestine on the basis of their suffering elsewhere, by providing historical justification for their predicament. Muhammad Jarbu'a, for instance, explains in the introduction to his *Exonerating Hitler* that his reason for writing the book, which both

---

1   Wolfgang Schivelbusch, *The Culture of Defeat: On National Trauma, Mourning, and Recovery*, New York: 2001, pp. 1–37. For broader analyses of the Arab responses to the defeat see Fouad Ajami, *The Arab predicament: Arab Political Thought and Practice since 1967*, Cambridge: 1982; idem, *The Dream Palace of the Arabs: A Generation's Odyssey*, New York: 1998; Issa J. Boullata, *Trends and Issues in Contemporary Arab Thought*, Albany: 1990.

justifies Hitler's anti-Jewish measures and denies the Holocaust (see above), is the call "kill the Jews wherever they are."[2]

"A people who does not know how to hate will not know how to win," wrote the conservative Palestinian politician Anwar al-Khatib in 1955, reflecting the fury and frustration of his people. Hatred (*hiqd*) of one's enemy is essential for achieving victory in war. He referred to Germany's response to the Versailles Treaty and Hitler's hatred of the Jews as the best model for harnessing hatred in the service of national recuperation after defeat. Citing heavily from Hitler's *Mein Kampf* to describe the inherent evil of the Jews, Khatib charged with vehemence:

God have mercy on Hitler. He knew the Jews and described them well; he revealed their wickedness (*lu'm*) and excelled in hating them …

Undoubtedly, the advocates of civility, universalism and peace will loathe those who call to pity Hitler, and will abhor my call for "hatred" and will disparage such calls as reactionary. To those I say, look at the Arabs of Palestine … look how they were and what is their current state and then judge.

God have mercy on Hitler … each time we wish to hate the Jews and detest them there is no better option than to turn to his book *Mein Kampf* to enhance our knowledge of that accursed people and light the fire of enmity (*baghda*) in our hearts.[3]

Khatib's glorification of hatred and presentation of Hitler's enmity to the Jews as the model to be followed reflect in a nutshell the logic behind the justification of the Holocaust in the Arab discourse. Blaming the drastic act of annihilating the Jews on their own alleged criminal activities and character was the ultimate form of demonization born out of the conflict, which did not distinguish between Zionists and Jews. Justifying Nazi hatred of the Jews was supposed to provide the definitive answer to the inherent Jewish character and mode of behavior. It provided the demonization of the Jews with "objective historical" validation by showing that the Arabs were not alone in detesting the Jews for the crimes which the latter had perpetrated, but were in fact part of a broader historical phenomenon.

Concurrently, in describing Jewish history as an uninterrupted sequence of persecutions, the Arab writers accepted, inadvertently, a common Jewish

---

2   Jarbu'a, *Tabri'at hitler*, pp. 6–7. All citations from this book in this chapter are taken from the Beirut edition. Significantly, the Riyad edition did not include the above passage.

3   *Filastin*, 27 August 1955. Khatib served in various administrative and ministerial positions in the Jordanian government and was Jordanian governor of the Jerusalem district from 1965. See also Nasir al-Nashashibi's candid admission that he visited the concentration camp Dachau because he wanted to respond to the feelings of hatred he felt toward the Jews, *al-Hilal*, January 1962.

historical narrative which highlighted Jewish suffering everywhere and at all times, or the "lachrymose view of Jewish history" in the words of the renowned Jewish historian Salo Baron.[4] However, whereas Baron criticized this narrative, since it ignored, in his view, the more positive elements of Jewish history, mainly cultural creativity and vibrant communal life, the Arab writers adopted it in order to create a "counter-history" designed to prove that the persecution and suffering of the Jews were their own fault. In addition, placing Nazi policy against the Jews as merely a link in a long historical chain helped to relativize it or belittle its scope, even though some Arab writers conceded that Nazi persecutions were worse than all previous ones.[5]

Justification of the Holocaust was less prevalent than its denial. Still, its very existence, scope, bluntness and the argumentation it contained had no parallel in any other post-war societies. Even old or neo-Nazi groups in Europe that sought to rehabilitate the image of Hitler and his regime tended to deny the Holocaust and minimize Nazism's other crimes, rather than to openly and explicitly justify and defend them.[6] As was the case with Arab denial, justification was not confined to marginal or radical circles and media, but appeared among mainstream producers of culture, and did not arouse any significant criticism or condemnation in the Arab public discourse, even from those who did not espouse it. Although expressions of justification declined since the 1970s, they never disappeared, but remained largely confined to Islamists. During periods of heightened tension with Israel, it was often reinforced by nationalists and leftists as well.

The preponderance of Islamists among advocates of justification was rooted in their unique view of the Arab–Israeli conflict. Islamists have considered the conflict first and foremost as a religious one between Jews and Muslims and, therefore, have lumped all Jews together as the enemy.[7] Identifying themselves

---

4   Robert Liberles, *Salo Wittmayer Baron: Architect of Jewish History*, New York: 1995, pp. 116–18.

5   In her book *A Past Without a Shadow: Constructing the Past in German Books for Children*, New York: 2005, pp. 55–6, Zohar Shavit points to a similar phenomenon whereby the placing of Hitler as one among a long list of mass murderers throughout history relativizes his crimes.

6   The uniqueness of the Arab justification of the Holocaust is also evident by the widespread Arab condemnation of the Armenian genocide that was carried out by the Muslim Ottomans during World War I, that is, by fellow Muslims against another non-Arab minority that was supposedly allied with Western countries during a war that ravaged the Middle East.

7   See Meir Litvak, "The Islamization of the Israeli–Arab Conflict: the Case of Hamas," *Middle Eastern Studies*, vol. 23, no. 1 (1998), pp. 148–63; idem, "The Islamic Republic of Iran and the Holocaust: Anti-Zionism and Anti-Semitism," *Journal of Israeli History*,

(like many other followers of monotheistic religions all over the world) with the only true divine revelation, Islamists have seen themselves as striving or fighting for the sake of God, *ipso facto* placing their opponents as enemies of God who deserve a severe divine punishment.[8] For Islamists, the emergence of Israel is perceived as the greatest defiance of God, since the Jews were condemned to humiliation and subjugation to the Muslims after they had rejected the noble message of the Prophet Muhammad.[9] By contrast, nationalist and leftist writers presented the conflict as one between Zionism and Arab nationalism and occasionally drew a distinction between Zionists and Jews in general. Some even claimed to sympathize with the Jews who suffered because of Zionism.

Since Islamists have often failed to draw sharply chiseled distinctions between the past and the present,[10] they perceived Jewish or Israeli evil in the modern age as the direct continuation of their wars against the Prophet Muhammad. Just as their wars against the Prophet of God justified their expulsion or elimination in the case of the Banu Qurayza tribe in Medina in the seventh century, so was their persecution in Europe, culminating in their extermination by the Nazis, a just punishment for their misdeeds or supposed enmity to Islam throughout history. As various Islamic movements have argued since the 1980s that the Jews had forfeited their right to life as a protected minority because they had waged war on the Muslims and on God, they justified in retrospect the killing of the Jews by the Nazis.[11] In addition, it seems that Islamists are less sensitive

vol. 25 (2006), pp. 245–66.

8   Bernard Lewis, "The Roots of Muslim Rage," *The Atlantic Monthly*, September 1990, pp. 47 – 60. For such descriptions of the Jews, see Green (ed.), *Arab Theologians*.

9   For this perception in Islamic tradition, see "Jews and Judaism," *Encyclopedia of the Qur'an*, vol. 3, Leiden and Boston: 2003, pp. 21–34.

10   For this observation and its manifestation in medieval and modern Islamic historiography, see Jacob Lassner, *The Middle East Remembered: Forged Identities, Competing Narratives, Contested Spaces*, Ann Arbor, MI: 2000, p. 28. See also Emmanuel Sivan, *Islamic Fundamentalism and Anti-Semitism*, Jerusalem: 1985 (Hebrew), who explains that modern fundamentalists seek to "settle historical accounts" with the enemies of Islam in earlier times.

11   On modern advocacies of the extermination of the Jews, see the Hamas Charter article 7 and Mukhlis Barzaq, *al-Wa'd min khaybar ila al-quds*, chapter 8 in http://www.al-eman.com/IslamLib/viewtoc.asp?BID=265. The 'supplications' to God in Friday sermons to exterminate the Jews and Christians became so prevalent that in 2002 Kuwaiti Minister of Religious Endowments Ahmad Baqir, and Saudi Deputy Minister for Religious Affairs 'Abd al-'Aziz al-'Ammar urged their cessation. See www.islamonline.net/Arabic/news 30 April and 15 May 2002; *al-Sharq al-Awsat*, 29 December 2002; Wistrich, *Muslim Anti-Semitism*, p. 16–17.

to the discourse of the Holocaust in the West, which abhorred any support for or legitimacy of genocide after World War II.

Justification of the Holocaust was often accompanied by denial of its scope as full-scale genocide and its minimization to mere large-scale persecutions or pogroms. This connection ostensibly diminished the gravity of the justification, by the argument that the writers were not actually justifying the extermination of the Jews, but something less gruesome. Still, in several such cases the same writer who denied the scope of the Holocaust would express his (or her) wish that Hitler had actually done what was attributed to him. On other occasions, writers justified the killing of Jews but blurred the extent of annihilation by not clarifying whether they meant the annihilation of millions or just of tens of thousands. That duality, both justifying and denying the Holocaust, could be interpreted as another example of cognitive dissonance, that is, the perception of incompatibility between two cognitions or the uncomfortable tension that comes from holding two conflicting thoughts or beliefs at the same time. The writers wish to express their animosity to the Jews while refusing to acknowledge Jewish victimhood, thus resorting to denial as well.

The arguments of justification borrowed heavily from western anti-Semitic literature, first and foremost the *Protocols of the Elders of Zion*, to explain Jewish depravity throughout history. Hitler's *Mein Kampf* and other Nazi arguments have often served as reliable historical sources rather than as ideological tracts reflecting a twisted world-view. As was the case with Holocaust denial, this is more an expression of selective cultural borrowing rather than lack of knowledge. While Islamists usually reject western cultural influence as an anathema to authentic Islamic culture, they did not hesitate to borrow anti-Zionist and anti-Jewish themes from the same West in the service of their cause.

Concurrently, writers of all ideological colors often use highly charged Islamic or modern Arabic terms to describe Jewish or German acts in order to make the European situation more familiar to their readers or in order to evoke their sympathy for the Nazi measures against the Jews. For example, they accuse the Jews of practicing usury, which is prohibited by Islam, or of fomenting sedition (*fitna*, pl. *fitan*), a term associated with traumatic events in early Islamic history and therefore an act abhorred by Muslims. Such allusions also conform with the popular view that attributes sedition in Islam to Jewish machinations and absolves Muslims from responsibility for it.[12]

---

12   For the significance of *fitna* in Muslim tradition, see L. Gardet, "Fitna," *Encyclopaedia of Islam*, Leiden: 2nd edn (hereafter *EI2*), vol. 2, pp. 930–1. See also the attribution of the outbreak of Shi'i-Sunni enmity to the Jew 'Abdallah bin Sabba in Isaac Hasson, "Les Šī'ites vus par les neo-wahhabites," *Arabica*, vol. 53, no. 3 (July 2006), pp. 299–330.

Categories and motifs

Muhammad 'Ali al-Zu'bi, a preacher at the Beirut Grand Mosque and a prolific writer, complained in the 1950s that the Jewish writers of history mention the persecutions, but ignore the reasons for them. They describe the outcome rather than addressing its background, in order to mislead their readers. People are surprised that the Germans and Russians punished the Jews at the beginning of the twentieth century, and regard these acts as an affront to the human spirit and the values of enlightenment, liberalism and reconciliation. But, he added, the Jews are a classic case of the popular proverb "He struck me and cried, and rushed ahead of me to complain" (*Darabani wa-baka, wa-sabaqani wa-ishtaka*). Expressing his doubts as to whether the Jews actually belong to the human race, Zu'bi explained that all nations in the world recognized their evil and, therefore, repeatedly expelled them from their countries of residence.[13]

With such views in mind, justification of Hitler's action fall into four categories: theological justification describing it as God's just punishment of the Jews for their moral transgressions; pseudo-historical descriptions of the activities of the Jews in Europe, particularly Germany, in the course of history; short-term explanations focusing on their alleged "activities" during the 1920s and 1930s; and advance retribution for the post-war conduct of the state of Israel – which became more prevalent as the Arab–Israeli conflict extracted a heavier toll from the Arabs. Unlike the case of Holocaust denial, which grew more sophisticated over the years, there is greater continuity in the arguments of the justification themes.

The theological justification

Several Islamist writers, most notably Sayyid Qutb, the "father" of radical Islamist thought in Egypt, and Muhammad al-Ghazali, a leading ideologue of the Muslim Brothers, sought a theological explanation for the Holocaust, out of a belief in divine reward and punishment. Qutb, who depicted the Jews as the eternal enemies of Islam, spoke of the cyclical pattern of Jewish history in which the Jews repeatedly commit acts of evil and corruption, with God punishing them. Following a series of such encounters, Qutb added, God had brought Hitler to dominate the Jews, thereby placing Hitler in the role of the Biblical "slave of God," that is, the gentile ruler who carries out God's will in punishing the people of Israel without being aware of the divine reason for his action. But, to Qutb's chagrin, the Jews once again "have returned to evil

---

13 Al-Zu'bi, *Isra'il*, pp. 114–15. See a similar argument by Muhammad Tal'at al-Ghunaymi, a lecturer in international law at the University of Alexandria, *Qadiyyat filastin amama al-qanun al-duwali*, Alexandria: n.d., pp. 39–40.

doing in the form of Israel," and he expressed his hope that God would once again bring upon the Jews the most horrible punishment.[14]

The idea of divine punishment also guided Anis Mansur. In a chapter titled "The Demons, Nazism and Zionism," which describes a weekly meeting in the early 1950s at the house of his mentor, the renowned liberal Islamic thinker 'Abbas Mahmud al-'Aqqad, Mansur explained to a Jewish student that the rumor of Hitler's Jewish origins was false, but the Jews kept disseminating it because they believed that every great person must be Jewish. Moreover, the Jews wished to claim that the "suffering Hitler had caused them, was a family matter. Because they had sinned, they deserved to be punished, and the punishment came from one of them." Just as the Jews had been punished in the distant past and cursed by the Prophet Moses, they had driven the entire world to hate and persecute them, he concluded.[15]

Ibrahim Khalil Ahmad, an Islamist writer, whose book received the endorsement of the Ministry of Religious Endowments in Egypt, describes the Jews as seeking world domination and therefore as "the cause for calamities all over the world." In another chapter, titled "Israel will cease to exist," Ahmad justifies the need of various societies in the past *and in the future* (emphasis added) to carry out the same measures that Hitler had implemented against the Jews, because the Jews, through their conduct, justify the Qur'anic passages predicting their perdition.[16]

Muhammad Jarbu'a, who combined theological and historical arguments to justify the Holocaust, stated that Hitler embarked upon the extermination of the Jews because they were a lowly, immoral nation. He treated them as guilty persons whose moral sins call for their death. Although some people would describe this collective guilt as racist, he maintained that it remained valid, in view of the hundreds of charges which the Jews faced from God, the prophets and from other nations throughout history.[17]

Jewish wickedness throughout history

Those who claimed that Nazi persecutions of the Jews were merely the last phase among many similar cases focused on alleged inherent Jewish traits and conduct

---

14   Sayyid Qutb, *Ma'rakatuna ma'a al-yahud*, Jedda: 1970, 2nd edn, cited in Ronald L. Nettler, *Past Trials and Present Tribulations: A Muslim Fundamentalist's View of the Jews*, Oxford: 1987, p. 63; Muhammad al-Ghazali, *al-Isti'mar: ahqad wa-atma'*, Cairo: 1957, p. 168.

15   Anis Mansur, *Fi salun al-'aqqad kanat lana ayyam*, Cairo: 1983, p. 312.

16   Ibrahim Khalil Ahmad, *Isra'il fitnat al-ajyal: al-'usur al-qadima*, Cairo: 1969, p. 29.

17   Jarbu'a, *Tabri'at hitler*, p. 6.

throughout history that aroused the just wrath of nations. In other words, they blamed the Jews for whatever befell them. These writers often employed contradictory arguments, typical of anti-Semitic arguments elsewhere. For instance, they charged that the Jews segregated themselves and refused to integrate into the societies in which they lived, and simultaneously complained that the Jews displaced non-Jews by taking over their professions and livelihoods, suggesting that the problem was actually rooted in their continued existence as Jews. Thus, a Syrian tenth grade textbook for national (*qawmi*) education published in 1998–99 [p. 104] attributed Nazi persecution of the Jews to their "inability to assimilate into the societies in which they lived,"[18] implying that the insistence on preserving their distinct identity was a crime or an act of aggression in itself.

'Aqqad maintained that "Hitler was not the first" who preached enmity to the Jews. Rather, the "pogroms against the Jews in East and Central Europe," including massacres and famine, occurred centuries beforehand, thereby reducing the Holocaust to a large scale pogrom. He attributed the persecutions which occurred time and again and in various places to a Jewish "chronic disease." Due to their inherent traits and their being an undeveloped nation, the Jews always collided with other nations, he explained, arguing that the major reasons for persecutions were entrenched in the Jews' self-imposed isolation, which was also among the psychological and social foundations of Zionism. Zionism was responsible for the persecutions it brought upon the Jews, he claimed, and at the same time it used the allegation of persecutions, particularly the Nazi one, as leverage on other nations to accept Zionist claims.[19]

In a chapter devoted to Nazism in his book on imperialism, Egyptian historian Mustafa al-Shihabi emphasized the charge that also appeared in Hitler's *Mein Kampf* on the role of the Jews as leaders of every anarchist movement in Europe. The Jews had taken over Marxist Communism and world capitalism in order to annihilate the Aryan state and rule humanity. "The Jew sucks the blood of the peoples among whom he lives and hides his racism," Shihabi says. But, if the Jew feels strong, as was the case under the British Mandate in Palestine, then his real fanatic, violent and unscrupulous face is revealed. Still, while borrowing from the Nazi anti-Semitic repertoire, Shihabi limited Hitler's actions against

---

18 Arnon Groiss (ed.), *Jews, Zionism and Israel in Syrian School Textbooks*, New York: 2001, p. 23.

19 'Abbas Mahmud al-'Aqqad, *Hitler fi al-mizan*, Beirut: 1971, p. 28; idem, *al-Sahyuniyya*, pp. 15–17, 43–7, 152. See a similar claim by Muhammad 'Ali Muhammad, *al-Wa'd al-batil, "wa'd balfur"*, Cairo: 1961, p. 11.

the Jews to expulsion from government position, confiscation of property and forcing many of them to emigrate from Germany.[20]

Egyptian army colonel Amin Sami al-Ghamrawi felt sorrow in the early 1960s for the injustice done to Hitler, who had supposedly tried to defend the Jews, but turned against them once he realized their evil and wickedness. The world is afflicted by the weakness of memory, Ghamrawi complained, and "remembers only the suffering (ta'dhib) which Hitler inflicted upon the Jews, without trying to fully comprehend the reasons that forced him to behave in this way." Even the Germans, who suffered in the past and who continue to suffer from the Jews, denounce Hitler, who sought to save them from being "a soft prey which the Jewish wolves keep devouring mercilessly." Based on this description, Ghamrawi asked his readers to decide for themselves "whether or not Hitler had been right in his measures against the Jews to defend himself and his people."[21] Writing after the 1967 war, Dissuqi and Salman agree with SS leader Heinrich Himmler, who declared on 4 October 1943 that the Nazis had the right and duty to fight the Jews who wanted to exterminate them. The truth, they conclude, is that Himmler's statements against the Jews were but a "minor observation" compared with the enormity of the crimes of the Jews against other peoples.[22] 'Abduh al-Rajih, an Egyptian lecturer at the university of Alexandria, who depicted the Jews as "enemies of humanity" for their racism towards others and their "insistence" on racial purity, which has caused so much bloodshed in history, describes their extermination as a justified act of European self-defense. When the peoples of Europe realized that the Jews' main goal was the destruction of Christianity, numerous ideological and philosophical movements urged their exclusion and extermination so that these societies would be able to live in peace.[23]

Anis Mansur offered in 1972 a vehement justification of the Holocaust and identified emotionally with Hitler in an article which discussed the changes in Hitler's image. During the early years after the war Hitler and the Germans were accused of brutality (wahshiyya), and Hitler was presented as a human savage whose "favorite food were Jews whom he had burned and drowned since they betrayed every country, and hated all countries." Subsequently, Mansur added, a new approach emerged which conceded that Hitler was indeed brutal, not only towards the Jews, but to all his enemies, Jews and Christians alike, and that the

20   Mustafa al-Shihabi, *Muhadarat fi al-isti'mar*, Cairo: 1955, pp. 70–1.

21   Amin Sami al-Ghamrawi, *Li-Hadha akrahu al-yahud*, Cairo: 1964, pp. 268–88.

22   Dissuqi and Salman, *al-Sahyuniyya*, pp. 73, 94–5. The authors mistakenly cite the date as 1940.

23   'Abduh al-Rajih, *al-Shakhsiyya al-isra'iliyya*, Cairo: 1969, pp. 42–3, 52–3, 119–20.

crematoria in Dachau, Buchenwald and Belsen were aimed not only at the Jews, but at anyone who disagreed with him. These approaches, Mansur explained, reflected the compassion people felt towards the Jews. The Jews, however, are not the poor people who deserve pity, but they are the enemies of humanity and what they commit in the Palestinian Occupied Territories could not have been done even by Hitler himself. Therefore, people throughout the world began to feel sorry for the "genius man who did not burn the rest of the Jews, since the Jews are traitors by their nature ... They sold Hitler and Germany to Russia and America." The entire world realized, he concluded, that "Hitler was right," as the Jews are "blood-suckers" who want to destroy the world.[24]

Following the visit by President Anwar Sadat to Israel in November 1977, which launched the Israeli–Egyptian peace process, Mansur mellowed somewhat and ceased to justify the Holocaust, although he continued to attack the Jews. However, with the outbreak of the "Second Intifada" in September 2000, he returned to his old views. Analyzing the perverted character of the Jews in modern times, Mansur concluded that it had "become clear to the world that what happened to the Jews of Germany, Poland, and Russia, was justified." Moreover, he claimed that he found support for this view from certain "sects in Israel that view the Jewish State as heretic," and believe that what Hitler did to European Jews was an appropriate punishment for their mistreatment of the Jews who had originated from Arab countries.[25]

Among those who continued to justify the Holocaust after the signing of the Israeli–Egyptian peace treaty were senior members of the Egyptian religious establishment, who described the sins of the Jews in Europe as an additional proof of Jewish treachery against Islam. Most prominent among them was Shaykh Muhammad Sayyid al-Tantawi, Rector of the prestigious al-Azhar University in Cairo, the highest religious authority in Egypt. His book *The Israelites in the Qur'an and the Sunna*, published in 1997 during his tenure as rector, is a broad, 700-page attack on the Jews based on Islamic sources. Tantawi, however, did not restrict himself to the description of alleged Jewish crimes against the Prophet Muhammad, but went on to review Jewish history in Europe, citing extensively from the *Protocols of the Elders of Zion* as a principal historical source.

---

24   *Al-Akhbar* (Cairo), 19 August 1972. See also his eight-part series devoted to attacks on the Jews in *Akhbar al-Yawm*, 2, 9, 16, 23, 30 August, 6, 13 and 20 September 1969.

25   *Al-Ahram*, 13 February 2001. A French translation of the article was published in the Cairo daily *Le Progrès Egyptien*. A "refined" version was published in the English-language *Egyptian Gazette*, in which the justification of the Holocaust was omitted, as were some of the more blatant anti-Semitic expressions. See Memri, Special Dispatch Series, no. 188, 22 February 2001.

In addition to fomenting the two world wars as a source for profiteering, the "most blatant example" of Jewish conduct was their "treasonous acts" in Germany during World War I, which caused the German defeat, Tantawi asserted. As a reward for their perfidy they received the Balfour Declaration (2 November 1917), which recognized the Zionist cause in Palestine. The Jews, he went on, had exploited the Germans in the vilest ways ever since they settled in Germany in the eighth century. They had achieved almost complete control of German finances through the practice of usury and other means of amassing illegal fortunes (*mal haram*). Little wonder that the Germans rose against them several times and employed all the means of killing, expulsion and pillage. Hitler was one of those who "added up all their acts of treachery" and acted against them. Tantawi ended by citing a statement attributed to Hitler that "should the Jews win that would be the funeral of the human race ... and when I protect myself from the Jew, I struggle to defend God's creation."[26]

The Jews were blood-suckers and Trojan horses in Germany, Jarbu'a concludes the list. It was they, through their conduct, who "provided the other nations with the reasons to burn them, and these reasons render their burning a just act (*taj'alu ihraqahum 'adala*)." This "wicked, corrupt, treacherous swindler people ... who allows itself to play with the money and blood of children, women and old of the gentiles... [and with] the fate of other nations ... gives the greatest justifications for others to exterminate it (*yu'ti akbar al-mubarrarat li-ghayrihi li-ibadatihi*)."[27]

Short-term explanation: the Jewish stab in Germany's back

The more popular theme of justification focused on the immediate context of the Nazi era as the culmination of Jewish machinations and evil doing against European societies. Proponents of this view adopt verbatim the "stab in the back" charge, which the German right had raised as an excuse for Germany's defeat in World War I.[28] They also adopt and employ the broad Nazi argument

---

26 Muhammad Sayyid Tantawi, *Banu isra'il fi al-Qur'an wal-sunna*, Cairo: 1997, pp. 623, 647–8, 651. The book was based on his doctoral dissertation submitted in 1967. See a similar description of the Jews by Mahmud Mazru'a, Dean of the Faculty of Principles of Religion and Propagation in Manufiya University in Egypt in his *Dirasat fi al-yahudiyya*, Cairo: 1987, pp. 131, 136–7; Ahmad, *Isra'il: fitnat al-ajyal*, p. 29; Shaykh Ibrahim Mudayras of the PNA in Special Information Bulletin, May 2005, www.intelligence.org.il/eng/sib/5_05/as_sermon.htm; and Hamas leader Mahmud al-Zahhar to al-'Arabiyya TV, 21 April 2004, www.memritv.org, clip No. 40.

27 Jarbu'a, *Tabri'at hitler*, pp. 27–8.

28 See, for instance, Ahmad Muhammad Ramadan, *Isra'il wa-masir al-insan al-mu'asir*, Amman: 1987, pp. 179–80, who claims that the Zionist leader Nahum Goldman took pride

against the Jews, relying on Hitler's *Mein Kampf* as an important historical source. Quite a few of these writers draw a direct link between the wrong done to Germany by the Versailles Treaty, which they blame on the Jews, and the injustice done to the Arabs in the post-war political settlements, thereby presenting the Germans and Arabs as joint victims of Jewish machinations.

"One stands perplexed by the cruelty which Hitler and his lieutenants had shown towards the Jews," the Egyptian publicist and nationalist thinker Muhammad 'Ali 'Alluba wrote, and wondered whence this hatred came. His conclusion was clear. The Jews turned their backs to the German homeland, and turned into a threat to nation and country alike. When the German Supreme Commander Hindenburg wanted to accept President Wilson's peace terms in November 1918, "in order to save humanity" and avoid the situation of victors and vanquished, 'Alluba claimed, the Jews threw away Wilson's ideas and imposed the Versailles Treaty, whose clauses, he alleges, matched those conditions adopted at a secret meeting of the Jews and the Free Masons. The treaty that was forged by "Jewish-Zionist inspiration" brought misery and suffering to the whole of Europe, particularly Germany and Austria, and eventually led to the outbreak of World War II. This predicament was the reason for Hitler's decision to take revenge against the Jews, and his first move after assuming power was to "eliminate Zionism and expel the Jews from his country. Hitler had to turn against them, as he wanted to save his nation and the world as a whole from this destructive evil and poison which had spread among the Christian nations."[29]

As an example of Jewish continuous efforts to sow sedition and destruction against the countries in which they lived, seen as a justified cause for their persecution, Asma' Fa'ur cites the story of the Jewish (but totally assimilated) communist leader Kurt Eisner in post-World War I Bavaria. Eisner, she says, "captured for himself the region of Bavaria, which had been a German principality for ten centuries, separated it from the greater homeland and declared it an independent republic." He appointed himself president of the new republic, congregated the Jews there, and put the management of its affairs in their hands. It was only natural, Fa'ur adds, that subsequently the Jews suffered persecutions, killings and expulsions by Hitler.[30]

The Syrian Sulayman Naji blamed the Jews for all the tragedies that had befallen Europe. In the chapter discussing Jewish crimes in Germany, Naji adopts *in toto* Nazi accusations against the Jews and presents all Germans as supporting

of that fact already in 1920.

29 'Alluba, *Filastin*, pp. 127–35; see a similar argument of Versailles as inspired by Zionists in Banaja, *Nazra*, pp. 101ff.

30 Asma' 'Abd al-Hadi Fa'ur, *Filastin wal-maza'im al-yahudiyya*, Beirut: 1990, p. 142.

Hitler for saving them from the Jewish menace. He describes Germany's misery after its 1918 defeat, which the Jews exploited to enrich themselves until they controlled 90 percent of all German wealth. He explains that the Jews sought to destroy Germany in the same way they had brought ruin on imperial Russia and the Ottoman Empire, because Germany "showed its disdain" to them and recognized their true aims. Fate prevented the Jews from realizing their evil plans against Germany, Naji declared, when Hitler emerged and "removed the veil" from their plots and plans. He established the National Socialist Party, which challenged the Jews, "shattered their hopes to enslave Germany," and saved his country "from their evil."[31] Adopting an ostensibly milder tone but granting it official governmental approval, the 1989 Syrian National-Socialist Education textbook (Grade 10, p. 104) attributed Hitler's "persecution" of the Jews to their "control and monopoly over currency exchange, banks and commercial financing" as well as their "treason toward their homeland, Germany," and their putting "themselves in the service of the Allies."[32]

Shaykh Muhammad Jami'a, former prayer leader of the Islamic Cultural Center and Mosque of New York and official representative of al-Azhar University in the US in 2001, was equally forthright. He explained Nazi policy against the Jews as a legitimate revenge for their betrayal of Germany and for violating their pact with it. Presumably, he alluded to the Islamic concept of the "Pact of 'Umar," which guaranteed security and religious autonomy to the non-Muslim minorities under Islamic rule as long as they accepted Muslim superiority, and which the Jews violated, according to the Islamist point of view, by establishing the state of Israel. Blaming the 11 September 2001 terrorist attack in the US on the Zionists, he complained that no one dared mention this fact, because of Jewish absolute control over the media and all foci of power, and concluded that had the Americans known the extent of Jewish control, "they would have done to the Jews what Hitler did."[33]

---

31 Sulayman Naji, *al-Mufsidun fi al-ard aw jara'im al-yahud al-siyasiyya wal-ijtima'iyya 'abr al-ta'rikh*, Damascus: 1966, pp. 281–4. See a similar justification of German "revenge" on the Jews for enriching themselves at German expense by Dissuqi and Salman, *al-Sahyuniyya*, pp. 71, 73, 94–5; 'Abd al-Latif al-Sahar, *Wa'd Allah wa-isra'il*, Cairo: 1967, pp. 108–9, 125; Mahmud, *al-Yahud*, pp. 192–3; Muhammad 'Abd al-'Aziz Mansur, *al-Yahud al-maghdub 'alayhim*, Cairo: 1980, p. 1; 'Abd al-Hamid al-Najjar, *al-Tatawwur al-ta'rikhi li-bani isra'il*, Cairo: 1973, pp. 74–5.

32 Groiss (ed.), *Jews*, p. 23.

33 www.lailatalqadr.com, 4 October 2001 – Memri, Special Dispatch 288, 17 October 2001. See a similar argument by Shaykh Muhammad Khidr of al-Azhar in *al-Akhbar*, 27 May 2001 and by the Jordanian journalist Mahmud al-Khatib in *al-'Arab al-Yawm*, 27 April 1998.

Hitler had carried out an intifada (popular uprising) against the Jews in Germany, Jarbu'a charged, implicitly equating Israeli rule over the Palestinians with Jewish "rule" over the Germans prior to 1933. Germany was subject to Jewish terrorism, and what Hitler had done was to carry out a just verdict against traitors. He had done what many others had wanted but failed to do, that is, save his country from the Jews.[34] In view of these heavy charges against the Jews, several writers who found warm words for Hitler "of blessed memory," were indignant at the Jewish or world reactions to his just desire to exterminate the Jews. According to Zu'bi the moment "Hitler tried to uproot the poisonous nails stuck inside the nation's body, the sons of the snakes cried and hollered 'Hitler is trying to eliminate us because we are Semites,'" instead of recognizing their guilt.[35] "Hitler, may he rest in peace," 'Ali Imam 'Atiyya concluded, "had done the world a service by destroying the Jews."[36]

Several writers portray Hitler as responding to alleged Jewish aggressive policies against Germany during the 1930s, particularly the efforts to organize an economic boycott in retaliation for Germany's anti-Jewish policies. Two Lebanese writers consider the resolutions of the Jewish Congress in Amsterdam in July 1933 as a declaration of economic war against Germany. "Although Hitler exerted strenuous efforts to reach an understanding with [the US], Jewish effort thwarted them," they claim, thereby magnifying Jewish power. Moreover, they attribute the US entry to the war in 1941 to Jewish incitement and influence, ignoring trifle events such as Pearl Harbour and Hitler's declaration of war against the US.[37]

Egyptian Mahmud Fawzi, echoing the nationalist German historian Ernst Nolte, focuses on the pledge of full and unconditional support to the British war effort which the Zionist leader Chaim Weizmann gave in a letter on 3 September 1939. It was only natural, Fawzi concludes, that the German reaction to the Jewish declaration of war was the arrest of the Jews in detention camps. The same fate awaited American citizens of Japanese origin when the US entered the war.[38]

---

34   Jarbu'a, *Tabri'at hitler*, pp. 8–9, 20, 54–5, 62, 65, 66, 72–3.

35   Muhammad 'Ali al-Zu'bi, *Dafa'in al-nafsiyya al-yahudiyya min khilal al-kutub al-muqaddasa: al-tawrat, al-injil wal-qur'an wal-ta'rikh wal-waqi'*, Beirut: 1973, 3rd edn, p. 113; 'Abd al-Hadi Muhammad Mas'ud, *Hitler wa-mussulini wal-adyan*, Cairo: 1951, pp. 174, 184.

36   'Ali Imam 'Atiyya, *al-Sahyuniyya al-'alamiyya wa-ard al-mi'ad*, Cairo: 1963, pp. 213–15.

37   Najjar and al-Hajj, *al-Sahyuniyya*, p. 55. Other writers, who want to prove Zionist collaboration with Nazism raise the opposite argument, claiming that these congresses foiled the international boycott against Germany (see Chapter 7). Either the Jews did both, or they were guilty regardless of any action they took.

38   Mahmud Fawzi, *Jarudi wal-islam wa-ghadab al-sahyuniyya*, Cairo: 1996, p. 100. See a

Fawzi ignored the fact that Weizmann's letter followed six years of Nazi persecution of the Jews, and that it was not the cause of Nazi policies but a response to them, blurring also the distinction between the extermination of the Jews by Germany and the unjustified and immoral incarceration of Japanese Americans in California. In a similar vein, Nasr Shimali explains that Hitler incarcerated the Jews in camps because they were a hostile minority that had to be kept away from the front lines. The German High Command feared that the Jews would carry out acts of espionage, propaganda, weapons smuggling and black-market activities, and all it wanted was to protect its soldiers from that menace.[39]

A popular theme of justification was the replacement of the term "Jews" with "Zionists" or the description of Hitler as reacting to Zionist policies, thereby finding a common cause between the Germans and the Arabs, but also giving greater legitimacy to the Holocaust by substituting the racist basis of anti-Semitism with political opposition to Zionism. Hajj Amin al-Husayni, the Palestinian leader who collaborated with the Nazis (see Chapter 9), explains in his memoirs that initially Hitler had no grudge against the Jews, but changed his mind when the Jews started plotting against the German army after receiving the Balfour Declaration from the British. Another reason that Hitler could never forgive the Jews, he adds, was severe eye injury that was caused by a British gas attack and his awareness that it was Chaim Weizmann who had invented poison gas and handed it to Britain to be used against Germany.[40]

"Those who are astonished by Hitler's hatred against the Jews," stated Muhammad Mu'nis, one of the leading Nasserist historians in Egypt during the 1960s, would be "less surprised when they realize the reasons for this deep and total hatred." The reason was the alliance between international Zionism and France to control Germany in eternal humiliation. Even President Hindenburg, the great war hero, could not sign one document without the signature

---

similar claim in Naʻnaʻa, *al-Sayhuniyya*, pp. 134–5. The German historian Ernst Nolte raised a similar claim in 1985, with the qualification that, following Weizmann's statement, Hitler could have regarded the Jews as potential enemy aliens and incarcerated them in detention camps for the duration of the war. Nolte's broader and highly problematic views provoked sharp criticism and debates as part of the famous "Historians' debate" (Historiker-streit) in Germany. See Charles S. Maier, *The Unmasterable Past: History, Holocaust, and German National Identity*, Cambridge: 1988.

39   Shimali, "al-Fariq bayna muʻaskar abu ghurayb wa-muʻaskar ushwitz," www.voltairenet. org/article136329.html.

40   Hajj Amin al-Husayni, "Safahat min mudhakkirat al-sayyid muhammad amin al-husayni," *Filastin*, no. 103, October 1969, p. 19; no. 105, December 1969, p. 5. Weizmann discovered a process for synthesizing acetone (a solvent used in the manufacture of munitions) which helped the British armament industry, but was not involved in the production of gas.

of the Jewish Minister Walter Rathenau, he says.[41] Mu'nis was not bothered
by the chronological discrepancy as Rathenau, who was an anti-Zionist Jew,
served as minister for reconstruction during 1919–21 and as foreign minister in
1922 until his assassination by right-wing officers, whereas Hindenburg served
as president from 1926 to 1935. Following a similar line, Brigadier (retired)
Hasan Mustafa of the Lebanese army comments that Hitler managed to eliminate Zionist influence in Germany, but failed to extricate himself from the evil
of world Zionism, as he himself conceded before his suicide that it was Zionism
that had driven him to the war.[42]

Historian Biyan al-Hut went a step further in justifying Hitler's war against
Zionism, although she did describe the extermination of the Jews as inhumane.
The struggle between Zionism and Nazism was actually a struggle between two
types of racism and tyranny, she said. Hitler was the only one among world
leaders who understood the danger to the world from the Zionist movement,
and therefore adopted inhumane measures to eliminate the Jews. However,
while eradicating the Zionist movement, he was not concerned with the welfare
of the rest of the world. Another major mistake Hitler committed, she adds, was
the methods he used and his failure to focus on the Zionists. Instead, he waged
a campaign against the Jews as a whole, a mistake that pushed many of the Jews
to adopt Zionism.[43]

Kamil Muruwwa, the Shi'i Lebanese journalist and founder of the influential *al-Hayat*, who went to Germany during the war, denounces the wholesale
extermination of the Jews, but expresses understanding for Nazi hatred toward
them as natural and inevitable, since it entailed a clash between two racist movements, Nazism and Judaism, each claiming its uniqueness and racial superiority.[44] In a similar vein, the Lebanese priest Ikram Lama'i criticizes Pope Pius XII
for failing to come out against the final solution, but blames the Jews for elicit-
ing anti-Semitism by their conduct, particularly their involvement in crime and
usury. He explains Hitler's hatred of the Jews as stemming from their dealings

41   Husayn Mu'nis, *October*, 12 September 1981. For another senior Egyptian historian who
     held a similar view, see Ahmad Badawi in *al-Quds*, May 1984, cited by Yadlin, *An Arro-
     gant Oppressive Spirit*, p. 83. See also 'Abd al-Wahhab Zaytun, *Yahudiyya am Sahyuniyya*,
     Beirut: 1991, p. 95.

42   Mustafa, *al-Musa'adat*, pp. 7, 16–17. In his will before committing suicide Hitler did
     blame the Jews for the war, but did not speak of Zionism.

43   Biyan Nuwayhad al-Hut, *al-Qiyadat wal-mu'assasat al-siyasiyya fi filastin 1917–1948*, Bei-
     rut: 1981, p. 460.

44   *Al-Hayat*, 14–15 October 1989. See the same argument in 'Ali al-Sayyid Muhammad
     Isma'il, *Mada mashru'iyat asanid al-siyasa al-isra'iliyya*, Cairo: 1975, p. 91.

with the slave (*'abid*) trade, and from the inevitable clash between his world-view and their desire to dominate the world.[45] Writers of the left were, on the whole, much more critical of Hitler and Nazi Germany than were nationalists and Islamists. Therefore, only a few of them justified Hitler's anti-Jewish policies by looking for acceptable socio-economic reasoning, which borrowed from Marx's association of the Jews with capitalism.[46] Egyptian intellectual Hasan al-Zayyat, in a 1947 article titled "God have mercy upon Adolf Hitler," maintained that Hitler came out against capitalism, represented by "the Jews and their pimps ... who live on the blood of society just as fleas and ants live on human blood." Conceivably, the emerging conflict in Palestine led al-Zayyat to shift from his sharp criticism of Nazism of the 1930s, to longing for it, stating that "had God enabled Hitler to be the judge [at Nuremberg], there would have been no problem in Palestine."[47] Egyptian Marxist Fathi al-Ramli denied the Jewish claim that the persecutions against them had been religiously motivated. Rather, he said, they had a class background, because Judaism was the vanguard of the exploitative system in all capitalist societies. Consequently, these persecutions were only a natural outcome of the hatred which the masses harbored against their exploiters.[48]

Writing many years later, Jurji Haddad, a Jordanian Christian journalist, describes Nazism and Zionism as twin movements born out of capitalism (see Chapter 7). The bloody clash between them during the war was merely "one manifestation of the struggle for world-wide domination," reflecting the contradictory trends within capitalism. Zionism, which represented international capitalism, allied itself with those who provided it with the greatest economic freedom and opportunity to penetrate the Nazi and fascist economies. Since the Nazis regarded Zionist penetration as an opening for foreign domination, they launched a racist offensive against the Jews as a *defensive* (emphasis added) move and as part of the war against other imperialist powers. Thus, while refraining from explicitly justifying Nazi activities, Haddad places the blame for the fate of the Jews on their own actions.[49]

---

45   Lamaʻi, *al-Ikhtiraq*, p. 85.

46   See his anti-Jewish diatribe "Zur Judenfrage" (On the Jewish Question), published in February 1844 in the Deutsch–Französische Jahrbücher.

47   *Al-Risala*, 27 January 1947, p. 1. For Zayyat's views during the 1930s, see Gershoni, *Light in the Shadow*, pp. 302–4, 321. For a similar view justifying Hitler's actions against "Jewish capitalism" which controlled and suffocated Germany, see Kilu, "al-Hulukast."

48   Al-Ramli, *al-Sahyuniyya*, pp. 113–14.

49   Jurji Haddad, *al-Masʼala al-yahudiyya wal-haraka al-wataniyya al-ʻarabiyya*, Beirut: 1976, p. 159.

As mentioned above, justification of Nazi policy against the Jews was often joined with denial of the scope of the Holocaust. Islamist writer Ahmad al-'Attar asserts that even if Hitler did kill a few thousand Jews, the claim that they were innocent is a myth. Although he does not wish to defend Hitler, he says, an objective view of history would show that the Jews had never been loyal to their German homeland. They stood against it throughout history, and had been a major cause of its defeat in the two world wars. 'Attar describes, as the prime example of the Jews' efforts to destroy the patriotic and nationalist spirit of the German people during the eighteenth century, the literary salons sponsored by Jewish women [who had in fact all converted to Christianity]. Money and "beautiful Jewish women" were used there in order to "trap the German youth in the net of debauchery (*fujur*), corruption and heresy."[50] Jordanian journalist Mahmud al-Khatib while denying the Holocaust concluded that "Hitler did not kill the Jews because they were Jews, but rather because they betrayed Germany."[51]

Justification as an advance retribution for Israeli policies

Expressions of justification decreased from the 1980s onwards, presumably owing to two complementing processes: the growing sophistication and prevalence of Holocaust denial, and the increasingly negative view of Nazi Germany in the Arab political and cultural discourse. It was very difficult to simultaneously justify and deny the Holocaust or to present Nazi Germany as the epitome of evil while justifying its actions against the Jews, although various writers managed to live with these contradictions. In addition, the decline of explicit calls for the annihilation of Israel and the Jews probably had an impact on retrospective justification of the Nazi extermination policy. It is not a coincidence that Islamists, who more than any other group continue to speak about eliminating the Jews, could justify the Holocaust as well.

Periods of crises in Arab–Israeli relations from the 1980s onwards elicited expressions of support for Hitler's deeds as a just retribution for Israel's actions. These statements were often a way of expressing frustration over Arab weakness and inability to retaliate against alleged Israeli acts of aggression, and taking

---

50   Al-'Attar, *al-Yahudiyya*, pp. 158, 164, 166–8. See also Shaykh Wafiq al-Qassar in Green (ed.), *Arab Theologians*, p. 52; Sa'fan, *al-Yahud*, p. 104, who implicitly justified the Holocaust while simultaneously denying it and accusing the Zionists of collaborating with Nazi extermination policies. 'Abd al-'Aziz, *Mawsu'at al-mashahir*, vol. 2, pp. 164–5, expressed his wish that the charge against Hitler for killing the millions of Jews would have been justified.

51   *Al-'Arab al-Yawm*, 27 April 1998.

comfort in the fact that someone else was able to punish the Jews. Support for Hitler's actions served as an outlet for the failure of the writers themselves to take actual measures against the Israelis. It may have also provided a sense of comfort in portraying the aggressive Israelis as weak and oppressed by a more powerful force. Dr. Yahya al-Rakhawi, for instance, reacting to the 1982 Israeli siege of Beirut, attributed the widespread support for Israel after its establishment as stemming from the universal wish to assemble as many Jews as possible in one place so that it would be easier to eliminate them at the right moment, adding that such a thought preoccupied many statesmen who were wiser but also more cowardly than Hitler. In this conflict with Israel, he continued: "We cannot but see the image of the great Hitler, God have mercy upon him, the wisest [of all] who had dealt with this problem, and attempted to annihilate them out of mercy for humanity, ... Now the Jews demonstrate in practice how correct was his intuition."[52]

The outbreak of violence between the Palestinians and Israel in September 2000 gave these calls a renewed surge. "Thanks to Hitler, of blessed memory," wrote Ahmad Rajab, a columnist in the semi-official Egyptian daily *al-Akhbar*, "who on behalf of the Palestinians revenged in advance against the vilest criminals on the face of the earth. Although we do have a complaint against him, for his revenge on them was not complete."[53]

Even more passionate was Fatima 'Abdallah Mahmud in her article "Accursed Forever and Ever," which combined denial with justification and depicted the Jews as a "catastrophe for the human race," and "the virus of the generation." As an example of Jewish treachery and lies, Mahmud invoked the invention of the Holocaust myth, which, she contended, was refuted by numerous French and British scholars. Hitler, she explained, was "no more than a modest pupil" in the world of murder and bloodshed. But "I," she exclaimed, "in light of this imaginary tale, complain to Hitler, even say to him from the bottom of my heart, 'If only you had done it, brother, if only it had really happened, so that the world could sigh in relief [without] their evil and sin.'"[54]

A corollary theme was the view of Hitler's treatment of the Jews as a model to be emulated by the Arabs. In a symposium hosted on 29 November 2005 (the 56th anniversary of the UN resolution on the partition of Palestine) by Hizbullah's Al-Manar TV at the Université Libanaise, Lebanon's largest state univer-

---

52   *Al-Ahrar*, 19 July 1982. See also Yadlin, *An Arrogant Oppressive Spirit*, p. 100.

53   *Al-Akhbar*, 18 April 2001. Lest he be misunderstood, Rajab repeated his statement a week
       later, ibid., 25 April 2001. See also: ADL, *Holocaust Denial in the Middle East: The Latest
       Anti-Israel Propaganda Theme*, New York, n.d., www.adl.org.

54   *Al-Akhbar*, 29 April 2002 – Memri, Special Dispatch Series, no. 375, 3 May 2002.

sity, one participant stated that "just like Hitler fought the Jews – We are a great Islamic nation of Jihad and we too should fight the Jews and burn them."[55]

Rare voices came out in explicit denunciation of the Arab justification of the Holocaust. In the late 1980s PLO official Marwan Kanafani criticized those who justify the Holocaust from an anti-Semitic or Fascist point of view as only helping Zionist propaganda. He also disapproved of those who tried to minimize the number of the Jewish victims, as if there was any moral significance whether only one million or six million Jews perished. Concurrently, he complained of a ceaseless Zionist campaign to instill a guilt complex into American society regarding the Holocaust, which prevented any "rational and objective" discussion of the reasons for the persecution of the Jews, and particularly of the "crimes committed by Zionism."

Conclusions

The Arab justification of the Holocaust, unlike the other major themes discussed in this study, has undergone significant changes in scope and intensity since 1948. Although always less prevalent than Holocaust denial, it was more rife among all political and intellectual trends during the 1950s and 1960s, when the Arab–Israeli conflict was perceived as an existential one. As the conflict changed in nature, at least partially, into a conflict between states, the justification theme declined and remained mostly, but never exclusively, the domain of writers from the Islamic camp – established clerics and members of radical organizations alike. These groups that continued to adhere to the strong ideological perception of the conflict, some of them even advocating the eventual extermination of the Jews, coupled with extreme intolerant attitudes toward their rivals, felt less compunction in explicit justification of Nazi policies against the Jews. A few nationalist writers occasionally resorted to justification during periods of heightened tension and crisis in the Arab–Israeli conflict.

However, continuity in the motifs and arguments has remained a salient characteristic of the Arab justification theme. The arguments, which rely heavily on European, including Nazi anti-Semitic literature, reflect, as was the case with denial, a selective reading of and borrowing from western culture. This is particularly significant considering the preponderance of Islamist proponents of justification, who are staunch opponents of western cultural influences in almost all other fields, but who readily absorb ideas and images from the same West whenever its suits their political goals or ideological convictions. The only

---

55   Memritv.org, clip no. 962. See similar statements in Chapter 9.

212

significant change has been the growing use of justification as advance retribution for Israeli military measures against the Arabs in times of crisis.

Justification appeared more common among Egyptians than among others, despite the signing of the Egyptian–Israeli peace treaty in March 1979. Moreover, opposition to the peace treaty may have even encouraged anti-Jewish writings in Egypt, as many intellectuals and writers who opposed the treaty as signifying their country's failure to realize its national aspirations gave vent to their frustration by increasing their diatribe against the Jews. Another reason may have been a sort of a tacit deal between the government and the intellectuals which allowed the latter to turn their anger and their pens against Israel, the Jews and the US in return for avoiding criticism of the government's domestic failures.[56] Contrary to the Egyptians, justification was far less common among Palestinian writers, particularly after the signing of the 1993 Palestinian–Israeli Declaration of Principles. Although their resentment towards Zionism was no less acute than the Egyptians', the Palestinians' political discourse seems to have been more refined, and attentive to the western discourse. In addition, the Palestinians may have feared that such statements would elicit harsh Israeli responses.[57]

While utterances of justification became far less common in the semi-official Arab press, they were to be found more in books which dealt with Jews or Judaism. It would be going too far to speak of two distinct discursive frameworks on the Holocaust, as denial was rife in the press and many journalists used harsh language regarding Israel and the Jews. Yet, it appears that Arab governments were more tolerant of such statements in books because of their lower circulation and because they did not implicate them in any way.

In addition to their historical fallacy, the charges against the Jews that were intended to justify their extermination reflect a typical anti-Semitic trait, which views all the Jews, all over the world and at all times, as acting in unison and blames all of them for the alleged actions of the few. Even if the false charge of a Jewish stab in the back were true, it did not explain why the Jews outside Germany had to pay for such misdeeds with their lives.

It is next to impossible to determine the extent of the dissemination and absorption of justification among broader strata of the Arab public. The preponderance of books rather than newspapers advocating this idea could point to a

---

56   For the proliferation of anti-Jewish writing in Egypt, see Rafael Israeli, *Peace is in the Eyes of the Beholder*, New York: 1985; Yadlin, *An Arrogant Oppressive Spirit*. For the "tacit deal," see Fouad Ajami, "The Orphaned Peace," in his *Dream Palaces*.

57   For a few exceptional justifications, see Muhammad Nasr Ahmad in *al-Hayat al-Jadida*, 7 November 1998, and the sermon broadcast on PNA TV, 13 May 2005 – PNW Bulletin, 16 May 2005.

smaller constituency, although the flow of ideas between books and newspapers cannot be denied. Concurrently, the use of this theme by various Islamist movements could mean that it reaches wider publics. Nizam 'Abbasi's stated intention of challenging the view that the extermination of the Jews benefited the Arab cause may indicate that such a view, which saw some positive elements in the Holocaust, was not rare.[58] Another indication is the response of 32 percent of the interviewees in Hilal Kashan's survey, who said that they felt no sympathy toward Holocaust survivors, because "the Jews deserved it."[59]

With these developments in mind, the justification of the Holocaust in the Arab media discourse could be excused as a mere manifestation of frustration caused by Israeli policies and as an extreme manifestation of a hyperbolic style in Arab public discourse, which exists in other fields as well. However, such a degree of demonization cannot be dismissed, in view of its potential influence on the minds of the audiences, regardless of the original intentions of its producers, just as other cases in history have shown, where words led to deeds.

---

58   'Abbasi, al-'Alaqat, p. 7.

59   Kashan, Arab Attitudes, p. 44. An anecdotal evidence, though problematic for drawing generalizations, may be found in notes written in Arabic by several visitors on 7 September 2003 at the SNP Museum in the Slovak town Banska Bystrica, which hosted a traveling exhibit of photographs of women, Jewish and non-Jewish, maltreated in Auschwitz and elsewhere during the Holocaust. A certain Khaled Zahariya [sic] from Saudi Arabia wrote in the exhibition's guestbook: "what Hitler did to the Jews is exactly what they deserve. Still, we would have wished that he could have finished incinerating all the Jews in the world, but time ran out on him and therefore Allah's curse be on him and on them." Ibrahim al-'Arimi from Oman commented: "The most beautiful sights of Jews." We are thankful to Dr. Mordechai Kedar for providing us with these photographs.

7

THE EQUATION OF ZIONISM WITH NAZISM

In the post-World War II era the branding of any enemy as equal to Hitler or Nazism became the ultimate verbal weapon of delegitimization. British Prime Minister Anthony Eden, for instance, described Egyptian President 'Abd al-Nasir as "Hitler on the Nile" prior to the 1956 Suez War. Years later, President George H. W. Bush equated Iraqi President Saddam Husayn with Hitler on the eve of the 1991 Gulf War.[1]

The equation of Zionism with Nazism, too, began shortly after the end of World War II as part of the Arab public debate on Zionism and Israel, among all ideological trends, and was raised by Arab spokesmen in various international forums. It was not the product of Soviet ideological and political influence, as previously thought, though it later borrowed themes from Soviet literature that presented Israel in the same vein during the 1970s and 1980s.[2] Still, it was broader and more intense than in most other places, not only due to the inclination toward inflammatory rhetoric in Arab public discourse. Rather, like Holocaust denial, the depiction of Zionism and Israel as Nazi became a major rhetorical means to delegitimize them. Arab writers were probably aware of the particular painful effect of such an equation on the Israeli psyche, in view of the past suffering of the Jews under the Nazis. They sought to deprive the Jews of their human dignity by equating them with their worst tormentors. Moreover, not only does this accusation transform victims into perpetrators, but it threatens them with the ultimate fate of the Nazis.

As in other themes, a high degree of continuity, alongside growing sophistication in arguments, characterizes the effort to equate Zionism with Nazism, employing pseudo-scholarly contentions, including the publication of academic

---

1   Keith Kyle, *Suez*, New York: 1991, p. 164; H. W. Brands, "George Bush and the Gulf War of 1991," *Presidential Studies Quarterly*, vol. 34, no. 1 (March 2004), note 53.

2   Lewis, *Semites and Anti-Semites*, pp. 162–3.

works at universities.[3] However, despite a broad consensus among various ideological trends in the Arab world on the alleged resemblance, there are disagreements over the given explanations. Proponents of the equation acknowledged Nazi atrocities committed against the Jews, but often minimized the number of Jewish victims or denied the Nazi policy of total annihilation of the Jews. The comparisons are often based on excessive exaggeration of alleged Israeli crimes as well as on distortion, if not outright falsification, of Zionist ideology with the occasional resort to citations that are either patently incorrect or taken out of context. First and foremost among these fallacies is that Zionism is based on racial ideology.

While reflecting the widespread notion that Nazism and Hitler were the epitome of evil, such equations – intentionally or not – demonstrate clear misunderstanding or conscious misrepresentation of the essence of Nazism, whose most salient feature and distinct character was murderous racism, by presenting it as merely one racist movement among many others. They often meant the downgrading of the horrors of Nazism itself to mere oppression, persecution or military aggression rather than large-scale genocidal policies. Consequently, the equation metaphor is used as one more tool of Holocaust denial. For instance, the Amman-based Lebanese journalist Hayat al-Huwayk 'Atiyya states explicitly that the Nazi "final solution" did not mean the extermination of the Jews, but merely removing them from Germany, just as the Zionists sought to remove the Palestinians from their land.[4]

Quite a few of these comparisons were logically flawed, pointing to common attitudes of both movements, such as their opposition to Communism, which apply to many other national or ideological movements, including in the Arab world, and rendering the equation totally meaningless. Other logically flawed equations argue that if a certain historical phenomenon preceded another one it must have produced it, or that if two historical movements – Zionism and Nazism in this case – emerged during the same historical period or in geographical proximity they must have been intertwined or identical.

3   See, for example, Nadiya Sa'd al-Din, *al-Sahyuniyya wal-naziyya wa-ishkaliyyat al-ta'ayush ma'a al-akhar*, Amman: 2004, which is based on her MA thesis approved by Al al-Bayt University in Jordan, and the numerous publications by 'Abd al-Wahhab al-Masiri discussed below.

4   Hayat al-Huwayk 'Atiyya, "al-'Alaqa al-sahyuniyya al-naziyya, 1933–1941," www.ssnp. info/thenews/daily/Makalat/Hayat/Hayat_25-12-05.htm. See also Tal'at Rumayh, "al-Sahyuniyya wal-fashiyya: jawhar fikri wahid," www.moqawama.tv/arabic/f_vzioni.htm, who solves the contradiction between the Nazi extermination of the Jews and the claim of their great similarity by minimizing the number of Jewish victims and highlighting the false charge of Zionist–Nazi collaboration.

The equation theme appears in the Arab public discourse in two major ways. The first purports to show substantive resemblance or even identity between Zionism or Judaism and Nazi ideology, best articulated in Mamduh al-Shaykh Ali's statement that a close examination of the two ideologies would show that "Zionism is nothing but Nazism with a Jewish face while Nazism is actually Zionism with a secular look."[5] The second equates Israel's policies, and particularly its treatment of the Palestinians, with those of the Nazis, or describes Israel as worse than the Nazis.[6]

The alleged ideological similarity

Various Arab writers claimed an alleged similarity between Zionism and Nazism in ideology, ambitions and practices already in the late 1940s, rejecting what they saw as Zionist attempts to mislead world opinion as to the hostility between the two movements. The resemblance allegedly stemmed first and foremost from the principle of racial purity, which guided both movements, and from their aggressive natures. Racism among the Jews was manifested in their self-perception as "God's chosen people," which was equivalent in essence to the Nazi concept of Aryan racial superiority. "The Jews sucked Nazism into their veins, and embraced a racist, wicked, and resentful culture," wrote Rakan al-Majali, a columnist in the semi-official Jordanian daily *al-Dustur*.[7] Some even contend that the very claim of the Jews that they constitute one nation is essentially a Nazi idea, since they are merely an amalgam of totally separate groups sharing nothing in common. Just as the Nazis emphasized racial purity, so does the imaginary (*maz'um*) Jewish race contend that it is the purest of all races, therefore forbidding intermarriages between Jews and non-Jews and believing in its right to dominate others.[8] These claims distort the basic tenets of

5 Al-Shaykh Ali, "Nahwu ru'ya."

6 In addition to the innumerable newspaper articles which employ this theme, there were several books fully dedicated to this comparison, e.g., 'Isam Shurayh, *al-Sahyuniyya wal-naziyya*, Beirut: 1969; Mu'in Ahmad Mahmud, *al-Sahyuniyya wal-naziyya*, Beirut: 1971; 'Abd al-Nasir Hurayz, *al-Nizam al-siyasi al-irhabi al-isra'ili: Dirasa muqarina ma'a al-naziyya wal-fashistiyya wal-nizam al-'unsuri fi janub afriqiya*, Cairo: 1997.

7 *Al-Dustur*, 9 March 2007.

8 For examples, see 'Abbas Mahmud al-'Aqqad, "al-Sahyuniyya wal-shuyu'iyya," in *al-Sahyuniyya*, pp. 84–5, 148; Hasan Sa'b, *Zionism and Racism*, Beirut: 1965, p. 9; Hifni Qadri, *Tajsid al-wahm: dirasa sikulijiyya lil-shakhsiyya al-isra'iliyya*, Cairo: 1971, p. 85; Mahmud, *al-Sahyuniyya wal-naziyya*, pp. 292, 296–7; Jam'iyyat al-kharijiyyin fi al-kuwait, *al-Qadiyya al-filastiniyya fi arba'in 'aman bayna darawat al-waqi' wa-tumu'at al-mustaqbal*, Kuwait, n.d., p. 12; Ramadan, *Isra'il*, pp. 185–200; Akram 'Atallah, "al-Sahyuniyya al-naziyya: bayna huriyyat al-bahth wa-tahrimihi," *Ru'ya*, no. 10 (July 2001), pp. 54–5; Hasan Hanafi in *al-Zaman*, 5 January 2005; Ahmad Anwar, *Mukhattatat al-yahudiyya*

Jewish beliefs and practices. Jews indeed opposed intermarriage – for religious not racial reasons, fearing their assimilation and extinction as a minority in the larger societies within which they lived, fears which characterized other religious minorities for centuries. Jews permit marriages once the non-Jewish spouse embraces Judaism, whereas racists oppose any intermarriage, based on the flawed notion of the resultant mixing of blood.[9]

The Jewish self-perception as the chosen people has aroused the wrath of many peoples throughout history, even though other nations saw themselves in the same vein.[10] Muslims, in particular, found this claim provocative. The main reason for this annoyance was the contrast between the Jewish belief and the Muslims' self-perception of being "the best nation that hath been raised up unto mankind" (Qur'an, Surat Al 'Imran 106), and the carriers of the true faith that superseded Judaism and Christianity. Moreover, according to Islamic tradition, the Jews were destined to humiliation and subjugation to the Muslims, due to their rejection of the Prophet Muhammad's message. Consequently, the emergence of Zionism and Israel's successes vis-à-vis the Arabs posed a theological and psychological problem for many Muslims, who saw them as an aberration or distortion of the correct cosmological order.[11]

Many of the Arab writers seemed to be unaware of or ignored the major difference between the Jewish notion of the chosen people and the Nazi ideal. The Jews were not chosen by God because of their inherent genetic superiority or other qualities, as the Bible makes explicitly clear, but rather as carriers of a divine mission "of making the world a better place (*Tikkun ha-olam*)."[12] Judaism, which considered all human beings as created in the image of God, was never a proselytizing religion, unlike Christianity or Islam. It did not reject converts,

lil-saytara 'ala al-'alam wa-kayfiyyat muwajahatiha, Cairo: 2006; Walid Muhammad 'Ali, "al-Sahyuniyya wal-naziyya takamul al-adwar," 16 June 2006, www.falasteen.com/article.php3?id_article=60. An exceptional view is offered by Egyptian academic al-Rajih, *al-Shakhsiyya*, p. 52, who criticizes the Jewish notion of the "chosen people," but explains its fundamental divergence from the Nazi idea.

9   Islamic law allows Muslim men to marry non-Muslim women because the children would be considered Muslim, but bans the marriage of Muslim women to non-Muslims.

10   For the prevalence of this phenomenon see Anthony Smith, *Chosen Peoples: Sacred Sources of National Identity*, Oxford: 2003, and Bruce Cauthen, "Covenant and Continuity: Ethno-Symbolism and the Myth of Divine Election," *Nations and Nationalism*, vol. 10, nos 1–2 (January 2004), pp. 19–33.

11   See for instance, Nettler, *Past Trials*, pp. 5–6, 19–23; Lewis, *Semites and Anti-Semites*, p. 185.

12   See, Gilbert S. Rosenthal, "Tikkun ha-olam: The Metamorphosis of a Concept," *Journal of Religion*, vol. 85, no. 2 (April 2005), pp. 214–27; David Novak, *The Election of Israel: The Idea of the Chosen People*, Cambridge: 1995.

whereas racist ideologies, and Nazism in particular, totally excluded the possibility of any member of the so-called "lower races" joining the "superior one." Ahmad Baha' al-Din explains the clash between Nazism and Zionism as natural and inevitable, in view of their common character as two racist movements. That the Nazis massacred the Jews rather than the other way around does not prove that the Jews were just or innocent and the Nazis were evil, but simply that the Nazis were stronger than the Jews. Had the Jews been more powerful, they would have committed the same massacres against the Germans. Such a statement is not intended to exonerate or justify the Nazis, he cautions, since Nazism is a black page in human history, but so is Zionism. Both ideologies are based on the same racist ideas and philosophies, "which have to be eradicated from the face of the earth." Similarly, Mamduh al-Shaykh Ali contends that this supposed resemblance was the real reason for Hitler's animosity towards the Jews, citing a [fictitious] statement by Hitler that "two chosen peoples cannot coexist, and we are the only true chosen nation."[13]

A corollary argument for the resemblance between Nazism and Zionism is that both are based on lies and deceits. Therefore, 'Abd al-Rahman Sulayman and Ahmad al-Hamli contend, just as science refuted the claim of Aryan racial superiority, it rejects the supposed Zionist claim that the Jews are a race entitled to sovereignty and rule over humanity and that Judaism is a racial identity (*jinsiyya*). According to Nadiya Sa'd al-Din, the Zionist case is even weaker. Nazism was influenced by the heritage of German and western thinkers and philosophers, whereas Zionism is a "borrowed" philosophy and strategy to be applied in a foreign environment, since the Jews are not a people and their link to Palestine is too fallacious to serve as the basis for a genuine national ideology.[14]

The UN General Assembly resolution of 1975 which equated Zionism with racism provided Arab writers with supposedly objective support for their claims. The Institute for Arab Research and Studies (*ma'had al-buhuth wal-dirasat al-'arabiyya*), which was affiliated with the Arab League, published a collection of articles on the essence of racism and Zionism which contained all the common motifs equating Zionism with Nazism. The overall conclusion of the contributors, all of whom were senior Egyptian academics and publicists, was that Zionism was a sub-type of Fascism, as it was a national idea based on racism. Whereas the liberal solution to the Jewish problem advocated the assimilation

---

13   Baha' al-Din, *Isra'iliyyat*, p. 170; al-Shaykh Ali, "Nahwu ru'ya."
14   'Abd al-Rahman Sulayman and Ahmad al-Hamli, *Isra'il ba'd al-zilzal*, Cairo: 1975, pp. 12–13; Sa'd al-Din, *al-Sahyuniyya wal-naziyya*, reviewed in www.aljazeera.net/NR/exeres/71628824-A250-4F24-86D9-00C867C3DA2B.htm. Dissuqi and Salman, *al-Sahyuniyya*, pp. 75, 85, 101, 103; Muhammad Faraj, *al-Sahyuniyya mashru' isti'mari*, Cairo: 1983, p. 3; Munir al-Ma'shush, *al-Sahyuniyya*, Beirut: 1979, pp. 80–4.

of the Jews into the societies in which they lived and the socialist solution advocated a social revolution, Zionism proposed a racist solution based on extremist nineteenth-century racist ideology and on the notion that the Jews are "God's chosen people." The closest European ideology to Zionism, they maintained, was racist Nazism. Moreover, as the "master race," each movement sought to impose peace and put the entire world at the service of its superior culture "through the sword."[15]

The Palestinian lawyer 'Issa Nakhle points to the "mutual admiration" between Nazism and Zionism and explains that both movements suffer from the same pathology, since their basic belief systems reject all morality and any concept of good and evil or any rational discourse. He equates Hitler's statement that only members of the German nation, i.e., those who have German blood, can be German citizens to the alleged Israeli principle that only those having Jewish blood belong to the nation. Consequently, he adds, no Arab can belong to this nation.[16] Islamist Kamal Sa'fan contends that both Zionism and Nazism went a long way in boasting in their national uniqueness and in their hatred and humiliation of the other. Based on Aryan racial uniqueness, the Nazis demanded the allegiance of all other Germans, wherever they resided. Similarly, Zionists require the allegiance of all dispersed Jews. Zionist thought on Palestine, he says, was the same as Julius Streicher's definition, of greater Germany as the land where all Germans and those having German blood should live. Moreover, many of the Zionist and Nazi ideas converge, he claims, such as the belief in the superman, focusing on the past and the future, contempt for slaves and for the diaspora, denial of real history, hostility toward free thought, and belief in a Godless religion.[17]

Racial purity, various Arab writers maintained, led Nazis and Zionists to believe not only in their racial superiority, but also in the unique historical and cultural mission they had to fulfill.[18] Zionism translated the idea of "the chosen people" and the aspiration to be "light unto the nations" into a mixture

---

15   Mufid, Yasin and Rizq, *al-Sahyuniyya wal-'unsuriyya*, pp. 13, 27, 35.

16   In addition to the false claim on Jewish blood as the precondition of belonging to the Jewish nation, as non-Jews could and did become Jews, Nakhle confuses Hitler's statement on citizenship in a state with the Jewish perception of belonging to a nation, and omits the fact that non-Jews can become and are citizens of Israel.

17   Sa'fan, *al-Yahud*, p. 103; Mahmud, *al-Sahyuniyya wal-naziyya*, p. 210; Nakhle, *Encyclopaedia*, vol. 2, pp. 870, 872.

18   Like other nationalist movements that were influenced by nineteenth-century German romanticism, Arab nationalism too regarded itself as having a historical mission to humanity. The slogan of the pan-Arab Ba'th party, for example, spoke of "One Arab nation with an eternal mission," referring to the cultural mission the Arabs carried for the entire world.

of racism and religious fanaticism and developed an exploitative and aggressive chauvinism out of the belief that God had created the gentiles to serve the Jews. As early as 1958, Palestinian Fayiz Sayigh charged that "the Zionist concept of the 'final solution' to the 'Arab problem' in Palestine and the Nazi concept of the 'final solution to the Jewish problem' in Germany consisted essentially of the same basic ingredient: the elimination of the unwanted human element in question." While he conceded that the Nazis used more ruthless means, he insisted that "behind the difference in techniques lay an identity of goals."[19] Therefore, Zionism saw no problem in the mass expulsion of the Palestinians, Sulayman and Hamli wrote. Nazism espoused the idea of "Germany above all" and claimed the right to expand and to dominate other "inferior" peoples, justifying its aggression with the motto of "living space (*Lebensraum*) for the German people." Zionism preceded Nazism but justified its expansionism by a similar terminology and the catchphrase of "secure borders."[20]

Several writers emphasize the close resemblance between the two movements by referring to common ideological origins in nineteenth-century romanticist nationalism, particularly the idea of "organic nationalism" (*qawmiyya 'udwiyya*), ignoring the fact that all ethnic nationalisms drew from the same roots, and that Nazism and Zionism subsequently developed in two very different directions.[21] Muhammad Khalid al-Az'ar points to the German background of many of the early Zionists as proof that both Nazism and Zionism "originated from the same ideological source," and emphasizes the Yiddish language, the "language of Zionist conspiracies," which grew out of German, as another significant indicator.[22]

Of particular importance within this shared ideological origin, according to some writers, was the belief in social Darwinism. The Palestinian Encyclopedia

19 Fayiz A. Sayigh, *Risalat al-mufakkir al-'arabi*, Beirut: 1955, pp. 26–7, cited in Harkabi, *Arab Attitudes*, p. 176.

20 Sulayman and Hamli, *Isra'il*, p. 13; Sa'b, *Zionism and Racism*; Bahjat Abu Gharbiyya, "Safahat min ta'rikh al-qadiyya al-filastiniyya hatta 'am 1949: al-ru'ya al-ta'rikhiyya wa-malamih al-tajriba al-dhatiyya," in Jam'iyyat al-kharijiyyin, *al-Qadiyya al-filastiniyya*, p. 12; *Filastin al-Thawra*, 30 April 1983; Marwan Darwish, *al-Judhur al-ta'rikhiyya li-hizb al-likud (takattul)*, Nablus: 1996, p. 10; *al-Ahram*, 18 April 1997; Al-Jazeera TV, 15 May 2001 – Memri, Special Dispatch Series, no. 225, 6 June 2001.

21 Masiri, "al-ibada," p. 62; al-Shaykh Ali, "Nahwu ru'ya." Radical Islamists employ the same argument against Arab nationalism, particularly the teachings of Michel 'Aflaq, ideologue of the Ba'th party. See Safar al-Hawali, "al-Qawmiyya," www.alhawali.com. inded; 'Umar 'Abd al-Hakim, "Abu Mus'ab al-Suri," *Da'wat al-Muqawama al-'alamiyya al-islamiyya*, www.megaupload.com/sa/?d=DL4T5CZK, pp. 592–3.

22 Muhammad Khalid al-Az'ar, "al-Tashabuh bayna al-'aqida al-sahyuniyya wal-fikr al-nazi," www.moqawama.tv/arabic/f_vzioni.htm.

claims that the central idea common to Zionism and other racist movements is the belief that the world is comprised of different nations that are in state of perpetual struggle, and that the superior ones must dominate the weaker and take over their wealth. The leftist columnist Jurji Haddad maintains that although both movements were influenced by Darwin's view of the struggle for survival, they did not adopt his progressive idea of development and evolution, as demonstrated by Zionist pride over the survival of the Jewish race through the centuries.[23] Haddad and 'Abd al-Wahhab al-Masiri also find shared ideological origins for both movements, since both draw upon the German philosophers Friedrich Nietzsche and Heinrich Trietschke.[24]

By contrast, Islamist writer Jawdat al-Sa'd sees Judaism as the source of the Nietzschean ideas, which gave birth to Nazism. He contends that the [non-existent] saying "God will uproot the weak and the useless with wool shears" acquired a sacred status among the Jews, as it was attributed to the Patriarch Isaac in the Torah, and consequently was accepted as a model for emulation in the Zionists' conduct toward themselves and others. This saying, which stresses the importance of power, justified the need to sever the weak limbs from the Jewish body and uproot the non-Jews in order to attain power, and its logic fits all racist ideas, particularly Nazism. Judaism, therefore, was the racist exemplar for chauvinistic movements. The Nazis and those like them borrowed their ideas from Judaism. Since Nazi theoreticians such as Alfred Rosenberg, in *The Myth of the Twentieth Century*, drew their ideas from Nietzsche, the tight link between Judaism as a religion and Nazi ideology was self-evident, he concluded.[25]

The Palestinian-Jordanian Fahd al-Rimawi attributed Jewish sensitivity to the equation with Nazism to two factors: Nazi persecution of the Jews, but also the Jewish origins of Nazism. *The Protocols of the Elders of Zion*, that personified Jewish philosophy, he says, served as the basis of Nazi ideas. The Islamist

23 *Al-Mawsu'a al-filastiniyya*, Damascus: 1974, vol. 4, q.v. "Al-Sahyuniyya wal-naziyya," pp. 431–4; Jurji Haddad, "al-Tamathul wal-ta'awun bayna al-sahyuniyya wal-naziyya," *Shu'un Filastiniyya*, no. 209 (August 1990), p. 62; al-Az'ar, "al-Tashabuh."

24 Haddad, "al-tamathul," pp. 64–5; Masiri, *al-Sahyuniyya*, p. 144. See also Mahmud, *al-sahyuniyya wal-naziyya*, p. 154.

25 Sa'd, *al-Shakhsiyya*, pp. 199–200. See also, Jarbu'a, *Tabri'at hitler*, p. 23. Anis Mansur, by contrast, argues that Nietzsche despised the Jews, but they had re-edited his books after World War II, removing all the anti-Jewish statements from them and blaming his sister for inserting them, *al-Musawwar*, 6 December 1963. For an analysis of Nietzsche's complex attitude toward Jews and Judaism, which distinguishes between his views on (1) pre-prophetic Judaism of the Old Testament, (2) prophetic Judaism which influenced Christianity, and (3) modern Judaism, see Michael F. Duffy and Willard Mittelman, "Nietzsche's Attitude Towards the Jews," *Journal of the History of Ideas*, vol. 49, no. 2 (April 1988), pp. 301–17.

Dr. Salah al-Zaru al-Tamimi goes further back in time and finds the origins of the Nuremberg laws in the edicts of the Second-Temple Biblical author Ezra.[26] These contentions found their logical conclusion in Dia' al-Hajiri's statement that "the fusion of the Jews and the Nazis created the Zionist demon."[27]

Dr. Khalid al-Adghar reiterated the claim that Zionism was "one of Nazism's ancestors," since its racism went earlier in time and was rooted in the Torah. Still, as Zionism had many thinkers, while Nazism had only one philosopher, Alfred Rosenberg, its philosophical basis was weaker. Nevertheless, Nazism was merely Zionism's "failing disciple," because it brought upon itself the wrath of the whole world, whereas Zionism managed to build a state and even win international support.[28] For the radical Saudi cleric Safar al-Hawali, the supposedly Jewish "Talmudic" roots of Nazism were the ultimate proof of the evil of that movement.[29]

Several writers, both leftists and Islamists, consider Zionism as the ideological source of Nazism. The Ba'thist writer 'Abd al-Wahhab Zaytun and the Algerian Ben Ashenhu claim that the Nazis drew from Zionism their idea of racial hierarchy which positioned the European whites at the top while placing the Arabs and blacks at the bottom, in order to facilitate their invasion of the lands of these inferior peoples and seize their lands for the Nazi "living space." The Lebanese Walid Muhammad 'Ali, citing the Soviet "thinker" Yevgeni Yevseyev, claims that Hitler himself conceded that he learned from the Zionists how to employ "political intrigues, secret tactics, terrorism, hidden secrets and manipulations."[30]

Writers of the left often allege resemblance between Zionism and Nazism as two capitalist phenomena hostile to Communism and Socialism. Like many Marxist writers in the West, they tend to underplay the racist elements of Nazism and present it as not much different from other types of Fascism.[31] Consequently, they tend to see German Nazism, Italian Fascism and Zionism as a manifestation of the "disgraceful decay" of European national thought resulting

---

26   *Al-Dustur*, 16 April 1997; *al-Sabil*, 8 March 1999; Zaytun, *Yahudiyya*, p. 105.

27   'Abd al-Wahhab al-Masiri, "Zahirat mu'adat al-yahud bayna al-haqiqa wal-haqa'iq," *Shu'un Filastiniyya*, nos. 225–6 (December 1991/January 1992), p. 82; idem, "al-ibada," p. 68. See a similar argument in al-Shaykh Ali, "Nahwu ru'ya"; Diya' al-Hajiri, *Isra'il min al-dakhil*, Cairo: 2002, p. 67.

28   *Al-'Arabi*, 6 May 2001.

29   Al-Hawali, *al-Qawmiyya*.

30   Ben Ashenhu, *Usul al-sahyuniyya*, pp. 64–5. See also al-Kaylani, *al-Irhab*, p. 7; 'Ali, "al-Sahyuniyya wal-naziyya."

31   For such views, see Kershaw, *The Nazi Dictatorship*, pp. 18–41.

from the crisis of capitalism, and adopt Marx's hostile stand toward Judaism as the epitome of bourgeois capitalism.[32]

Qasim Hasan, an Iraqi communist, finds three major similarities between Zionism and Nazism which demonstrate the Fascist essence of Zionism. First, German, Italian and Japanese Fascism were all terrorist dictatorships created by capitalism as an instrument of political control and as part of the imperialist drive for colonial expansion. Likewise, Zionism is a foreign invasion of western capitalists into the Arab East, designed to set up a capitalist Jewish state, supported by international capitalism, in order to dominate the Arab economies. Like them, Zionism cannot exist without terror designed to displace the Palestinians. Second, European and Japanese Fascisms used nationalism in order to appeal to the masses and seduce them into supporting imperialism and the domination of the Arab world. Similarly, Zionism uses nationalism to acquire the support of international Jewry and transform it into an auxiliary force in the struggle against the Arab liberation movement. Third, Fascism does not have a new economic theory that would replace capitalism and is merely a tool of those who support violence in order to impose their will on others. In the same vein, Zionism is a tool of western imperialism against the Arabs. Zionism, he concludes, contains all the attributes of a Fascist system in both its economic outlook and its resort to terror.[33] Like Qasim, Hamad Maw'id stresses the centrality of violence and power in Zionism and Fascism. He describes Zionism as one of the most extremist manifestations of Fascism because it seeks to carry out a genocide of the Palestinian people, or at least ethnocide, that is, the complete destruction of their economic, cultural and social life, in order to facilitate the establishment of a pure Jewish state.[34]

Echoing crude Marxist analyses of Nazism as merely one facet of Fascism, Jurji Haddad rejects the depiction of Nazism and Judaism as racist entities based on belief in genetic superiority and national exclusiveness. Rather, adapting Marx's *Zur Judenfrage* to the post-World War II period, he regards both ideologies as two currents which developed out of capitalism and typify it, but which are being depicted in racist terminology. The first one is the isolationist approach of nationalist chauvinism that gave birth to Nazism, and the second is sectoral or class exploitation of cosmopolitan anti-nationalism represented by Zionism. The result of both was the emergence of national and international

32   'Adnan 'Abd al-Rahim, *al-Idi'ulujiyya al-sahyuniyya bayna al-tazayyuf al-nazari wal-waqi' al-isti'mari*, Beirut: 1978, p. 43; Mahmud 'Abbas, "al-Sahyuniyya taw'am al-naziyya wal-yahud awwal dahayaha," *Shu'un Filastiniyya*, no. 112 (March 1981), p. 6.

33   Qasim Hasan, *al-'Arab wal-mushkila al-yahudiyya*, Beirut: 1949, pp. 103–4.

34   *Al-Hurriyya*, 11 March 1990.

capitalist markets during the imperialist phase of capitalism, i.e., the highest form of capitalism, according to the Leninist concept. Although both represent the two faces of capitalism, Zionism is the worst. That is because the historical sin of the Jews is to be the incarnation of capitalism, which is the "vilest form of exploitation." Nazi ideology is German-born, but the difference between the German ideology and the German personality is very wide, whereas there is complete identity between Judaism and Zionism. The blame on the Jews for this historical sin does not stem exclusively from their chronological precedence in capitalism, or from the fact that Jewish ideology is "the mother of all exploitative ideologies," but from present-day materialistic reality. In other words, the Jews represent the group that leads, or stands at the top of the pyramid of capitalist exploitation. At the time, Nazism was the enemy in front, but it was less dangerous to the world's progressive liberation movement from the long-term historical point of view. Had Zionism succeeded in subjugating Germany politically and economically and forging a worldwide imperialist alliance such as present-day NATO against the Soviet Union and the Chinese Revolution, the universal liberation movement would have been much worse off today, he concludes.[35]

Some writers emphasize the "identity" in the Nazi and Zionist attitudes toward the status of the Jews in European societies. Masiri depicts anti-Semitic hatred toward the Jews as a "clear cut Zionist position." Both Zionism and Nazism saw the Jew as an exceptional person who did not belong to the nation in which he lived and was independent of any social obligations. Both believed that the Jews always stood opposite to the gentiles and that they possessed ingrained characteristics that precluded their assimilation.[36] What the proponents of this point ignore is the fact that the Zionist view of Jewish alienation came in response to the failure of Jewish emancipation and integration in Europe, and to growing anti-Semitism.[37]

---

35   Haddad, *al-Mas'ala al-yahudiyya*, pp. 151–8, 160, 245–6.

36   Masiri, "al-Ibada," p. 67; 'Atallah, "al-Sahyuniyya;" Darraj, "al-Talfiq wal-'udwaniyya," claims that Zionism "invented" anti-Semitism in order to advance its idea of the Jews' "otherness."

37   Post-Zionist historians in Israel criticized Zionism for unconsciously adopting various anti-Semitic stereotypes regarding Diaspora Jews; see, for instance, Rina Rekem-Peled, "Zionism as Reflection of Anti-Semitism: On the Relations between Zionism and Anti-Semitism in Germany of the Second Reich," in Jacob Borut and Oded Heilbruner (eds.), *German Anti-Semitism*, Tel Aviv: 2000 (Hebrew), pp. 133–56. The difference, however, between this criticism, which focused on culture and behavior rather than on racist foundations, and Masiri's accusations, is that Zionists believed they could transform the Jews into a healthier nation, whereas the much more violent, Fascist and crude Nazi depiction of the Jews served as justification for annihilating them.

Munir Ma'shush finds great resemblance between Hitler's statement on the need to "annihilate the intelligentsia as a law of life however cruel," and a [fabricated] statement by the Zionist leader and future prime minister Menahem Begin that "there should be no mercy in killing the enemy until we destroy the so-called Arab civilization and build our own unique culture on its ruins." Just as the Nazis dreamed of building an empire based on their ancient empire on which the sun never sets, so do the Zionists dream of rebuilding greater Israel from the Nile to the Euphrates.[38]

Such arguments were not confined to radical Islamists or intellectuals writing in obscure publications. The late Syrian President Hafiz al-Assad (d. 2000) summed up these motifs in a speech that was quoted verbatim in a Syrian school textbook. Assad asserted that, in essence, there is no difference between Nazism and Zionism, in view of their indistinguishable claims to racial superiority, adding that the Nazis justified the occupation of other countries by their need for "living space," while the Zionists occupy Arab lands under the guise of securing their state. The Nazis persecuted and expelled [but did not exterminate, he implies] other people and the Zionists do the same today to the Arab peoples and to the Muslim peoples in the future. Another Syrian school textbook, citing a document of the ruling Ba'th party, defined Zionism as "a racist Nazi movement that seeks to settle in parts of the Arab homeland." Textbooks used by the Palestinian Authority also compare the two movements and conclude that Zionism and Nazism are "the most blatant examples of racist belief and discrimination."[39]

Several among those who make the equation insist that Zionism is worse than Nazism. Most prominent is Syrian President Bashar al-Assad, who stated that "Zionism is racism, which exceeded Nazi racism."[40] Dissuqi and Salman argue that Zionism went further than Nazism in its aspiration to take over the whole world under one Jewish government until the Day of Judgment. The Nazis were satisfied by Aryan domination in and exploitation of Eastern Europe, whereas the Zionists seek to "control the fate of humanity." In 1975, *Filastin al-Thawra* claimed that the Nuremberg Laws were less stringent than the laws of the Jewish Talmud, while the Hamas Charter maintained 13 years later that Zionism represented Nazism in its worst form, implying that there were better

---

38   Ma'shush, *al-Sahyuniyya*, pp. 80–1, 83.

39   *National (Pan-Arab) Socialist Education for the Tenth Grade: 1998–1999*, p. 93, citing Assad's speech to the Islamic Summit in Kuwait, 27 January 1981; *National (Pan-Arab) Socialist Education for the Eight Grade 1999–2000*, p. 96. Both quoted in Meirav Wurmeisser, *The Schools of Ba'athism: A Study of Syrian Schoolbooks*, Tel Aviv: 2000, p. 13; *Yedi'ot Aharonot* Friday Supplement, 23 July 1999.

40   *Al-Thawra*, 16 February 2006.

forms of Nazism. "When we compare Zionism to the Nazis we are actually doing the Nazis a disservice although we condemn their acts; this is because the horrific crimes against humanity committed by the Nazis do not equate with Zionist terrorism against the Palestinian people," concluded then Hamas leader 'Abd al-'Aziz al-Rantisi on 19 August 2003, on the same day that Hamas carried out a suicide attack in Jerusalem.[41]

'Abd al-Wahhab al-Masiri and the "scientific equation"

Undoubtedly the most consistent, complex and comprehensive equation of Zionism with Nazism since the 1970s was made by 'Abd al-Wahhab al-Masiri. Unlike others, Masiri sought to extricate the Arab discussion of the Holocaust from the strict Arab-Israeli context and examine it in a larger context of historical critique of western culture. In that sense he shares the long line of Muslim writers who contrasted the "rationalist-materialist" West with "spiritual" and "moral" Islam. At the same time, he seeks to endow his analysis with a philosophical-historical basis. Unlike other writers, he makes extensive use of western scholarly literature on the Holocaust and Nazism in addition to the writings of various Holocaust deniers. In the course of 30 years of writing his arguments underwent significant evolution and became more sophisticated from crude Holocaust denial during the 1970s to the acceptance of the destruction of the Jews as an historical fact, while giving it his unique interpretation and significance. Unlike his earlier writings in which he rejected the "fallacious 6,000,000 figure," and belittled the extent of the Holocaust, in his later works Masiri came out against the preoccupation with numbers as missing the main historical problem concerning Nazism, but continued to reject the findings of the western academic research on the Holocaust.

Masiri explains in the introduction to his book *Zionism, Nazism and the End of History* that his aim is to conduct a comprehensive reassessment of Nazism and the Holocaust, which would undermine the hegemonic Zionist approach to these issues. His main conclusion is that Nazism is not an aberration or distortion of core western values and culture, as the flawed common western scholarship claims, but rather it is a central and fundamental element within Western civilization and western modernity, as is Zionism. Hence, in his view the great similarity between the two movements.

---

41   Dissuqi and Salman, *al-Sahyuniyya*, pp. 75, 85, 101, 103; *Filastin al-Thawra*, 12 January 1975; *The Hamas Charter*, articles 20, 31, www.palestinecenter.org/cpap/documents/charter.html; Rantisi in *al-Risala* (Gaza), 21 August 2003. See also, 'Abbas, "al-Sahyuniyya," p. 6; Jam'iyyat al-kharijiyyin, *al-qadiyya al-filastiniyya*, p. 22; Ma'shush, *al-Sahyuniyya*, pp. 80–4; al-Shimali, "al-Fariq."

To prove his point, Masiri adopts the "counter-history" (*tawthiq mudad*) methodology or deconstruction, whose main goal, in his words, is to take out from the vast array of facts and evidence (*qara'in*) anything that will render the hegemonic western Zionist explanatory model totally objectionable or at least hardly acceptable. He has no intention, he says, to carry out a construction effort that is supposed to clarify what happened in Nazi society or inside the camps. Rather, he seeks to understand the civilizational, historical, cultural and political framework of the Nazi phenomenon. He assures the readers that he would strive to reach these goals without diminishing the extent of Nazi crimes against the Jews, the Slavs, the Roma and others, as that would be a cognitive and moral failure, even though Zionism used the Nazi extermination for its own purposes of plundering other nations and to justify the Israeli occupation. At the same time he promises not to become a victim of prejudicial views, ideas and epistemological categories that exist in the Western discourse. Clarifying the truth, he adds, would foil Zionist efforts to instrumentalize (*tawzif*) the Western-Nazi crime in the service of Zionist crimes.

As his point of departure, Masiri contrasts the traditional Islamic and modern western concepts of the human condition. Similarly to most modern Islamic thinkers, he presents Islam as a spiritual world-view that subordinates human beings to a transcendental moral system centered on God, providing a comprehensive system of absolute moral values and principles. By contrast, the secular and materialistic mind-set has taken the lead in the West. This materialistic view and the new western philosophies that reject all metaphysical truths also freed humanity from its commitment to absolute values, mainly religion and religious morality. Western modernity, which focuses on a continuous and rapid change, rejects any permanence in every aspect of life including values, and is in fact a "value-free" modernity, which espouses total moral relativism. Consequently, religion was replaced by biological and racial characteristics as the basic criterion for classifying human beings. Through this development, Masiri contends, Western civilization eliminated the traditional person who believed in moral philosophical transcendental values that stood above history and the materialistic world. In the political sphere, western modernity gave birth to totalitarian secularist ideologies such as Marxism, Fascism and Nazism. Moreover, "both Nazism and Zionism are the ultimate manifestation of this type of modernity."[42] In his analysis Masiri presents a superficial and essentialist picture

---

42   Masiri, *al-Sahyuniyya*, pp. 26, 29, 33; idem, "al-Sahyuniyya wal-naziyya wal-ijra'at al-munfasala 'an al-qimma," 29 March 2005, www.aljazeera.net/NR/exeres/C875A445-A238–4349–884B-3BCC33AF6ECE.htm. Masiri ignores the fact that the same western culture also produced liberalism and democracy, which were missing from traditional religious societies.

of western culture that ignores its wealth and diversity, in addition to a totally distorted picture of Zionism which is based on a skewed reading of some Zionist sources and total disregard of all evidence that undermine his arguments. Likewise, his presentation of Nazism disregards the anti-modernist components and, more importantly, the anti-enlightenment core of this ideology.

Masiri concedes that western secularism and materialism gave birth to a humanistic tendency, which put human beings at the center of the human experience. Yet, their more important outcome, he asserts, was the emergence of other attitudes that glorified utilitarianism, achievements and progress regardless of the human and moral cost they entailed. This western utilitarian approach, shared by the left and the right as well as by "the Nazis and the Zionists," related to human beings as "human material," a "common Zionist–Nazi term" judging every person according to the benefit he brings to society, and served as the philosophical and emotional criterion for mass murder. It is this idea that has become dominant in the West, and as a result liberated human beings from any moral responsibility for their actions. The change was most poignantly manifested in the rise and dominance of Social Darwinism that espoused the idea that "might is right." Both, Nazism and Zionism, he claims, without bringing any credible evidence, insist that only the law of nature, that is, the "survival of the fittest," rather than morality, dominates human society. Thus, both justify the exploitation of the weak for the sake of the powerful and regard violence as a legitimate and absolute value.

Just as Nazi ideology divided Germans into those who were or were not useful, i.e., "mouths that eat but are not useful," he says, so was the emphasis on the usefulness of man a central theme in Zionist and western literature regarding the Jews. Its practical implication was the idea that he who did not benefit society did not deserve to live, hence the readiness in western civilization to get rid of undesired elements by organized extermination. In this way, he links the Darwinist-Nazi approach to the tendency among the Jews to highlight their contribution to the world and to the idea of turning the Jewish people into a productive collective, espoused by the socialist Zionist thinker Bear Borokhov.[43] The Zionists, Masiri claims, sought to fuse Darwinism with Judaism and some

---

43   Masiri, "al-Ibada," p. 63. Borokhov spoke of the need to turn the Jews into a productive people, but referred mainly to the needed transformation from merchants and pedlars in Eastern Europe to peasants and workers in their historic homeland out of the belief that physical work, particularly in agriculture, has positive psychological effects and would heal the Jewish people from the malaise of the Diaspora, an idea that had nothing to do with Masiri's interpretation. See Avraham Yassour, "Philosophy – Religion – Politics: Borochov, Bogdanov and Lunacharsky," *Studies in East European Thought*, vol. 31, no. 3 (April, 1986), pp. 199–230.

of their thinkers interpreted the wandering of the Israelites in the desert not as a punishment for their sins and moral corruption but as a divine application of the principle of natural selection in which God eliminated the weak so that only the strong, "the supermen," could enter the land of Canaan.

The western utilitarian Darwinist approach produced a hierarchy of superior and inferior races, in which the whites stood on top, while the blacks, the Arabs and the Jews were at the bottom, thereby serving as the scientific basis for imperialism.[44] The potential for extermination that had existed in this approach, according to Masiri, was realized in a gradual historical process, which transformed human beings into a commodity and led to the displacement of whole populations. The Zionist settlement in Palestine was part of the European "population transfer" idea of exporting the European problem to Third World countries, as well as a means to get rid of the Jews by sending them to Asia.[45] Concurrently, the exterminationist potential was fully realized in Nazi Germany, when it resorted to it in order to solve its domestic problems, he adds, reiterating in a way the arguments of a few western scholars who found the deep cause of the Holocaust in various aspects of western modernity and western culture.[46] Nazism exterminated the Jews and the Roma because they were useless and unproductive. Germany sought to rid itself of this useless mob by sending them to other countries, but those, including the US, refused to take them. By rejecting the Jewish immigration the West facilitated the Nazi crime and in fact agreed with its basic philosophy, even if it did not adopt the radical conclusion that evolved from it. In addition to the economic reasoning for extermination, Masiri finds a broader psychological and cultural framework for it, rooted in

---

44   Masiri, *al-Sahyuniyya*, pp. 27–30; idem, "al-Ibada," p. 63.

45   Masiri, *al-Sahyuniyya*, pp. 33, 35–9.

46   For scholarly views linking Nazism to western modernity, see Richard L. Rubenstein, "Modernization and the Politics of Extermination," Michael Berenbaum (ed.), *"A Mosaic of Victims," Non Jews Persecuted and Murdered by the Nazis*, London and New York: 1990; Zygmunt Bauman, *Modernity and the Holocaust*, Oxford: 1989. Historian Yehuda Bauer points to the failure of these contentions to explain why modernity did not produce Nazi-like regimes and murderous ideologies in other modern countries, e.g., the US and France, and why murderous regimes rose in countries like Ruwanda and Cambodia, *Rethinking*, pp. 68–92. For those who link Nazi extermination to economic thinking, see Goetz Aly and Susanne Heim, *Vordenker der Vernichtung, Auschwitz und die deutschen Plaene fuer new europäische Ordnung*, Hamburg: 1991 and idem, "The Economics of the Final Solution: A Case Study from the Generalgouvernment," *Simon Wiesenthal Center Annual*, no. 5 (1988), pp. 3–48. For criticism of this approach, see Dan Diner, "On Rationality and Rationalization: An Economic Explanation of the Final Solution," in his *Beyond the Conceivable: Studies on Germany, Nazism, and the Holocaust*, Berkeley: 2005, pp. 138–58; David Bankier, "Modernization and the Rationalization of Extermination," *Yad Vashem Studies*, vol. 24 (1995), pp. 79–98 (Hebrew).

German philosophy and in a Protestant cultural concept which combines ethical and religious elements.[47]

Masiri maintains that the Nazi solution to the Jewish problem was not substantially different from other western imperialist solutions offered to similar problems. Both Nazism and imperialism are rooted in the belief of white and Aryan supremacy over other races. This supremacy gives the Aryans the moral justification to solve their problems by exporting them to other countries, even if that means the elimination of their indigenous populations. When the Nazis failed to transfer the Jews to other countries, they removed them, together with the Slavs and Roma, to the death camps.[48] As proof for this argument, Masiri cites the Nazi ideologue Alfred Rosenberg, who spoke during his trial at Nuremberg about the integral link between Nazism and European colonialism, blurring the gap between colonialism that sought economic exploitation and the genocidal essence of Nazism.[49] Masiri adopts the self-justification of Nazi leaders as a reliable historical testimony as part of his critique of western culture. However, whereas the Nazis used such arguments to exculpate themselves, Masiri uses them to condemn western civilization as a whole. Thus, he asserts that those who sought revenge from Germany after the war shared with the Nazis the same concept of extermination.

In criticizing western culture for its utilitarianism and emphasis on technological development, Masiri claims that Nazism was the ultimate manifestation of western modernity, as shown in the concentration camps, which were designed to extract maximum labor and productivity under the worst possible conditions, a mentality which is the complete opposite of the humanism of Islam. Yet, while he gives a fairly reliable description of the horrible conditions in these camps, he totally ignores the extermination camps that were intended solely for the murder of the Jews and the absence of any economic logic in killing large numbers of people who could have worked and served the German war economy. Moreover, he ignores the irrational racial and anti-Jewish foundation of Nazism.[50]

Having "demonstrated" that Nazism and western culture are one and the same, Masiri proceeds to place them in opposition to Islam, thereby transform-

---

47   Masiri, *al-Sahyuniyya*, p. 45.

48   Slavs were not sent to death camps. The Nazis did use Russian PoWs for their horrific "medical" experiments and sent many thousands of members of the Polish intelligentsia and clergy as well as underground activists to Auschwitz, where they suffered like all prisoners. Many of them perished under the horrible conditions there or were executed on various excuses or occasions. But they were not sent to extermination, as the Jews.

49   Masiri, *al-Sahyuniyya*, pp. 13, 40.

50   Masiri, ibid., pp. 109–13.

ing Islam and Muslims into Nazism's opposite moral pole and, therefore, true victims. As a proof, he contends that the western response to the death camps and to the extermination of the Jews was no different from Nazism, from the moral point of view. The West sought to solve the Jewish problem and to compensate the Jews for what the Nazis did to them by establishing a state on the dead bodies of the Palestinians, as if the crime of Auschwitz could be erased by the crimes of Deir Yasin and Beirut.

To further prove that the Muslims and Islam, who had always been the ultimate "other" for the West ever since the eleventh-century Crusades, represent the true antithesis to western civilization, and to Nazism in particular, Masiri highlights the use of the term *Muselmann* ("Muslim" in German) during the Holocaust. The term described those camp inmates who had lost their will to live, due to starvation, and were in the process of dying. Masiri points to the explanation of this term given in the *Encyclopedia Judaica*, describing the victims sitting crossed-legged in an "oriental fashion," staring into the air, as a prelude to their death. This type of sitting is associated with Muslims, Masiri states, and he charges the *Encyclopedia* with racism, since the word "oriental" is interchangeable with "Muslim". Hence, when the Nazis came out against the Jews, they in fact directed their hatred and violence against the Muslims, who were their ultimate target and victims.[51] Masiri's reasoning, however, disregards the fact that the Jews not the Muslims were those who were murdered

This claim of describing the Muslims as the real victims of Nazism (and, in his view, of Zionism) enables Masiri to complete his overall argument. Western civilization bred imperialism, Darwinism, Nazism and Zionism, which are all linked to each other. Nazism is the genuine heir of western civilization, as it carries within itself the essence of western culture and psychology, and it represents western civilization in its confrontation with Islamic civilization. The Muslim or *Muselmann* has thus become the symbol of the ultimate "other" for Nazism, and only then was it applied to others, such as Jews and Slavs. Masiri further contends that the association of the *Muselmann* with the Muslims not only reflects the western view of the Muslims, but also clarifies why the West hastened to solve the crime of Auschwitz by the crimes of Deir Yasin and similar events. In all those cases, the crime was aimed at Muslims. This argument, he believes, takes away the monopoly of the Jews of the status of being the only victims of Nazism and exposes their control over knowledge. Otherwise, it would be difficult to understand why this important term, which proves the victimhood of the Muslims, had been hidden from the world.[52]

---

51   Masiri, ibid., p. 227.

52   Masiri, ibid., p. 228.

The series of linkages that Masiri makes between Nazism and western civilization, between the camp inmates and the Muslims, and between Auschwitz and the alleged equivalent Israeli crimes, enable him to demonstrate the more important association between Zionism and Nazism: the structural and essential similarity that led them to cooperate with each other.[53] Many of his claims are historically invalid; some are valid to all national movements, including Arabism, and as such misconstrue the true meaning of Nazism and the so-called negative aspects of Zionism. Others contradict each other. Masiri classifies these alleged similarities into four major categories: (1) organic nationalism, that is, the link between land and blood which leads to the enslavement of the other; (2) racial theories; (3) sanctification of the state; (4) the Darwinist Nietzschean origins. The similarities, Masiri maintains, are not coincidental, but rather they are the logical outcome of numerous historical factors. He notes that many of the late nineteenth-century Zionist thinkers saw German culture as the fulcrum of European culture, and points to the similarity between Yiddish and German. Both points are true, but are totally irrelevant. Zionist leaders, notably Herzl, like many Europeans at the time, admired German philosophy, poetry and music, but not the racist *Volkish* ideas of the extreme German right, whereas the similarity between languages does not reflect resemblance between ideologies. Hebrew and Arabic are close Semitic languages, but that does not imply that Zionism and Arabic nationalism drew from each other.

Masiri's first major argument is that Zionism stems from a mythological perception of reality which rejects reason and sanctifies emotion, and that as such it is identical with radical European romanticism and Nazi radicalism. The radicalism of Zionism, as well as its secularism, is of an irrational Fascist type. The Nazis emphasized the importance of Nordic folklore and popular legends, which they turned into a religion and an absolute source for values. The Zionists, Masiri insists, have done the same. They regarded Judaism as a sacred folklore of the so-called Jewish people that should not be discussed or questioned. The idea of the covenant between God and "the chosen people," in which God promised the sacred land of Palestine, was a popular myth from which Ben-Gurion [who was an avowed secularist] drew much benefit, and used for organizing his state borders, even though he himself did not believe in it. The "Prophetic trend," Masiri claims, is common to both Nazism and Zionism, as both see the prophet as a superman and both seek to realize absolute ideals. Concurrently, he adds, both movements believe in the pantheist idea of the "unity of being"

---

53 For the claim that similarity led to collaboration, see also al-Shaykh Ali, "Nahwu ru'ya"; Rumayh, "al-Sahyuniyya wal-fashiyya"; al-Az'ar, "al-Tashabuh"; and *al-Thawra*, 16 February 2006.

(*wahdat al-wujud*), which blurs the boundaries between the divine and earthly and replaces them with infinite and absolute vagueness.[54]

While presenting irrational mythology as the basis of Zionism and Nazism, Masiri makes the completely opposite assertion that a common characteristic of the two movements is rationalism (*'aqlana*), which is the opposite of the spirituality of Islam. This rationalism refers to the "means" that those movements employ, whereas "rationalism of the goals," apparently the moral aspect in his view, is left to the individual to decide.[55] The concentration camps in Germany, and allegedly those that exist in Israel, are the best manifestations of rationalism in western culture. Thus, he claims that what had happened in the "Nazi hell" of the camps is not different from what takes place in the "Zionist paradise" of Israeli prisons. Likewise, he claims that Germany's relations with the Jewish ghettoes were essentially "colonial," not different from Britain's relations with its own colonies or with Israel's treatment of the Palestinian Authority. The ghetto was a small and easily controlled entity "enjoying" autonomy to run its internal affairs, similar to the situation of the Palestinian Territories. The Israelis, he concludes, drew the lessons of the Jewish experience in Europe, and aspire to forge their relations with the Arabs along the lines of the Nazi relations with the *Judenräte*. These claims, in addition to their historical fallacy, contain more than an implicit denial of the Holocaust, which Masiri claims to acknowledge.[56]

The racial foundation is another common denominator between the two movements, according to Masiri. The pan-German ideology is based on the premise that the primary allegiance of all members of the German race should be to the German homeland, and that they should all become citizens of the German state, even if their parents and ancestors were born in other countries. This idea, he claims, influenced Zionism, which speaks about the mystical unity of the Jewish people. The Jew remains Jewish wherever and whenever he is, and his primary loyalty belongs to the Jewish state. Zionism preceded Nazism with the idea that the Jews were not integrated members of the societies

---

54   In addition to the fuzziness of the entire argument, Masiri is oblivious to the strong antipantheist elements in Jewish tradition.

55   He probably refers to the philosophical terms "Zweckrationalitat" and "Wertrationalitat" respectively.

56   Masiri, *al-Sahyuniyya*, p. 163. One can criticize Israeli policies in the Palestinian Territories, but the false comparison ignores the basic facts that the Palestinians are not subject to starvation policies, which the Jews had suffered from, and, more importantly, were not and are not subject to random murder and organized extermination. Among other differences one can mention the sizeable armed forces and political institutions of the PNA, a wide web of international relations, foreign aid exceeding $1 billion annually (up to 2006), and the freedom to emigrate. All of these were missing in the ghettoes, whose inhabitants were prisoners destined for extermination.

in which they lived. It revolved around the idea of anti-Semitism and examines every issue from that point of view, as was the case with Nazism. Consequently, both lead their adherents to hate the "other."[57] As in other cases, there is a grain of truth in Masiri's claims, which is then used to make utterly false comparisons. Jews indeed remained Jewish wherever they were, as long as they did not convert or assimilate, but that is a far cry from the racist idea that denies the possibility of a change in identity.[58] Zionism emerged in Europe in response to anti-Semitism and in response to the failure of Jewish integration into European societies. Thus, it came to accept the anti-Semitic premise that the Jews indeed did not belong in Europe but needed a state of their own. That was far a cry from any resemblance to Nazism. Whereas the Zionists wanted the Jews to emigrate from Europe in order to spare them from persecution, the Nazis wanted to get rid of them and, when that failed, they mass-murdered them. Moreover, Masiri takes a phenomenon common to all nationalist movements, including Arab nationalism, i.e., the demand for the primary allegiance of their members, and presents it as unique to Nazism and Zionism. He also fails to show why Jewish belief in the unity of the Jews is any different from Arab belief in the unity of the Arab nation or of any other nation.

Hegelian dialectic, according to Masiri, is another common basis for Nazi and Zionist thinking and for the way in which the thinkers of both movements justify their political plans. Thus, both movements regard the state as the realization of the absolute idea in human spirit, but Zionists are worse than the Nazis in this respect because they did not have a state at all.[59] Masiri further contends that many Zionist leaders expressed their admiration to Nazism as a national liberation movement and longed for its success in Germany. As a proof, he claims, without citing his source, that the *Judische Rundschau*, the Zionist newspaper in Germany, supposedly justified the Nazi burning of books, arguing that many of those authors whose books were burned betrayed their Jewish roots and sought to take part in German culture rather than contribute to Jewish culture. In fact, the newspaper lamented that men of "pure German blood" were "judged only for their deeds," whereas for the

---

57   Masiri, *Nihayat al-ta'rikh*, pp. 113–14. See a similar claim by al-Az'ar, "al-Tashabuh."

58   The Palestinian National Covenant (article 5) also maintains that Palestinian identity is passed through the father, regardless of time and geographic location, www.mideastweb.org/plocha.htm.

59   Masiri, ibid., p. 117. Hegelian thinking characterizes Socialism and Communism as well, thereby rendering his argument completely meaningless.

Jews "there is no need for specific reason; the old saying goes: 'The Jew will be burnt'."[60]

The Israeli Law of Return is another indication for Masiri for the similarity between Zionism and Nazism, as it is based on a religious–racial definition that enables every Jew to settle in Israel, while denying the displaced Arabs the same right, and as it seeks to establish an Arab-free living space. Although the Law of Return was the "legal framework for the racial Zionist expansionism and the source of the false (*maz'uma*) Jewish identity of the Zionist state," he lamented the fact that none of the Arab peace treaties with Israel demanded its removal or change in the same manner that the Palestinians were required to amend their National Charter and remove the clauses that called for the elimination of Israel.[61] Masiri distorts the text and the meaning of the Law of Return, adopted in 1950, granting Jews worldwide the right to settle in Israel as citizens. The Law of Return does not affect the rights of citizenship of Arabs residents, and it does not contradict international law.[62] Moreover, Masiri does not fathom the absurdity of equating a law intended to provide refuge to Jews with clauses that call for the elimination of a state.

Masiri won widespread praise in the Arab media for his writings on Zionism, and particularly for writing an encyclopedia on Zionism and Judaism. The encyclopedia also won him President Mubarak's Award for writings on the social sciences during the 1999 Cairo International Book Fair. The official Palestine Authority newspaper *al-Hayat al-Jadida*, for example, published a 12-part series of his articles called "Zionism and Violence," in which he summarized his main arguments against Zionism. In many press interviews he explained the importance of his writings in facilitating greater recognition of Zionism so that the Arabs would cease fearing it and understand that Israel was destined to be defeated and disappear from history.[63]

---

60   Saul Friedlander, *Nazi Germany and the Jews*, New York: 1997, p. 58.

61   Masiri, *al-Sahyuniyya*, pp. 141–4; see also his statements in *al-'Arabi*, 6 May 2001.

62   The 1965 UN International Convention against all forms of discrimination explicitly enables states to regulate immigration and granting of citizenship; it bans discrimination against a specific group but allows granting preference to a specific group. The EU stipulated in the Venice conference in 2001 that states have the right to grant preferred status in immigration and citizenship to members of their nation. Such laws exist in several European and Asian countries, such as Hungary, Germany, Greece, Finland, Ireland and South Korea. Amnon Rubinstein and Alexander Yakobson, *Israel and the Family of Nations*, Tel Aviv: 2003, pp. 222–40. The Israeli law was never based on race and enabled persons with mixed Jewish and non-Jewish parentage to immigrate and attain citizenship. Finally, Israel never was and never intended to be an Arab-free state, as more than 22 percent of its citizens at the beginning of the twenty-first century were Arabs.

63   *Filastin al-Thawra*, 13 August 1979, 10 July 1988; *al-Liwa'*, 31 July 1996, 20 Octo-

The so-called similarity in policies and practice

After "proving" the shared ideological origins and foundations between Zionism and Nazism, various writers sought to demonstrate their perfect resemblance in practical policy as well. Such charges against Zionism and Israel of implementing Nazi policies and measures against the Arabs, particularly the Palestinians, have been rife since the end of World War II. They will be dealt with here only briefly, due to their repetitive nature.

For 'Issa Nakhle, the smear campaigns and the violence which the Nazis employed against their rivals before reaching power were the same techniques that the Zionists employed against their non-Zionist rivals in Palestine. Likewise, the systematic "inch-by-inch" way in which the Zionists took over various Jewish organizations in America is no different from the way the Nazis took over Germany. He disregards the fact that the Zionists prevailed in free elections, whereas the Nazis resorted to terror against their rivals before and after assuming power. Just as the Nazis separated children from their parents in order to raise a "new race of the German super man," Nakhle added, so did the Zionists abduct the children of Jews who came from Yemen during the early 1950s. For all of these reasons, Zionists and Nazis were not "strange bed-fellows" during the Third Reich, he concluded.[64]

The Palestinian educator Wa'il al-Qadi found similarities between the educational systems of Nazi Germany and of Israel as instruments of socialization and shaping national consciousness. The Zionist belief in the importance of education as securing Israel's long-term survival equals that of Nazi Germany, Fascist Italy, militaristic Japan and ancient Sparta. All of these regimes advocated the cultivation of extremist nationalism in shaping the personality of their citizens in a cruel manner. Jewish-Zionist consciousness and the idea of a shared Jewish fate do not stand on a genuine national basis, such as Arab nationalism, he explains, but on an extremist nationalistic view revolving around the notion of the chosen people, just as the Nazi educational system was based on German racial superiority.[65]

---

ber 1999; *al-Hayat al-Jadida*, 9 January–10 February, *al-Hayat*, 23 January, 6 February, *al-Ahali*, 10 February 1999; *Filastin al-Muslima*, July 1997, March 1999; *The Egyptian Gazette*, 9 March, *al-Sha'b*, 26 March, *al-Ahram al-'Arabi*, 17, 24 April, 14 August, *al-Ahram*, 5 October 1999; *Sutur*, September 2001.

64 Nakhle, *Encyclopedia*, pp. 870, 872, 874. During the mass wave of Jewish immigration in 1949–51, when Israel more than doubled its population, several dozens children of Yemenite origin disappeared from hospitals amidst the general disorganization in the country. They either died or were given to adoption after contact with their parents was lost. The entire tragic affair has remained a source of controversy and agony in Israel ever since.

65 Wa'il al-Qadi, *al-Tarbiyya fi isra'il*, Nablus: 1994, pp. 1, 55.

Munir Ma'shush claims that the Germans and the Zionists were alike in violating all international laws and norms of conduct. Both were hostile to Communism, Socialism and acts of resistance and self-sacrifice (a'mal fida'iyya) by their opponents. Hitler used the Partisan activities against German troops as an excuse to annihilate anyone who challenged him, and so do the Zionists when they exploit any act of sacrifice against them to "totally eradicate" the inhabitants of the adjacent areas.[66]

Following an official Israeli protest over the representation of then Israeli Foreign Minister Shimon Peres as a Nazi in the Egyptian newspaper al-'Arabi, the editors published in May 2001 a series of responses by Egyptian intellectuals and historians, who reiterated the claim while downplaying its main features. The prominent historian Yunan Labib Rizq maintained, while citing French Holocaust denier Roger Garaudy, that Hitler was the one who should protest the equation, and not Peres. That was because Nazism was part of the extremist European historical heritage, but it was still a philosophy, even if one might disagree with it. Nazism was partially racist, whereas Zionism is harsher and completely racist. "I have read a lot about Nazism," he wrote, "but I have never heard that Hitler's artillery aimed at houses, refugee camps and civilian neighborhoods. All the Nazis did was put people in detention camps, but they did not commit what Israel is doing now." Moreover, Nazism never contained the colonizing element that Zionism has, he added.

Beside media articles and reportage containing such accusations, caricatures are the most prevalent tool for disseminating them. Unlike written materials, caricatures are open for appropriation by both literate and illiterate people. They enable viewers to acquire political awareness, and reflect the cultural norms of society.[67] To highlight the alleged cruelty and brutality of Israelis a swastika is added to the helmets and uniforms of Israeli soldiers or on the foreheads of politicians. Israeli leaders are depicted in Nazi uniform or with Hitlerian moustaches and hair styles. Many of the anti-Israeli caricatures also use stereotypic anti-Semitic motifs, often borrowing from the Nazi repertoire, and portray the modern Israeli as a bearded, hooked-nose and hunchbacked Jew dressed in a black coat.

Prior to the 1967 war, caricatures in the Arab press tended to present Israel and Israelis as weak, miserable and despicable creatures who were about to be punished by the proud, self-confident Arabs. After the 1967 defeat, the Israeli

---

66   Ma'shush, al-Sahyuniyya, pp. 82–6.

67   For the importance of caricature in analyzing modern Arab discourse, see Gershoni, Light in the Shadow, p. 53. For Arab caricatures of Israel, see Arye Stav, Peace: Arab Caricatures – An Anti-Semitic Profile, Tel Aviv: 1996 (Hebrew).

image changed to menacing, brutal and aggressive Nazi-type oppressors. This change partly reflected the impact of Soviet propaganda, but was mainly part of process that transformed the image of Israel from a weakling into a bully threatening the entire Middle East, and from David to Goliath. Another common practice of these equations is the increasing use since the 1980s of the terms "Judeo-Nazi" (*Yahu-nazi*) or "Zionazi" (*Sahyu-nazi*).[68]

The ramifications and aims of the equation of Zionism with Nazism are quite clear to those who make it. In her book dedicated to the equation, Nadiya Sa'd al-Din argues that both movements are inherently incapable of peaceful coexistence with "the other," as both "thrive on violence, racism" and territorial expansionism, and both seek "control and hegemony." She rejects Israel's peace overtures toward the Arabs and peace treaties with Egypt and Jordan (in which Israel gave up territories) as identical with Hitler's conniving policies during the 1930s, which were designed to mislead European leaders as to his true intentions. Her conclusion is that Arab concessions and attempts to please Israel have all failed, just as European appeasement failed to tame Nazi Germany.[69] In a similar vein, Muhammad Jabir Sabah, who states that Nazism and Zionism are "two sides of the same coin," equates Arab advocates of peace with Israel with the "appeasement policy" of British Prime Minister Chamberlain vis-à-vis Hitler in 1938.[70]

Most others who make the equation reach more radical conclusions. Just as Nazism found its demise because it was inherently faulty and because the whole world united against it in war, so should and would be the end of Zionism. Khalid al-Shimali ends his pseudo-historical article that denies the killing of Jews in the gas chambers by expressing the hope that the world that "took pride in being the world of culture and civilization, that fought the Nazis during the war, would now fight Israeli Zionism, because it carries extremist Nazi ideas that are more dangerous to human civilization than Nazism during the World War."[71]

68　See for instance, *Filastin al-Thawra*, 27 December 1992; Mustafa Ikhmis, *al-Sahyunazi-yya: qatiluha qabla an taqtulakum*, Bethlehem: 2000. Frequent use of the term "Zionazi" is found in the publications of the "Drive the Zionists to the Sea" association which appeared in msanews@msanews.mynet.net during 2000 and 2001. See also *Takbir*, no. 12 (February 1993).

69　See three favorable reviews on the book by Ibrahim Gharabiyya, "al-Sahyuniyya wal-naziyya wa-ishkaliyyat al-ta'ayush ma'a al-akhar," www.aljazeera.net/NR/exeres/71628824-A250-4F24-86D9-00C867C3DA2B.htm, on the Islamic website www.islammemo.cc/article1.aspx?id=23226; www.akhbarelyom.org.eg/adab/issues/610/0800.html.

70　*Al-Wasat*, 18 June 2006.

71　*Al-Istiqlal*, 20 December 1989. See also Anis Qasim, "The Rule of Principles" in AJAZ (American Jewish Alternatives to Zionism) and EAFORD (International Organization for the Elimination of All Forms of Racial Discrimination), *Judaism or Zionism: What*

For Egyptian writer Fathi Ghanim, who reflected on the 1988 Palestinian uprising (Intifada), "Zionist racism is a type of madness whose end is certain, since deviant human societies cannot survive for long. Due to their racism they are forced to persist in their aggression until they are fought against and eliminated," as was the case with Nazi racism. Muhammad Dawudiyya, who also compared Israeli policy during the Intifada to that of Nazi Germany, maintained that there was no point in equating Zionism with Nazism, as the two movements "went hand in hand" since the 1930s. Still, he expressed his confidence that the balance of power between Zionism and the Arabs would change, because the "power of Zionism was less than that of Nazism." In a similar vein Ibrahim al-Qa'ud, writing on the Palestinian–Israeli confrontation in 2001, called to "reveal the integral and mental link between Zionism and Nazism as two racist movements," and to try Israeli leaders for crimes they had committed against humanity, as was the case with the Nazi leaders.[72]

Even the writer 'Umar Masalha, who ends his discussion of a possible peace between Jews and Arabs with the conciliatory note that Israel is a fact of life, turns to the equation between Nazism and Zionism and to its inevitable conclusion. The twentieth century witnessed the fall of the "empires of the Czars, the Ottomans, the Nazis, the colonialists and the Communists." "Sooner or later," the author, a former PLO representative to UNESCO, adds, "Zionism will follow the same way."[73]

While Zionism was the major target of the charges of Nazism, similar accusations were raised against other enemies of the Arab nation. Dr. Hilmi Mahmud al-Qa'ud posited the "Nazism of the Zionists" as equal to the "Nazism of the Crusaders," (i.e., the West). The "Nazism of the Crusaders," he says, is not restricted to Hitler and [the extremist right wing Austrian leader] Yörg Haider, but also applies to then US President Clinton and French Prime Minister Lionel Jospin, as they all believe in racism and the superiority of the European race.[74] Following the 2003 US invasion to Iraq, US President George W. Bush became a favorite target of equations with Hitler, among others by Syrian Foreign Minister Faruq al-Shara'. Conversely, a few liberal writers equated the al-

Difference to the Middle East, London: 1986, p. 258.

72 *Al-Masa'*, 8 September, *Sawt al-Sha'b*, 2 March 1988; *al-Jumhuriyya*, 7 June 1989; *Akhir Sa'a*, 25 April 2001; Sa'd al-Din, *al-Sahyuniyya wal-naziyya*.

73 Omar Masalha, *Towards the Long-Promised Peace*, London: 1994, pp. 281–4.

74 *Al-Sha'b*, 3 March 2000; Jamaaluddin al-Haidar, "Legalized War on Islam," bayan@vistus.net; *Ha'aretz*, 28 September 2001.

Qa'ida organization with Nazism, as both are "based on hatred and physical elimination of the other."[75]

Conclusions

The pervasive equation in Arab Holocaust discourse between Judaism or Zionism and Nazism is based on a gross misreading of the two movements and contains implicit if not explicit denial of the Holocaust. While it belittles or disregards the murderous and genocidal essence of Nazism, it attributes to Judaism and Zionism articles of faith or distorted ideological principles which are foreign to them. Occasionally, it attributes to Judaism supposedly unique elements which are shared by many other nations, including Arabs. These equations have evolved from mere statements to whole pseudo-academic books and studies, best manifested in Masiri's prolific writings, which sought to transform the so-called identity between Zionism and Nazism into a broader condemnation of western civilization.

However, several Arab intellectuals have questioned the equation between Nazism and Zionism. During a debate on al-Jazeera TV held on 15 May 2001, the 53rd anniversary of the Palestinian Nakba, on the question "Is Zionism worse than Nazism?", the Tunisian liberal intellectual 'Afif al-Akhdar agreed that "there is no doubt that there is a commonality between Nazism and Zionism," but, "this commonality exists between Nazism and all nationalist movements," which are based on one principle, namely the centrality of ethnic and racial elements. That is why they use expressions like "the chosen people" or the phrase common among Islamists: "We are the greatest nation delivered to mankind."[76]

Dalal al-Bizri, in response to a spate of articles equating Israel with Nazi Germany, criticized the short memory of the writers by pointing to the fact that only a few years earlier many Arabs had seen Nazi Germany as their "enemy's enemy," and therefore as their friend who would liberate them from French and British rule. Although al-Bizri finds one significant commonality between Israel and Nazi Germany, that is, their inclination toward collective suicide, she sees the equation between the two as a case of demonization of the other, which reflects the frustration and anger of the Arabs over their weakness and inferiority *vis-à-vis* Israel. Those who make this equation, she adds, are well aware how

---

75   For a few examples, see *Al-Ahram Weekly*, 15 May, *al-Ra'y al-'Am*, 13 April, Reuters, 12 April 2003; *al-Sharq al-Awsat*, 15 April 2004; *al-Wasat*, 10 May 2005; *al-Jazeera*, 10, 24 July 2005 – Memri, Special Dispatch Series, no. 1007, 17 October 2005; *al-Jumhuriyya*, 27 April, *Majallat al-'Asr*, 30 July 2006.

76   Al-Jazeera TV, 15 May 2001 – Memri, Special Dispatch Series, no. 225, 6 June 2001.

FROM EMPATHY TO DENIAL

sensitive the Jews are to this type of comparison. Therefore, she warned that inflaming hatred toward Israel would not weaken it, but on the contrary would augment its cruelty and would only worsen the plight of the Arabs.[77]

Yet, the continuing extensive use of the equation indicates widespread reception. In an internet poll carried out at the end of the al-Jazeera discussion mentioned above, 84.6 percent of 12,374 participants maintained that Zionism was worse than Nazism; 11.1 percent said that Zionism was equal to Nazism, and only 2.7 percent (the remaining 1.6 percent were not accounted for) still believed that Nazism was worse. All that is left for me to do, said the moderator, Dr. Faysal al-Qasim (who had sided with the Holocaust deniers), "is to congratulate the Zionists for this painful result; indeed, they have excelled in exceeding the Nazis."[78]

77   *Al-Hayat*, 20 May 2001.
78   Al-Jazeera TV, 15 May 2001, ibid.

242

8

THE ALLEGED NAZI–ZIONIST COOPERATION

The accusation of the Zionists of colluding and collaborating with the Nazis in the extermination of European Jewry emerged shortly after World War II. It intensified over the years, especially following the Eichmann trial (see Chapter 3) and the tightening Soviet–Arab relations in the 1960s, and developed from sporadic statements by politicians and journalists to more sophisticated pseudo-academic articles and books. According to this narrative, the supposed determination of the Zionists "to get rid" of their political rivals and push the mass of the Jews, most of whom rejected Zionism, to emigrate to Palestine converged with the Nazi desire to rid themselves of the Jews at all costs. This joint interest allegedly drove the two parties to a close collaboration on a variety of levels, culminating in the extermination of non-Zionist, poor or old Jews. Some writers go even further, saying that the "Zionists were the people who killed the Jews in Europe," or that the Nazis carried out the murders at the behest of the Zionist leaders.[1] The Zionist leaders allegedly kept secret their contacts with the Nazis in order to exploit the extermination of the Jews for the mobilization of international support for Israel, and in order not to embarrass the sons of those collaborators, many of whom were said to have held high positions in Israel.

Contacts between Zionist activists and Nazi officials indeed took place during the 1930s, up to the war period, deriving from the need to save as many Jews as possible from the claws of the Nazi regime, and not out of support for or identification with it. The 1933 "Transfer (Ha'avara) agreement," signed between Haim Arlozorov, head of the Political Department of the Jewish Agency, and the German government facilitated the emigration of around 55,000 Jews from Germany to Palestine.[2] So long as the Nazis sought to rid Germany of the

---

1   *Akhbar al-Usbu'*, 23 June 1965; ZCCF, "The Zionist Movement and Its Animosity to Jews," 11 October 2001, in Memri, Special Report, no. 16, 16 May 2003; *al-Thawra*, 12 December 2003.

2   On the agreement, see Nicosia, *The Third Reich*, pp. 29–50, 126–40; David Yisraeli, *The Palestine Problem in German Politics 1889–1945*, Ramat Gan: 1974 (Hebrew), pp.

Jews and did not embark on their policy of extermination, the Zionist movement in Germany enjoyed greater freedom of action than its political rivals, who had advocated the full integration of the Jews into German society.[3] Such contacts ceased completely once the war broke out and the Zionist leadership mobilized its meager resources to support the British war effort.[4] However, The Zionist–Nazi contacts are presented in the Arab writings in a distorted way, often through patent falsification of the evidence in order to vilify the Zionist movement and leadership and present them as ruthless and harmful to their own people.

Proponents of the "collaboration" theme were quite frank about the political aims behind their accusations. Thus Khalid Jamal al-Mutawa' laments the Arab and Muslim failure "to take advantage of this trump card in smearing the Zionist executioner (*jallad*)," and in "embarrassing the greatest plunderer" despite the ease with which it could be done. Likewise, the Egyptian Mamduh al-Shaykh 'Ali contends that instead of immoral and harmful reliance on Holocaust deniers, the Arabs would gain more by focusing on those Zionists who were involved in the Nazi extermination crime.[5]

The charges of Zionist–Nazi cooperation make Arab–Nazi collaboration seem less serious, and enhance the equation between Zionism and Nazism. Not only did Zionism resemble Nazism in its ideology and conduct, according to this claim, but it even cooperated with it in the crime against the very people it pretended to save from anti-Semitism. Thus the Palestinian Encyclopedia stated that:

The activities of the representatives of the Zionist movement who collaborated with the Nazis in Eastern Europe reflected official Zionist policy, and constituted part of the Zionist plan that sought to establish a racist Zionist entity in the land of Palestine. In order to achieve this goal, the Zionist movement insisted on full collaboration with the

---

122–51; Yifaat Weiss, "The 'Transfer Agreement' and the 'Boycott Movement': A Jewish Dilemma at the Eve of the Holocaust," *Yad Vashem Studies*, vol. 26 (1998), pp. 129–71, internet edition.

3   For elaborate discussions on Zionist contacts with the Nazis to save Jews, see Bauer, *Jews for Sale?*; Nicosia, *The Third Reich*, pp. 29–50; 126–40; Yisraeli, *The Palestine Problem*, pp. 122–51; Ernest Marcus, "The German Foreign Office and the Palestine Question in the Period 1933–1939," *Yad Vashem Studies*, vol. 2 (1958), pp. 179–204.

4   During the war, the ca. 600,000 Jewish community in Palestine sent 27,000 volunteers to the British army. The Jewish Brigade, formed in 1943, represented only a segment of the Zionist war effort. See Howard Blum, *The Brigade: An Epic Story of Vengeance, Salvation and World War II*, New York: 2001.

5   *Akhbar al-Khalij*, 3 September 2005, cited in Hamas website www.palestine-info.net/arabic/terror/sijil/2005/malame7.htm; Al-Shaykh Ali, "nahwu ru'ya"; 'Abd al-Wahhab al-Masiri, "al-I'lam al-'arabi wa-qadiyyat al-ta'awun bayna al-naziyyin wal-sahayina," www.elmessiri.com/ar/modules.php?name=News&file=article&sid=16.

Nazis and on giving them any assistance to get rid of the Jews who opposed emigration to Palestine in return for allowing the emigration of the Zionists.[6]

Mahmud 'Abbas presented a similar argument, ostensibly from the German point of view, saying that the Nazis regarded the Zionists as their natural allies. This supposed collaboration continued until the end of the war in various ways "including massacres against the Jews ... and the transfer of tens of thousands of Jews to Palestine." Undoubtedly, he concludes, through these activities the Nazis sought to establish a national state for the Jews on which they could rely and secure their interests in the Middle East.[7] All of these claims, however, have been thoroughly refuted by all serious historical studies of Nazi political and ideological attitudes towards Zionism. As Jeffrey Herf pointed out, "Nazi support for emigration of German Jews to Palestine stemmed from the anti-Semitic motivation of removing Jews from Germany, not from a desire to see them found their own new state."[8]

The charge of collaboration helps those who find it difficult to totally deny the occurrence of the Holocaust, by accepting the death of some Jews while blaming the Zionists for it. It deprives the Holocaust of any moral or political meaning and thus undermines the Zionist scheme to accrue financial or political profits, since, if the Zionists had a hand in it, it could no longer be regarded as a legitimate tragedy and certainly not carry the meaning of the term "Holocaust" (i.e., religious offering, see Chapter 5).

The alleged collaboration theme is particularly prevalent among Palestinians of all political shades, and Syrians. This theme can be regarded as a central component in the semi-official Palestinian discourse on the Holocaust.[9] Two major

---

6   "Al-Naziyya wal-sahyuniyya," in *al-Mawsu'a al-filastiniyya*, vol. 4, p. 434. See also Na-khle, *Encyclopaedia*, p. 892ff.

7   'Abbas, "al-Sahyuniyya," p. 6; Muhammad 'Ali Sirhan, "Man yahtakiru hurriyyat al-ra'y wal-haqiqa fi al-gharb," www.baath-party.org/monadel/no-339/almonadil339_8.htm. Sirhan's story, in addition to being factually false, is plagued by anachronisms. He had Menahem Begin operating in Berlin during the 1930s, whereas Begin was the leader of the Beitar movement in Poland during that period. See also Habib Qahwaji, *Isra'il hanjar amrika*, Damascus: 1979, p. 33; 'Arafa 'Abduh 'Ali, "'Ada' 'alani wa-sadaqa sirriyya," *al-Mawqif al-'Arabi*, no. 92 (June 1988), p. 100.

8   Yisraeli, *The Palestine Problem*, pp. 154ff; Francis R. Nicosia, "Zionism in National Socialist Jewish Policy in Germany, 1933–39," *Journal of Modern History*, vol. 50, no. 4 (1978), pp. 1253–82; idem, *The Third Reich*, stating that the Nazis totally opposed the establishment of a Zionist state as a major threat to their interests; Jeffrey Herf, "Convergence: The Classic Case Nazi Germany, Anti-Semitism and Anti-Zionism during World War II," in idem (ed.), *Anti-Semitism and Anti-Zionism in Historical Perspective*, London: 2006, p. 51.

9   In addition to Mahmud 'Abbas, *al-Wajh al-akhar*, see Salman Rashid Salman, "Almaniya al-naziyya wal-qadiyya al-filastiniyya," *Shu'un Filastiniyya*, no. 31 (March 1974), pp. 92–

reasons may account for its central place among the Palestinians. Jewish immigration during the 1930s, particularly from Germany, which was facilitated by the "Transfer Agreement," had a decisive impact in tipping the economic and strategic balance in favor of the Jews in Palestine. In addition, the collaboration of the Palestinian leader Hajj Amin al-Husyani with the Nazis, which the Zionist and Israeli discourse highlighted, is projected onto the Zionists as a mirror image of the Zionist charges, thereby purifying the Palestinian side (see Chapter 9). Psychological projection denotes a shift of the border between the self and the world in favor of the self, attributing to the "other" those repulsive or harmful aspects of the self.[10] Still, the official website of the Palestinian Authority refrained from adopting this position. In other words, what the PLO could afford to do as an organization, the PNA as a surrogate state maintaining [tense] relations with Israel was more inhibited in doing.[11] Since the 1990s, the collaboration theme has acquired growing popularity among other Arab nationalities as well.

As was the case with Holocaust denial, the allegations of Nazi–Zionist collaboration may be found in a variety of contexts and are not confined to publications devoted to the Israeli–Arab conflict. A political-science encyclopedia published in Jordan, for example, assigned special entries to this issue immediately after the entry on Nazism. Significantly, it gave more space and detail to this alleged collaboration than to the discussion of Nazism.[12]

The so-called collaboration, which is often related in a typical "conspiracy theory" fashion, enhances the sophistication and Machiavellian nature of Zion-

104; Mahmud al-Labadi, "Jawla fi al-'aql al-i'lami al-sahyuni," *Shu'un Filastiniyya*, no. 94 (September 1979), p. 123; Haddad, "al-Tamathul", p. 69; al-Sa'd, *al-Shakhsiyya*, p. 201; Hisham Dajjani, *al-Yahudiyya wal-sahyuniyya*, Beirut: 1985, p. 96; Fawwaz Tuqqan, *al-Isti'mar al-sahyuni lil-ard al-filastiniyya: qissat al-sahyuniyya wal-ard wal-muqawama mundhu 1870*, Amman: 1987, p. 31; Maw'id, *al-Sahyuniyya*, p. 33; Hasan 'Abd al-'Al, *al-Hurriyya*, 28 January, 11 February 1990; Faris Yahya [Glubb], *Zionist Relations with Nazi Germany*, Beirut: 1978. Glubb, the son of former British commander of the Jordanian army John Bagot Glubb, converted to Islam. The PLO published his works both in English and in Arabic. The English version appears under the name Yahya, while the Arab version in *Shu'un Filastiniyya*, nos. 84 and 85 (November, and 1978), pp. 67–94 and 119–38 carries the name Glubb.

10   Projection may also be the reason for the endorsement of this theme by the Iraqi media in the 1980s. in view of the enthusiasm for Nazi Germany in Iraq during the 1930s and the flight of Iraqi leaders to Germany in 1941, *Alif Ba*, 7 May to 26 July 1995; *al-Dustur*, (Paris), 6 February 1984.

11   PNA, Ministry of Information, "Siyasat al-qiyada al-sahyuniyya," www.minfo.gov.ps/index.php?scid=2&pid=269.

12   "Al-Naziyya" and "al-Naziyya wal-sahyuniyya," in 'Abd al-Wahhab al-Kiyali et al. (eds.), *al-Mawsu'a al-siyasiyya*, Amman: 1995, vol. 6, pp. 545–8.

ism, thereby helping to explain Palestinian failure to confront it. This is also a likely reason why it became popular among Islamists, who often resort to conspiracy theories.

There are two major differences between proponents of the collaboration theme and those who either justify or deny the Holocaust. The first is the distinction made between Jews and Zionists, as the former claim to identify with Jewish suffering caused by the Zionists, while the latter view both categories as identical. Thus, 'Abbas describes the Jews as the first victims of Zionism and stresses the need to sympathize with them.[13] Second, all of these writers condemn the Nazis, partly because their policies eventually harmed the Arabs.

Although the accusation of Nazi–Zionist collaboration implies recognition of the Holocaust as a historical event, many of those who raise it simultaneously deny the Holocaust or minimize the number of Jews who perished. Mahmud 'Abbas devoted his book to proving Zionist–Nazi collaboration in the extermination of the Jews, but at the same time, citing Faurisson as a source, he casts doubts on the six million figure as a Zionist invention, and claims that sending the Jews to concentration camps after the 1938 Kristallnacht was done for their protection.[14] Likewise, Rafiq Natshe contends, after his denial of the killing of Jews, that the Zionists cooperated with the Nazis in sending "hundreds of thousands" of Hungarian Jews to Auschwitz and to certain death. Egyptian history professor 'Arafa 'Abduh 'Ali praises Garaudy and David Irving for exposing the myth of the Holocaust and gives in detail Henry Roques' claims that the gas chambers were used to combat epidemics in Germany, but at the same time accuses the Zionists of helping the Nazis in exterminating the Jews.[15]

A similar position was expressed by the three official Syrian dailies, *Tishrin*, *al-Thawra* and *Syria Times*. Dr. 'Imad Mahmud Habib acknowledges that the Nazis did kill some Jews, but hastens to say that "every Jew murdered in an organized manner by the Nazis was in fact murdered on request from the Zionists," as part of a series of secret agreements between the two parties.[16] The Egyptian journalist Lutfi Nasif solves the contradiction in a similar vein by saying that while gas chambers did not exist, the Zionist movement collaborated with the Nazi SS in terrorizing the Jews in order to force them to emigrate and

13 'Abbas, "al-Sahyuniyya". See also Nadhir Juzmani, in *al-Hurriyya*, 24 June 1990; Hadi al-'Alawi, in *al-Hurriyya*, 18 October 1992.

14 'Abbas, *al-Wajh al-akhar*, pp. b, g, 30.

15 Natshe, *al-Isti'mar*, p. 151; 'Abduh 'Ali, in *al-'Arabi*, May 2000, pp. 108–10. See also Hawatima, "al-Sahyuniyya"; al-Masiri, "al-Ibada," p. 61; Akram 'Atallah, "al-Sahyuniyya," pp. 54–73; Muhammad Mahalla, *al-Tahaluf al-yahudi al-nazi*, Damascus: 2001, pp. 114, 119.

16 *Tishrin*, 31 January 2000. See also *Syria Times*, *al-Thawra*, 12 December 2002.

in planning and organizing the massacre of "several thousand" Jews in German "detention camps." Thus, the Zionists come out guilty on two counts: they collaborated with the Nazis, and later raised false accusations against them, thereby obtaining through deceit international support for establishing their state.[17]

Like most Holocaust deniers, the advocates of the collaboration theme exert considerable efforts to endow their allegations with academic respectability by relying on some documentary evidence as well as on previous historical studies or journalistic reports. However, in addition to fabricating evidence which does not exist, while ignoring all evidence which refutes their allegations, they often misquote genuine historical sources, use partial citations which distort the content of the original data, pick details out of context, or present a complex historical situation in a very simplistic and therefore deceitful way. They rely on anti-Zionist Soviet and East German as well as ultra-Orthodox Jewish publications whose reliability as historical sources is extremely questionable and problematic.[18] Yahya-Glubb, for instance, says explicitly that he relied solely on Jewish sources so that no one would be able to accuse him of anti-Semitism – a ploy used later by Garaudy and other Arab writers.[19]

A major characteristic of the a-historical approach of these writers, carried out in order to vilify the Zionists, is the intentional blurring of various types of collaboration discussed in the academic scholarship on World War II and the Holocaust. The first type is proactive or voluntary collaboration, motivated by ideological identification with the political or ideological goals of the Nazi regime, as was the case with the Fascist Ustasha in Croatia, the Iron Guard in Romania or the Arrow Cross in Hungary. It could also stem from financial or other personal considerations, as was the case with many ordinary people who turned Jews over to the Nazis for the financial reward. The second type is collab-

---

17   *Al-Jumhuriyya*, 4 March 2000. See a similar pattern in 'Abd al-Qadir's articles in *Alif Ba*. In three of the series installments, on 14, 21 and 28 June 1995, he enumerates Faurisson's arguments denying the Holocaust, while the article published on 7 May titled "Ben Gurion ordered the killing of Germany's Jews," speaks of Zionist–Nazi collaboration in the killing of Hungarian Jews. See also Hamas leader 'Abd al-'Aziz al-Rantisi in *al-Risala*, 21 August 2003.

18   See, for example, Yuri Ivanov's book *What is Zionism?*, Moscow: 1967, which was translated to Arabic and Y. Yevseyev, *al-Fashiyya taht al-najm al-azraq*, Moscow: 1971. See also Klaus Polkehn, "The Secret Contacts: Zionism and Nazi Germany, 1933–1941," *Journal of Palestine Studies*, vol. 5, nos. 3/4 (Spring–Summer 1976), pp. 54–82. The Hamas website cites the article "Zionism and The Third Reich," by Holocaust denier Mark Weber of the IHR, www.palestine-info.net/arabic/terror/sijil/2005/malame7.htm. Most popular of the ultra-orthodox sources is Moshe Shonfield, *The Holocaust Victims Accuse*, New York: 1977.

19   Yahya-Glubb, *Zionist*, p. 7.

oration under duress, threats or for lack of any other choice, the "collaboration of the hanged man with the rope" in Vidal-Naquet's words. In this case, the collaborator did not identify with the goals of the Nazi regime and even opposed them, but believed, rightly or wrongly, that his approach was the best way to foil these goals, or at least to minimize their effect. Often, such collaborators acted under constant threat to their lives, and therefore had to conduct themselves submissively vis-à-vis the ruler. For example, most leaders of the Jewish Councils (*Judenräte*) in the Jewish ghettoes in occupied Europe during the war had to comply with Nazi demands while fulfilling their thankless tasks, in the futile hope that they would be able to spare their communities from extermination. All of them faced horrible moral dilemmas as to the limits of such collaboration. Yet, most tried as best as they could to circumvent Nazi demands, many of them were executed for refusing to comply and quite a few actively helped the Jewish undergrounds in their ghettoes. Some, indeed, failed the moral test while trying to save themselves or their communities, as would happen in any group subjected to such inhumane circumstances. All of them eventually perished during the war.[20] The proponents of the collaboration theme ignore these differences and avoid making any effort to understand the insoluble dilemmas and the actual difficulties which these Jews faced or the tragedy of their situation. Rather, they prefer to create a simplistic and false image of Zionist power to fit their own political agenda.

A common approach of the proponents of the collaboration theme is to take a true historical case or fact and twist it in order to prove their claims. A prominent example is pointing to the impact of anti-Jewish Nazi policies in the 1930s which transformed the Zionist movement into the major political and ideological force within German Jewry, in order to contend that the Zionists welcomed or even supported the rise of Nazism.[21] In addition to presenting Zionism in Machiavellian terms as a far-sighted leadership possessing power and sophistication, this claim stems from a logical flaw, typical of conspiracy theories in general, which attributes intent, often a sinister one, to historical developments. Accordingly, if a certain historical development advanced the goals or policy of a specific group, then the latter must have initiated this development or backed it. Thus, if Nazi policies shattered the Jews' illusions of full integration into

---

20   For an extensive discussion of this problem, see Isaiah Trunk, *Judenrat: The Jewish Councils in Eastern Europe under Nazi Occupation*, Lincoln, NE: 1996; Aharon Weiss, "Jewish Leadership in Occupied Poland – Postures and Attitudes," *Yad Vashem Studies*, no. 12 (1977), pp. 335–65.

21   See, for instance, Muhammad Khalaf in *al-Dustur* (Paris), 6 February 1984, and Hasan 'Abd al-'Al in *al-Hurriyya*, 28 January 1990.

German society, thereby proving right the Zionist arguments, then the Zionists must have been behind those policies.

Consequently, many of the Arab writers claim that the Zionist leaders welcomed the rise of Nazism, since they hoped that Nazi persecution would force the Jews to leave Germany and thereby advance the Zionist goal of establishing the Jewish state. Zionism was facing a slow death during the 1920s, Akram 'Atallah asserts, and Hitler's rise to power extended it "priceless aid" with its anti-Semitic propaganda and subsequent massacres. The Zionist movement was happy with the persecution of the Jews, claimed Jurji Haddad, which provided "a golden opportunity that would force the Jews to go to Palestine and realize the Zionist maxim that Jews should not be part of non-Jewish society." The worse these persecutions became, the greater the number of Jews who sought emigration, and "this is what the Zionists had always aspired to," since their main priority was not to save Jews but immigration to Palestine. Mahmud 'Abbas claims that Jewish leaders organized demonstrations against Germany in western countries, while simultaneously supporting German persecution of the Jews as part of their overall scheme to expedite Jewish emigration. Nasir Damj goes further in saying that the "gangs affiliated with the Jewish Agency," aided by the Gestapo, carried out the Kristallnacht pogroms on 9–10 November 1938 in order to intimidate the Jews and drive them to emigrate. *Filastin al-Thawra* extended the blame to all Jews, not just the Zionists, claiming that, on the day Hitler assumed power, Jewish synagogues waved the Nazi flags and until the mid-1930s Jewish rabbis in Germany held prayers for Hitler's well-being. Hitler, 'Atallah concludes, became one of the most important executors of the Zionist scheme.[22]

Muhammad Faraj provides a Marxist explanation of the Zionist–Nazi collaboration. Zionism, he says, was a creature of the prosperous Jewish bourgeoisie in Europe, but also an opposition to Jewish assimilation. Since Europe lacked the necessary material, scientific and historical conditions for the emergence of Jewish nationalism, Zionism assumed a reactionary imperialist character from the start. Consequently, the Zionists shifted their support from one reaction-

---

22 Ahmad Jabir in *Filastin al-Thawra*, 13 December 1986; 'Abbas, *al-Wajh al-akhar*, pp. 3–4, 43; Haddad, "al-Tamathul," p. 69; Nasir Damj, *Tahawwulat minhajiyya fi masir al-sira' al-'arabi al-isra'ili*, Acre: 1996, p. 67; 'Atallah, "al-Sahyuniyya." See also Wiliam Fahmi, *al-Hijra al-yahudiyya ila filastin*, Cairo: 1974, p. 31; Nasr Shimali, *Iflas al-nazariyya al-sahyuniyya*, Beirut: 1981, p. 118; 'Abd al-'Al, in *al-Hurriyya*, 28 January 1990, 28 January 1990. Khalaf, in *al-Dustur* (Paris), 6 February 1984; *Filastin al-Thawra*, 1 June 1985; 'Abd al-Qadir, in *Alif Ba*, 25 May 1995. *Alif Ba*, without noticing the irony of its action, inserted in the article a picture of the Palestinian leader Hajj Amin al-Husayni having an amicable conversation with Hitler.

ary leader to the other in order to achieve their aims: from the Russian Czar,[23] through the German Kaiser, all the way to Hitler in order to carry out their imperialist schemes. Since the Jewish masses rejected the Zionists, the latter needed anti-Semitism to advance their aims and they collaborated with leaders of the reactionary Fascist governments, most notably Hitler, whom they described as a "God given gift." Moreover, the imperialist vantage point of the Zionists pushed them to take an active part in the persecution of the Jews. They knew about these persecutions in advance, but preferred to keep silent or to lie, since the end always justified their means to realize their imperialist goals.[24]

Some writers claim that the Zionist–Nazi collaboration preceded the Nazi rise to power. The Palestinian Encyclopedia, glossing over the difference between the two world wars, contends that Jewish–German intimacy existed already during World War I, when Germany protected Jewish interests in Palestine and Ze'ev Jabotinsky, leader of the right-wing Zionist Revisionist Movement, was active in Berlin (even though he was actually in England, mobilizing troops to fight with the British army [the authors]). Similarly, Kamal Sa'fan mentions Alfred Nossig, a Jewish-Austrian artist who attended the first Zionist Congress and who allegedly worked as a spy for Germany during World War I, as proof of the close links between the two movements, even though the Nazis emerged only after the war. Muhammad Mahalla extends the blame to Zionists and non-Zionists alike, whom he labels "Talmudic Jews," and 'Abduh 'Ali asserts that "Jewish monopolies and banks" gave Hitler substantial financial support that was essential to paving his way to power. 'Abd al-'Al, on the other hand, blames Zionism for not doing anything to prevent Hitler from assuming power, thereby attributing to it greater power than it ever had. Most German Jews, he claims, urged the formation of a unified anti-Nazi German front, but the Zionists opposed any cooperation with non-Jews, because they had already planned to set up an alliance with the Nazis in order to put an end to the liberal and "Red" presence in Germany and to Jewish assimilation. Nasir Damj adds that when the "Nazi Christian-Democratic party led by the Fuehrer Adolph [Israeli PM] Sharon Hitler assumed power in the Reichstag," the two movements established "close relations," since Hitler needed Jewish support in order to overcome the

---

23   He probably refers to the efforts of the Zionist leader Herzl to solicit the support of the Russian Interior Minister Vyacheslav von Plehve for the Zionist enterprise in 1903, but fails to mention that Herzl wanted to save Russian Jews from further pogroms and persecutions by getting them out of Russia.

24   Faraj, al-Sahyuniyya, pp. 64–6.

domestic crisis in Germany. The Zionists, the Egyptian *al-Liwa'* concluded, citing the anti-Zionist writer Lenny Brenner, "produced Hitler."[25]

The essence of the alleged Zionist–Nazi collaboration, according to the various Arab writers, was to promote the emigration of "rich capitalist" Jews, who were mostly anti-Zionist, and of young people "who would serve as fighters and workers" in Palestine. The Zionist organizations, they allege, did not wish to "buy" the poor and the weak, and left them for extermination. Levi Eshkol (the future prime minister of Israel), head of the "Palestine Office" in Germany during the 1930s, supposedly "knew in advance of the plan to exterminate the Jews," but pledged to the Nazis to keep it a secret in return for saving fewer than a hundred Zionist activists, thereby "forsaking the half a million that perished."[26] Sa'd uses the book *The Secret Roads* by the Kimche brothers to build the case, which they did not do, that the Jewish emissaries came to Germany during the 1930s not in order to save Jews, but merely to select the young and healthy, who would come to Palestine. According to Palestinian historian Basheer Nafi, the so-called collaboration led to the "ethnic cleansing" of German Jewry,[27] an inherently negative term implying that the alternative of staying in Germany was morally the better choice.

The 1933 "Transfer Agreement" is naturally presented as the cornerstone of the Zionist–Nazi collaboration. Yahya-Glubb says that non-Zionist Jews all over the world hoped to impose a total boycott on Germany in order to help their brethren, but the Zionist Congress in Prague declined the calls in order not to foil the agreement. Thus, he charges that a regrettable precedent was created of sacrificing the interests of the Jewish masses in Europe for the sake of Zionist political interests. The Germans, he adds, "realized the importance of this precedent" for future collaboration. The agreement enabled them to break

25   *Al-Mawsu'a al-filastiniyya*, vol. 4, p. 432; Nakhle, *Encyclopaedia* vol. 2, pp. 873–4; Sa'fan, *al-Yahud*, p. 105; 'Abduh 'Ali, in *al-Mawqif al-'Arabi*, p. 100; Mahalla, *al-Tahaluf*, pp. 93, 102ff; Haddad, "al-Tamathul," pp. 63, 68; Khalaf, in *al-Dustur*, 6 February 1984; Anon, "Bank ferenheim al-yahudi mawwala su'ud al-haraka al-naziyya," *Filastin al-Thawra*, 1 June 1985; 'Abd al-'Al, in *al-Hurriyya*, 11 February 1990; *al-Khalij*, 4 January 2005; Damj, *Tahawwulat*, p. 67; *al-Liwa'*, 27 October 1999.

26   Ma'shush, *al-Sahyuniyya*, p. 75. In addition to the fact that he awards Eshkol the foresight, which the Germans did not have at the time, as they were not planning extermination during the 1930s, he omits the fact that Arab opposition to Jewish immigration, manifested in the 1936–9 Rebellion, was the major reason for the low number of Jewish emigrants. He also minimizes the scale of subsequent Nazi extermination of the Jews from six million to 500,000.

27   Sa'd, *al-Shakhsiyya*, p. 203; Basheer Nafi, "The Arabs and the Axis: 1933–1940," *Arab Studies Quarterly* (Spring 1997, electronic edition). See also Dajjani, *al-Yahudiyya*, p. 96; 'Abd al-'Al, in *al-Hurriyya*, 11 February 1990; Shamil 'Abd al-Qadir, in *Alif Ba*, 24 May 1995; *al-Hayat*, 29 January 1998.

the boycott and to get the Jews out of Germany, while it enabled the Zionists to get Jews and property to Palestine, again implying that their remaining in Germany was the right moral choice, regardless of the future outcome.[28] Other writers insist that the Transfer Agreement was highly instrumental in helping Germany to break the boycott organized by the non-Zionist Jews and other anti-Fascist groups.

In order to emphasize the gravity of the Zionist conduct, other writers inflate the power of Jewish organizations worldwide as if the Jewish boycott could have brought about the downfall of the Nazi regime. In addition, they complain that the agreement flooded Palestine with German goods, to the detriment of the local Arab economy. Whereas they present non-Zionist Jews as principled, moral persons, they portray the Zionists as cynical manipulators who cared only for their selfish, narrow interests.[29]

Haddad contends that the Transfer Agreement enabled the Zionists to reap political gains by justifying their contention of the permanent nature of anti-Semitism. Sam'an and 'Abd Al-'Al assert that the training camps which the Zionists were allowed to set up in Germany to prepare youth for emigration (which provided training in agricultural work [the authors]), enabled the Zionists to rid themselves of their liberal rivals in the Jewish community, who advocated integration in German society, implying that this was still a realistic option during the late 1930s. As part of this cooperation, 'Abduh 'Ali says, the Zionists launched a massive propaganda campaign in Europe, fully coordinated with the Gestapo, that accused the Nazis of arresting Zionist activists in order to enhance Zionist prestige among the Jews for allegedly risking their lives on behalf of their brethren.[30]

---

28 Yahya, *Zionist*, pp. 21ff. See also *al-Mawsu'a al-filastiniyya*, vol. 4, pp. 432–4. Yahya and others ignore the facts that many leaders of German Jewry feared that boycott would make Jewish emigration more difficult and that the Zionist Congress issued a strong public protest against the attacks on German Jews. See Weiss, "The Transfer Agreement," pp. 8, 20.

29 Natshe, *al-Isti'mar*, p. 152; al-Sa'd, *al-Shakhsiyya*, p. 203; Ma'shush, *al-Sahyuniyya*, p. 74; Sa'fan, *al-Yahud*, p. 105; 'Abd al-'Al, in *al-Hurriyya*, 11 February 1990; Haddad, "al-Tamathul," p. 69. Nicosia, *The Third Reich*, pp. 34–5, 150 and 195, agrees that the Transfer Agreement helped to break the boycott, but explains that the boycott encountered great difficulties even without the agreement, and would not have lasted for long anyway, in view of Germany's economic power and the marginal power of the Jews at the time. The reluctance of all governments to take in Jewish refugees in the later 1930s and the fear of the American Jewish community to pressure the US government to help the Jews during the war attest to the weakness of the Jews and the Zionists and to the difficulties, if not impossibility, of a prolonged Jewish-sponsored boycott against Germany.

30 Haddad, "al-Tamathul," p. 69; Jabir in *Filastin al-Thawra*, 13 December 1986; Naji Sam'an, "Banuramat," p. 244; 'Abd al-'Al, in *al-Hurriyya*, 28 January 1990; 'Abduh 'Ali, in *al-Mawqif al-'Arabi*, p. 100.

Some writers stress the price which the Palestinians and Arabs paid as a result of these relations, implying that they are the true victims of Nazism. In addition to alleging the provision of military training to Jewish youth, Dr. 'Imad Habib invents a story that the Nazis transferred to the Zionists blueprints for the production of weapons and ammunition and that, consequently, Arabs were killed by Zionists armed by Hitler and Himmler.[31] In a flight of wild imagination, the Islamist Majdi Ibrahim Muharram asserts that the Gestapo, aided by Menahem Begin, sent Jewish youth who looked like Arabs from East European ghettoes to Egypt for espionage missions.[32]

The Zionists, according to these descriptions, also sought economic and financial gain from their relations with the Nazis. Yahya-Glubb accuses the Zionist emissaries of making substantial personal profits from their collaboration with the Nazis at the expense of ordinary Jews. He takes a true fact, that the Nazis allowed the dispatch of emissaries to various Jewish communities to raise money for German Jews, citing for that purpose a respectable authority as Hanna Arendt, but then adds from his own imagination that the Zionists sold to the German Jews the foreign currency they had raised charging them inflated rates. This "charity" act of the Jewish Agency, he adds sarcastically, became extremely profitable, since the entire goal of these "so-called rescue operations" and agreements with the Nazis was not to save Jews but to advance their main goal of establishing the Zionist state.[33]

'Abbas rejects the argument that the Transfer Agreement helped the Germans to obtain foreign currency and undermine the boycott against them, and insists that Jewish capitalists were the only ones who benefited from it. He denies the assertion that the agreement was designed to reduce the Jewish presence in Germany, insisting that only the wealthy Jews left, whereas the poor and the workers stayed behind. German persistence in keeping the agreement, despite the reservations voiced by the German community in Palestine, stemmed from one reason only, and that was German commitment to help the Zionists in establishing "a national homeland" for the Jews that would be linked to German imperialism and would serve its interests.[34]

---

31   *Al-Thawra*, 12 December 2002; Glubb in *Filastin al-Thawra*, 1 January 1981. See also Sam'an, "Banuramat," p. 244. Both stories are completely baseless.

32   "Kulluhum khidam lil-sahayina," http://alarabnews.com/alshaab/2004/22–10–2004/8. htm.

33   Yahya-Glubb, *Zionist*, pp. 31–2. See also "al-naziyya wal-sahyuniyya," *al-Mawsu'a al-filastiniyya*, vol. 4, p. 432, which states that "Zionist emigration organizers took, in collaboration with the Nazis, their share in Jewish property at the expense of ordinary Jews."

34   'Abbas, *al-Wajh al-akhar*, pp. 13, 22; Salman, "Almaniya al-naziyya," pp. 100–3.

Consequently, several Palestinian writers conclude that this alleged collaboration was motivated not only by pragmatic considerations but also by the ideological affinity between the two movements, "representing a worldview and conduct rooted in the Torah."[35] 'Issa Nakhle, who attributes the "mutual admiration" between Nazis and Zionists to the great resemblance between the two movements, "cites" Eichmann as saying that had he been Jewish, he would have become an ardent Zionist. The Syrian-produced TV drama *al-Shatat* (Diaspora) showed the Hungarian-Jewish activist Rudolf (Yisrael Reszoe) Kasztner explaining to Eichmann the great similarity between Zionism and Nazism as the basis for the proposed collaboration between the two parties.[36]

Salman Rashid Salman, who criticizes Hitler's policy towards the Arabs, presents a complex picture of disagreements within the Nazi leadership between the "dominant" group that ostensibly supported Zionism and the Transfer Agreement and those who opposed the agreement because they feared it would lead to the establishment of a Jewish state. He concedes that Germany opposed the 1936 Partition plan proposed by the Peel Commission, although it did not change its emigration policy. He concludes, however, that Hitler "did not see any danger in Zionism," but on the contrary regarded Zionism as a useful tool for German policy.[37] 'Abbas, on the other hand, claims that the Nazis sought the establishment of a Jewish state in Palestine. As proof, he cites from David Yisraeli's book a document sent by then German Foreign Minister von Neurath to the German ambassador in London, supposedly saying that Germany wished the establishment of a state in Palestine led by the Jews under British sovereignty. In addition to totally distorting the content of the cable quoted by Yisraeli, which actually said that Germany unequivocally opposed the establishment of any Jewish state, he ignores all other German statements enumerated in the book and by other scholars that demonstrate Nazi opposition to Jewish statehood.[38]

Quite a few writers point to the [truly shameful] efforts by the small LEHY organization to establish links with German representatives in Syria during

35 Hasan, *al-'Arab*, pp. 103, 106; al-Sa'd, *al-Shakhsiyya*, p. 202; *al-Mawsu'a al-filastiniyya*, vol. 4, p. 434; Masiri, "al-I'lam al-'arabi."

36 Nakhle, *Encyclopaedia*, vol. 2, pp. 873–4; www.memritv.org, Clip 896, 21 October 2005. *Al-Shatat* described in 23 installments the alleged Jewish conspiracy to take over the world, based on *The Protocols of the Elders of Zion*. It was first aired on Hizbullah's al-Manar TV during the month of Ramadan 2003, on two Iranian channels during Ramadan 2004, and on the Jordanian al-Mamnu' TV channel during Ramadan 2005.

37 Salman, "Almaniya al-naziyya," p. 103.

38 'Abbas, *al-Wajh al-akhar*, pp. 18–19, citing David Yisraeli's *The Palestine Problem*, pp. 160–1.

1940–41 as a proof for the ambitions of all Zionist circles to forge such links.[39] Edward Said states that the "Revisionists [i.e., the Revisionist party led by Jabotinsky], the Irgun [IZL], and the Stern Gang [LEHY] and other Zionists" maintained contacts with the Nazis "hoping to emulate their Reich in Palestine," thereby projecting a singular act of a marginal group onto the Zionist mainstream, even though they pursued an opposite line. An Islamist publication goes further, saying that during the war "Zionist terror organizations" forged links with Hitler in order to help the German campaign in North Africa in return for German concessions in Palestine that would assist the establishment of a "Nazi Israel."[40]

Keeping silent and collaborating in the extermination

Among the most serious accusations leveled against the Zionists was their alleged passive and active cooperation in the extermination of non-Zionist Jews, or those Jews that were of no use to the Zionist enterprise, in order to push the remaining Jews to Palestine. The view that Zionism was indifferent to the fate of the Jews and did not do all that was possible in order to save European Jewry was buttressed by post-Zionist and Jewish right-wing criticism against the Zionist leadership during World War II. Both the Israeli and Arab criticism tend to overestimate the influence of the Zionist movement during that period. Right-wing Zionist critics believed that persuasive propaganda or loud cries of anguish could have changed Allied policies toward thwarting the extermination of the Jews. By contrast, post-Zionists underestimated the indifference or often hostility of wide circles in the Allied camp toward the fate of the Jews. However, both types of critics never accused the Zionist leadership of actual complicity in the destruction of the Jews.[41] Arab writers, on the other hand, take these arguments further, accusing the Zionist leadership of keeping silent over the extermination of the Jews or even of actively supporting or initiating this policy.

In contrast to these accusations, and despite its meager means and inhospitable international environment, the Zionist leadership made several unsuccessful

39   'Abd al-Hafiz Muharib, *Hagana, Etzel, Lehy: al-'alaqat bayna al-tanzimat al-sahyuniyya al-musallaha, 1937–1948*, Beirut: 1981, pp. 159–63; *al-Hayat*, 23 February, 5 September 1989; 'Abd al-Qadir in *Alif Ba*, 7 May 1995.

40   Edward W. Said, "An Exchange on Edward Said and Difference," *Critical Inquiry*, vol. 15 (Spring 1989), p. 644; *Takbir*, no. 112, February 1993. Contrary to Said's claims, the IZL supported the British war effort and its commander, David Raziel, was killed in Iraq on 20 May 1941 on a mission on behalf of the British army.

41   For right-wing criticism, see Yechiam Weitz, "Revisionist Criticism of the Yishuv Leadership during the Holocaust," *Yad Vashem Studies*, vol. 23 (1993), pp. 369–96; Ben Hecht, *Perfidy*, New York: 1961. For post-Zionist views, see Tom Segev, *The Seventh Million*.

efforts to advance projects to save Jews. Tragically, however, the Zionists were a weak movement, in a distant country under British rule, that could do very little without British and American consent and support.[42] The Allies, for their part, refused to divert resources from the war effort to save Jews. The US launched hesitant measures to help Jews escape from extermination only in 1944, while Britain actually exerted efforts to prevent any rescue operation that might have led the Jews to Palestine. In addition to legitimate military considerations, indifference and sometimes outright anti-Semitism played a role in their policy.[43]

Nadhir Juzmani and Munir Ma'shush change historical roles between the British and the Zionists by asserting that Chaim Weizmann rejected a British offer made by the 1936 Peel Commission to save six million Jews from Nazi terror by bringing them to Palestine. Distorting Weizmann's anguished answer that Zionism was unable to help most of the suffering Jews in Europe at the time and should at least focus its efforts on saving the younger generation, they claim instead that Weizmann declared "Let the old people perish as they are a moral and economic burden to the world, while ... we will save the young and the wealthy in Palestine."[44]

The Zionist leadership outside Europe during the war

The myth of Zionist crimes is intensified when the war period is discussed. According to Yahya-Glubb, the Zionists chose to continue their cooperation with Hitler, even after he had decided to eliminate the Jews, in order to save a limited number of their co-religionists, while forsaking a larger number of Jews to die, rather than lead a Jewish struggle against the Nazis alongside progressive Jews and non-Jews, because that alternative would have meant conceding the failure of their philosophy.[45] As a proof of Zionist complicity, Ma'shush cites an

---

42   For these efforts, see Bauer, *Jews for Sale*; Porat, *The Blue and the Yellow Stars*. For refutations of the criticism against the Zionist leadership, see note 35 in the Introduction.

43   For Allied reluctance and procrastination in helping the Jews during the war, see, *inter alia*, David S. Wyman, *The Abandonment of the Jews: America and the Holocaust, 1941–1945*, New York: 1984; Aronson, *Hitler, the Allies, and the Jews*; Bernard Wassertein, *Britain and the Jews of Europe, 1939–1945*, London: 1999.

44   Juzmani, in *al-Hurriyya*, 24 June 1990; Ma'shush , *al-Sahyuniyya*, pp. 74–6. The British did not offer to save the Jews, but rather asked Weizmann what the Zionists would do with the six million European Jews. For the authentic texts of Weizmann's statement, see *The Letters and Papers of Chaim Weitzmann, Series B Papers*, New Brunswick, NJ: 1983–84, vol. 2, pp. 276–87. Following the renewed outbreak of the Arab rebellion, the British began to restrict Zionist immigration despite the growing exhortations of the Zionists and the increasing plight of European Jews.

45   Yahya-Glubb, *Zionist*, pp. 33–5. The alleged dilemma never existed. The Transfer Agreement was invalidated once the war broke out in September 1939. The Nazis banned

article allegedly written in 1933 by a Zionist leader called Reifer in Bukovina, who defined the foundations of the bloody collaboration between the Zionists and the Nazis that was the cause of death for so many Jews. Reifer supposedly explained [foreseeing the Nazi extermination plan before the Nazis themselves] that the Jews should be patient and realize that not all of them would survive. Only the chosen few, i.e., the Zionists, would survive, and the Zionist leadership was negotiating with the Germans to that effect. How strange, Ma'shush concludes, that the Jews who mourn their dead today and take money from the Germans "ignore the fact that the Zionist leadership was the one that launched the conspiracy against them."[46]

Consequently, according to Yahya-Glubb and 'Abbas, the Jewish leaders, particularly the Zionists, who stayed in "safe havens" outside Nazi-occupied Europe, did not issue any call for their brethren in Europe to rebel against the Nazis, nor make any effort to smuggle weapons to the besieged Jews in the ghettoes. The reason for that conduct, they both charge, was the exclusive preoccupation of the Zionists in setting up their own state. While presenting the Zionists as much more powerful and influential than they ever were, 'Abbas goes further in saying that not only did the Zionist leadership fail to give any assistance to the Jews, but it did its utmost to conceal the facts of the extermination and to suppress the spirit of rebellion that emerged in the ghettoes. The Zionists, he concludes, carried out a selection process in their rescue operations in order to decide who would live and who should perish.[47]

Yahya-Glubb and Khalaf reject the argument that the Zionist movement lacked the means to aid the Jews in the ghettoes or to pressure the Allies to bomb the gas chambers or the railroads to the death camps, insisting that the Zionists had "the financial means, political connections and influence over the centers of power" all over the western world. While the Jews in Europe pleaded

---

Jewish emigration on 27 October 1941, independently of any Zionist actions, and the Allies were extremely reluctant to let Jews in, as shown convincingly in the studies mentioned in note 43. More importantly, the Zionist leadership sided unequivocally with Britain once the war started. Nor does Glubb ask why the "good" Europeans, who are contrasted with the "evil" Zionists and who had been supposedly aware of Nazi intentions, did not do anything to save the Jews.

46   Ma'shush , *al-Sahyuniyya*, ibid.

47   Yahya-Glubb, *Zionist*, pp. 52–6; 'Abbas, *al-Wajh al-akhar*, pp. 47–8, 151; Shimali, *Iflas*, p. 119, citing 'Abbas. As elsewhere, the question of Jewish resistance was much more complex than the superficial and distorted picture which the Arab writers portray. They ignore the fact that news of the mass extermination of Jews reached Palestine only after most of the Jews had perished. Likewise, they do not bother to ask how the Zionist leadership could have instructed or called the Jews to rebel during the war and why the Jews, most of them anti-Zionist according to the Arab allegation, would heed these calls.

for help, both say, the Zionists came out with the Biltmore program in May 1942, which reflected their immense power over US policy. The plan demonstrated that the Zionists sought to take advantage of the massacre of the Jews, most of whom were anti-Zionist, in order to advance their plan.[48]

A similar distortion of historical realities, was the charge that Zionists intentionally thwarted all attempts to save Jews by sending them to other countries except Palestine, since their main goal was not to save Jews but to use them as "raw material" for the Zionist state. Ahmad Jabir maintains that the Zionists signed secret agreements with the American and British governments to prevent the entry of Jews into their countries. However, since not all Jews could come to Palestine, the Zionists "condemned them to death without any hesitation." The US-based Islamic organization al-'Aqida, alleged that many Jews who did not immigrate to America because of Zionist "exhortations," chose to stay in Germany "only to be killed in the Holocaust," adding that millions of Jews died for that reason.[49] Another alleged Zionist crime was the sinking in the Black Sea of the *Struma* on 23 February 1942, which carried 700 refugees, in order to slander Britain.[50]

Arab writers also charge the Zionists with foiling a deal which the Jewish rabbi from Slovakia, Michael Dov Weissmandel, had reached with the Nazis to spare one million Jews for three million dollars. They listened to his anguished pleas, Yahya-Glubb writes, ostensibly in sympathy, but refused to send him that amount. Those nationalists, he adds sarcastically, who had all the means and power at their disposal, refused to hand in the money that had been collected

---

48 Yahya-Glubb, *Zionist*, pp. 55–6; Khalaf, in *al-Dustur*, 6 February 1984. The Biltmore program, named after the New York hotel where it was formulated, called for the establishment of a Jewish state as the goal of the Zionist movement for the post-war period. The US government at the time opposed a Jewish state and the resolutions did not influence its policy at all.

49 Jabir in *Filastin al-Thawra*, 13 December 1986; Haddad, "al-Tamathul," p. 72; *al-Tali'a*, November 1971; Masiri, "al-Ibada," p. 69; Yahya-Glubb, *Zionist*, pp. 51ff; 'Abd al-'Al, in *al-Hurriyya*, 28 January 1990; Juzmani, in *al-Hurriyya*, 24 June 1990; Aqidah Islamic Information Service MSANEWS, 22 October 2000. Hasan Sabri al-Khuli, *Siyasat al-isti'mar wal-sahyuniyya tujah filastin fi al-nisf al-awwal min al-qarn al-'ishrin*, Cairo: 1973, p. 753.

50 Dr. Ahmad Tarabayn, *Filastin fi khitat al-sahyuniyya wal-isti'mar: amrika fi khidmat al-dawla al-yahudiyya 1939–1947*, Beirut: 1972, p. 40; Ma'shush, *al-Sahyuniyya*, p. 76; 'Abduh 'Ali, in *al-Mawqif al-'Arabi*, p. 102; *Filastin al-Thawra*, 17 January 1993; Elyas Shufani, *al-Mujaz fi ta'rikh filastin al-siyasi mundhu fajr al-ta'rikh hatta sanat 1948*, Beirut: 1996, p. 492; *al-Hayat al-Jadida*, 24 June 2003. The *Struma* was sunk by a Soviet submarine, see Douglas Frantz and Catherine Collins, *Death on the Black Sea: The Untold Story of the Struma and World War II's Holocaust at Sea*, New York: 2003.

in order to save Jews.[51] Going even further, Shaykh Bassam Jarrar of Hamas claimed in a widely distributed audio-cassette in late 2005 that the "Elders of Zion" had written a book called *The Victims of the Crematorium of Zion*, which purported to show how the Jewish Agency refused to save 30,000 Jews from the crematoria in return for $50,000, claiming that women, children and the aged could not reach Israel. Jarrar states that one can learn the level of the Jews' moral turpitude from the book, since they were not willing to pay a dollar and a half [*sic*] to save their brothers.[52]

Writing inside Israel, Emil Tuma, ideologue of the Israeli Communist party, took a milder position, either because he was more exposed to the Israeli historical discourse or because he feared strong public reaction to blunt, false charges. He, therefore, only accused the Zionist leadership of focusing its efforts on establishing a state rather than on helping European Jews. Still, even he does not abstain from inflating Zionist power by concluding that "had the Zionist leadership shown any interest in saving the Jews, it could have spared hundreds of thousands from death."[53] In similar vein, Palestinian historian 'Abd al-Rahman 'Abd al-Ghani concedes the open hostility between the Zionists and the Nazis, but blames the Zionists for not providing help to the Jews out of fear of conflict with the Allies.[54]

In order to further vilify the Zionists, several writers falsely attribute to the Allied leaders intentions and plans to rescue Jews during the war. Some claim that the Zionists thwarted President Roosevelt's "deep ambition" to save 500,000 Jews by settling them in Alaska, because they insisted on Palestine as their sole destination. Others speak of foiling "sincere" British efforts to save Jews by sending them to the Indian Ocean island of Mauritius. 'Abbas also speaks of Zionist attacks on the rescue committees set up in the US toward the end of the war. Likewise, Nakhle claims that the Zionists refused to use the quota of

---

51   Yahya-Glubb, *Zionist*, pp 53–4. The "working group," in which Zionists played a leading role alongside non-Zionist Jews, did not reach an agreement with the Nazis, but made the offer in 1942 to local Nazi officials to save Jews in return for $3 million in what became known as the Europa Plan. In contrast to Yahya-Glubb's accusations, the Zionist leadership tried to raise the necessary funds, even though it had no idea how serious the offer was and how it would transfer them to Slovakia. The negotiations with the Nazis faltered in 1943 and most Slovak Jews were deported to the death camps. See Bauer, *Jews for Sale*, pp. 91–101.

52   www.intelligence.org.il/eng/eng_n/incitement_e1205.htm. Jarrar probably refers to Shonfield's, *The Holocaust Victims*, but in an anti-Semitic fashion he considers him as one of "the Elders of Zion," and lumps him together with his Zionist political rivals.

53   Emil Tuma, *Judhur al-qadiyya al-filastiniyya*, Jerusalem: 1976, p. 275. The PNA official website www.minfo.gov.ps/index.php?scid=2&pid=269 adopted Tuma's position.

54   'Abd al-Ghani, *Almaniya*, pp. 362–3.

30,000 immigration certificates to Palestine allotted by the British during the war because they knew that most Jews would only use them to move later to other countries. In a different turn, Mu'in Mahmud describes the plan to transfer Jews to the island of Madagascar as a joint Nazi–Jewish plan.[55] All of these allegations were totally baseless.

The Zionist leadership under Nazi occupation

Discussing the Jewish resistance movements in Nazi-dominated Europe, Yahya-Glubb makes a clear distinction between two groups: the Zionists, who supposedly collaborated with the Nazis in order to save themselves and some of their followers, versus the non-Zionist Jews, who chose the moral and courageous path of resistance. Unfortunately, he adds self-righteously, most members of the Jewish councils in the ghettoes were Zionists, who believed that they were doing the right thing in collaborating with the Nazis. The Nazis, on the other hand, found in those Zionists "loyal and obedient servants, who led the Jewish masses to their destruction in their lust for power and money."[56] Indeed, many *Judenräte* leaders believed that obeying the Germans would help to save from death as many Jews as possible, but Yahya-Glubb falsely attributes their attitude to Zionist ideology, as many of them were not Zionists. He ignores the facts that most of them were unaware of the true aims of the Nazis until it was too late and that they lacked viable alternatives that could save a large number of Jews.

Masiri, too, claims that the Nazis appointed many Zionists to the Jewish councils due to the great ideological affinity between their two respective movements (see Chapter 7). Masiri quotes the *Encyclopedia Judaica*, ostensibly in agreement, that the councils' members should not be accused of collaboration, being under the threat "of the butcher's knife" and that they had to follow a policy with which they disagreed. He insists, however, that the same criterion should be applied to all those who collaborated with the Nazis, including mid- and low-level Nazi officials, since they too lived under Nazi terror, again blurring the distinction between voluntary and involuntary collaboration.[57]

Masiri rejects the argument that armed Jewish resistance was futile. It is highly conceivable, he maintains, that millions of Jews and non-Jews would

---

55   'Abbas, *al-Wajh al-akhar*, pp. 48, 56–7, 69; Shimali, *Iflas*, p. 119, citing him; 'Abduh 'Ali, in *al-Mawqif al-'Arabi*, p. 101; Jabir, in *Filastin al-Thawra*, 13 December 1986; Haddad, "al-Tamathul," p. 72; Masiri, "al-Ibada," p. 69; Yahya-Glubb, *Zionist*, pp. 51ff; 'Abd al-'Al, in *al-Hurriyya*, 28 January 1990; al-Balwi, "al-Hulukast."

56   Yahya-Glubb, *Zionist*, pp. 37–8, 44–5. See a similar argument in al-Shaykh 'Ali, "Nahwu Ru'ya."

57   Masiri, *al-Sahyuniyya*, pp. 157–8.

have opposed being loaded onto the trains to the death camps, and that such action would have foiled the German efforts, or at least made it more difficult to carry them out. The absence of resistance was due to the Zionist *Judenräte*, who calmed the fears of the Jews and advocated subservience until the extermination plan was all but completed. As an example, he points to the *Judenrat* at Theresienstadt in Czechoslovakia, whose members "enjoyed" great freedom and cooperated with the Germans in misleading a Red Cross delegation that visited it in 1943.[58] Masiri goes even further, saying that, compared with other groups in Germany or with other nations, the Jews as a whole, not just the Zionists, did not show any opposition or resistance to the Nazis. Even Jewish resistance in Warsaw, in which the Jews constituted 45 percent of the population, started only in 1943, after Berlin had decided to liquidate the Jewish ghetto, when it was no longer possible to save the inmates of the Nazi camps and when the war was tilted in favor of the Allies. This timing, he says, demonstrates the opportunistic dimension of Jewish and Zionist conduct during the war. By contrast, he praises the non-Zionist Jews as the real heroes of the ghettoes who led whatever resistance there was.[59] Masiri is supposedly willing to understand the abstention of German Jews from active opposition to the Nazis, considering their small numbers, the broad support for the Nazi regime in Germany and the efficiency of the Nazi system of repression. But he refuses to accept the submissiveness of the Jews in Poland and Hungary, where, he claims, Jews constituted a much greater force and could join the Polish and Hungarian peoples toward the end of the war and rebel.[60]

These accusations demonstrate the a-historical and propagandist vantage point of Masiri and other advocates of the collaboration theme. In addition to totally ignoring the horrible conditions of the unarmed, starving and terrorized Jews in the ghettoes, who faced much more powerful armed German forces, which rendered resistance almost impossible, Masiri disregards the fact that most Jews were unaware of the Nazi extermination policy until it was too late. He overlooks the historical reality that the Jews were isolated from the Polish and Hungarian populations, which were by and large hostile to them and often assisted the Nazis in their anti-Jewish measures. Consequently, armed resistance in the ghettoes was more an act of defiance to the Nazis in order to redeem Jewish honor than actually foiling the powerful Nazi repressive apparatus. Moreover, Masiri disregards the fact that during the war there were around

---

58   Ibid., pp. 158, 160–1. He too does not explain why non-Zionist Jews would obey the so-called Zionist exhortations.

59   Masiri, ibid., p. 128.

60   Masiri, ibid., p. 129.

1,000 Jewish rebellions motivated by Zionist ideology and that thousands of Jews escaped to the forests to fight the Germans.[61] He also gets his chronology wrong. By the time the Poles rebelled against the Germans in 1944 (also when the tide turned against Germany) most Jews were already dead. In addition, he does not ask why around four million Soviet PoWs, who were held under horrific conditions, did not rebel, even though they had been able-bodied men (unlike the Jewish population, which had children and elderly people), and were not misguided by Zionism. Finally, he omits the fact that the leaders of the resistance movements in the ghettoes were mostly members of the Zionist youth movements, who cooperated with the non-Zionist organizations.[62]

'Abbas is even less generous toward the *Judenräte*, which he describes as thoroughly Zionist. He claims that the Nazis gave them "complete freedom of action regarding Jewish affairs as part of their overall policy, which operated in complete harmony with the Zionist leadership." In other words, he charges that the *Judenräte* were not forced to carry out their duties, but were volunteers whose conduct brought Zionist–Nazi collaboration to its highest level, manifested in committing "numerous horrendous crimes against the Jews." Both he and 'Abduh 'Ali depict the Jewish police force set up by the Nazis as a "Zionist organization" that helped the Nazis deport the Jews to the death camps as part of the Zionist action plan.[63]

In similar vein, 'Abd al-Fattah 'Atallah quotes "documents" published by the Soviet Anti-Zionist Committee that "prove" Zionist responsibility for the "heinous crimes" committed against the Jewish population. As an example, he mentions the "Zionist *Judenrat*" in the Lvov Ghetto in Western Ukraine that exerted efforts to save the Zionists and the rich while sending to the death camps (allegedly voluntarily and of their own desire) tens of thousands of working-class Jews. He even extends Zionist crimes to the non-Jewish population when he charges the Zionists of cooperating with the German and Ukrainian police against the anti-Nazi movement.[64]

---

61   On the activities of the Zionist youth movements in the struggle against Nazis, see Meir Grubsztein (ed.), *Jewish Resistance during the Holocaust*, Jerusalem: 1971; Rivka Knoller, *The Activities of Religious Zionist Youth Groups in Europe during the Holocaust, 1939–1945: A Summarized Review of Limited Archive Sources*, Ramat-Gan: 1989.

62   Among the many studies on Jewish resistance and the difficulties it encountered, see Yehuda Bauer, *They Chose Life: Jewish Resistance in the Holocaust*, New York: 1973; Dov Levin, *Fighting Back: Lithuanian Jewry's Armed Resistance to the Nazis, 1941–1945*, New York: 1997; Michael Robert Marrus, *Jewish Resistance to the Holocaust*, Westport, CT: 1989.

63   'Abbas, *al-Wajh al-akhar*, p. 192; 'Abduh 'Ali in *al-'Arabi*, p. 112.

64   'Atallah in *Filastin al-Thawra*, 23 March 1985.

Mu'in Mahmud relies on Polish communist sources to lay his charges against the Jewish leaders who helped the Germans to exterminate their brethren. The Poles, he states, would never be able to forget the shameful role which the *Judenrat* and the Jewish police played. In addition to identifying with Polish horror over Jewish crimes, Mahmud invents a story of a Zionist unit set up by the Germans inside the Warsaw Ghetto in order to spy on the Polish underground and expose the efforts of "those noble Poles" to supply the Jews with weapons and food. The Polish underground, he goes on, even managed to smuggle 500 Jews from the ghetto into the forests, but the *Judenrat* intervened through one of the rabbis and managed to persuade these Jews to return to the ghetto, whence they were sent to the death camps.[65]

An anonymous contributor to *Filastin al-Thawra* accuses the entire Jewish bourgeoisie of collaborating with the Nazis in Germany, Poland and France. He charges Jewish leaders in France with attaining the status of "honorary Aryans" for themselves, while helping the Nazis to send thousands of other Jews to Auschwitz.[66] Seeking to demonstrate the overarching Jewish–Zionist collaboration with the Nazis, Akram 'Atallah and Masiri point to the service of a few thousand soldiers and officers of mixed Jewish descent in the German army during the war. This is the reason, they comment, why the Zionists insist on rejecting and persecuting any historians who examine their "dark history."[67]

Since Jews did rebel against the Nazis in various ghettoes, in death camps and in the forests, 'Abbas and Yahya-Glubb solve the problem by insisting that none of these acts was organized by Zionists. Rather, they claim, many non-Zionist Jews who were truly anti-Fascist took part in the anti-Nazi resistance, whereas the Zionist leaders sought to foil these attempts. In a few cases,

---

65 Mahmud, *al-Sahyuniyya wa-naziyya* pp. 300–1. The historical facts were very different. The major Polish underground, the Armia Krajowa, refused to accept Jews who fled from the ghettoes and on many occasions murdered them. It gave the Warsaw ghetto fighters only sixty pistols and some ammunition. The right-wing Narodowe Siły Zbrojne [NSZ] murdered thousands of Jews who fled the war and even after liberation. Only the much smaller communist Gwardia Ludowa (People's Guard) extended some help to the Jews. See Yisrael Gutman and Shmuel Krakowski, *Unequal Victims: Poles and Jews During World War Two*, New York: 1986.

66 *Filastin al-Thawra*, 1 June 1985.

67 'Atallah in *al-Haqiqa*, no. 1 (May 1997), pp. 40–1; 'Abd al-Wahhab al-Masiri, "Junud naziyyun yahud," 16 January 2007, www.aljazeera.net/NR/exeres/1F29F6E0-0D3E-4332-B82E-31044645E852.htm. On this story, see Bryan Mark Rigg, *Hitler's Jewish Soldiers: The Untold Story of Nazi Racial Laws and Men of Jewish Descent in the German Military*, Lawrence: 2002. Apart from the fact that none of these soldiers was Zionist, as most if not all of them saw themselves as Germans rather than Jews, or that some of them simply sought to survive, 'Atallah and Masiri seem to accept the Nazi view that a Jew remains a Jew even though his ancestors had converted to Christianity.

Yahya-Glubb concedes, the "Zionist groups" had no choice but to resist the Nazis. Since both authors could not ignore the Zionist affiliation of many of the rebellion leaders, most notably Mordechai Anielewicz, commander of the Warsaw Ghetto rebellion, they assert that they acted on an individual or local basis, in violation of the policies of their movements.[68]

'Abd al-Ghani takes a somewhat different and more genuine historical approach when referring to the isolation of the Jews in ghettoes in his broader discussion of the role of Hajj Amin al-Husayni in the Holocaust. Unlike the others who rely on fabricated sources, he cites historian Lucy Dawidowicz, who criticized *Judenrat* leaders for making it easier for the Germans to exterminate the Jews by their calls to cooperate with them, and affirms that, rather than harboring malice against their fellow Jews, they hoped to circumvent the Nazis' killing apparatus.[69]

Many Arab writers point to the activities of Kasztner, who headed the Aid and Rescue Committee in Budapest in 1944, as the most prominent manifestation of the alleged Zionist–Nazi collaboration.[70] They all attribute Kasztner's activities to his Zionist ideology, which supposedly sought to save a few "useful" Zionists, who would immigrate to "Israel," while charging him of misleading the Jews and helping the Germans to transfer hundreds of thousands of others to Auschwitz.[71] Both Masiri and al-Shaykh 'Ali turned Kasztner into an agent of the Hungarian and Nazi espionage services even before the war. When Eichmann came to Budapest in 1944, Masiri contends, he was accompanied by only 150 German

<hr/>

68   Yahya, *Zionist*, pp. 37–50; 'Abbas, *al-Wajh al-akhar*, pp. 172ff.

69   'Abd al-Ghani, *Almaniya*, p. 361.

70   When Germany occupied Hungary in 1944, the committee's leaders divided up responsibilities in an attempt to save Hungarian Jews. Otto Komoly worked on procuring support for the Jews from Hungarian political and church leaders, while Kasztner and Joel Brand began negotiating with SS officers Eichmann and Kurt Becher. The rescue deals they discussed were based on the Slovak Working Group's Europa Plan. While Brand traveled to Turkey to convince the Allies of the Germans' proposition, Kasztner immersed himself in one specific part of the negotiations: the Germans' offer to let hundreds of Hungarian Jews leave Hungary by train, as a proof of the Nazis' goodwill. Eventually, over 1,600 Jews left on the "Kasztner train" and ultimately reached safety in Switzerland. Although negotiations with the SS continued until early 1945, a bargain was never reached. Nonetheless, 21,000 Hungarian Jews were transferred to a safer camp in Strasshof, Austria in mid-1944, where most survived. Early in 1945 Kasztner and Becher traveled to several concentration camps where Becher convinced the commanders to hand over the Jews to the Allies. See Bauer, *Jews for Sale*, pp. 145–71.

71   *Al-Mawsu'a al-filastiniyya*, vol. 4, pp. 432–3; Sa'fan, *al-Yahud*, p. 105; Nakhle, *Encyclopaedia*, p. 875; 'Abbas, *al-Wajh al-akhar*, pp. 59; Sa'd, *al-Shakhsiyya*, p. 206; Khalaf, in *al-Dustur*, 6 February 1984; 'Abd al-'Al, in *al-Hurriyya*, 28 January 1990; 'Atiyya, "al-'Alaqa."

officials and several thousand Hungarian soldiers. Confronting this small force, stood half a million Jews, but they did not resist the German actions, because the Zionist Kasztner misled them in return for saving 2,000 Zionists.[72]

Natshe, who flatly denied the extermination of the Jews in one part of his book, points to the Kasztner affair as the ultimate proof of Zionist–Fascist alliance. He describes Eichmann's proposal to the Allies to spare some Jews in exchange for trucks and other commodities as a pro-Zionist scheme to enable the emigration of wealthy Jews and members of the Zionist youth organizations. In return, Kasztner was supposed to guarantee Jewish obedience in the detention camps in Hungary, whence the Jews were taken to Auschwitz. *Al-Shatat* TV series which featured the Kasztner–Eichmann deal, showed Kasztner promising to mislead Hungarian Jews about the true German intentions behind their deportation to Auschwitz in exchange for Eichmann allowing the emigration of 2,000 Jews, "among our best biological specimens." He also intimated to his "friend" Eichmann that, in return for helping the Nazis to "annihilate the Jews of Hungary," the Zionists would benefit from the huge funds which those Jews had hidden in Switzerland, while the Germans would "benefit from the annihilation of the Hungarian Jews." In similar vein, Akram 'Atallah accused the Zionists of supplying equipment to the German armies during the war.[73]

The Kasztner affair elicited a heated political commotion in Israel in the mid 1950s, with right-wing parties accusing him of collaborating with the Nazis in order to save himself. Kasztner was assassinated on 4 March 1957 by right-wing activists. The Israeli Supreme Court later cleared him of collaboration, and later-day historians of the Holocaust tend to agree that, under the inhumane constraints which faced him, he in fact saved the lives of thousands of Jews.[74] Several Arab writers, however, maintain that the Israeli security services killed Kasztner in order to "prevent the dissemination of more facts on the collaboration between the Jewish Agency and the Nazis," and out of fear of losing "worldwide support of which the Zionists took advantage."[75]

According to Jabir, Kasztner was not the only Zionist leader who had served the Nazis. Citing the East German writer Julius Mader, he mentions a (fabri-

---

72   Masiri, *al-Sahyuniyya*, pp. 172–3; al-Shaykh 'Ali, "Nahwu ru'ya;" Sirhan, "Man yah-takiru."

73   www.memritv.org, Clip 896, 21 October 2005; 'Atallah, "Al-Sahyuniyya." See also Natshe, *al-Isti'mar*, pp. 150–1, and *al-Safir*, 15 November 1988, which both emphasize the point of saving wealthy Jews at the expense of the poor.

74   Yechiam Weitz, *The Man who was Murdered Twice: The Life, Trial and Death of Yisrael Kasztner*, Jerusalem: 1995 (Hebrew).

75   Nakhle, *Encyclopedia*, p. 875; Yahya-Glubb, *Zionist*, pp. 57–64; *al-Mawsu'a al-filastini-yya*, p. 433–4; 'Abbas, *al-Wajh al-akhar*, pp. 56–7; 'Abduh 'Ali, in *al-'Arabi*, p. 112.

cated) 16-page Gestapo list of well-known Zionists, many of whom became senior leaders in Israel, e.g., president Chaim Weizmann and prime ministers David Ben-Gurion, Moshe Sharett and Yitzhak Shamir, who cooperated with the Gestapo. Hamid bin ʿUqayl even claims that Shamir took part in the extermination act itself.[76] Khalaf extends the alleged Zionist–Nazi collaboration to the post-war period as well. The Nazi war criminal Claus Barbie, who lived in Bolivia, was engaged from 1967 in purchasing large quantities of weapons for Israel, he fulminates, and even served as an export agent of the Israeli armament industries.[77]

The abduction of Eichmann by Israeli agents in 1960 serves as the final proof for many Arab writers of the secret Zionist–Nazi ties. Although Eichmann was not the most senior Nazi official who remained alive, they contend, he was the one official who knew the most about the close contacts, particularly those related to the Kasztner affair. He was therefore abducted in order to prevent him from publishing the incriminating material on Zionism. His trial enabled the Zionist leaders to divert attention from the negative political impact of the Kasztner affair, and "many of his secrets were buried with him" following his speedy execution, they maintain. Sirhan had Eichmann escaping to the Middle East together with several other high-ranking Nazi officers who were all privy to the alleged secret Zionist–Nazi collaboration, fearing that Begin and Shamir might kill them in order to eliminate the secret. The conspiracy theory about the Zionists finds its logical conclusion, and the "plot," which had started during the 1930s, ends by 1962.[78] The Zionist–Nazi collaboration, the Palestinian Encyclopedia concluded, assumed the shape of the "worst dangerous devilish alliance between the two most racist and brutal movements in modern time."[79]

The Zionists as promoters of extermination

A much harsher charge leveled at the Zionists is that of actually instigating the mass murder of the Jews. Maʿshush claims that emigration from Germany ceased in 1937 because Jews were no longer persuaded by the Zionist idea; but

---

76 Jabir, in *Filastin al-Thawra*, 13 December 1986. See also ʿAbduh ʿAli, in *al-Mawqif al-ʿArabi*, p. 103 and *Syria Times*, 6 September 2000.

77 Khalaf, in *al-Dustur*, 6 February 1984; *Filastin al-Thawra*, 12 March 1983. As mentioned in Chapter 9, there is evidence that Barbie actually maintained contacts with Arab organizations after the war.

78 Yahya-Glubb, *Zionist*, pp. 65–8; ʿAbbas, *al-Wajh al-akhar*, p. 207–14; Sirhan, "Man Yahtakiru"; Saʿd, *al-Shakhsiyya*, pp. 206–7; Ramadan, *Israʾil*, pp. 203–5.

79 *Al-Mawsuʿa al-filastiniyya*, vol. 4, p. 434. See a similar phrasing in *al-mawsuʿa al-siyasiyya*, vol. 6, p. 548.

he also concedes that Britain began to restrict Jewish immigration to Palestine. Therefore, he contends that the Zionists turned to the Nazis for help. In response to their plea, Himmler authorized the SS to implement its obligation to the Zionists and pressure the Jews by exterminating six million of them.[80]

Several Islamist writers go even further, attributing the very idea of exterminating the Jews to the Zionists. Al-Sa'd contends that two (non-existent) Zionist leaders in Poland, Carter Rubin and Jacob Tehon, devised a plan together with the Nazis to exterminate sick and elderly Jews. Sa'fan and Masiri maintain that the Nazis drew the idea of extermination from Alfred Nossig, who was acting on behalf of the Zionists. In return, the Nazis appointed him as head of the Jewish affairs section and Jewish art in the Warsaw Ghetto.[81] In addition to their false nature, the accusations based on Nossig's case follow a typical anti-Semitic pattern, whereby the alleged activities of an individual, regardless of the circumstances, are projected onto the entire community as supposedly reflecting its inherent nature and policies.

'Abbas joins the charge that the Zionist leadership incited the Nazis to take revenge on the Jews, concocting a more elaborate scheme. While collaborating with the Nazis in secret, the Zionist leadership in Palestine and the US assumed a public hostile and provocative stand toward the Nazis, which exacerbated the intensity of the "heinous" Nazi attacks against the Jews. The most glaring example of the Zionist incitement was the 1942 Biltmore Conference, in which the Zionist leadership decided on the establishment of a Jewish state and at the same time declared war on Germany in the name of the Jewish people. When Hitler heard of the resolution through his ambassador in the US, 'Abbas adds, he became furious and declared "I shall now destroy them." Later Hitler convened all the senior officials in Germany to work out a detailed plan for the extermination of the Jews. While 'Abbas concedes that the Biltmore Conference was not the sole reason leading Hitler to order the extermination, he insists that it played a major role in bringing about the tragic fate of the Jews.[82] In addition to contradicting every serious scholarly

---

80 Ma'shush , al-Sahyuniyya, p. 74.

81 Sa'd, al-Shakhsiyya, p. 202; Sa'fan, al-Yahud, p. 105; Masiri, al-Sahyuniyya, pp. 166–7. Nossig was close to the Zionists during his youth, but distanced himself from them years later. He was appointed to these positions in the ghetto and sought to advance Jewish *emigration* from Nazi-ruled Poland (but not extermination). He was executed by the predominantly Zionist underground in the ghetto as a suspected Gestapo informer. Needless to say, the Nazis did not need the fabricated suggestion of a lone old Jew to arrive at the idea of exterminating the Jews. For his activities, see Shmuel Almog, "Alfred Nossig: Reappraisal," *Studies in Zionism*, no. 7 (Spring 1983), pp. 1–31.

82 'Abbas, al-Wajh al-akhar, p. 48; Shimali, Iflas, p. 119.

study on the origins of the process that led to the actual extermination of the Jews, 'Abbas' story contains several basic factual errors that demonstrate the crudity of the absurd plot. In May 1942, Germany and the US had been at war for six months, so Hitler could not have had an ambassador in Washington. The Wannsee Conference, which discussed the implementation of the Final Solution, took place on 20 January 1942, while mass murder operations against the Jews in the Soviet Union had started already in July 1941, long before the events 'Abbas talks about. His intention, however, was clear. Not only were the Zionists guilty of collaborating with the Nazis, but the decision to establish a Jewish state was directly responsible for the deaths of the Jews. The stress on the Zionist Biltmore program either as a "cause" for the extermination or as a proof of Zionist sacrificing European Jews is illuminating. For the Palestinians, the Biltmore program, which called for a Jewish state, was a great threat, and therefore it had to be associated with a clearly negative act or process that would decisively tarnish Zionism.

Finally, some writers maintain that the Zionists played a leading role in the actual planning and execution of the extermination process and in running the operation room and death camps that were set up to exterminate the millions European Jews.[83]

Egyptian scholar 'Aysha 'Abd al-Rahman (better known by her pseudonym Bint al-Shati) and Nadhir Juzmani cite an alleged confession of the Jews of their role in facilitating the extermination. Both describe a secret meeting of Jewish rabbis, reminiscent of those attributed to the Elders of Zion, that was supposedly held on 12 January 1952 in Budapest (then under the Communist anti-Zionist regime), in which a rabbi called Emmanuel Rabinovich stated that, in order to achieve their goal of world domination, the Jews would have to carry out "the same activities" that they did during Hitler's days. We ourselves, he supposedly said, would "sacrifice part of our people through actions that we would direct behind the scenes."[84]

The TV drama series al-Shatat also charged the Jews with starting the two world wars, the dropping of the atomic bombs on Hiroshima and Nagasaki

---

83   Mahmud 'Abbas, in *Filastin al-Thawra*, 5 April 1986; 'Abd al-'Al, in *al-Hurriyya*, 28 January 1990; ZCCF, "The Zionist Movement and Its Animosity to Jews," 11 October 2001 – Memri, Special Report, no. 16, 16 May 2003; *al-Thawra*, 12 December 2002.

84   William Brinner, "An Egyptian Anti-Orientalist," in G. Warburg and U. Kupferschmidt (eds.), *Islam, Nationalism and Radicalism in Egypt and the Sudan*, New York: 1986, p. 235; Juzmani, in *al-Hurriyya*, 24 June 1990; 'Abd al-Rahman cites *Pawns in the Game* by the Canadian naval officer Richard G. Carr, a prolific writer on Jewish-Communist plots to take over the world. The book itself came out in four editions during 1954–62, and was translated into Arabic as *Ahjar 'ala ruq'at al-shitranj*, Beirut: 1979. The "speech" also appears on the neo-Nazi website www.aryan-nations.org.

269

and with helping Hitler to annihilate the Jews of Europe. Episode 22 showed the "global Jewish government" convening to *celebrate* [authors' emphasis] the deaths of one million Jews in World War II, and its head explains why their death served the leaders' goals.

The higher the number of Jews killed in this war, the more we will be able to convince the world that the *Protocols of the Elders of Zion* is nothing more than a lie invented by the Christian world to increase people's hatred for the Jews. After public opinion is persuaded that this book is nothing more than a lie, we will launch a secret and quiet offensive to prove the truth of this book, until the world again fears us deep inside, and will be defeated by us without a war.[85]

Conclusions

Unlike other themes in the Arab Holocaust discourse, the charges of Zionist–Nazi collaboration rest on some factual basis. Limited and temporary shared interests which led to contacts were subsequently inflated and distorted with outright fabrications in order to create a false picture of ideological closeness and large-scale voluntary collaboration serving "sinister" Zionist political goals. With the passage of time, there was an increasing effort to endow these charges with pseudo-academic foundations, employing a-historical approaches with little regard to the complexity of the inhuman situation which Jews experienced under Nazi rule, and attributing naive or mistaken policies of some Jews, who were forced to abide by Nazi orders, to their "vicious" Zionist ideology.

The charges of collaboration were in some ways an act of psychological projection onto the Zionists of opposite charges against Arab leaders, particularly the Palestinian Hajj Amin al-Husayni, who did collaborate voluntarily with the Nazis. They enabled Arab writers who could not close their eyes to the actual occurrence of the extermination of the Jews to downgrade its historical significance by laying part of the blame on the Zionists. During the 1960s and 1970s the collaboration theme was associated mainly with Palestinians, but it has been recreated and reproduced by other Arab writers in recent years, particularly Syrians and Islamists.

---

85   Memri, Special Dispatch Series, no. 627, 12 December 2003.

9

ARAB RETROSPECTIVE PERCEPTIONS
OF NAZI GERMANY

World War II is among the few wars in history in which there is an almost uni-versal consensus on the identity of the villainous parties, with Nazi Germany perceived as the epitome of evil. Consequently, many of the post-war European countries tended to construct a more heroic and positive "past" for that period for themselves, which highlighted resistance to Nazism, while minimizing if not totally obliterating manifestations of collaboration with the Nazis. The Holo-caust, thus, is marginal in these narratives.[1]

Arab attitudes toward Nazi Germany and the war were more complex, due to increasing resentment toward Britain and France, the imperial powers that had dominated the Middle East since World War I, and due to the fact that imperial Germany, and later the Weimar republic, had no direct imperialist designs in the Middle East. Britain's responsibility for the Balfour Declaration in support of Zionism and its subsequent policy in Mandatory Palestine, which the Arabs perceived as favoring the Jews, exacerbated these resentments and enhanced Arab sympathy toward Germany during the 1930s, particularly in Iraq and among the Palestinians. Nazi enmity toward the Jews was never a disadvantage in the eyes of many Arabs.[2] As mentioned above (see Chapter 5), resentment toward western hegemony over the writing of history, which according to some

---

1   Judt, *Postwar*, pp. 803ff. In some of the countries whose rulers had collaborated with Hitler and which later fell under Communist rule, e.g., Lithuania, Slovakia, Romania and Hungary, there were attempts following the fall of Communism to advance partial rehabilitation of these collaborators.

2   On Iraq, see Lukasz Hirszowicz, *The Third Reich and the Arab East*, London: 1966, pp. 95–172. On Syria, see Philip S. Khoury, *Syria and the French Mandate: The Politics of Arab Nationalism, 1920–1945*, Princeton: 1987, pp. 566, 590–2; Goetz Nordbrunch, *Nazism in Syria and Lebanon*, London: 2008. On the Palestinians, see Nicosia, *The Third Reich*, pp. 84–5, 109–10, 185–6; 'Abd al-Ghani, *Almaniya*, pp. 189–97; Yisraeli, *The German Reich*, pp. 188ff.

271

Arab writers did not do justice to the Arabs and Germans alike, contributed to these ambivalent attitudes to the war.

Israel Gershoni has maintained that the commonly held view of broad popular support in Egypt for Nazi Germany during the 1930s, based on the notion of "the enemy of my enemy is my friend," had largely been the invention of the revolutionary Nasserist regime. The young officers who seized power in July 1952, he says, sought to create a new collective memory in order to establish for themselves a long record of resistance going back to the 1930s. In the effort to highlight their opposition to Britain during the war, these officers boosted their identification with the Axis powers and portrayed it as a broad-based phenomenon.[3] This narrative has remained the official one in Egypt up to the present, as shown in Egyptian high-school textbooks and it still retains popularity in Egyptian public discourse, suggesting that it appealed to many.[4]

Except in North Africa, the Arabs did not experience Nazi rule and the horrors of the war.[5] They were ruled by the Allied powers, which were reluctant to award them with independence even after the war had ended. Thus, in his testimony to the Anglo-American Committee Jamal Husayni, secretary of the AHC, stated that "the Germans were not our enemies, but enemies of the Jews."[6] Moreover, since the Arabs perceived the birth of Israel as the direct outcome of the war, the Allies' victory always carried with it a bitter taste, which was aggravated by growing opposition to the post-war policies of the US and Britain.

Arab dealing with past attitudes toward Nazi Germany was part of a broader grappling with their past and collective memory. It was heavily influenced by the degree of exposure and acceptance of western cultural and ideological influences and by universal conventions that regarded Nazism and Nazi Germany as inherently evil. While the mainstream Arab discourse adopted the prevalent western view of totally abhorring Nazi Germany as evil incarnate, there was always another view – not insignificant – which found positive points in Nazi Germany.

There is a complex correlation between Arab representations of the Holocaust and attitudes towards World War II and Nazi Germany. Animosity toward Zionism and the Allies produced sympathy toward Germany and facilitated a broader acceptance of Holocaust denial. It also served as a cause for justification of Nazi measures against the Jews. Many of those who criticized Nazi Germany

---

3   Gershoni, *Light in the Shadow*, pp. 20ff.

4   Sa'adallah Suryal Yusuf, *al-Mu'allim fi ta'rikh misr wal-'arab al-hadith*, Cairo: 1995, p. 133.

5   The Arab writers that we encountered in this research rarely related to North Africa in their discussion of Arab attitudes towards Nazi Germany.

6   Karlibakh, *The Anglo-American Commission*, vol. 1, pp. 354–5, 362.

ignored or minimized its racist and murderous nature when it applied to the Jews, or even justified Hitler's anti-Jewish policies, and confined their criticism only to Nazi policies against other European nations. Others did not see Nazism as significantly different from other imperial western powers. Only proponents of the "alternative discourse" on the Holocaust (see Chapter 11) condemn Hitler and simultaneously acknowledge the Holocaust, to various degrees.[7]

This chapter seeks to discern continuity and change in post-war attitudes and representations of Nazi Germany, World War II in general and the Arab positions in the war as manifested in the Arab public discourse rather than to analyze the "actual" Arab attitudes toward Nazi Germany during the 1930s and early 1940s. The chapter discusses six themes: the debate whether World War II was an imperialist war or a just one; attitudes towards Nazism; Nazi Germany as an alleged victim of Zionist warmongering; retrospective reflection on Arab attitudes towards Germany during the Nazi period; Palestinian evaluations of Hajj Amin al-Husayni's collaboration with Nazi Germany; and views of Nazi Germany in internet fora. The chapter focuses mainly on Egypt and the Palestinians, not only because they have been two major producers of discourse on these issues, but also because they represent two very different poles: the Palestinians, who have to grapple with the consequences of their leader's collaboration with Germany, and the Egyptians, whose intellectual elites were least favorable towards Nazi Germany during the 1930s.

An imperialist or a just war?

Egyptian historian Salah al-'Aqqad stated in 1966 that the question of the Arabs and World War II was not a thing of the past, as it continued to elicit passionate debates whenever it was raised.[8] Egyptian diplomat Butrus Butrus-Ghali also stressed the continuous relevance of this topic in the introduction he wrote to Muhammad 'Adil Shukri's study on Nazi ideology, which was published in the same year. In particular, he pointed to the "imperialist" and Zionist "propaganda," which "sought to harm the reputation of the [Egyptian] revolution by claiming that it was partially influenced by Nazism."[9]

Still, the number of historical studies on Nazi Germany and the war published in the Arab world is strikingly low, especially when compared with the

---

7   See for instance, Farouk Mohamed [sic], "Tasawwur 'an film adulf hitler," www.ra2yak.com/Articles/Article.aspx?articleid=510, who sharply attacks Hitler, including his genocidal policies against the Jews.

8   Salah al-'Aqqad, *al-'Arab wal-harb al-'alamiyya al-thaniya*, Cairo: 1966, p. 14; idem, *al-Harb al-'alamiyya al-thaniya: dirasa fi ta'rikh al-'alaqat al-duwaliyya*, Cairo: 1963, p. 211.

9   Shukri, *al-Naziyya*, p. 9.

FROM EMPATHY TO DENIAL

"explosion" of such publications in the West, lamented 'Aqqad. In an attempt to explain this paucity, 'Aqqad pointed to the common misperception of Arab passivity during the war as compared with their more important role during World War I and the cultural–ideological shift which they had experienced then, from Ottoman-Islamic identity to nationalism, as well as lack of historical perspective – though he himself found the latter reason unsatisfactory, considering the sources available to Arab historians. However, it seems that this situation has not changed substantially in subsequent decades,[10] perhaps due to the deep absorption of Arab writers in their own affairs and lack of curiosity about the history of other peoples,[11] or due to a reluctance to deal with less glamorous periods of Arab history.

The mainstream Egyptian political–historical discourse in the immediate aftermath of the war presented the country decidedly on the side of the Allies in the fight against Nazi tyranny. However, as it became clearer during the late 1940s that Egypt's road to full independence and the complete evacuation of British troops from its soil were far away, this attitude changed. Instead, Egypt's sacrifices and costs were increasingly emphasized alongside British deception, which cast a heavy shadow on the war's essence and goals. While Nazi Germany was still perceived as deserving all condemnation for its transgressions and crimes, these were now belittled in comparison to Britain's misdeeds.[12] Both motifs, highlighting Egypt's war effort and the moral equation between Nazi Germany and Britain, marked a change in the representation of the war and became more prominent in Egypt as well as in the rest of the Arab world.

The moral equation between the Allies and Nazi Germany reflected both a deep-seated animosity toward the former imperial powers and a certain belittling of Nazi crimes, but also a rejection of Nazism as inherently evil. This duality

---

10   Only a handful of books were published in Egypt on Nazism or the war, among them: Salah al-'Aqqad, *Dirasa muqarina lil-harakat al-qawmiyya fi almaniya, italiya, al-wilayat al-muttahida wa-turkiya*, Cairo: 1957; idem, *al-Harb*; Jalal Yahya, *al-'Alam al-'arabi al-hadith mundhu al-harb al-'alamiyya al-thaniya*, Cairo: 1967; Al-Dissuqi, *al-Harb*. See also a later group of publications, Muhammad Jamal al-Din al-Masdi et al., *Misr wal-harb al-'alamiyya al-thaniya*, Cairo: 1978; 'Isam Muhammad al-Dissuqi, *Misr fi al-harb al-'alamiyya al-thaniya*, Cairo: 1976; 'Atiq, *al-Malik faruq*. A few biographical sketches of Hitler and Goebbels appeared on Arabic websites, e.g., 'Abdallah Khalifa, "Tadakhkhul al-hitleriyya wal-staliniyya," www.arabrenewal.com; Muhammad Dissuqi, "Goebbels: al-'abqari al-maghrur," www.20at.com/article2.php?sid=654.

11   United Nations Development Programme, *The Arab Human Development Report 2002*, New York: 2002, p. 78, put the annual number of books translated to Arabic in all fields at 330, or 20% of what Greece translates.

12   *Al-Ahram*, 28 August 1959; *al-Hilal*, January 1956, pp. 28–34; Farid 'Abdallah Jurji, *Isra'il al-za'ifa*, Cairo: 1965, p. 41;

274

enabled Arab writers to forge texts that accepted the universal basic paradigms of the war and include credible historical descriptions, while simultaneously expressing contradicting views on the essence and meaning of the war. The latter aimed mainly at creating a discourse that would fit into the broader historical and political narratives in the Arab world that shape Arab collective memory.[13]

According to Anwar Sadat, one of the leaders of the revolutionary regime, Egypt had wanted to avoid the war, but it could not determine its own fate. Therefore, he added, "our land had turned into a huge field that absorbed the sweat of fathers and brothers, who tilled it in order to supply flour to the usurpers (*ghasibin*)." The army was in a great predicament, and the question that divided its ranks was "on which side to fight."[14] 'Abd al-Nasir, too, spoke in the late 1950s of the "imperialists and oppressors on whose side we fought during World War II; we supplied them with all their needs," and consequently, we "have turned into booty (*ghanima*) in this war."[15]

The moral equation between Nazi Germany and the Allies was made possible by disregarding or belittling the racist and genocidal component of Nazi ideology and practice, particularly the Holocaust. It was not a coincidence, therefore, that most writers who made it were also engaged in Holocaust denial. Ahmad Baha' al-Din, the Egyptian leftist writer, asserts that Germany should not be blamed for the imperialist war, in which two capitalist regimes fought for world dominance. Just as the Germans had destroyed and killed in the countries which they occupied, so did the Allies cause great destruction in Germany, "and that should suffice to settle the account," he concludes.[16] The 1962 National Charter, the major ideological program of Nasserist Egypt, stated that the "people expressed itself by its adamant refusal to take part in a war that was nothing but a conflict over colonies and markets between Nazi racism and Franco-British imperialism, which brought upon humanity as a whole unlimited disasters of mass killing and destruction." The Egyptian people rejected the slogans that both sides voiced "in order to deceive world nations."[17]

Writing in the late 1960s, Egyptian historian Muhammad Kamal al-Dissuqi, of the nationalist camp, denounced both Allied and German historians for not taking an objective position and for presenting themselves as fighting for high moral values. He described Nazism as a racist expansionist movement and referred to

---

13   See a similar phenomenon in post-war German children's literature in Shavit, *A Past without Shadow*, pp. 45–55.

14   Anwar al-Sadat, *Safahat majhula*, Cairo: 1954, pp. 30–1.

15   *Al-Ahram*, 21 March 1958, 30 June 1959.

16   Baha' al-Din, *Isra'iliyyat*, pp. 174, 202–4, 226.

17   Hamdi Hafiz, *Thawrat 23 yuliu: al-ahdath, al-ahdaf, al-injazat*, Cairo: 1964, p. 304.

the Nazi system of oppression – the concentration camps, the plans to Germanize large areas of Europe by exterminating the local population and settling Germans, and the murder of invalids and mental patients in Germany.[18] Yet, for Dissuqi, the evil inherent in Nazism did not justify the Allies, as the war was a struggle between two imperialist forces whose economic interests clashed. The difference between them was mainly in the terminology they used, not in their deeds. Churchill, the French and the Japanese used the term "colonies" (*musta'marat*) unabashedly; Hitler spoke of a "living space"; Stalin demanded territorial gains; while Roosevelt spoke of "financial profits." The true meaning of all of these terms was one: the enslavement and plundering of the small nations. Worst of all was world Zionism, which played a leading role in pushing the world toward war and incited the other states against Hitler. Dissuqi expressed his solidarity with the German people, explaining that he fully shared their "pains and hopes." Moreover, he equated the Allies' deeds with those of the Nazis and found the latter wanting. Had historians objectively described the atrocities that the Allied forces committed in Germany, he says, "we would have seen more severe crimes beyond anything that the human mind could describe."[19] Years later, the leftist journalist Jurji Haddad adopted a similar historiographic approach and complained that only the Allied version of the war, which presented the Axis in the most negative fashion and themselves in a positive light, was heard.[20]

The moral equation between Nazi Germany and the western Allies continued in later years, as well. Referring in 1990, to the atrocities carried out during the war, Rim Arnuf highlights the Allied bombing of German cities and particularly the nuclear bombings of Hiroshima and Nagasaki as the greatest crime of the war, thereby identifying the "American barbarian" rather than Germany as the true villain of the war.[21] In a similar vein, and probably reflecting growing Arab animosity toward the US following its 2003 invasion of Iraq, the Qatari *al-Sharq* described the war as an imperialist one over spheres of influence and sources of wealth. Although many war crimes were committed by both sides, it added, the US managed to lay the responsibility on Nazism and Fascism. It scored a "cultural victory" by creating a positive image for itself, as if it were the defender of democracy and the liberator of Europe from the forces of evil.[22]

---

18   Dissuqi, *al-Harb*, pp. 249–50, 278.

19   Dissuqi, ibid, pp. l–t (introduction), 281, 284.

20   *Al-Dustur*, 22 February 2006.

21   Arnuf, "al-Khadi'a," pp. 69–75. See a similar argument that views Hiroshima and Nagasaki as the greatest crime of the war in Husayn, *Bara'at hitler*, p. 201.

22   *Al-Sharq*, 22 November 2006.

Shaykh Mahmud Muhammad Khadr of al-Azhar University was even blunter in his evaluation of the two sides. In an article titled "In Defense of Hitler," which casts doubt on the "dubious fact" of six million Jewish victims, he conceded that "no one was sorry when Hitler vanished from the world" together with his henchmen. The Nazi leaders committed suicide, Khadr explained, "so that they wouldn't have to see the faces of the old ape, Churchill, and the big bear, Stalin, who would sentence them to death with no one to defend them," asserting that each one of them had the right of defense, whatever their infractions might have been. He wondered what would have happened to Churchill, de Gaulle and Roosevelt, had Hitler won, since "perhaps the crimes for which they deserve the death sentence would have been much worse than all that Hitler had done."[23]

Left-wing writers justified the war against Nazi Germany but distinguished between the Soviet Union and the western Allies. Writing in the early 1970s, Emil Tuma, followed the Soviet line in describing the war as a battle between the Axis led by German Nazism and the anti-Nazi-Fascist-militarist front. The Axis' main goal was the fight against Communism and Socialism, the destruction of the Soviet Union and the formation of the "new order." By contrast, the opposing front was not unified. While the Soviet Union and other revolutionary forces sought to defeat the Fascist–Nazi Axis and promote freedom and progress, the western Allies endeavored to eliminate the rival imperialist camp, while preserving their own capitalism and imperialism.[24]

Attitudes toward Nazism: between admiration and rejection

The Arab discourse wavered between rejection and appreciation, or even admiration, in its attitude toward Nazi Germany and Hitler personally. It is possible to discern a shift from the early years after the war, when more negative references toward Nazi Germany prevailed, to increasing manifestations of sympathy with the growing resentment toward the western powers. Various foreign journalists spoke of a "pro-German cult" in Egypt, which only increased after the 1952 revolution. Among other things, they pointed to statements by then-

---

23   *Al-Akhbar*, 27 May 2001 – Memri, Special Dispatch Series, no. 231, 20 June 2001. See a similar claim by Egyptian journalist Muhammad Sa'id, saying that Hitler's negative image is inflated by western writers, whereas recent studies have demonstrated that Churchill's weak points had "even surpassed those attributed to Hitler," www.memritv.org, Clip no. 726, 26 April 2005.

24   Emil Tuma, *Sittun 'aman 'ala al-haraka al-qawmiyya al-'arabiyya al-filistiniyya*, Jerusalem: 1978, pp. 215–16. See also, *Filastin al-Thawra*, 11 May 1975, 10 October 1976

president Muhammad Naguib on the great faith of the new regime in Germany and the admiration of German efficiency, science and technology.[25]

During the 1950s and 1960s Egypt offered a safe haven to Nazi war criminals. Most notable among them were Johann von Leers, a senior official in the Nazi propaganda ministry, who arrived in Egypt in 1956, changed his name to 'Umar Amin, and was appointed as director of the Institute of the Study Judaism and Zionism in Cairo; Heinrich Sellmann, a former Gestapo officer, who changed his name to Mahmud Sulayman and was employed by the Egyptian police; and Franz Bartell, deputy Gestapo chief in the Katowice Ghetto, who was employed in the Jewish department of the Egyptian War Ministry. In response to western criticism of their employment, 'Abd al-Nasir was quoted as saying "we will use the services of those who know the mentality of our enemies."[26] The neo-Nazi publisher Helmuth Kramer received political asylum in Egypt in 1965 after being convicted in a German court of "spreading Nazi ideas." Kramer stated that 'Abd al-Nasir personally complied with his asylum request and allowed him to continue publishing his books. Syria gave political asylum to Fritz Stangl, the commandant of Treblinka extermination camp, and to Alois Brunner, Adolf Eichmann's aide who played a central role in the extermination of 130,000 Jews from Slovakia and Greece, as well as to the Nazi General Otto Ernst Remer.[27]

The Egyptian press, under both the monarchy and the republic, occasionally published the memoirs of Nazi leaders and generals.[28] President Naguib gave his support to a documentary film on the German General Erwin Rommel, and in 1982 Egypt opened a museum in the Western Desert dedicated to Rommel's

---

25   Sedar and Greenberg, *Behind the Egyptian Sphinx*, pp. 52–8, 109–18, 129–49. See also an article by a Swiss journalist in *al-Misri*, 24 August 1946.

26   David Trafford, "Beyond the Pale: Nazism, Holocaust denial and the Arab world," *Searchlight* (May 2000), pp. 18–19. Trafford does not mention the date of 'Abd al-Nasir's statement. The article also reports on several Nazi doctors who had conducted experiments in concentration camps and who found employment in Egypt. See also Lewis, *Semites and anti-Semites*, p. 160.

27   Immanuel Brand, "Nazis in the Service of Nasserism," *Yad Vashem News*, no. 38 (August 1967, Hebrew), p. 13; Trafford, "Beyond the Pale"; *Ha'aretz*, 6 January 1992; *Der Spiegel*, cited in *Ma'ariv*, 2 December 1996. During the 1960s Egypt also employed German engineers and scientists who had formerly worked for the Nazi government as part of its efforts to develop Egyptian missiles. However, since both the US and the USSR employed German scientists too, no ideological attitude can be attributed to this policy.

28   See for instance, "Goebbels' Diaries," *al-Misri*, 13 March–12 April 1948; "Rommel's Memoirs," *al-Ahram*, January–March 1950, 19 April–19 May 1953; *al-Hilal*, April 1955, pp. 62–9; and war stories in *al-Ahram*, 26 January 1954, 11 May 1955, 31 August 1955, 27, 28 May 1956, 18 October 1956, 1 August 1957, 28 June 1960.

memory.[29] Hitler's book *Mein Kampf* was translated in full into Arabic in 1963 and a second edition was issued in 1995. Earlier, Luis Heiden, a former Nazi propaganda official, had prepared a pocket-sized Arabic translation of *Mein Kampf* that was distributed as a gift to Egyptian army officers. Two abridged translations came out in Beirut in 1974 and 1975.[30] The introduction to the 1955 edition emphasized Hitler's efforts in the struggle against Communism, in view of the conflict between the Communist and capitalist camps. Hitler, it explained, was not an ordinary man, who lost a war and caused great suffering to his people. He took part in history, changed its face and left behind him a tremendous legacy in all fields.[31]

The introduction to the 1963 edition was even more reverential. The translator, Luis al-Hajj, explained that Hitler "was not an ordinary person who would be forgotten in the course of history ... Adolf Hitler did not belong only to the German people, but he is one of those great persons who had almost stopped the movement of history, altered its course and changed the world, and therefore his place belongs to history." Hitler, he added, was a soldier who not only left behind him a legend stained in the tragedy of a country whose dreams were shattered, but also left an ideological legacy whose demise is incomprehensible. It encompassed politics, society, science and war as a science and culture. The National Socialism, which Hitler had advocated, "did not die with the death of its flag bearer, and its seeds spread under every star." We insisted on transmitting Hitler's theories on nationalism, governments and ethnicity verbatim, he concludes, so that they should serve as a model and inspiration for the Arab reader.[32] The citation of *Mein Kampf* as a historical source to describe Jewish misdeeds by many writers may also reflect appreciation of the book and its author, at least so far as his attitude toward the Jews is concerned.

A good example of the dual representation of Nazism in the public discourse during the early 1950s was a poll that the Egyptian weekly *al-Musawwar* conducted in September 1953, following rumors that Hitler was alive, in which it asked several public figures and journalists to address a letter to Hitler. Among them was Anwar Sadat, then Speaker of Parliament, who wrote: "My dear Hit-

---

29   *October*, 6 June 1982.

30   Adolf Hitler, *Kifahi*, translated by Luis al-Hajj, Beirut: 1963; Trafford, "Beyond the Pale." Israeli Prime Minister David Ben-Gurion stated on 28 November 1956 that copies of the pocket-size translations were found in the possession of Egyptian officers during the 1956 Suez Campaign – ISA, HZ/5558/g–z; *Droit de Vivre*, November 1988. The 1995 edition was distributed in the Palestinian Authority territory, "Hitler's Mein Kampf in East Jerusalem and PA Territories" -Memri, Special Dispatch, no. 48, 1 October 1999.

31   Hilter, *Kifahi*, p. 3–4.

32   Ibid.

ler! I congratulate you from the bottom of my heart, because, though you appear to have been defeated, in reality you were the victor. You succeeded in sowing dissension between Churchill, the old man, and his 'satanic ally,' the Soviet Union." Sadat conceded that Hitler committed "some mistakes, such as opening too many fronts," but added, "you are forgiven on account of your faith in your country and people. That you have become immortal in Germany is reason enough for pride, and we should not be surprised to see you again in Germany, or a new Hitler in your place."[33] Nur al-Din Tarraf, the student leader of the Young Egypt Party, who served as minister of health in the first revolutionary cabinet, hailed Hitler as an "eternal leader" particularly in view of his "heroic" suicide.

The other respondents, among them three former ministers, expressed reservations and aversion toward Hitler's deeds, although none of them referred to his anti-Jewish policies. Ihsan 'Abd al-Qudus, editor of the left-wing weekly *Ruz al-Yusuf*, was the boldest. There was no place to dictators in the free world, he said, and reminded Hitler of his responsibility for the death of millions, for the gas chambers and bloodbaths, and sent Hitler back to his hiding place. Similarly, Hifni Mahmud blamed Hitler for launching the war, which harmed his people and humanity as a whole, while Ahmad Murtada al-Maraghi concluded that the German people now understood that it was better to forget Hitler's violent past.[34] The same issue of *al-Musawwar* contained another article that proposed to learn from Hitler and to prepare a book on the corruption of the Egyptian old regime, just as Hitler had done regarding German democracy.

In an earlier poll that *al-Musawwar* held among leading public figures, asking who they thought were the most prominent leaders during the ten previous years, Hitler and Rommel appeared in four lists, and Mussolini in two. Ahmad Baha' al-Din sharply condemned as abhorring (*mufza'*) Tarraf's choice of Hitler as a model for an admired leader who lived for his country and people. He sought to undermine this belief by enumerating the oppressive means that Hitler used in order to impose his "mad plans" on the German people.[35] While attacking Hitler's positive image, Baha' al-Din implicitly referred to the ongoing debate in Egypt at the time over the formation of the new (non-democratic) Nasserist regime, which encompassed questions such as the meaning of democracy, political pluralism, civil liberties and the role of the army in politics. However, none of his points addressed the genocide against the Jews, thereby ignoring one of Nazism's worst manifestations.

---

33   *Al-Musawwar*, 18 September 1953.

34   *Al-Musawwar*, ibid.

35   *Ruz al-Yusuf*, 24 August 1954.

In another intellectual duel at that time, Egyptian columnist and writer Muhammad al-Tabi'i, who advocated a one-party rule in Egypt, argued that the single parties in Nazi Germany, Fascist Italy and Kemalist Turkey implemented all the goals which their leaders had set up to rebuild their respective countries. They unified the people behind defined targets – first and foremost removal of the causes of weakness and corruption – while raising the standard of living and introducing momentum in every aspect of life. Tabi'i was particularly impressed by the power of the German state, which Hitler restored within six years. The German people loved Hitler and rallied behind him, and no one in Germany suspected him or his regime, except the Jews, he concluded.[36]

Salah al-'Aqqad pointed in 1957 to the crushing German defeat in 1945 and to the disasters that had befallen the Germans as proofs of the fallacy of Nazism and its concept of racial superiority. He addressed the Holocaust only in passing and disregarded its central place in Nazi ideology and practice. Instead, he stressed the [fabricated] motif of Nazi–Zionist collaboration, which served the official narrative of the war.[37] Conversely, Egyptian historian Ibrahim Wanus, writing on the historical ties between Egypt and the Arabian Peninsula, chose to cite "Nazi race scientists" who had found real physical links between the ancient Egyptians and the Arab civilizations of Yemen and Jordan. Regrettably, he adds, the "enemies of Nazism," destroyed these books after their victory over Germany, because "these theories refuted all rival contemporary ideologies, particularly Communism and Capitalism."[38] In other words, Wanus did not reject Nazi "science" and "scientific theories," but turned his criticism against Nazism's enemies.

Several Egyptian school textbooks issued during the 1950s portrayed Hitler as a great leader and Nazism as a legitimate ideology. In one such book, Najib al-Kaylani wrote an autobiographical short story called "the long road to the revolution," which recounts his adolescence during the inter-war period. The major protagonist is Hitler, "the noble person, who harbors great respect to Islam and the Arabs, and who is, therefore, so different from the filthy English."[39] This representation of Hitler, which stood in sharp contrast to Salah al-'Aqqad and others, who described Hitler as hostile to the Muslims and Arabs, was un-

---

36   *Akhir Sa'a*, 19 August, 2 September 1953. Tabi'i went on to express sympathy for Germany in his memoirs, *Min asrar al-sasa wal-siyasa: misr ma qabla al-thawra*, Cairo: 1970, p. 321, telling of his great yearning for Rommel's victory in 1942.

37   'Aqqad, *Dirasa muqarina*, pp. 55–60.

38   Ibrahim Wanus, in *al-Adab*, April 1960, p. 65.

39   Najib al-Kaylani, *Al-Tariq al-tawil*, Cairo: 1956, pp. 5–6, cited in Gershoni, *Light in the Shadow*, p. 365 note 55. Gershoni adds that the book won an award from the Ministry of Education and was reissued twice.

doubtedly intended to facilitate his acceptance by readers. Another high-school history textbook, published in 1966, took a more neutral line, presenting Nazism as a dictatorial system embodied by Hitler. The book described Hitler's seizure of power, his taking over of central Europe and the events that led to the war. Yet, implicitly it projected appreciation of Hitler's ability to unify the German people, to harness the state resources and build a strong army and his determination to nullify the Versailles treaty.[40] Readers could not have escaped the parallels between Germany's situation after World War I and Egypt's after World War II.

A twisted ambivalence toward Hitler appeared also outside Egypt. An article in the Lebanese Muslim weekly *al-Sayyad*, following the 1956 Suez war, chose *Mein Kampf* as its source to "criticize" Egypt for merely expelling the Jews in Biblical times, instead of eliminating them. While implicitly recognizing Hitler's overall evil, it maintained that the free world holds one point in Hitler's favour, that he waged a campaign to purge the world of the "Israeli plague." The world began to feel sorry for him for dying without completing his "humanitarian mission."[41]

The 1960s and 1970s witnessed continuity in Arab representations of Nazism, despite the rising influence of the Arab left on Arab thought and the closer ties between various Arab countries and the Soviet Union. While the mainstream sharpened its criticism of Nazism as the ultimate symbol of evil – a racist, aggressive and fanatic movement, more positive views continued to appear. A major manifestation of this phenomenon was the systematic and ubiquitous equation between Nazi Germany and Israel, the ultimate enemy at the time. While the equation of Israel with Nazi Germany aimed at representing it as the epitome of evil, it also gave the Arab consumer of this discourse a clearer feeling of Nazism as identical to the more familiar enemy, Israel and Zionism. Still, denunciation of Nazism as an historical phenomenon did not necessarily entail condemnation of its policies against the Jews, or acceptance of the Holocaust as a historical fact.

The Arab left was consistent in its absolute rejection and condemnation of Nazism from the war onwards. Emil Tuma emphasized the imperialist class nature of Nazism, which represented the German militarist monopolies, and criticized those who viewed Fascism as the movement of the petty bourgeoisie.

40 Ahmad 'Abd al-Karim et al., *Ta'rikh al-'arab al-hadith wal-mu'asir*, Cairo: 1966, pp. 264–7. See a similar approach in 'Aqqad, *Dirasa Muqarina*, pp. 55–60 and in al-Qiyada al-'amma lil-quwwat al-musallaha, *Hitler wa-qadatihi al-bahriyyin*, Cairo: 1966, Introduction, pp. a, b.

41 *Al-Sayyad*, 15 November 1956.

Concurrently, he failed to recognize the uniqueness of Nazi racism, presenting it as essentially not different from Italian or Spanish Fascism.[42] The impact of the Soviet discourse was evident in the frequent use by PLO publications of the Soviet term "Fascism" to denote Nazism. It reflected a broader, Marxist-inspired analytical concept that regarded Nazism as one version of a broader historical phenomenon – European Fascism – which was linked to capitalism as an economic and political system as well as to the crisis of the industrialist–capitalist classes, thus minimizing the racist and anti-Semitic essence of Nazism.[43] Moreover, it enabled the Soviets to use the broader term "victims of Fascism," denying the uniqueness of the Nazi extermination of the Jews. It also enabled Yasir 'Arafat to lay a wreath in East Berlin to the memory of the "victims of Fascism," which in the East German context referred to communists and citizens of the Soviet Union, but not to Jews explicitly.[44] Still, while the PLO often condemned neo-Nazi activity in Germany and depicted Israel as a manifestation of Nazism, its officials held contacts with the Nazi war criminal Claus Barbie, and German neo-Nazi activists, led by Karl Heinz Hoffman, underwent training in PLO camps in Lebanon. Over twenty activists in various PLO organizations chose for themselves *noms de guerre* that contained the word "Hitler" or "Abu-Hitler."[45]

Contrary to the left, nationalist public figures on occasion expressed favorable views towards Nazism. In an interview with *Der Spiegel*, probably in the hope of appealing to German public opinion after the 1967 war, Sharif Nasir bin Jamil, deputy commander-in-chief of the Jordanian army and King Husayn's uncle, stated that "since Hitler's time, we are admirers of the German people."[46] A leading Egyptian historian, Husayn Mu'nis, denounced Hitler in 1981 for having brought upon Germany defeat and tragedy, due to his megalomania, and for being recorded in history as one of those mad murderers. Yet, he insisted that it is "world Zionism," which describes Hitler as "the most hideous murderer in history." Aside from his understanding of Hitler's hatred of the Jews and his actions against the Versailles Treaty, Mu'nis insisted that only in the

---

42   Tuma, *Sittun 'aman*, pp. 215–16; idem, *Ta'rikh masirat al-shu'ub al-'arabiyya al-haditha*, Haifa: 1995, pp. 255–6. See also Qasim Hasan, *al-'Arab*.

43   For the historiographic debate whether Nazism was primarily a brand of Fascism or a *sui generis* phenomenon, see Kershaw, *The Nazi Dictatorship*, pp. 18–41.

44   *Filastin al-Thawra*, 10 October 1976, 14 May 1979, 13, 20 April, 18 May 1981, 13 October, 7 December 1985; *al-Hurriyya*, 1 February, 15 November 1987.

45   *Der Spiegel*, 17 July 1981; *Ma'ariv*, 14 September 1984; *Der Tag*, 19 July 1985; *Observer*, 5 February 1989; Barry Rubin, *The PLO Between Anti-Zionism and Antisemitism*, Acta no. 1, Jerusalem: 1993, p. 11; *New York Times*, 22 January 2006.

46   *Der Spiegel*, 3 July 1967, cited in Brand, "Nazis," p. 13.

distant future would people understand that Hitler had accomplished certain things during the 1930s that "excite the mind of every person."[47]

An illuminating manifestation of split visions of Nazism along generational lines is the case of the renowned Syrian poet Nizar Qabani and his niece. Writing in *al-Hayat* in 1995, the poet described the admiration which the 1940s generation felt toward Nazi Germany, whose name had a "beautiful ring, arousing one's imagination and dreams" and inspiring calls to "power, valor and national prosperity (*zahw qawmi*)", recalling his father, who wanted Germany to win the war and who listened only to Radio Berlin. Qabani's niece, in a responding article, criticized this approach among Arabs, "who suffered from dangerous illusions," the worst of which was that "the enemy of our enemies is our friend."[48] Commenting on this affair on the second anniversary of the poet's death, Jihad al-Khazin, a columnist and editor of *al-Hayat*, wrote that most of the readers' responses sided with the poet against his niece. Khazin also mentioned the poem that Qabani had sent him after the 1996 massacre in the Lebanese village Qana, in which he strongly attacked the Jews and mentioned Hitler: "may God have mercy upon him, who burned them." Khazin, who belongs to a younger generation and acknowledges the Holocaust, proposed to use the term "Hitler, may God curse him," because Hitler did not deserve mercy, but Qabani insisted that he would not curse Hitler. Eventually, they compromised on the wording: "Hitler did not find the time to exterminate them," which represented Hitler's acts in a more neutral fashion. Reflecting on the story in retrospect, Latifa Sha'lan of the Saudi weekly *al-Majalla* commented critically that Arab fascination (*i'jab*) for Hitler continues to the present (the year 2000), deriving its false legitimacy from anger at Israel's policy.[49]

Similarly, admiring voices of Nazi Germany could be found among regimes or groups that remained insensitive to the western or Soviet discourse. According to a German intelligence officer, Libya asked his country during the 1980s to train its experts "like the SS." Libyan President Mu'ammar Qadhdhafi chose to motivate the readers of his essay on Communism by citing Hitler's statement on the need for perseverance in order to achieve victory. Likewise, Swedish security sources claimed that Hizballah in Lebanon trained neo-Nazis in its camps.[50]

Greater ambivalence may be found among Islamists. Some of them denounced Nazism as the most blatant manifestation of western culture and, as such, as the

---

47   *October*, 12 September 1981.

48   *Al-Hayat*, 21 July 1995, 11 May 1998; *al-Majalla*, 17–23 December 2000.

49   *Al-Hayat*, 11 May 1998.

50   *Ma'ariv*, 5 January 1995, 28 September 1999; Benni Landau, *Ha'aretz Book Supplement*, 8 July 1998.

complete opposite of Islam. In a series of publications criticizing nationalism, including its Arab version, Shaykh Safar al-Hawali, a radical Saudi cleric, depicted Nazism (alongside Zionism) as the culmination of racist European nationalism. He used the link between Nazism and European nationalism to criticize secular Arab nationalism, particularly the Baʿthist ideology, for having borrowed its ideas from the same cultural sources.[51] In 1999 Hizballah, which had persistently denounced Nazism, accused the Jews of "producing" (*intaj*) Hitler by their ruthless and greedy financial practices, just as Jewish financiers in post-Communist Russia were the cause of the emergence and rise of Nazim in that country during the 1990s.[52]

An anonymous radical Sunni polemic claims that "Adolf Hitler had become a hero in the eyes of many people, particularly the Arabs, out of hatred and animosity of the Jews." Likewise, the Saudi cleric Saʿd al-Burayk, while attacking the alleged hypocrisy of the European idea of freedom of speech, complained that "freedom does not extend to anyone who mentions one good thing about Hitler. He is immediately accused of racism."[53] Even more revealing was Zuhayra Jamal Nimr in *al-Sabil*, organ of the Jordanian Muslim Brotherhood, whose admiration for Hitler stemmed from her frustration over Arab weakness, expressing her wish that the Arabs would have Hitler's ambition.

He lived in poverty and therefore hated the rich Jews who held positions unjustly. His hatred was kindled because of exploitation ... He took revenge against them and regained his rights. But we, the Arabs, want peace with those who ... took away our land ... Hitler took revenge on the Jews because he knew they were profiteers, traitors and blood suckers. He got rid of them in a sinful way and fulfilled his dream and regained his stolen rights. Is not such a person worthy of admiration? Hitler achieved what the Arabs failed to achieve, even though he started his career as a lowly official. He cleansed his country of Jews in his own way and the Jewish historians lied when they said it was a Holocaust. I contemplate history and see Hitler, the Nazi leader, I learn from his mistakes, his firm resolve and desire, I adopt what is suitable for my principles and my Arabism and ask you to rethink correctly. Hopes and dreams are not easy concepts, but are achieved through work, effort and optimism. We must learn from the mistakes of others and know that nothing is impossible. Look at Hitler and do not change the fate of Jerusalem and Palestine to that of Spain.[54]

---

51 Al-Hawali, "*Al-Qawmiyya.*"

52 *Al-ʿAhd*, 18 June 1999.

53 Anon., "Hizballah am hizb al-shaytan," http://arabic.islamicweb.com/shia/hizb_allah. htm; www.memritv.org, Clip no. 1110, 9 March 2006.

54 *Al-Sabil*, 7 December 1999.

Nazi Germany as victim of Jewish–Zionist warmongering

Animosity toward the Allies as imperial powers, and particularly toward the Israelis and the Jews, prompted various writers, mostly Islamists, to present Nazi Germany as an innocent victim of a broad Jewish-Zionist conspiracy, an argument that was also used to justify Hitler's anti-Jewish policies (see Chapter 6). These claims appeared already during the 1960s, but increased from the 1970s and even more so from the 1990s, with the emergence of the Islamist movements as a major political force in the Middle East. The dominance of Islamists among the proponents of this theory is not coincidental, in view of their deeper cultural and political opposition to the US and Britain, their tendency to explain historical events by conspiracy theories and their open hatred toward the Jews. Islamist websites, which proliferated toward the end of the twentieth century, were particularly instrumental in disseminating these views. Writers of the left were absent from this group, as they could not clear Nazi Germany of its responsibility for the war.

This theme also presents Zionism as a powerful force that caused the death of millions of innocent people in order to achieve its sinister goals, either to avenge Germany's refusal to support it in the past, or as part of more elaborate scheme to take over the world. Thus, Nazi Germany is portrayed as a harmless or innocuous state.[55] As was the case with Holocaust denial, which resorted to European deniers in order to grant its arguments a pseudo-academic respectability, advocates of this theme relied first and foremost on the *Protocols of the Elders of Zion* as their main source, and on books such as William Guy Carr's conspiratorial and anti-Semitic tract *Pawns in the Game*, which was translated into Arabic and whose chapters appear on numerous Islamist websites.

Egyptian writer Mahmud Naʿnaʿa, an early advocate of this view, explained that the Zionists, who felt during the 1930s that Britain could no longer guarantee their project, concluded that a new world war would assure them political gains similar to those they had achieved following World War I, and would enable them to establish a state "from the Nile to the Euphrates." Naʿnaʿa cites Hitler's ominous "prophecy," made on 30 January 1939, that "if the international Jewish financiers in and outside Europe should succeed in plunging the nations once more into a world war, then the result will not be the Bolshevization of the earth, and thus the victory of Jewry, but the annihilation of the Jewish race in Europe," as a proof not of Hitler's evil intentions, but of the

---

55   Naji, *al-Mufsidun*, p. 396; ʿAbdallah al-Tal, *Judhur al-balaʾ*, Beirut: 1971, pp. 158–9, Mahalla, *al-Tahaluf*, p. 103.

real Zionist machinations to which Hitler merely reacted.[56] Muhammad Kamal al-Dissuqi, who completed his PhD in history in Germany, constructs a dual conspiracy of capitalist Jews and "world Zionism" that led to the war. While the Jewish capitalists pushed President Roosevelt into the war in order to make windfall profits, "World Zionism" pushed the US into a war which was not of her concern, in order to help hard-pressed Britain and thereby gain British political support for the Zionists after the war.[57]

Other writers claim that the Jews maintained historical enmity toward Germany, in addition to their persistent efforts to sow discord among the nations, in order to enable Zionism to play a leading role in the international arena. Mustafa Sa'dani details the success of the *Kehila* (code name for the Jewish leadership in the *Protocols of the Elders of Zion*) to manipulate the White House, the CIA, the Pentagon (neither of which existed at the time), and the FBI in order to incite American public opinion against Germany and push the US into the war. They instigated a war of vengeance that exposed the world to great risks, threatening humanity with nuclear destruction. The millions who had fallen prey to this war, 'Abd al-Hamid Wakid concluded, "perished as victims" of world Zionism, "the devil's ally."[58]

Husayn al-Turayki, head of the Arab League mission to Latin America during the 1960s, attributed Jewish activities against Germany to economics and vengeance. Using several anti-Semitic publications, including the *Protocols*, he accepted the Nazi claim of "Jewish capitalist domination over the economies, banks and stock exchanges all over the world." Nazi Germany's success in rebuilding its economy without resort to gold or to Jewish bankers "had serious repercussions for the Jews," who feared that other countries would follow suit. The way out of this predicament was to "break Germany." If we add to that Germany's success in pressuring and expelling (*tard*) the Jews from its territory, Turayki adds, we could understand "the hellish hostility that world Judaism developed toward Germany." World Zionism declared war on the Nazi regime as early as 7 August 1933 by declaring a boycott against it. Zionism's first goal was to bring the US into the war, just as it had done during World War I. Its task was easier since the American capitalist system was based on the gold standard or, in other words, "the system that the Nazis sought to demolish was the

56 Na'na'a, *al-Sayhuniyya*, pp. 134–5.
57 Dissuqi, *al-Harb*, pp. 226, 235. See also Najjar, *al-Tatawwur*, p. 75, who links Zionist activity to produce the two world wars with the attainment of the Balfour declaration.
58 Sa'dani, *al-Fikr al-Sahyuni*, p. 270; 'Abd al-Hamid Wakid, *Nihayat isra'il wal-sahyuniyya*, Cairo: 1971, pp. 484–5. See also, Yusuf Mahmud Yusuf, *Isra'il al-bidaya wal-nihaya*, Cairo: 1997, pp. 207, 209.

same one that the Jews sought to preserve."[59] Shaykh Ibrahim Mudayras, of the Hamas movement, presented Germany as a double victim of Jewish machinations in a Friday sermon in which he accused the Jews of inciting the major European countries to wage an economic war against Germany, while provoking Germany to launch a war against the whole world.[60]

Several writers, most prominently Shaykh Tantawi, dean of al-Azhar University, 'Abdallah 'Azzam, the leading ideologue of the radical Islamist-Salafi trend, as well as the Hamas movement, present the Jewish role in bringing about both world wars as part of a broader Jewish behavioral pattern of fomenting wars throughout history. By instigating the two world wars, the Jews "made huge financial gains by trading in armaments, and paved the way for the establishment of their state."[61] In his tract *Merchants of War* (*Tujjar al-hurub*), devoted to this legend, 'Azzam claimed that the Jews had declared an economic war on Hitler the day he assumed power, and managed to persuade Britain and France to declare war on Germany on the pretext of defending Poland, which was itself pushed into war by the Jews over the Danzig corridor. 'Azzam charges that the Jews pushed Neville Chamberlain to enter the war, but later forced him to resign so that they could appoint Churchill, "their biggest collaborator" as prime minister. Further, the Jews, through their representatives in the US administration, were those who persuaded Roosevelt to enter the war. Roosevelt, he goes on to say, had actually been a Jew, whose family changed its original name from Rosenberg after immigrating to the US from Spain.[62]

Others explain that the Zionists planned to launch three world wars. The first intended to topple the Czarist regime in Russia and transform it into the bastion of the atheistic Communist movement. The second was designed to destroy the Nazi system and pave the way for the establishment of a Zionist state in Palestine, assigning Roosevelt and Churchill to carry it out. The third would break out between the entire Muslim world and Israel. Similarly, the Saudi daily *al-Madina*, which charged the Zionists of collaborating with the Nazis in kill-

59 Husayn al-Turayki, *Hadhihi Filastin*, Tunis: 1971, pp. 154–7; Ahmad 'Awdi, *al-Sahyuniyya: nishatuha, tanzimatuha wa-anshitatuha*, Amman: 1993, p. 130, citing Turayki. See also Fahim, "al-'Alaqat," who describes the German people as victim of a Jewish plot.

60 PNA TV, 13 May 2005, www.intelligence.org.il/eng/sib/5_05/as_sermon.htm.

61 Tantawi, *Banu isra'il*, p. 623; Mahmud, *al-Sahyuniyya wal-naziyya*, pp. 85–6; The Hamas Charter 1988, article 22; al-Nadwa al-'alamiyya lil-shabab al-islami, *al-Mawsu'a al-muyassara fi al-adyan wal-madhahib wal-ahzab al-mu'asira*, www.alkashf.net.

62 'Abdallah 'Azzam, *Tujjar al-hurub*, www.tawhed.ws/a?i=77. See a similar wild conspiracy in Banaja, *Nazra*, pp. 124–8.

ing the Jews, accused the Jews of instigating World War II as part of a series of conspiracies against Islam which ended with the 11 September 2001 attack.[63]

Yasir Husayn's *Exonerating Hitler* (*Bara'at Hitler*), whose cover shows a demon with Stars of David manipulating the four Allied powers to turn their weapons against a sad-eyed Hitler, presents the most elaborate attempt to represent Hitler as a peace-seeking victim of joint Jewish conspiracies and Allied intransigence. The author explains that he has no desire to defend dictatorship or tyranny, military aggression or war crimes, but simply to set straight the historical injustice perpetrated by Zionist-inspired historiography. The Jews, he says, had "brainwashed" the world in baseless accusations and slander against Hitler.[64] Husayn, who rejects all current historical sources on the Nazi period – e.g., German archival documents and testimonies in German war-crime trials – as forged by the Jews, accepts Hitler's own words in *Mein Kampf* and Nazi apologetics as the true version of historical events.[65] He portrays Hitler as exerting continuous efforts to resolve Europe's problems peacefully, only to be rebuffed, time and again, by British and French stubbornness. All Hitler sought was to restore peacefully the German territories that had been usurped illegally and immorally after World War I and reunite their oppressed German inhabitants with their brethren inside Germany. Hitler merely wanted for his people a "living space" that was miniscule compared to the territories Britain controlled. "Had Britain and France" accepted Hitler's peace offers in 1936, Husayn states, "the war would not have broken out and humanity could have enjoyed peace for many years."[66]

Husayn practically reiterates the Nazi narrative on the 1938 Czechoslovakia crisis and praises British Prime Minister Chamberlain for recognizing Germany's rightful claims. The Jews, he charges, were responsible for portraying the "just and moral" Munich agreement as capitulation to Germany. Consequently, France provoked Czechoslovakia to assume an aggressive posture against Germany, and Hitler had no other choice but to take over this "ostensible state" (*dawla maz'uma*) that not only had oppressed Germans but now posed a security threat to Germany. The Jews also played a major role in pushing Britain and France to incite Poland against Germany's rightful claim to the Danzig corridor and foiled all of Hitler's sincere attempts to reach a peaceful settlement of the issue and avert war. Husayn repeatedly argues that, in contrast to Hitler's constant pursuit of peaceful solutions, Britain and France violated the

---

63   Ahmad 'Abd al-Ghafur 'Attar, *al-Masuniyya*, Beirut: 1974, pp. 5, 47; *al-Jumhuriyya*, 3 March 1989; *al-Madina*, 5 October 2004.

64   Husayn, *Bara'at Hitler*, pp. 58–60.

65   Ibid, pp. 32–9, 45–7.

66   Ibid, pp. 68–80, 200.

tenets of the Munich agreement and were therefore responsible for the outbreak of the war.[67] Typically of Nazi anti-Jewish propaganda, he projects Nazi aims and goals onto the Jews, accusing them of seeking to take over the world. The Jews, he claims, understood that Hitler was the one person who dared to come out against their control of the world media and threatened their worldwide schemes, and therefore they "exerted all their financial and psychological efforts to eliminate Hitler." The war, Husayn asserts, citing Hitler's testament as his proof, was waged between Hitler and the Jews, rather than between Hitler and the Allies. "It remains to be asked who the criminal is?" he poses in conclusion.[68] The growing popularity of this theme was reflected in the TV drama *al-Shatat*, which charged the Jews with starting the two world wars and with the dropping of the atomic bombs on Hiroshima and Nagasaki.[69]

The reversal of roles between perpetrators and victims culminated in the presentation of Nazi war criminals as victims of Zionist conspiracies. In his book dedicated to Holocaust denial, Muhammad Nimr Madani expresses his sympathy to Nazi officers who were "persecuted cruelly" for imaginary crimes they had never committed. Numerous senior officials in former Nazi detention camps, he explained, were executed or had to commit suicide, due to false charges over the existence of the gas chambers.[70]

The harshest condemnation is reserved to the Nuremberg Trials as a manifestation of unjust judgment of the victors over the vanquished, primarily because the Zionists stood behind them. Sulayman Naji, who justified Hitler's policy against the Jews, describes the trials in his book, published under the left-wing Ba'th regime in Syria during the mid-1960s, as a mockery to justice carried out under Jewish-Zionist inspiration. Naji reconciles the contradiction in his statement by denying the charges that Hitler sought to exterminate the Jews. Wars were conducted throughout history, he says, according to universally recognized rules of gallantry and mutual respect that demonstrated magnanimity toward the losers. The only exception was the Jews, who treated their defeated enemies with cruelty and vengeance. The Zionists were those who pushed for the Nuremberg trials, since the Allies themselves had nothing against Germany apart from ordinary victor–vanquished relationships. The destruction of Germany, which had opposed Zionism, was one of the long-term strategic aims of the

---

67   Ibid, pp. 83–90, 108–16, 153ff. See similar claims by Shaykh Nasir al-Ahmad, "al-Yahud wa-nar al-hurub," 11 June 2002, www.islammemo.cc/filz/one_news.asp?IDnews=70.

68   Ibid., pp. 152–6, 199–201.

69   Memri, Special Dispatch Series, no. 627, 12 December 2003; Clip no. 897, 21 October 2005, www.memritv.org. Husayn, *Bara'at Hitler*, pp. 153–4, repeats the story too.

70   Madani, *Hal uhriqa*, pp. 4, 18, 38–9, 41–8.

1897 Zionist Congress, and the Nuremberg trials were the means to achieve these goals. Hence the innovation (*bidʿa*)[71] of holding "the most unusual trials of their kind." Concurrently, the initiative to hold the trials came from the US, which was the real criminal in the war, having used nuclear weapons, which killed hundreds of thousands of innocent civilians. Naji expresses his anger that the Nazi leaders were brought to the court in chains "as if they were murderers and robbers." They were tried for "their conduct in the battlefield for services and sacrifices rendered for their nation and homeland," and over the fact that their "commendable traits and beneficial deeds were regarded as crimes and aggression." In this legal travesty, he concludes, "human dignity was executed and hanged."[72] Rim Arnuf denounced the trials in similar terms and highlighted the purported central role of the Jews behind them. The person who masterminded the whole affair was "the Jew Samuel Rosenman, legal advisor to President Roosevelt; the chief judge was Robert Jackson, well known as a friend of the Jews; his legal advisor was the Jew Sheldon Gluck, while the Jewish colonel, B. J. S. Andrews was responsible for executing the verdict.[73]

Another inversion of the criminal–victim role is Misbah Hamdan's story of the Jewish Brigade during the war. Hamdan argues that the Jewish Brigade did not participate in any important battle, but merely followed the Allied armies in order to "massacre children and old people ... to purge villages ... and satisfy their desires." Ahmad Shalabi, who enumerates cases of Jewish espionage and subversion against the rest of humanity throughout history, notes that the Germans suffered the lion's share of murders committed by Jewish terrorist organizations, but fails to mention the reason for these alleged actions. Thirty years later, in 1998, *al-Ahram al-ʿArabi* continued to harp on this theme, quoting British historian Morris Buckham [*sic*], who alleged that "western Jews" massacred 15,000 German PoWs after the war.[74] In similar vein, Madani mentions Jewish "death

---

71   An Islamic term denoting an unfavorable innovation.

72   Naji, *al-Mufsidun*, pp. 393–5.

73   Arnuf, "al-khadiʿa," pp. 72–3. While Rosenman and possibly Gluck were Jewish, the others were not. Donald Bloxham, *Genocide on Trial. War Crime Trials and the Formation of Holocaust History and Memory*, Oxford: 2001, p. 68, states that Jackson did not wish the Jewish issue in the trials to be presented by Jews and that his overall approach to the Holocaust was universalist and did not seek to overemphasize the Jewish component. Arnuf also ignores the non-Jewish origins of all prosecutors and judges from the other Allied countries.

74   Muhammad Misbah Hamdan, *al-Istiʿmar wal-sahyuniyya al-ʿalamiyya*, Beirut: 1967, pp. 227–9; Ahmad Shalabi, *Muqaranat al-adyan: al-yahudiyya*, Cairo: 1966, p. 299; *al-Ahram al-ʿArabi*, 26 December 1998. The quoted historian was most probably Morris Beckman, whose book *The Jewish Brigade: An Army with Two Masters 1944–45*, Staplehurst: 1988 praises the Brigade for its role in battle and does not mention such massacres. In 1945

squads" which specialized in the abduction and assassination of hundreds of anti-Zionist intellectuals and military thinkers in post-war Germany and France. Like Germany, he goes on to say, France suffered from widespread purges, carried out by supporters of Zionism, which led to the execution of over 48,000 people in 1945–46 alone. These purges paved the way for the establishment of Israel and the shipping of hundreds of thousands of Jews to Israel after the war. The circle that had started with the invention of the Holocaust lie as a Zionist ploy and continued with the terrorist operations in Germany ended up with the establishment of the Jewish state, he concluded.[75]

Sympathy with Germany and opposition to Nazism

As a result of the growing rejection of Nazi Germany since the 1970s, Arab intellectuals and historians attempted to re-examine Arab attitudes toward and relations with Nazi Germany both before and during the war, and to exonerate the Arabs from the charge of ideological identification with it. The debate had started already in the 1950s as part of the contest over the formulation of Arab collective memory on the struggle for independence during the 1930s and 1940s. The accusations by western and Israeli writers of broad Arab support for Germany,[76] which appeared as serving the Israeli case, also required an Arab response. Almost all of these writers contend that Arab sympathy and support for Germany was primarily instrumentalist, based on the well-known Arab notion of "the enemy of my enemy is my friend," while insisting that ideological identification with Nazism was minimal.[77]

Despite this trend, candid admissions of various memorialists on widespread sympathy and even enthusiasm for Germany during the 1930s and the war continued to be part of the public discourse. Ahmad Shuqayri, then a young political activist and future founder of the PLO, described in his memoirs how he used to listen to German and Italian radio broadcasts during the war:

the news on German victories in Europe filled our hearts with great hope. I used to sit in front of the map holding a pencil, listening to the military communiqués of Radio Berlin and rejoice to German victories ... I celebrated the new year 1942 with the great

---

soldiers from Jewish-Palestinian units in the British army did execute several dozen Nazi war criminals hiding in Germany. On the Brigade see also Michael J. Cohen (ed.), *The Rise of Israel*, vol. 29: *Jewish Military Effort 1939–1944*, New York: 1987.

75 Madani, *Hal uhriqa*, pp. 184–6.

76 See Sedar and Greenberg, *Behind the Egyptian Sphinx*, pp. 52–8, 109–18, 129–49.

77 Naji 'Allush, *al-Haraka al-wataniyya al-filastiniyya amam al-yahudiyya wal-sahyuniyya 1882–1948*, Beirut: 1974, p. 109; 'Aqqad, *al-Harb*, p. 4; Dissuqi, *al-Harb*, pp. 285–6; 'Ali al-Mahbubi, *Judhur al-isti'mar al-sahyuni fi filastin*, Tunis: 1990, p. 84.

Axis victories in Europe and North Africa. We only talked about Rommel and waited for the entry of his victorious army to Egypt and Palestine.[78]

Sami al-Jundi, one of the early members of the Ba'th party in Syria was more forthright in his memoirs:

We were racists, admiring Nazism, reading its books and the source of its thought, particularly Nietzche.... Fichte and H. S. Chamberlain's *Foundations of the Nineteenth Century*, which revolved on race. We were the first to think of translating *Mein Kampf.*

Whoever lived during this period in Damascus would appreciate the inclination of the Arab people to Nazism, for Nazism was the power which could serve as its champion, and he who is defeated will by nature love the victor.[79]

Years later, the prominent Islamist thinker Shaykh Yusuf al-Qaradawi recalled how almost all residents of his native Egyptian village, "like most people in Egypt," welcomed Hitler and viewed him as "sword of divine fate on Britain's neck to avenge its tyranny and crimes against the Muslims."[80] That the writers did not see any problem, moral or otherwise, in recalling and presenting these sentiments unapologetically years later, and that they did not arouse criticism, suggest that such attitudes were not perceived as inappropriate. Moreover, the persistence of retrospective expressions of sympathies toward Nazi Germany in the post-Nasserist period, and more importantly, their perpetuation by Islamists like Qaradawi, who opposed 'Abd al-Nasir and his ideology, may indicate that this was more than an invented myth, as Israel Gershoni asserted, and that it may have represented prevalent views among non-elite groups.

---

78   Ahmad Shuqayri, *Arba'un 'amman fi al-hayat al-'arabiyya wal-duwaliyya*, Beirut: 1973, p. 137. See also Bahjat Abu Gharbiyya, *Fi khidam al-nidal al-'arabi al-filastini: mudhakkirat al-munadil Bahjat Abu Gharbiyya, 1916–1949*, Beirut: 1993, p. 137.

79   Sami al-Jundi, *al-Ba'th*, Beirut: 1969, pp. 27ff., cited in Lewis, *Semites and anti-Semites*, pp. 147–8. See also 'Izzat Tanus, *al-Filastiniyyun: madi majid wa-mustaqbal bahir*, Beirut: 1982, p. 291, who explains that the people's admiration for heroic acts everywhere in the world led them to glorify the Germans; and Elyas Farah, *al-Watan al-'arabi ba'd al-harb al-'alamiyya al-thaniya*, Beirut: 1975, pp. 6, 31–3, who speaks of the hatred and bitterness that pushed various Arab groups to sympathize with the Fascist regimes and pray for their success.

80   "Al-Qaradawi: sira wa-masira," www.islamonline.net/Arabic/personality/2001/11/article12.SHTML. See also the Islamist Mas'ud, *Hitler wa-Musulini*, p. 6, who believed that World War II was a divine mission to destroy the West. Hasanayn Haykal, editor of *al-Ahram* during the 1950s and 1960s, says that ordinary Egyptians supported the Germans out of their enmity toward the British and the French, "Mudhakkirat Hasanayn Haykal," *al-Shira'*, 22 December 1997; Ibrahim Ibrash, *al-Bu'd al-qawmi lil-qadiyya al-filastiniyya: filastin bayna al-qawmiyya al-'arabiyya wal-wataniyya al-filastiniyya*, Beirut: 1987, p. 74.

In a book he wrote under the auspices of Jordan's King Husayn (who had always been pro-western and espoused a moderate position in the Arab–Israeli conflict), Sami al-Jundi presented a very different view from the one he had produced in his memoirs. He distinguished between Arab sympathy to the German people as a kind, loyal, brave people who had contributed to civilization more than any other people in history, and Arab opposition to Nazism. The Germans, he added, were victims of the post-World War I treaties, and the Arabs supported their just demand to revoke the Versailles Treaty, because they too resented the post-war settlement that divided them and subjected them to European rule. Yet, this did not mean that the Arabs had ever agreed with Nazi ideology, or were ever satisfied with the fact that the Nazis placed them on a low rung in their racial classification. Furthermore, sympathy to the Germans, due to the treachery of the Allies, did not mean that the Arabs supported the "acts of injustice perpetrated against the Jews."[81] The Saudi writer Fahd Marik, who justified Arab support for Hitler, countered this type of criticism by purporting to have "documentary proof" that Hitler had supported Arab national aspirations.[82]

Unlike the nationalist writers, Communists criticized Arab popular support for Germany during the war. Iraqi Qasim Hasan acknowledged the success of Fascist propaganda among the Arab masses that exploited their natural opposition to Britain and France, but weakened their opposition to the "new imperialism" manifested by Zionism.[83] Emil Tuma conceded that the people who were subject to western imperialist control should have understood the nature of the fateful global conflict while they were waging their own struggle for independence. They should have risen above their narrow national interests and supported the Soviet Union, even though it fought alongside their imperialist oppressors. He criticized the "patriotic forces," i.e., supporters of the Rashid 'Ali movement in Iraq and Hajj Amin al-Husayni in Palestine, who associated themselves with the Fascists, based on the wrong principle of "the enemy of my enemy is my friend."[84] Few Palestinian writers indirectly criticized Hitler's positive image among Arabs and the prevalent view that his success would have prevented the establishment of Israel. They maintained that Hitler despised the Arabs, saw them as an inferior race and supported continued British control over their lands.[85]

81   Sami al-Jundi, *al-'Arab wal-yahud: al-'ada' al-kabir*, Beirut: 1968, pp. 70–5.

82   Fahd al-Marik, *Kayfa nantasiru 'ala isra'il*, Beirut: 1966, pp. 247–9.

83   Qasim Hasan, *al-'Arab*, pp. 176, 105. See also Haddad, *al-Mas'ala*, p. 124.

84   Tuma, *Sittun 'aman*, pp. 216–19.

85   Salman, "Almaniya al-naziyya," pp. 101–3; Khalil Budayri, *Ta'rikh ma aghfalahu al-*

A counter theme, though a less common one, raised by those who had felt uncomfortable with the problematic past, has highlighted since the 1980s Arab support for the Allies.[86] Jurji Haddad took this argument much further, attributing to the Arabs a decisive role in Germany's defeat. He conceded that Nazi Germany had enjoyed the sympathy of various Arab circles during the 1930s, and claimed that Hitler had hoped for massive Arab support during the war. Yet, despite these "honeyed" German promises, the vast majority of the Arabs refused to support Germany. The Palestinians had voluntarily ceased their armed rebellion in 1939 so as to facilitate the British war effort while "hundreds of thousands" North Africans volunteered for the Free French forces and indeed constituted most of the casualties among these forces. Moreover, it was the Arab refusal to support the Germans that left Rommel's forces isolated in North Africa and enabled the British to defeat him in the decisive battle of El Alamein. Without that victory, he adds, the Soviets could not have defeated the Germans in Stalingrad in 1942–43, and the Allies could not have landed in Normandy in 1944. "We will not be exaggerating," he concluded, "if we said that the entire world, let alone Western Europe and America are indebted to the shift in the Arab position" which ensured their victory in the war.[87]

The Islamist Mustafa Tahhan offered a similar description, but fused it with criticism, typical of Islamist disapproval of Arab leaders. The Jews viewed the war positively and benefited from it because they understood its international dimensions, whereas the Arab position was timid and mistaken. While the Arabs cultivated useless sympathy for the Axis, the Jews worked diligently to build their armed forces and industry. The Arab leaders were all "products of British decision and policy," and therefore Britain could set up numerous military units of Arab volunteers and enlist many of them to the British and US navies. The Arabs doubled their agricultural output to help the British, but the latter fooled them by floating futile plans for Arab union, which only harmed Islamic unity.[88]

---

ta'rikh: sitta wa-sittun 'amman ma'a al-haraka al-wataniyya al-filastiniyya wa-fiha, Jerusalem: 1982, pp. 101–2.

86   Filastin al-Thawra, 1 January 1981; Tanus, al-Filastiniyyun, pp. 291–2; Ya'qub Kamil al-Dajjani and Lina Ya'qub al-Dajjani, Filastin wal-yahud: jarimat al-sahyuniyya wal-'alam, n.p.: 1993, p. 314; Elyas Sa'd, al-Hijra al-yahudiyya ila filastin al-muhtalla, Beirut: 1969, p. 34. Tanus and Dajjani ignore Husayni's siding with Germany.

87   Jurji Haddad, "al-'Alam al-'arabi wal-islami wa-da'wat dimitroff li-iqamat al-jabha al-muwahhada did al-fashiyya," al-Hiwar al-Mutamaddin, no. 1311, 8 September 2005, www.rezgar.com/debat/show.art.asp?aid=45036.

88   Mustafa Tahhan, Filastin: al-mu'amara al-kubra, Kuwait: 1994, pp. 224–5. Tahhan probably refers to units of the Jordanian army that guarded British installations in the Middle East, but no Arabs were enlisted to the two navies.

The stress on the pragmatic aspect in Arab–German relations also appears in several academically oriented studies published since the 1980s. Jordanian historian 'Ali Muhafaza, who had noted Hitler's deep hatred of the Jews, showed that Hitler's rise to power aroused great interest among Arab nationalists. Most saw Germany as a possible ally in the struggle for independence, while several viewed it as a model for emulation, e.g., the Iron Shirts and National Guard in Damascus, the Arab Youth in Aleppo, the Patriotic Youth in Hamma, the Najjada and Kata'ib in Lebanon, the Futuwwa and Jawwala in Iraq and the Syrian Social Nationalist Party in Syria and Palestine. Still, he maintained that this "Arab high regard" for German military organization did not mean the adoption of Nazi racist ideas, as many historians claim.[89] Discussing the war period, Muhafaza justified popular Arab opposition to Britain and France for their imperialist conduct and for British responsibility in relation to Zionism. Yet he chided the Arabs for failing to understand Germany's policy, which regarded the Middle East as of secondary importance compared with Europe. Moreover, the Germans exploited the Arab leaders, particularly Husayni, who worked hard to serve German military and political goals, because they regarded the Arabs as racially inferior and gave higher priority to accommodating Italian, Spanish and French interests.[90]

'Abd al-Rahman 'Abd al-Ghani's study on German policy in Palestine follows Muhafaza's line, though it is a more comprehensive work and makes greater use of German, British and Zionist archival material. Unlike other writers, 'Abd al-Ghani did not evade the more problematic aspects of the Palestinian attitudes toward Germany. His review of the Palestinian press does not gloss over the many expressions of sympathy and support for Hitler, yet he insisted that the newspaper editors did not wish to establish Fascist governments in the Arab world.[91] 'Abd al-Ghani criticized some of the Palestinian newspapers, particularly *al-Karmil* and Husayni's *al-Jami'a al-'Arabiyya*, which belittled the persecution of the Jews in Germany and continued to praise the Nazi regime without understanding the causal link between its racist policy and increasing Jewish immigration. He attributed this short-sightedness to their erroneous belief that a wide coverage of Jewish suffering would appear as justifying Zionist arguments.[92] By contrast, an 11th grade Palestinian history textbook published

89   Muhafaza, *al-'Alaqat*, p. 230.

90   Muhafaza, ibid., pp. 230, 237, 244, 169–270. See also Nafi, "The Arabs," and a favorable review of a study analyzing Saudi Arabia's King 'Abd al-'Aziz relations with the Germans, which raises similar arguments, *al-Hayat*, 31 March 2000.

91   'Abd al-Ghani, *Almaniya*, pp. 189–97.

92   'Abd al-Ghani, ibid., p. 53. See a similar conclusion in Moshe Shemesh, "The Position

in 2002 admitted openly that Arab inclination toward the Axis powers was accompanied by an "Arab awareness of the dangers that threatened the region" and the Arab peoples because of the Zionist mass immigration to Palestine that was permitted by the British government.[93]

Hajj Amin al-Husayni and Germany: a contested collaborator or a misunderstood hero?

Arab reassessment of past relations with Germany faced a particular problem in dealing with the most prominent Palestinian leader under the British Mandate, Hajj Amin al-Husayni, who had served as the Mufti of Jerusalem, Head of the Supreme Muslim Council in Palestine from 1922 to 1937 and AHC chairman in 1936–37. He reached Germany on 6 November 1941, fleeing from Iraq after the failure of the Rashid 'Ali movement and unsuccessfully sought Hitler's public support for Arab independence. Throughout the war he broadcast pro-German propaganda on Radio Berlin and worked to recruit Muslim-Bosnian volunteers to the SS. While in Germany, he urged the foreign ministries of Germany, Italy, Hungary and Bulgaria not to allow Jews to emigrate from their territories, lest they reach Palestine. On 23 June 1943, for example, he suggested to the Hungarian authorities that they send their Jews to Poland "where they would find themselves under active control," in order to "protect oneself [sic] from their menace and avoid the consequent damage,"[94] a clear euphemism for extermination in those days. At the end of the war, Husayni fled to Paris, arriving in Egypt in March 1946 as a result of Arab pressure on France to reject British and Yugoslav requests for his extradition for trial for war crimes. When the news of his arrival broke, it aroused a wave of sympathy and enthusiasm, manifested in numerous press articles and pilgrimage to his home.

Husayni's war-time collaboration with Germany, which was raised in the Nuremberg trials, served Zionist efforts to undermine the image of the Palestinian national movement in the early post-war years.[95] His actions positioned them no

---

of the Jaffa Newspaper, 'Filastin,' on the Axis State and the Democracies," *Iyunim betekumat Yisrael*, vol. 2, 1992 (Hebrew), pp. 245–78.

93   Palestinian National Authority, *History for Public High School*, Grade 11 (2002), p. 259, cited in Center for Monitoring the Impact of Peace, www.edume.org/reports/13/43. htm.

94   The letters are cited in full, including photocopies of the original in 'Umar, *Mudhakkirat*, pp. 188–97.

95   For Husayni's activities in Germany, see Hirszowicz, *The Third Reich*, pp. 214–16, 250–65; Elpeleg, *The Grand Mufti*, pp. 63–78, 'Abd al-Ghani, *Almaniya*, pp. 318–74, and 'Umar, *Mudhakkirat*, pp. 93–229.

longer as "reluctant bystanders" in the Holocaust, as they saw themselves, but as collaborators, a status which the Arab discourse and historiography on the Holocaust vehemently opposed. The debate over his role in World War II was heavily influenced by the ambivalence with which Arab, particularly Palestinian, historiography viewed Husayni as the person responsible to the 1948 defeat.

The initial Arab reaction to the accusations of Husayni's collaboration with the Nazis in the extermination of Jews was outright rejection. 'Abd al-Rahman 'Azzam, Secretary General of the Arab League, told the British Chargé d'Affaires that the Yugoslav demand was made under "Jewish inspiration," and former Egyptian minister Muhammad 'Ali 'Alluba denied the charges against Husayni as "a major Zionist plot."[96] The Egyptian press, reporting on the revelations on Husayni's war-time activities during the Nuremberg trials, argued that he was not the one to advise SS chief Himmler to exterminate the Jews, since he had arrived in Germany while mass extermination was already in full swing. Moreover, the Egyptian press stressed the fact that Britain did not regard Husayni as a war criminal, and that his name did not appear on the lists of war criminals which the Allies had prepared.[97]

The Palestinians, for their part, had to address the political ramifications of Husayni's activities. Jamal al-Husayni, Hajj Amin's nephew, explained to the Anglo-American Committee (see Chapter 1) that Hajj Amin's stay in Germany did not contradict the struggle for democracy during the war. He accused the British of pushing him to Germany when they deposed him from his positions and persecuted him for his leading role in the 1936 Arab rebellion, and insisted that, had Britain given the Arabs their rights, Hajj Amin would have become a "second General Smutts" – the South African premier known for his support of the British. Jamal Husayni further argued that Hajj Amin's activities in Germany could not be considered collaboration, since he could not refuse his German hosts, but he did not work for German victory. Comparing Hajj Amin's actions with Churchill's willingness to cooperate with totalitarian Russia against Germany, Jamal Husayni emphasized that Hajj Amin only worked for his own people and aspired to ensure political gains should the Germans win the war. Hajj Amin was in Germany, he added, but his heart was with his people, whose support for the British war effort far exceeded that of the Jews, who stabbed Britain in the back.[98]

---

96   FO 141/1062, 'Abd al-Rahman Pasha to the Ambassador, 14 July 1945; ibid., Chargé d'Affaires to London, 24 August 1945; *The Egyptian Gazette*, 3 December 1945; ISA, HZ 21/2566, "Egypt's Newspapers," 2–8 Deccember 1945.

97   *Al-Ahram*, 26 February, 25 March, 16, 29 April, 11, 21 June, 30 July 1946.

98   Karlibach, *The Anglo-American Commission*, vol. 1, pp. 360–2.

Hajj Amin himself was much more candid in explaining his relations with the Germans. In addition to claiming that he had to flee from the British, who threatened his life, he justified his choice of Germany by patriotic reasoning. He viewed Germany as a "friendly state" that had no imperialist record and never harmed any Muslim or Arab state, while it fought the British and the Jews, adding that:

I was certain that a German victory would have completely saved our country from imperialism and Zionism ... I did not cooperate with Germany for the sake of Germany, nor because of a belief in Nazism. I do not accept its principles, and this never crossed my mind. Still, I was, and continue to be, convinced that had Germany and the Axis been victorious, no remnant of Zionism would have remained in Palestine.[99]

Husayni also reviewed at length his efforts to prevent the emigration of the Jews from Axis territory, citing the "attempts of world Jewry in 1944" to facilitate emigration of East-European Jews to Palestine. He boasted that he wrote to Ribbentrop, to Himmler and to Hitler until he "succeeded in foiling the attempt." This success, he stressed, was the reason why the Jews launched a complaint against him to the UN in 1947 on the charge that his efforts had led to the death of these Jews. Yet, he insisted that he never sought the extermination of the Jews, arguing that the Germans "settled their accounts with the Jews" before his arrival and they "needed no encouragement." While Husayni was correct in saying that the Nazis did not need his prodding to exterminate the Jews, he must have been aware of their policies, as he himself recalled earlier in his memoirs that Hitler had told him in their meeting on 28 November 1941 of his mission to destroy world Jewry.[100]

Contrary to Husayni's own story, his biographers – both Palestinians and other Arabs – particularly those targeting western readers, were either apologetic or tried hard to minimize the significance of his activities. The Iraqi-American historian Majid Khadduri cited briefly the various charges against Husayni, but countered them by quoting his public denials, while ignoring the written memoirs.[101] Another biographer, Taysir Jbara, pointed to Husayni's pragmatic motivations in supporting Germany, and reviewed his efforts to obtain the Axis support for Arab independence. Jbara did not touch upon Husayni's activities regarding the Jewish issue aside from mentioning that the British wanted to try him as a war criminal and various Zionists threatened to kill him. Apparently, Jbara did not feel that these acts harmed the Palestinian cause and he therefore

99   'Umar, *Mudhakkirat*, p. 164; Elpeleg, *The Grand Mufti*, p. 65.

100   'Umar, ibid., pp. 109–11, 128, 188–96,

101   Majid Khadduri, *Arab Contemporaries: The Role of Personalities in Politics*, Baltimore: 1973, p. 81.

concurred with the writer 'Ajjaj Nuwayhad's statement that Husayni had been "God's gift" to the Palestinians.[102]

US-based Palestinian historian Phillip Mattar conceded that Hajj Amin's stay in Germany was the most controversial and "distorted" period of his career. The Zionists were "so eager to prove him guilty of collaboration and war crimes, that they exaggerated his connections with the Nazis," he charged, and he asserted that the "thousands of captured German documents" used by the many writers on the subject failed to produce hard evidence of Husayni's participation in atrocities, beyond his attempts to stop the Jewish emigration to Palestine. Conversely, the Mufti and other Arabs were so busy justifying his statements and actions in the Axis countries that they ignored the overwhelming fact that he had cooperated with the "most barbaric regime in modern times." Yet, Mattar argued that by "focusing on Arab-Nazi ideological affinity, writers have misrepresented the central goal of Arab nationalist cooperation with the Axis: the defeat of a common enemy."[103]

Salah Khalaf, PLO second-in-command, offered a more apologetic view of Husayni's actions in his own French-language autobiography. Khalaf rejected the Zionist claim that Hajj Amin sympathized with the Nazis. By siding with Germany, he was merely an Arab nationalist who implemented "in a distorted way" the Palestinian strategy of seeking external alliances. Like many other Arab nationalists, he believed that the Axis powers would win the war and grant the Palestinians independence in gratitude for their support. Husayni had committed "a major error, which we all condemn decisively," Khalaf added, and claimed that he personally told him that these illusions were based on naive considerations, since Hitler had ranked the Arabs very low in his racial hierarchy. Had Germany won, it would have imposed an occupation much more cruel than the British. Hajj Amin was not a Nazi, just as those leaders who supported the British were not imperialists, Khalaf concludes, thereby placing both choices on the same moral ground.[104]

The debate in Arabic publications was far less apologetic. Historian Biyan al-Hut flatly rejected the charges of collaboration with the enemy against Husayni, on the grounds that the Palestinians did not see the Germans as their enemies. She denied as a Zionist slander all accusations of Husayni's participation in the

---

102   Taysir Jbara, *Palestinian Leader Hajj Amin al-Husayni: Mufti of Jerusalem*, Princeton: 1985, pp. 182–6, 192.

103   Philip Mattar, *The Mufti of Jerusalem: Al-Hajj Amin al-Husayni and the Palestinian National Movement*, New York: 1988, p. 107.

104   Abou Iyad, *Palestinien sans patrie: Entretiens avec Eric Rouleau*, Jerusalem: 1979 (Hebrew), pp. 63–4.

extermination of Jews, and dismissed as fabricated citations from his speeches in Radio Berlin in which he urged the killing of Jews. She maintained that his activities against Jewish emigration from Europe during the war were not morally wrong, but a political necessity, since such emigration meant the dispossession of the Palestinians.[105]

'Ali Muhafaza and Mufid 'Abd al-Hadi justified Husayni's activities as not different from those of other leaders. Muhafaza equated them with British and American readiness to collaborate with another devil, Stalin, while 'Abd al-Hadi equated them with the collaboration of Sharif Husayn, leader of the 1916 Arab Rebellion against the Ottomans with the British.[106] None of them addressed the moral differences between the Nazis and these other leaders. The Lebanese Hayat 'Atiyya al-Huwayk was even blunter. She contended that Husayni's contacts with the Nazis were only intended to stop the "Nazi-Zionist" Transfer Agreement, which was implemented long before there was any Holocaust, and insisted that this was what the Arabs should focus on.[107]

By contrast, 'Abd al-Ghani, who had analyzed at length Palestinian political contacts with the Nazis, criticized Husayni's escape to Germany as motivated more by personal considerations than national ones, since the alternative was the cessation of his political activity. He discussed Husayni's effort to advance Arab national goals, but conceded that they were futile, even though Husayni left a deep impression on Hitler.[108] Husayni's enmity toward Zionism led him to blur the difference between Jews and Zionists and to hate all Jews, explained 'Abd al-Ghani, who also rejected the charge that Husayni actively supported their extermination. 'Abd al-Ghani claimed apologetically that the phrase "solution of the Jewish problem" that appeared in Husayni's correspondence with the German Foreign Ministry in 1944 was not written by him but by the former German ambassador to Iraq Fritz Grobba, and that its actual meaning was vague at the time. While he minimized Husayni's role in the "Final Solution," he conceded that from a moral point of view his cooperation with the Axis was not something to be proud of.[109] 'Abd al-Ghani's main criticism is not moral but political. It is directed against Husayni's failure as a national leader, who

---

105   Al-Hut, *al-Qiyadat*, pp. 460–2. See a similar argument in Huwayk, "al-'Alaqa," and in *al-Hayat*, 1–2, July 1989.

106   Muhafaza, *al-'Alaqat*, pp. 259, 269; Mufid Abdul Hadi, *The Other Side of the Coin: A Native Palestinian Tells his Story*, Nablus: 1998, p. 61.

107   "Mudakhala hawla muhadarat al-filistiniyyun wal-muhraqa al-yahudiyya," www.almunta-da.org.jo/arabic/iss1922001sep06.htm.

108   'Abd al-Ghani, *Almaniya*, pp. 326–34.

109   'Abd al-Ghani, ibid., pp 361, 366, 369–71, 403.

missed the fundamental differences between Arab national interests and those of the Axis, and who deluded himself that he could be an ally of the Germans, while they saw him as an agent in their service. 'Abd al-Ghani did not belittle the enormity of the Holocaust, but stressed its impact in swaying world public opinion in favor of the Zionists, portraying Zionism as the major beneficiary of the war.[110]

The official Palestinian view of Husayni's legacy was much more ambiguous, at least partly because the PLO leadership sought to diminish his stature while presenting itself as a reaction to the type of leadership that he had represented. An obituary written in *Filastin al-Thawra* after his death on 4 July 1974 praised his support for the Iraqi national movement in 1941 and his efforts on behalf of the Palestinian cause after his arrival in Cairo in 1946, while glossing over his war-time activities. The Palestinian Encyclopedia mentioned briefly that he stayed in Europe for four years, during which he established offices for the Arab national movement in Berlin and Rome and worked for the Palestinian and Arab causes in the spheres of diplomacy and propaganda, and noted that the British, Yugoslav and American governments wanted to try him for war crimes, but without mentioning what these were.[111] The PNA official website is more candid. While generally criticizing Arab "reactionary" circles for siding with Germany, it concedes that Husayni "joined the Nazi Axis and served its goals," but insists that the Palestinian people did not heed his calls to rebel against the British.[112] Again, the mantle of surrogate statehood apparently obliged it to take a more realistic position.

The newly emergent Palestinian Islamist historiography of the 1990s rehabil-itated Husayni's image from that of a failed leader to a devout one, who waged the struggle against Zionism from an Islamic vantage point. Consequently, and because Islamist writers were far less concerned with universal criteria regarding Nazism, they treated his relationship with Germany in a different light. Najib al-Ahmad praised Husayni's efforts to forestall Jewish emigration from Europe during the war. Ahmad Nawfal and Jadu' al-'Abidi go further, asserting that he "chose well" in cooperating with Germany. They explain that the Palestinian people could not have defended themselves, because Britain had concealed its aim to grant Palestine to the Jews, and no Arab leader except Husayni under-stood this situation. Hence, he had no choice but to look for help from a more powerful player than Britain. Both agree that, had Germany and Italy prevailed

110   Ibid., 401–4.

111   *Filastin al-Thawra*, 10 July 1974 and 8 March 1986; *al-Mawsu'a al-filastiniyya*, vol. 4, p. 160. See also, *al-Quds*, 28 July, *al-Hayat al-Jadida*, 8 August 2003.

112   www.minfo.gov.ps/index.php?scid=2&pid=269.

in the war, "Palestine's fate would have been much better than its present state under Zionist rule." The authors deny the assertion that Husayni's arrival in Germany meant agreement with its ideology, reiterating the comparison of Stalin's alliance with Churchill and Roosevelt. In conclusion, they denounce the claim that Husayni served Germany as one of the greatest lies, using the negative term *Isra'iliyyat* – that refers to false Jewish traditions, which erroneously entered Islamic tradition.[113]

Mustafa Tahhan also praises Husayni for his foresight, and criticizes him only for focusing on seeking gains in the foreign arena, which proved ephemeral, while neglecting the domestic scene. Reviewing Husayni's dealings with Hitler, Tahhan expressed his anger at the Jews, who dared to blame him for massacres against Jews and demanded his trial as a war criminal.[114] In a joint Jewish–Arab debate, Abdallah Nimr Darwish, former leader of the Islamic Movement in Israel, took the middle way, attributing Husayni's actions to his deep resentment over British mistreatment of the Arabs. But why, he asked, did everyone focus on Husayni and ignore the "dozens of Jewish leaders who maintained tight links with the Nazis" and served them faithfully? All of these leaders, Jews and Arabs alike, who maintained close ties with the Nazis, should be asked whether they knew in advance of Hitler's intentions to destroy the Jews.[115] Thus, while inventing a myth of "dozens" of Jewish collaborators, Darwish exonerated Husayni by circumventing his actual activities.

The only writer who advocated a principled position against Husayni was 'Azmi Bishara, in an article directed to European and Israeli audiences. Bishara described Husayni's conduct as a "serious failure" which required "far reaching Palestinian self-criticism." He insisted that Husayni was the exception among Palestinian leaders, most of whom supported the British, and claimed that the scope of his ties with the Germans remained controversial.[116] Bishara's radical political approach obviously affected his ability to question some Palestinian political myths, but he did not go that far as to deal with the non-Arab accusations against Husayni or examine the level of Arab and Palestinian support that Husayni received after the war – which might have indicated that Husayni was not so exceptional.

---

113   Najib al-Ahmad, *Filastin; ta'rikhan wa-nidalan*, Amman: 1985, pp. 295–8; Ahmad Nawfal and 'Awni Jadu' al-'Abidi, *Safahat min hayat al-hajj amin al-husayni mufti filastin al-akbar wa-qa'id harakatiha al-wataniyya*, Zarqa': 1985, p. 134–6; Husayn Adham Jarrar, *al-Hajj amin al-husayni: ra'id jihad wa-batal qadiyya*, Amman: 1987, pp. 213, 218–36.

114   Tahhan, *Filastin*, pp. 226–9.

115   *Al-Mithaq*, 20 April 2001.

116   Bishara, "The Arabs," p. 55.

Internet discussion forums: radical voices from below

The spread of discussion forums in the internet since the 1990s, particularly Islamist ones, provides an insight into the reception of views on Nazi Germany among broader constituencies. These debates came out primarily in response to short and fairly dispassionate biographies of Hitler published in 2005–6. There is no way of assessing how representative these responses are, as use of the internet is not widespread in the Arab world and it could be argued that participants in such forums are usually more outspoken or radical than most people. Yet, the types of response or their absence could indicate the acceptance or rejection of certain views.

Most of the responses did not address the Holocaust, but focused on Hitler's qualities as a leader and the particular lessons the Arabs and Muslims should draw from his historical role. The minority view sharply criticized Hitler as a dictator who had brought nothing but destruction and death to his country. One contributor, who condemned Hitler as a "war criminal and dictator, who deserved to be put on trial," added that Hitler was the same as George W. Bush. That "ignorant corporal," wrote another respondent, "led an entire nation to oblivion, and because we Arabs experience a high level of ignorance, we glorify such a boorish person." Some of us admire him because he killed the Jews, "a horrible thing in itself," he said, but he cautioned that the figures of Jewish victims were highly inflated. "Should we admire his killing of the Jews, simply because the Jews are our enemies?" asked a third, who condemned Hitler as a murderer (saffah).[117]

Most respondents, however, had a more positive view of Hitler, describing him as a "hero," "an artist," "a great military leader who had led his country through great economic hardships," as "the most noble leader the world had known," a "leader who was devoted to his country," "the only truly democratic leader," "a great man who was slandered by Britain and the US as a disturbed personality," and as someone who "deserves to be remembered forever." A few others presented a less intimidating Hitler by minimizing his ambitions. He only wanted to unify all German speakers in one country, one writer contended, but international circumstances foiled his efforts and led to a world war. A strong German state is in fact a "service to humanity." We have no idea whether he truly wanted to conquer the world, wrote another, while a third explained that Hitler was not different

---

117   The citations for the following passages are taken from http://bouhout.blogs.ma/tb.php?id=25, March to July 2006; www.akhawia.net/archive/index.php/t-8895.html, July 2005; www.resala.org/forum/archive/index.php/t-2127.html; "Hail Hitler," in http://shkbta.be/?p=33; www.omanidream.net/vb/archive/index.php/t-1285.html; www.narwanour.com/cen/Hitler.jpg;   www.alhandasa.net/forum/archive/index.php/t-8240.html; "Hitler, almaniya wal-murabbun al-yahud," www.egyptiantalks.org/invb/index.php?showtopic=11462&st=90.

from Bismarck, and the only difference between them was that during his time the Jews had occupied foci of power all over the world.

Several of those who praised Hitler emphasized his service to humanity in targeting the Jews. He was the only leader who was aware of the extent of the Zionist treachery and threat to the world, and he ceaselessly warned Chamberlain that the Zionist lobby and the Jewish money-lenders were manipulating the policies of all other countries – but to no avail. He understood the Jewish threat and "carried out genocide to save his country from the Jews," wrote one participant. Many people slander Hitler for burning the Jews, wrote another, but it was not without reason, as they had endangered his country. Many believe that the Holocaust was a myth or that the Jews greatly inflated the number of their deaths, wrote a third, while "I believe that Hitler had done humanity a great service in burning several thousands of them."

Another exchange on Hitler in an Islamist forum drew 8,453 entries from 1 October 2000 to 6 October 2006. A certain 'Aziz recalled Hitler's words from *Mein Kampf* on his dream of avenging Germany's defeat as he lay wounded in hospital in November 1918, and comments that the world had paid a heavy price for that dream. Yet, he concludes, "May a second Hitler arise ... the best thing he did was to burn the Jews." In response, another participant, Serdal, agreed that Hitler had caused great harm and destruction, but criticized the statement on Hitler's burning the Jews, not on a moral basis, as he agreed that the Jews were the most "despicable people," but, as he said, because the killing of the six million Jews was a lie they had invented. Another contributor also expressed his hope that a second Hitler would arise in the West, so that western countries would fight each other. None of the participants, however, condemned 'Aziz's call to burn the Jews.[118]

Conclusions

The Arab discourse persistently reflected ambivalent attitudes toward Nazi Germany. On the one hand, Nazism definitely became the symbol of evil incarnate, as shown by the frequent use of the term "Nazi" as a pejorative against Israel, the US and various internal rivals. In using this representation, the Arab critics focused on Hitler's policies toward the people of Europe, that is, military aggression and vicious state terror against civilian populations, while minimizing the centrality of his anti-Jewish ideology and genocidal actions against the Jews. In other words, they distinguished between their negation of Hitler and Nazi

---

118   www.swalif.net/sforum1/showthread.php?threadid=66580. The same description of Hitler's dream appeared on another website, www.uaearab.com/DREAM/53.htm, but its director omitted the last passage on the Jews.

Germany and their attitudes toward the Holocaust for political reasons related to the conflict with Israel.

Concurrently, a minority view, which found positive points in Nazi Germany, has continued to appear throughout the years since the end of World War II. Proponents of this view do not praise Hitler's racism or aggression. Rather, they find Hitler's anti-Jewish policy the positive or attractive element in his regime or a factor that atones for his crimes in other fields. Others view him positively out of hatred for the western Allies, who were deemed the historical enemies of the Islamic world. While definitely less pervasive than the dominant view, the persistence of this view suggests that it may not have been negligible, since those who raised it have come from a variety of places and political backgrounds, and from the mainstream of society. Equally important, they did not seem uncomfortable in airing their views, nor have they been subject to harsh criticism or arouse fierce debates.[119] All of these points suggest that the proponents of the sympathetic view have assumed that they have a wider audience, which agrees with them. The repeated stress by various writers on Hitler's disdain toward the Arabs, and the warnings that his victory would not have served their interests may also indicate that they considered such views to be widespread.

Most Arab writers deny any Nazi ideological appeal as the basis for past links with Nazi Germany and attribute them to political pragmatism or emotional expression of animosity toward the western imperial powers. Two opposite ideological poles emerge on this issue. Communists were the most persistent in their rejection of Nazi Germany, and unequivocal in their criticism of Arab links with it. Conversely, some Islamists had no qualms over regretting Germany's defeat, out of their opposition to western culture, and insensitivity to western cultural conventions.

While most Arab writers accept their pro-German inclinations or past search for German alliance as a legitimate endeavor born out of political necessity, they use the (largely false) allegations of Zionist cooperation in order to delegitimize Zionism. The contradiction is typical of conflict situations "whereby the actions of one's own country are attributed to altruistic motives, but the identical actions taken by an enemy are attributed to self-serving motives."[120] Yet, most Arab writers who have created this false equation go further. They claim a bogus ideological affinity between Zionism and Nazism when discussing Zionism,

119   See, for instance, the memoirs of Yunus al-Bahri, *Huna Birlin, hayy al-'arab*, Beirut: 1955, recalling his time in Berlin, where he broadcast propaganda on behalf of Nazi Germany on Radio Berlin, and Abdul Hadi, *The Other Side*, which did not arouse any criticism.

120   Sande et al., "Value Guided Attributions," p. 91.

but belittle or blur the menacing essence – the murderous racism – of Nazism when discussing the Arab side. In addition to the psychological element, this phenomenon reflects a broader problem of insufficient self-criticism in Arab historiography. This problem is particularly visible in the Palestinian grappling with Hajj Amin al-Husayni's collaboration with Nazi Germany. That the Zionist movement used it in order to advance its own goals prompted many Arab writers to adopt an apologetic posture that sought to minimize the extent or significance of this collaboration. Some criticized him for the harm he caused the Palestinians themselves by his activities. But almost none addressed the moral issue, probably because they still viewed the problem through the prism of the Arab–Israeli conflict.

10

THE PALESTINIAN CATASTROPHE (NAKBA) VERSUS THE HOLOCAUST

The Holocaust was rarely raised as an independent subject in the Arab public discourse up until the mid-1990s but was, as we have seen, frequently invoked, explicitly or implicitly, in the writings on and discussions of historical and political issues such as Jewish history and the Jewish problem, the Palestine problem, and the Zionist enterprise. There existed a correlation between the narratives which evolved around those issues, and certain motifs of Holocaust representation. The context affected the nature of the reference to the Holocaust. For example, in the debate on Jewish history and the Nazi atrocities justification emerged as a major motif, whereas in the discussion on the Palestine problem the comparisons between the Palestinian catastrophe and the Holocaust and between the attitude of the Jews toward the Arabs and Nazi behavior toward the Jews were prominent.

The Zionist premise that the solution to the Jewish problem could be achieved only by the creation of a Jewish national home in Palestine (Eretz Yisrael) had been acknowledged by the international community after World War II, when the UN adopted its 29 November 1947 resolution on the partition of Palestine. The Holocaust served as a catalyst and provided further justification for the establishment of the Jewish state, hence interlocking on the one hand the Jewish problem and the Palestine problem and on the other hand the tragedies of the Jewish and Palestinian peoples. The Arab governments and public discourse rejected the linkage between the solutions of the Jewish problem and the Palestine problem (see also Chapter 1), and presented in its stead a link between the Holocaust and the Palestinian catastrophe, introducing two parallel human tragedies. The Palestinians strove to gain recognition of their tragedy, with all it entails for rights of self-determination and restoration of justice. This striving for victimhood status constituted the backbone of the narrative from which various motifs developed, starting with the equation of the extent and gravity of the tragedies, through denying the tragedy of "the other" and turning him from victim to perpetrator. This equation not only ignored the differences between the two but completely distorted the perception of the Holocaust in the Arab world. In Israeli society, on the other hand, the Holocaust became a founding myth, as Israeli historian Anita Shapira pointed out, underscoring the causal relationship between the Holocaust and the birth of Israel and the Arab–Israeli conflict.[1]

Even before the occurrence of the actual events, the tragedy inflicted on the Jews by the Germans was compared to the tragedy that might be caused by the establishment of the Jewish state (see also chapter 1).[2] The war of 1948, launched by Arab states as a result of their rejection of the UN partition resolution, brought in its wake what came to be known in Arab historiography and discourse as the Nakba (catastrophe). It represented the defeat, displacement, dispossession, exile, dependence, insecurity, lack of statehood and struggle to survive. The coining of the term was attributed to Syrian scholar Custantin Zurayq in his book, *The Meaning of the* Nakba, published as early as August 1948,[3] even before the real dimensions of the Arab defeat in Palestine became evident. But, perusing Egyptian papers from 1945 revealed that already then, Egyptian intellectuals used the term to describe the developments in Palestine. Ibrahim 'Abd al-Qadir al-Mazini blamed British policy for the catastrophe befalling Palestine and other Arab countries,[4] and Mahmud 'Izzat 'Arafa reflected on the evolving Palestinian tragedy, comparing it to the historical Arab Nakba in Spain[5] – a comparison which was often made in the discourse of the Arab–Israeli conflict. Although other words were also used to describe the 1948 defeat, like *ma'asa, karitha, naksa, hazima*, the term Nakba struck roots in the Palestinian and Arab discourse to mark the uniqueness of the Palestinian tragedy.

Traditionally, Arabs used the word Nakba in reference "to strong misfortunes caused by external forces they could not confront,"[6] explained Egyptian sociologist Saad Eddin Ibrahim. The connotative significance of the word and

---

1   Anita Shapira, "Politics and Collective Memory: The Debate over the 'New Historians' in Israel," *History and Memory*, vol. 7, no. 1 (Spring/Summer 1995), pp. 17–19. See also, Don-Yehia, "Memory"; Yehiam Weitz and Avital Saf (eds.), *Major Changes Within the Jewish People in the Wake of the Holocaust*, Jerusalem: 1996, pp. 497–518. The term "founding myth" points to an inspiring or patriotic story, real or imagined, which becomes a national symbol and shapes national collective memory.

2   *Al-Ahram*, 4 November 1945, 11 January 1946.

3   Custantin Zurayq, *Ma'na al-nakba*, Beirut: 1948.

4   *Al-Risala*, 5 November 1945.

5   *Al-Risala*, 19 August 1946.

6   *Civil Society*, vol. 7, no. 77 (May 1998), p. 4.

its Arabic synonyms, added Palestinian columnist Hassan Khidr, is "firstly, a deference to nature, with all its latent violence and its impetuosity; secondly, a resignation to the vicissitudes of fate; and thirdly, a relinquishment of responsibility for the catastrophe."[7] Indeed, over the years the Nakba seemed to express the enormity of the disaster which inexplicably and unexpectedly was inflicted on the Palestinian people (and its Arab allies) by an outside force – a catastrophe or "a cataclysm" that "led to the dual injustice of the dispossession and exile," thus exonerating the Arabs and the Palestinians from any responsibility for its occurrence.[8] However, it also provided the ground for the development of a special Palestinian narrative and a vast body of literature of longing and return to the "lost paradise,"[9] and played a crucial role "in shaping and expressing a separate Palestinian identity,"[10] especially due to the high sense of exclusion and alienation that the Palestinians encountered in the hosting Arab countries.[11]

In 1998, when Israel celebrated its fiftieth anniversary, the Nakba was officially commemorated in the PNA for the first time since its occurrence. It was marked in public rallies, processions, seminars and exhibits in the major towns of the West Bank and the Gaza Strip, triggering a public debate on its meaning, significance and place in Palestinian national identity. The events which took place on this occasion, and the many publications and articles in the Palestinian and Arab press, threw light on a process of change in the discourse on the Nakba. Although the Nakba always played an essential role in the Palestinian public agenda, the barrage of writing in 1998 was unprecedented and denoted a crossroads in its perception.

---

7   *Al-Ahram Weekly*, 2 April 1998.

8   Ibrahim Abu Lughud, "From Catastrophe to Defeat, Two Terms for Big Events," in Y. Harkabi (ed.), *The Arabs and Israel: A Collection of Translations from Arabic*, no. 1, Tel-Aviv: 1975 (Hebrew), p. 34. See also Ibrahim Abu Lughud, "The Nakba: This is What Happened," *Alpayim*, no. 16 (1998), pp. 152–7 (Hebrew); Fawwaz Turki, "To be a Palestinian," *Journal of Palestine Studies*, vol. 3, no. 3 (Spring, 1974), p. 4; *The Palestinian People's Appeal on the 50th Anniversary of the Catastrophe* "Al-Nakba", www.pna.org/mininfo/nakba. On the evasion of responsibility see also Sadiq Jalal al-'Azm, *al-Naqd al-dhati ba'd al-hazima*, Beirut: 1969, p. 20. See also Harkabi, *Arab Attitudes*, p. 381.

9   Abd al-Latif Tibawi, "Visions of the Return. The Palestinian Arab Refugees in Arabic Poetry and Art," *Middle East Journal*, vol. 17, no. 5 (1963), pp. 507–26; Reuven Snir, "'One Wound of his Wounds' – The Palestinian Arab Literature in Israel," *Alpayim*, no. 2 (1990) (Hebrew), pp. 244–68; Danny Rubinstein, *The People of Nowhere. The Palestinian Vision of Home*, Jerusalem: 1991.

10   Rashid Khalidi, *Palestinian Identity. The Construction of Modern National Consciousness*, New York: 1997, p. 19; Kimmerling and Migdal, *Palestinians*, p. 182.

11   For a discussion of the meaning of the Nakba, see Webman, "The Evolution."

The discussion of the reconstruction of the meaning of the Nakba is beyond the scope of this study. Rather, this chapter seeks to highlight the usage of Holocaust metaphors in the Arab, and particularly Palestinian, discourse and to discern the trends and consequences emerging from juxtaposing the Nakba with the Holocaust. The Nakba, epitomizing the Palestinian suffering, was being reconstructed as a founding myth in the Palestinian national identity, fulfilling, wittingly or unwittingly, a similar role to that of the Holocaust, the epitome of Jewish suffering, in Israeli society. "In the construction of identity, both Arabs and Jews have used the leverage of very similar arguments, projecting an image of themselves that refers to the same stereotypes and putting into practices strategies of the same kind."[12] However, this process was not confined to the narratives of Jews and Palestinians. Scholars of history and memory point to the development of a "culture of victimhood" in the West, especially since the 1980s and 1990s, as part of ethnic and national identity and collective memory that involves the recognition and rectification of past evils.[13] Holocaust consciousness has spread in the Third World as well, and is reflected in the spheres of "theology, negritude, human rights, diaspora studies, popular culture, genocide scholarship, historical contextualism, racial analysis."[14] Yet, the Palestinian discourse, which has preceded this trend, was naturally influenced by it and matured by the end of the 1990s, due to the peace process, the changing circumstances of the Arab–Israeli conflict and the emergence of the new discourse on the Holocaust (see below). This maturation was manifested in the discussion over the Nakba in 1998.

The analogy between what befell the Jews and Palestine's Arabs was a major motif in the Palestinian and Arab discourse on the Holocaust. The comparison between the tragedies of the Jewish and Palestinian peoples seemed compelling from the Arab, and particularly Palestinian, point of view, since the Palestinians, as Rami Khouri explained, "have experienced many of the same historical pains that Jews have suffered over the past two and a half millennia."[15] Palestin-

---

12   Ada Lonni, "Parallel Strategies in Israeli and Palestinian Experiences," *Palestine-Israel Journal*, vol. 8/4–9/1 (2001–2), pp. 71–83.

13   Charles S. Maier, "A Surfeit of Memory? Reflections on History, Melancholy and Denial," *History and Memory*, vol. 5, no. 2 (Fall/Winter 1993), pp. 136–7; Gulie Neeman-Arad, "A History of Memory: The Changing Status of the Holocaust in the Conscious of the Jews in the United States," *Zmanim*, no. 57 (Winter 1996–97) (Hebrew), p. 19; Jean-Michel Chaumont, *La concurrence des victims, génocide, identité, reconnaissance*, Paris: 1997, pp. 160–80; *New York Review of Books*, 8 April 1999, p. 6.

14   William F. S. Miles, "Third World Views of the Holocaust," *Journal of Genocide Research*, vol. 6, no. 3 (September 2004), p. 379.

15   *Jordan Times*, 15 May 1998.

ian activist Ata Qaymari admitted that many Palestinians perceive the Holocaust through the prism of their Nakba, "the counterpart of the Holocaust in Palestinian history, in which their whole social, economic and cultural fabric was destroyed and uprooted." Thus, there are significant similarities in the ways in which both communities address their catastrophe, in commemoration and historiography, and "the Palestinians are trying, just as the Jews did and are still doing, to gather a kind of collective memory that preserves their own social, cultural and historical fabric."[16] Palestinian scholar Rashid Khalidi went even further, seeing the Holocaust as "our benchmark for man's inhumanity to man," claiming that, if it has any universal relevance, "it teaches that we should not be allowed to forget or forgive wrongs committed against a whole people."[17]

In the preface to the Arabic translation of Robert Faurisson's articles in the book *The Historical Lie: Were Six Million Jews Killed?* the translator Majid Hillawi bitterly complained that the Arabs and Palestinians accepted the Holocaust as a criterion for many of their political, cultural and artistic decisions and repeated "the Zionist lies in order to gain international sympathy" by describing the suffering of the Palestinian people in terms invented by the Jews such as "Holocaust," "massacre," "victimhood," "diaspora" and "memory."[18] A similar view was expressed by Palestinian poet Mahmud Darwish, who warned that the acceptance of these "tempting metaphoric images" reflected the Israeli success to domineer Palestinian identity.[19]

Indeed, the terminology and discourse of the Holocaust highly affected the Arab discourse on the Nakba from the mid-1940s, when immigration to Palestine emerged as the solution for the displaced Jews in Europe. The Palestine problem was perceived as a refugee catastrophe and not as a problem of a persecuted people in search of a haven, as the Jews claim.[20] It was presented as "worse than the problem of the Nazi persecution in Europe,"[21] which was said to be exploited for the justification of the persecution and uprooting of another peo-

---

16   Ata Qaymari, "The Holocaust in the Palestinian Perspective," in Paul Scham, Walid Salem and Benjamin Pogrund (eds.), *Shared Histories. A Palestinian-Israeli Dialogue*, Jerusalem: 2005, p. 149.

17   Rashid Khalidi, "Truth, Justice and Reconciliation: Elements of a Solution to the Palestinian Refugee Issue," in Ghada Karmi and Eugene Cotran (eds.), *The Palestinian Exodus 1948–1998*, Reading: 1999, p. 227.

18   Furisun, *al-Ukdhuba*, p. 18. See also, Hazim Saghiya, *Difa'an 'an al-Salam*, Beirut: 1997, p. 69; *Ha'aretz*, 21 March 1997.

19   Mahmud Darwish, "The Identity of Absence," *Mifgashim*, 7–8 (Autumn 1987), p. 47 as quoted in Gur-Ze'ev, *Philosophy*, p. 105.

20   *Al-Ahram*, 19 September 1948.

21   *Al-Misri*, 7 December 1952.

ple for the absorption of displaced Jews. No one can claim that it was the Arabs' duty to allow immigration of Jews to Palestine in view of their suffering, wrote Egyptian sociologist Rashid al-Barrawi. Sympathy feelings "do not provide a special moral right to Palestine"[22] (see also Chapter 1). The narrative formulated a contrast between the settlement of displaced Jews in Palestine and the deportation of the Arabs from Palestine and a causal relation between the two. The Jews had become the oppressors who caused the suffering of the Arab refugees, "after being trodden under the oppressors' feet in the past." They were tortured by the nations and found refuge in Arab lands but the Arabs "were paying today the price of their hospitality."[23] The Jews who suffered from the West adopted its despicable methods and directed them against an innocent people who were not guilty for what had happened in Europe, asserted Suwaylim al-'Umri, a lecturer in the department of international relations at Cairo University in the mid-1950s.[24] The Arabs' moral standing in that narrative appeared to be higher than that of the West and the Jews, since they were innocent of systematic persecution of the Jews and had provided them with shelter in the past. Hence, the oppression caused to them was regarded as an imploring injustice and ingratitude on the part of the Jews, which had not gained international recognition.

Competing for victimhood status

The issues of victimization and victimhood, which played and are still playing a crucial role in the representation of Jewish history and identity, are also major elements in the national Palestinian narrative, that considers the moment of the establishment of the State of Israel as the moment of defeat and displacement of the Palestinian people. Whereas the events of 1947 and 1948 – partition, and the War of Independence – mean for Israelis a national rebirth after the Holocaust and a cause for national celebration, for Palestinians "the same events are seen as an unmitigated disaster and are the focus of national mourning."[25] "What has been a success for one party has been a failure for the other party," explained Ibrahim Dakkak, a leading PLO activist from Jerusalem.[26] About a

22   Rashid al-Barrawi, *Mushkilat al-sharq al-awsat*, Cairo: 1948, pp. 40–2.

23   *Al-Misri*, 6 July 1949. See also: *al-Ahram*, 3 May 1949.

24   Al-'Umari, *al-Sharq al-awsat*, p. 45. The theme of Arab hospitality toward the Jews appears occasionally in the discourse without elaboration. It is unclear which hospitality they were referring to. Indeed Jews found refuge in the Ottoman Empire after their deportation from Spain in 1492, and in the mid-1930s in Turkey.

25   Khalidi, "Truth," p. 224.

26   "1948–1998 in the Eyes of Two Peoples. A Roundtable Discussion," *Palestine-Israel Journal of Politics, Economics and Culture*, vol. 5, no. 2 (1998), p. 24. See also, Joseph Samaha, *Salam 'abir. Nahwu madd 'arabi lil-"mas'ala al-yahudiyya"*, Beirut: 1993, p. 28; *al-Sharq*

decade earlier, Israeli Arab communist activist Emil Habibi elaborated, in an article entitled "Your Holocaust Our Catastrophe," that although the suffering experienced by the Jews of Europe should not be compared to the suffering of the Palestinians, the Palestinians were still suffering. The Holocaust was perceived by the Arabs "as the original sin" which enabled the Zionist movement to convince millions of Jews that theirs was the right course. "If not for your – and all of humanity's – Holocaust in World War II, the catastrophe that is still the lot of my people would not have been possible."[27] Israeli Arab lawyer Khalid Kassab Mahamid presented a similar view, claiming that the Palestinian Nakba was small relative to the horrible events of the Holocaust, but that the Palestinian people bore the brunt of its political consequences. "The magnitude of the Palestinian people's catastrophe stems from the magnitude of the Holocaust, whereas the problem of Israel is smaller than the Palestinian problem because it receives aid due to the Holocaust, while the Palestinians pay the price with their homeland and tough life."[28]

The Palestinians perceived themselves as the victims of "the victims of the greatest act of horror of the 20th century."[29] The Nakba has been represented as a unique and acute unprecedented historical experience. On a virtual scale of suffering or a crimes graph, the Palestinian tragedy was graded higher than the Jewish suffering. "It is the biggest mark of disgrace on the forehead of the twentieth century," was a recurrent assertion.[30] The Arab refugees' problem was said to surpass the Jewish refugees' problem,[31] Israel was accused of perpetrating "the biggest crime that history had ever known,"[32] and its leaders were depicted as murderers and Nazi criminals.

---

al-Awsat, 7 April 1998.

27 Emil Habibi, "Your Holocaust Our Catastrophe," *Politica*, no. 8 (June–July 1986) (Hebrew), pp. 26–7. See also quote from the *Jerusalem Post*, 28 April 1989, in Linn and Gur-Ze'ev, "Holocaust," p. 200. This phrase was repeatedly invoked in various forms. See, for instance, "Their Holocaust, Our Cemetery," *al-'Arab al-Yawm*, 4 July 1998.

28 Khalid Kassab Mahamid, *al-Filastiniyyun wa-dawlat al-muhraqa*, Umm al-Fahm: 2006, p. 11.

29 Rashid Khalidi, "Fifty Years after 1948: A Universal Jubilee?," *Tikkun*, vol. 13, no. 2 (March/April 1998), pp. 54–6; Edward Said, *The Politics of Dispossession*, New York: 1994, p. 121; *al-Hayat*, 5 May, *al-Quds*, 6 May, *al-Ahram Weekly*, 14 May 1998.

30 See, for instance, Muhammad Safwat, *Isra'il al-'aduw al-mushtarak*, Cairo: 1952, p. 187. See also, 'Abd al-Rahman al-Rafi'i, *Fi a'qab al-thawra al-misriyya. Thawrat 1919*, Cairo: 1989, part 3, p. 245; statement by Syrian Prime Minister Faris al-Khuri, *Majallat al-Azhar*, 24 January 1955, p. 606; *al-Quds*, 15 May 1998.

31 Safwat, ibid, p. 195. For a similar claim, see 'Alluba, *Filastin*, p. 10; Ramli, *al-Sahyuniyya*, p. 167.

32 Al-Qusari, *Harb filastin*, p. 41. See also, Muhammad Farid Abu Hadid, *al-Thaqafa*, 24

Hazim Saghiya, a Lebanese liberal intellectual and editor of the daily *al-Hayat*, who is one of the leading propagators of a new Arab approach toward the Holocaust, contended that the Palestinians were envious of the Jews, who became the "model of victimhood" and of their "profitable" tragedy. Hence, the Palestinians strove to be recognized as victims and at the same time denied the Holocaust, tried to minimize it, and adopted western propagandists who cast doubt on it.[33] Hillawi, Darwish and Saghiya contend that, by embracing this approach, whether they admitted it or not, the Palestinians "inherited the Jewish ideology of justice in regard to victimhood," as Ruth Linn and Ilan Gur-Ze'ev explained. "They aspire to become the 'David of the Holocaust with a stone in their hand,' and wish to demonstrate "the mutation of the 'Jew as victim.' Being in exile has created the Palestinian collective consciousness, and they see themselves as the real Jews, victims in exile."[34] Therefore, they have preserved the refugee camps as the visible presentation of victimhood, and a living symbol of both Israeli oppression and universal injustice and aggression.[35]

The predominant public opinion outside Israel, explained Lebanese commentator Jihad al-Khazin in May 2006, is that "the real victims today are the Palestinians, who took the place of the Israelis as a persecuted, dispersed and humiliated minority," and even the Holocaust does not generate the same feelings of compassion toward them.[36] In his two visits to Yad Vashem, Palestinian activist Ghasan 'Abdallah admitted that he couldn't but feel a sense of "déjà vu," realizing the resemblance between the images exhibited and what happened to the Palestinians. The dehumanization of the enemy, especially the victim, is the same, just "change the word 'Arab' in Israel with 'Jewish' in Germany," the 'yellow star' with the orange identity card or the special car-plate number, and the artificial division of the Palestinians into Druze and Muslims, Bedouins and Christians, displaced and unrecognized, pre-

---

November 1952, pp. 3–5.

33 Saghiya, *Difa'an*, pp. 67–8. See also, Samir Kassir, "La Nakba recommence?" *Revue d'Etudes Palestinnienes*, vol. 17, no. 69 (automne 1998), pp. 61–3; Qaymari, "The Holocaust," pp. 150–1.

34 Linn and Gur-Ze'ev, "Holocaust," p. 195. See also Gur-Ze'ev, *Philosophy*, p. 105.

35 Gur-Ze'ev, *Philosophy*, p. 203; Qaymari, "The Holocaust," pp. 151–2.

36 *Al-Hayat*, 15 May 2006. According to Jordanian Islamist weekly *al-Liwa'*, 'Ali Sa'ada published in 2001 a book entitled "The Palestinian Holocaust. The History of Violence against the Palestinians ... The Collective Annihilation" (*al-Hulukust al-filastini. Ta'rikh al-'unf didd al-filastiniyyin ... al-ibada al-jima'iyya*). Sa'ada, who reportedly relies on "western historians and particularly Norman Finkelstein," began his book with a discussion of the Holocaust industry after the 1967 Arab–Israeli war. *Al-Liwa'*, 27 June 2001.

1967 and after, he suggested, ignoring the differences between the two cases and implicitly minimizing the Holocaust. Even the illegal Jewish immigration after World War II and the Warsaw uprising in 1943 reminded him of the illegal attempts of Palestinians to return to their homes and villages after 1948–49 and of the situation of the refugee camps in Lebanon.[37]

The comparison between the sufferings of the two peoples was dominant in the discussion of the German reparations to Jewish survivors and the State of Israel. The Arab countries tried to connect this issue to the compensation of Arab refugees who lost their property in Palestine (see Chapter 2).[38] Moreover, the Jews raised a hue and cry over their grievances and were being compensated with money and sympathy, whereas the Palestinian Arabs received neither fair treatment nor compensation.[39] The renewed Jewish effort for the restitution of Nazi victims' property in the mid-1990s gave rise to similar demands for compensation in the Arab discussion of the issue (see also below). Who would compensate the Palestinians for their loss of lands and assets, wondered *al-Ahram* editor Ahmad Bahjat.[40] Rami Khouri, who expressed his admiration for the Jewish determination to pursue Nazi criminals and demand moral and material compensation, expected "a significant body of Jews and Israelis" to acknowledge the valid Palestinian claim for compensation or return of property and other assets that they lost during the establishment of the State of Israel.[41] London-based Palestinian scholar Ghada Karmi emphasizes the "striking contrast" between the moral attitudes and practical steps taken towards resolving the issue of compensation for Jewish victims of Nazism and those towards rectifying outstanding Palestinian losses from 1948 onwards,"[42] overlooking the Arab role and responsibility in creating the refugee problem, and the parallel refugee problem resulting from the Jewish exodus from Arab countries.

---

37   Ghasan 'Abdallah, "Filastini fi al-sarh al-tadhakkuri lil-hulukust", *Hawliyyat al-Quds*, 1 (Autumn 2003), pp. 57–8. The same article was published also in *Jerusalem Quarterly File*, no. 15 (Winter 2002).

38   *Al-Ahram*, 12 September 1951, 16 November, 15 December 1952.

39   Mahmud, *al-Yahud wal-jarima*, p. 193. This argument had been repeatedly raised almost in the same wording. See, for instance, *al-Ahram*, 6 February 2001; *al-Dustur*, 10 October 2004.

40   *Al-Ahram*, 5 May 1997. Similar themes appeared in Hizballah's *al-'Ahd*, 11 April, *al-Majd*, 5 May, 15 December, *al-Watan* (Qatar), 6 March 1997.

41   *Jordan Times*, 25 February 1997.

42   Ghada Karmi, "The Question of Compensation and Reparations," in Karmi and Cotran (eds.), *The Palestinian*, p. 197.

Recognition and apology

In the public debate on the Nakba in 1998 it was argued that the motif of victimhood should turn into a call to the world to recognize its guilt towards the Palestinians, and a demand to be added "to the list of Holocaust victims" and to be entitled to restitution. For the Palestinians, as for the Jews, Karmi asserted, the quest for recognition was a moral one – of which material compensation was but one aspect. Recognition entailed also the acknowledgment of the responsibility for the Nakba by Israel and by the West, which was blamed for hastening to relieve its conscience after the Holocaust by granting a state to the Jews. "The essence of the Palestinian grievance is not only that they lost their homeland, but that the perpetrators have consistently refused to make reparation or even to acknowledge their responsibility in the matter."[43] The Palestinian tragedy became invisible, she maintained, and "no one understood the full human cost of that ethnic cleansing."[44] Rashid Khalidi also points to the "unremitting pressure from the Israeli side for more than 50 years to ignore, diminish and ideally to bury the whole question of the Palestinians made refugees in 1948," and writes that "the key requirement for a solution is not so much compensation (important as it is), as acceptance of responsibility and some form of atonement."[45] The denial of the Palestinian tragedy is similar to denial of the Holocaust, "with all the allowances necessary when making comparisons between situations which are inherently dissimilar," he concludes.[46]

Nadim Rouhana, another Palestinian scholar, who claims that Israel denies both the means of which the project of establishing a Jewish state was achieved and the consequences for the Palestinian people, explained that "in order to avoid the moral implications," Israel developed "a massive and sophisticated denial mechanism" for dealing with its own history.[47] Both sides identify themselves as victimized by the other, and "there is an underlying fear that the acknowledgement of the tragedy of the 'other' will justify moral superiority and imply acceptance of their collective rationale. For the Palestinians, accepting the

43 Ibid., p. 201.

44 *Al-Ahram Weekly*, 15 April 1999. See also *al-Ahram Weekly*, 6 April 2000.

45 Khalidi, "Truth," in Karmi and Cotran (eds.), *The Palestinian*, pp. 221–2.

46 Ibid., p. 225–6.

47 Nadim Rouhana, "The Holocaust and Psychological Dynamics of the Arab-Israeli Conflict," paper submitted to the Third World Views of the Holocaust Conference, Boston, April 2001, www.violence.neu.edu/Nadim.Rouhana.html. See also Nadim N. Rouhana, "Zionism's Encounter with the Palestinians: The Dynamics of Force, Fear, and Extremism," in Robert I. Rotberg (ed.), *Israeli and Palestinian Narratives of Conflict. History's Double Helix*, Bloomington: 2006, p. 115.

Jewish pain around the Holocaust means accepting the moral ground for the creation of the State of Israel. For the Israelis, he claims, accepting the pain of the 1948 Palestinian refugees means sharing the responsibility for their plight and their right of return."[48]

The denial of the Palestinian catastrophe was also introduced as a motive behind the denial of the Holocaust by the Palestinians.[49] Joseph Massad compared the "obscene number games on the part of holocaust [sic] deniers" to Zionist Jewish denial of the Palestinian Nakba and to the continued Zionist tendency to play down the number of Palestinian refugees. "While the Nakba and the holocaust are not equivalent in any sense," he contended, "the logic of denying them is indeed the same." He falsely claimed that the PLO and most Palestinian intellectuals had expressed since the 1960s their solidarity with Jewish Holocaust victims and had attacked those who denied it, unlike the official and unofficial Israeli denial of the expulsion of the Palestinians.[50] Following the cancellation of Palestinian Authority chairman Yasir 'Arafat's visit to the Holocaust Memorial Museum while on a visit to Washington in January 1998, Bilal al-Hasan, in al-Sharq al-Awsat, identified the debate over this issue among the Palestinians not with their refusal to acknowledge that the Holocaust took place, but "because the Israelis refuse to acknowledge the holocaust they have inflicted on the Palestinians." No one in Europe and America had yet acknowledged that "they set in motion this new holocaust," he said.[51] Reporting on an American administration's fund for Holocaust survivors, Egyptian paper al-Akhbar accused the United States of ignoring the Palestinian victims' rights and turning a blind eye to Israel's crimes against the Palestinians, which are no less barbaric than the "so-called crematoria."[52]

The Holocaust as an excuse for Israel to shun responsibility for its actions toward the Palestinians was also implied in Edward Said's claim that Israel should recognize its historical responsibility in relation to the Palestinian tragedy.[53] The Palestinian People's Appeal, issued during the commemoration of the Nakba in 1998, called upon the world "to undertake not only recognition of guilt and ad-

---

48   Dan Bar-On and Saliba Sarsar, "Bridging the Unbridgeable: The Holocaust and Al-Nakba," *Palestine-Israel Journal*, vol. 11, no. 1 (2004), p. 67.

49   Mahamid, *al-Filastiniyyun*, p. 9.

50   *Al-Ahram Weekly*, 9 December 2004.

51   *Al-Sharq al-Awsat*, 27 January 1998. For additional views in this vein see Ray Hanania, "Arafat and the Holocaust Museum," *Palestine Times*, January 1998. The Ingenious Circle in Washington, www.Hebron.com.

52   *Al-Akhbar*, 2 April 1999.

53   *L'Orient le Jour*, 5 July 1999.

mission of culpability in relation to the Palestinian people, but also to undertake an active and massive process of rectification to secure the implementation of Palestinian rights."[54]

Another moral aspect deriving from the acknowledgment of the Palestinian tragedy was the demand for an official apology as part of the reconciliation process. The apologies made to the Jews by Spain, France and Portugal and by Pope John Paul II in his 16 March 1998 document "We Remember: Reflections on the Shoah" prompted an expectation among Arab writers of an explicit apology by Israel and Britain to the Palestinians.[55] The contention that "the Nakba is the moral heir of the Holocaust,"[56] and that Israel should acknowledge its responsibility for the Palestinian tragedy, apologize for it and pay compensation, exactly as the Germans did, was also raised in the wake of the Stockholm International Forum on the Holocaust held in January 2000, and the Pope's visits to Egypt, Jordan, Israel and the Palestinian Authority in February and March 2000. Ghasan 'Abdallah asserted that such an apology resulting in Palestinian forgiveness was imperative to the acceptance of Israel as a normal state among the nations (see also Chapter 4).[57]

The argument that the Palestinian Nakba is being ignored by the international community (despite the extensive preoccupation of the UN with the Palestinian issue), whereas a great attention is given to the Holocaust, was dominant in the Arab debate over the UN decision to commemorate sixty years since the liberation of Nazi concentration camps in January 2005 and the resolution to designate 27 January as the international Holocaust Memorial Day (see below). Linking "Auschwitz and Palestine," al-Hayat editor 'Abd al-Wahhab Badrakhan complained that the event and Kofi Annan's failure in his speech to mention the Palestinians, who had paid the price for Israel's ascent from the ashes, constituted an organized denial of the Palestinian catastrophe.[58] Why had Annan decided to commemorate the "so-called" Holocaust when so many scholars and European

54   *The Palestinian People's Appeal*. See also *al-Hayat*, 20, 21 January, 15 May, *al-Ahram Weekly*, 14 May, *Jordan Times*, 9 May, *al-Sharq al-Awsat*, 27 January, 11, 18, 25 May, *al-Quds*, 16 February, 15 May 1998; "1948–1998 in the Eyes of Two Peoples," pp. 24, 31, 33.

55   *Al-Ahram*, 22 March, *Al-Quds*, 24 April 1998; interview with Rashid Ghannoushi, 10 February, MSANEWS, 12 February 1998.

56   *Al-Hayat*, 21 May 2000.

57   'Abdallah, "Filastini," p. 59.

58   *Al-Hayat*, 27 January 2005. For a discussion of the Arab reaction to the international Holocaust Memorial Day, see also chapters on Arab Countries in *Antisemitism Worldwide* 2004, 2005, www.antisemitism.tau.ac.il.

researchers doubted it and when the Palestinian Nakba was totally ignored, wondered Nawwaf al-Zaru.[59]

More militant Palestinians called for the establishment of a special tribunal to sentence Israeli "war criminals" for crimes committed against Palestinians.[60] In mid-July 2001, the fourth "Arab regional conference against racism" was held in Cairo, with the participation of about seventy Arab and international human rights organizations. The conference, which convened under the slogan "together to put an end to the last racist regime," dealt extensively with so-called "Israeli racism," and called for the establishment of an international court for the trial of "Israeli war criminals."[61]

With this goal in mind, the Arab and Muslim delegations sought to turn the World Conference against Racism, Racial Discrimination, Xenophobia and Related Intolerance, which convened in Durban, South Africa at the beginning of September 2001, into an international tribunal against Zionism and Israel. Hence, they concentrated their efforts on removing references to anti-Semitism, trivializing the Holocaust and, most of all, reintroducing the equation between Zionism and racism into the conference's resolutions. The Arab media coverage supported these attempts by publishing countless articles stressing the "Zionist crimes" against the Palestinian people and the Arabs.[62]

Redemption and reconstruction

Other aspects of Holocaust terminology have been cast into the Palestinian discourse. "Destruction and redemption" (*shoah u-geula*), "Holocaust and rebirth" (*shoah u-tehiya*), turn into "Nakba and resistance" (*nakba wa-muqawama*), "perseverance and resistance" (*israr wa-nidal*).[63] Zurayq and other early

---

Al-Dustur, 27 January 2005. See also, al-Dustur, 30 January 2005.

60   Al-Hayat, 28 April, al-Hayat al-Jadida, 11 May 1998.

61   Al-Sharq al-Awsat, 18, 21, 22, 23 July, al-Ahram al-'Arabi, 21 July, al-Hayat, 23 July 2001.

62   Michael Colson, "Durban and the Middle East: Challenges for U.S. Policy," Washington Institute for Near Eastern Policy, *PolicyWatch*, no. 548, 1 August 2001; al-Sharq al-Awsat, 10, 16 August, al-Ba'th, 26 August, Tishrin, 1, 3, 4, 6, 8 September, al-Akhbar, 2 September 2001. See also the declaration of the International Conference of Non-Governmental Organizations Defending Palestinian Rights adopted in Tehran on 23 April 2001, *Middle East Affairs Journal*, vol. 7, nos. 1–2 (Winter/Spring 2001), pp. 235–9. William Miles gave a rather different interpretation to the position of Arab and certain Muslim states on the Holocaust at Durban. He falsely assessed that their vitriolic linkage of the Holocaust to the Arab–Israeli conflict did not reflect "Holocaust denial or dismissal," since their delegations invoked the Holocaust "in apparent (if propagandistic) sympathy for its European Jewish victims." Miles, "Third World," p. 372.

63   Al-Hayat, 19 April, al-Quds, 15 May 1998.

writers on the Nakba, as well as Arab leaders such as Egyptian president 'Abd al-Nasir, referred to the potential of the Nakba to turn into a cathartic experience leading to reform and reconstruction.[64] The idea of the refugees' return and the emphasis on the temporary life in exile (*ghurba*) were a central theme in Palestinian national narrative, despite the growing vagueness, as time went by, of the feasibility and extent of the return and the ways of its implementation. The concept of "the right of return" (*haqq al-'awda*) can also be seen in relation to its Israeli counterpart, "the law of return" recognizing the legitimate right of each and every Jew to immigrate to the ancestral homeland.

The increasing belief in the realization of national aspirations in the wake of the 1993 Oslo Agreements affected the Palestinian perception of victimhood. From marking the demise of the Palestinians, in contrast to the establishment of the state of Israel, the Nakba was reconstructed as a founding myth to shape the memory of the past as well as to serve as a springboard for a hopeful future. It was identified as an event with "a great emotional charge and strong legitimizing value," which "has the taste of tragedy" needed for building collective identity.[65] "We do not seek to be captives of history or victims of the past. The Palestinian people have launched a redemptive journey to the future. From the ashes of our sorrow and loss, we are resurrecting a nation celebrating life and hope."[66] These words of the official Palestinian People's Appeal, issued on 14 May 1998 by the PNA and read by Palestinian poet Mahmud Darwish at the end of the march commemorating the fiftieth anniversary of the Nakba, speak for themselves.

Commemoration and memorialization

"The feeling of 'being victims' is normally based on solid individual and collective experiences during protracted violent conflict. These experiences gain a powerful grip on identity construction, however, when they are transformed in the collective memory into myths and transmitted from one generation to the next through memoirs and family stories, school books and national symbolic acts and festivals."[67] The Jewish experience of documentation and memorialization has undoubtedly set an example for the Palestinians, as for other ethnic groups. The commemoration of the fiftieth anniversary of the Nakba seemed to

---

64   See, for instance, Zurayq, *Ma'na*; Walid Kamhawi, *al-Nakba wal-bana'. Nahwu ba'th al-watan al-'arabi*, Beirut: 1956; Nadim al-Bitar, *al-Fa'iliyya al-thawriyya fi al-Nakba*, Beirut: 1965; Harkabi, *Arab Attitudes*, pp. 381–3.

65   Ada Lonni, "Parallel Strategies," p. 76.

66   *The Palestinian People's Appeal.*

67   Bar-On and Sarsar, "Bridging the Unbridgeable," pp. 64–7.

provide an appropriate point of departure for the documentation and memorialization of the Palestinian story. Scholarly accounts on the 1948 war, as well as personal testimonies of survivors, were published during the early months of 1998 in series of articles in Palestinian periodicals and dailies. Special sections on the internet sites of the Palestinian Authority and the Khalil Sakakini Cultural Center were devoted to events and testimonies of 1948, and young Palestinians in refugee camps engaged in making films and video diaries about the refugees and camp life.[68] Historian Walid Khalidi, who was one of the first to embark on the project of documenting Palestinian history, published a new book entitled in Arabic *Lest We forget* (*Kay la nansa*) (in English *All That Remains*), in which he surveyed the 418 Arab villages in Palestine destroyed in the wake of the 1948 war. Oral history was part of the campaign of history recording. This included personal accounts, especially of Palestinian refugees, and even engaged in investigating Palestinian camp women as tellers of history[69] – perhaps also reflecting the shift from high rhetoric to the personal experience in the memorialization of the Holocaust in Europe and in Israel.

Another means of memorialization of the Holocaust is the museums and the memorials. Probably agreeing that the subtext of a memorial museum is "that by virtue of prior suffering, collective existence should be recognized and honored by the wider civic culture,"[70] Palestinians have become increasingly aware of the need to have a museum or memorial which records their suffering. Attempts are being made to build up a national museum to restore the heritage and formulate the national ethos, both as a political tool for preserving the national entity and as an effective way to mobilize the people into a process of national struggle to gain their legitimate rights. Palestinians stress folklore, costumes and wedding traditions, in addition to preserving symbols of the Nakba – keys of the refugees' original houses and original names of villages and towns. "All this and other forms of identification recall the Israeli attempts to create a part of their national ethos out of the Holocaust."[71] Hence, some writers suggested erecting a Palestinian center to commemorate the Palestinian catastrophe and heroism, or an Arab museum for "Zionist victims," as a suitable answer to all the Jewish memorials "effectively used by the

---

68   *Al-Ahram Weekly*, 19 February 1998; Rosemary Sayigh, "Dis/Solving the Refugee Problem," *Middle East Report*, no. 207 (Summer 1998), pp. 19–23.

69   Rosemary Sayigh, "Palestinian Camp Women as Tellers of History," *Journal of Palestine Studies*, vol. 27, no. 2 (Winter 1998), pp. 42–58; "Reflections on al-Nakba," *Journal of Palestine Studies*, vol. 28, no. 1 (Autumn 1998), pp. 5–35; *Palestine Times*, no. 84 (June 1998); *Jordan Times*, 20 April 1999; *Ha'aretz*, 16 November 1999.

70   Charles Maier, "A Surfeit of Memory?" p. 145.

71   Qaymari, "The Holocaust," p. 151, 159.

Israelis and Zionists to keep the world's conscience agitated and troubled."[72] Following the Pope's visit to Yad Vashem, Palestinians called again for the establishing of a parallel museum – "a Nakba museum" as "a mute expression" to play a similar role in convincing the world of their tragedy.[73] Impressed by the Jewish devotion to remembrance, Ghasan 'Abdallah suggested that the way the Jews honor their dead should serve as a lesson for the Palestinians when they establish their memorial.[74]

The major effort in this direction was made by a group of Jews and non-Jews in 1995. They launched the Deir Yasin Remembered project, aiming at building a permanent memorial at the site of the former village of Deir Yasin, within sight of the Yad Vashem Holocaust memorial center. "Deir Yasin Remembered has grown out of the voice and vision of those, like Elie Wiesel, who extol the virtues of remembering and never forgetting the suffering of any people," wrote Daniel McGowan in the preface of his book *Remembering Deir Yassin*. He defined the goal of the project as "the resurrection of ... [an] important piece of Palestinian history as a way to create a future where Israelis and Palestinians can live together in a just and equitable way."[75] Deir Yasin, which was constructed over fifty years as a symbol of the Nakba, "a key element in the Palestinian transformation of the events of 1947–49 into a cosmic injustice,"[76] was becoming the focus of memorialization and another manifestation of the changing perception of the Nakba. Rami Khouri, considered the proposed venture as part of a necessary process of mutual rehumanization and transformation of the cycle of mutual denial into "a more morally responsible and historically constructive cycle of acknowledgement of the past, understanding, compassion and ultimately, forgiveness and reconciliation."[77] Khouri's words on the Deir Yasin Remembered project are perhaps the most explicit expression, linking the reconstruction of the meaning of the Nakba and the revision of the Holocaust representation in the Arab world (see below). The two processes developed simultaneously and independently but were interrelated, deriving from the peace process and the changing perception of the Arab-Israeli conflict.

72   *Al-Hayat*, 4 February, *al-Ahram*, 27 May 1998; Khalidi, "Universal Jubilee," p. 56.

73   *Al-Hayat al-Jadida*, 25 March 2000.

74   'Abdallah, "Filastini," p. 58.

75   Daniel A. McGowan and Marc H. Ellis (eds.), *Remembering Deir Yassin. The Future of Israel and Palestine*, New York: 1998.

76   Kimmerling and Migdal, *Palestinians*, p. 152.

77   *Jordan Times*, 22 April, *Ha'aretz*, 24 April 1997.

Conclusions

The usage of Holocaust metaphors brings to the fore a crucial question in the discussion of the Holocaust as a unique Jewish experience versus its universalistic meaning. The controversy over this issue continues unabated as the corollary of the process of turning the Holocaust into a yardstick of all evil and of universalizing its memory by the international community, which reached its peak with the designation of 27 January as international Holocaust Memorial Day. Quoting David Newman, an Israeli scholar from Ben Gurion University, *Syria Times* argued that "a country that continually uses, and all too often manipulates, Holocaust imagery to justify its policies of self-defense and 'never again,' cannot complain when the rest of the world uses those same standards to make judgments concerning its own policies."[78]

Renowned Israeli Holocaust scholar Yehuda Bauer contends that the term "Holocaust" has become flattened in the public mind because any evil that befalls anyone anywhere becomes a Holocaust – Vietnamese, Soviet Jews, blacks in American ghettoes, women suffering inequality, and so on. The Holocaust is both the name of a specific, unique event in recent history, and also a generic concept: the planned total annihilation of a national or ethnic group on the basis of a general ideology. The uniqueness of the Holocaust does not lie in numbers and not in the method of mass destruction, he explains, but in the existence of two elements: planned total annihilation of a national or ethnic group, and the quasi-religious, apocalyptic ideology that motivates the murder. Hence, "the universal implications of this unique event are precisely in its uniqueness."[79] A similar view was introduced by American Jewish historian Lucy Dawidowicz in her criticism of American curricula which expanded in the 1980s the list of victims of Nazi genocide and applied the history of the Holocaust to the American civil rights movement and other social action groups.[80] Researcher Wendy Zierler even showed that Holocaust comparison in the African American context has led, in some instances, to some hateful results.[81] American Jewish writer Cynthia Ozick was quoted as commenting, on the growing trend of using the Holocaust as metaphor in American literature and political discourse,

---

78   *Syria Times*, 25 February 2004.

79   Yehuda Bauer, "Whose Holocaust?" *Midstream*, vol. 26, no. 9 (November 1980), p. 45.

80   Lucy S. Dawidowicz, "How They Teach the Holocaust," *Commentary*, vol. 90, no. 6 (December 1990), pp. 25–32. For an analysis of the invocation of the Holocaust in the African American history, see Wendy Zierler, "'My Holocaust Is Not Your Holocaust': 'Facing' Black and Jewish Experience in *The Pawnbroker*, *Higher Ground* and *The Nature of Blood*," *Holocaust and Genocide Studies*, vol. 18, no. 1 (Spring 2004), pp. 46–67.

81   Zierler, "'My Holocaust Is Not Your Holocaust'", p. 49.

that "Jews are not metaphors," whereas American Jewish scholar Edward Alexander defined it as "stealing the Holocaust from the Jews," claiming that the exigencies of politics make it convenient to use Jews as metaphor for other people's sufferings.[82] This process began with small, innocent acts of distortion, he wrote, "with references to the curtailment of free lunch programs in Harlem as genocide, or its casual descriptions of Watts as a concentration camp, and of the ordinary black neighborhood anywhere as a ghetto." But since the Israeli victory in the June 1967 War, he maintained, "the rage and resentment against the Jews for refusing to be passive victims" has expressed itself mainly in the depiction of Israelis as Nazis and Palestinians as Jews. "The triumphant stroke in the campaign to steal the Holocaust from the Jews" by inverting the roles of the victim and the predator was the Arab and Soviet-inspired "Zionism is racism" UN resolution in 1975,[83] aiming at delegitimizing the Jewish state and the Jewish people.[84] "To make of the murdered Jews of Auschwitz and all the other killing centers metaphors for all humanity," he affirmed, "is not to exalt but to degrade them ... Those who deprive the dead Jews of their death are of necessity in collusion with those who seek to deprive the living Jews of their lives."[85] Likewise, he considered the efforts to recreate Palestinian Arabs as Jews "as a powerful symbolical statement of their resentment against the Jews" and of their wish to share *ex post facto* the Jews' Holocaust suffering.[86]

In contrast to Bauer, Dawidowicz and Alexander, William Miles[87] boasted that the Third World indigenized the Holocaust and its legacies in diverse manners. Eurocentric accounts of World War II and the Holocaust, he explained, "generally ignore linkages to the non-western world whereas Third World perspectives underline the relevance of the Holocaust to their own condition." The Holocaust resonates strongly with lethal outcomes of racism, and hence concepts associated with it, such as diaspora, reparations, concentration camps, became fundamental to the study of many Third World peoples and were incorporated into their narratives and literature.[88] He agrees that the Holocaust has become "a 'standard' of historical injustice; a 'touchstone of a consciousness of

82 Edward Alexander, *The Holocaust and the War of Ideas*, New Brunswick: 1994, pp. 6, 195.
83 Edward Alexander, "Stealing the Holocaust," *Midstream*, vol. 26, no. 9 (November 1980), p. 48–9; Alexander, *The Holocaust*, p. 197.
84 Alexander, *The Holocaust*, p. 197.
85 Alexander, "Stealing," p. 50.
86 Alexander, *The Holocaust*, p. 202.
87 Miles, "Third World Views," p. 375. The article presented the gist of deliberations of a conference under this title held at Northeastern University in April 2001.
88 Ibid., p. 379.

catastrophe'; an exemplary [case] for those who have suffered violence and degradation elsewhere" beyond the Euro-Atlantic world. Reparations for survivors turned into a model of legal justice, whereas the invocation of "H/holocaust parallelism" refers to collective self-identification with the Holocaust for instrumental reasons, such as "inciting western intervention, justifying punishment against perpetrators, constructing comparable memorials and garnering postgenocidal aid."[89] Although Miles is aware that "H/holocaust parallelism" can have a perverse instrumental dimension, he assumes that the indigenization of Holocaust study "is not only inevitable but, conducted with the appropriate caveats and sensitively, ought to be welcomed."[90]

Philosopher and sociologist Jean-Michel Chaumont, on the other hand, challenged the issue of Holocaust uniqueness and singling out of the Jewish suffering. This tendency, he warned, raises indignation among other groups of victims who interpret it as the banalization of their suffering and the monopolization of public attention by Jewish memory.[91] By analyzing the role of victimhood perceptions in "identity conflicts," he demonstrated the linkage between the struggle for recognition, assumption of responsibility and demand for compensation.[92] Historian Peter Novick and professor of educational psychology David Moshman go even further. Novick considers the claim of Holocaust uniqueness as an attempt to downplay the catastrophes of others, whereas Moshman contends that the Holocaust-based conceptions of genocide restrict the ability to recognize and understand genocides. Construed as the prototypical instance of genocide, the Holocaust has become the standard against which all other genocides, and purported genocides, are measured.[93] "Evaluating the relative evil and horror of specific mass atrocities is for the most part an impossible and pointless enterprise,"[94] he claims. Yet, to acknowledge other genocides "is not to deny the horror of the genocide that has most shocked the conscience of the world."[95]

This view is shared by Gur-Ze'ev, who believes that acknowledging the holocaust of others "does not imply forgetfulness of the Jewish Holocaust, nor

89   Ibid., p. 382.
90   Ibid., p. 389.
91   Chaumont, *La concurrence*, pp. 9–18.
92   Ibid., pp. 322–42.
93   Peter Novick, *The Holocaust and Collective Memory*, Bloomsbury: 2000, p. 9; David Moshman, "Conceptual Constraints on Thinking about Genocide," *Journal of Genocide Research*, vol. 3, no. 3 (2001), p. 433. See also Joseph Massad's review of his book, "Deconstructing Holocaust Consciousness," *Journal of Palestine Studies*, vol. 32, no. 1 (Autumn 2002), pp. 73–83.
94   Moshman, "Conceptual Constraints," p. 443.
95   Ibid., p. 448.

any diminution in the understanding of its uniqueness in the history of human evil."[96] Gur-Ze'ev derives his conclusion mainly from the Israeli–Palestinian encounter. Writing with Ruth Linn in a joint paper, he points to "a dialectic of negation" between the ways Palestinian and Israeli communities constructed their collective consciousness of the Holocaust. Each community has attempted to deconstruct the other's symbolic power and to reconstruct its own unique narrative of suffering, claiming to the self-righteous higher ground of ultimate victimhood, he contended.[97]

However, in contrast to Gur Ze'ev's claim, the competition for victimhood status, which naturally typified particularly the Palestinian national identity discourse, and the adoption of Holocaust metaphors, distorted the Arabs' perceptions of the Holocaust and drove them almost automatically to take a contentious stand over issues related to it. They created a moral equivalence between what happened to the Jews in Europe under Nazi domination and what is happening to the Palestinians at the hands of Israel, diminished the significance of the Holocaust and challenged its uniqueness. Whereas the wrong-doings toward the Jews were minimized, the injustice toward the Palestinians was magnified, leading to the dehumanization of Israel, Zionism and the Jews.[98]

To borrow from Miles' definitions, the Arabs have indigenized the Holocaust long before other Third World countries, despite the extensive extant denial discourse. Joseph Massad rejects the linkage between the Jewish Holocaust and the Palestinian Nakba. "It is Israeli and Zionist propagandists who make the link rhetorically, and many Palestinians accept the link at face value," he charges.[99] From a different vantage point, Ibrahim 'Allush also challenges the advisability of comparing the Palestinian suffering to the Holocaust. Yet, unlike Massad, who does not deny the Holocaust but contests what he considers as its appropriation by Zionism and Israel, 'Allush propagates Holocaust denial and regards the comparison of the Palestinian tragedy to the Jewish one as a confirmation of "the Holocaust's uniqueness myth."[100] The Arab discourse does not corroborate 'Allush's conclusion, but the comparison between the two tragedies unwittingly

---

96   Ilan Gur-Ze'ev, "The Morality of Acknowledging/Not-acknowledging the Other's Holocaust/Genocide," *Journal of Moral Education*, vol. 27, no. 2 (1998), pp. 171–2.

97   Linn and Gur-Ze'ev, "Holocaust", pp. 197, 203.

98   For a discussion of the representation of the Holocaust in the Palestinian discourse, see Meir Litvak and Esther Webman, "Perceptions of the Holocaust in Palestinian Public Discourse," *Israel Studies*, vol. 8, no. 3 (Fall 2003), pp. 123–41.

99   Joseph Massad, "Palestinian and Jewish History: Recognition or Submission?" *Journal of Palestine Studies*, vol. 30, no. 1 (Autumn 2000), p. 63.

100   *Al-Sabil*, 27 April 2004.

recognizes the Holocaust as a benchmark for evil and acknowledges that it took place, and at the same time minimizes its dimensions. The Arab response to the UN decision to commemorate the Holocaust is a case in point. Commentators did not deny the occurrence of the Holocaust, but rejected its uniqueness and compared it to other human tragedies, and specifically to the Palestinian one, accusing Israel and Zionism of manipulating its memory and of racism.[101] Syrian columnist and Minister of Information Buthayna Sha'ban contended that the slogan "never again" was important, but the manifestations of discrimination, aggression and violation of human rights continued in the European continent against Muslims, who were considered a security threat.[102] "Yes to humane commemoration, no to racism"[103] and to "the Holocaust industry,"[104] were typical titles and themes of editorials. Egyptian permanent representative at the UN ambassador Majid 'Abd al-Fattah even demanded the designation of another day for the commemoration of other genocides, such as in Rwanda, Bosnia and Cambodia.[105] The expanding Holocaust consciousness and learning around the globe[106] enhances the integration of its concepts and symbols into the Arab historical and moral framework as well as into the global contexts of racism, genocide and anti-imperialism, and may usher in a change in the perception of Holocaust uniqueness and universalism.

---

101 See for example: *al-Sabil*, 8 November, *al-Dustur*, 16 November, *Tishrin*, 22 November, *al-Badil*, 3 December, *al-Hayat al-Jadida*, 18 December, *al-Mustaqbal*, 19 December 2005.

102 *Tishrin*, 31 January 2005.

103 *Al-Sharq al-Awsat*, 5 November 2005.

104 *Al-Khalij*, 7 November 2005.

105 *Al-Ahram al-'Arabi*, 12 November 2005.

106 Miles, "Third World Views," pp. 373–9.

11

BREAKING TABOOS: THE NEW ARAB
DISCOURSE ON THE HOLOCAUST

In the wake of the collapse of the Soviet Union, which gave rise to the notion of
a new world order, the signing of the Israeli–Palestinian accords and the 1994
Israeli–Jordanian peace agreement, a revision of the Arab traditional approach
towards the Jewish Holocaust seemed to be emerging among liberal Arab intellectuals. Criticizing the prevalent Arab perceptions of the Holocaust, they called
for the unequivocal recognition of the suffering of the Jewish people, which
eventually would lead to the recognition of the Palestinian tragedy by the Israelis
and facilitate reconciliation and coexistence between the two peoples. The gist of
this new approach is the acknowledgement of the Holocaust as an undisputed
historical fact, a crime against humanity, and the separation of its human aspects
from its political repercussions. Prior to this call, a few Arab intellectuals and
activists, such as Israeli author and communist activist Emil Habibi and Palestinian Christian theologian Naim Stefan Ateek, referred to the Jewish tragedy,
recognizing its occurrence and its importance to the Jews. Ateek even urged the
Palestinians to understand it, while insisting that the Jews understand the importance of the tragedy of Palestine for them.[1] But it seems that these calls went
unheeded, whereas the new wave of writings in the mid 1990s, mainly by Arab
intellectuals living in the West and closely familiar with its culture, caused a rip-
ple effect and aroused a wide range reaction all over the Arab world.

The debate on the new approach coincided with, and was exacerbated by,
certain events and issues in the first half of 1998: the controversy over the proposed visit of 'Arafat to the Holocaust Memorial Museum in Washington in
January; Garaudy's trial in February and his subsequent tour to the Middle

---

1   Habibi, "Your Holocaust Our Catastrophe," pp. 26–7; Naim Stifan Ateek, *Justice and
     only Justice. A Palestinian Theology of Liberation*, New York: 1990, pp. 168–70. See also:
     Stephen Wicken, "Views of the Holocaust in Arab Media and Public Discourse," *Yale
     Journal of International Affairs*, vol. 1, no. 2 (Winter/Spring 2006), pp. 108–14.

East; and the response to the Pope's document "We Remember: Reflections on the Shoah" of 16 March.[2] This chapter examines the Arab response to these episodes and others which have surfaced since then, such as the restitution of Jewish property and the international initiatives to commemorate the Holocaust, and seeks to establish that the new discourse marked a significant turning-point in the Arab discussion of the Holocaust, expanding its dimensions and legitimizing variegated views. It brought the Holocaust to the fore and turned it into a major subject in the general Arab public discourse, yet it did not succeed in undermining the traditional and dominant approach, which considered it a matter that does not concern Arabs and continued to waver between denial and even justification of the suffering which befell the Jews.

Liberal Lebanese writer and one of the first propagators of the new approach, Hazim Saghiya, challenged the traditional Arab notion of "the Holocaust does not concern us" in a book supporting peace with Israel, contending that this notion resulted from a limited understanding of European history and modernity, laziness, lack of curiosity and a certain degree of opportunism. He blamed the Palestinians for concentrating on the adverse political dimensions of the Jewish tragedy. Since they failed to get recognition for their own tragedy, they were blinded and could not identify with the human aspect of the Jewish tragedy or show any sympathy.[3] The Arabs, claimed Saghiya, could surely not be blamed for the Holocaust, but as members of the international community they should not exclude themselves from responsibility for the calamity. In order to understand western and world sympathy toward Israel, the Arabs should try to understand the Holocaust. They should show more sensitivity toward and understanding of the Jewish tragedy in order to gain worldwide respect and sympathy for the Palestinian tragedy. Mutual sensitivity would help to overcome the barriers on the road to peace.[4]

"The history of the modern Arab world – with all its political failures, its human rights abuses, its stunning military incompetence, its decreasing production, the fact that, alone of all modern peoples, we have receded in democratic and technological and scientific development – is disfigured by a whole series of outmoded and discredited ideas, of which the notion that the Jews never suffered and that the Holocaust is an obfuscatory confection created by the

---

2   For a discussion of the Arab response to the document, see Chapter Four and *Anti-Semitism Worldwide 1998/9*, pp. 19–21.

3   Saghiya, *Difa'an*, pp. 63–9. Faysal Jalul, a Lebanese journalist living in Paris agreed with this criticism in his review of Saghiya's book, *al-Nahar*, 29 December 1997. See also: Kassir, "La Nakba recommencee?," pp. 61–3.

4   Saghiya, ibid., pp. 63–94; *Ha'aretz*, 21 March 1997; *al-Hayat*, 10, 14, 15, 18, 28 November, 18 December 1997.

Elders of Zion is one that is acquiring too much, far too much, currency," explained Edward Said.[5] He called for an act of comprehension that "guarantees one's humanity and resolve that such a catastrophe should never be forgotten and never again recur." Seeking bases for coexistence, Said claimed that a link existed between what happened to the Jews in World War II and the catastrophe of the Palestinian people, and unless this connection was recognized there would be no foundation for coexistence. He insisted that he did not attach conditions to the comprehension of and compassion for the Jewish tragedy; however, he believed that "such an advance in consciousness by Arabs ought to be met by an equal willingness for compassion and comprehension on the part of the Israelis and Israel's supporters."[6] Said, who accused Zionism and Israel of instrumentalizing the Holocaust for their ends, falls into the trap of instrumentalization by connecting the recognition of the two tragedies. "We must recognize the realities of the Holocaust not as a blank check for Israelis to abuse us, but as a sign of our humanity, our ability to understand history, our requirement that our suffering be mutually acknowledged." The Holocaust does not excuse Zionism for what it has done to Palestinians, he goes on to say. Hence, "by recognizing the Holocaust for the genocidal madness that it was, we can then demand from Israelis and Jews the right to link the Holocaust to Zionist injustices towards the Palestinians, link and criticize the link for its hypocrisy and flawed moral logic."[7]

The motif of mutual recognition of the Jewish and the Palestinian tragedies as a paramount element in any reconciliation between the two peoples is central to this approach, shared by Palestinian, Lebanese and North African writers and intellectuals. An acknowledgment of its centrality was expressed in the official Palestinian People's Appeal on the fiftieth anniversary of the Nakba, published in May 1998 (see Chapter 10). "While we extend a compassionable recognition of the unspeakable Jewish suffering during the horror of the holocaust [sic], we find it unconscionable that the suffering of our people be denied or even rationalized."[8] A historical reconciliation does not only mean recognition of past suffering and its importance to the collective memory of each people, but requires the creation of a new narrative which takes into account the histories of both peoples. "While neither people should be expected to change its national narrative, it will be necessary for both to take account of elements of

---

5   *Al-Ahram Weekly*, 25 June, *al-Hayat*, 30 June1998.

6   *Al-Hayat*, 5 November, *al-Ahram Weekly*, 6 November 1997; *Ha'aretz*, 20 February, *Le Monde Diplomatique*, August-September 1998.

7   *Al-Ahram Weekly*, 25 June, *al-Hayat*, 30 June 1998.

8   *The Palestinian People's Appeal.*

the other's," wrote Rashid Khalidi.[9] Said propagated the idea of a new joint Israeli–Palestinian narrative "free of ethnocentrism and religious intolerance."[10] Reading Palestinian and Jewish history together, he suggested, "not only gives the tragedy of the Holocaust and of what subsequently happened to the Palestinians their full force but also reveals how, in the course of interrelated Israeli and Palestinian life since 1948, one people, the Palestinians, have borne a disproportional share of pain and loss."[11] Sahgiya and Tunisian writer Salih Bashir pondered on the idea of a joint narrative of the vanquished and the victors. Reconciliation, they claimed, necessitated the assimilation of the history of each other and of their respective Holocausts.[12]

Another theme which is apparent in this new approach is the universalization of the Holocaust. The lessons from the Holocaust become universal moral values that serve as a bulwark for democracies against the threats of fundamentalism, extremism and racism, which target Jews and Muslims alike, argued Saghiya and Bashir. In recent years, they claimed, the Jews, whose consciousness had been shaped by the Holocaust, were losing the "monopoly" they held on human suffering. The increasing recognition of the Holocaust's significance, the expansion of the sphere of memory and the participation of other peoples in it, pointed to the expropriation of the Holocaust from limited Jewish possession, and its assuming a meaning and a message for all humanity. Only this broader perception of the Holocaust by the Jews, accompanied by a similar recognition by the Arabs, could lead to a real reconciliation in the Middle East. Defining the Holocaust as "the most complex and intractable knot in the Middle East conflict," they insisted on the "dissociation between the acknowledgment of the Holocaust and what Israel is doing," for the development of a discourse which says that "the Holocaust does not free the Jewish state or the Jews of accountability" for the Palestinian tragedy. Any injustice perpetrated by Israel against the Palestinians, they add, or any denial of their rights "will be tantamount to an infringement of the sanctity of the Holocaust, which has become a yardstick for universalistic values." Moreover, "if the memory of the Holocaust" comes between the Jews and "their capacity to coexist with that other people at whose expense the 'Jewish question' was solved, it will be a victory for Hitlerism after its defeat."[13]

---

9   Khalidi, "A Universal Jubilee?," p. 55. See also Bishara, "Response," p. 102.

10   *Al-Ahram Weekly*, 15 January, *Mitzad Sheni* (Monthly, Hebrew), May 1998.

11   *Al-Ahram Weekly*, 14 January 1999.

12   *Al-Hayat*, 18 December 1997, 15 May 1998.

13   *Al-Hayat*, 18 December 1997. The article entitled "Universalizing the Holocaust or breaking the Jewish monopoly over it," gained them the "Common Ground Award for

The new Arab approach gradually gained the support of further Arab intellectuals and writers, and evoked an intensive debate on the Holocaust in the Arab press. The readiness to accept the occurrence of the Holocaust is infiltrating into the Arab discourse, although not necessarily acknowledging its dimensions, uniqueness and meaning. Young Palestinians admitted, in an interview with an Israeli paper, that only after the beginning of the peace process did they begin to realize and understand the human tragedy experienced by the Jewish people.[14] In Egypt, whose intellectuals lagged behind the Palestinians and Lebanese in adopting the new approach, Amin al-Mahdi, a writer and one of the founders of the small Egyptian peace movement, proposed in his book *The Democracy Crisis and Peace*, published in 1999, the formation of a parliament for peace that would adopt in its founding proclamation an unequivocal denunciation of the "Holocaust and the suffering inflicted on the Jews," and at the same time denounce the "acts of terrorism" perpetrated by Zionist circles and the State of Israel.[15]

The outbreak of the al-Aqsa intifada at the end of September 2000, the stalling peace negotiations and the growing antagonism between Israelis and Palestinians curtailed the continued development of the new approach. The voices propagating it were on the defensive but did not disappear, and their impact had been reflected in statements, Arabs visiting Auschwitz and Holocaust museums, and Arab scholars participating in conferences dealing with the Holocaust. Jordan's Prince Hasan Bin Talal, brother of the late King Husayn, was among the special guests invited to a ceremony marking the rededication of the lone remaining synagogue in the Polish town of Oswiecem in September 2000.[16] Sayf al-Islam al-Qadhdhafi, the son of the Libyan President Mu'ammar al-Qadhdhafi, criticized on 7 January 2005 in Davos, Switzerland, those Arabs who deny the Holocaust, because it was a historical fact, discovered by the Red Army which liberated Auschwitz.[17] Several Palestinian scholars discussed the Holocaust from a Palestinian perspective in different academic forums. Nadim

Journalism in the Middle East" in 1999 (*Ha'aretz*, 21 February 2000). See also Bishara, "Response," p. 104; Salma Khadra Jayyusi, "The End of Innocence," in McGowan and Ellis, *Remembering*, p. 33; Matthijs Kronemeijer, *An Arab Voice of Compromise. Hazem Saghieh's "In Defence of Peace" (1997)*, Ultrech University: 2005, pp. 46–50 – igiturarchive.library.uu.nl/student-theses/2006–0324–082630/UUindex.html.

14   *Ha'aretz* magazine, 28 May 1999.

15   Amin al-Mahdi, *Azmat al-dimuqratiyya wal-salam*, Cairo: 1999, p. 258; *Ha'aretz*, 28 May 1999.

16   Satloff, *Among the Righteous*, pp. 182–3. Oswiecem had a thriving Jewish community before the Germans built the nearby death camp, Auschwitz, and turned it into the industrial core of the final solution.

17   *Al-Quds al-'Arabi*, 8 January 2005.

Rouhana, an Israeli Arab scholar, participated along with other Muslims in the "Third World Views of the Holocaust" conference, which took place in Boston in April 2001; Palestinian activist Ata Qaymari presented a paper on the Palestinian perspective at a conference held in Cyprus in 2004. The conference, co-sponsored by the Yakar Center for Social Concern, the Palestinian Center for the Dissemination of Democracy and Community Development (Panorama) and the Truman Institute at the Hebrew University, brought together sixteen Israeli and Palestinian academics and journalists to discuss shared histories. US-based Palestinian scholar Saliba Sarsar also wrote a paper on the Holocaust and the Nakba in cooperation with Dan Bar-On.[18] Moreover, according to an Israeli report from December 2005, the number of non-Jewish schools in Israel teaching the Holocaust was growing and Arab students from the Galilee were increasingly participating in workshops on the subject organized by the Ghetto Fighters' Museum (Beit lohamei hagetaot).[19] However, when the issue of teaching the Holocaust was raised in April 2000 in a symposium on "How to Strengthen Peace through Education," the Chairman of the Education Committee of the Palestinian Legislative Council (PLC), Musa al-Zu'but, rejected any attempt to include the history of the Holocaust in the Palestinian curriculum. "If the purpose is to express sympathy," added Ziyad Abu 'Amr, chairman of the PLC Political Committee, "this is useless for us ... We are in dire need of studying our own heritage." Hatim 'Abd al-Qadir, another PLC member and Fatah leader went even further, considering teaching the Holocaust "a great danger to the developing Palestinian mentality." If such a decision is made "it will undoubtely ruin the Palestinian dream and aspirations. It will entirely obliterate the past, present and future of the Palestinians."[20]

Two additional events symbolize the change in the attitude toward the Holocaust. Perhaps naturally, both occurred among Israeli Arabs, despite resistance and criticism from their peers. In December 2002, Christian Arab educator Father Emil Shoufani declared in Paris his initiative to launch a campaign "memory for peace" to learn "the Jewish pain" and "the origins of anxiety" which determined the Israelis' attitude toward the "other," to share the pain and eventually pave the way for better understanding and coexistence. Realizing the

18 Rouhana, "The Holocaust and Psychological Dynamics"; Qaymari, "The Holocaust;" Bar-On and Sarsar, "Bridging the Unbridgeable." The first academic paper on the Arab attitude toward the Holocaust was presented by Azmi Bishara in Germany in 1993 and later translated into Hebrew, see Bishara, "The Arabs."

19 Israel Radio, reshet b' site, 15 December 2005 – bet.netvision.net.il.

20 *Al-Risala*, 13 April, *al-Istiqlal*, 20 April 2000. For an extensive report on the controversy around this issue, see: *al-Quds al-'Arabi*, 11 April, *al-'Arabi*, 20 April 2000; Memri, Dispatch no. 187, 21 February 2000.

significance of the Holocaust in the Israeli psyche, he believed that "the memory of the Holocaust is the key for reopening the dialogue" between the Palestinians and the Israelis, which had been severed due to the intifada. He embarked on a venture that brought together 250 Arab and Jewish Israelis and a group of Muslims, Christians and Jews from France at the death camp of Auschwitz-Birkenau. The trip, which took place between 26 and 30 May 2003 after a period of joint learning about the Holocaust and exposure to the personal experiences of Jewish survivors, received the blessing of Egyptian as well Palestinian officials, including Yasir 'Arafat.[21] Shoufani's initiative was criticized particularly by Israeli Arabs who considered it a betrayal of the Palestinian cause for taking place at that specific time of Israeli–Palestinian fighting and ignoring a reciprocal Jewish recognition of the Palestinian tragedy.[22] Shoufani's views were not only a natural outcome of the new approach, but perhaps a further extension of its limits. Inspired by the philosophical writings of Emmanuel Levinas, particularly his conception of one's ethical obligation to the Other, Shoufani rejected any linkage between his will to share the Jewish pain and the acknowledgement of Palestinian suffering, insisting that the act of compassion is unilateral in order to "break the cycle of give and take that proved to be a vicious circle."[23] Similarly, Palestinian activist Ata Qaymari suggested that the Palestinians learn not to mix up their anger against occupation with a human reaction to the suffering of the other. "Such an attitude will help Jews not only overcome their trauma, but also to identify with the three forms of the Palestinian agony, namely, racial discrimination, occupation and exile."[24]

Unlike Shoufani, Israeli Arab lawyer Khalid Kassab Mahamid, who erected the first and only Arab museum of the Holocaust in April 2005, is not shy to link acknowledgement of the Holocaust with mutual recognition of the Palestinian tragedy. In the one-room museum in his law offices in Nazareth hang posters from Yad Vashem exhibiting the horrors of the Holocaust as well as posters displaying the flight of Palestinian refugees during the 1948 war and symbols of the Nakba, such as the key. He urges the Palestinians as well as all Arabs to learn about the Holocaust in order to understand the deep Israeli concern with security, assuming that such an understanding will enable them

---

21   *Ha'aretz*, 3, 5, 7 February, 27 May, *al-Sinara*, 7 February, 14 March, *Kul al-'Arab*, 7 February, 5 June, *Panorama*, 7 February, 30 May, 11 June, *al-Mashhad al-Isra'ili*, 2 May, *al-Sharq al-Awsat*, 25 May, *Ma'ariv*, 28 May, *Yedi'ot Aharonot*, 30 May 2003. A comprehensive account of Shoufani's worldview and initiative, see: Jean Mouttapa, *Un Arabe Face à Auschwitz. La mémoire partagée*, Paris: 2004.

22   Mouttapa, ibid., pp. 39–40; *Fasl al-Maqal*, 21, 28 February, 7 March 2003.

23   Mouttapa, ibid., p. 271.

24   Qaymari, "The Holocaust," pp. 152–3.

to counter Israeli argumentations and thus help the Palestinians achieve their political objectives.[25] Mahamid's instrumentalization of the acknowledgement of the Holocaust accurately reflects the new approach.

'Arafat's proposed visit to the US Holocaust Memorial Museum

In mid-January 1998, on the eve of a renewed round of talks between the Palestinians and Israelis in Washington, members of the State Department's Middle East team initiated the idea of 'Arafat's visit to the Holocaust Museum as a gesture of reconciliation that could improve the atmosphere of the Washington talks. 'Arafat agreed to the visit but the museum's board of directors refused to extend an official VIP invitation to him, thus creating a diplomatic blunder leading to the dismissal of Walter Reich, the museum's manager.[26] The cancelled visit turned into a subject of debate in Palestinian and Arab circles. Should 'Arafat visit the Holocaust Museum, and what did the visit signify? There were those who believed that the visit should take place so as to promote understanding and reconciliation; those who conditioned the visit on a mutual gesture of acknowledgement by Israel of the suffering it inflicted on the Palestinians; and those who absolutely rejected the visit.

'Arafat had reportedly a genuine interest in the Holocaust and was keen to visit the museum and witness for himself the woes suffered by the Jews during the war. The visit could give him an opportunity "to share with the Jewish people its historical pains and to bring the two peoples closer to each other," said his adviser and Israeli Arab Member of Knesset, Ahmad Tibi,[27] whereas journalist Bilal al-Hasan thought that if the visit had gone ahead it would have meant "bestowing a right on the Jews without obtaining a major right which they are withholding from him."[28] Considering the acknowledgement of the humanism of the other as "a civilizational imperative," American sociologist of Palestinian origin Halim Barakat wondered "why is it always necessary that the weak and the victim should acknowledge first the humanism of his strong, oppressor, ar-

25 Mahamid, *al-Filastiniyyun*; *Jerusalem Post*, 18 March, *Boston Globe*, 6 May, *Independent*, 17 May 2005; *Ha'aretz*, 24 February 2006. See also: www.alkaritha.org; Satloff, *Among the Righteous*, pp. 184–5.

26 *Ha'aretz*, 19, 25 January, 20 February, *Washington Post*, 21 January, *al-Hayat*, 25, 27 January 1998.

27 *Al-Hayat al-Jadida*, *al-Nahar*, 21 January 1998; Haitham Ibrahim, "'Arafat's Holocaust Museum Visit Lopsided Gesture" – Arol (Arabia on-line), www.arabia.com.

28 *Al-Sharq al-Awsat*, 27 January 1998. For additional views in this vein see: Ray Hanania in *Palestine Times*, January 1998; Fadwa Fawwaz, "Holocaust doesn't Justify Israeli Aggression – MSANEWS, 24 January 1998; The Ingenious Circle in Washington – www. Hebron.com.

rogant and relentless enemy?"[29] Saghiya praised 'Arafat's readiness to visit the museum and called on the Palestinians to intensify the demand for their inclusion in the list of the Holocaust's victims and, as such, for their compensation.[30] Rami Khouri, who visited the Holocaust Memorial Museum out of his belief that such a visit was "important to better understand the meaning and the place of the Holocaust in the lives of the Jews, Israelis, Arabs," saw the episode as "a missed opportunity." The key to resolving the Arab–Israeli conflict, he maintained, lay in acknowledging, addressing and removing the fears of both sides.[31] 'Arafat's acceptance of the invitation to visit the museum did not stem from his personal desire to do so but from a wise political calculation, claimed *al-Sharq al-Awsat*'s editor, 'Abd al-Rahman al-Rashid. The Holocaust, he argued, certainly happened and was a repugnant act, whether one soul was victimized or five million, and there was no base for its justification. Al-Rashid made a link between neo-Nazi activity and Hitler's Nazism, claiming that those among Muslims who doubted the Holocaust did not grasp that by doing so they concealed the persecution of Muslims by neo-Nazi racist groups in Germany and elsewhere in Europe. "We disagree with the Israelis almost on everything ... but we find ourselves with them in the rejection of Nazism."[32]

But, there were those who also dismissed the importance of the visit, based on the traditional Arab approach to the Holocaust. The Holocaust is not "an Arab complex," wrote *al-Hayat*'s editor, 'Abd al-Wahhab Badrakhan. "The Arabs do not have Holocaust accounts in their wars with Israel. It's the opposite way around. Israel used the Holocaust to justify its aggression against the Arabs." Dismissing the dynamic force of Holocaust denial in Arab thought, he complained that the suffering of the Jews was found in museums, whereas the suffering of the Palestinians under the Jews was a living reality, yet people were required to acknowledge the suffering in museums and ignore the living one.[33] Shafiq al-Hut, Palestinian member of the Palestine National Council (the PLO's parliament) and an opponent of the Oslo process, thought that 'Arafat was ill advised when he agreed to visit the museum. Al-Hut criticized the Arab writers who believed that changing the Arab position toward the Holocaust would lead to the end of the Arab–Israeli conflict and to historical reconciliation. The Holocaust became a problem for the Arabs with its politicization and sanctification, he claimed. However, no Arab or Palestinian could contest it

29   *Al-Hayat*, 27 January 1998.
30   *Al-Hayat*, 20 January 1998.
31   *Jordan Times*, 27 January 1998.
32   *Al-Sharq al-Awsat*, 22, 24, 25 January 1998.
33   *Al-Hayat*, 21 January 1998.

from a human or a religious perspective.[34] Twelve Jordanian opposition parties issued a statement on 17 January in which they berated Jewish claims about the Holocaust. If it materialized, 'Arafat's visit could deepen the gulf between the opposition and the establishment in the Middle East and expose the discrepancy between public opinion in the region and official policy, they warned.[35]

The Garaudy affair

The episode which triggered the most extensive debate was the publication of Roger Garaudy's book *Les Mythes fondateures de la politique Israelienne* in 1996, and his subsequent visits to the Middle East during that year and again at the beginning of 1998. It was the first Holocaust-related issue to arouse such an extensive debate since the Eichmann affair. Garaudy, a French philosopher and a former official of the Communist Party who converted to Islam in 1982, became a staunch critic of Israeli policies following the Israeli invasion to Lebanon. His book sought to tarnish what he considered as accepted and uncontested Zionist claims, and provided a comprehensive, systematic analysis of the allegedly erroneous historical roots of the Zionist-Jewish state from the Biblical period to Israel's political thought and praxis. The second part of the book, which deals with "the myths of the 20th century" – the myth of Zionist anti-Fascism, the myth of the Nuremberg trials, the "myth of the Holocaust" – aroused a great controversy in France, leading to his indictment according to the anti-racist Gayssot Law of 1990 banning Holocaust denial, and to his trial in February 1998.[36]

In contrast to the western reaction to Garaudy and his book, Arab intellectuals, writers, journalists, politicians and clergy embraced the man and his book, and he became a household name in discussions involving Holocaust denial. The book was translated into Arabic and several other publications containing compilations of his lectures, newspaper articles, and reflections on his writings were published in Beirut and Cairo.[37] The main themes that emerged in the discussions in 1996 included: the dangers of Zionism to the world; international Zionism's domination of world affairs; the racist traits of the Jewish state; Zionist collaboration with the Nazi regime; the fabrication of the Holocaust

34   *Al-Watan al-'Arabi*, 6 February 1998.

35   Arol, 21 January 1998 – arabia.com.

36   For a survey on Garaudy's visit to the Middle East and the debate in the Arab press in 1996, see *Antisemitism Worldwide 1996/7*, pp. 193–204; Esther Webman, "Rethinking the Holocaust. An Open Debate in the Arab World, 1998," in Porat and Stauber (eds.), *Antisemitism Worldwide 1998/9*, pp. 16–30.

37   See for example: Fawzi, *Jarudi wal-islam*; Wizarat al-I'lam, *Jarudi*, Cairo, no date.

myth for the financial and mental extortion of the West; the right of freedom of speech; the affair as part of the West's attack on Islam.

However, already in 1996 those themes which reflected the traditional attitude to Zionism and the Holocaust were accompanied by several exceptional voices that signaled the changing nature of the discussion over these issues. A Lebanese sociologist, Wadah Sharara, was perhaps the first to pose self-critical questions, although he did not suggest an alternative approach. "Why are we fascinated by people like Garaudy?" Since all the revisionist sources which deal with the Jewish question in World War II, as well as those which deal with the establishment of Israel, flatter the Arabs, is the Arab fascination a kind of revenge, reflecting hatred toward the West or a search for self-praise, he wondered.[38] An Egyptian member of the University of Hilwan called for the establishment of an international study group composed of experts in history, political science and the humanities, including Arabs, to research and reach a final conclusion on "the lie of the gas chambers."[39] Although intended to challenge the Jewish/Israeli narrative and even deny the Holocaust, this call for allegedly learning the facts was unprecedented and was voiced also by other Egyptians such as poet Ahmad 'Abd al-Mu'ti Hijjazi and 'Abd al-Wahhab al-Masiri. The latter, criticized the limited scope of Arab studies on the issue, their political nature and their linkage to the Arab–Israeli conflict. The concern with numbers of victims, the gas chambers and Israel's political exploitation of the Holocaust, he argued, lacked depth and complexity and did not touch upon the really important questions.[40] The Arabs and the Muslims "do not care if six million Jews were killed or more or less. This is a western problem," he elaborated in an interview.[41]

Garaudy was also condemned by some Arab writers. 'Abd al-Rahman al-Rashid criticized the unbalanced Arab approach to Garaudy. Nowhere in the world did people relate to his book as the Arabs did, he reasoned, while those familiar with Nazi history denounced it. Unfortunately, he concluded, the support of Garaudy stemmed from political considerations and from his hatred of the Jews.[42] Edward Said criticized Arab efforts "to enlist people like the degraded Roger Garaudy in order to cast doubt on the six million victims,"[43] and

---

38 *Al-Hayat*, 1 July 1996.

39 *Al-Sha'b*, 9 August 1996.

40 *Al-Ahram*, 16 October 1996; al-Masiri, *al-Sahyuniyya*, p. 11. For a discussion of his views, see above.

41 *Al-Liwa'*, 31 July 1996.

42 *Al-Majalla*, 29 December 1996. See also responding letter, *al-Majalla*, 26 January 1997.

43 *Al-Hayat*, 5 November, *al-Ahram Weekly*, 6 November 1997.

Hazim Saghiya referred to him as the anti-Christ and a crook – statements which provoked responses defending Garaudy and his brave stance.[44]

Two years after the publication of his book, on 7 January 1998, Garaudy's trial opened in Paris on charges of Holocaust denial and incitement for anti-Semitism according to the Gayssot law. The trial lasted for three days and the verdict was given on 27 February. He was convicted on the charge of disputing crimes against humanity and was fined 120,000 francs (US$20,000). He filed an appeal but lost and the appeal court even toughened the sentence, in mid-December, to a nine months' suspended jail term and a fine of 160,000 francs (US$28,000).[45]

The first quarter of 1998 witnessed "the second Garaudy wave" in the Middle East, as Wadah Sharara termed the plethora of articles in the Arab press in the wake of the trial opening and Garaudy's new round of visits to the Middle East to rally moral and financial support.[46] Under the slogan "Garaudy you are not alone," coined by Egyptian journalist Salah 'Isa,[47] the campaign of solidarity with Garaudy aroused an overwhelming reaction, far exceeding the warm embrace of 1996. Arab intellectuals, human rights activists, professional unions and political organizations were engaged in this campaign – setting up funds and gathering donations; issuing statements of support; submitting protests to the French embassies in Arab capitals; organizing rallies and marches; and holding seminars. An Arab lawyers' delegation, which included Egyptian 'Ali Hamid al-Ghatit and Moroccan Khalid al-Sufyani, reinforced Garaudy's defense team, and a Palestinian living in Switzerland, Tahir Shukri, gave a defense testimony. In his appearance before the court al-Ghatit compared Garaudy to Voltaire, Jean-Jacques Rousseau, Emile Zola and Egyptian writer Taha Husayn, all considered brave thinkers who defended truth and their beliefs. He attacked France for condemning a person seeking the truth and the Gayssot law as an infringement of free speech and thought.[48]

In the period between the hearings and the verdict Garaudy conducted a tour in the Middle East during which he visited Qatar, the United Arab Emirates

---

44   *Al-Hayat*, 12, 18 November, 4 December 1997.

45   *Al-Ahram*, 26 September 1998.

46   *Al-Hayat*, 28 February 1998.

47   *Al-Nahar*, 10 January 1998.

48   *Al-Ahram*, 10, 17, 19 January, 28 February, *al-Hayat*, 8, 9 January, 28 February, *al-Safir*, 9, 17 January, *al-Sha'b*, 13, 14, 20 January, *al-'Ahd*, 16 January, *al-Nahar*, 16, 28 January, 24, 28 February, *al-Da'wa al-Islamiyya*, 21 January, *Ha'aretz*, 26 January, 1 March, *al-Tasawwuf al-Islami*, February, *al-Ayyam*, 8 Februay, *al-'Alam*, 21 February, *al-Quds al-'Arabi*, 28 February, *Majallat Filastin*, March 1998; Arol, 11, 12, 15, 26 January, 28 February, AFP, 17 December 1998 – arabia.com.

(UAE) and Egypt. After the trial he also made a visit to Iran at the beginning of April.[49] Qatar was a major stop in his trip and the base of the Committee in Defense of Garaudy. The UAE papers called on their readers to send donations and messages of support to Garaudy and explained that the aim of the donations would be "to debunk Zionist allegations and to resist the Zionist influence in France."[50] The Arab Lawyers Federation, based in Cairo, raised funds independently and mobilized lawyers, journalists, writers, workers and doctors to join the committee in support of Garaudy.

In addition to the solidarity demonstrations held in Cairo, Jerusalem and Gaza in January, which ended with the submission of protest letters to the French embassy and consulate,[51] Garaudy attracted large audiences in each of the countries he visited. In Qatar a well-covered conference, under the auspices of Shaykha Muza, the wife of the Emir of Qatar, brought together several Arab Islamists, among them Shaykh Yusuf al-Qaradawi and the Egyptians Fahmi Huwaydi and Muhammad 'Amara. Qaradawi stressed the support of one billion Muslims for Garaudy's struggle against Zionism. Huwaydi compared the controversies evoked by Salman Rushdie and Garaudy in the West, a theme which was also raised by Garaudy and emerged in the many articles written on the affair.

The other major gathering which reportedly attracted huge masses was a seminar held at the Cairo International Book Fair. In his talk, as in most of his public appearances during his tour, Garaudy refrained from touching upon the issue of the Holocaust. He mainly concentrated on the US, Zionism and their unholy alliance, which could allegedly lead to a third world war and to a clash between the Judeo-Christian civilization and the Islamic civilization, perceived by them as barbaric and backward. He accused Zionism of controlling 95 percent of the world media, and attacked the Gayssot law as an unjust law that would inevitably lead to his condemnation.[52]

Among the staunch supporters of Garaudy were Islamic organizations and notable religious leaders. Garaudy met with Shaykh al-Azhar Muhammad al-Tantawi and with Egyptian Mufti Nasr Farid Wasil, the two highest religious authorities in Egypt. Wasil stated that it was incumbent upon every Muslim

49 Al-Sha'b, 9 January, Kayhan International, 20 April 1998. For a discussion of the affair in Iran, see: Litvak, "The Islamic Republic," pp. 261–3.

50 Arol, 12, 26 January; Independent, 1 February, al-Ayyam (Dubai), 12 February, al-Hayat al-Jadida, 10, 13 February 1998.

51 Al-Sha'b, 16 January, al-Risala, 22 January 1998.

52 Al-Hayat, 9, 17 February, al-Hayat al-Jadida, 13 February, Egyptian Gazette, 16 February, al-Ahram, 15, 16, 17 February, al-'Alam, 28 February, Ha'aretz, 19 February, al-Ra'y, 16 March 1998.

to defend Garaudy and stand by his side. Syria's Grand Mufti, Shaykh Ahmad Kuftaro, also expressed total support for Garaudy, saying he was "a free thinker who does not compromise his principles."[53] Hamas leader Shaykh Ahmad Yasin sent a support letter to Garaudy "the French Muslim intellectual," to stress that all the intellectuals in the world and all Muslims were behind him. He pointed to the double standards and the contradiction between the attitude of the West to Salman Rushdie, the author who defamed Islam but was embraced by the West as "a man of intellect" and to Garaudy who was being tried for speaking of the Jews.[54] Islamists tended to emphasize the dichotomy between Islam and the West and to present the trial as another manifestation of the hatred of the West and Zionism toward Islam and Muslims. Another proof brought up in this context was the attitude of the West to the Egyptian professor Hamid Nasr Abu Zayd (banished from Cairo University in 1995 for his modernist interpretation of the Qur'an) in comparison to the attitude to Garaudy.[55] Syrian Muslim scholar Muhammad Sa'id Ramadan al-Buti also attacked the West for its uneven treatment of Rushdie and Garaudy, and urged the Arabs and Muslims to adopt a unified stand and condemn the West.[56] The trial was "a badge of honor" on Garaudy's chest, wrote Muhammad 'Amara. Both 'Amara and Buti disputed Garaudy's interpretation of Islam but asserted that this controversy did not contradict the feeling of pride that every Arab and Muslim should feel toward him as he defended "our right cause in face of western hegemony and Zionist blackmail."[57] Garaudy's real crime, claimed Egyptian Rajab al-Banna, was his conversion to Islam.[58] In response to a question during his weekly Qur'anic lesson, Shaykh Muhammad Husayn Fadlallah also argued that Garaudy's problem was his "crossing all the red lines." First, he became a Muslim, arousing the European complex against Islam. Second, since the Jews control the European media, it was only natural that the freedom of speech in many western states corresponded to the freedom of the Jews to preserve their myths and fairy tales.[59]

---

53   *Al-Safir*, 13 January, *al-Sabil*, *al-Quds*, 13 January, *Independent*, 1 February, *al-Hayat*, 12 February, *al-Ayyam*, 19 February 1998, Reuters, 19 February 1998 – arabia.com.

54   *Filesteen al-Yawm* on line, 15 January 1998 – www. Palestine-info.org.

55   *Al-Sabil*, 13 January, *al-Sha'b*, 16, 20 January, 7 April, *al-Bilad*, 17 January, *Ha'aretz*, 20 January, *al-Risala*, 22 January, *al-'Alam*, January 1998.

56   *Al-Hayat*, 28 February 1998.

57   *Al-Ahram*, 20 March, *al-'Arabi*, May 1998.

58   *October*, 25 January 1998.

59   *Al-'Ahd*, 20 February 1998.

Garaudy's views were introduced to the Arab reader in various translations of his works. A translation of his book, with a preface by Muhammad Hasanayn Haykal, was published in 1998[60] and distributed at the Cairo book fair during Garaudy's visit. Chapters of the book were published in the Libyan paper *al-Jamahiriyya* during January. The full text of the Gayssot law, including Garaudy's critical view of the law, was published,[61] and Garaudy's book with his lawyer Jacques Verges on the trial's proceedings, *The Process of Liberty* was also translated into Arabic and published in several papers.[62] In addition to exposing Garaudy's views and expressing almost unconditional support, a major portion of the articles turned into a debate on the meaning and ramifications of the trial and the significance of his struggle.

Several themes seemed to emerge in the discussion: The trial and the Gayssot law were seen as flagrant violations of the basic freedoms of expression and thought, as an indictment against the West for its defunct democracy and moral double standards; the trial was said to be directed against Islam, since Garaudy was a Muslim thinker who defended an Arab and Muslim cause; and Garaudy was presented as both the persecuted Dreyfus and the savior of truth Emile Zola. "International Zionism" was accused of controlling world media and manipulating them for its needs; and the Jews of sanctifying the Holocaust in order to allow them to continue the mental and financial exploitation of the West – leading to the conclusion that research and revision of data on the Holocaust was legitimate, since there was no subject so sacred as to defy inquiries.

The statement of the twelve Jordanian opposition parties, which also referred to the proposed visit of 'Arafat to the Holocaust Museum in Washington mentioned above, described the trial as a "theatrical farce," exposing Zionism's influence on western media and society. It urged the public to condemn the trial and demanded that the Arab and Islamic media expose the so-called Zionism's plots and crimes, as well as propagate Garaudy's writings.[63] The Egyptian journalists' union announced on 10 January that the trial was conducted in contradiction to France's historical role as the cradle of civil liberties. A day later, the Palestinian Writers Association expressed support for Garaudy's "brave struggle" for the

60 Jarudi, *al-Asatir*. See also: Salih Zahr al-Din, *al-Khalfiyya al-ta'rikhiyya li-muhakamat rujih gharudi*, Beirut, 1998; Rujih Jarudi, *Muhakamat al-sahyuniyya al-isra'iliyya*, Cairo: 1999.

61 *Al-Nahar*, 14, 17 February 1998.

62 *Al-Ahram*, 9–23 February, *al-Hayat al-Jadida*, 10–22 February, *al-Dustur*, 9–25 February 1998. The versions were identical, differing only in the titles and sub-titles of the chapters.

63 *Al-Dustur*, 18 January 1998; Arol, 18 January 1998.

freedom of thought and called for donations to assist him.[64] The general manager of the Palestinian Authority Information Ministry, Sa'd Basisu, explained that Garaudy symbolized the French people's conscience and that he was tried for defending the truth.[65] Another PNA official, Ahmad 'Abd al-Rahman, stated that Garaudy should have the right to express his point of view on any subject, especially since no one argued with all the books and films about the Holocaust which "have told what happened to the Jews in an unbelievable and exaggerated manner."[66]

Garaudy's trial gave new impetus to the conspiracy theory of Jewish forces maneuvering behind the scenes of regional and international affairs. The Jews rule the world by laws, claimed Egyptian journalist 'Adil Hammuda.[67] The Gayssot law, explained lawyer 'Ali al-Ghatit, was enacted to incriminate anyone who demanded the return of occupied Arab lands.[68] The same Jewish hand that was behind the trial was behind the Monica Lewinsky affair and behind the banishment of British historian and Holocaust denier David Irving from various countries, wrote Egyptian editor of the French-language daily al-Ahram Hebdo, Muhammad Salmawi.[69]

The main discussions thus focused on the political aspects and implications of the affair for the Arab world. "Where are we in Garaudy's trial?" was the topic of a debate held by a Lebanese paper with Lebanese journalists – a topic which accurately reflected the questions raised in this debate and in interviews with a range of Egyptian intellectuals and journalists. "Is the trial a French affair or a democratic affair or another phase in our war with Israel?" Three positions seemed to emerge among the Lebanese. One considered the affair an internal French affair; one considered that the Arabs should take a stand on its more general aspects, such as the issue of freedom of expression; and one considered it an Arab affair, strongly connected to the Arab–Israeli conflict.[70] It is impossible to introduce the full range of opinions, but it can be safely assessed that the third position, which sought to focus on and expose Zionism and Israel's deeds

64   *Al-Hayat al-Jadida*, 11 January, *al-Hayat*, 15 January, *al-Safir*, 16 January, *Jerusalem Post*, 20 January, *al-Nahar*, 21 January, *Filastin al-Muslima*, February 1998.

65   *Al-Ayyam*, 16 January 1998.

66   *Reuters*, 19 January 1998. Similar statements of support were issued by other writers, lawyers, journalists, women and youth organizations in Lebanon, Syria, Morocco, Kuwait and Iran. *Al-Nahar*, 13 January, *al-Safir*, 14,15 January, *al-Ittihad* (Morocco), 28 January, *al-'Ilm* (Morocco), 4 February, *al-Bilad*, 21 March 1998.

67   *Ruz al-Yusuf*, 19 January 1998.

68   *Al-Ahram*, 24 January 1998.

69   *Al-Ahram*, 2 February, *al-Ahram Hebdo*, 4 February 1998.

70   *Al-Nahar*, 14, 16 January, *al-Safir*, 23 January 1998.

in "Palestine and South Lebanon," was the dominant one. This is even more strikingly so in relation to the Egyptians, among whom a stronger agreement prevailed. They emphasized the role of the Zionist lobby in hatching the trial and criticized the violation of civil liberties in France.[71] A few Egyptian writers even gloated over the exposure of the dubious democracy of the West.[72]

This consensus was broken by dissenting voices, mainly among Lebanese, Palestinian and North African intellectuals who rejected the support of Garaudy, questioned its motives and advisability, and found it at odds not only with the western position but also with the Arab and Palestinian cause. "The trial taking place in Paris does not involve the Arabs, the Muslims or even the Zionists," wrote Hasan Nafaa, a professor of political science at Cairo University, who wrote his PhD dissertation on Garaudy in the 1970s. "The Garaudy issue should be viewed in its true context: the trial of an independent-minded French citizen and the suppression of free opinion in a society which allows for the establishment of political parties such as the National Front."[73] Amina Rashid, the head of the Department of French Culture at Cairo University, also shared the view that the Gayssot law strengthened the Fascist trends in France.[74] Some critics saw the overwhelming Arab sympathy for Garaudy as an embarrassment, urging his supporters not to attack France or belittle the Holocaust. Others lashed out at Arab human rights activists campaigning in solidarity with Garaudy, while failing to raise their voices on countless rights violations on their own turf.[75]

Although there were scant direct references to Garaudy's views on the Holocaust in these discussions, they were perceived by several writers as endorsing Holocaust denial. Among them were the Lebanese Ibrahim al-'Ariss, Samir Kassir, Hazim Saghiya, Wadah Sharara, Hasan al-Shami and Faysal Jalul; Palestinians Edward Said, Majid 'Asqalani, Ray Hanania and Mahmud al-Rimawi; Tunisian poet Tahir al-Bakri and Saudi 'Abd al-Rahman al-Rashid. Rejecting the Holocaust-denial motifs, which appeared in Garaudy's book, these writers and academicians considered support of Garaudy to be a miserable choice of an inappropriate weapon in the struggle against Israel. Solidarity with Garaudy meant agreement with the European extreme right, which propagated Garaudy's views on Holocaust denial and harbored the same feelings of hate toward Ar-

---

71   *Al-Safir*, 23 January, *al-Nahar*, 28 January, *al-Ayyam*, 19 February 1998. See also Kassir, "La Nakba recommencee?," p. 62.

72   *Al-Ahram*, 31 January 1998.

73   *Al-Ahram Weekly*, 22 January 1998.

74   *Al-Nahar*, 28 January 1998.

75   *Al-Ahram*, 22 January, 18 February, *al-Ayyam*, 19 February, *al-Hayat*, 24 March 1998.

abs and Jews. Moreover, the adoption of his views, they warned, did not serve the Arab cause. It not only put the Arabs in opposition to the main prevailing current in the world but also perpetuated ignorance and error. Cherishing the myth of Holocaust denial could easily lead to the denial of the Palestinian cause. Attacks on Israeli policies or Zionism should hence be separated from the issue of the Holocaust, which was a historical fact and a deplorable crime against humanity.[76] Egyptian author Jamal al-Ghaytani thought the Arabs should not belittle the brutality of the Nazis against humanity,[77] and Christian Lebanese writer Joseph Samaha contended that what was done to the Jews by the Nazis should be deplored and that it was positive that Europe, which committed this crime, suffered from a guilt complex. Samaha, who believes that with the right approach the Arabs can bring their cause to the consciousness of the nations, also criticized the prevalent claim that the Holocaust established the State of Israel.[78]

There is no doubt, admitted Egyptian leftist writer Muhammad Sid Ahmad, that the Jews were persecuted in Western and Eastern Europe – persecutions which reached their peak with the Holocaust. But it was also true that after the war the Jews managed to exploit their advantage in the western media to expose the racist crimes against them and when the State of Israel was established the Palestinians became the oppressed of the second half of the twentieth century.[79] Several writers argued that the subject of the Holocaust became "a black box" or "a forbidden zone" for research and was capitalized by the Jews. If it was a closed subject, wrote Egyptian-based Palestinian writer Muhammad Khalid al-Az'ar, then its political and mental exploitation should also stop.[80]

A memorandum from Palestinian writers stressed that in no way did their solidarity with Garaudy mean belittling the sufferings of the Jews under the Nazis. Nevertheless, they implicitly engaged in relativization and soft denial when claiming that various peoples were the victims of the Nazis, and that the number of victims and the way they were victimized were legitimate subjects for revision.[81] Likewise, Palestinian Fu'ad Zaydan, who pointed to the millions

---

76 *Al-Jadid*, no. 22, Winter 1998, p. 40; *al-Hayat*, 13, 15, 20, 22, 23 January, 28 February, 12 March, 22 April, 11 May, *al-Bilad*, 26 February, *al-Nahar*, 16 January, 28 February, *al-Safir*, 19 January, *al-Sharq al-Awsat*, 24, 25 January, *al-Ahram Weekly*, 25 June 1998. For an analysis of Garaudy's opponents views, see *al-Nahar*, 27 January 1998.
77 *Al-Ayyam*, 19 February 1998.
78 *Al-Safir*, 23 January 1998.
79 *Al-Ahram, al-Ahram Weekly, al-Nahar*, 22 January, *al-Hayat al-Jadida*, 23 January 1998.
80 *Al-Quds*, 19 January, *al-Hayat*, 16 February 1998.
81 *Al-Risala*, 22 January 1998.

348

of non-Jewish victims of World War II, stressed that "the struggle against racist Zionism is also a struggle against the falsification of history in order to preserve its real place in the memory of humanity."[82] The Arabs, said 'Abd al-Wahhab Badrakhan, "do not deny this Holocaust but they put it in parentheses until the world (and Israel) will acknowledge the other holocausts which Israel perpetrated against the Arab world."[83] A US-based Jordanian academician, Ayman Hanna Haddad, found similarities in the approaches of Garaudy and Daniel Goldhagen to the Holocaust. They both dealt with a historical fact but while one diminished it, the other exaggerated it. They both presented a radical interpretation and reached unscientific conclusions. Haddad discerned a great deficiency in the articles on the affair published in the Arab press, since most of the writers, supporters and critics alike did not adopt a critical approach with regard to the facts, testimonies and conclusions brought up by Garaudy.[84] This observation was criticized by Egyptian Salah 'Izz, who agreed that there was no expert on the subject of the Holocaust in the Arab world who was able to provide a critical review of the book. If we are to exert effort in the research of extermination, he went on to say, we would be better off starting with what is happening to Muslims in Bosnia or in other parts of the world.[85]

The debate over Garaudy and the manifestations of solidarity with him stemmed not only from a deep belief in his views on the Holocaust. His attack on Zionism attracted much more attention and was readily incorporated into the hostile discourse against Israel and Zionism. The stalemate in the peace process and other political developments in the region, such as the Iraqi crisis, polarized the dichotomy between "us" – the Arabs and Muslims on the defensive – and the "others" – Israel, Zionism and the West – and encouraged the identification with Garaudy's cause. The debate went beyond a mere discussion of the trial. It dealt with the theoretical aspects related to the trial – freedom of expression, freedom of research, the legitimacy of historical revision and the role of intellectuals in public life, reflecting a typical deniers' argumentation. The trial was perceived as part of a larger political struggle between Israel and Zionism, on the one hand, and the Arabs and Muslims, on the other hand. "His views are an inspiration for the Arab struggle against religious extremism and the Zionist occupation," concluded Salah 'Izz.[86]

---

82 *Al-Hayat al-Jadida*, 13 February 1998.
83 *Al-Hayat*, 15 January 1998.
84 *Al-Hayat*, 7 February 1998.
85 *Al-Hayat*, 12 February 1998.
86 *Al-Nahar*, 10 January 1998.

The positions expressed reflected also on the supposedly moral values of the writers. "We are with Zola in his defense of Dreyfus as we are with Garaudy for his right to expose the myths and deceptions on which Israel bases its policy, regardless of who is the persecuted, the Jews in the case of Dreyfus or the Palestinians in the case of Garaudy," argued Sid Ahmad.[87] As Arabs and Muslims, explained 'Izz, our approach to the Holocaust derives from the Islamic tenet that whether one million were killed or six million or more, the crime against humanity is the same.[88]

However, despite the overwhelming sympathy toward Garaudy, some contended that, in defending Garaudy, the Arabs and Muslims proved incompetent again, as expressions of sympathy were far from being effective.[89] Criticism was also raised against the opponents of solidarity with Garaudy.[90] While some sought to translate the campaign into a political action against Zionism and Israel, others wished that the Arabs would have Garaudy's courage in criticizing their own societies and manifesting the same zeal in defense of similar cases before Arab courts.[91]

The debate at times reflected personal feuds, claimed Samir Kassir, who was pleased, in the final analysis, that the general unanimity in the Arab press, especially the Lebanese, had been broken and that it was possible for the first time to defend the universalistic view of the Jewish extermination.[92] The Arab embrace of Garaudy served also as a catalyst for Edward Said's article "Bases for Coexistence,"[93] which was a cornerstone for the new Arab approach to the Holocaust.

The Swiss banks affair and restitution of Jewish property

The emergence of the new approach toward the Holocaust converged with another issue of contention – the new wave of claims for the restitution of Jewish property lost during the Nazi era. Fifty years after the Holocaust and with the ending of the Cold War, generational change and the opening of archives of old documentation created a need to re-examine the fate of Jewish victims' property. Almost fifty government-appointed commissions and organs were es-

87   *Al-Ahram*, 22 January 1998.

88   *Al-Hayat*, 12 February 1998. This point was also raised in the memorandum of the Palestinian writers, *al-Risala*, 22 January 1998.

89   *Al-Sha'b*, 9 January, *Ruz al-Yusuf*, 12 January, *October*, 18 January, *al-Risala*, 22 January, *al-'Alam*, 28 February 1998.

90   *Al-Nahar*, 21 January, *Filastin al-Muslima*, February, *al-Hayat*, 22 April 1998.

91   *Al-Nahar*, 17, 28 January, *al-Safir*, 20 January 1998.

92   Kassir, "La Nakba recommencee?," p. 63.

93   *Ha'aretz*, 20 February 1998.

tablished in the mid-1990s in Western Europe, Latin America and the former republics of the Soviet Union with the task of investigating the issue. The exposure of the Swiss deposits affair drew special attention, in light of previous Swiss reluctance to respect property claims after returning 12 percent of the stolen gold to the Allies according to the Washington Agreement of 1946. As a neutral, democratic state surrounded by Axis powers, Switzerland's financial institutions were used by victims of persecution as safe havens for assets and by the Nazis for laundering stolen assets, including gold taken from the central banks of German-occupied Europe. Hence, what started as an investigation of the dormant accounts of victims turned into a comprehensive examination of all Swiss economic transactions with the Nazis.[94] As a result of mounting Jewish and international pressure, the Swiss Bankers Association entered an agreement with the World Jewish Congress and the World Jewish Restitution Organization in May 1996 to establish the "Independent Committee of Eminent Persons," headed by Paul A. Volcker, whose task it was to carry out a thorough audit of the dormant accounts of victims of Nazi persecution.[95] In May 1997 a report coordinated by Stuart E. Eizenstat, US Under-Secretary of Commerce for International Trade, on the "US and Allied Efforts to Recover and Restore Gold and other Assets Stolen or Hidden by Germany during WWII" was published, and in December 1997 the British government convened an international conference on Nazi gold. It was only natural that these issues should arouse interest in the Arab media.

The German reparations and western economic and financial support to the State of Israel have preoccupied the Arab discourse on the Holocaust continuously since the early 1950s, as we have seen above. These were perceived as saving Israel from collapsing and strengthening its security vis-à-vis the Arabs, and laid the ground for a major motif in Holocaust representation – the alleged moral and financial exploitation of the West by Israel and the Jews. This in turn led to the vilification of the Jews in old, anti-Semitic stereotypic terms and prompted minimization of the magnitude of the events and the number of Jewish victims. The debate, however, which revolved around the new campaign for property restitution, reflected, as did the previous cases discussed in

---

94   For further details see: Avi Becker, "The Evil Face of 'Neutralism'," *Masuah*, vol. 25 (April 1997), pp. 129–41 (Hebrew); Institute of the World Jewish Congress, *Reevaluating European History: Committees of Inquiry on the Restitution of Jewish Property*, Policy Dispatch no. 41, April 1999; Itamar Levin, *The Last Deposit. Swiss Banks and Holocaust Victims' Accounts*, Westport: 1999.

95   The Committee completed its report three years later. See: Independent Committee of Eminent Persons (ICEP), *Report on Dormant Accounts of Victims of Nazi Persecution in Swiss Banks*, Berne: 1999.

this chapter, the cracks in the traditional Arab approach toward the Holocaust. The responses encompassed the entire spectrum of Arab attitudes toward the Holocaust, demonstrating once again the continued evolution of the repertoire of terms and ideas which sustains this discourse. On the one hand, one could find articles describing the affair as one more manifestation of Jewish-Zionist achievement in imposing its will and in exploiting the Holocaust in order to "plunder" Europe financially and politically. On the other hand, one could find neutral reporting on the negotiations over the claims[96] and on the controversy among the Jews about the distribution of recovered assets,[97] as well as nuances on the meaning of the Holocaust and the practical implications which the Arabs should draw from the affair. Since Jewish organizations, rather than the Israeli government, took the lead in the claims and negotiations with the Swiss, the distinction between Jews and Zionists was blurred, often giving way to crude anti-Jewish statements. In addition, a few commentaries revealed deep-seated resentment toward the West for unfair treatment and exploitation of Third World nations. Twenty-three Swiss of Palestinian origin reportedly sent a letter to the Swiss president at the beginning of 1997, asking him to intervene with the Israeli authorities in order to help them in their demand for compensation,[98] a move that did not bear fruit.

Several Palestinian writers focused on perceived similarities between Jewish and Palestinian suffering and claims for moral and financial restitution. Tamim Mansur of the nationalist Arab-Israeli party Balad criticized the Zionist policy of "wailing and crying," which instilled the memory of the Holocaust in western minds to such an extent that many other similar tragedies of other peoples, including the Palestinians, did not receive the same universal attention. Using the same term *karitha* (catastrophe) in reference to both the Holocaust and the Palestinian tragedy, Mansur criticized the Israeli government for emphasizing the humanitarian and moral aspects of demanding financial remuneration for Jewish funds stored in Switzerland, while simultaneously refusing to return the property of displaced Palestinians. He also accused Israel of playing on European feelings of guilt and compassion by raising the Swiss banks affair in order to cover up its obstruction of the Middle East peace process.[99] In similar vein,

---

96   *Al-Hayat*, 25 February, 26, 27 March 1997.

97   *Al-Hayat*, 25 November 1997.

98   *Al-Hayat*, 7 March 1997.

99   *Fasl al-Maqal*, 8 November 1996. The persistence of the Israeli-Palestinian conflict and Israeli claims for Jewish property left in Arab countries are the reason for the situation about which Mansur complains, while Switzerland and Israel were not in a state of conflict. Similar themes appeared in: *al-Watan*, 6 March, *al-'Ahd*, 11 April, *al-Ahram*, 5 May, *al-Majd*, 5 May, 15 December 1997.

Ghada Karmi, who had denied the Holocaust when writing in Arabic, emphasized in an article aimed at western readers the "striking contrast" between the moral attitudes and practical steps taken towards resolving the issue of compensation for Jewish victims of Nazism and "those towards rectifying outstanding Palestinian losses from 1948 onward."[100]

Palestinian translator Isma'il al-Baqqawi took the argument a step further, in both denying the Holocaust and emphasizing the charge of the "Holocaust industry." He insisted that Jews died, like Poles, Hungarians and Russians, but only "as a result of the war, and not due to a prior plan." He apologized for using the term Holocaust, because the Israelis attach it "only to the Jews who were killed," whereas he preferred to use "this expression in the human sense." Baqqawi accused "the Zionist leadership" of turning "this truly tragic historical event into an industrial enterprise" designed to bring them "a lot of capital, a fortune of wealth." They started in Germany in the 1950s with what they called "reparations," and suddenly, in the second half of the 1990s they turned to other countries and to Switzerland and began to invent their lies, according to which the Swiss bought the gold fillings of the Jewish victims that the Nazis had taken." Eventually, they forced the Swiss government to pay them large amounts of money, but Swiss society was extremely hurt "by having discovered the [Jewish] robbery."[101]

The presentation of the affair as Jewish robbery,[102] amplifying the "Jewish pressure on Switzerland to finance Israeli projects,"[103] and Switzerland as surrendering to "Zionist-American blackmail and paying out billions of dollars,"[104] was highlighted in the Islamist Hamas organ *Filastin al-Muslima*, which had continuously advocated a harsh anti-Jewish line. In an article entitled "Europe – A Prisoner of the Gold Fantasy and the Jewish Holocaust," the author Mahmud al-Khatib contended that European governments fell one after the other under the guilt complex, which the "international Jewish lobby" had created, pointing out to Germany's repentance for its sins with "massive and continued support to the Zionist state." The Jews, he claimed, were only a fraction of the war's casualties as compared with other people, and they were not exterminated for

100 Karmi, "The Question of Compensation," pp. 197, 201. See also her article in *al-Hayat*, 31 July 1998, which describes the Holocaust as a fabricated Israeli myth.

101 PA TV, May 27, 2003 – *www.pmw.org.il*, 29 May 2003. See similar claims in Nidal Hamad, "Amrakat al-'alam ta'ni sahyanatihi" – http://www.falasteen.com/article.php3?id_article=100.

102 *Al-Sha'b*, 28 January 1997.

103 *Al-Sha'b*, 7 February 1997.

104 *Al-Sha'b*, 14 March 1997.

being Jews but because they were "more treacherous and conspiratorial" than other groups vis-à-vis the Nazi regime.[105]

A host of articles described the affair as affirming the claims of the controversial Jewish American academic Norman Finkelstein regarding what he termed as "the Holocaust industry." His claims lent greater validity to Arab arguments, particularly as they were made by a Jew. Germany was the first victim of the "Holocaust industry," as it was forced to pay exorbitant amounts, commented *al-Watan*, but although "Shylock" did not end his war on Germany, he had opened a new front against Switzerland. However, whereas Finkelstein did not deny the historical veracity of the Holocaust (even though he complained that too many Jews claimed to have survived), many of the Arab writers used his contentions to advance its denial.[106] Jamil 'Atiyya Ibrahim defined the affair as "the biggest operation of political robbery in the 20th century." What interests us as Arabs, he concluded, is to avoid this heinous robbery, since the Arabs have already paid the price of the compensation that Israel received from Germany.[107]

Al-Ahram also linked the restitution issue with Jewish power to exert pressure on international organizations and with their drive to control world economy. Writer Muhammad 'Abd al-Mun'im described the Holocaust as an affair of "great public success" for the Jews, who managed to implant their suffering in the world's consciousness; nevertheless, the Swiss banks affair revived their "Shylock" image, which they had sought to marginalize for many years.[108]

According to Muhammad al-Khuli, the Jewish-Zionist tactic of reviving "old files" from the Nazi period and linking them to banks and corporations all over the West had turned their previous "subtle" mode of plunder into an "open pillage." Justice had become a "legendary sucking machine," which managed billions of dollars for the sake of a small group called "Holocaust victims," provided they were only Jews. Fusing together relativization of the Holocaust and strong resentment against the West, he wondered why Western countries singled out the Jews for compensation for hard labor, while refusing to compensate "Egyptian workers, Blacks in America and the sons of Angola, Congo or Johannesburg," who had died under their exploitation.[109]

105 *Filastin al-Muslima*, March 1999.
106 See for example, *al-Wafd*, 18 March 2001; *al-Watan*, 6 June 2002; *al-Mujtama'*, 19 January 2002. See also: *al-Liwa'*, 27 June 2001.
107 *Al-Musawwar*, 10 January 1997.
108 *Al-Ahram*, 3 August 1997. see also: *al-Ahram*, 7 December 1997; Anon. "Radakhat laha uruba wa-rafadaha al-sadat" – http://us.moheet.com/asp/report/amlak.yahood.htm
109 *Al-Bayan*, 17 December 1998.

Others turned the affair into an indictment of Western hypocrisy in general. Thus, one writer complained why Europe paid the Jews, whereas it ignored the "millions of Muslims" who perished in the torture chambers of the Spanish Inquisition, or millions of Africans who were enslaved in the West. Eliyas 'Aqila decried "Western hypocrisy," that forced Germany and Switzerland to pay compensation for the Jewish victims, while other states were not forced to do the same for their own victims, such as the US and its native Americans. Moreover, adopting neo-Nazi claims, he transformed the perpetrators into victims while wondering why Germany itself did not receive compensation for its soldiers, as thousands of them had allegedly died under the inhuman conditions of the British and American PoW camps.[110]

Several writers viewed the affair in the context of Jewish collective traits and turned it into a broader condemnation of the Jews. Islamist writer Tawfiq al-Sami'i emphasized that the Jews have always excelled in the use of propaganda and were never restrained from using "deceit, excesses and lies" (al-kidhb wal-fahsh wal-dajl). The most glaring example of this conduct, he added, was their success in bringing the entire western world to sympathize with them, particularly when "they concocted the story of the Holocaust."[111] The Holocaust had turned into a "hen laying golden eggs," and although over fifty million people from all religions "died" during the war only a few of their descendants thought of "trading their bones in the way the Jews do," commented Muhammad al-Qasabi.[112] The Jews were those who invented the bank interest and established "the exploitation of other peoples as one of their basic characteristics," claimed Tal'at Shahin, who considered the literary figure of Shylock as the epitome of their personality. Ever since the end of World War II, the Jews had invested all their "weapons" in order to plunder others. They were not satisfied with the funds they had forcibly extracted in the past and they sought compensation from countries that had fought Hitler for their sake or from those that took no part in the war. The Jews had reverted to their old ways of "searching in their old accounting books," this time the alleged dormant accounts in the Swiss banks. The entire idea of bank secrecy, Shahin added, was a Jewish invention intended to protect criminals or corrupt leaders who steal the wealth of their countries, but later to deprive them of the money on the pretext that it was accrued il-

---

110 "Al-Saha al-'arabiyya," 7 May 2000 – http://alsaha.fares.net/sahat?14@81.Ru87oSx-5P2l.0@.ee8e18a; "al-Hulukast wal-nifaq al-'alami" – http://www.alsbah.net/alsbah_nuke/modules.php?name=News&file=article&sid=6170.

111 "Al-I'lam al-'arabi wa-ghiyab al-ta'thir fi al-saha" – http://www.islamselect.com/index.php?pg=cats&CR=151&offset=30&pglist=10&ln=1.

112 *Akhbar al-Yawm*, 22 August 2001. See similar themes in *al-Watan*, 6 June 2002, *al-Sharq al-Awsat*, 9 August 2003.

legally. "I cannot imagine that non-Jews could invent such a mechanism," he concluded and called upon the Arabs to use these Jewish weapons of keeping old scores in order to extract compensation from the imperialist West for its exploitation of the Arabs.[113] Similarly, 'Abd al-Bari 'Atwan, editor of *al-Quds al-'Arabi*, as well as Palestinian activist Salman Abu Sitta, urged the Palestinians to learn from the Jews and demand compensation for their property lost as a result of the 1948 war.[114] Abu Sitta presented Jewish "squeezing" of European society as a successful campaign for restitution, even though its legal and moral basis was much less firm than the Palestinians' claims. This policy reached the level of "plunder" vis-à-vis Switzerland, as there was no evidence, he claimed, that the Swiss banks actually held any Jewish gold or funds.[115]

In accord with his views on the integral place of the Arabs in the European social, political and cultural fabric, Hazim Saghiya assessed the broader implications of the affair, suggesting that it be viewed from a neutral and more moral stance. The Arabs should not see the affair as "a Jewish conspiracy" in the context of the conflict with Israel, but rather should learn from European repentance in order to enlighten the Palestinians so that they would not continue to pay a price for the sins committed by others.[116] After attending an Amman meeting entitled "Fear and Peace" organized by the Royal Institute for Inter-Faith Studies in February 1997, Rami Khouri expressed his admiration for the Jewish determination to pursue Nazi criminals and demand moral and material compensation. "Seen within an Arab-Israeli perspective, this effort is both heroic and problematic," he stated, suggesting that "both sides must recognize, accept and respond to the fears of the other." Although he was pleased, as an Arab, "that those who participated in the crimes of the Holocaust are still being identified, hunted, prosecuted, punished, chastised and made to pay moral and material compensation for their evil-doing," he also felt disappointed "that this takes place in an international political and moral environment that seems to set two standards of rights, guilt, indemnification and atonement," since there was no parallel effort to acknowledge the Palestinian claim for compensation.[117]

---

113   *Al-Bayan*, 11 February 2000. Our colleague Prof. Ofra Bengio drew our attention to a common Arab proverb denoting that "the Jew, once he is bankrupt searches for his accounting books."

114   "Al-Laji'un wal-bidd al-fasid" – http://www.hussamkhader.org/internal/maqal/7.htm, 15 July 2003. See also *al-Zaman*, 12 May 2003.

115   *Al-Dustur*, 3, 4, 10 13 September 1997.

116   *Al-Hayat*, 1, 23 February 1997.

117   *Jordan Times*, 25 February, *Ha'aretz*, 27 February 1997.

Holocaust denial making new inroads in the Middle East

The outbreak of the al-Aqsa intifada at the end of September 2000 in the PNA territories intensified the references to the Holocaust. Crude Holocaust denial re-emerged as a means for delegitimizing Israel and Zionism, along with motifs that had typified the discourse of the early years of the Arab–Israeli conflict, such as regret that Hitler had not finished the job (see Chapters 5 and 6). The PNA semi-official paper *al-Hayat al-Jadida* published on 13 April 2001 an article by Khayri Mansur, "Marketing Ashes," in which he raised recurring themes of Holocaust denial: the claim of political and economic exploitation by Zionist propaganda; the deflated number of the exterminated Jews; and the lack of scientific evidence on the use of gas.[118] Hizballah's website disseminated the "Holocaust Lie," quoting from Richard Harwood's book *Did Six Million Jews Really Die?* and referred readers also to the Leuchter Report.[119]

Norman Finkelstein's book *The Holocaust Industry* drew considerable attention in the Arab media. It was translated into Arabic, reviewed and discussed, while Finkelstein himself became a welcome interviewee.[120] Although it does not deny the Holocaust, the book was perceived as an anti-Jewish/anti-Zionist tract, confirming Arab claims of exploitation of the Holocaust for political Zionist ends. Although these and other manifestations dealt a blow to the nascent alternative approach to the Holocaust, it did not disappear and remained a factor to be reckoned with in every discussion. Three events triggered renewed debates over the Holocaust during 2001: a cancelled conference of western deniers scheduled to take place in March in Beirut; a follow-up Arab forum on "historical revisionism" in May in Amman; and the World Conference against Racism, Racial Discrimination, Xenophobia and Related Intolerance in Durban, South Africa in September. They all highlighted the resistance to change in the attitude towards the Holocaust and in its conceptualization in ideological terms. The Durban conference became the stage of the first official Arab and Muslim attempt to institutionalize the trivialization of the Holocaust by eliminating its Jewish uniqueness and turning it into one among many "holocausts," whereas the other two were the first public fora of denial and cooperation with western deniers.

The conference on "Revisionism and Zionism," co-sponsored by two Holocaust denial organizations, the California-based IHR and the Swiss-based radi-

---

118   *Al-Hayat al-Jadida*, 13 April, *Jerusalem Post*, 18, 19 April, 8 June, Ma'ariv, 19 April 2001.

119   Resistance.homepage.com. On the Leuchter Report see Chapter 4.

120   *Al-Ahram al-'Arabi*, 24 February, *al-Sharq al-Awsat*, 13 March, *al-Hawadith*, 16 March, *al-Adab*, March-April, *Annashra*, April, *Daily Star*, 3 July 2001.

cal right-wing Truth and Justice Association, was scheduled to be held between 31 March and 3 April 2001 in the Lebanese capital Beirut. Jürgen Graf, founder of Truth and Justice, who fled to Iran to avoid a fifteen-month prison sentence for denying the Holocaust, was a driving force in its organization. If it had taken place, it would have been the first such conference in the Middle East. The choice of the Middle East was not incidental. The organizers wanted to exploit the anti-Israeli mood in the Arab world, due to the ongoing intifada, in order to promote their cause in a favorable atmosphere. French Holocaust deniers Roger Garaudy and Robert Faurisson and German neo-Nazi lawyer Horst Mahler were among the scheduled speakers. No Arab participant was named in the program. Suspicions that Iran and Hizballah were behind the conference were never substantiated. In fact, the conference was not even mentioned in the Arab media until the US State Department intervened with the Lebanese government at the beginning of March, at the urging of American Jewish organizations the Wiesenthal Center, the World Jewish Congress and the Anti-Defamation League.[121]

Recognizing the potential damage to the Arab cause, a group of fourteen Arab intellectuals – North Africans, Lebanese and Palestinians, including Edward Said, poet Mahmud Darwish and author Elias Khouri – published an open letter to Lebanese Prime Minister Rafiq al-Hariri, calling for its cancellation. Arab Knesset member Ahmad Tibi also wrote to Hariri, urging the Arabs to reject any expression of understanding for Nazism, which had committed crimes against many peoples, including the Jews.[122] Most press criticism was voiced in Lebanese papers. In a harsh editorial entitled "The Protocols of the Elders of Beirut," prominent Lebanese writer Joseph Samaha branded the conference "a dishonor for Lebanon." Holding the conference of "the falsifiers of history" in Lebanon, he warned, would be interpreted by Israel and her supporters "as the prolongation of the Nazi extermination project," and this would harm the Palestinian cause and the Palestinian victims.[123] Indeed, the international pressure bore fruit and Hariri canceled the conference on 23 March.[124] Lauding Hariri's decision, the Lebanese *Daily Star* editorial argued that "few moves could place this country [Lebanon] in a poorer light than to host their [the deniers] detest-

121 US Newswire, *Jerusalem Post*, 12 February; *Ma'ariv*, *Ha'aretz*, 13 February; ihr.org/conference/beirutconf; *Tishrin*, 24 February; *al-Nahar*, *al-Safir*, 3 March; *Tehran Times*, 4 March 2001.
122 *Le Monde*, 15 March, *Ha'aretz*, 19, 20, 23 March 2001.
123 *Al-Hayat*, 13 March, *Le Monde*, 15 March 2001.
124 *Al-Nahar*, 23, 24 March, *Jerusalem Post*, 23, 25 March, *al-Hayat*, 24, 25 March, *Daily Star*, 24, 26 March, *Ha'aretz*, 25, 29 March 2001.

able gathering. The very real challenges posed to the Arab world by the Jewish state demand far too much attention to let a cabal of hate-mongers distract the authorities in Lebanon or elsewhere in the region ... Arguments about whether the Nazis murdered six million Jews or 'only' five million are legitimate but essentially irrelevant in the big picture ... those who deny that the Holocaust took place at all are worthy of nothing but universal scorn."[125]

Hariri's statement canceling the Beirut conference neither mentioned the organizers' identity nor denounced their goals. Reaction in the Arab press and in the Lebanese parliament was divided, some supporting the conference and hence critical of the intellectuals' letter and the cancellation, and others opposing the conference. The public debate, as in previous cases such as the Garaudy affair in 1996 and 1998, revolved around the benefits Zionism and Israel would have accrued if the conference had taken place and the potential damage to Lebanon and to the Palestinian cause. Those arguing in favor of the conference pointed out the importance of discussing the "Israeli robbery in relation to the Holocaust," especially in light of the ongoing state of conflict with Israel. Those opposing it made it clear that their opposition did not mean "defending Israel and its use of the Nazi Holocaust for the financial exploitation of states."[126] "The denial of the Holocaust ... is equivalent to the denial of the Palestinian right of return ... Moreover, it amounts to the unjust exoneration of the Nazis, and might lead to the equal denial of crimes committed by Israeli war criminals," wrote 'Abd al-Wahhab Badrakhan.[127] On the other hand, the fourteen intellectuals were attacked for conceding unconditionally to the Zionist narrative and exerting pressure on Arab leaders to adopt their approach, while ignoring the adverse effects of their actions, such as infringement of freedom of speech.[128] Such attacks prompted Edward Said to retract. In a message dated 2 April, he explained that he had appended his signature to the letter "on condition that there would be no appeal to any government concerning the banning of the conference."[129] Similarly, three months later Mahmud Darwish claimed that the cancellation was "a violation of human rights and of the rights of scien-

---

125   *Daily Star*, 24 March 2001.

126   *Al-Nahar*, 20, 23 March, *al-Wasat*, 26 March 2001. See also: Nordbruch, "An Attempt to Internationalize the Denial of the Holocaust," *SICSA Annual Report* 2001, Jerusalem: 2001, pp. 9–11.

127   *Al-Hayat*, 19 March 2001.

128   *Al-Anwar*, 21 March, *al-Akhbar*, 13 April 2001; Ibrahim Alloush, "Between Public Relations and Self-Alienation: Arab Intellectuals and the 'Holocaust'," *the Journal of Historical Review*, May/June 2001, pp. 23–44.

129   ihr.org/conference/beirutconf.

tific research of revisionist historians."[130] In the context of this discussion, some commentators criticized the Arab attitude toward the extreme right in Europe. Lebanese liberal writer Samir Kassir, for example, regretted that the Lebanese government had not seized the opportunity to explain to the world that the anti-Israeli and anti-Zionist position had nothing to do with the racist atmosphere in Europe.[131] Yet, it seemed that the increased usage in the Arab discourse of alleged Zionist exploitation of the Holocaust and the equation of Zionism with racism and Nazism converged with the denial discourse and argumentation. "The existence of the Zionist entity itself is not only a crime against the Arabs, but against humanity as well," concluded the statement of the Jordanian Writers Association on 10 April denouncing the cancellation of the Beirut conference. Hence, "the liberation of humanity from neo-Nazism is its liberation from Zionism."[132]

The bitter controversy aroused by the intellectuals' letter, as well as the cancellation of the conference, culminated in an initiative to hold an alternative gathering in Amman. A group of Arab intellectuals led by Ibrahim 'Allush, a member of the Jordanian Writers Association (JWA) who had returned to Jordan after thirteen years in the US, decided to organize a convention in Amman to discuss "what happened to the revisionist historians' conference in Beirut?" The meeting, which was postponed twice owing to the intervention of Jordanian security authorities, finally took place, in cooperation with the Association against Zionism and Racism (AZAR), on 13 May, coinciding with the commemoration of the Palestinian Nakba. In contrast with the Beirut conference, where all the speakers were to have been Western Holocaust deniers, the principal participants in the Amman conference were Arab journalists and members of anti-normalization professional associations. They sought, first and foremost, to demonstrate opposition to the intellectuals who had called for the cancellation of the Beirut conference. The two main speakers were Hayat al-Huwayk 'Atiyya and Jordanian journalist 'Arafat Hijjazi. 'Atiyya, who appeared two days later in an al-Jazeera talk show which dealt with the question "Is Zionism Worse than Nazism?" (See also Chapter 7), emphasized the alleged parallels between Zionism and Nazism and argued that "historical revisionism" was not an ideology but a well-documented research project, and Hijjazi reiterated common themes of Holocaust denial. The speakers also praised Roger Garaudy's contribution to popularizing "revisionism", outlined the speech Robert Faurisson had

---

130   MSANEWS, 16 July 2001.

131   *Al-Nahar*, 23 March 2001.

132   ihr.org/conference/beirutconf.

intended to deliver at the Beirut conference and proposed to establish an Arab Committee of Historical Revisionism.[133]

The meeting in Amman was the first of its kind, signaling a developing trend of cooperation between Arabs and western deniers. Ibrahim 'Allush, who directs the Free Arab Voice website, asserted in an interview to the *JHR* that Arabs should be interested in the Holocaust and should take an active role in its denial. He argued that "most Arab regimes and leaders would not dare embrace 'Holocaust' revisionism openly," but "the Arab world is fertile ground for revisionist seeds."[134]

Indeed, 'Allush's assertion was reflected in the Arab and Muslim activities at the UN conferene in Durban. Encouraged by the "Declaration of the International Conference of NGOs Defending Palestinian Rights" adopted in Tehran on 23 April,[135] Arab and Muslim delegations sought to turn the Durban conference into an international tribunal against Zionism and Israel. They concentrated their efforts on removing references to anti-Semitism, trivializing the Holocaust, and above all, reintroducing the equation between Zionism and racism into the conference resolutions. The Arab media coverage supported these attempts by publishing countless articles stressing the "Zionist crimes" against the Palestinian people and the Arabs.[136] In keeping with Syria's traditional emphasis on this equation, Foreign Minister Faruq al-Shara', in his speech at the conference, described Israel as "the last racist bastion," and the Syrian delegation made a last-minute concerted effort to brand Israel a racist state in the final conference declaration.[137]

The American walkout from the conference was denounced by Arab League Secretary, former Egyptian Foreign Minister 'Amr Musa, and by Arab commentators. The US step was viewed not only as "a Zionist defeat" but as a further proof of American bias toward Israel and unconditional support "for

133   "The Jordanian Writers Association Sets a New Date for Its Forum," The Free Arab Voice Online (FAV), 15 April 2001, "Why the 'Holocaust' is important to Palestinians, Arabs and Muslims?," FAV, 28 April – http://www.freearabvoice.org; *Jerusalem Post*, 17, 23 April, *Jordan Times Online*, 15 May 22 May, *al-Safir*, 20 April, *al-Hayat al-Jadida*, 15 May 2001; E. Yaghi, "Exclusive Interview with Dr. Ibrahim Alloush," Middle East News Online, 7 May 2001; al-Jazeera TV, 15 May – Memri, Dispatch no. 225, 6 June 2001; Revisionist Historian Forum a Great Success, Middle East News Online, 16 May; AZAR, 18 May – MSANEWS, 18 May 2001.

134   "Why the 'Holocaust' is important," ibid.; Alloush, "Between Public Relations." See also his series of articles in *al-Sabil*, 1–22 May 2001.

135   *Middle East Affairs Journal*, vol. 7, Nos. 1–2 (Winter/Spring), pp. 235–9.

136   Colson, "Durban and the Middle East;" *al-Sharq al-Awsat*, 10, 16 August, *al-Ba'th*, 26 August, *Tishrin*, 1, 3, 4, 6, 8 September, *al-Akhbar*, 2 September 2001.

137   *Tishrin*, 3 September, South Africa News Agency (SAPA), 8 September 2001.

its aggressive and racist practices."[138] The American positions on the issues of slavery and racism were perceived as demonstrating its "double standards," and complete Zionist control over American decision making.[139]

The revoking in 1994 of UN resolution 3379 (1975), which branded Zionism as a kind of racism and racial discrimination, elicited strong Arab protests. However, the new crisis in Israeli–Palestinian relations, which adversely affected Israeli foreign relations, seemed to converge with Arab/Muslim assertiveness and to encourage blatant utilization of this motif in the struggle against Israel in international fora. From early 2001 Arab representatives were reportedly trying to revive UN resolution 3379.[140] By March, about one thousand Arab intellectuals of all political stripes had signed a petition to this effect.[141] A similar call was issued by 'Ali 'Aqla 'Arsan, president of the Syrian Arab Writers Association, who also suggested establishing a documentation center for Zionist crimes and carrying out studies on the relations between Nazis and Zionists.[142]

The three waves of debates in 2001 exposed the fragility of the new approach toward the Holocaust. Although its propagators continued to express their opinions in times of crisis, they were more apprehensive, and the old traditional themes dominated the discourse. The Durban deliberations were further proof of the significance of the equation of Zionism with racism in the Arab discourse on the Holocaust and the close linkage between anti-Zionism and anti-Semitism. In summing up the Arab performance in Durban, 'Amr Musa confided that he could not say that Arabs had achieved all they had hoped for, "especially as regards the racist Israeli practices ... But we were able to drop all indications to the Holocaust, except one."[143]

The UN decision to commemorate the Holocaust

An additional episode which reflected the continuity and change in the Arab discourse on the Holocaust was the UN special session on 27 January 2005, the anniversary of the liberation of Auschwitz, commemorating sixty years since the liberation of the Nazi concentration camps and the end of World War II, and the decision to designate 27 January as International Holocaust Remembrance Day. Two waves of debate evolved in the media in January and November

138   MENA, 4 September, *Tishrin*, 5, 6, 9 September, *Syria Times*, 8 September 2001.
139   *Jedda Arab News* (Internet version), 2, 19 August, *Tehran Times*, 5 September 2001.
140   *Al-Ahram al-'Arabi*, 24 February, *Annashra*, April, *al-Istiqlal*, 2 August 2001.
141   *Al-Istiqlal*, 24 March 2001.
142   *Al-Usbu' al-Adabi*, 5 May 2001.
143   MENA, 8 September 2001.

2005, revealing once again that the Arab discourse on the Holocaust had become less monolithic and more complex than it used to be. Yet, it still failed to separate the human aspects of the Holocaust and the perceived resultant political gains of Zionism and Israel, and persisted in linking the Jewish tragedy to the plight of the Palestinians. Already in January 2004, the commemoration of Holocaust Memorial Day in Europe had elicited such reactions. The Jews were continuing to exploit the European feelings of guilt, accused 'Abd al-Wahhab Badrakhan, in order to mobilize support and mute criticism of Israel's policies. It was an occasion for Jewish writers to settle scores with deniers and brand as anti-Semitic any description of a Jew as a Nazi. The Jews, he complained, preferred that "the Holocaust affair" should remain between them and the West, despite its human and universal aspects, and rejected the participation of Arabs and Muslims in shouldering this human responsibility, yet they continued to persecute the Palestinians, trampling on all the lessons that should have been derived from the Holocaust.[144]

The UN initiative to mark the sixtieth anniversary of the end of World War II was supported by several Arab and Muslim countries, such as Jordan, Morocco and Pakistan,[145] but the decision to commemorate the Holocaust was met with reservations and rejection. The Egyptian Parliament, for instance, unanimously rejected it and the Muslim Council of Britain, the umbrella organization of British Muslim representative organizations, headed by Iqbal Sacranie, refused to take part in the British official Holocaust Remembrance Day unless it included the "holocaust" of the Palestinian intifada.[146] Undoubtedly, the liberation of the concentration camps was an important historical event, wrote Ghada Fakhri, but did it really represent the end of the war? Why did the UN General Assembly decide to commemorate only one aspect of the horrors which caused millions of deaths in Europe, Asia and Africa? Why had it not commemorated, a year earlier, ten years since the genocide in Rwanda? "It is clear," she concluded, "that this initiative conceals the agenda of President George Bush's administration."[147]

Badrakhan, as well, considered it natural for the UN to engage in memory of the Holocaust, which concerned all humanity, but its exploitation to exonerate Israel's "bloody record" was a different matter. Any confusion between Israel and the Holocaust was a manipulation of its memory and detrimental to its lessons. Israel considered worldwide solidarity with the Jews in remembrance of

---

144   *Al-Hayat*, 29 January 2004.

145   *Al-Hayat*, 13 January 2005.

146   *Sunday Times*, 23 January 2005.

147   *Al-Sharq al-Awsat*, 21 January 2005.

the Holocaust as sympathy for its crimes against the Palestinian people, he contended.[148] Many other commentators agreed that the UN decision reflected an American dictate and handed a victory to Israeli Prime Minister Ariel Sharon, who would continue his "aggressive and murderous policies" toward the Palestinians. By continually highlighting the Holocaust, they added, Europe would remain "stuttering" and indecisive in its response to the Palestinian problem. Lebanese commentator Muhammad al-Sammak, in *al-Mustaqbal*, went further, accusing Israel of turning the West Bank and Gaza into a second Auschwitz. Sammak, who asserted that the enemies of Nazism were equally culpable of the genocide at the concentration camps for not attacking them and for closing their doors to Jews trying to flee, was at pains "to see those same countries which one day failed to stand up to Nazi crimes against the Jews, failing again to confront Israeli crimes against the Palestinians."[149]

Several Egyptian writers also accused Israel of exploiting the memory of the Holocaust and slighting other persecutions, including African slavery and the persecution of non-Jews by the Nazis, and assessed that the UN decision reflected the change in the global balance of power and a victory for Israel. The Israeli governments in the last six decades, claimed Nawwaf al-Zaru, who denied the Holocaust in the Jordanian *al-Dustur*, "succeeded in exploiting 'the Holocaust' in a Shylockian racist and imperialist manner which exceeded any reason, logic and justice." Why had Annan decided to commemorate the "so-called" Holocaust when so many scholars and European researchers doubted it and when the Palestinian Nakba was totally ignored, he wondered.[150] The same UN which "a few years ago had denounced Zionism as a racist movement," wrote Egyptian ambassador Sayyid Qasim al-Misri in the mainstream daily *al-Akhbar*, not only revoked its decision but succumbed to Zionist pressures. Even leftist intellectual Muhammad Sid Ahmad, who fully supported the preservation of the memory of the German death camps, viewed the commemoration as attesting "to Zionism's ability to mobilize public opinion at the global level." In an article in *al-Ahram Weekly*, he lamented that the message of the triumph of the values of humanity over the dark forces unleashed by the Nazi ideology had not been conveyed in the celebrations. Jews are entitled, he claimed, "not to be persecuted by reason of their ethnic identity," but "are not entitled to exploit their victimization by the Nazis to justify depriving the Palestinian people of their basic human and political rights."[151]

---

148   *Al-Hayat*, 27 January 2005.

149   *Al-Mustaqbal*, 31 January 2005.

150   *Al-Dustur*, 27 January 2005. See also: *al-Dustur*, 30 January 2005.

151   *Al-Akhbar, al-Ahram Weekly*, 3 February 2005.

Hazim Saghiya justified Arab writers who criticized Israel's exploitation of the Holocaust. Their concern, he said, was understandable in view of the denial of the Palestinian suffering. However, he stressed that the link made by either Israel or the Arabs between the Holocaust and the conflict in the Middle East was unacceptable. Saghiya referred to another aspect raised in the discussion when he added that today's Europe desisted from seeing the Jew as "the other." "'The other' today is first of all the Muslim and then the non-European immigrants and minorities." The lessons of the Holocaust had led to the unification of Europe, especially its human rights values and pluralism. Sanctification of the Holocaust in Europe was a spiritual need which transcended religion, he wrote, and its political and material exploitation should not cancel out the rich and valid findings about the Holocaust that were continually coming to light.[152] In similar vein Syrian Minister of Culture Buthayna Sha'ban contended in the daily *Tishrin* that the slogan "never again" was important but that the manifestations of discrimination, aggression and violation of human rights continued in the European continent against Muslims, who were considered a security threat.[153]

Islamists, on the other hand, mostly denied the Holocaust. Hizballah's mouthpiece *al-'Ahd - al-Intiqad* referred often to "alleged" massacres of "large numbers" of Jews in gas chambers and crematoria in Auschwitz, and to the persecution of "revisionist" historians who claimed that "the so-called Holocaust" was invented to perpetuate European feelings of guilt toward the Jews and to cover up "the unprecedented crimes" against the Arabs, and in particular the Palestinians. Commemoration of the sixtieth anniversary had no symbolic meaning, the paper added, whereas Hayat 'Atiyya al-Huwayk defined it in the Islamist Jordanian weekly *al-Sabil* as "hysteria."[154] "Today the world celebrates the security of Israel," asserted Ibrahim 'Allush in the same paper. Notorious for his ideational support of Holocaust denial, 'Allush reiterated that the Holocaust was "an invented lie" and "a global ideology" of the Zionist movement. Jews died in World War II, like the other 45 million who died due to the war, hunger and diseases. If we accept that Jews were exterminated in gas chambers as a result of a predetermined extermination policy that caused the annihilation of six million out of 15 million Jews, then we acknowledge the "amazing Holocaust story." Each of these three claims, he concluded, was refuted by revisionist scholars.[155] Islamist scholar Ahmad Nawfal complained that, like the interna-

---

152   *Al-Hayat*, 29 January 2005.

153   *Tishrin*, 31 January 2005.

154   *Al-'Ahd – al-Intiqad*, 24 January, *al-Sabil*, 18 January 2005.

155   *Al-Sabil*, 1 February 2005. See also an interview with 'Allush aired on al-Jazeera TV on

tional community which failed to commemorate other holocausts, "the para-lyzed" Muslim world failed to mark "the special holocausts" in the Muslim past and present. Munir Shafiq, a Jordanian-based Palestinian Islamist scholar, who assessed that the UN decision aimed at rallying support for exonerating Annan from corruption accusations, claimed that the Palestinian people sympathized with the Nazi victims more than any other people because they were exposed to similar atrocities, despite the differences, by the State of Israel, its army and leaders. Therefore, he did not understand how Kofi Annan "dared saying that 'Israel' emerged from the Holocaust ashes." By this he not only sympathized with the Holocaust, wrote Shafiq, but linked it to the establishment of the state, "forgetting history altogether," which showed that the project of state building started before Nazism and the Holocaust.[156]

The second wave of discussion of the Holocaust took place following the actual adoption of the UN resolution on 1 November 2005.[157] Similar motifs were reiterated. Most articles did not deny the occurrence of the Holocaust but rejected its uniqueness and equated it to other human tragedies and specifically to the Palestinian one, accusing Israel and Zionism of racism and of manipulating its memory.[158] "Yes to humane commemoration, no to racism"[159] and to "the Holocaust industry,"[160] were typical titles and themes. Egyptian permanent representative at the UN ambassador Majid 'Abd al-Fattah demanded the designation of another day for the commemoration of other genocides, such as in Rwanda, Bosnia and Cambodia, and made a call to "set up a comprehensive agenda for the combat of ideologies and extremist national movements as well as violence against foreigners and hatred of Islam and other religions."[161] Palestinian Islamic Jihad organ al-Mujahid described the new resolution as "a new crime" which reflected the Zionist campaign to control minds and Judaize the world. The real Holocaust was World War II itself, said one article, "a European war launched by European peoples against each other and involving others. Not only the Jews were afflicted by it … but Zionist deceit monopolized the Holocaust and expropriated the discourse on its behalf." Doubting the Holocaust

---

23 August – Memri, Special Dispatch, no. 976, 31 August 2005; *al-Sabil*, 8 November 2005.

156   *Al-Sabil*, 1 February 2005.

157   *Ha'aretz*, 2 November 2005.

158   See for example: *al-Sabil*, 8 November, *al-Dustur*, 16 November, *Tishrin*, 22 November, *al-Badil*, 3 December, *al-Hayat al-Jadida*, 18 December, *al-Mustaqbal*, 19 December 2005.

159   *Al-Sharq al-Awsat*, 5 November 2005.

160   *Al-Khalij*, 7 November 2005.

161   *Al-Ahram al-'Arabi*, 12 November 2005.

was forbidden and whoever denied it was brought to trial, whereas in the name of freedom of speech one could doubt religion and any scientific proven truth, the paper said, alluding to the attitude to Muslims in the West.[162]

Holocaust denial also appeared in statements made by Iranian president Mahmud Ahmadinejad at the end of 2005 in an interview with Iranian TV during the Islamic Conference Organization meeting in Saudi Arabia on 8 December and on 15 December, triggering again a spate of responses. "We do not accept the claim" of some European countries, he said, that during the war Hitler killed millions of innocent Jews in furnaces and sent them to concentration camps. The Holocaust was "a legend" invented by the Jews, who held it in higher esteem than religion, he explained. Linking the Holocaust to the Palestinian cause, he wondered why innocent Palestinian people had to pay the price for a crime they had not committed, and proposed that western countries allocate part of their lands for the establishment of the Jewish state.[163]

Arab reactions to these statements demonstrated support, on the one hand, and rejection, on the other. Naturally, Islamist movements such as Hamas, the Palestinian Islamic Jihad and the Egyptian Muslim Brothers, as well as Egyptian opposition papers such as *al-Wafd*, identified with Ahamdinejad's vision and goals. Khalid Mash'al, head of Hamas' political bureau, praised him, and the Muslim Brotherhood General Guide, Muhammad Mahdi 'Akif, supported his claims.[164] "We have had enough of the lies and the falsification of facts," wrote Egyptian columnist Hisham 'Abd al-Ra'uf, asserting that the most serious lie was the Jews' Holocaust.[165] "He said out loud what millions of Muslims think," was a recurring theme. Ahamdinejad's argument was hardly a surprise to the Arab audience, wrote Rasha Saad in *al-Ahram Weekly*, quoting 'Abd al-Wahhab Badrakhan's editorial, which considered the statements as a reminder to the West and Israel "that the historical facts do not match up to the image they have been portraying and which they work hard to sustain."[166] Ahamdinejad had only spoken the truth about the Arab–Israeli conflict and did not retract, despite angry reactions, applauded Islamist Yasir Za'atra in *al-Dustur*. The Iranian president "drove us to rethink why the Jews came to our lands," added

---

162   *Al-Mujahid*, December 2005.

163   ABC News, 8 December, *Ha'aretz*, 9, 11, 15 December, Reuters, *The Independent*, 9 December, *Die Welt*, 14 December, *Washington Post*, 15 December 2005; David Menashri, "What lies behind Ahmadinejad's hate speech?," *Tel Aviv Notes*, no. 155, 21 December 2005.

164   *Ha'aretz*, 16, 25 December, *al-Hayat*, 23, 24 December 2005.

165   *Al-Masa'*, 12 December – Memri, Special Dispatch, no. 1052, 20 December 2005. See also: *al-Jumhuriyya*, 12 December 2005.

166   *Al-Ahram Weekly*, 15 December 2005. See also: *al-Dustur*, 30 October 2005.

'Isam Kamil in *al-Jumhuriyya*.[167] Moreover, asserted Egyptian Islamist intellectual Fahmi Huwaydi in *al-Sharq al-Awsat*, Palestine had been erased from the map with the consent of the same countries that had been upset by the Iranian president's statements. Western reactions were "the epitome of terrorism, hatred and hypocrisy," concluded Rakan al-Majali.[168]

The worldwide condemnation of the Iranian president's declarations was seen by other commentators as serving Israel's interests, and although they agreed with his messages, especially the call to wipe Israel off the map, considered his tactics to be wrong, unrealistic and even potentially detrimental to Iran itself.[169] An *al-Ahram* editorial rejected the statements categorically, fearing that they could only lead to further disasters. Israel was a UN member and a fact, which could not be changed by such declarations, wrote another editorial on 10 December, whereas the issue of the Holocaust was determined by the international organization in its commemoration resolution.[170] Acknowledging that the Holocaust was a despicable historical fact, Jerome Shahin thought that "like any other fact of history," it must be "amenable to objective scientific analysis if need be." He also wondered how the Arabs could make the West understand that "while exterminating the Jews was wrong, so was expiating the guilt of the Holocaust at the expense of another people."[171]

Rejection of Ahamdinejad's approach to the conflict and to the Holocaust was in some cases intertwined with criticism of Arab society, regimes and culture, and particularly Islamist movements. Saghiya deplored the fact that Ahmadinejad's words had been received enthusiastically by many Arab writers and expressed his disappointment that Holocaust denial had become "a disease" that infected the Middle East's rulers, whereas in the past it had been confined to the fanatic margins of society.[172] Holocaust denial, warned Ahmad al-Rabi'i, exonerated Adolf Hitler and was antithetical to Islamic values. "We should differentiate between the innocent Jews who were exposed to death and the exploitation of the Holocaust by the Zionist movement ... The Islamic political contentions about the Holocaust aim at patting the people's sentiments, while

---

167 *Al-Dustur*, 31 October, 20 December, *al-Jumhuriyya*, 12 December 2005.

168 *Al-Dustur*, 1 November, *al-Sharq al-Awsat*, 2 November 2005.

169 *Al-Dustur*, 29 October, 1, 3 November, 11 December, *al-Sharq al-Awsat*, 1 November, *al-Hayat al-Jadida*, 7 November, *al-Ayyam*, 11 December, *al-Jumhuriyya*, 14 December 2005.

170 *Al-Ahram*, 30 October, 10 December 2005. See also: *al-Jumhuriyya*, 10 December 2005.

171 *Al-Mustaqbal*, 20 December 2005.

172 *Al-Hayat*, 24 December 2005.

damaging our reputation and moral standing."[173] A similar view was voiced by others, such as Palestinian intellectual George Catan, Lebanese writer Nissim Dhahir and Egyptians Murad Wahba and 'Amr Hamzawi, who acknowledged its significance as a moral lesson for all humanity in dealing with contemporary human tragedies.[174]

The Arab debate on the Holocaust was not confined to the above-mentioned affairs. There were a few other events during the decade following the emergence of the new approach which triggered discussion of the Holocaust in the Arab media.[175] In all those discussions the traditional themes of the representation of the Holocaust continued to dominate the discourse. However, they also consistently contained dissenting voices, challenging the dominant approach and suggesting an alternative reading of the Holocaust, mainly out of the belief that it was detrimental to the Arabs and weakened their cause. Egyptian journalist and intellectual Muhammad Sid Ahmad, for instance, viewed the Arab attempt to downplay the threat that the Freedom Party leader Jörg Haider represented as "extremely dangerous." The Arab stand, he said, "should not be determined as necessarily the opposite of the stand taken by Israel."[176] Haider's rise, he warned, "is chillingly similar to Hitler's rise," and he was a populist hero who exploited his countrymen's "insecurities and xenophobia."[177] In the same vein, Lebanese writer and researcher Raghid al-Sulh warned that "Jörg Haider will not help the Arabs."[178]

Intellectuals and writers such as Egyptians Rida Hilal, 'Abd al-Mun'im Sa'id and Khalid al-Mubarak, and Lebanese Joseph Samaha and Jihad al-Khazin criticized Arab identification with western Holocaust deniers. This stand, they said, played into the hands of Israel and ignored the racist tendencies of those historians who targeted Jews and Muslims alike. Instead, the Arabs needed to stress the irony of the fact that the Jews, after surviving Nazi atrocities, had themselves become oppressors.[179] It was in the Arab interest, concluded Joseph Samaha,

---

173   *Al-Sharq al-Awsat*, 24 December 2005.

174   George Catan, "The Jewish Holocaust: Reality or Myth" – www.metransparent.com/texts/george_catan, 25 May 2005; *al-Hayat*, 8 February, *al-Musawwar*, 25 March 2005; *al-Sharq al-Awsat*, 1 January 2006.

175   For a discussion of those affairs, see chapters on Arab countries in Porat and Stauber (eds.), *Antisemitism Worldwide, 1998–2006*.

176   The Austrian support of the Freedom Party and the possibility of Haider's joining the Austrian cabinet were met with harsh criticism in the West and particularly Israel and Jewish organizations. See: *Antisemitism Worldwide, 1999/2000, 2000/2001*.

177   *Al-Ahram Weekly*, 17 February 2000.

178   *Al-Hayat*, 5 March 2000.

179   *Al-Hayat*, 15, 16, 22, 30 April; *Jerusalem Post*, *al-Ahram al-'Arabi*, 2 May; *al-Ahram Week-*

"for the world to universalize some sort of moral limitation to any oppression or vile action." This would enable the Arabs "to profit from any apology for a crime committed against the Jews or others."[180] Complaining about or opposing "the apology of the West to the Jews on the Holocaust or anti-Semitism," added Palestinian writer Marwan Bishara, contradicted the Arabs' interests and values. He also criticized the link between the Holocaust and the establishment of the state of Israel which the Arabs make as reflecting the acceptance of the Zionist narrative.[181]

Upon becoming prime minister of the PNA, Mahmud 'Abbas, whose PhD dissertation accused Zionism of collaborating with Nazism and contested the number of Jewish victims (see Chapter 8), retracted the assumptions of his thesis in an interview with Israeli daily *Ha'aretz*. "The Holocaust was a terrible, unforgivable crime against the Jewish nation," he said, and added that it "was a terrible thing that nobody can claim I denied it." Abu Mazin, who sought to put an end to the intifada, reiterated this view in his concluding statement on 4 June 2003, at the end of the Aqaba summit between himself and Israeli Prime Minister Sharon.[182] Those Arabs who deny the Holocaust "accept the Zionist logic as correct," contended Joseph Massad, and he stressed that they had no position inside the PLO, nor any legitimacy among the Palestinian intelligentsia. "Palestinians and other Arabs were called upon to accept the Jewish holocaust [sic] and Israel's 'right to exist' as a package deal," wrote Massad. Their response to Israel's linkage varied, he elaborated. "Some, falling into the Zionist ideological trap, reasoned that accepting the Jewish holocaust meant accepting Israel's right to be a colonial-settler racist state, then the holocaust must be denied or at least questioned."[183] Some Arab intellectuals started to acknowledge the Holocaust and sympathize with the Jewish people, wrote Hashim Salih in *al-Sharq al-Awsat*. This did not mean surrender to Zionist ideology or Israeli propaganda, but "admitting the truth ... and condemning organized crime against humanity in every time and place."[184]

ly, 11 May 2000.

180 *Al-Hayat*, 2 April 2000.
181 *Al-Hayat*, 6 April 2000.
182 *Ha'aretz*, 28 May, *The Guardian*, 29 May 2003; "PM Abbas and Israeli PM Ariel Sharon statements following the Aqaba summit," Aqaba, Jordan, 4 June 2003, *Journal of Palestine Studies*, vol. 33, no. 1 (Fall 2003), p. 150.
183 *Al-Ahram Weekly*, 9 December 2004. See also article by Ibrahim 'Allush, *al-Sabil*, 27 April 2004.
184 *Al-Sharq al-Awsat*, 25 February 2004.

Drawing lessons from the Holocaust would be a sublime goal, argued Palestinian London-based writer Khalid al-Harub, were it not for the Jewish organizations' attempts to exploit it. There was an excessive preoccupation with the Holocaust, which had been the end result of brute racism. Hence, despite the growing centrality of the Holocaust in western consciousness, racism toward the "other" was increasing, he contended. al-Harub opposes the legal limitation of Holocaust denial and advocates freedom of speech, fearing that the trend of shattering sacred myths most prevalent in the West would also impinge upon the Holocaust.[185] Similarly, Dalal al-Bizri reproached the Arabs for ignoring the anti-Semitic core in Nazism, which considered the Arabs, too, as the scum of nations. The Arabs, she said, should ask themselves several questions: "If the Holocaust was a historical fact, how does it affect our cause?" "Does the veracity of the event negate the depiction of Zionism as executioners?" "Shouldn't we understand for ourselves and not through intermediaries the dimensions of the Holocaust?" She therefore called on the Arabs to conduct independent research on the Holocaust and Jewish history in Europe. Such studies would establish them as "the present victims of past victims," she maintained.[186]

Conclusions

The barrage of articles generated by the Holocaust-related episodes discussed above, and especially by the Garaudy affair and later the adoption of International Holocaust Memorial Day, touched upon issues beyond the immediate limited questions stemming from them: should 'Arafat visit the Holocaust Museum? Should the Arabs support Garaudy, Haider and Irving? What should be the Arab stand toward International Holocaust Memorial Day? The discussion among intellectuals has evolved into an unprecedented examination of the Arab attitude toward the Holocaust, and especially its denial, in an attempt to explain its origins and motives. From the particularity "of being totally innocent of any responsibility for the Holocaust, that terrible catastrophe of the Jewish people, which ended with a metaphorically identical Catastrophe of their own," expounded Ata Qaymari, "stems the whole reaction, response and stand of the Palestinian people."[187] Leiptzig-based Egyptian scholar Omar Kamil explained that the Arab intellectual refused to acknowledge the Holocaust out of the erroneous perception that acknowledgment of the suffering of the other diminishes the meaning of the Pal-

---

185   *Al-Hayat*, 18 February 2000.

186   *Al-Hayat*, 30 April 2000.

187   Qaymari, "The Holocaust," p. 148.

estinian suffering,[188] whereas others, such as Ray Hanania and Joseph Massad, contended that the Arab attitude to the Holocaust, and particularly denial, was a reaction to the use of the Holocaust in justifying Israel's existence and political stand vis-à-vis the Palestinians.[189] Moreover, analyzing the Arab approach toward the Holocaust reflected on the image of Arab societies and occasionally incorporated harsh criticism of their social, political and moral situation.

The debates reveal that the unanimity of the traditional Arab discourse on the Holocaust has been broken and that a small but growing number of writers dare to defend its universal meaning and to call for its recognition as a traumatic Jewish experience which shapes the Jewish people's psyche. This group of writers was consistent in defending 'Arafat's decision to accept the invitation to the Holocaust Museum, in condemning the Arab embrace of Garaudy, Irving and Ahmadinejad, and in welcoming the Pope's document for providing "constructive moral and political guidelines" as a standard of behavior and universal morality for all human beings,[190] as well as International Holocaust Memorial Day. They also rejected Holocaust denial and criticized the indiscriminate translation of western deniers' publications into Arabic.[191]

In a way, one can see the new approach as a return to the earlier diversified discourse of the 1940s, when the Arabs made an attempt to separate the political from the humanitarian aspects of the Jewish tragedy. Realizing the potential gains that Zionists could derive from this tragedy, they also tried, as we have shown in the first chapter, to disconnect the immediate causal link between the establishment of the State of Israel and the Holocaust. Both motifs typify the new Arab approach.

The readiness to accept the Holocaust and isolate its human implications from what is perceived as its political consequences – namely, the establishment of the State of Israel and the suffering inflicted on the Palestinian people – is gradually infiltrating into the Arab discourse. Even opponents of the new approach, who continued to maintain that the Holocaust did not concern the Arabs, to relativize it by comparing it to the Nakba, to stress that the Holocaust was and is being exploited by Israel and Zionism, or to adhere to the equation of Zionism with Nazism, point out that, notwithstanding, no one could ig-

188 *Al-Sharq al-Awsat*, 30 January 2004; Massad, "Palestinian and Jewish History," p. 53. For similar opinions, see Muhammad Haddad, *al-Hayat*, 8 February 2004; Na'il Bal'awi, *al-Quds al-'Arabi*, 4 May 2006.

189 Ray Hanania, "Morality and Principles in the Palestinian Struggle for Nationhood," 5 August 1998 – www.hanania.com; Massad, ibid.

190 *Jordan Times*, 21 April 1998; *Ha'aretz*, 23 April 1998.

191 See for instance Saghiya, *Difa'an*, p. 68; *al-Nahar*, 29 December 1997.

nore or deny that the Holocaust was a deplorable crime. Among these one may mention people such as PLO council member Shafiq al-Hut, Egyptian writer Muhammad Hasanayn Haykal, Egyptian Marxist thinker Muhammad Sid Ahmad, *al-Hayat*'s editor 'Abd al-Wahhab Badrakhan, Palestinian scholar Joseph Massad and others.[192] Some writers have been keen to show that Islamic civilization was by definition opposed to such an extermination crime. As Arabs and Muslims, explained Egyptian writer Salah 'Izz, "our approach to the Holocaust derives from the Islamic tenet that whether one million were killed or six million or more, the crime against humanity is the same."[193] Moreover, Muslims who doubt the Holocaust fail to grasp that they are concealing the persecution of Muslims by neo-Nazi racists in Germany and elsewhere in Europe.[194]

Yet, the deconstruction of the new approach by the conventional terms of Holocaust historiography can easily show that it is charged, in different degrees, with sophisticated motifs of Holocaust denial discourse as well as elements of relativization and political instrumentalization. The recognition of the Holocaust by Saghiya, Said, Khouri, Bishara and others is instrumental. The persecution of the Jews is acknowledged, but at the same time is linked to the Palestinian tragedy and its acknowledgment by Israel and the West. The comparison between the two, either directly or by inference, involves by definition the minimization and relativization of the Holocaust. The recognition of the Holocaust is a basis for reconciliation and a means for the realization of Palestinian national aspirations. Haykal considers it a mistake to leave "the genuine part of the Holocaust myth" to the scheming of the Zionist movement. The opposition to Garaudy, Haider, Irving or Ahmadinejad stemmed not only from their denial of the Holocaust, but also from the damage the Arab support might inflict on the Palestinian cause. The solidarity with them was perceived as an inappropriate choice of weapon in the struggle against Israel, which "discredits us more than we already are discredited in the world's eyes." Similarly, embracing the myth of Holocaust denial was rejected because it could easily lead to the denial of the Palestinian cause and strengthen Israel's monopoly over the Holocaust.[195]

---

192   *Al-Hayat*, 21 January, *al-Ahram*, *al-Ahram Weekly*, *al-Nahar*, 22 January, *al-Watan al-'Arabi*, 6 February 1998; Preface by Muhammad Hasanayn Haykal, Jarudi, *al-Asatir*, pp. 5–11; Massad, "Palestinians and Jewish History."

193   *Al-Hayat*, 12 February 1998. See also *al-Ahram Weekly*, 29 January 1998.

194   *Al-Sharq al-Awsat*, 22, 24, 25 January 1998.

195   Haykal, Jarudi, ibid.; *Al-Jadid*, no. 22 (Winter 1998), p. 40; *al-Hayat*, 13, 15, 20, 22, 23 January, 28 February, *al-Safir*, 19 January, *al-Nahar*, 27 January, *Al-Ahram Weekly*, 25 June, *Le Monde Diplomatique*, August-September 1998; *al-Hayat*, 8 February 2005; *al-Quds al-'Arabi*, 4 May 2006.

In response to ʿAzmi Bishara's article on the Arabs and the Holocaust, Dan Michman, a renowned Israeli expert on Holocaust studies, questioned the motives of those who propagate the need to derive universal lessons from the Holocaust and to resist its denial. Does their attitude reflect a humanistic, liberal and enlightened approach or an attempt to be politically correct? Is the universalization of the Holocaust the only legitimate interpretation, and is it not itself a manipulation, he challenged. Michman believed that universalization neutralizes the Holocaust from its Jewish context.[196] Bishara categorically rejected Michman's interpretation and insisted that his attitude emanated from an unequivocal rejection of Holocaust denial, relativization or belittling the Holocaust, yet he argued that the Bible sanctified the idea of genocide, implicitly attributing the origins of this phenomenon to the Jews.[197] The new approach indeed contains basic elements of post-Zionist discourse, which seeks to separate the discussion of the Holocaust from that of the Israeli–Palestinian conflict and to create a new, joint Israeli–Palestinian narrative of the victors and the vanquished.[198]

Is it proper to label the proponents of the new approach to the Holocaust as deniers, for what is conceived as relativization, or to dismiss the significance of their conciliatory move, for their political instrumentalization of the Holocaust? Does universalization of the Holocaust necessarily mean undermining the uniqueness of the Jewish experience? These are questions which continue to preoccupy scholars of the Holocaust as well as scholars of genocide studies who use Holocaust metaphors to represent their cases, as we have shown in the previous chapter. The new approach derived from the terminology and reasoning of the discourse in the West, as Holocaust denial and other motifs of Holocaust representation in the traditional Arab discourse were partially adopted from western and Soviet literature. Arab intellectuals who participated in the debates on the Holocaust, propagating the new approach, such as Edward Said, Hazim Saghiya, Salih Bashir, Samir Kassir, Ray Hanania, Omar Kamil, ʿAmr Hamzawi and others, live in the West and are highly conversant with its culture and values. They are mainly Palestinian, Lebanese, North African and Egyptian scholars, writers and journalists, liberals and secularists. Perhaps not surprisingly, Christians were prominent among the Palestinians and the Lebanese. They genuinely advocate a change in the Arab attitude toward the Holocaust and do not deny its uniqueness, although some implicitly minimize it, and most of them fail to isolate the political dimension from their discourse, despite their declared aspiration to do so. "Keeping the Holocaust in

---

196   Dan Michman, "Responses," p. 119.

197   Bishara, "Response," p. 102.

198   Shapira, "Politics," p. 19.

the thoughts of all of us," wrote Samah Jabr, "is useful in terms of reminding us of the wrong that can be wrought in the name of right ... Jewish groups in Palestine today who place possession of land above globally recognized laws of human rights are capable of generating endless holocaust and catastrophe."[199] Thus, there was no contradiction between the recognition of the Holocaust and the condemnation of Israel and Zionism as a Nazi racist state or movement doomed to destruction.

The debates on the Holocaust and its universal moral lessons can be seen as part of an attempt to come to terms with history, desperately needed in times of reconstructing national identity and paving the way for a historical compromise and reconciliation. The identification in the Arab world of the Holocaust as the crucial factor in the establishment of the State of Israel led, in the effort to del-egitimize the state, to the denial of the Holocaust. The changing circumstances of the Arab–Israeli conflict, the legitimacy bestowed on Israel by entering into negotiations and a peace process with it, created a cognitional dilemma and made the attitude toward the Holocaust obsolete and in need of rehabilitation. These developments are also closely connected with global political and cultural trends. Thus, the discussions also involved a penetrating examination and reas-sessment of the past, present and future place and role of the Arab world and Islamic culture among the nations and in civilization in general, as exemplified by Said and Saghiya. "We face again here a comprehensive world-view which denies history, monopolizes the human being and contradicts the democratic essence, based on the acceptance of the other and the advancement of the val-ues of coexistence, tolerance and pluralism," wrote Washington-based Egyptian scholar 'Amr Hamzawi in response to the Arab embrace of Ahmadinejad's de-nial of the Holocaust.[200]

The taboo on the Holocaust has been partly lifted. Calls for original Arab research and for spreading knowledge of the Holocaust, Arabs admitting to visiting the death camps and the Washington Museum, are a far cry from the past ban on information. The new approach, however, has also ushered in a reaction and a spate of new publications dealing with Holocaust denial.[201] Such was the case of Egyptian journalist Hasan Rajab, who remained unconvinced that six million Jews were gassed, even after his visit to Auschwitz;[202] Masiri,

---

199   Samah Jabr, "History in Repetition," in Al-Awda archives – http://groups.yahoo.com/group/al-awda-news.

200   *Al-Sharq al-Awsat*, 1 January 2006.

201   See for example: Ramsis 'Awad, *al-hulucast bayna al-inkar wal-ta'kid*, Cairo: 2000; *Taqrir Luchter*, Cairo: 2000.

202   *Al-Akhbar*, 14 July 1998.

whose studies on Judaism and Zionism only further strengthened his conviction of the alleged symbiotic relations between Zionism and Nazism;[203] and Ibrahim 'Allush's ideological embrace of Holocaust denial.[204] 'Allush continued to claim that acknowledgment of the Holocaust is an acknowledgment of its uniqueness as a Jewish tragedy that diminishes the Palestinian one and constitutes recognition of Israel's right to exist, or even a submission "to the Zionization of the holocaust and to its appropriation by Israeli propagandists for their own purposes."[205] In similar vein, the new approach was criticized for failing to mention the Palestinian suffering and explicitly call for a mutual recognition.[206]

The discourse on the Holocaust in the Arab world is still weak and apprehensive, claims Muhammad Haddad. The Arab intellectual is either silent or mixes up between the Holocaust and the Palestinian affair, resorts to denial, anti-Semitism and the myth of the *Protocols of the Elders of Zion* – three dangerous positions which do not serve Arab interests. It is about time, he concludes, that Arab intellectuals adopt a clear view composed of three aspects: the Holocaust is a historical fact and not an invention; neither the Arabs nor the Palestinians took part in it; and the sympathy of the Arabs with Hitler during World War II had nothing to do with the Holocaust. The western world, he adds, has no intention to renew the persecution of the Jews and encourage anti-Semitism in its midst. Yet, it seeks to atone for his second feeling of guilt and find a just solution for the Palestinian problem.[207] It is hard to predict whether the new approach to the Holocaust would bring about a sweeping shift in the representation of the Holocaust in the Arab world. Meanwhile, it seems that its mark on the discourse is greater than its real weight among writers or the public at large.

---

203 See his book *al-Sahyuniyya wal-naziyya* discussed above (Chapter 7).

204 *Al-Sabil*, 27 April 2004, 8 November 2005.

205 Massad, "Palestinians and Jewish History," pp. 61–2.

206 See for example: Rub'i al-Madhun, *al-Hayat*, 20 January 1998; Muhammad Jabir al-Ansari, "Edward Said: muraja'a am taraju'," *al-Nashra*, 13/1 (January 1998), pp. 21–4 (The same article was published in two installments in *al-Hayat*, 11, 12 November 1997).

207 *Al-Hayat*, 8 February 2004.

CONCLUSIONS

The Arab Holocaust discourse had begun by the end of World War II and was shaped, from its inception, by the political developments related to the Jewish–Arab conflict in Palestine. Following the 1948 war and the escalation of the conflict, it became an integral part of the broader Arab anti-Semitic discourse, which evolved under the shadow of the conflict. The demonization of Israel, the Jews and Zionism and the use of images and symbols from the Nazi era sought, on the one hand, to undermine the victims' claims and the basis of legitimacy of Israel and Zionism, and reflected, on the other hand, Arab will to dissociate themselves from the Nazi ideology by attributing Nazi principles and conduct to the "enemy," "the other," who happened to be Nazism's main victim.

Since the prevalent view in the Arab discourse regarded the Holocaust as the major source of international legitimacy and support for Israel, it developed a dual approach toward it: dissociation and intensive preoccupation. "We, the Arabs found ourselves, despite our will, a party to anything that is related to the Jews, including the story of anti-Semitism," explained Ahmad Baha' al-Din in 1964, adding that the suffering of the Jews in Europe, which "culminated in the gas chambers that Hitler had set up to eliminate the Jewish race," led them to adopt an ideology "which is no less racist than Hitlerism."[1] Baha' al-Din's statement epitomizes the still valid Arab position that, although the Holocaust did not concern the Arabs, they had to confront it and pay the price for it. Consequently, they felt the need to challenge its universal perception and status by employing simultaneously an entire spectrum of themes and arguments. These included: acknowledgment of and some sympathy toward Jewish suffering; justification; accusing Zionism of collaborating with the Nazis in exterminating European Jews; equation between Zionism and Nazism, reversing the role of the Jews from victims to persecutors and presenting the Palestinians as the true victims of the Holocaust; minimization and relativization of the Holocaust; and ultimate denial.

---

1   Baha' al-Din, *Isra'iliyyat*, pp. 95–6. For the persistence of this approach, see for instance, *al-Sabil*, 3 January, *al-Quds al-'Arabi*, 3 February, *al-Sharq al-Awsat*, 6 February 2006.

This categorization does not rank the various motifs by their severity, nor does it establish their frequency and importance, which fluctuated over time. Most of these themes appeared already in 1945, and have shown remarkable continuity ever since, creating a repertoire of terms, arguments and concepts which writers resorted to on different occasions and in a variety of contexts. In certain cases, even the same wording that appeared in the early 1950s was used by different writers in the 1990s, either as a direct borrowing or, more likely, reflecting a prevailing intellectual climate. This continuity, however, did not mean stagnation or a-historicity. All of these themes were perceived as equally legitimate and useful, with the emphasis shifting from one motif to another, according to the nature of historical events related to the Holocaust, and incorporating more sophisticated arguments along the years.

Similarly to the western and Communist discourses, the Arab discourse underwent evolution on several complementary and intertwined levels: the political–historical, the theological and the philosophical. Its point of departure dictated its boundaries, which rarely allowed any deviation from them. The political–historical debate held a major place in the public discourse, representing all political shades from the left to the Islamists. It was preoccupied with the nature and history of the Jews, with the characteristics and ideology of the Zionist movement, with anti-Semitism and its effect on the Holocaust, and with the evolution of the Arab–Israeli conflict. Certain themes within this discussion touched upon moral and cultural aspects such as the supposed equation between Zionism and Nazism and the charge of Zionist–Nazi collaboration. Those not only pointed to the negative traits of the "other," the enemy, but *ipso facto* highlighted the moral superiority of the Arabs and their culture. The philosophical debate was rather limited and incorporated into the historical one, as it hardly dealt with the universal ethical meaning of the event. Its main focus was the search for explanations for the Holocaust and for their connection to historical, social and cultural causes that were embedded in the character of the Jews and their relations with surrounding societies. The theological debate was conducted mostly by Islamists and derived from determinist religious perceptions and from the belief in divine reward and punishment. It dealt mainly with the moral responsibility of the Jews for their fate and for raising divine wrath against them. Moreover, it contrasted Arab Islamic civilization with the western Christian civilization which perpetrated the Holocaust, contending that under Islam such persecutions could have never taken place.

The formative period up to 1948 witnessed three major themes: acknowledgment of Jewish suffering, coupled with the attempt to separate it from the Palestine problem; minimization of the scope and historical significance of the

Holocaust; and blaming the Jews for what had befallen them. The separation between the Jewish and Palestine problems ceased to be relevant with the establishment of the State of Israel. The signing of the German–Israeli reparations agreement in the early 1950s prompted a shift in emphasis toward the charges of Israeli and Jewish instrumentalization of the Holocaust in order to cultivate guilt complexes in the West and extract political and financial gains. The ambiguity towards Nazi Germany during the 1950s receded, increasingly turning Nazism into a symbol of ultimate evil, manifested *inter alia* by its growing equation with Zionism, the ultimate enemy, and occasionally with other enemies of the Arab nation.

The Eichmann trial, which served as a watershed in the attitudes of Israelis and westerners to the Holocaust, had a parallel though opposite effect on the Arab world, prompting Arab writers to intensify their efforts to either deny the Holocaust or accuse the Zionists of collaboration in the extermination of the Jews. References to the Holocaust as a Jewish tragedy or as a wholesale genocide became scarce. Instead, the Holocaust was deprived of its uniqueness with its equation with the Nakba, the victims were turned into perpetrators, or were even held responsible for their own destruction. The exacerbation of the Arab–Israeli conflict after 1967 and the growing activities of western Holocaust deniers from the late 1970s boosted Arab references to the Holocaust. In addition to the rising volume of denial literature, and the growing sophistication of the argumentations, greater effort was made to "prove" by pseudo-academic publications Zionist–Nazi collaboration and the resemblance between the two movements. While blatant justifications of the Holocaust became less common after the 1970s, they have resurfaced in times of crisis in Arab–Israeli relations such as the 1982 war in Lebanon or the Palestinian–Israeli confrontation since 2000.

The 1990s ushered a new phase in the Arab intellectual discourse. The collapse of the Soviet Union raised the notion of a new world order; the signing of the 1993 Israeli–Palestinian accords and the 1994 Israeli–Jordanian peace agreement gave rise to a new critical Arab intellectual discourse on the state of the Middle East which encompassed the issue of Arab attitudes towards the Holocaust. It criticized the prevalent Arab perceptions of the Holocaust, calling for unequivocal recognition of the suffering of the Jewish people, which eventually would lead to the recognition of the Palestinian tragedy by the Israelis and facilitate reconciliation and coexistence between the two peoples. The new approach was triggered by Arab intellectuals living in the West and closely familiar with its culture, and aroused a wide range of reactions all over the Arab world, leading to a counter-trend of ideological Holocaust denial. While it remained a minority trend, the new approach contributed to a broader recognition of the occurrence of the Holocaust, albeit intertwined with "soft" denial.

The Arab Holocaust discourse was not engaged in a systematic study of facts and their meanings, but comprised of eclectic references to events and preoccupation with their political ramifications in the Middle East. This discussion did not relate to the historiographic debates on the Holocaust or on its moral and universal meanings, but rejected the norms adopted in the West regarding the study of the Holocaust. The point of departure was the establishment of Israel and the injustice done to the Arabs, thereby distorting the historical perspective of the Holocaust and narrowing it down to the end result of a political process that had started fifty years earlier and that had no connection to it. This approach was not the outcome of lack of information and knowledge of the historical events, but derived from ideological motives and political needs. The selective references to western historical and intellectual scholarship reflect an intimate acquaintance with and deliberate choice of those motifs that could serve the Arab cause. However, over the years ignorance increasingly spread among the public at large, due to the intentional disruption of the free flow of information, such as western Holocaust textbooks, and the banning of documentaries, feature films and teaching of the Holocaust. This ignorance facilitated the reception and entrenchment of a distorted view of the Holocaust.

Still, a new authentic discourse emerged parallel to the western and Soviet ones, though lacking a single coherent narrative. The various motifs which appear in it derived from indigenous sources and from Soviet and western radical, right-wing inspiration, thus producing a discourse that constitutes and reflects a symbiosis between European and Middle Eastern anti-Semitism and anti-Zionism. This borrowing unwittingly revealed subtle or unconscious esteem for the West or western sources, even on the part of those who reject western cultural influence as anathema to authentic Muslim or Arab culture. In a few cases, such as the equation between Zionism and Nazism and the charge of Zionist-Nazi collaboration, Arab writers even preceded their Soviet counterparts, whereas the justification theme was never prominent in either Soviet or western extreme right literature.

At times, Arab references to the Holocaust reflected broader grievances toward the "West" over its conduct vis-à-vis the Arabs and Muslims. Such was the case in the discussion of German reparations to Israel, which were described as unduly favoring the Jews over the Palestinians, or the resentment over Pope John Paul II's 1998 apology to the Jews, which was contrasted with Christian refusal to apologize for western aggression against the Muslims from the time of the Crusades. Moreover, the Holocaust was used to tarnish western civilization as a whole. It was described, as 'Abd al-Wahhab al-Masiri articulated, as one in a long series of genocides perpetrated against inferior "non-whites" and as the essence and culmination of a western materialist, immoral and secular mind-set. Such a view naturally led to the perception of the Allies' war activities, particularly the Americans', rather than Germany's, as the real crime of the war.

Aiming primarily against Zionism and Israel, the discourse progressively turned anti-Semitic. While denial was motivated by the desire to undermine Israel's legitimacy, it distorts and denies Jewish history. Moreover, it deprives the Jews of their human dignity by presenting their worst tragedy as a scam and appeals to the tendency of both European and Middle Eastern anti-Semitism to charge the Jews with unscrupulous machinations designed to achieve illegitimate and immoral goals, mainly financial extortion. Likewise, the equation between Zionism and Nazism harbored anti-Jewish motifs, as various groups, particularly Islamists, never distinguished between Zionism and Judaism. Furthermore, many writers claimed that Jewish "racist" theology begets Nazism. The vilification of Zionists as Nazis is intended to offend the most painful feelings of the Jews by equating them with their worst tormentors. Not only does it transform victims into perpetrators, but it threatens them with the ultimate fate of the Nazis. The convergence between the two themes culminated in the justification of the Nazi murder of the Jews due to their alleged character and activities. As such, the demonization of the Jews exceeded parallel manifestations of post-war anti-Semitism elsewhere in the world.

Since its inception, the Arab Holocaust discourse has contained inherent contradictions. Most glaring has been the simultaneous denial of the Holocaust and its appropriation as a criterion for suffering and evil and the accusation of Zionism as taking an active role in its execution, thereby unwittingly implying its occurrence. An article published in *al-Hayat al-Jadida* in 1997, criticizing Israeli policy, provides an illuminating example by incorporating almost all themes employed by the discourse. It accused the Zionist movement of encouraging the rise of Nazism in Germany, adding that the great similarity in ideology and practice between the two movements was the cause of the animosity between them, but also the proof of their collaboration, which in itself refutes Zionist allegations of Nazi massacres against the Jews and renders the Palestinians as the actual victims.[2] Such contradictions, which are typical of classical anti-Semitism and of belief systems in societies engaged in intractable conflicts, were acknowledged by Arab writers from the late 1980s, particularly the proponents of the new approach. The shift during the 1990s to a more sophisticated

---

2   *Al-Hayat al-Jadida*, 3 September 1997.

"soft" denial enabled Arabs to reconcile denial with allegations against Zionism, or with blaming the Jews for their fate.

Up to the 1970s, a significant convergence existed between official state positions toward the Holocaust, particularly those of Egypt and Jordan, and the public discourse, with the latter consistently being less inhibited. Several studies have shown that, by and large, Arab school textbooks disregarded the Holocaust, but this void was filled by the public discourse that shaped popular perceptions of the Holocaust.[3] After the signing of the peace treaty with Egypt in 1979 a certain gap evolved between the official and public discourses. While, for instance, 'Abd al-Nasir questioned the Holocaust, his successor, Anwar Sadat, visited the Israeli Yad Vashem memorial during his 1977 trip to Israel and Husni Mubarak's close adviser Usama al-Baz publicly denounced Holocaust denial. Likewise, Mahmud 'Abbas, in his capacity as a senior PLO official, denied the Holocaust and accused Zionism of collaborating with the Nazis during the early 1980s, but once he became the PNA's prime minister he retracted his position. Representing a surrogate state, the PNA official website also was more restrained than the PLO in its pronouncements about the Holocaust. However, such a gap could not be discerned in Syria, which persisted in its hard-line position in the conflict. President Hafiz al-Assad's speech equating Zionism with Nazism was reproduced verbatim in a school textbook. Similarly, his son and successor, Bashar, consistently referred to Israel and Zionism as the new Nazism, claiming that their ideological roots lay in the ancient Jewish holy books, the Torah and the Talmud, and lent his support to western Holocaust deniers.[4]

The changing status of the conflict following the peace agreements with Israel did not ameliorate the public discourse, and perhaps even exacerbated its hostile references to Jews, Zionism and the Holocaust. Arab writers and intellectuals, particularly Egyptians, gave vent to their frustration at the peace treaties by resorting to harsh anti-Israeli and anti-Jewish rhetoric. The various governments gave their tacit agreement as a compromise with increasingly restive public opinion and as a means to divert political criticism and discontent away from their own policies to external players. Yet, governments continued to set the boundaries of the discourse. While expressions of justification became far less

3   Hava Lazarus-Yafeh, "An Inquiry into Arab Textbooks," *Asian and African Studies*, vol. 8, no. 1 (1972), pp. 1–19; Avner Giladi, "Israel's Image in Recent Egyptian Textbooks," *The Jerusalem Quarterly*, 7 (Spring 1978), pp. 88–97; Elie Podeh, "Recognition without Legitimization: Israel and the Arab-Israeli Conflict in Egyptian History Textbooks," *Internationale Schulbuchforschung*, vol. 25, no. 4 (2003), pp. 371–98; Groiss (ed.), *Jews, Zionism and Israel*; idem (ed.), *Jews, Israel and Peace in the Palestinian Authority Textbooks*, New York: 2005.

4   *Al-Safir*, 27 March 2003.

common, various degrees of denial became more prevalent, with the Syrians, Palestinians and Islamists emphasizing Nazi–Zionist collaboration. Justification received a certain stamp of approval in Syrian school textbooks, whereas it was rare among Palestinians, conceivably due to their greater contacts with Israeli society and possible fear of Israeli reaction.

Throughout most of the period under discussion there were no significant differences in arguments and images used by nationalists and Islamists. Conversely, a clearer difference existed between those groups and leftist writers, particularly regarding Nazi Germany and Holocaust denial. While various nationalists and Islamists were ambiguous toward Nazi Germany, or regarded the Allies as equally repulsive, the leftists, under the influence of the Soviet position, adopted an unequivocally hostile position toward Nazi Germany. Likewise, justification of the Holocaust, or its outright denial, were less prevalent among leftists than among nationalists and Islamists. This divergence also stemmed from differing attitudes toward the conflict. While the left accepted a two-state solution, the Islamists were adamant in viewing the conflict as an existential religious struggle between Jews and Muslims necessitating the elimination of Israel. Up to the early 1950s and since the 1990s, liberal Arab intellectuals wanted the Arabs to share the values of the universal human community and viewed its culture as a "term of reference" that had to be taken into consideration, whereas the Islamists resented this approach. During this period, outright denial replaced justification as the prominent motif among Islamists, while "soft denial," that is, relativization of the Holocaust, the blurring of the victims' Jewish identity, the minimization of the number of victims or their distinct targeting by the Nazis became common among leftists and nationalists alike.

Historians at times point to the limitations of written texts in reflecting the emotional and behavioral complexities of political attitudes. However, we believe that the wealth and diversity of the texts, which have dealt with the Holocaust over a sixty- year period, succeeded in transmitting the multi-faceted Arab approach to the Holocaust and in echoing the political, cultural and moral dimensions which shaped it. The present study has dealt mainly with the production of representations of the Holocaust, and has only occasionally touched upon their reception by the public – an issue that deserves its own comprehensive examination. Although such a task is difficult to pursue in non-democratic societies, various indicators can point to dissemination and reception of the dominant discourse. The growing number of references to the Holocaust in varying contexts and media, such as newspapers, books, TV programs and the internet, as well as the reiteration of the same motifs, could reinforce the reception of the inculcated perceptions and indicate their widespread acceptance. The large number of contributors to the public debate from all walks of life – politicians, academicians, intellectuals, journalists and ordinary people, is another indicator to the spread and absorption of these representations. The limited political liberalization in some Arab countries and the appearance of opposition publications which allowed writers a greater leeway to express their views indicate that the Arab Holocaust discourse was not dictated from above, but was overwhelmingly spontaneous, reflecting prevalent views and opinions. Moreover, up to the emergence of the new approach, the consumers of the discourse, who had already been predisposed to view Zionism and often Judaism in negative terms, due to the ongoing conflict, were not exposed to alternative views that challenged the dominant discourse, and therefore had no reason to question it. The enthusiastic welcome given to Garaudy in Arab capitals in 1996 and 1998, Hillal Kashan's survey and the frequent use of Holocaust images and metaphors serve as further testimony. "We were educated from childhood that the Holocaust is a big lie," admitted Muhammad al-Zurqani, former editor-in-chief of *al-Liwa' al-Islami*, the organ of the ruling party in Egypt, in a discussion on Egyptian television dedicated to Holocaust denial.[5]

The subjective vantage point of the Arab discourse determined the scope and nature of the explanations of the Holocaust. German-based Egyptian historian Omar Kamil attributed the narrow Arab view of the Holocaust to the different historical experiences and expectations in Europe and the Arab world, which shaped their respective collective memories. As a result, he contended there exists an epistemic barrier which hinders the Arab intellectual's ability to grasp the depth of the Holocaust's significance, and therefore he perceives it through the prism of his colonial experience.[6] Undoubtedly, the Holocaust discourse was intertwined with the broader anti-colonial one. Yet, the epistemic barrier to understanding the Holocaust is not primarily rooted in Arab historical memory of colonialism, but in a deliberate rejection of the western and Jewish Holocaust scholarship. Various Arab arguments on the Holocaust related to concrete historical events, which were tendentiously interpreted. Over the years, they drew apart from the historical basis, either as a result of the disruption of the free flow of information, or due to selective and unbalanced intake of data, creating a fertile ground for ignorance. In its turn, ignorance played a major psychological role in the reception and entrenchment of those arguments, so much so that

---

5   Special Dispatch Series, No. 782, 10 September 2004, www.memri.org.

6   Omar Kamil, "Araber, Antisemitismus und Holocaust zur Rezeption der Shoah in der Arabischen Welt (Teil 1 + 2)," in *Israel, Palästina und die Deutsche Linke, 26–28 March 2004*, pp. 38–45, www.buko.info/dokumentation/pdfs/reader_ratschlag2004.pdf.

even the knowledge of the facts did not necessarily lead to acknowledging them or their legitimacy.

The debate over the Holocaust remained dominated by the politics of the Arab–Israeli conflict and affected by the political realities of the Middle East. The fact that the Holocaust continues to generate both sympathy and international support for Israel is a deep cause of Arab frustration. There was a strong correlation between the growing role of the Holocaust in the Israeli and Jewish identity and the frequency of Arab reference to it. The more central it became in Jewish consciousness, the more antagonism it aroused among Arabs and Muslims. Similarly, it seems that intensified international interest in the Holocaust in the wake of the new millennium elicits an adverse Arab and Muslim reaction.

BIBLIOGRAPHY AND SOURCES

ARCHIVAL SOURCES

Israel State Archives

HZ/5/217
HZ/6/217
HZ/10/217
HZ/7/3544
HZ/21/2566
HZ/41/10
HZ/2445/8a
HZ/2517/19
HZ/2530/3a
HZ/2545/8a
HZ/2548/18
HZ/2593/3
HZ/2530/3a
HZ/3100/1
HZ/3112/22
IHZ/3753/6
HZ/3757/12
HZ/3766/32

UK National Archives (formerly the Public Record Office)

CO 733/463
CO 733/482
FO 371/45237
FO 371/51198
FO 371/61956
FO 371/96848 (JE1013/40)
FO 371/97867 (C1041/3)
FO 371/98518 (E18210/7)
FO 371/98519 (E18210/27,31)

FO 371/102842 (E11318/2)
FO 371/103955 (CW1041/16)
FO 371/103955 (CW1041/19)
FO 371/103956 (CW1041/9)
FO 371/157811-ER 1661/12
FO 953/2023
WR 985/985/48
WR 1682/985/48

US National Archives

LM 089, Roll 37, 1950–1954 International Relations (674.84A/8–2853).

Newspapers & periodicals

Al-Adab
Al-Ahali
Al-'Ahd - al-Intiqad
Al-Ahram
Al-Ahram Hebdo
Al-Ahram Weekly
Al-Ahrar
Al-Akhbar
Akhbar al-Khalij
Akhbar al-Usbu'
Akhir Sa'a
Al-'Alam
Alif Ba
Alpayim
The American Journal of Sociology
Aqidah Islamic Information Service
Arab News
Arab Observer
Arab Studies Quarterly
Al-'Arab al-Yawm
Al-'Arabi
Arabica
Asian and African Studies
The Atlantic Monthly
Al-Ayyam (Dubai)
Al-Ayyam (Ramallah)
Al-Badil
Balsam
Al-Ba'th

Al-Bayan
Al-Bilad
Bi-Shvil Ha-Zikaron
Boston Globe
La Bourse Egyptienne
Civil Society
The Canadian Islamic Congress Bulletin
Commentary
Critical Inquiry
Daily Star
Al-Da'wa al-Islamiyya
Droit de Vivre
Al-Dustur (Amman)
Al-Dustur (Paris)
Egyptian Gazette
Fasl al-Maqal
Al-Fikr al-'Arabi
Filastin (Beirut)
Filastin (Jerusalem)
Filastin al-Muslima
Filastin al-Thawra
Filesteen al-Yawm online, www.Palestine-info.org.
The Guardian
Ha'aretz
Al-Haqiqa
Hatzofeh
Al-Hawadith
Al-Hayat
Al-Hayat al-Jadida
Hawliyyat al-Quds
Al-Hilal
History and Memory
History of European Ideas
al-Hiwar al-Mutamaddin
Holocaust and Genocide Studies
Al-Hurriyya
Al-'Ilm (Morocco)
The Independent
International Herald Tribune
Internationale Schulbuchforschung
Israel Studies
Al-Istiqlal
Al-Ittihad (Morocco)
Iyunim be-tekumat Yisrael

Al-Jadid
Jedda Arab News (internet version)
Jerusalem Post
The Jerusalem Quarterly
Jerusalem Quarterly File
Jewish Social Studies
Jordan Times
Journal of Genocide Research
Journal of Historical Review
Journal of Israeli History
Journal of Modern History
Journal of Moral Education
Journal of Palestine Studies
Journal of Social Issues
Al-Jumhuriyya
Al-Katib
Kayhan International
Al-Khalij
Kul Al-'Arab
Al-Liwa'
Al-Liwa' al-Islami
Ma'ariv
Al-Majalla
Majallat al-'Asr
Majallat al-Azhar
Majallat Filastin
Al-Majd
Maroc Hebdo International
Al-Masa'
Al-Mashhad al-Isra'ili
Metaphor and Symbolic Activity
Middle East Affairs Journal
Middle East Journal
Middle East Quarterly
Middle East New Online
Middle East Report
Middle Eastern Studies
Mideast Mirror
Al-Misri
Mitzad Sheni
Modern Judaism
Le Monde
Le Monde Diplomatique
Al-Mujahid

Al-Mujtama'
Al-Musawwar
Al-Mustaqbal (Beirut, daily)
Al-Nahar
Al-Nashra (Annashra)
National Zeitung
New York Review of Books
New York Times
Observer
October
L'Orient le Jour
Palestine-Israel Journal
Palestine Times
Panorama
Policy Watch
Politica
Presidential Studies Quarterly
Le Progrès Egyptien
Al-Quds
Al-Quds al-'Arabi
Rabitat al-'Alam al-Islami
Al-Ra'y
Revue d'Etudes Palestinnienes
Al-Risala (Cairo)
Al-Risala (Gaza)
Al-Ru'ya
Ruz al-Yusuf
Al-Sabil
Al-Safa'
Al-Safir
Sawt al-Haqq wal-Hurriyya
Sawt al-Sha'b
Searchlight
Al-Sha'b
Al-Shams
Al-Sharq
Al-Sharq al-Awsat
Al-Shira'
Shu'un Filastiniyya
Al-Sinara
Al-Siyasa
Al-Siyasa al-Duwaliya
Skira Hodshit
Der Spiegel

Studies in Contemporary Jewry
Studies in Zionism
Al-Sunna
Sutur
Syria Times
The Tablet
Tel Aviv Notes
Der Tag
Takbir
Al-Tasawwuf al-Islami
Tehran Times
Al-Thaqafa
Al-Thawra (Syria)
Tikkun
Tishrin
Al-Usbu' al-Adabi
Al-Wafd
Al-Wasat
Washington Post
Al-Watan (Qatar)
Al-Watan al-'Arabi
Die Welt
Die Welt des Islams
The Wiener Library Bulletin
Yad Vashem News
Yad Vashem Studies
The Yale Journal of International Affairs
Yedi'ot Aharonot
Zmanim

News Agencies

ABC News
Agence France Presse (AFP)
Associated Press (AP)
MENA
Reuters
South Africa News Agency (SAPA)
US Newswire

BOOKS AND ARTICLES

Arabic

'Abbas, Mahmud, "Al-Sahyuniyya taw'am al-naziyya wal-yahud awwal dahayaha," *Shu'un Filastiniyya*, no. 112 (March 1981), pp. 3–7.

'Abbas, Mahmud, *Al-Wajh al-akhar: al-'alaqat al-sirriyya bayna al-naziyya wal-sahyuniyya*, Amman: 1984.

'Abbasi, Nizam, *Al-'Alaqat al-sahyuniyya – al-naziyya wa-athriha 'ala filastin wa-harakat al-taharrur al-'arabi, 1933–1945*, Kuwait: 1984.

Al-'Abbasi, Ramadan (tr.), *Usturat ghuraf al-gaz al-naziyya: utruhat nant wa-qadiyyat ruk*, Beirut: 1997.

'Abdallah, Abu Islam Ahmad, "Ba'd rahil Jan Paul al-thani," http://albayan-magazine.com/bayan-212/bayan-21.htm.

'Abdallah, Ghasan, "Filastini fi al-sarh al-tadhakkuri lil-hulukast," *Hawliyyat al-Quds*, no. 1 (Autumn 2003), pp. 56–9.

'Abd al-'Aziz, Magdi Sayyid, *Mawsu'at al-mashahir*, vol. 2, Cairo: 1996.

'Abd al-Ghani, 'Abd al-Rahman, *Almaniya al-naziyya wa-filastin 1933–1945*, Beirut: 1995.

'Abd al-Karim, Ahmad et al., *Ta'rikh al-'arab al-hadith wal-mu'asir*, Cairo: 1966.

'Abd al-Rahim, 'Adnan, *Al-Idi'ulujiyya al-sahyuniyya bayna al-tazayyuf al-nazari wal-waqi' al-isti'mari*, Beirut: 1978.

'Abd al-Wahhab, Ahmad. *Isra'il harrafat al-anajil*, Ba'abdin: 1972.

'Abd al-Wahid, Husayn, *Brutukulat hukama' sahyun*, Cairo: 2002.

'Abduh 'Ali, 'Arafa, "'Ada' 'alani wa-sadaqa sirriyya," *al-Mawqif al-'Arabi*, no. 92 (June 1988), pp. 98–103.

'Abduh 'Ali, 'Arafa, "Usturat al-hulukast: ta'awun mashbuh bayna al-sahyuniyya wal-naziyya," *Al-'Arabi*, no. 498 (May 2000), pp. 108–14.

'Abidu, Muhammad, "Al-Sahayina wal-hulukast cinima'iyyan," *al-Hiwar al-Mutamaddin*, no. 1534, 28 April 2006, www.rezgar.com/debat/show.art.asp?aid=63372.

Abu Gharbiyya, Bahjat, *Fi khidam al-nidal al-'arabi al-filastini: mudhakkirat al-munadil Bahjat Abu Gharbiyya, 1916–1949*, Beirut: 1993.

Abu Hasana, Nafidh, "Al-Fatikan wal-quds," www.Palestine-info.info.

Abu al-Rus, Ilya, *Al-Yahudiyya al-'alamiyya wa-harbuha 'ala al-masihiyya*, Beirut: 1993.

Ahmad, Ibrahim Khalil, *Isra'il fitnat al-ajyal: al-'usur al-qadima*, Cairo: 1969.

Al-Ahmad, Najib, *Filastin ta'rikhan wa-nidalan*, Amman: 1985.

Al-Ahmad, Nasir, "Al-Yahud wa-nar al-hurub," 11 June 2002, www.islammemo.cc/filz/one_news.asp?IDnews=70.

'Ali, Muhammad 'Ali and Muhammad Hina'i 'Abd al-Hadi, *Dawlat al-irhab*, Cairo: n.d. [probably 1963].

'Ali, Walid Muhammad, "Al-Sahyuniyya wal-naziyya takamul al-adwar," 16 June 2006, www.falasteen.com/article.php3?id_article=60.

Al-'Aliyan, 'Abdallah, "Al-Fatikan bayna al-i'tidhar lil-yahud wa-'adam al-i'tidhar lil-'arab wal-muslimin: dirasa fi al-khalfiyyat al-thaqafiyya al-idi'ulujiyya," www. islamicfeqh.com/almenhaj/Almen26/min26001.htm.

'Alluba, Muhammad 'Ali, *Filastin wa-jaratuha*, Cairo: 1954.

'Allush, Ibrahim, "Man hum al-mu'arrikhun al-muraji'un wa-limadha ta'nina al-muhraqa al-yahudiyya," www.freearabvoice.org/arabi/index.htm.

'Allush, Naji, *Al-Haraka al-wataniyya al-filastiniyya amam al-yahudiyya wal-sahyuniyya 1882–1948*, Beirut: 1974.

'Allush, Naji, *Al-Muqawama al-'arabiyya fi filastin, 1917–1948*, Acre: 1979.

Anon, "Akbar ukdhuba ta'rikhiyya yuhawilu al-yahud tamriruha: hiyya ukdhubat al-hulukast aw al-muhraqa fa-hal laha asl?" http://3asfh.net/vb/showthread. php?t=40811.

Anon, "Al-Baba al-jadid wa-mustaqbal al-infitah wal-hiwar," www.aljazeera.net/NR/ exeres/29633E6E-2196-4CF0-9DB2-DA4DC000B8B7.

Anon, "Hitler, almaniya wal-murabun al-yahud," www.egyptiantalks.org/invb/index. php?showtopic=11462&st=90.

Anon, "Hizballah am hizb al-shaytan," http://arabic.islamicweb.com/shia/hizb_allah. htm.

Anon, "Al-Hulukast wal-nifaq al-'alami," www.alsbah.net/alsbah_nuke/modules.php?n ame=News&file=article&sid=6170.

Anon, "Al-I'lam al-'arabi wa-ghiyab al-ta'thir fi al-saha," www.islamselect.com/index.p hp?pg=cats&CR=151&offset=30&pglist=10&ln=1.

Anon, "Al-Kanisa al-kathulikiyya bayna al-mumana'a wal-ikhtiraq al-sahyuni," www. balagh.com/islam/4q0vkqaa.htm.

Anon, "Kulluhumkhidamlil-sahayina," http://alarabnews.com/alshaab/2004/22-10-2004/8. htm.

Anon, "Al-Laji'un wal-bidd al-fasid," 15 July 2003, www.hussamkhader.org/internal/ maqal/7.htm.

Anon, "Mantiq al-ibada aw al-khuruj 'ala al-fitra," www.alqlm.com/index. cfm?method=home.con&contentID=305.

Anon, "Mudakhala hawla muhadarat al-filastiniyyun wal-muhraqa al-yahudiyya," www. almuntada.org.jo/arabic/iss1922001sep06.htm.

Anon, "Qisat al-ikhtiraq al-yahudi lil-fatikan," www.khayma.com/hedaya/news/fat-his. html.

Anon, "Radakhat laha uruba wa-rafadaha al-sadat," http://us.moheet.com/asp/report/ amlak.yahood.htm.

Anon, "Al-Saha al-'arabiyya," 7 May 2000, alsaha.fares.net/sahat?14@81.Ru87oSx-5P2l.0@.ee8e18a.

Anon, "Shakhsiyyat sana'at al-ta'rikh: al-baba yuhana Bulus al-thani," www.alshamsi. net/man/mel/yohana_bolls.html.

Anon, "Tahwid al-nasraniyya: qissat al-ikhtiraq al-yahudi lil-fatikan," www.alsaha.com/ sahat/Forum1/HTML/003888.html.

Anon, "Ya shaykh al-azhar al-istiqala akram bika," www.marsad.org.uk/arabic.

Anwar, Ahmad, *Mukhattatat al-yahudiyya lil-saytara 'ala al-'alam wa-kayfiyyat muwaja-hatiha*, Cairo: 2006.

Al-'Aqqad, 'Abbas Mahmud, *Al-Sahyuniyya wa-qadiyyat Filastin*, Beirut, Sidon: n.d.

Al-'Aqqad, 'Abbas Mahmud, *Hitler fi al-mizan*, Beirut: 1971.

Al-'Aqqad, Salah, *Dirasa muqarina lil-harakat al-qawmiyya fi almaniya, italiya, al-wila-yat al-muttahida wa-turkiya*, Cairo: 1957.

Al-'Aqqad, Salah, *Al-Harb al-'alamiyya al-thaniya: dirasa fi ta'rikh al-'alaqat al-duwali-yya*, Cairo: 1963.

Al-'Aqqad, Salah, *Al-'Arab wal-harb al-'alamiyya al-thaniya*, Cairo: 1966.

Arnuf, Rim, "Al-Khadi'a allati sahamat fi sun' isra'il," *Balsam*, no. 181 (July 1990), pp. 69–75.

'Atiq, Wajih 'Abd al-Sadiq, *Al-Siyasa al-duwaliyya wa-khafaya al-'alaqat al-misriyya al-almaniyya, 1952–1965*, Cairo: 1991.

'Atiq, Wajih 'Abd al-Sadiq, *Al-Malik faruq wa-almaniya al-naziyya: hams sanawat min al-'alaqa al-sirriyya*, Cairo: 1992.

'Atiyya, 'Ali Imam, *Al-sahyuniyya al-'alamiyya wa-ard al-mi'ad*, Cairo: 1963.

'Atiyya, Hayat al-Huwayk, "Al-'Alaqa al-sahyuniyya al-naziyya, 1933–1941," www.ssnp.info/thenews/daily/Makalat/Hayat/Hayat_25-12-05.htm.

'Atallah, Akram, "Al-Sahyuniyya – al-naziyya: bayna hurriyyat al-bahth wa-tahrimihi," *al-Ru'ya*, no. 10 (July 2001), internet edition, pp. 54–73.

'Attar, Ahmad 'Abd al-Ghafur, *Al-Yahudiyya wal-sahyuniyya*, Beirut: 1972.

'Attar, Ahmad 'Abd al-Ghafur, *Al-Masuniyya*, Beirut: 1974.

'Awad, Ramsis, *Al-Hulukast bayna al-inkar wal-ta'kid*, Cairo: 2000.

'Awdi, Ahmad, *Al-Sahyuniyya: nishatuha, tanzimatuha wa-anshitatuha*, Amman: 1993.

Al-Az'ar, Muhammad Khalid, "Al-Tashabuh bayna al-'aqida al-sahyuniyya wal-fikr al-nazi," www.moqawama.tv/arabic/f_vzioni.htm.

Al-'Azm, Sadiq Jalal, *Al-Naqd al-dhati ba'd al-hazima*, Beirut: 1969.

'Azzam, 'Abdallah, *Tujjar al-hurub*, www.tawhed.ws/a?i=77.

Baha' al-Din, Ahmad, *Isra'iliyyat*, Cairo: 1965.

Al-Bahri, Yunus, *Huna birlin, hayy al-'arab*, Beirut: 1955.

Al-Balwi, Sa'd Khalif, "Al-Hulukast: ukdhuba qamat 'alayha isra'il," www.adabihail.com/pages.php?pageid=61.

Banaja, Sa'id, *Nazra hawla al-mu'amarat al-duwaliyya al-yahudiyya wa-asl al-thawrat*, Beirut: 1985.

Al-Barrawi, Rashid, *Mushkilat al-sharq al-awsat*, Cairo: 1948.

Ben Ashenhu, 'Abd al-Hamid, *Usul al-sahuyniyya wa-ma laha*, Algiers: 1974.

Al-Bitar, Nadim, *Al-Fa'iliya al-thawriyya fi al-nakba*, Beirut: 1965.

Bu'ayni, Shirbil, "Al-Fatikan wal-i'tidhar min al-yahud," www.elaph.com/ElaphWrit-er/2005/1/36397.htm.

Budayri, Khalil, *Ta'rikh ma aghfalahu al-ta'rikh: sitta wa-sittun 'amman ma'a al-haraka al-wataniyya al-filastiniyya wa-fiha*, Jerusalem: 1982.

Dajjani, Hisham, *Al-Yahudiyya wal-sahyuniyya*, Beirut: 1985.

Al-Dajjani, Ya'qub Kamil and Lina Ya'qub al-Dajjani, *Filastin wal-yahud: jarimat al-sahyuniyya wal-'alam*, n.p., 1993.

Damj, Nasir, *Tahawwulat minhajiyya fi masar al-sira' al-'arabi al-isra'ili*, Acre: 1996.

Darraj, Faysal, "Al-Talfiq wal-'udwaniyya fi al-idi'ulujiyya al-sahyuniyya," www.wahdah.net/zionideology.html.

Darwish, Marwan, *Al-Judhur al-ta'rikhiyya li-hizb al-likud (takattul)*, Nablus: 1996.

Al-Dissuqi, 'Isam Muhammad, *Misr fi al-harb al-'alamiyya al-thaniya*, Cairo: 1976.

Dissuqi, Muhammad, "Goebbels: al-'abqari al-maghrur," www.20at.com/article2.php?sid=654.

Al-Dissuqi, Muhammad Kamal, *Al-Harb al-'alamiyya al-thaniya: sira' isti'mari*, Cairo: 1968.

Al-Dissuqi, Muhammad Kamal and 'Abd al-Tawwab 'Abd al-Raziq Salman, *Al-Sahyuniyya wal-naziyya. Dirasa muqarina*, Cairo: 1968.

Fahim, Fa'iq, "Al-'Alaqat al-khassa bayna almaniya wa-isra'il," www.aleqtisadiah.com/article.php?do=show&id=1021.

Fahmi, Wiliam, *Al-Hijra al-yahudiyya ila filastin*, Cairo: 1974.

Farah, Elyas, *Al-Watan al-'arabi ba'd al-harb al-'alamiyya al-thaniya*, Beirut: 1975.

Faraj, Muhammad, *Al-Sahyuniyya mashru' isti'mari*, Cairo: 1983.

Fa'ur, Asma' 'Abd al-Hadi, *Filastin wal-maza'im al-yahudiyya*, Beirut: 1990.

Fawzi, Mahmud, *Jarudi wal-islam wa-ghadab al-sahyuniyya*, Cairo: 1996.

Furisun, Rober, *Al-Ukdhuba, al-ta'rikhiyya: hal fi'lan qutila sitta malayin yahud*, Beirut: 1988.

Ghalima, Nasir, *Saytarat isra'il 'ala al-wilayat al-muttahida al-amrikiyya*, Beirut: 1981.

Al-Ghamrawi, Amin Sami, *Li-Hadha akrahu al-yahud*, Cairo: 1964.

Gharabiyya, Ibrahim, "Al-Sahyuniyya wal-naziyya wa-ishkaliyyat al-ta'ayush ma'a al-akhar," www.aljazeera.net/NR/exeres/71628824-A250-4F24-86D9-00C867C3DA2B.htm.

Al-Ghazali, Muhammad, *Al-Isti'mar: ahqad wa-atm'a*, Cairo: 1957.

Al-Ghunaymi, Muhammad Tal'at, *Qadiyyat filastin amama al-qanun al-duwali*, Alexandria, n.d.

Haddad, Jurji, *Al-Mas'ala al-yahudiyya wal-haraka al-wataniyya al-'arabiyya*, Beirut: 1976.

Haddad, Jurji, "Al-Tamathul wal-ta'awun bayna al-sahyuniyya wal-naziyya," *Shu'un Filastiniyya*, no. 209 (August 1990), pp. 54–77.

Haddad, Jurji, "Al-Qadiyya al-armaniyya," *al-Hiwar al-Mutamaddin*, 25 April 2005, www.rezgar.com/debat/show.art.asp?aid=36126.

Haddad, Jurji, "Al-'Alam al-'arabi wal-islami wa-da'wat dimitroff li-iqamat al-jabha al-muwahhada didda al-fashiyya," *Al-Hiwar al-Mutamaddin*, no. 1311, 8 September 2005, www.rezgar.com/debat/show.art.asp?aid=45036.

Hafiz, Hamdi, *Thawrat 23 yuliu: al-ahdath, al-ahdaf, al-injazat*, Cairo: 1964.

Al-Hajiri, Diya', *Isra'il min al-dakhil*, Cairo: 2002.

Hallaq, 'Abdallah, "Nahwa jabha masihiyya-islamiyya li-muwajahat al-sahyuniyya," www.alwahdaalislamyia.net/13th/jabha.htm.

Halumi, Muhammad Najm and Ahmad Muhammad Saqr, *Al-Sahyuniyya madiha wa-hadiruha*, Cairo: 1961.

Hamad, Nidal, "Amrakat al-'alam ta'ni sahyanatihi," www.falasteen.com/article. php3?id_article=100.

Hamdan, Muhammad Misbah, *Al-Isti'mar wal-sahyuniyya al-'alamiyya*, Beirut: 1967.

Hasan, Qasim, *Al-'Arab wal-mushkila al-yahudiyya*, Beirut: 1949.

Al-Hawali, Safar, "Al-Qawmiyya," in www.alhawali.com.inded.

Hawatima, Na'if, "Al-Sahyuniyya wa-sina'at al-karitha," *Al-Hiwar al-Mutamaddin*, no. 1204, 21 May 2005, www.rezgar.com/debat/show.art.asp?aid=37761.

Hitler, Adolf, *Kifahi*, translated by Luis al-Hajj, Beirut: 1963.

Hurayz, 'Abd al-Nasir, *Al-Nizam al-siyasi al-irhabi al-isra'ili: Dirasa muqarina ma'a al-naziyya wal-fashistiyya wal-nizam al-'unsuri fi janub afriqiya*, Cairo: 1997.

Husayn, Yasir, *Bara'at Hitler wa-tazwir al-ta'rikh*, n.p., 1995.

Al-Hut, Biyan Nuwayhad, *Al-Qiyadat wal-mu'assasat al-siyasiyya fi filastin 1917–1948*, Beirut: 1981.

Ibrash, Ibrahim, *Al-Bu'd al-qawmi lil-qadiyya al-filastiniyya: filastin bayna al-qawmiyya al-'arabiyya wal-wataniyya al-filastiniyya*, Beirut: 1987.

Ikhmis, Mustafa, *Al-Sahyunaziyya: qatiluha qabla an taqtulakum*, Bethlehem: 2000.

Al-Imam, Mahmud Rif'at, "Ibadat al-jins: nash'at al-mafhum wa-mu'adalat al-tatbiq," *al-Siyasa al-Duwaliyya*, no. 151 (January 2002), pp. 54–72.

Islamonline, "I'tidharat al-fatikan wa-mawqifihi min al-quds mawdu' al-hiwar," 14 March 2000, www.islam-online.net/livedialogue/arabic/Browse. asp?hGuestID=y680k4.

Isma'il, 'Ali al-Sayyid Muhammad, *Muda mashru'iyyat asanid al-siyasa al-isra'iliyya*, Cairo: 1975.

Al-Jamal, Ahmad 'Abd al-Qadir, *Min mushkilat al-sharq al-awsat*, Cairo: 1955.

Jam'iyyat al-kharijiyyin fi al-kuwayt, *Al-Qadiyya al-filastiniyya fi arba'in 'aman bayna dawrat al-waqi' wa-tumu'at al-mustaqbal*, Kuwait: n.d.

Jarbu'a, Muhammad, *Tabri'at hitler min tuhmat al-hulukast*, Beirut: 2002.

Jarbu'a, Muhammad, *Tabri'at hitler min tuhmat al-hulukast*, Riyad: 2004.

Jarrar, Husayn Adham, *Al-Hajj amin al-husayni: ra'id jihad wa-batal qadiyya*, Amman: 1987.

Jarudi, Rujih, *Al-Asatir al-mu'assisa lil-siyasa al-isra'iliyya*, Cairo: 1998.

Jarudi, Rujih, *Muhakamat al-sahyuniyya al-isra'iliyya*, Cairo: 1999.

Al-Jaza'iri, Abu Hamza, "Al-Hulukast: al-ukdhuba allati sadaqnaha," www.maktoob-blog.com/abuhamza_aljazairi?post=80368.

Al-Jazeera network, "I'tidhar al-fatikan 'an al-hurub al-salibiyya'" 25 January 1999, www.aljazeera.net/channel/archive/archive?ArchiveId=89739

Al-Jiyar, 'Abd al-Ghaffar, *Filastin lil-'arab*, Cairo: 1947.

Al-Jundi, Sami, *Al-'Arab wal-yahud: al-'ada' al-kabir*, Beirut: 1968.

Jurji, Farid 'Abdallah, *Isra'il al-za'ifa*, Cairo: 1965.

Kafuri, Michel, *Al-Sahyuniyya: nishatuha wa-athruha al-ijtima'i*, Cairo: 1947.

Kamil, 'Abd al-'Aziz, "Ziyarat baba al-fatikan: khutuwat jadida 'ala tariq al-ikhtiraq," www.islamweb.net/aqeda/big_religen/crist/13.htm.

Kasha, Suhayl, "Al-Turath al-babili al-dini: sirqatuhu wa-tashwishuhu," www.ssnp. info/thenews/daily/Kasha.htm.

Khalaf, Ghazi, "Al-Hulukast: 'muhraqa' naziyya am 'muhraqa' naziyya-sahyuniyya mushtaraka," www.alwahdaalislamyia.net/40/ghazi%20khalaf.htm.

Al-Kaylani, Haytham, *Al-Irhab yu'assisu dawla: namudhaj isra'il*, Beirut: 1997.

Al-Kaylani, Musa Zayd, *Sanawat al-ightisab: isra'il 1948–1965*, Amman: 1965.

Khalifa, 'Abdallah, "Tadakhkhul al-hitleriyya wal-staliniyya," www.arabrenewal.com.

Khallaq, Husayn 'Ali, *Al-Wajiz fi ta'rikh al-'alam al-mu'asir*, Beirut: 1980.

Al-Khuli, Hasan Sabri, *Siyasat al-isti'mar wal-sahyuniyya tujah filastin fi al-nisf al-awwal min al-qarn al-'ishrin*, Cairo: 1973.

Kilu, Michel, "Al-Hulukast: 'arabiyan," www.moqawama.tv/arabic/articles/holocost.htm, June 2000.

Al-Kiyali, 'Abd al-Wahhab et al. (eds.), *Al-Mawsu'a al-siyasiyya*, vol. 6, Amman: 1995.

Al-Labadi, Mahmud, "Jawla fi al-'aql al-i'lami al-Sahyuni," *Shu'un Filastiniyya*, no. 94 (September 1979), pp. 122–33.

Lama'i, Ikram, *Al-Ikhtiraq al-sahyuni lil-masihiyya*, Beirut: 1991.

Lawand, Ramadan, *Al-Harb al-'alamiyya al-thaniya*, Beirut: 1965.

Luchter, Fred, *Taqrir luchter*, Cairo: 2000.

Al-Madani, Muhammad Nimr, *Hal uhriqa al-yahud fi afran al-ghaz?* Damascus: 1996.

Mahalla, Muhammad, *Al-Tahaluf al-yahudi al-nazi*, Damascus: 2001.

Mahamid, Khalid Kassab, *Al-Filastiniyyun wa-dawlat al-muhraqa*, Umm al-Fahm: 2006.

Al-Mahbubi, 'Ali, *Judhur al-isti'mar al-sahyuni fi filastin*, Tunis: 1990.

Al-Mahdi, Amin, *Azmat al-dimuqratiyya wal-salam*, Cairo: 1999.

Mahmud, 'Abd al-Munsif, *Al-Yahud wal-jarima*, Cairo: 1967.

Mahmud, Hamid, *Al-Di'aya al-sahyuniyya: wasa'iluha wa-asalibuha wa-turuq mukafahatiha*, Cairo: 1966.

Mahmud, Mu'in Ahmad, *Al-Sahyuniyya wal-naziyya*, Beirut: 1971.

Mansur, Anis, *Fi salun al-'aqqad kanat lana ayyam*, Cairo: 1983.

Mansur, Muhammad 'Abd al-'Aziz, *Al-Yahud al-maghdub 'alayhim*, Cairo: 1980.

Al-Marik, Fahd, *Kayfa nantasiru 'ala isra'il*, Beirut: 1966.

Markaz filastin lil-dirasat wal-bahth, *Al-Fatikan wal-sira' al-'arabi al-sahyuni*, Gaza: 2000.

Al-Masdi, Muhammad Jamal al-Din et al., *Misr wal-harb al-'alamiyya al-thaniya*, Cairo: 1978.

Al-Ma'shush, Munir, *Al-Sahyuniyya*, Beirut: 1979.

Al-Masiri, 'Abd al-Wahhab, *Nihayat al-ta'rikh: dirasat fi bunyat al-fikr al-sahyuni*, Beirut: 1979.

Al-Masiri, 'Abd al-Wahhab, "Al-Ibada al-naziyya lil-yahud wa-asbabiha: asbabuha al-ta'rikhiyya wal-hadariyya," *Shu'un Filastiniyya*, no. 183 (June 1988), pp. 59–70.

Al-Masiri, 'Abd al-Wahhab, "Al-I'lam al-'arabi wa-qadiyyat al-ta'awun bayna al-naziyyin wal-sahayina," www.elmessiri.com/ar/modules.php?name=News&file=article&sid=16.

Al-Masiri, 'Abd al-Wahhab, *Al-Sahyuniyya, al-naziyya wa-nihayat al-ta'rikh*, Cairo: 1997.

Al-Masiri, 'Abd al-Wahhab, "Al-Sahyuniyya wal-naziyya wal-ijra'at al-munfasala 'an al-qimma," 29 March 2005, www.aljazeera.net/NR/exeres/C875A445-A238-4349-884B-3BCC33AF6ECE.htm.

Al-Masiri, 'Abd al-Wahhab, "Zahirat mu'adat al-yahud bayna al-haqiqa wal-haqa'iq," *Shu'un Filastiniyya*, nos. 225–6 (December 1991/January 1992), pp. 82–92.

Mas'ud, 'Abd al-Hadi Muhammad, *Hitler wa-mussulini wal-adyan*, Cairo: 1951.

Maw'id, Hamid, *Al-Sahyuniyya ta'lim al-hiqd: qira'a fi tashkil al-'aql al-sahyuni*, Nicosia: 1993.

Mazru'a, Mahmud, *Dirasat fi al-yahudiyya*, Cairo: 1987.

Mohamed, Farouk, "Tasawwur 'an film adulf hitler," www.ra2yak.com/Articles/Article.aspx?articleid=510.

Mu'assasat al-dirasat al-filastiniyya, *Al-Kitab al-sanawi lil-qadiyya al-filastiniyya, 1964*, Beirut: 1966.

Mufid, Shihab al-Din, al-Sayyid Yasin and Yunan Labib Rizq, *Al-Sahyuniyya wal-'unsuriyya: al-sahyuniyya ka-namat min anmat al-tafriqa al-'unsuriyya*, Cairo: 1997.

Muhafaza, 'Ali, *Al-'Alaqat al-almaniyya al-filastiniyya min insha' mutraniyyat al-quds … wahatta nihayat al-harb al-'alamiyya al-thaniya, 1841–1945*, Beirut: 1981.

Muhammad, Muhammad 'Ali, *Al-Wa'd al-batil, "wa'd balfur"*, Cairo: 1961.

Muharib, 'Abd al-Hafiz, *Hagana, Etzel, Lehy: al-'alaqat bayna al-tanzimat al-sahyuniyya al-musallaha, 1937–1948*, Beirut: 1981.

Munir, Michel, *Kanis fi al-kanisa: al-'alaqat al-masihiyya al-yahudiyya*, Damascus: 2001.

Al-Muradi, Nuri, "Al-Hulukast (madhabih al-yahud) – haqiqa am khiyal," 31 October 2002, www.alkader.net/Man_alkader/Alholakost.htm.

Al-Musaymiri, Riyad ibn Muhammad, "Al-Baba fi qubdat al-malik," http://saaid.net/Doat/almosimiry/15.htm.

Mustafa, Hasan, *Al-Musa'adat al-'askariyya al-almaniyya li-isra'il*, Beirut: 1965.

Al-Nabulsi, Muhammad Ahmad, "Al-Sahyuniyya wal-harb al-nafsiyya," www.baheth-center.org/arabic/sahyouniyyat/almasonya_alnfsia.htm.

Al-Nadwa al-'alamiyya lil-shabab al-islami, *Al-Mawsu'a al-muyassara fi al-adyan wal-madhahib wal-ahzab al-mu'asira*, www.alkashf.net.

Nafi', 'Abd al-Majid, *Baritaniya al-naziyya*, Cairo: 1947.

Naji, Sulayman, *Al-Mufsidun fi al-ard aw jara'im al-yahud al-siyasiyya wal-ijtima'iyya 'abr al-ta'rikh*, Damascus: 1966.

Al-Najjar, 'Abd al-Hamid, *Al-Tatawwur al-ta'rikhi li-bani isra'il*, Cairo: 1973.

Al-Najjar, 'Abdallah and Kamal al-Hajj, *Al-Sahyuniyya bayna ta'rikhayn*, Beirut: 1972.

Na'na'a, Mahmud, *Al-Sahyuniyya fi al-sittinat: al-fatikan wal-yahud*, Cairo: 1964.

Nasrallah, 'Abd al-Rahim, *Imbiraturiyyat al-fawda wa-hulukast al-'iraq*, http://iraqk.com/modules.php?name=News&file=article&sid=3321.

Natshe, Rafiq Shakir, *Al-Isti'mar wa-filastin: isra'il mashru' isti'mari*, Amman: 1984.

Nawfal, Ahmad and 'Awni Jadu' al-'Abidi, *Safahat min hayat al-hajj amin al-husayni mufti filastin al-akbar wa-qa'id harakatiha al-wataniyya*, Zarqa': 1985.

399

"Nida' lil-'alamayni al-islami wal-masihi min ajl al-quds," 16 June 1996, www.kuftaro. org/Arabic/Kuftaro_Book/4-2-2.htm.

Nikitina, Galina, *Dawlat isra'il. Khasa'is al-tatawwur al-siyasi wal-iqtisadi*, Cairo: n.d.

PNA, Ministry of Information, "Siyasat al-qiyada al-sahyuniyya," www.minfo.gov.ps/ index.php?scid=2&pid=269.

Qadah, Mahmud 'Abd al-Rahman, "Mujaz ta'rikh al-yahud wal-radd 'ala ba'd maza'imihim al-batila," www.iu.edu.sa/Magazine/107/5.htm.

Al-Qadi, Wa'il, *Al-Tarbiyya fi isra'il*, Nablus: 1994.

Qadri, Hifni, *Tajsid al-wahm: dirasa sikulijiyya lil-shakhsiyya al-isra'iliyya*, Cairo: 1971.

Qahwaji, Habib, *Isra'il hanjar amrika*, Damascus: 1979.

Qamhawi, Walid, *Al-Nakba wal-bana'. Nahwu ba'th al-watan al-'arabi*, Beirut: 1956.

"Al-Qaradawi: sira wa-masira," www.islamonline.net/Arabic/personality/2001/11/article12.SHTML.

Al-Qasim, Anis, *Nahnu wal-fatikan wa-isra'il*, Beirut: 1966.

Al-Qiyada al-'amma lil-quwwat al-musallaha, *Hitler wa-qadatihi al-bahriyyin*, Cairo: 1966.

Qubaysi, Bishri and Musa Makhul, *Al-Hurub wal-azamat al-iqlimiyya fi al-qarn al-'ishrin: uruba, asia*, Beirut: 1997.

Al-Qusari, Muhammad Fa'iz, *Harb filastin, 'am 1948: Al-sira' al-siyasi bayna al-sahyuniyya wal-'arab*, Cairo: 1961.

Al-Quwwat al-musallaha: Qiyadat al-jaysh al-awwal, *Al-Sahyuniyya*, Cairo: 1960.

Al-Rafi'i, 'Abd al-Rahman, *Fi a'qab al-thawra al-misriyya. Thawrat 1919*, Cairo: 1989.

Al-Rajih, 'Abduh, *Al-Shakhsiyya al-isra'iliyya*, Cairo: 1969.

Ramadan, Ahmad Muhammad, *Isra'il wa-masir al-insan al-mu'asir*, Amman: 1987.

Al-Ramli, Fathi, *Al-Sahyuniyya a'la marahil al-isti'mar*, Cairo: 1956.

Al-Ramli, Fathi, *Al-Sahyuniyya al-'alamiyya wa-ma'rakat al-masir al-'arabi*, Cairo: 1968.

Rif'at, Kamal al-Din, *Al-Isti'mar wal-sahyuniyya wa-qadiyyat filastin*, Cairo: 1967.

Rif'at, Muhammad, *Qadiyyat Filastin*, Cairo: 1947.

Al-Rimadi, Jamal al-Din, *Al-Sahyuniyya al-'alamiyya wa-ma'rakat al-masir al-'arabi*, Cairo: 1968.

Rumayh, Tal'at, "Al-Sahyuniyya wal-fashiyya: jawhar fikri wahid," www.moqawama. tv/arabic/f_vzioni.htm.

Sa'd al-Din, Nadiya, *Al-Sahyuniyya wal-naziyya wa-ishkaliyyat al-ta'ayush ma'a al-akhar*, Amman: 2004.

Sa'd, Elyas, *Al-Hijra al-yahudiyya ila filastin al-muhtalla*, Beirut: 1969.

Sa'dani, Mustafa, *Al-Fikr al-yahudi wal-siyasa al-yahudiyya*, Cairo: 1971.

Al-Sadat, Anwar, *Safahat majhula*, Cairo: 1954.

Sadq, Najib, *Qadiyyat filastin*, Beirut: 1946.

Sa'fan, Kamal, *Al-Yahud: ta'rikh wa-'aqida*, Cairo: 1988.

Safwat, Muhammad, *Isra'il al-'aduw al-mushtarak*, Cairo: 1952.

Saghiya, Hazim, *Difa'an 'an al-Salam*, Beirut: 1997.

Al-Sahar, 'Abd al-Latif, *Wa'd allah wa-isra'il*, Cairo: 1967.

Salama, Husayn, "Al-Mazhar al-hulukasti: 'al-'aql al-qurbani lada al-yahud," www.al-wahdaalislamyia.net/53/salamah.htm.

Salman, Rashid Salman, "Almaniya al-naziyya wal-qadiyya al-filastiniyya," *Shu'un Filastiniyya*, no. 31 (March 1974), pp. 92–104.

Samaha, Joseph, *Salam 'abir. Nahwu madd 'arabi lil-"mas'ala al-yahudiyya"*, Beirut: 1993.

Sam'an, Naji, "Banuramat al-'unf al-isra'ili wa-'unf al-gharb," *al-Fikr al-'Arabi*, nos. 85–6 (Summer–Fall 1996), pp. 242–53

Sayigh, Fa'iz A., *Risalat al-mufakkir al-'arabi*, Beirut: 1955.

Sayyid Ahmad, Rif'at, *Qissati ma'a ukdhubat al-hulukast*, Cairo: 2005.

Shalabi, Ahmad, *Muqaranat al-adyan: al-yahudiyya*, Cairo: 1966.

Al-Shaykh 'Ali, Mamduh, "Nahwu ru'ya 'arabiyya jadida lil-hulukast: Inkaruha khata' wa-ihtikaruha khati'a," 12 May 2004, www.islamdaily.net/AR/Contents.aspx?AID=2115.

Al-Shihabi, Mustafa, *Muhadarat fi al-isti'mar*, Cairo: 1955.

Shimali, Nasr, *Iflas al-nazariyya al-sahyuniyya*, Beirut: 1981.

Shimali, Nasr, "Al-Fariq bayna mu'askar abu ghurayb wa-mu'askar auschwitz," www.voltairenet.org/article136329.html, 6 May 2004.

Shimali, Nasr, "Al-Qada al-yahud fi al-jaysh al-almani al-nazi," 6 May 2004, www.arabrenewal.net/index.php?rd=AI&AI0=4073.

Shimali, Nasr, "'Indama iqtaraha hitler madaghaskar watanan lil-yahud," www.albasrah.net/maqalat_mukhtara/arabic/0205/shemali_050205.htm.

Shufani, Elyas, *Al-Mujaz fi ta'rikh filastin al-siyasi mundhu fajr al-ta'rikh hatta sanat 1948*, Beirut: 1996.

Shukri, Muhammad Fu'ad, *Almaniya al-naziyya. dirasa fi al-ta'rikh al-urubbi al-mu'asir (1939–1945)*, Cairo: 1948.

Shuqayri, Ahmad, *Arba'un 'amman fi al-hayat al-'arabiyya wal-duwaliyya*, Beirut: 1973.

Shurayh, 'Isam, *Al-Sahyuniyya wal-naziyya*, Beirut: 1969.

Shurayh, Ismahan, "Al-Hulukast iquna urubiyya," www.alhourriah.org/?page=ShowDetails&table=articles&Id=469&Issue=.

Sirhan, Muhammad 'Ali, "Man yahtakiru hurriyyat al-ra'y wal-haqiqa fi al-gharb," www.baath-party.org/monadel/no-339/almonadil339_8.htm.

Sulayman, 'Abd al-Rahman and Ahmad al-Hamli, *Isra'il ba'd al-zilzal*, Cairo: 1975.

Al-Tabi'i, Muhammad, *Min asrar al-sasa wal-siyasa: misr ma qabla al-thawra*, Cairo: 1970.

Tahhan, Mustafa, *Filastin: al-mu'amara al-kubra*, Kuwait: 1994.

Al-Tal, 'Abdallah, *Judhur al-bala'*, Beirut: 1971.

Tantawi, Muhammad Sayyid, *Banu isra'il fi al-qur'an wal-sunna*, Cairo: 1997.

Tanus, 'Izzat, *Al-Filastiniyyun: madi majid wa-mustaqbal bahir*, Beirut: 1982.

Tarabayn, Ahmad, *Filastin fi khitat al-sahyuniyya wal-isti'mar: amrika fi khidmat al-dawla al-yahudiyya 1939–1947*, Beirut: 1972.

Tawfiq, Ra'uf, *Sinimat al-yahud: dumu' wa-khanajir*, Cairo: 1997.

Al-Thaghlabi, Suhayl, *Al-Sahyuniyya tuharrifu al-injil*, Damascus: 1999.

Tuma, Emil, *Judhur al-qadiyya al-filastiniyya*, Jerusalem: 1976.

Tuma, Emil, *Sittun 'aman 'ala al-haraka al-qawmiyya al-'arabiyya al-filastiniyya*, Jerusalem: 1978.

Tuma, Emil, *Ta'rikh masirat al-shu'ub al-'arabiyya al-haditha*, Haifa: 1995.

Tuqan, Fawwaz, *Al-Isti'mar al-sahyuni lil-ard al-filastiniyya: qissat al-sahyuniyya wal-ard wal-muqawama mundhu 1870*, Amman: 1987.

Al-Turayki, Husayn, *Hadhihi filastin*, Tunis: 1971.

Al-'Umar, 'Abd al-Karim (ed.), *Mudhakkirat al-hajj muhammad amin al-husayni*, Damascus: 1999.

Al-'Umari, Ahmad Suwaylim, *Al-Sharq al-awsat wa-mushkilat filastin*, Cairo: 1954.

Wakid, 'Abd al-Hamid, *Nihayat isra'il wal-sahyuniyya*, Cairo: 1971.

Wizarat al-I'lam, *Jarudi*, Cairo: n.d.

Yahya, Jalal, *Al-'Alam al-'arabi al-hadith mundhu al-harb al-'alamiyya al-thaniya*, Cairo: 1967.

Yuhana, D., "Hiwarat Hayya: i'tidharat al-fatikan wa-mawqifihi min al-quds," Islamonline.org, 14 March 2000.

Yusuf, Mahmud Yusuf, *Isra'il al-bidaya wal-nihaya*, Cairo: 1997.

Yusuf, Sa'adallah Suryal, *Al-Mu'allim fi ta'rikh misr wal-'arab al-hadith*, Cairo: 1995.

Zahr al-Din, Salih, *Al-Khalfiyya al-ta'rikhiya li-muhakamat rujih gharudi*, Beirut: 1998.

Zaytun, 'Abd al-Wahhab, *Yahudiyya am Sahyuniyya*, Beirut: 1991.

Ziedan, Yousef, "Al-Internet: al-shabaka al-duwaliyya wal-dafira al-ma'lumatiyya," www.ziedan.com/English/memory.asp.

Al-Zu'bi, Muhammad 'Ali, *Isra'il. Bint baritaniya al-bakr*, Cairo: n.d.

Al-Zu'bi, Muhammad 'Ali, *Dafa'in al-nafsiyya al-yahudiyya min khilal al-kutub al-muqaddasa al-tawrat, al-injil wal-qur'an wal-ta'rikh wal-waqi'*, Beirut: 1973, 3rd edn.

Zurayq, Custantin, *Ma'na al-nakba*, Beirut: 1948.

Other languages

Abdul Hadi, Mufid, *The Other Side of the Coin: A Native Palestinian Tells his Story*, Nablus: 1998.

Abou Iyad, *Palestinien sans patrie: Entretiens avec Eric Rouleau*, Jerusalem: 1979, Hebrew.

Abu Lughud, Ibrahim, "From Catastrophe to Defeat, Two Terms for Big Events," in Y. Harkabi (ed.), *The Arabs and Israel: A Collection of Translations from Arabic* no. 1, Tel-Aviv: 1975, Hebrew, pp. 34–46.

Abu Lughud, Ibrahim, "The Nakba: This is What Happened," *Alpayim*, no. 16, 1998, Hebrew, pp. 152–7.

Ajami, Fouad, *Dream Palaces of the Arabs: A Generation's Odyssey*, New York: 1998.

AJAZ (American Jewish Alternatives to Zionism) and EAFORD (International Organization for the Elimination of All Forms of Racial Discrimination), *Judaism or Zionism: What Difference to the Middle East?* London: 1986.

Alexander, Edward, "Stealing the Holocaust," *Midstream*, vol. 28, no. 9 (November 1980), pp. 46–51.

Alexander, Edward, *The Holocaust and the War of Ideas*, New Brunswick: 1994.

Alloush, Ibrahim, "Between Public relations and Self-Alienation: Arab Intellectuals and the 'Holocaust'," *the Journal of Historical Review*, (May/June 2001), pp. 23–44.

Almog, Shmuel, "Alfred Nossig: Reappraisal," *Studies in Zionism*, no. 7 (Spring 1983), pp. 1–31.

American Jewish Committee, Institute of Human Relations Press, *The Eichmann Case in the American Press*, New York: 1962.

Anawati, G. C, "'Isa," *Encyclopaedia of Islam,* vol. 4, 2nd edn. Leiden, pp. 81–4.

Ankersmith, F. R., *Historical Representation*, Stanford, CA: 2001.

Anon, "The Ingenious Circle in Washington," www.Hebron.com.

Arad, Yitzhaq, "The Holocaust in Soviet Historiography," in Y. Gutman and G. Greif (eds.), *The Historiography of the Holocaust Period*, Jerusalem: 1988, pp. 187–216.

Arendt, Hannah, *Eichmann in Jerusalem. A Report on the Banality of Evil*, New York: 1963.

Aronson, Shlomo, *Hitler, the Allies, and the Jews*, Cambridge: 2004.

Ateek, Naim Stifan, *Justice and only Justice. A Palestinian Theology of Liberation*, New York: 1990.

Bach, Gavriel, "Thoughts and Reflections 30 Years after the Eichmann Trial," *Bi-Shvil Ha-Zikaron*, no. 41 (April–May 2001), Hebrew, pp. 4–15.

Bar-On, Dan and Saliba Sarsar, "Bridging the Unbridgeable: The Holocaust and Al-Nakba," *Palestine–Israel Journal*, vol. 11, no. 1 (2004), pp. 63–70.

Bar-Tal, Daniel et al. (eds.), *Stereotyping and Prejudice. Changing Conceptions*, New York: 1989.

Bar-Tal, Daniel, "Societal Beliefs in Times of Intractable Conflict: The Israeli Case," *International Journal of Conflict Management*, vol. 9 (1998), pp. 22–50.

Bar-Tal, Daniel, "From Intractable Conflict Through Conflict Resolution to Reconciliation: Psychological Analysis," *Political Psychology*, vol. 21, no. 2 (June 2000), pp. 351–65.

Barari, Hasan, "Arab Scholarship on Israel: A Critical Assessment," US Institute of Peace: Project Report Summary, 2 May 2007, www.usip.org/fellows/reports/2007/-5-2_barari.html.

Bartov, Omer, *Murder in Our Midst: The Holocaust, Industrial Killing, and Representation*, New York: 1996.

Bauer, Yehuda, "Whose Holocaust?" *Midstream*, vol. 26, no. 9 (November 1980), pp. 42–6.

Bauer, Yehuda, "'Revisionism' – The Repudiation of the Holocaust and its Historical Significance," in Y. Gutman and G. Greif (eds.), *The Historiography of the Holocaust Period*, Jerusalem: 1988, pp. 697–708.

Bauer, Yehuda, "In Search of a Definition of Antisemitism," in Michael Brown (ed.), *Approaches to Anti-Semitism*, New York: 1994, pp. 10–24.

Bauer, Yehuda, *Jews for Sale? Nazi-Jewish Negotiations, 1933–1945*, New Haven: 1994.

Bauer, Yehuda, *Rethinking the Holocaust*, New Haven: 2001.

Becker, Avi, "The Evil Face of 'Neutralism'," *Masuah*, vol. 25 (April 1997), Hebrew, pp. 129–41.

Beckman, Morris, *The Jewish Brigade: An Army with Two Masters 1944–45*, Staplehurst: 1988.

Beinin, Joel, "Nazis and Spies: Representations of Jewish Espionage and Terrorism in Egypt," *Jewish Social Studies*, no. 2 (1996), pp. 54–84.

Bilsky, Liora, "Like a Phoenix: Arendt in Jerusalem: 2000," *Bi-Shvil Ha-Zikaron*, no. 41 (April–May 2001), Hebrew, pp. 16–23.

Bishara, 'Azmi, "The Arabs and the Holocaust: The Analysis of a Problematic Conjunctive Letter," *Zmanim*, no. 53 (Summer 1995), Hebrew, pp. 54–71.

Bishara, 'Azmi, "Response," *Zmanim*, no. 55 (Spring 1996), Hebrew, pp. 102–7.

Bloxham, Donald, *Genocide on Trial. War Crime Trials and the Formation of Holocaust History and Memory*, Oxford: 2001.

Bohlen, Charles, *Witness to History*, New York: 1973.

Brands, H. W., "George Bush and the Gulf War of 1991," *Presidential Studies Quarterly*, vol. 34, no. 1 (March 2004).

Braun, Robert, "The Holocaust and Problems of Historical Representation," *History and Theory*, vol. 33, no. 2 (May 1994), pp. 172–97.

Brinner, William, "An Egyptian anti-Orientalist," in G. Warburg and U. Kupferschmidt (eds.), *Islam, Nationalism and Radicalism in Egypt and the Sudan*, New York: 1986, pp. 228–48.

Bronner, Stephen Eric, *A Rumor about the Jews: Reflections on Antisemitism and the Protocols of the Learned Elders of Zion*, New York: 2000.

Browning, Christopher R., "German Memory, Judicial Interrogation, and Historical Reconstruction: Writing Perpetrator History from Post-War Testimony," in S. Friedlander (ed.), *Probing the Limits of Representation*, Cambridge: 1992, pp. 22–36.

"The Canadian Islamic Congress Bulletin," 9 October 1999, http://msanews.mynet.net.

Cartus, F. E., "Vatican II and the Jews," *Commentary*, vol. 30, no. 1 (January 1965), pp. 19–29.

Catan, George, "The Jewish Holocaust: Reality or Myth," 25 May 2005, www.metransparent.com/texts/george_catan.

Chaumont, Jean-Michel, *La Concurrence des Victims, Génocide, Identité, Reconnaissance*, Paris: 1997.

Cohen, Michael J. (ed.), *The Rise of Israel*, vol. 29: *Jewish Military Effort 1939–1944*, New York: 1987.

Cohen, Michael J., *Truman and Israel*, Berkeley: 1990.

Cohen, Mark, *Under Crescent and Cross: The Jews in the Middle Ages*, Princeton: 1994.

Cohn, Norman, *Warrant for Genocide: The Myth of the Jewish World Conspiracy and the Protocols of the Elders of Zion*, Choco, CA: 1982.

Colson, Michael, "Durban and the Middle East: Challenges for U.S. Policy," Washington Institute for Near Eastern Policy: *PolicyWatch*, no. 548, 1 August 2001.

Dawidowicz, Lucy S., *The War against the Jews, 1933–1945*, New York: 1975.

Dawidowicz, Lucy S., *The Holocaust and the Historians*, Cambridge, MA: 1981.

Dawidowicz, Lucy S., "How They Teach the Holocaust," *Commentary*, vol. 90, no. 6 (December 1990), pp. 25–32.

"The Declaration of the International Conference of NGOs Defending Palestinian Rights," *Middle East Affairs Journal*, vol. 7, nos. 1–2 (Winter/Spring 2001), pp. 235–9.

Don-Yehia, Eliezer, "Memory and Political Culture: Israeli Society and the Holocaust," *Studies in Contemporary Jewry*, vol. 9 (1993), pp. 139–62.

"Drive the Zionists to the Sea," association which appeared in msanews@msanews.mynet.net 2000.

Eddy, William A., *F.D.R. Meets Ibn Saud*, New York: 1954.

Elpeleg, Zvi, *The Grand Mufti: Haj Amin al-Hussaini, Founder of the Palestinian National Movement*, London: 1993.

Fackenheim, Emil L., *God's Presence in History: Jewish Affirmations and Philosophical Reflections*, New York: 1970.

Fawwaz, Fadwa, "Holocaust doesn't Justify Israeli Aggression," MSANEWS, 24 January 1998.

Finkielkraut, Alain, *The Future of a Negation: Reflections on the Question of Genocide*, Lincoln, NE: 1998.

Frankel, Jonathan, *The Damascus Affair: "Ritual Murder," Politics and the Jews in 1840*, Cambridge: 1997.

Free Arab Voice, "Why the 'Holocaust' is important to Palestinians, Arabs and Muslims," 28 April 2001, www.freearabvoice.org.

Friling, Tuvia, "Ben Gurion and the Holocaust of European Jewry 1939–1945: A Stereotype Reexamined," *Yad Vashem Studies*, vol. 18 (1987), pp. 199–232.

Friling, Tuvia, *An Arrow in the Mist: Ben-Gurion, the Yishuv Leadership and Rescue Efforts during the Holocaust*, 2 vols., Beer Sheva: 1998, Hebrew.

Friedlander, Saul (ed.), *Probing the Limits of Representation: Nazism and the "Final Solution"*, Cambridge: 1992.

Friedlander, Saul, *Nazi Germany and the Jews*, New York: 1997.

Friedmann, Yohanan, *Tolerance and Coercion in Islam: Interfaith Relations in the Muslim Tradition*, New York: 2003.

Funkenstein, Amos, "History, Counter History and Narrative," in S. Friedlander (ed.), *Probing the Limits of Repesentation*, Cambridge: 1992, pp. 66–81.

Gardet, L., "Fitna," *Encyclopaedia of Islam*, vol. 2, 2nd edn., Leiden, pp. 930–1.

Gelber, Yoav, "Zionist Policy and the Fate of European Jewry," *Yad Vashem Studies*, vol. 13 (1979), pp. 169–210.

Gelber, Yoav, *Jewish Palestinian Volunteers in the British Army during the Second World War*, Jerusalem: 1981, Hebrew.

Gershoni, Israel, *Light in the Shadow: Egypt and Fascism, 1922–1937*, Tel Aviv: 1999, Hebrew.

Gershoni, Israel and James P. Jankowski, *Redefining the Egyptian Nation, 1930–1945*, Cambridge: 1995.

Giladi, Avner, "Israel's Image in Recent Egyptian Textbooks," *The Jerusalem Quarterly*, no. 7 (Spring 1978), pp. 88–97.

Gilbert, Arthur, *The Vatican Council and the Jews*, Cleveland, OH: 1968.

Gilbert, Martin, *Exile and Return: The Emergence of Jewish Statehood*, London: 1978.

Gilbert, Martin, *Auschwitz and the Allies*, New York: 1981.

Gilbert, Martin, *The Holocaust: The Jewish Tragedy*, London: 1986.

Glenn, Mark, "One Less Than Six Million," www.ipc.gov.ps/ipc_e/ipc_e-1/e_Articles/2004/articles-008.html.

Gorman, Anthony, *Historians, State and Politics in Twentieth Century Egypt: Contesting the Nation*, London: 2003.

Gorni, Yosef, *Between Auschwitz and Jerusalem*, Tel Aviv: 1998, Hebrew.

Grauman, Carl F. and Serge Moscovici (eds.), *Changing Conceptions of Conspiracy*, London and Berlin: 1987.

Green, D. F. (ed.), *Arab Theologians on Jews and Israel: Extracts from the Proceedings of the Fourth Conference of the Academy of Islamic Research*, Geneva: 1971.

Griffin, L. J., "Narrative, Event-Structure Analysis, and Causal Interpretation in Historical Sociology," *The American Journal of Sociology*, vol. 98, no. 5 (1993), pp. 1094–133.

Groiss, Arnon (ed.), *Jews, Zionism and Israel in Syrian School Textbooks*, New York: 2001.

Groiss, Arnon (ed.), *Jews, Israel and Peace in the Palestinian Authority Textbooks*, New York: 2005.

Grossman, Kurt R., *Germany's Moral Debt: The German-Israel Agreement*, Washington: 1954.

Grubsztein, Meir (ed.), *Jewish Resistance during the Holocaust*, Jerusalem: 1971.

Gur-Ze'ev, Ilan, "The Morality of Acknowledging/Not-acknowledging the Other's Holocaust/Genocide," *Journal of Moral Education*, vol. 27, no. 2 (1998), pp. 161–78.

Gur-Ze'ev, Ilan. *Philosophy, Politics and Education in Israel*, Haifa: 1999, Hebrew.

Gutman, Yisrael (ed.), *Encyclopedia of the Holocaust*, New York: 1990.

Gutman, Yisrael and Gideon Greif (eds.), *The Historiography of the Holocaust Period: Proceedings of the Fifth Yad Vashem International Conference, Jerusalem, March 1983*, Jerusalem: 1988.

Habibi, Emil, "Your Holocaust Our Catastrophe," *Politica*, no. 8 (June–July 1986), Hebrew, pp. 26–7.

Haim, Sylvia G., "Arab Anti-Semitic Literature," *Jewish Social Studies*, vol. 17, no. 4 (1955), pp. 307–12.

The Hamas Charter 1988 (18 August 1988), www.yalc.edu/lawweb/avalon/mideast/hamas.htm.

Hanania, Ray, "Morality and Principles in the Palestinian Struggle for Nationhood," 5 August 1998, www.hanania.com.

Harkabi, Yehoshafat, *Arab Attitudes Toward Israel*, Jerusalem: 1972.

Harle, Vilho, "On the Concepts of the 'Other' and the 'Enemy'," *History of European Ideas*, vol. 19, nos. 1–3 (1994), pp. 27–34.

Hasson, Isaac, "Les śi'ites vue par les neo-wahhabites," *Arabica*, vol. 53, no. 3 (July 2006), pp. 299–330.

Hecht, Ben, *Perfidy*, New York: 1961.

Herf, Jeffrey (ed.), *Anti-Semitism and anti-Zionism in Historical Perspective*, London: 2006.

Herf, Jeffrey, "Convergence: The Classic Case Nazi Germany, Anti-Semitism and Anti-Zionism during World War II," in J. Herf (ed.), *Anti-Semitism and Anti-Zionism in Historical Perspective*, London: 2006, pp. 50–70.

Hilberg, Raul, *The Destruction of the European Jews*, London: 1961.

Hilberg, Raul, *Perpetrators, Victims, Bystanders. The Jewish Catastrophe 1933–1945*, London: 1995.

Hirszowicz, Lukasz, *The Third Reich and the Arab East*, London: 1966.

Hopkins, Harry, *Egypt the Crucible: The Unfinished Revolution of the Arab World*, London: 1969.

Hurewitz, J. C., *The Struggle for Palestine*, New York: 1951.

Ibrahim, Haitham, "Arafat's Holocaust Museum Visit Lopsided Gesture," Arol (Arabia online) (1998), www.Arabia.com.

Independent Committee of Eminent Persons (ICEP), *Report on Dormant Accounts of Victims of Nazi Persecution in Swiss Banks*, Berne: 1999.

Institute of the World Jewish Congress, *Reevaluating European History: Committees of Inquiry on the Restitution of Jewish Property*, Policy Dispatch no. 41, April 1999.

"Interview with Rashid Ghannoushi, 10 February," MSANEWS, 12 February 1998.

Israel Studies Special Issue: Israel and the Holocaust, vol. 8, no. 3 (Fall 2003).

Israeli, Rafael, *Peace is in the Eyes of the Beholder*, New York: 1985.

Jabr, Samah, "History in Repetition," in Al-Awda archives, 13 February 2001, www.mediamonitors.net/samah11.html.

Jasen, G. H., *Zionism, Israel and Asian Nationalism*, Beirut: 1971.

Jayyusi, Salma Khadra, "The End of Innocence," in D. A. McGowan and M. H. Ellis (eds.), *Remembering Deir Yassin*. New York: 1998, pp. 25–34.

Jbara, Taysir, *Palestinian Leader Hajj Amin al-Husayni: Mufti of Jerusalem*, Princeton: 1985.

Jelinek, Yeshayahu, *The Parish Republic: Hlinka's Slovak People's Party, 1939–1945*, New York: 1976.

John, Robert and Sami Hadawi, *The Palestinian Diary*, Beirut: 1970.

"The Jordanian Writers Association Sets a New Date for Its Forum," The Free Arab Voice Online, 15 April 2001, www.freearabvoice.org.

Journal of Historical Review, "A Conversation with Dr. Ibrahim Alloush," vol. 20, no. 3 (May/June 2001), electronic edition.

Judt, Tony, "Epilogue: From the House of the Dead an Essay on Modern European Memory," in idem, *Postwar: A History of Europe since 1945*, New York: 2005.

Judt, Tony, "Europe – Rising from the House of the Dead," 25 October 2005, www.theglobalist.com/StoryId.aspx?StoryId=4874.

Kahtany, Abdallah, *Zionism*, Riyad: 2000.

Kamil, Omar, "Araber, Antisemitismus und Holocaust zur Rezeption der Shoah in der arabischen Welt (Teil 1 + 2)," in *Israel, Palästina und die deutsche Linke, 26–28 March 2004*, pp. 38–45, www.buko.info/dokumentation/pdfs/reader_ratschlag2004.pdf.

Karlibakh, Azriel (ed.), *The Anglo-American Commission on Palestine*, Tel Aviv: 1946, 2 vols, Hebrew.

Karmi, Ghada, "The Question of Compensation and Reparations," in G. Karmi and E. Cotran (eds.), *The Palestinian Exodus 1948–1998*, Reading: 1999, pp. 197–220.

Karmi, Ghada and Eugene Cotran (eds.), *The Palestinian Exodus 1948–1998*, Reading: 1999.

Kashan, Hilal, *Arab Attitudes toward Israel and Peace*, Washington Institute Research Memorandum no. 40, Washington, August 2000.

Kassir, Samir, "La Nakba recommence?" *Revue d'Etudes Palestinnienes*, vol. 17, no. 69 (automne 1998), pp. 59–65.

Katz, Jacob, *From Prejudice to Destruction: Anti-Semitism, 1700–1933*, Cambridge, MA: 1982.

Kempner, Robert, *Profession: Annihiliation – Eichmann's Way*, Jerusalem: 1963, Hebrew.

Kershaw, Ian, *The Nazi Dictatorship: Problems and Perspectives of Interpretation*, London: 1985.

Khadduri, Majid, *Arab Contemporaries: The Role of Personalities in Politics*, Baltimore: 1973.

Khalidi, Rashid, *Palestinian Identity. The Construction of Modern National Consciousness*, New York: 1997.

Khalidi, Rashid, "Fifty Years after 1948: A Universal Jubilee?" *Tikkun*, vol. 13, no. 2 (March/April 1998), pp. 8–17.

Khalidi, Rashid, "Truth, Justice and Reconciliation: Elements of a Solution to the Palestinian Refugee Issue," in G. Karmi and E. Cotran (eds.), *The Palestinian Exodus 1948–1998*, Reading: 1999, pp. 221–42.

Khoury, Philip S., *Syria and the French Mandate: The Politics of Arab Nationalism, 1920–1945*, Princeton, NJ: 1987.

Kimmerling, Baruch and Joel S. Migdal, *Palestinians. The Making of a People*, New York: 1993.

Knoller, Rivka, *The Activities of Religious Zionist Youth Groups in Europe during the Holocaust, 1939–1945: A Summarized Review of Limited Archive Sources*, Ramat Gan: 1989.

Kramer, Gudrun, "Anti-Semitism in the Muslim World: A Critical Review," *Die Welt des Islams*, vol. 46, no. 3 (2006), pp. 243–76.

Kronemeijer, Matthijs, *An Arab Voice of Compromise. Hazem Saghieh's "In Defence of Peace" (1997)*, Utrech University, 2005, igitur-archive.library.uu.nl/student-theses/2006–0324–082630/UUindex.html.

Kyle, Keith, *Suez*, New York: 1991.

Lang, Berel (ed.), *Philosophy and the Holocaust*, New York: 1984/85.

Lassner, Jacob, *The Middle East Remembered: Forged Identities, Competing Narratives, Contested Spaces*, Ann Arbor, MI: 2000.

Lazarus-Yafeh, Hava, "An Inquiry into Arab Textbooks," *Asian and African Studies*, vol. 8, no. 1 (1972), pp. 1–19.

Levi, Neil and Michael Rothberg, *The Holocaust: Theoretical Readings*, New Brunswick: 2003.

Levin, Itamar, *The Last Deposit. Swiss Banks and Holocaust Victims' Accounts*, Westport, VA: 1999.

Lewan, Kenneth M, "How West Germany Helped to Build Israel," *Journal of Palestine Studies*, vol. 4, no. 4 (Summer 1975), pp. 41–64.

Lewis, Bernard, *The Jews of Islam*, Princeton, NJ: 1984.

Lewis, Bernard, "The Roots of Muslim Rage," *The Atlantic Monthly* (September 1990), pp. 47–60.

Lewis, Bernard, *Semites and Anti-Semites: An Inquiry into Conflict and Prejudice*, London: 1997.

Liberles, Robert, *Salo Wittmayer Baron: Architect of Jewish History*, New York: 1995.

Linn, Ruth and Ilan Gur-Ze'ev, "Holocaust as Metaphor: Arab and Israeli Use of the Same Symbol," *Metaphor and Symbolic Activity*, vol. 11, no. 3 (1996), pp. 195–206.

Lipstadt, Deborah, *Beyond Belief: The American Press and the Coming of the Holocaust 1933–1945*, New York and London: 1986.

Lipstadt, Deborah, *Denying the Holocaust: The Growing Assault on Truth and Memory*, New York: 1993.

Litvak, Meir, "The Islamization of the Israeli–Arab Conflict: The Case of Hamas," *Middle Eastern Studies*, vol. 23, no. 1 (1998), pp. 148–63.

Litvak, Meir, "The Islamic Republic of Iran and the Holocaust: Anti-Zionism and Anti-Semitism," *Journal of Israeli History*, vol. 25 (2006), pp. 245–66.

Litvak, Meir and Esther Webman, "Perceptions of the Holocaust in Palestinian Public Discourse," *Israel Studies*, vol. 8, no. 3 (Fall 2003), pp. 123–41.

Lonni, Ada, "Parallel Strategies in Israeli and Palestinian Experiences," *Palestine–Israel Journal*, vol. 8/4–9/1 (2001–2), pp. 71–83.

Maddy-Weitzman, Bruce, "Islamism, Moroccan-Style: The Ideas of Sheikh Yassine," *Middle East Quarterly*, vol. 10, no. 1 (Winter 2003), pp. 43–51.

Maier, Charles S., *The Unmasterable Past: History, Holocaust, and German National Identity*, Cambridge: 1988.

Maier, Charles S., "A Surfeit of Memory? Reflections on History, Melancholy and Denial," *History and Memory*, vol. 5, no. 2 (Fall/Winter 1993), pp. 136–51.

Marcus, Ernest, "The German Foreign Office and the Palestine Question in the Period 1933–1939," *Yad Vashem Studies*, vol. 2 (1958), pp. 179–204.

Marrus, Michael R., "The Holocaust at Nuremberg," *Yad Vashem Studies*, vol. 26 (1998), pp. 5–41.

Masalha, Omar, *Towards the Long-Promised Peace*, London: 1994.

Massad, Joseph, "Palestinian and Jewish History: Recognition or Submission?" *Journal of Palestine Studies*, vol. 30, no. 1 (Autumn 2000), pp. 52–67.

Massad, Joseph, "Deconstructing Holocaust Consciousness," *Journal of Palestine Studies*, vol. 32, no. 1 (Autumn 2002), pp. 73–83.

Mattar, Philip, *The Mufti of Jerusalem: Al-Hajj Amin al-Husayni and the Palestinian National Movement*, New York: 1988.

McGowan, Daniel A. and Marc H. Ellis (eds.), *Remembering Deir Yassin. The Future of Israel and Palestine*, New York: 1998.

Memorandum of the Institute of Arab American Affairs on the Recommendations of the Anglo-American Committee of Inquiry, New York, August 1946.

Michman, Dan, "'The Holocaust' in the Eyes of Historians: The Problem of Conceptualization, Periodization, and Explanation," *Modern Judaism*, vol. 15, no. 3 (October 1995), pp. 233–64.

Michman, Dan, "Responses," *Zmanim*, no. 54 (Winter 1995), Hebrew, pp. 117–19.

Michman, Dan (ed.), *Post-Zionism and the Holocaust*, Ramat Gan: 1997, Hebrew.

Menashri, David, "What Lies behind Ahmadinejad's Hate Speech?" *Tel Aviv Notes*, no. 155, 21 December 2005.

Miles, William F. S., "Third World Views of the Holocaust," *Journal of Genocide Research*, vol. 6, no. 3 (September 2004), pp. 371–93.

"Mohamed Hassanein Heikal: Reflections on a Nation in Crisis, 1948," *Journal of Palestine Studies*, vol. 18, no. 1 (August 1988), pp. 112–20.

Moshman, David, "Conceptual Constraints on Thinking about Genocide," *Journal of Genocide Research*, vol. 3, no. 3 (2001), pp. 431–50.

Mouttapa, Jean, *Un Arabe face à Auschwitz. La mémoire partagée*, Paris: 2004.

Nafi, Basheer, "The Arabs and the Axis: 1933–1940," *Arab Studies Quarterly* (Spring 1997), electronic edition.

Nakhle, Issa, "Memorandum to the President," *Journal of Historical review*, vol. 3, no. 3 (Fall 1982), electronic edition.

Nakhle, Issa, *Encyclopaedia of the Palestinian Problem*, vol. 2, New York: 1991.

Neeman-Arad, Gulie, "A History of Memory: The Changing Status of the Holocaust in the Conscious of the Jews in the United States," *Zmanim*, no. 57 (Winter 1996–7), Hebrew, pp. 14–22.

Nettler, Ronald L., "Arab Images of Jews and Israel," in William Frankel (ed.), *Survey of Jewish Affairs, 1989*, Oxford: 1989, pp. 33–43.

Nettler, Ronald L., *Past Trials and Present Tribulations: A Muslim Fundamentalist's View of the Jews*, Oxford: 1997.

Nettler, Ronald L., "Early Islam, Modern Islam and Judaism: The Isra'iliyyat in Modern Islamic Thought," in Ronald L. Nettler and Suha Taji-Faruki (eds.), *Muslim–Jewish Encounters. Intellectual Traditions and Modern Politics*, Amsterdam: 1998, pp. 1–14.

Nevo, Yosef, "The Attitude of Arab Palestinian Historiography toward the Germans and the Holocaust," in *Remembering for the Future*, vol. 2, Oxford: 1989, pp. 2241–50.

Nicosia, Francis, "Zionism in National Socialist Jewish Policy in Germany: 1933–39," *Journal of Modern History*, vol. 50, no. 4 (1978), pp. 1253–82.

Nicosia, Francis R., *The Third Reich and the Palestine Question*, London: 1985.

Nordbruch, Goetz, "An Attempt to Internationalize the Denial of the Holocaust," *SICSA Annual Report 2001*, Jerusalem: 2001, pp. 9–11.

Novak, David, *The Election of Israel: The Idea of the Chosen People*, Cambridge: 1995.

Novick, Peter. *The Holocaust and Collective Memory*, Bloomsbury: 2000.

Oron, Yitzhak (ed.), *Middle East Record*, London: 1960.

"The Palestinian National Covenant," www.mideastweb.org/plocha.htm.

Papadatos, Peter, *The Eichmann Trial*, London: 1964.

Penkower, M. N., *The Holocaust and Israel Reborn: From Catastrophe to Sovereignty*, Urbana, IL: 1994.

Perlman, Moshe, *How Eichmann Was Caught*, Tel Aviv: 1961.

Petrie, Jon, "The Secular Word 'Holocaust': Scholarly Sacralization, Twentieth Century Meanings," www.berkeleyinternet.com/holocaust.

Pipes, Daniel, *The Hidden Hand: Middle East Fears of Conspiracy*, New York: 1996.

"PM Abbas and Israeli PM Ariel Sharon statements following the Aqaba summit, Aqaba, Jordan, 4 June 2003," *Journal of Palestine Studies*, vol. 33, no. 1 (Fall 2003), p. 150.

PNA, Ministry of Information, *The Palestinian People's Appeal on the 50th Anniversary of the Catastrophe "Al-Nakba"*, www.pna.org/mininfo/nakba.

Podeh, Elie, "Recognition without Legitimization: Israel and the Arab–Israeli Conflict in Egyptian History Textbooks," *Internationale Schulbuchforschung*, vol. 25, no. 4 (2003), pp. 371–98.

Poliakov, Leon, *Brévaire de la haine: Le IIIe reich et les juifs*, Paris: 1951.

Polkehn, Klaus, "The Secret Contacts: Zionism and Nazi Germany: 1933–1941," *Journal of Palestine Studies*, vol. 5, nos. 3/4 (Spring–Summer, 1976), pp. 54–82.

Porat, Dina, *The Blue and the Yellow Stars of David: The Zionist Leadership in Palestine and the Holocaust, 1939–1945*, Cambridge: 1990.

Porat, Dina, "*The Protocols of the Elders of Zion*: New Uses of an Old Myth," in R. S. Wistrich (ed.), *Demonizing the Other*. Amsterdam: 1999, pp. 322–35.

Porat, Dina and Roni Stauber (eds.), *Anti-Semitism Worldwide, 1994*–2005, Tel Aviv: 1995–2007.

Qaymari, Ata, "The Holocaust in the Palestinian Perspective," in Paul Scham, Walid Salem and Benjamin Pogrund (eds.), *Shared Histories. A Palestinian–Israeli Dialogue*, Jerusalem: 2005, pp. 148–53.

"Reflections on al-Nakba," *Journal of Palestine Studies*, vol. 28, no. 1 (Autumn 1998), pp. 5–35.

Reitlinger, Gerald, *The Final Solution: The Attempt to Exterminate the Jews of Europe, 1939–1945*, London: 1953.

Rekem-Peled, Rina, "Zionism as Reflection of Anti-Semitism: On the Relations between Zionism and Anti-Semitism in Germany of the Second Reich," in Jacob Borut and Oded Heilbruner (eds.), *German Anti-Semitisim*, Tel Aviv: 2000, Hebrew, pp. 133–56.

Rembiszewski, Sarah, *The Final Lie: Holocaust Denial in Germany: A Second Generation Denier as a Test Case*, Tel Aviv: 1996.

"Revisionist Historian Forum a Great Success," *Middle East News Online*, 16 May 2001.

Rouhana, Nadim, "The Holocaust and Psychological Dynamics of the Arab–Israeli Conflict," paper submitted to the *Third World Views of the Holocaust Conference*, Boston, April 2001, www.violence.neu.edu/Nadim.Rouhana.html.

Rouhana, Nadim, "Zionism's Encounter with the Palestinians: The Dynamics of Force, Fear, and Extremism," in Robert I. Rotberg (ed.), *Israeli and Palestinian Narratives of Conflict. History's Double Helix*, Bloomington, IN: 2006, pp. 115–41.

Rubin, Barry, *The PLO Between Anti-Zionism and Antisemitism*, Acta no. 1, Jerusalem: 1993.

Rubin, Uri, "Jews and Judaism," *Encyclopedia of the Qur'an*, vol. 3, Leiden and Boston: 2003, electronic edition.

Rubinstein, Amnon and Alexander Yakobson, *Israel and the Family of Nations*, Tel Aviv: 2003, Hebrew.

Rubinstein, Danny, *The People of Nowhere. The Palestinian Vision of Home*, Jerusalem: 1991.

Rubinstein, Robert A. and Mary LeCron Foster (eds.), *The Social Dynamics of Peace and Conflict. Culture in International Security*, Boulder, CO: 1988.

Rychlak, Ronald J., *Hitler, the War, and the Pope*, Indiana: 2000.

Sa'b, Hassan, *Zionism and Racism*, Beirut: 1965.

Sagi, Nana, *German Reparations, A History of The Negotiations*, Jerusalem: 1980.

Said, Edward W., "An Exchange on Edward Said and Difference," *Critical Inquiry*, vol. 15 (Spring 1989), pp. 611–46.

Said, Edward W., *The Politics of Dispossession*, New York: 1994.

Sande G. N. et al., "Value Guided Attributions: Maintaining the Moral Self Image and the Diabolical Enemy-Image," *Journal of Social Issues*, vol. 45 (1989), pp. 91–118.

Satloff, Robert, *Among the Righteous: Lost Stories from the Holocaust's Long Reach into Arab Lands*, New York: 2006.

Sayigh, Rosemary, "Dis/Solving the Refugee Problem," *Middle East Report*, no. 207 (Summer 1998), pp. 19–23.

Sayigh, Rosemary, "Palestinian Camp Women as Tellers of History," *Journal of Palestine Studies*, vol. 27, no. 2 (Winter 1998), pp. 42–58.

Schiffrin, Deborah, Deborah Tannen and Heidi E. Hamilton (eds.), *The Handbook of Discourse Analysis*, Malden, MA: 2001.

Schivelbusch, Wolfgang, *The Culture of Defeat: On National Trauma, Mourning, and Recovery*, New York: 2001.

Sedar, Irving and Harold J. Greenberg, *Behind the Egyptian Sphinx*, Philadelphia: 1960.

Segev, Tom, *The Seventh Million, Israelis and the Holocaust*, Jerusalem: 1991, Hebrew.

Shafir, Michael, *Between Denial and "Comparative Trivialization": Holocaust Negationism in Post-Communist East Central Europe*, ACTA, no. 19, Jerusalem: 2002.

Shapira, Anita, "Politics and Collective Memory: The Debate over the 'New Historians' in Israel," *History and Memory*, vol. 7, no. 1 (Spring/Summer 1995), pp. 9–40.

Shapira, Anita, "The Eichmann Trial: Changing Perspectives," *The Journal of Israeli History*, vol. 23, no. 1, 2004, pp. 18–39.

Shavit, Zohar, *A Past Without a Shadow: Constructing the Past in German Books for Children*, New York: 2005, Hebrew.

Shemesh, Moshe, "The Position of the Jaffa Newspaper, 'Filastin,' on the Axis State and the Democracies," *Iyunim be-tekumat Yisrael*, vol. 2 (1992), Hebrew, pp. 245–78.

Shermer, Michael and Alex Grobman, *Denying History: Who Says the Holocaust Never Happened and Why Do They Say It?* Berkeley: 2000.

Shils, Edward, *The Intellectuals and the Powers and Other Essays*, Chicago: 1972.

Shinar, Eliezer, *Under the Burden of Necessity and Emotions, on a National Mission. Israeli-German Relations, 1951–1966*, Tel Aviv: 1967, Hebrew.

Sivan, Emmanuel, "A Resurgence of Arab Anti-Semitism," in William Frankel (ed.), *Survey of Jewish Affairs 1988*, London: 1989, pp. 78–95.

Sivan, Emmanuel, *Islamic Fundamentalism and Anti-Semitism*, Jerusalem: 1985, Hebrew.

Skinner, Quentin, "Meaning and Understanding in the History of Ideas," *History and Theory*, vol. 8, no. 1 (1969), pp. 3–53.

Smith, Anthony, *Chosen Peoples: Sacred Sources of National Identity*, Oxford: 2003.

Snir, Reuven, "'One Wound of his Wounds' – The Palestinian Arab Literature in Israel," *Alpayim*, no. 2 (1990), Hebrew, pp. 244–68.

State of Israel, *The Attorney General of the State of Israel vs. Adolf Eichmann: Testimonies*, 2 vols., Jerusalem: 1974.

Stark, Freya, *The Arab Island*, New York: 1946.

Stauber, Roni. "*Realpolitik* and the Burden of the Past: Israeli Diplomacy and the 'Other Germany'," *Israel Studies*, vol. 8, no. 3 (Fall 2003), pp. 100–22.

Stav, Arye, *Peace: Arab Caricatures – An Anti-Semitic Profile*, Tel Aviv: 1996, Hebrew.

413

Stern, Kenneth, *Holocaust Denial*, New York: 1993.

Taji-Farouki, Suha, "A Contemporary Construction of the Jews in the Qur'an: A Review of Muhammad Sayyid Tantawi's *Banu Isra'il fi al-Qur'an wa al-Sunna* and 'Afif 'Abd al-Fattah Tabbara's *al-Yahud fi al-Qur'an*," in Ron Nettler and Suha Taji-Farouki (eds.), *Muslim–Jewish Encounters, Intellectual Tradition and Modern Politics*, Oxford: 1998, pp. 15–37.

Tamimi, Azzam, "Questions on the 50th Anniversary of Israel's Creation," www.ptimes.com/articles/htm.

Teveth, Shabtai, *Ben-Gurion and the Holocaust*, New York: 1996.

Tibawi, Abd al-Latif, "Visions of the Return. The Palestinian Arab Refugees in Arabic Poetry and Art," *Middle East Journal*, vol. 17, no. 5 (1963), pp. 507–26.

Trunk, Isaiah, *Judenrat: The Jewish Councils in Eastern Europe under Nazi Occupation*, Lincoln, NE: 1996.

Turki, Fawwaz, "To Be a Palestinian," *Journal of Palestine Studies*, vol. 3, no. 3 (Spring 1974), pp. 3–17.

United Nations Development Programme, *The Arab Human Development Report 2002*, New York: 2002.

Vidal-Naquet, Pierre, *Assassins of Memory: Essays on the Denial of the Holocaust*, New York: 1992.

Volkov, Shulamit, "Anti-Semitism as a Cultural Code: Reflections on the History and Historiography of Anti-Semitism in Imperial Germany," *Yearbook of the Leo Baeck Institute*, vol. 23 (1978), pp. 25–46.

Wasserstein, Bernard, *Britain and the Jews of Europe, 1939–1945*, London: 1999.

Webman, Esther, "Rethinking the Holocaust. An Open Debate in the Arab World, 1998," in D. Porat and R. Stauber (eds.), *Anti-Semitism Worldwide, 1998/9*, pp. 16–30.

Webman, Esther, "The Adoption of *The Protocols* in the Arab Discourse on the Arab–Israeli Conflict, Zionism and the Jews" in idem (ed.) *The Protocols of the Elders of Zion: The One-Hundred Year Myth and its Impact* (forthcoming).

Webman, Esther, "The Evolution of a Founding Myth – The Nakba and Its Fluctuating Meaning," in Meir Litvak (ed.), *Palestinian Collective Memory and National Identity* (forthcoming), New York: 2009.

Webman, Esther and Sara Rembiszewski, "The Unholy Alliance between Muslim Fundamentalists and Holocaust Deniers," Occasional Paper, Tel Aviv University, October 1993.

Weiss, Aharon, "Jewish Leadership in Occupied Poland – Postures and Attitudes," *Yad Vashem Studies*, no. 12 (1977), pp. 335–65.

Weiss, Yifaat, "The 'Transfer Agreement' and the 'Boycott Movement': A Jewish Dilemma at the Eve of the Holocaust," *Yad Vashem Studies*, vol. 26 (1998), pp. 129–71, electronic edition.

Weitz, Yechiam, "Revisionist Criticism of the Yishuv Leadership during the Holocaust," *Yad Vashem Studies*, vol. 23 (1993), pp. 369–96.

Weitz, Yechiam, *The Man Who was Murdered Twice: The Life, Trial and Death of Yisrael Kasztner*, Jerusalem: 1995, Hebrew.

Weitz, Yehiam and Avital Saf (eds.), *Major Changes within the Jewish People in the Wake of the Holocaust*, Jerusalem: 1996.

Weitzmann, Chaim, *The Letters and Papers of Chaim Weitzmann, Series B Papers*, New Brunswick, NJ: 1983–84.

Wicken, Stephen, "Views of the Holocaust in Arab Media and Public Discourse," *Yale Journal of International Affairs*, vol. 1, no. 2 (Winter/Spring 2006), pp. 108–14.

Wiesel, Elie, *Night*, New York: 1960.

Wistrich, Robert S., *Anti-Zionism and Anti-Semitism in Our Time*, Jerusalem: 1985, Hebrew.

Wistrich, Robert S. (ed.), *Demonizing the Other: Anti-Semitism, Racism, and Xenophobia*, Amsterdam: 1999.

Wistrich, Robert S., *Muslim Anti-Semitism: A Clear and Present Danger*, New York: 2002.

Wodak, Ruth and Martin Reisgl, "Discourse and Racism," in D. Schiffrin, D. Tannen and H. E. Hamilton (eds.), *The Handbook of Discourse Analysis*, Malden, MA: 2001, pp. 372–97.

Worsley, Peter, "Images of the Other," in R. A. Rubinstein and M. LeCron Foster (eds.), *The Social Dynamics of Peace and Conflict. Culture in International Security*, Boulder, CO: 1988, pp. 69–80.

Wurmeisser, Meirav, *The Schools of Ba'athism: A Study of Syrian Schoolbooks*, Tel Aviv: 2000.

Wyman, David S., *Paper Walls: America and the Refugee Crisis, 1938–1941*, Amherst, MA: 1968.

Wyman, David S., *The Abandonment of the Jews: America and the Holocaust, 1941–1945*, New York: 1984.

Yablonka, Hanna, *The State of Israel vs. Adolf Eichmann*, Jerusalem: 2001, Hebrew.

Yablonka, Hanna, "The Eichmann Trial and Israelis, 40 Years Later," *Bi-Shvil Ha-Zikaron*, no. 41 (April–May 2001), Hebrew, pp. 24–31.

Yablonka, Hanna, "The Development of Holocaust Consciousness in Israel: The Nuremberg, Kapos, Kastner and Eichmann Trials," *Israel Studies*, vol. 8 no. 3 (Fall 2003), pp. 1–24.

Yadlin, Rivka, *An Arrogant Oppressive Spirit: Anti-Zionism as Anti-Judaism in Egypt*, New York: 1989.

Yaghi, E., "Exclusive Interview with Dr. Ibrahim Alloush", Middle East News Online, 7 May 2001.

Yahya [Glubb], Faris, *Zionist Relations with Nazi Germany*, Beirut: 1978.

Yakira, Elhanan, *Post-Zionism, Post Holocaust: Three Essays on Denial, Repression and Delegitimation of Israel*, Tel Aviv: 2006, Hebrew.

Young, James, "Towards a Received History of the Holocaust," *History and Theory*, vol. 36, no. 4 (1997), pp. 21–43.

Young, James E., *Writing and Rewriting the Holocaust. Narrative and the Consequences of Interpretation*, Bloomington, IN: 1988.

Zierler, Wendy, "'My Holocaust Is Not Your Holocaust': 'Facing' Black and Jewish Experience in *The Pawnbroker, Higher Ground* and *The Nature of Blood*," *Holocaust and Genocide Studies*, vol. 18, no. 1 (Spring 2004), pp. 46–67.

Zur, Ofer, "The Love of Hating: The Psychology of Enmity," *History of European Ideas*, vol. 13, no. 4 (1991), pp. 345–69.

Zweig, Ronald W., *German Reparations and the Jewish World. A History of the Claims Conference*, London: 2001.

"1948–1998 in the Eyes of Two Peoples. A Roundtable Discussion," *Palestine–Israel Journal*, vol. 5, no. 2 (1998), pp. 23–34.

Websites

http://abbc.com/islam.

www.akhawia.net/archive/index.php/t-8895.html, July 2005.

www.alhandasa.net/forum/archive/index.php/t-8240.html.

www.alkaritha.org.

www.arabrenewal.com/index.php?rd=AI&AI0=7376.

bayan@vistus.net.

http://bouhout.blogs.ma/tb.php?id=25 - March to July 2006.

www.ihr.org.

www.intelligence.org.il/eng/sib/5_05/as_sermon.htm.

Israel Radio, reshet b' site – bet.netvision.net.il.

www.lailatalqadr.com.

www.memri.org.

Middle East News Online.

www.narwanour.com/cen/Hitler.jpg.

Nizkor Project Shofar FTP Archive File: people/r/rami.ahmed/antizionist-congress.

www.omanidream.net/vb/archive/index.php/t-1285.html.

Palestinian National Authority, www.minfo.gov.ps.

www.pmw.org.il.

www.resala.org/forum/archive/index.php/t-2127.html.

Resistance.homepage.com

shkbta.be/?p=33.

www.swalif.net/sforum1/showthread.php?threadid=66580.

www.tau.ac.il/Anti-Semitism.

www.uaearab.com/DREAM/53.htm.

INDEX

Abaza, Fikri, 43

'Abbas, Mahmud (Abu Mazin) 8; and alleged Nazi-Zionist collaboration, 245, 247, 250, 254, 255, 258, 260, 263, 264, 268, 269, 370, 382; and denial, 161, 164, 184, 187, 382

'Abbasi, Nizam, 214

'Abd al-'Al, Hasan, 251

'Abd al-'Aziz ibn Sa'ud, King, 44, 45, 306n

'Abd al-'Aziz, Zaynab, 149, 150

'Abd al- Fattah, Majid, 339, 376

'Abd al-Ghani, 'Abd al-Rahman, 9, 260, 265, 296, 301

'Abd al-Hadi, Mufid, 300, 301

'Abd al-Hadi, Muhammad Hinna'i, 88

'Abd al-Mun'im, Muhammad, 150, 354

'Abd al-Nasir, Jamal, 94, 293; and denial, 161, 186, 382; equation with Hitler, 215, 278; and Nakba, 322; on World War II, 275

'Abd al-Qadir, Hatim, 336

'Abd al-Qadir, Shamil, 174, 176

'Abd al-Qudus, Ihsan, 78, 80, 114, 124, 280

'Abd al-Rahman, Ahmad, 346

'Abd al-Rahman, 'Aysha, 269

'Abd al-Ra'uf, Hisham, 367

'Abdallah, Ghasan, 316, 320, 324

'Abduh 'Ali, 'Arafa, 247, 251, 253, 263

'Abidi, Jadu' al-, 302,

Abu 'Amr, Ziyad, 336

Abu Dhikra, Wajih, 176

Abu Jadid, Muhammad Farid, 48

Abu al-Majid, Sabri, 116

Abu Mazin (*see* 'Abbas Mahmud)

Abu al-Rus, Ilya, 144

Abu Sa'da, Salwa, 166

Abu Sitta, Salman, 356

Abu Zakariya, Yahya, 149

Abu Zayd, Hamid Nasr, 344

Abu Ziyad, Hilmi, 98

Adenauer, Konrad, 107, 126; and Eichmann trial 105, 106; and reparations 61, 64, 66, 70, 72, 73, 77, 81, 84, 87

Adghar, Khalid al-, 223

Afghanistan, 190

Ahmad, Ibrahim Khalil, 199

Ahmad, Najib al-, 302

Ahmadinejad, Mahmud, 367, 368, 372, 373, 375

417

Bashir, Salih, 334, 374
Basisu, Sa'd, 346
Ba'th Party, 220n, 221n, 223, 285; Syrian, 226, 290, 293
Bauer, Yehuda, 230n, 325, 326
Bavaria, 204
Baz, Usama al-, 382
Bea, Augustin Cardinal, 133, 138, 139
Begin, Menahem, 77, 90, 107, 108n, 180, 226, 245n, 254, 267
Beirut, 115, 192, 198, 211, 232, 279, 340, 358; Holocaust denial conference in, 179, 357, 358, 359, 360, 361
Belgium (Belgians), 29, 165
Ben Ashenhu, 'Abd al-Hamid, 223
Ben-Gurion, David, 46, 87, 233, 267, 279; and Eichmann affair, 93, 95, 96, 97, 98, 99, 100, 101, 103n, 105, 108, 109, 113, 114, 115, 116, 117, 121, 122, 123
Ben Zvi, Yitzhak, 111
Benigni, Roberto, 182
Bergen Belsen, 26, 50
Bergmann, Hugo, 111
Bevin, Ernest, 39, 40
Bible, 163, 218, 374
Biltmore Program, 259, 268, 269
Birkenau, 175, 337
Bishara, 'Azmi, 1, 2, 9, 303, 373, 373
Bishara, Marwan, 370
Bismarck, Otto von, 304
Bizri, Dalal al-, 241, 371
Bonn, 65n, 66, 68, 70, 75
Böker, Alexander, 71
Borokhov, Baer, 229
Bosnia, 182, 297, 329, 349, 366
Brand, Joel, 106, 110, 265n
Brecht, Bertold, 144
Brenner, Lenny, 252
Britain, 36, 56, 59, 71, 85, 102, 107, 108n, 110n, 138, 234, 258n, 297, 298, 299,

300, 302, 304, 320, 363; and Arab attitudes toward, 3, 23, 28, 49, 51, 64, 77, 79, 141, 167, 187, 189, 241, 271, 272, 274, 275, 286, 289, 293, 294, 295, 296, 301, 303, 310; Foreign Office of, 62, 76; and rescue of Jews, 38, 39, 106, 110, 257, 259, 260; and German reparations, 62, 63, 64, 73; Jews of, 44, 48; Muslim Council of, 363; and Nazi Germany, 77, 79, 80, 112, 137, 141, 167, 206, 207, 239, 244, 274, 288, 289, 291, 301, 351, 355; White Paper (see Palestine); and Zionism, 35, 38, 39, 41, 43, 48, 53n, 54n, 150n, 207, 244, 251, 256, 257, 261, 268, 286, 287, 302 (see also Balfour Declaration)
Boycott, Arab, 40, 68, 69, 73, 74, 76, 80, 81, 86, 115, 186
Boycott of Nazi Germany, 86, 206, 252, 253, 254, 287
Browning, Christopher, 18
Brunner, Alois, 278
Bu'ayni, Shirbil, 148
Buber, Martin, 111, 127
Buchenwald, 26, 29, 30, 202
Budapest, 265, 269
Bulgaria, 30, 297
Buenos Aires, 86, 93, 97
Bul'awali, Tijani, 189
Bundestag, 61n, 72
Bunduk, Mazin al-, 120, 122
Burayk, Sa'd al-, 285
Buti, Muhammad Sa'id Ramadan al-, 344
Butrus-Ghali, Butrus, 121, 187, 273
Buwayz, Faris, 146, 161, 184
bystanders, 11, 24, 36, 297

Cabot-Lodge, Henri, 100

Cairo, 64, 68, 70, 71, 72, 75, 85, 109, 113, 118, 121, 161, 202, 278, 302, 321, 340, 343; Radio Cairo, 95, 112

Cairo International Book Fair, 168, 236, 343, 345

Cairo University, 121, 128, 314, 344, 347

Cambodia, 230n, 329, 366

Camp David Summit (2000), 3

Canadian Islamic Congress, 149

capitalism, 1, 160, 164, 200, 224, 225, 277, 281, 283; and Jews, 209, 225

Carr, William Guy, 269n, 286

Cassidy, Edward Cardinal, 147

Catan, George, 369

Catholic Church (see Church)

Chamberlain, Neville, 239, 288, 289, 293, 304

Chaumont, Jean-Michel, 327

Children of Israel, 4

Chosen People, 41, 51, 119, 128, 148, 217, 218, 219, 220, 233, 237, 241

Christianity: relations with Islam, 4, 145, 148, 149, 150, 196n, 380; relations with Judaism, 4, 15, 42, 54, 131-153, 201, 204, 270, 331, 378;Scriptures, 135, 144, 159

Church: Anglican, 136; Catholic, 15, 42, 131-153, 265; and Zionism, 133, 142, 143, 151; Coptic, 137, 161; Eastern, 132, 134, 137, 145, 147, 161; Melchite, 136; Orthodox, 134, 135; Protestants, 132; Vatican II Council, 15, 131-153

Churchill, Winston, 31, 38n, 276, 277, 280, 288, 298, 302

CIA (Central Intelligence Agency), 151, 287

Clinton, Bill, 240

Cold War, 109n, 350

concentration camps, 7, 25, 28, 29, 30, 33, 46, 56, 79, 80, 110, 141, 165n, 167, 169, 171, 172, 175, 187, 194n, 202, 207, 231, 234, 247, 265n, 276, 278n, 320, 326, 362, 363, 364, 367 (see also detention camps)

Communism, 155, 187, 200, 216, 223, 235n, 238, 271n, 277, 279, 281, 284

Concordat, 146

conspiracy theories, 6, 7, 142, 143, 151, 158, 177, 246, 247, 249, 255n, 267, 286, 287, 288n, 346, 356

counter history, 195, 228

Croatia, 165n, 248

crucifixion, 131, 133, 134, 136, 138, 140, 141, 142, 144, 148

Crusades, 148, 149, 189, 232, 380

culture of defeat, 193

Czechoslovakia, 30, 34, 104, 186, 262, 289

Dachau, 29, 30, 33, 170n, 175, 194n, 202

Dakkak, Ibrahim, 314

Damascus, 63, 97; Blood Libel, 4n, 182, 293, 295

Damj, Nasir, 250, 251

Daqqaq, Basil, 115, 121, 143

Danzig Corridor, 288, 289

Darraj, Faysal, 158

Darwinism, 188, 230, 232; and Zionism, 221, 222, 229, 233

Darwish, Mahmud, 313, 316, 322, 358, 359

Darwish, 'Abdallah Nimr, 303

Daud, Muhammad, 177

Da'uk, Faris Ahmad, 70

Davos, 335

Dawidowicz, Lucy, 174, 265, 325, 326

Dawudiyya, Muhammad, 240

death camps, 7, 25, 28, 30, 32, 93, 118, 143n, 155, 165, 167, 169, 171, 172, 173, 175, 176, 177, 190, 228, 231, 232, 233, 234, 258, 260n, 262, 263, 264, 269, 278, 335n, 337, 364, 375 (*see also*, Auschwitz, Maidanek and Treblinka)
Deir Yasin, 103, 116, 232, 324; Remembered project, 324
DeLorme, Roger, 165
Democratic Front for the Liberation of Palestine (DFLP), 187
Deputy (Der Stellvertreter), the, 142, 143
detention camps, 30, 169, 187, 190, 206, 207n, 238, 248, 266, 290
Dhahani, Mahmud, 121
Dhahani, Salah al-, 47
Dhahir, Nissim, 369
Dhu al-Faqar, Husayn, 103, 104n, 121, 125, 128
diaspora, 313, 326; Arab, 180; Jewish, 127, 128, 137, 220, 225n, 229n, 255, 312
Dissuqi, Muhammad Kamal al-, 162, 177n, 201, 226, 275, 276, 286
Dixon, Pierson, 100
Dönitz, Karl, 31
Dresden, 164, 167, 175
Dreyfus, Alfred, 345, 350
Durban World Conference, 14, 321, 357, 361, 362

Eddy, William, 36
Eden, Anthony, 215
Egypt, 10, 17, 23, 59, 95, 106, 108, 115, 119, 198, 202, 203n, 207, 254, 280, 292, 297, 322, 337, 361; and the Eichmann affair, 95, 96, 98, 99, 103, 112, 113, 115, 118, 121, 122, 123, 124, 125, 126, 128; Ministry of Re-

ligious Endowments, 199; and Jewish refugees, 37, 38, 41, 43, 44, 45, 49, 150n; and World War II, 9, 23, 25, 27, 28, 109n, 141n, 273, 274, 275; attitudes towards Nazi Germany, 27, 28, 31, 32, 33, 108, 272, 273, 277, 279, 280, 281, 282, 293; and Nazi experts, 60, 84, 85, 86, 105n, 278; and denial, 161, 181, 186, 329, 343, 345, 346, 361, 366, 382, 384; 1962 National Charter, 275; 1952 revolution, 63, 273; peace with Israel, 3, 9, 18, 202, 213, 239, 335, 364; and reparations, 62, 64-76, 86, 87, 90, 91; and Vatican II Council, 135n, 136, 137, 320
Eichmann, Adolf, 15, 32, 166, 176, 255, 265, 266, 278; affair, 14, 93-129, 267, 340; Trial, 102-122, 133, 142, 156, 174, 243, 379; execution, 93, 95, 110, 111, 121, 122
Einsatzgruppen, 32
Eizenstat, Stuart E., 351
Eisner, Kurt, 204
El Alamein, 295
Elie Lillie, 186
Eshkol, Levi, 252
Europe, 1, 4, 11, 17, 27, 34-53, 55, 56, 57, 82, 83, 109, 111, 120, 131, 135, 138, 139, 145, 146, 148, 149, 155, 156, 163, 167, 169, 170, 171, 175, 180, 183, 184, 188, 196, 197, 201, 203, 204, 223, 225, 234, 238, 239, 253, 258, 271, 273, 282, 286, 288, 289, 292, 294, 295, 302, 303, 305, 314, 319, 323, 329, 332, 339, 351, 355, 356, 364, 367, 384; culture and ideology, 134, 135, 137, 140, 141, 143, 144, 220, 223, 225, 230, 231, 233, 240, 276, 283, 285, 344, 360, 373, 380, 381; guilt complex, 1, 87,

Hindenburg, Paul von, 204, 207, 208
Hiroshima, 148, 164, 168, 269, 276, 290
Hitler, Adolf, 30, 31n, 44, 55, 83, 86n, 97, 160, 162, 176, 188n, 195, 215, 216, 271n, 334, 355; and Jews, 13, 28, 29, 44, 45, 47, 51, 52, 54, 57, 78, 79, 80, 82, 83, 84, 88, 89, 100, 115, 118, 137, 140, 141, 146, 165, 167, 171, 172, 173, 177, 181, 182, 189, 190, 191, 194-214, 219, 250, 251, 252, 254, 255, 256, 257, 268, 269, 270, 273, 277, 281, 282, 283, 284, 285, 286-292, 294, 295, 299, 303, 304, 305, 339, 357, 367, 368, 377; and Allies, 54, 239, 276, 277, 286-292; Arab assessments of, 29, 43, 45, 46, 84, 98, 99, 107, 108, 118, 120, 123, 125, 138, 146, 147, 148, 152, 156, 164, 167, 170, 173, 175, 183, 189, 192, 193-214, 219, 220, 223, 226, 238, 239, 240, 274n, 276, 277-307, 368, 369, 376
Hizballah, 146, 150, 211, 284, 285, 357, 358, 365
Hlinka, 132
Hochhuth, Rolf, 142, 143, 144
Hoffman, Karl Heinz, 283
Hoffman, Michael, 179
Holland, 29, 30, 59, 64
Hourani, 'Abdallah, 159
Höss, Rudof, 32, 33, 176
Human Factor (film), 181
Hungary, 29, 30, 236n, 248, 262, 266, 271n, 297, 353; Jews, 32, 101, 106, 110, 177, 247, 255, 262, 265, 266
Husayn, King, 283, 293, 335
Husayn, Magdi, 179
Husayn, Muhammad al-Khadr, 83
Husayn, Saddam, 215
Husayn, Sharif, 301

Husayn, Yasir, 288, 289, 290
Husayn, Taha, 342
Husayni, Hajj Amin al-, 16, 23, 97, 108, 109n, 123, 207, 250n, 265, 270, 273, 294, 296, 297-303, 306
Husayni, Jamal, 42, 46, 272, 298
Hut, Biyan al-, 208, 300
Hut, Shafiq al-, 339, 373
Huwaydi, Fahmi, 150, 343, 368

Ibrahim, Jamil 'Atiyya, 354
Ibrahim, Saad Eddin, 310
Imam, Muhammad Rif'at al-, 189
'Inan, Muhammad 'Abdallah, 85
Inquisition (Spanish), 142, 149, 355
International Holocaust Remembrance Day, 362, 363
International Jewry, 51, 77, 224
Institute for Arab Research and Studies, 219
Institute for Historical Review (IHR), 178, 179, 180, 357
Intifada, 3, 202, 206, 240, 335, 337, 357, 358, 363, 370
Iran, 178, 255n, 343, 358, 367, 368
Iraq, 38n, 41, 43, 45, 62, 109, 150n, 174, 175, 185, 215, 240, 246n, 256n, 271, 276, 294, 297, 301, 302, 349
Irgun Zeva'i Leumi (IZL), 53, 54, 103n, 256
Iron Guard, 248
Irving, David, 168n, 176, 178, 247, 346, 371, 372, 373
'Isa, Salah, 342
Islam, 134, 150, 295, 340, 341, 350; and Judaism, 5, 119n, 134, 140, 196, 197, 198, 202, 205, 212, 218, 288, 302, 344; and the West, 66, 83, 149n, 197, 218, 227, 228, 231, 232, 234, 281, 285, 306, 343, 344, 345, 366, 368, 373, 375, 378

Islamic Conference Organization, 367

Islamic Cultural Center, New York, 205

Islamic Jihad of Palestine, 159n, 366, 367

Islamic Movement, Israel, 159n, 303

Islamists, 13, 17, 28, 78, 127, 146, 148, 149n, 151, 153, 284, 295, 343, 344, 378, 383; and denial, 82, 83, 159, 170, 177, 178, 179, 180, 365, 367, 368; and justification, 195, 196, 197, 198, 205, 209, 210, 212, 214; and relativization, 118n; equating Zionism with Nazism, 221, 223, 226, 241, 381; and alleged Nazi-Zionist collaboration, 247, 256, 268, 270, 383; perceptions of Nazism, 284, 285, 286, 288, 293, 295, 302, 303, 305, 306

Isma'il, Ahmad Sulayman, 69

Istanbul, 110, 132

Italy, 30, 53n, 237, 281, 297, 302

'Izz, Salah, 349, 350, 373

Jabir, Ahmad, 259, 266

Jabotinsky, Ze'ev, 251, 256

Jabr, Samah, 375

Jackson, Robert, 291

Jalul, Faysal, 332n, 347

Jamali, Fadil, 41, 45

Jamati, Habib, 115

Jami'a, Muhammad, 205

Jankowski, James, 14

Jarbu'a, Muhammad, 183, 193, 199, 203, 206

Jarrar, Bassam, 260

Jawwala al-, 295

Jawdat, Salih, 121

Jazeera TV al-, 241, 242, 360

Jbara, Taysir, 299

Jewish Agency, 30, 37, 47, 56, 110, 167, 243, 250, 254, 260, 266

Jewish Councils, (see Judenräte)

"Jewish problem," 2, 12, 24, 39, 40, 43, 47, 49, 50, 53, 56, 98, 101, 107, 171, 181, 219, 221, 231, 232, 301, 309

Jewish refugees, 26, 27, 35, 37, 41, 44, 46, 48, 51, 53, 56, 61, 67, 150, 253, 259, 315

John XXIII, Pope, 100, 133, 139

John Paul II, Pope, 15, 131, 145, 151, 320, 380

Jo Mard, 'Abd al-Jabir, 54

Jordan, 10, 18, 62, 73, 74n, 95, 98, 104n, 109, 136, 145, 162n, 163, 166, 192, 194n, 216n, 246, 281, 283, 293, 295n, 320, 335, 340, 345, 360, 363, 382; Muslim brotherhood, 285; peace with Israel, 3, 239, 331, 379; Writers Association, 180, 360

Jospin, Lionel, 240

Judaism, 8, 13, 33, 127, 132, 134, 145, 152, 159, 163, 209, 213, 224, 225, 229, 233, 236, 241, 278, 287, 376, 381, 384; charges of racism, 208, 217, 218, 219, 222, 224, 241

Judenräte, 234, 249, 261, 262, 263, 264, 265

Judgment Day, 134, 226

Judt, Tony, 1

Jundi, Sami al-, 292, 293

Jurassic Park (film), 182

Juzmani, Nadhir, 257, 269

Kafar Qasim, 116

Kagan, Ra'ya, 174

Kahtany, 'Abdallah, 176

Kaltenbrunner, Ernst, 32

Kanafani, Marwan, 212

Kamil, 'Isam, 368

Kamil, Omar, 371, 374, 384

Karmi, Ghada, 317, 318, 353

Kashan, Hilal, 192, 214, 384

Kassir, Samir, 347, 350, 360, 374